PREFACE TO THE EIGHTH EDITION

In this edition the title has been altered since the description "new" is no longer appropriate to a principal Act which reached the statute book more than thirty years ago. In general, the style of previous editions has been retained, though much of the historical material relating to events prior to 1944 has been deleted both from the Introduction and from the text. Although the reorganisation of local government (following the Local Government Act 1972) has not substantially altered the law of education, it has had profound effects on the internal organisation of local government, bringing the education service into a closer relationship with other local government services. This development together with the current reduction in public expenditure may well, in due course, affect the law of education.

Part I consists of an introduction to the law of education; Division A of Part II consists of the annotated texts of the Education Acts 1944–76 together with the Education (Handicapped Children) Act 1970; Division B of Part II contains the annotated texts of other statutory provisions of importance to local education authorities.

Part III contains all the relevant statutory instruments made under the statutory provisions in Division A of Part II which were in force on 31st December, 1975. These are arranged in chronological order.

Part IV consists of a selection of circulars and administrative memoranda which appear to be of sufficient importance to print in full. The copyright of these belong to the Crown and they are printed by permission of the Controller of Her Majesty's Stationery Office.

Part V deals with a number of cases important to administrators and teachers in connection with their common law responsibilities.

We wish to thank the Department of Education and Science for allowing the use of their copyright material, and the publishers who have been so helpful to us; and also Mr. J. D. Mann, Deputy Education Officer of Sheffield for his critical and constructive comments on the Introduction; our indebtedness to Mrs. Nellie Taylor, who has participated in our work at all stages is immense.

June 1976

GEORGE TAYLOR
JOHN B. SAUNDERS

THE LAW OF EDUCATION

EIGHTH EDITION

THE LAW OF EDUCATION

EIGHTH EDITION

BY

GEORGE TAYLOR, ESQ., M.A.

OF GRAY'S INN, BARRISTER, FORMERLY CHIEF EDUCATION OFFICER, CITY OF LEEDS

AND

JOHN B. SAUNDERS, ESQ.

OF LINCOLN'S INN, BARRISTER

LONDON

BUTTERWORTHS

1976

ENGLAND: BUTTERWORTH & CO. (PUBLISHERS) LTD.
LONDON: 88 KINGSWAY, WC2B 6AB.

AUSTRALIA: BUTTERWORTH & CO. (AUSTRALIA) LTD.
SYDNEY: 586 PACIFIC HIGHWAY, CHATSWOOD, NSW 2067.
Also at MELBOURNE, BRISBANE, ADELAIDE and PERTH.

CANADA: BUTTERWORTH & CO. (CANADA) LTD.
TORONTO: 2265 MIDLAND AVENUE, SCARBOROUGH M1P 4S1

NEW ZEALAND: BUTTERWORTH & CO. (NEW ZEALAND) LTD.
WELLINGTON: 26–28, WARING TAYLOR STREET, 1.

SOUTH AFRICA: BUTTERWORTH & CO. (SOUTH AFRICA) (PTY.) LTD.
DURBAN: 152–154 GALE STREET.

U.S.A.: BUTTERWORTH & CO. (PUBLISHERS) INC.
BOSTON: 19 CUMMINGS PARK, WOBURN, MASS. 01801.

ISBN 0 406 39640 x

PREFACE TO THE FIRST EDITION

Although the Education Act 1944, is entitled simply " An Act to reform the law relating to Education in England and Wales " the effect of its 122 sections and 9 schedules is to render obsolete every work on the law relating to education which has ever been written.

The Act is the first step in the Government's programme of post-war reconstruction and reform, and Mr. R. A. Butler, who is now the first Minister of Education, is to be congratulated heartily on piloting his Bill through Parliament in so satisfactory a manner. It may well be said that no Education Bill since the creation of the national system of education in 1870 has had so smooth a passage, in spite of the expected storms of opposition and dissension which at one time seemed likely to arise not only on the religious issues, but also on the proposal to abolish the 169 " Part III " authorities and to concentrate the administration of education in the hands of the county and county borough councils.

On the religious question there is little to say. The religious provisions of the Act appear, at least to a mere administrator, as a fair compromise between the various interests involved, though, as is inevitable with a compromise, no one has been completely satisfied. From an administrative point of view, the change from a " dual " system to one in which there are four types of school, county, aided, special agreement and controlled, each with their peculiar rights and duties, to say nothing of " transferred " and " substituted " schools and " schools for displaced pupils ", means a considerable increase in the complexity of the administrative arrangements. One can only hope that this will be justified by a rapid improvement in the schools.

The administrative system created by the Act has naturally caused a great deal of heartburning to those authorities who lose their educational functions on 1st April, 1945. It does, in fact, seem inequitable that an authority with a population of 180,000 should lose its status as an education authority simply because it has not hitherto seen fit to seek county borough status, whilst others with less than 50,000 people retain their functions because they have the status of a county borough or a county. But, as Mr. Butler rightly pointed out in the House, he was compelled to take the local government system as he found it and the solution of such problems must be related to local government as a whole and not merely to education. He has made some concessions to the smaller authorities by the creation of a body, the divisional executive, which is new to local government, and to the larger non-county boroughs and urban districts by enabling them to claim exemption from any general scheme of divisional administration for a county and to prepare their own schemes. By these means he claims that local interest in education, which was the main peg upon which the Part III authorities hung their claims, will not only be preserved but stimulated, since the system of divisional administration may cover the whole of the county and not merely the old Part III areas.

The system proposed is both novel and ingenious and will be of considerable value, given goodwill and tolerance on both sides. The relationship in the past between many of the smaller local authorities in the country and their respective county councils has, however, not been entirely happy. It is often felt by the smaller authorities that their position in relation to the county councils is not fully appreciated in Whitehall. Indications have been given both in Parliament and elsewhere, that the administrative system created for education may be regarded as a model for the reconstruction of other local government services, and in fact the Minister of Health has recently begun conversations on the subject of local government reform within, as he put it, the scope of the existing county and county borough system. The future constitution and functions of local authorities, other than county and county borough councils, is therefore in question. Those who believe that size does not necessarily mean efficiency or that the most democratic form of local government is not that which is furthest removed from the electorate, must now agree on a common policy which would enable the smaller communities to play a responsible part in the administration of their own affairs. In a world in which government control seems bound to increase, it may be that the smaller authorities should have even more important functions than hitherto.

If the Education Act 1944, is regarded merely as the framework of a new and progressive educational service, and if all those who are to administer its provisions do everything in their power to provide a better and a fuller education for all, it is likely that the Act will prove to be one of the greatest social reforms of the century. The implementation of its provisions would take a considerable time, even if the only problems were the provision of the necessary buildings and the supply of the required number of teachers. This Act has had priority over other measures of social reconstruction in the Parliamentary time-table. What priority will it have after the war? No doubt there will be set-backs and disappointments. Patience, courage and ability will be needed, especially by those privileged to serve the people in administering the new law. Local authorities and their staffs have risen whole-heartedly to the demands of war and will assuredly face the problems of peace no less worthily.

The purpose of this commentary upon the new Act is to provide an easy and satisfactory way by which all who are concerned with the administration of the educational services may become familiar with the new Act and its various provisions, with its relation to the provisions which it replaces, and with its practical and every-day application. The work has not been burdened with long descriptions of the facts and judgments of decided cases—since a large proportion will in any event now become obsolete—nor has the Act been merely cross-referenced and indexed. What has been attempted, however, is a clear exposition of the Act and its relation to the old law in as concentrated a form as possible. Reference is made to cases which are likely to have any relevance to the new law, as well as to the various Reports issued in recent months which will be of major importance in their relation to educational administration.

Certain circulars dealing with the new administrative system are quoted in full, including the Memorandum issued by the then Board of Education on the Government of Maintained Secondary Schools and Circular 5 of the Ministry which deals with Local Administration and Schemes of Divisional Administration.

The date of writing has been generally assumed to be 1st April, 1945, except in the case of provisions coming into operation or on which action has to be taken before that date.

It is impossible to conclude without expressing thanks to our publishers for their kindness and assistance in the preparation of this book, without which its publication so soon after the Royal Assent to the Act could not have taken place.

October, 1944.

D. J. BEATTIE.
P. S. TAYLOR.

TABLE OF CONTENTS

TABLE OF CASES

In the following Table references are given where applicable to the English and Empire Digest where a digest of the case will be found.

TABLE OF STATUTES

References in this Table to "*Stats*" are to Halsbury's Statutes of England (Third Edition) showing the volume and page at which the annotated text of the Act will be found. Page references printed in bold type indicate where the Act is set out in part or in full.

PART I

INTRODUCTION

INTRODUCTION

1. THE EDUCATION ACT, 1944

The law of education is embodied in the Education Act 1944 as amended by subsequent acts. It repealed virtually all previous legislation relating to education, while retaining the basic administrative structure created at the turn of the century (a).

The Education Act 1944 was the first of the major Acts of reconstruction to reach the statute book for implementation in the post-war world. Prepared and drafted in the latter years of the war, it sought to eliminate grave educational inequalities and injustices by creating a substantially new system of education to be planned and executed by Local Education Authorities in accordance with national policy. Unlike most statutes, it is mainly concerned with general principles and wide aspirations; it provided a grand design to be implemented over a long period. Because of its nature, the 1944 Act has enabled radical developments unforeseen by its progenitors to take place and it has served successive generations without the need for a major review.

Post-war shortages of manpower, materials and financial resources together with a sudden increase (the " bulge ") in the school population made progress slower than was hoped for (b). In fact, some of the provisions (e.g., the raising of the school leaving age to sixteen) have only recently been implemented while the important concept of county colleges has been ignored.

In retrospect, the three main achievements of the Act appear to be: (1) the resolution of the religious conflict which had bedevilled educational progress for over a century; (2) the recognition of the need for secondary education for all; (3) the establishment of an administrative system that distributed duties and powers in such a way that the two main partners were able to contribute: to the Secretary of State was assigned the duty to determine and promote national policy and to the Local Education Authorities the opportunity to plan and develop their systems at all levels.

As with other strategic planning, the education service envisaged in the 1944 Act has evolved in unexpected ways. To remove ambiguities, to iron out inconsistencies and to take into account new thinking, seventeen amending acts have been required. Because the general powers and duties conferred by the principal act upon both central and local government were so far reaching, important developments have occurred without further legislation, e.g. the establishment of polytechnics and the assumption of responsibility for the universities by the Secretary of State for Education and Science.

2. EDUCATION AUTHORITIES

CENTRAL

The Department of Education and Science.—The administration of education has during the past 140 years become progressively the responsibility of central government and Local Authorities. But not until the Education Act 1899 was the administration (excluding that of universities) centralised in one government department (the Board of Education headed by a President) responsible for the *superintendence* of matters relating to education, a limitation continued by the Education Act 1921. Its task was essentially regulatory and not dynamic.

Administratively the Education Act 1944 is of the utmost significance since it introduced a profound change in the status and duties of the central

(a) Board of Education Act 1899; Education Act 1902.

(b) Mr. R. A. Butler, now Lord Butler, principal architect of the Act, remarked at the time that " full implementation of the Act would take a generation ".

department; the Board was abolished and the political head of the Department of Education became a Minister. Further legislation in 1964 added to the importance of the Department in replacing the Minister of Education by the Secretary of State for Education and Science (c) and the merging of the Ministries of Science and Education into the Department of Education and Science. The Secretary of State acquired responsibility for the universities (previously undertaken by the Chancellor of the Exchequer) and later for the Arts and Sport (the latter being subsequently transferred to the Department of the Environment) and for the planning and establishment of the Open University. Ministers of State are usually appointed to assist the Secretary of State in various aspects of the work of the Department.

There is little doubt that the alterations of 1944 and 1964 in the title of the Head of the Department and in the extent of his duties have added to the prestige of the office and have effectively guaranteed him a place in the Cabinet. These changes reflect the increased importance and growing cost of education in the national life and economy.

Even more importantly, the Education Act 1944 increased the powers of the head of the central department in relation to educational policy in general and over local education authorities in particular. No longer limited to superintending the work of local authorities, he is charged with the duty to promote " the education of the people of England and Wales . . . and to secure the effective execution by local authorities, under his control and direction, of the national policy " (d). To underline the nature of this power, s. 68 enables him to give directions to an authority which, in his opinion, is acting unreasonably or proposes so to act despite the fact that the issue lies within the discretion of the authority. There is no machinery for appeal against a decision made under this section.

It is true that these extensive ministerial powers have been sparingly used (though recourse to this section by the Secretary of State has been more frequent in the current decade), but the powers given to the Secretary of State under numerous sections of the Education Acts and Local Government Acts (e) to issue regulations (statutory instruments) have proved an effective way of exercising detailed control over local authorities. The frequent issue of circulars and administrative memoranda provide further opportunities for the direction of education at local level. Furthermore, s. 67, reinforcing s. 68, enables the Secretary of State to act as arbiter in a variety of situations; s. 92 gives him the power to call for any reports or information he requires.

Students of the Education Acts 1944–75 can be in no doubt as to who is the senior partner in the educational system. Shortage of financial resources, materials and teachers with movements of population during the decade immediately following 1944 made inevitable the Department's intervention in the work of local authorities; the more recent policies of reorganising secondary education and teacher training (among others) have served to emphasise the transfer of initiative from local to central government. The Secretary of State does, of course, often consult local authorities and teachers before making changes in policy or detail but he is under no obligation to do so.

It should be noted that two appeals have been made to the courts against decisions made by the Secretary of State (f). From these it is evident (as it is in similar appeals against decisions made by local authorities) that the courts, refusing to become involved in policy, are solely concerned to ensure that procedures adopted by the Secretary of State, as well as by local

---

(c) The Secretary of State for Education and Science Order 1964, S.I. 1964 No. 490 made under the Ministers of the Crown (Transfer of Functions) Act 1946.

(d) Education Act 1944, s. 1.

(e) E.g. Local Government Acts 1958, 1966 and 1972.

(f) *Lee* v. *Secretary of State for Education and Science* (1967), 111 Sol. Jo. 756, see p. 262; *Legg* v. *Inner London Education Authority*, [1972] 3 All E.R. 177 in which the method of making a decision by the Secretary of State was criticised in the course of the judgment.

authorities, are in accordance with the provisions of the acts and do not offend against natural justice.

Advisory Bodies.—The Act established two central advisory councils, (g) one for England and the other for Wales. The Chairman and members were to be appointed by the Secretary of State and they were required to advise him upon such matters as they thought fit and upon any questions referred to them by him. In the years immediately following 1944 the councils' reports were of limited significance and it was not until the late fifties that specific subjects were referred to them. The resulting reports—*The 15–18s* (Crowther 1959–60), *Half Our Future* (Newsom 1963), *Children and their Primary Schools* (Plowden 1967) and *Primary Schools in Wales* (Gittins 1967)—had a major influence on future planning. A novel feature of all these reports was the extensive programme of research commissioned and published by the councils.

The intention of this section of the Act was almost certainly that the central advisory councils should be permanent bodies, but this intention has not been fulfilled. For the four reports mentioned above the councils were specially constituted and were disbanded at the conclusion of their enquiries. Since 1967 the councils have not been reconstituted (h).

However, a number of other councils, not constituted under the Act, have been set up to advise on specific issues, e.g. The National Advisory Council for Industry and Commerce and the National Advisory Council for the Training and Supply of Teachers which, after issuing nine reports, was disbanded in 1966. The Business Education Council and the Technician Education Council were both created in 1973 on the recommendation of the Hazlegrave report (1969) (i).

More recently the Secretary of State has adopted the procedure of appointing a variety of committees of enquiry, advisory committees, working parties and special units to enquire into particular areas of the educational system. Committees of enquiry have investigated such subjects as higher education (Robbins report 1963), teacher education and training (James report 1972), adult education (Russell report 1973), the pay of non-university teachers (Houghton report 1974) and the teaching of reading and the use of English in schools (Bullock report 1975).

The Joint Advisory Committee on Agricultural Education presented a report (the Hudson report) in 1973, the latest of eleven reports on the subject issued between 1948 and 1973 by various committees. An advisory committee on the supply and training of teachers was established in 1972; this committee was asked, unusually, to outline to the Secretary of State any difference of opinion among its members instead of presenting a majority view.

Working parties studied such subjects as educational technology (1972), and school transport (1974). The Secretary of State adopted in 1974 the somewhat revolutionary policy of appointing two special units to study educational as opposed to administrative matters; one is investigating educational disadvantage and the education of immigrants, and the other problems of educational under-achievement.

A comparatively recent development has been the establishment of Parliamentary specialist committees to explore specific areas of administration in government departments. One of these, the Select Committee on Education and Science, reported on the Inspectorate (1968) and on student/staff relations (1969). These committees have now been replaced by the

---

(g) Education Act 1944, s. 4.

(h) For a discussion of advisory councils and committees see *Advisory Councils and Committees in Education*, Maurice Kogan and Tim Packwood, London, Routledge and Kegan Paul, 1974.

(i) A report of a committee of the National Advisory Council on Education for Industry and Commerce.

Expenditure Committee of the House of Commons (1970–71) of which there is an Education and Arts sub-committee. It has reported on Further and Higher Education (1972–73) and on maintenance allowances for pupils and students aged 16–19. This sub-committee takes evidence, written and oral from officials and from bodies and individuals outside government departments, which is published with its reports.

Annual Report to Parliament.—An annual report by the Board of Education has been required since 1870, and the Education Act, 1921, required an annual report of their proceedings. This included a short general review of educational activity and a large number of statistics of great value. The Education Act, 1944, obliges the Secretary of State to make an annual report to Parliament giving an account of the exercise and performance of the powers and duties conferred and imposed upon him by the Act and of the composition and proceedings of the Central Advisory Councils for Education (k). The reports were issued in this form from 1947 until 1961, when the actual report and the statistics were separated; the latter are now much more fully and attractively presented and appear at more frequent intervals.

Educational Research.—The Act gave general powers to the Secretary of State to aid educational research, and the regulations (l) made under the relevant section (m) mention specifically his powers to make grants to recognised persons for

(*a*) the development of special educational methods;
(*b*) the maintenance of special educational services of an advisory or organising character;
(*c*) research.

Initially these powers were virtually unused, but more recently the Secretary of State has aided various bodies (including local education authorities) undertaking research.

The National Foundation for Educational Research was established in 1945 and from the outset was a teacher, local authority, university and Ministry of Education partnership though the main source of finance was from local authorities. Owing to a restricted budget until 1958 research was limited, but since that date the Foundation's work has expanded through the commissioning of research by government and other agencies. Major long term sponsored studies into various aspects of education have been initiated (for example, comprehensive education, streaming, the teaching of reading and the evaluation of the primary French project).

Late in the fifties and in the early sixties experiments and developments were taking place in the teaching of science, modern languages and mathematics in primary and secondary schools and of reading in the primary school, and these were supported by voluntary bodies—the Nuffield Foundation, the associations of teachers of science and mathematics, and in some cases were initiated by individual teachers and local authorities. Not until 1962 did the Ministry enter this field with its establishment of the Curriculum Study Group.

But in response to the deep concern felt by teachers and local authorities that the work of the Group might lead to central direction of the curriculum in schools, the Secretary of State agreed to the replacement of the Curriculum Study Group by the Schools Council which is representative of the whole education service. Established in 1964, the Schools Council is an independent body, jointly financed by local education authorities and the Secretary of State and controlled by teachers (who form the majority of its members)

(k) Education Act, 1944, s. 5.
(l) S.R. & O. 1946 No. 424.
(m) Education Act 1944, s. 100.

and by representatives of the local education authorities and of the Department of Education and Science.

The functions of the Schools Council are to promote and encourage curriculum study and development, to sponsor research which will contribute to the solution of immediate and practical problems, and to co-ordinate secondary school examinations in England and Wales. Areas of enquiry include the development of new teaching materials and methods relevant to the curriculum of primary and secondary schools: a study of the sixth form curriculum and examinations particularly in relation to entry into higher and further education: the teaching of English as a second language and the problems of the curriculum in multi-racial schools. It has a Welsh Committee charged with the responsibility of studying the special needs of schools in Wales.

While the Schools Council has made a considerable impact on curricular development it has not yet solved the problem of widespread dissemination of its work among schools. The freedom of the teacher, greater in this country than in other European countries, enables him to ignore or reject the research and development work of the Council.

THE LOCAL EDUCATION AUTHORITIES

As outlined above, the Secretary of State is required to secure the effective execution by Local Authorities of the national policy for education; it is virtually through Local Authorities that the statutory educational system is administered.

Prior to the Education Act 1944, the county councils and county borough councils were the Education Authorities for elementary, secondary and further education with the exception that borough and urban district councils above a certain size had powers for administering elementary education. The 1944 Act eliminated the two latter and the only Education Authorities were county councils and county borough councils. Provision was made, however, for schemes of administration in county authorities for the exercise of certain functions (specified in the schemes) in primary and secondary education by local bodies (excepted districts and divisional executives) on behalf of the county council.

A major change was made by the Local Government Act 1972 (n). Excluding Greater London, the new Local Education Authorities are now the non-metropolitan county councils and the metropolitan district councils. Divisional executives were abolished and no provision is made for the delegation by Local Education Authorities of any of their functions to a lower level of administration (o).

Education Committees: Chief Education Officer.—The provision (p) in the 1944 Act that required every Local Education Authority to appoint such education committees as they think expedient for the efficient discharge of their duties was continued after some controversy by the Local Government Act 1972 (q).

Two or more Local Education Authorities may join in appointing a committee to advise the appointing authorities on any matters relating to the discharge of their functions (r); these joint committees can only be advisory and are distinct from sub-committees set up by the education committee of the authority (s).

(n) Section 192 (1).
(o) *Ibid.*, s. 192 (2) and see section on Education Committees.
(p) Education Act 1944, Sch. 1, Part II, para. 1.
(q) Section 101 (9) (a).
(r) Local Government Act 1972, s. 102 (4).
(s) See DES Circular 1/73.

In cases where it appears to the Secretary of State desirable that two or more Local Education Authorities should combine for the purpose of exercising some but not all of their functions and that those Authorities should establish a joint education committee for that purpose, he may by order establish a joint education committee of those Authorities and provide for reference to the committee of such questions as he shall specify (t).

Every education committee must include persons of experience in education and persons acquainted with the educational conditions prevailing in the area for which the committee acts, but at least a majority of the committee must be elected members of the Authority (u). It is usual for committees to co-opt representatives of the teaching profession, of the main religious denominations, of industry, commerce and, where appropriate, of agriculture (a).

A teacher employed by a Local Authority is ineligible to be an elected member of the authority; this disqualification applies also to teachers in schools and colleges maintained but not established by the authority and to non-teaching members of staff (b). A teacher in a school, college or other educational institution maintained or assisted by a county council may, however, be an elected member of a district council and a teacher in a school, college or other educational institution maintained or assisted by a metropolitan district council may be an elected member of the metropolitan county council (c).

A Local Education Authority may not exercise any of their educational functions until they have received a report from one of their education committees, unless in their opinion the matter is urgent (d). The authority may authorise any of their education committees to exercise on their behalf any of their educational functions except the power to borrow money or raise a rate (e). An education committee, subject to any restrictions imposed by the authority, may appoint sub-committees and may authorise these sub-committees to exercise any of their functions on their behalf (f). The Secretary of State has been advised that an education committee may not set up sub-committees on an area basis and delegate functions to them (g) but education committees are not precluded from setting up area advisory committees.

Every Local Education Authority must appoint a chief education officer (h).

The minutes of the proceedings of an education committee must be open to inspection by any local government elector (i) and, in common with all other committees of Local Authorities, meetings of the education committee must be open to the public and the press (k).

The Commissions for Local Administration may not investigate complaints concerning any action taken by a Local Education Authority relating to secular instruction in schools (l) nor any action taken concerning instruction (secular or religious), curriculum, internal organisation, management or discipline in any school, college of education or college of further education

---

(t) Education Act 1944, Sch. 1, Part II, para. 3; Local Government Act 1972, s. 192 (5). The Welsh Joint Education Committee is an example of such a committee.

(u) Education Act 1944, Sch. 1, Part II, paras. 5, 6.

(a) It is of interest to note that the education committee is the only committee of a local authority which regularly has co-opted members and the only one which has ever co-opted employees.

(b) Local Government Act 1972, s. 80.

(c) *Ibid.*, s. 81 (4).

(d) Education Act 1944, Sch. 1, Part II, para. 7; Local Government Act 1972, Sch. 30.

(e) Education Act 1944, Sch. 1, Part II, para. 8.

(f) *Ibid.*, para. 10.

(g) See DES Circular 1/73.

(h) Education Act 1944, s. 88; Local Government Act 1972, Sch. 30.

(i) Education Act 1944, Sch. 1, Part II, para. 9.

(k) Public Bodies (Admission to Meetings) Act 1960.

(l) Under Education Act 1944, s. 23.

maintained by the authority (m). It should be noted that the Commissions investigate complaints (n) of maladministration, e.g. unjustifiable delay, incompetence, neglect or prejudice.

The Greater London Area.—As a result of the London Government Act, 1963, the administration of education in the Greater London area has, from the 1st April, 1965, been radically changed. In Greater London (covering the area of the London and most of the area of Middlesex County Councils, both of which ceased to exist, and parts of Essex, Kent and Surrey and a small part of Hertfordshire) the local education authorities are the twenty outer London boroughs and a special committee of the Greater London Council known as the Inner London Education Authority; the latter covers the area previously administered by the London County Council with the exception of North Woolwich. Membership of the special committee consists of the councillors of the Greater London Council representing the inner London boroughs together with one representative of each inner London borough council and of the Common Council.

Not later than 31st March, 1970, the Secretary of State for Education and Science was required to lay before Parliament a report or review of education in the Inner London Education area; in the light of this review, the Secretary of State may, by regulation, make provision for the transfer of all or any of the functions of the Inner London Education Authority in part or parts of the area to the Common Council and the inner London boroughs, or to a body including a member or members appointed by them, but a draft of these regulations must be approved by resolution of each House of Parliament. However, the need for review and for any subsequent action was removed by legislation in 1967 (o).

The arrangements for the inner London area were a compromise; the Royal Commission on Local Government in Greater London (Herbert Commission) recommended that the Greater London Council should be the education authority and that all the new London boroughs should be responsible for the day to day administration of the service. The Government White Paper (Cmnd. 1562) proposed that the outer London boroughs should become local education authorities but that in the centre of London there should be one education authority with a population of the order of two million; however, such was the quality of the education service provided by the London County Council in an area where education had from the outset been planned as a unity that this proposal to dismember it aroused much opposition from many quarters.

The outer London boroughs were required by 1st April, 1966, to prepare revised development plans for primary and secondary education after consulting contiguous areas and after ensuring that account had been taken of children living in one area and attending school in another. Section 31 (8) is concerned with the question of " free trade " between areas for primary, secondary and further education. The new authorities were also required to submit a re-statement of the schemes for further education.

The administration of education in Greater London was unchanged by the Local Government Act 1972, and the provisions with regard to the appointment of education committees and chief education officers apply to the ILEA and the outer London boroughs as they do to other local education authorities. A teacher employed in a school, college or other educational institution maintained or assisted by the ILEA is not disqualified from being a councillor of the Greater London Council for an electoral area in an outer

---

(m) Local Government Act 1974, s. 26, Sch. 5, para. 5.

(n) Among those dealt with have been parental complaints relating to allocation of children to secondary schools.

(o) Local Government (Termination of Reviews) Act, 1967, s. 2.

London borough or from being a member of the council of an inner London borough (p).

General Duties and Powers.—Section 7 of the 1944 Act outlines in general terms the duties of Local Education Authorities as does s. 1 for those of the Secretary of State. They are required " to contribute towards the spiritual, moral, mental and physical development of the community by securing that efficient education " at all stages shall be available to meet the needs of their areas. The stages to be provided are primary, secondary and further education though subsequent legislation enables Local Authorities to organise their educational system in stages other than primary and secondary.

More specifically, Local Authorities must secure that there are sufficient schools in their area and that these must be sufficient in number, character and equipment and offering such variety of instruction and training as may be desirable in view of the different ages, abilities and aptitudes of the pupils. In carrying out this duty they must have regard to the need for providing nursery education, special educational treatment and boarding education for pupils for whom it is considered desirable by their parents and the authority (q). In the exercise of their duties Local Authorities must have regard to the general principle that, so far as is compatible with the provision of efficient instruction and the avoidance of unreasonable public expenditure, pupils should be educated in accordance with the wishes of their parents (r).

In addition to providing education at school, Local Authorities are required to ensure that adequate facilities for further education for persons over compulsory school age are provided (s) and to carry out the directions of the Secretary of State with regard to establishing, maintaining or assisting colleges of education or other institutions for the training of teachers (t).

The remaining duties of Local Education Authorities may be briefly summarised as follows:

1. To appoint a fit person to be chief education officer to the local authority (u).
2. To secure that the school premises of every school maintained by them conform to standards prescribed by the Secretary of State and to provide for the health and safety of staff and pupils (a).
3. To ascertain which children in their area require special educational treatment (b).
4. To provide facilities to the Secretary of State for Health and Social Security for the medical and dental inspection of pupils in schools and students in establishments of further education (c).
5. To make instruments and rules of management for every county primary school and instruments and articles of government for every county secondary school, special school, establishment of further education and college of education maintained by the authority (d).
6. To provide for collective worship and religious instruction in every county school in accordance with an agreed syllabus and to provide facilities for denominational religious instruction in certain cases in a county secondary school (e).

(p) Local Government Act 1972, s. 81 (3).
(q) Education Act 1944, s. 8.
(r) *Ibid.*, s. 76.
(s) *Ibid.*, s. 41.
(t) *Ibid.*, s. 62.
(u) *Ibid.*, s. 88; Local Government Act 1972, Sch. 30.
(a) Education Act 1944, s. 10. In certain circumstances the Secretary of State may accept lower standards: Education (Miscellaneous Provisions) Act 1948, s. 7 (1); Education Act 1968, s. 3 (3).
(b) *Ibid.*, s. 34.
(c) National Health Service Reorganisation Act 1973, s. 3.
(d) Education Act 1944, s. 17; Education (No. 2) Act 1968, ss. 1, 2.
(e) Education Act 1944, ss. 25, 26.

7. To provide, in accordance with regulations, milk, meals and other refreshments in schools maintained by the authority (f).
8. To require parents to cause their children of compulsory school age to receive efficient full-time education and to enforce the regular attendance of their children at school (g).
9. To secure that the person or clothing of any pupil found to be infested with vermin or in a foul condition shall be cleansed at suitable premises by suitable persons with suitable appliances (h).
10. To make arrangements for the provision of such free transport as the authority thinks necessary or as the Secretary of State may direct to facilitate the attendance of pupils at schools, colleges or classes or to pay the reasonable expenses of such pupils (i).
11. To provide a careers service for those attending, full or part time, educational institutions other than a university (k).
12. To make awards, in accordance with regulations, to students attending university or comparable courses, undertaking training for teaching and pursuing full time courses for the diploma of higher education or the higher national diploma (l).
13. To supervise the employment of children under the upper limit of compulsory school age (m).
14. To make arrangements to ensure the health and safety of pupils, students and teachers at educational institutions maintained by the authority (n).

In addition to these *duties* local education authorities are given certain *powers* which they may exercise if it seems to them desirable; subject in most cases either to the approval of the Secretary of State, or in accordance with regulations made by him.

1. To establish a new school, to maintain as a county school a school not at the time such a school or to cease to maintain a school (o).
2. To arrange for the grouping of schools under one management (p).
3. To give directions as to the use of the premises of a voluntary school subject to the limitations imposed by the Act (q).
4. To control the secular instruction in every county school and every voluntary school except an aided secondary school, save in so far as may be otherwise provided in the rules of management or articles of government (r).
5. To control the appointment of teachers in county schools, and subject to the provisions with regard to religious education, in controlled and special agreement schools, save in so far as may be otherwise provided by the rules of management or articles of government (s).
6. To provide board and lodging for a pupil if in their opinion education suited to his age, ability and aptitude can best be so provided (t).
7. To provide such clothing as is necessary to enable a pupil to take full advantage of the education provided at a school maintained by them (u).
8. To make special arrangements for the education of a child or young person otherwise than at school where owing to extra-

(f) *Ibid.*, s. 49. (g) *Ibid.*, ss. 37, 40.
(h) *Ibid.*, s. 54. (i) *Ibid.*, s. 55.
(k) Employment and Training Act 1973, ss. 8–10.
(l) Education Act 1962, s. 1; Education Act 1975, s. 1.
(m) Employment of Children Act 1973, s. 2.
(n) Health and Safety at Work etc. Act 1974, ss. 4, 52.
(o) Education Act 1944, s. 13. (p) *Ibid.*, s. 20.
(q) *Ibid.*, s. 22. (r) *Ibid.*, s. 23.
(s) *Ibid.*, s. 24. (t) *Ibid.*, s. 50.
(u) Education (Miscellaneous Provisions) Act, 1948, s. 5.

ordinary circumstances he is unable to attend a suitable school (a).

9. To cause an inspection to be made of any educational establishment maintained by them, such inspections to be made by officers appointed by the authority (b).
10. To arrange with the proprietor of a school in their area not maintained by them, upon such financial and other terms as may be agreed, for providing milk, meals and other refreshments at the school, or for providing clothing for any pupil at the school who is inadequately clothed (c).
11. To defray such expenses of children at schools maintained by them, or at special schools, as may be necessary to enable them to take part in any school activities, to pay the fees and expenses of children at schools at which fees are payable (d).
12. To bestow awards on persons over compulsory school age attending, full or part-time, courses of further education (e).
13. To arrange for work experience for pupils in the last year of their compulsory attendance at school (f).
14. To make such provision for conducting or assisting the conduct of research as appears to them desirable for improving the educational facilities provided for their area and to participate in the organisation of conferences for the discussion of questions relating to education (g).
15. To provide financial assistance to any university or university college (h).
16. To accept gifts for educational purposes (i).
17. To purchase compulsorily any land which is required for the purposes of their functions under the Act (k).

3. THE DUTY OF THE LOCAL EDUCATION AUTHORITY TO PROVIDE EDUCATION

Between 1902 and 1944 there were two parallel forms of education provided by Local Education Authorities—elementary and secondary. The former catered for the majority of the nation's children from the age of 5 to 14. In those authorities which had implemented the recommendations of the Hadow report (l) there were senior schools for pupils aged 11–14 and junior schools for the age groups up to 11. Where reorganisation had not taken place, children received all their education from the age of 5 to 14 in the same school. Secondary schools were attended by fee-paying children together with a minority who were admitted to free places on selection by examination at the age of 11. In addition there were in large urban areas a number of technical and trade schools, normally housed in the local technical college, providing a general education combined with vocationally oriented courses for pupils over the age of 11.

This socially and academically divisive system was transformed by the 1944 Act which stated that the statutory system of education was to be organised in three successive stages to be known as primary, secondary and further education (m). The first two stages, based on the Hadow principle

---

(a) Education Act, 1944, s. 56.
(b) *Ibid.*, s. 77 (3).
(c) *Ibid.*, s. 78 and Education (Miscellaneous Provisions) Act 1948, s. 5.
(d) Education Act 1944, s. 81. Education Act 1962, s. 4 (4).
(e) Education Act 1962, s. 2.
(f) Education (Work Experience) Act 1973, s. 1.
(g) Education Act 1944, s. 82.
(h) *Ibid.*, s. 84.
(i) *Ibid.*, s. 85.
(k) *Ibid.*, s. 90.
(l) Report of the Consultative Committee on the Education of the Adolescent 1926.
(m) Education Act 1944, s. 7.

that children should change schools at about the age of 11, were to provide free schooling for all children up to the age of 15 and ultimately to the age of sixteen. Local Authorities were required to arrange for the transfer of children from primary to secondary schools between the ages of ten years six months and twelve years.

As a preliminary, they were required to prepare development plans (n) for the approval of the Secretary of State showing how they proposed to implement this part of the Act together with proposals for nursery education, special schools and boarding accommodation. In addition the plans had to show which school buildings with suitable alterations could be made to conform to the prescribed standards, which needed replacement—inevitably the majority since many schools dated back to the previous century—and what new schools were required.

In preparing their development plans, Local Education Authorities encountered three separate problems: lack of information about future patterns of settlement arising out of the growth and movement of population; the difficulty of separating primary from secondary education without additional buildings: and finally, lack of time to consider their future policy with regard to the structure desirable for mass secondary education. Until the early sixties, development plans remained the framework within which Local Education Authorities were required to draw up building programmes; movements of population and changing ideas about education rendered them virtually obsolete thereafter. The following pages outline the structure of nursery, primary and secondary education as it has developed since 1944.

It should be noted that the duty of the authority to secure that there shall be sufficient schools available for their area does not necessarily mean that they must themselves provide or even maintain all such schools. Before submitting their Development Plan to the former Minister they had to take into consideration *all* schools available for providing primary and secondary education (o). The interpretation clause (p) defines " school " as an institution . . . maintained by a local education authority, an independent school, or a school in respect of which grants are made by the Secretary of State to the proprietor of the school; and the expression " school " where used without qualification includes any such school, or all such schools as the context may require. The authority may, therefore, establish schools themselves (q) (and if no other persons or bodies establish or have established sufficient schools they *must* establish sufficient schools themselves); they may maintain schools established by other persons or bodies in which case they are responsible for all the expenses of maintaining the school, except, in the case of an aided or special agreement school, any expenses which under the provisions of the Act are payable by the managers or governors (r); they may assist any school established by other persons or bodies, by making to the proprietor a grant or payment in consideration of the provision of facilities at the school (s). They may nominate pupils to occupy " free " or " reserved " places at schools to which the Secretary of State makes grants (t) and they may pay the fees of pupils at independent schools. If they send a pupil to an independent school because they cannot provide suitable education for him at one of their own schools, or at a school maintained by another authority, they must pay the whole of the school fees, including the boarding fees where necessary. In other cases, to avoid hardship, they may assist the parent by paying the whole or part of the fees according to his income (u). The powers of an authority under the Act

(n) *Ibid.*, s. 11.
(o) Education Act 1944, s. 11 (2).
(p) *Ibid.*, s. 114.
(q) *Ibid.*, s. 9 (1).
(r) *Ibid.*, s. 114 (2) (*a*).
(s) *Ibid.*, ss. 9 (1), 114 (2) (*b*); see also s. 11 (2) (*d*).
(t) *Ibid.*, s. 100 (1) (*b*).
(u) Scholarships and other Benefits Regs., S.R. & O. 1945 No. 666; and Education (Miscellaneous Provisions) Act 1953, s. 6, but see p. 31 for recent developments.

include power to establish, maintain and assist schools outside as well as inside their areas (a).

Nursery education.—Recent developments make it desirable to consider nursery education, which is part of primary education, separately from the other stages of schooling.

It is defined in the Act as education for children over two years of age but under five years of age: it may be provided in nursery schools or in nursery classes attached to primary schools (b). Prior to 1944, Local Education Authorities had the power but not the duty to provide for this age group. Between the wars, a number of nursery schools had been established by local authorities, mainly in areas which would now be regarded as areas of social priority and there were also nursery classes in elementary schools. During the war there was a great expansion in the provision of nursery classes in order to enable the mothers of young children to work.

By the 1944 Act (c), it became the duty of Local Education Authorities to provide nursery education, and their development plans included proposals for it. However, shortage of resources after the war precluded any implementation of these proposals. Instead of an expansion in nursery education there was a great reduction because the increased birth rate led to pressure on accommodation in primary schools with the consequence that nursery classes virtually disappeared.

As late as 1960 the Secretary of State, in reply to a campaign for nursery education, stated that he could not approve any increase in nursery places (d). Four years later, a shortage of teachers led to a concession whereby local authorities were permitted to establish nursery classes if they contained a proportion of children of married women teachers wishing to return to teaching and provided that no new building was required.

In 1967 a new era began when the Plowden and Gittins (e) reports made strong recommendations for a considerable expansion of nursery education; for the first time a number of proposals for nursery places, specifically for educational priority areas, were approved in that year's building programme. In the following year, the Urban Aid programme, designed to assist areas of stress (i.e. areas of overcrowded housing or with a substantial proportion of immigrants on the school roll) in inner city areas, included the provision of further nursery places as did the Urban Aid programmes in succeeding years (f).

National policy changed radically in 1973 when the Secretary of State announced her intention (g) of expanding nursery education at a rate which would permit provision to be made by 1982 up to the limit recommended by the Plowden report (for 90% of four year olds and 50% of three year olds). Places were to be available for three and four year old children only, preferably in nursery classes attached to primary schools; the Secretary of State suggested that the majority of pupils should attend part-time. She also expressed the hope that means would be found of encouraging the further development of voluntary playgroups, at least until nursery education became more widely available, and of enlisting the active co-operation and support of parents whose children attended nursery schools and classes.

Despite the enthusiasm of Local Education Authorities for the expansion of nursery education, it is doubtful whether the economic climate of the late seventies will permit them to achieve the target by 1982.

(a) Education Act 1944, s. 9 (6).
(b) *Ibid.*, s. 8 (2) (*b*) and s. 9 (4).
(c) *Ibid.*, s. 8 (2) (*b*).
(d) DES Circular 8/60.
(e) *Children and their Primary Schools* 1967; *Primary Education in Wales* 1967.
(f) Some authorities increased their pre-school provision by giving interest-free loans to voluntary groups wishing to set up nurseries: others gave grants to pre-school playgroups and some experimented with joint day nurseries and nursery school projects.
(g) *Education: A Framework for Expansion* 1972, Cmnd. 5174. See also DES Circular 2/73.

Primary and secondary education.—The Education Act 1944 defines *primary* education as full-time education suitable for junior pupils and *secondary* education as full-time education appropriate to the needs of senior pupils other than full-time education which may be provided for senior pupils in institutions of further education (h).

Children become of statutory school age at the beginning of the term after that in which they attain the age of five; they cease to be of statutory school age at sixteen (i). Schools or classes mainly for children under eight years of age must provide a minimum of three hours secular instruction daily, divided into two sessions; for children over eight the minimum is four hours similarly divided (k).

Until 1964 primary and secondary schools were organised on the basis of a break at about the age of eleven, thus fulfilling the requirements of the Act that there should be two distinct stages of education—primary followed by secondary. In that year amending legislation (l) permitted the establishment of schools with special age limits, i.e. schools for children ranging in age from under ten years six months to over twelve years. Subsequent legislation (m) extended this provision by allowing Local Education Authorities to convert an existing school into a school with these age limits. These schools are termed middle schools. They are administered either as primary or secondary schools, since, in approving proposals for middle schools, the Secretary of State directs that they shall be deemed either a primary or a secondary school (n). Normally middle schools provide a four-year course extending from eight years to twelve, or nine years to thirteen.

Local authorities were, in 1944, faced with an enormous task in providing education for children over the age of eleven in secondary schools; most authorities maintained grammar schools which admitted special place holders and fee-payers while the remaining children of secondary school age attended senior elementary schools with a few transferring at the age of thirteen to technical schools often housed in the local technical colleges; some authorities, however, had not reorganised their elementary schools into junior and senior schools and were quite unable to provide education for senior pupils in schools separate from primary schools.

The nature of secondary education required to meet the needs of all children was a matter which had not seriously been considered; the only sources of ideas available were the Spens (o) and Norwood (p) reports and the White Paper of 1943, all of which appeared to envisage what has become known as the tripartite system: grammar schools for " bookish " children who would complete a seven-year course; technical high schools for children with a practical bent; modern schools for the rest.

It was generally realised that to select children at the age of eleven for one or other of these types of schools was a difficult and invidious task, but owing to lack of time authorities had little alternative other than to draw up their plans on the basis of a tripartite scheme with their existing secondary schools forming a ready-made system of grammar schools. Several authorities decided to leave the question open by planning to build different

(h) Education Act 1944, s. 8; Education (Miscellaneous Provisions) Act 1948, s. 4. A junior pupil is a child who has not attained the age of twelve; a senior pupil is a person who has attained the age of twelve but has not attained the age of nineteen (Education Act 1944, s. 114).

(i) Education Act 1944, s. 35; Education (Miscellaneous Provisions) Act 1948, s. 4. The term in which a child ceases to be of statutory school age depends on the date of his sixteenth birthday (Education Act 1962, s. 9, modified by the Education (School Leaving Dates) 1976: see DES circular 4/76). The school-leaving age was raised to sixteen in the school year 1972–73.

(k) Schools Regulations, S.I. 1959 No. 364.

(l) Education Act 1964, s. 1 (1).

(m) Education Act 1968, s. 2.

(n) Education Act 1964, s. 1 (2). In practice, schools for pupils aged 8–12 years are deemed primary schools while those for pupils aged 9–13 years are deemed secondary schools.

(o) *Secondary Education with Special Reference to Grammar Schools and Technical High Schools* 1938.

(p) *Curriculum and Examinations in Secondary Schools* 1943.

types of schools on the same campus; others adopted a policy of bilateral (grammar/technical, technical/modern) schools; and the London County Council, looking to the U.S.A., planned large comprehensive schools providing education for all ranges of ability and courses of all types.

Meanwhile, with the abolition of fees, authorities were confronted with the problem of ensuring that entrants to grammar schools had the appropriate abilities and aptitudes for the academic courses provided there. To prevent primary schools from " cramming " and to give better opportunities to children from less cultured homes, most authorities adopted very similar types of selection examination, consisting of standardised tests, known in popular language as " the eleven-plus ". The procedure for selection was gradually modified and most authorities adopted, in addition to or instead of tests, the child's school record and teachers' assessments. The method of transfer from primary to secondary schools was entirely a matter for local authorities and the central authority has never given any guidance or overruled an authority's decision about a child.

Technical high schools were not established on the scale envisaged although there were a few highly successful schools of this type. Modern schools, particularly those in new buildings, showed that there were real possibilities of providing a sound and challenging education for the majority of children, and the creative work done in these schools was often of a high order. Provision of a genuine secondary education for all children was however retarded by the inability of local authorities, owing to a shortage of resources, to replace or improve the old senior elementary schools or even in some cases to make possible the division of education into primary and secondary stages. Moreover, during the late fifties and early sixties dissatisfaction was growing in many quarters with the selective basis of the organisation of secondary education. The Leicestershire Plan attracted much attention and the Croydon proposals for sixth-form colleges aroused lively discussion. Comprehensive schools were established by a number of authorities particularly in areas where a large demand for new secondary places had been created by the building of large new housing estates. Other authorities decided to reorganise their schools on comprehensive lines as and when new buildings made this possible.

The initiative for developing new forms of secondary education was removed from local authorities in 1965 with the issue of DES Circular 10/65. In this circular the Secretary of State requested all authorities to submit for his approval schemes of reorganisation designed to eliminate selection at eleven plus and to provide education for all levels of ability (except the handicapped) in comprehensive schools. Various ways in which this might be achieved were outlined in the circular. Once again authorities encountered great difficulties in drawing up schemes when they had at their disposal only buildings intended for other types of organisation: the necessity to include voluntary aided schools in their schemes was another major source of difficulty. In the year after the issue of this circular local authorities were informed that no new secondary building projects could be approved which were incompatible with the introduction of a non-selective system of education (q).

Although reorganisation is as yet far from complete, various distinctive patterns are emerging:—

—all through schools for children aged 11–18
—first schools for children up to the age of 8 or 9 years, middle schools for children aged 8 or 9 to 12 or 13 years and upper schools for older pupils
—schools for children aged 11–16 followed by education either in a sixth form college or a college of further education.

(q) DES Circular 10/66.

Owing to local preference or the nature of the buildings available, a number of county authorities have adopted different methods of organisation in different parts of their area.

Because a minority of authorities were reluctant to submit schemes under Circular 10/65 or submitted schemes retaining an element of selection, the then Secretary of State proposed, in 1969, to introduce compulsion by means of legislation. His intentions were frustrated by a change in Government. The new Secretary of State reversed this policy by issuing Circular 8/70, removing from authorities any obligation to submit schemes or to implement such schemes as had been approved but not carried out.

With the next change in Government, this circular was withdrawn in 1974; authorities and governors of voluntary schools were requested to submit (r) to the Secretary of State by the end of that year schemes for the organisation of secondary education on a non-selective basis. At the same time the governors of voluntary schools were informed that they could not " expect to continue to receive the substantial financial aid which their schools enjoy through being maintained by the local education authority if they are not prepared to co-operate with that authority in settling the general educational character of the school and its place in a local comprehensive system ". The Secretary of State also indicated that, contrary to previously held opinion, there was no need for a comprehensive school to be large and that proposals for small schools would be acceptable. At the time of writing (s) some authorities are still unwilling to submit schemes and a Bill is passing through Parliament which will compel all local authorities to organise their secondary education on comprehensive lines.

Some new authorities created by the Local Government Act 1972 have inherited on amalgamation a variety of patterns of secondary education from previous authorities; the Secretary of State left it to authorities to decide whether to unify their system or whether to continue with different systems in different parts of their area.

Special education.—Local education authorities are required to make provision for children who suffer any disability of mind or body by providing for them special educational treatment, i.e. education by special methods appropriate to their handicap (t). Schools which are specially organised for this purpose are known as special schools (u), but it should be noted that special educational treatment is not confined to that given in special schools and that not all special schools are maintained by local authorities, though schools not so maintained must be recognised as special schools by the Secretary of State.

Under the Education Act 1944 (a), there were certain children whose disability of mind or body was so severe that they were regarded as unsuitable for education in any school; this provision no longer obtains and all children of school age, however severely handicapped, are now the responsibility of the local education authority (b).

The establishment and discontinuance of schools.—Decision-making as to the opening and closure of schools has long proved contentious. Procedures for publication of public notices, registration of local objections, and exercise of ministerial direction were first laid down in the Education Act 1902 and redefined in various acts prior to 1944. Section 13 of the

---

(r) DES Circular 4/74.
(s) February, 1976.
(t) Education Act 1944, s. 8.
(u) *Ibid.*, s. 9.
(a) *Ibid.*, ss. 57 followed by 57A, 57B (inserted by the Mental Health Act 1959), all repealed—see note (b).
(b) Education (Handicapped Children) Act 1970. For a more detailed discussion of special educational treatment, see p. 28.

Education Act 1944, the section concerned with these procedures, has proved to be one of the Act's most controversial sections; only s. 76 dealing with parental rights in the choice of school has provoked more argument and public debate.

In calling upon Local Education Authorities to prepare development plans indicating the new schools they proposed to establish and the obsolete or redundant ones they intended to close, the Education Act 1944, presented an early example of structural planning (incidentally the concept of periodic review was not followed up: movements of population rendered development plans obsolete but there was no provision for their up-dating). Section 13, on the other hand, was backward-looking: it was conceived in terms of conflict of interest between Local Education Authorities and the managers of voluntary schools: it did not take into account the plans of an authority for the whole or part of its area, and it has remained unaltered in substance despite changes in the nature of disputes that arose.

In its original form, the section requires local authorities proposing to (1) establish a new county school (2) maintain as a county school a school not previously so maintained or (3) cease to maintain a county or voluntary school, to submit proposals to that effect to the Secretary of State. Similarly any persons proposing that a school not being a voluntary school established by them should be maintained as a voluntary school must, after consultation with the local authority, submit proposals to the Secretary of State. Public notice must be given of the proposals after they have been submitted. It is open to the managers or governors of any voluntary school likely to be affected by the proposals or any ten or more local government electors (c) to lodge objections with the Secretary of State within two months (d) of the publication of the notice. At the conclusion of this period the proposals may be approved by the Secretary of State after making such modifications, if any, as appear to him to be desirable.

A local authority may not do anything in relation to these proposals until they are approved; after approval has been received, the Authority or the persons proposing to establish a school must submit specifications and plans of the school premises to the Secretary of State. When these have been approved by him, the local authority or the persons responsible for the proposals are under an obligation to implement them.

Where the proposals for the maintenance of a voluntary school are approved by the Secretary of State, the Authority is required to maintain the school but is under no obligation to maintain any school after proposals for ceasing to maintain it have been approved by the Secretary of State.

It is clear, therefore, that the respective duties of the Secretary of State and the local authority in relation to the establishment of new schools and the closure of existing ones are well defined in s. 13. Few problems arose until the middle of the sixties when reorganisation of secondary education on comprehensive lines caused considerable controversy concerning the interpretation of s. 13, resulting in appeals to the courts and amendments to the section. Reorganisation involved not only the opening and closing of schools but also the enlargement of existing schools or a change in their character or both, changes for which public notice was not required by s. 13. The amendments to the section were concerned with this aspect of reorganisation.

The main amendments made by the Education Act 1968 are:

(1) where a significant enlargement of an existing school is proposed by an authority or by managers or governors; the same procedure must be followed as in the establishment of a new school (e).

(c) See note (i).
(d) Education (Miscellaneous Provisions) Act 1953, s. 16.
(e) Education Act 1968, s. 1 (2) *(a)* *(b)*.

(2) where a significant change in the character of a school is proposed by an authority or the managers or governors, the same procedure as for the establishment of a new school applies (f),

(3) a significant change in the character of a school includes altering the age limits of children attending the school, converting the school from a single sex to a co-educational school or vice versa, and changing the basis of admission to the school (g),

(4) the question as to whether an enlargement or a change in the character of a school is significant is a matter for determination by the Secretary of State (h).

Despite these clarifying amendments, s. 13 remains an obstacle to the planned use of resources because it perpetuates a procedure of public notice and approval based on each school being regarded as " an island to itself ". For example, when an authority propose to merge two schools, public notice must be given of the closure of one school and the enlargement of the other. If an authority's plans affect an area containing several schools, s. 13 allows local government electors (i) to object to one or more changes proposed in the plan; similarly it enables the Secretary of State to reject one unit in the plan or to make modifications for an individual school as seem desirable to him. Such modifications can have the effect of nullifying the plan as a whole (k).

The managers or governors of a voluntary school who propose to discontinue the school may not do so except after serving not less than two years' notice of their intention on the Secretary of State and on the local education authority and, if expenditure has been incurred on the premises by the Secretary of State or by a local education authority or a former authority, they may not serve notice that they propose to discontinue the school without leave of the Secretary of State, who may impose such requirements as he thinks just in regard to the repayment of grants made by him, to the conveyance of the premises to the authority, to the payment by the authority for the premises conveyed, and, if the premises are not conveyed to the authority, in regard to payments to be made by the managers or governors to the authority (l). Once notice has been given it may not be withdrawn except with the consent of the local education authority. If, while the notice is in force, the managers or governors inform the authority that they are unable or unwilling to carry on the school until the expiration of the notice, the authority may conduct the school as a county school during the unexpired period of the notice. During that time, the authority must keep the school in good repair, and the interest in the school premises will be deemed to be vested in the authority, but the managers or governors will be entitled to the use of the premises when not required for the purposes of the school to the same extent as they would if they had continued to carry on the school. When the period of the notice has expired the duty of the local education authority to maintain the school will be extinguished. The two years' notice is needed in order that the local education authority may, during that time, make provision for alternative school accommodation for the pupils attending the school it is proposed to discontinue, if such

---

(f) *Ibid.*

(g) *Ibid.*

(h) *Ibid.*, Sch. 1.

(i) In August 1973 the Secretary of State issued a press statement asserting that she was entitled to take into account objections to proposals from persons or bodies other than local government electors, managers or governors even if these were received after the lapse of two months. This interpretation of the Secretary of State's powers has not been tested in the courts.

(k) See *Legg* v. *Inner London Education Authority*, [1972] 3 All E.R. 177. In the judgment it was held that the ministerial " modification " had eaten away so much of the original proposals made by the ILEA that what the Secretary of State purported to approve amounted to decisions so different from the proposals originally submitted that they could no longer be regarded as modifications: consequently approval was invalid. Furthermore it was held that the public notice of proposals must provide adequate information not only of a local authority's intentions but also of the implications of the proposals. See DES Circular 6/70 Addendum No. 1.

(l) Education Act 1944, s. 14 (1), as amended by the Education Act 1946.

accommodation is necessary. It is important to remember that though proposals to establish or discontinue a school may have been included in the Development Plan, and may have been approved in that Plan, that will not render it unnecessary to submit the proposals to the Secretary of State and give public notice in the way just described. A local education authority may not, without the leave of the Secretary of State, even undertake to establish or cease to maintain a school unless proposals are submitted to the Secretary of State in this way (m).

It may be convenient here to mention the power of a local education authority, by means of an order confirmed by the Secretary of State, to purchase compulsorily any land for a school or college which the authority propose to maintain. They may thus use this power not only for schools which they propose to establish, but also for voluntary and assisted schools and colleges, so long as no expenditure that should be borne by the managers or governors ultimately falls to be borne by the authority in the case of land purchased for a voluntary school. The compulsory acquisition of land is now governed by the Acquisition of Land (Authorisation Procedure) Act, 1946, and the Secretary of State for Education and Science, who is the authority having the power to authorise the purchase, is the authority to whom the compulsory purchase must be submitted for confirmation. An authority may also purchase land by agreement for the purpose of a voluntary or assisted school (n).

4. THE CLASSIFICATION OF SCHOOLS AND THEIR ADMINISTRATION

One of the principal characteristics of schooling in England and Wales is the wide variety of types of schools; this can be accounted for only by its history. Long before the state took upon itself the obligation to make provision for the education of children, churches, private individuals, city companies (particularly in London), and other philanthropic bodies had established and maintained schools. Many schools still preserve a distinctiveness due to their origins; it may be observed that some of their distinctive features appear to be inappropriate in the egalitarian climate of the last quarter of the twentieth century and are being eroded.

Grammar schools before 1944.—Prior to 1944, schools could be broadly classified as either elementary or secondary, each containing widely differing types of schools. Let us consider the latter first. Until 1902, secondary education was provided in endowed grammar schools. Some of these were boarding schools and had become known as " public " (o) schools (though not all boarding schools were public schools and not all public schools were boarding schools). After 1902, local authorities had the power to supply or aid the supply of secondary or " higher education " as it was termed during this period. As a result they themselves provided many new day secondary schools whose methods and outlook were based on those of the endowed schools. By 1944 these secondary schools, which provided an ever-increasing proportion of free or " special " places, had proved highly successful academic institutions. Some endowed grammar schools admitted a number of children from elementary schools and in return received financial assistance from local authorities; others, admitting a smaller proportion of

---

(m) Education Act, 1944, s. 13 (5).

(n) *Ibid.*, s. 90, as amended by the Education (Misc. Prov.) Act, 1948, s. 10. The forms to be used in the case of a compulsory purchase made by a Local Education Authority are set out in the Compulsory Purchase of Land Regulations, 1946 (S.R. & O. 1946 No. 573 as amended by S.R. & O. 1947 No. 121). See also Circular 2/60 (1.3.1960) and Admin. Memo. No. 1/60.

(o) As to the terms public school and direct grant school generally, see chapters 1 and 2 and chapters 4 and 5 of the First and Second Reports respectively of the Public Schools Commission (1968 and 1970).

such children, received a grant from the Board of Education; others accepted grants from the local authority and from the Board, while many retained their complete independence and accepted no assistance from rates or taxes.

Elementary schools before 1944.—Early in the nineteenth century, religious bodies founded schools for the elementary instruction of the "labouring poor"; they received their income from voluntary subscriptions and fees, assisted after 1833 by annual grants from the state. In 1870 school boards were set up with power to levy a rate for the purpose of establishing and maintaining schools in districts not served by a voluntary school. Consequently between 1870 and 1902 there was a dual system of board schools and of church schools completely separate in control and finance one from the other.

The Education Act 1902 gave responsibility for the maintenance costs (teachers' salaries, books, equipment etc), of all public elementary schools, i.e. provided and non-provided schools, to the new Local Education Authorities, leaving the managers of the non-provided schools to find the money for repairs, alterations and improvements to their buildings. The Local Education Authority was made responsible for the efficiency of the secular education given in these schools, but the managers retained the right to appoint teachers (subject to the approval of the authority which could not be withheld except on educational grounds) and to control the religious instruction, which was given in accordance with the trust deed of the school.

During the period 1902–1944, serious problems arose owing to the growing divergence between the standards of premises of schools provided by the Local Education Authority and of non-provided or voluntary schools, many of which, often older than the former board schools, were substandard. Their managers, dependent on parish funds, were generally unable to fulfil their obligations for repairs and improvements. In addition, owing to lack of financial resources, managers could not consider building new senior schools for reorganisation on Hadow lines; to overcome this difficulty the Education Act 1936 enabled Local Education Authorities to enter into agreements with managers to make grants of between 50% and 75% of the cost of erection or extension of non-provided schools for senior pupils. In order to build senior schools of an economical size, it was necessary for the managers of two or more schools to co-operate in proposals for a new school; co-operation was slow in forthcoming and little progress in entering into agreements had been made by 1939 when the war stopped all new building.

Types of schools since 1944.—Under the Education Act 1944, the system of two overlapping types of elementary and secondary schools was replaced by the two successive stages of primary and secondary schools. But the dual system of provided and non-provided schools was continued in a new form and with a new nomenclature. The term "provided" was replaced by "county".

County schools.—County schools may be defined as those schools maintained by a Local Education Authority and established by the Authority or by an education authority under previous statutes (p). The whole cost of providing the premises, improving or enlarging them and of keeping them in good repair is, of course, borne by the Authority. It should be noted that the majority of primary and secondary schools in England and Wales are county schools (17,420 county and 8657 voluntary schools in 1974).

Voluntary schools.—A school maintained by a Local Education Authority but not established by them is known as a voluntary school (q).

(p) Education Act 1944, s. 9 (2).
(q) *Ibid.*, s. 9 (3).

There are three types of such schools according to the method selected for receiving financial assistance for the cost of repairs, alterations and improvements to their buildings and, in the case of a new school, for the cost of establishing it.

The three types are controlled schools, aided schools and special agreement schools (r). The managers or governors of voluntary schools already in existence in 1944 seeking aided or special agreement status had to satisfy the Secretary of State within a prescribed period of their ability to observe the conditions attaching to schools in these categories; if they were able to do so, the Secretary of State was required to direct that the school should be an aided or special agreement school (s). The remaining voluntary schools became controlled schools (t). Whatever category was chosen, no transfer of property or ownership was involved.

Apart from the method of receiving financial assistance these three types of schools differ in other respects, e.g. the nature of religious education given, the appointment and dismissal of teachers and the use of premises outside school hours. These differences are dealt with later under the appropriate headings.

Controlled schools.—The managers or governors of a controlled school are not usually responsible for any expenditure in connection with the school (u). It is the duty of the local education authority to maintain the school, to provide any site and playing fields in addition to or in substitution for the existing site and to provide any buildings which are to form part of the school premises. If the authority provide a site they must convey their interest in it to such persons as the Secretary of State may direct to be held in trust for the purposes of the school; playing fields, however, provided by the authority remain the property of the authority (a).

The premises of a controlled school may not be enlarged significantly without the consent of the local authority and the Secretary of State. Before approving a proposal for enlargement, the local authority and the Secretary of State must be satisfied that the enlargement is mainly required for pupils for whom places would have been available in another voluntary school if that school had not ceased to be available, or that the enlargement is required for the better provision of primary or secondary education at the school, or for the provision of additional primary or secondary places in the area served by the school. If the proposal for enlargement is approved, the Secretary of State may direct that the expenses incurred shall be paid by the local authority (b).

A new controlled school may be established with the approval of the local authority and the Secretary of State provided that the latter is satisfied that the new school is required for the purpose of providing places for pupils who would have attended other voluntary schools if they had not ceased to be available (c). The exception to this provision relates to a new controlled middle school where it must be shown that the new school will accommodate pupils who, or a substantial proportion of whom, would have attended other voluntary schools if they had not ceased to be available (d). In either case the Secretary of State may direct that the local authority meet the whole or part of the cost of the school (e).

(r) *Ibid.*, s. 15 (1).
(s) *Ibid.*, s. 15 (2).
(t) *Ibid.*, s. 15 (2) proviso.
(u) *Ibid.*, s. 15 (3).
(a) Education Act 1946, Sch. 1.
(b) Education Act 1946, s. 1 (1); Education (Miscellaneous Provisions) Act 1953, s. 3; Education Act 1967, s. 2; Education Act 1968, Sch. 1.
(c) Education Act 1953, s. 2.
(d) Education Act 1967, s. 3.
(e) Education Act 1953, s. 2.

The managers or governors of a controlled school (or any other person so entitled by the trust deed) may determine the use to which the school premises (including the playing fields) shall be put on Saturdays unless they are required for the school or for any purpose connected with education or with the welfare of the young for which the local authority desire to provide accommodation. The foundation managers or governors have the right to determine the use made of the premises on Sundays. Subject to these conditions the local authority may give directions as to the occupation and use of the premises (f).

The caretaker and cleaners at a controlled school are appointed and dismissed by the local education authority (g).

Aided schools.—The managers or governors of an aided school are responsible for external repairs and alterations to the school buildings and receive a contribution of 85% towards the cost involved from the Secretary of State. The local authority are responsible for internal repairs to the school buildings and also for the repair and alterations to any other buildings and school grounds and for the maintenance of the playing fields and any buildings connected with them (h).

Capital expenditure in connection with the enlargement or improvement of the school is the responsibility of the managers or governors who receive from the Secretary of State a maintenance contribution of 85% of the cost (i). Any other capital expenditure, e.g. an addition to the existing site, the provision or extension of playing fields is met by the local authority (k).

When an existing school is transferred to a new site, the local authority must provide the new site, meet the cost of the school grounds and of any other buildings other than the school buildings and convey their interest in the site to the managers or governors (l). The managers or governors are required to provide the school buildings; after taking into account any sums received from the disposal of the original site and school premises, the Secretary of State will make a grant of 85% of the cost of the new school buildings (m).

Where a new aided school is established in substitution for one or more existing schools, the new site, school grounds and school buildings must be provided by the managers or governors; the arrangements for grant are similar to those for the transfer of an existing school to a new site. In the case of such a substitution the Authority provide the playing fields and any buildings connected with them (n).

When a new aided school is established, the site, school grounds and school buildings are provided by the managers or governors who will receive a grant of 85% of the cost from the Secretary of State. The Authority must provide any other buildings on the site required for the school, the playing fields and any other buildings required in connection with them (o).

The managers or governors control the occupation and use of the premises when they are not being used for the purposes of the school, but the Authority may direct the managers or governors to provide free of charge accommodation on the school premises for any educational purpose or youth activities for which the Authority wish to provide accommodation.

(f) Education Act 1944 s. 22 (1). See Education Act 1946, s. 4 as regards sums received for letting or hiring of premises.

(g) Education Act 1944, s. 22 (4).

(h) Education Act 1944, s. 15 (3); *ibid.*, s. 102 amended by Education Act 1975, s. 3.

(i) *Ibid.*

(k) Education Act 1946, Sch. 1.

(l) *Ibid.*

(m) Education Act 1944, s. 103 amended by Education Act 1975, s. 3.

(n) Education Act 1944 s. 16 (2).

(o) Education Act 1944, s. 13 (7) amended by Education Act 1968, s. 3 (1) (*b*); Education Act 1967, s. 1 (2) amended by Education Act 1975, s. 3.

The Authority must, however, be satisfied that there is no suitable alternative accommodation and must limit their use to not more than three days a week (p).

The local authority may give directions to the managers or governors as to the number and conditions of service of persons employed for the care and maintenance of the school premises (q); staff employed for the school meals service are appointed to the service of the authority. The method of appointing other non-teaching staff is a matter for agreement between the authority and the managers or governors.

Special agreement schools.—Provision was made in the 1944 Act (r) for proposals, suitably modified where necessary, for new voluntary senior schools made under the Education Act 1936 to be revived. Under this provision Local Education Authorities entered into an agreement with the governors to meet between 50% and 75% of the cost of establishing " special agreement " schools.

There are 131 such schools and all are, of necessity, secondary schools. Since there is no provision in the 1944 Act for the establishment of additional special agreement schools, the only financial arrangements for such schools which need to be considered are for the alteration of an existing school or the significant enlargement of such a school. In both cases the liabilities of governors, the Secretary of State and of the local authority are the same as for aided schools (s). The arrangements for the maintenance of school buildings, playing fields and other buildings are also the same as for aided schools (t). The non-teaching staff, e.g. caretaking and maintenance staff (u), clerical and school meals staff are appointed and dismissed by the local authority which also determines their conditions of service.

The managers or governors of a special agreement school may at any time repay to the local education authority the grant made to them by the authority in accordance with the agreement. They can then apply to the Secretary of State for an order revoking the previous order by which the school became a special agreement school, and if the Secretary of State is satisfied that they will be able and willing with the assistance of the maintenance contribution to defray the expenses for which they would be liable, he must direct that the school shall be an aided school (a). If at any time the managers or governors of either an aided school or of a special agreement school are unable or unwilling to carry out their obligation to pay the expenses of any necessary alterations or repairs for which they are liable, it is their duty to apply to the Secretary of State for an order revoking the order by which the school became an aided school or a special agreement school, and the school will then become a controlled school (b).

It should be noted that the managers and governors of all voluntary schools are required to make available such accommodation as is appropriate for the medical and dental inspection of pupils attending the schools (c) and they must give the local authority the facilities required to provide milk and meals. For this purpose they must allow the Authority to make such use of the premises and equipment at the schools as the Authority considers necessary (d).

(p) Education Act 1944, s. 22 (2) (5).
(q) *Ibid.*, s. 22 (4).
(r) *Ibid.*, s. 15, Sch. 3 amended by Education (Miscellaneous Provisions) Act 1948, s. 11 (1).
(s) Education Act 1944, s. 15 (3).
(t) *Ibid.*
(u) *Ibid.*, s. 22 (4).
(a) *Ibid.*, s. 15 (5).
(b) *Ibid.*, s. 15 (4).
(c) National Health Reorganisation Act 1973, s. 3 (4).
(d) Education Act 1944, s. 49; Provision of Milk and Meals Regulations 1969, S.I. 1969 No. 483.

General.—If any local education authority, or the managers or governors of any county school or any voluntary school fail to discharge any duty imposed upon them by or for the purposes of the Education Act, 1944, the Secretary of State may make an order declaring the authority, the managers or the governors, as the case may be, to be in default. The order will then give directions for the purpose of enforcing the performance of the duty, and such directions are enforceable, on an application made on behalf of the Secretary of State, by mandamus (e). Any person interested may complain to the Secretary of State of the default in question, or he can act upon his own initiative.

If complaint is made that the managers or governors of a school have acted or are proposing to act unreasonably, the Secretary of State may give such directions as he thinks expedient even though the law allows them discretion to act according to their opinion (f). If there is a dispute between the local education authority and the managers or governors in connection with their powers and duties under the Act, the matter may be referred to the Secretary of State and determined by him even though the power or duty is contingent on the opinion of the authority or the managers or governors (g).

The Education Act 1973 has given the Secretary of State powers to modify the trust deeds of schools where it appears to him that modification is necessary in consequence of proposals relating to the establishment of and changes affecting schools (h), or in the case of special schools, to meet requirements imposed by the Secretary of State (i). The managers, governors or proprietor of the school must first be consulted (k).

Where the premises of a voluntary school have ceased, or are likely to cease, to be used as a school the Secretary of State may by order provide for the use of any endowment held, wholly or partly, in connection with the provision of religious education in accordance with a particular denomination. Such an order may only be made on the application of persons appearing to the Secretary of State to be the appropriate authority of the denomination concerned. The order may require or authorise the disposal by sale or otherwise of any land or other property forming part of the endowment including the school premises and teacher's dwelling house. In the case of land liable to revert, the Secretary of State may exclude the operation of the reversion if he is satisfied that the person to whom the land would revert cannot be found or that, if he is found, he has consented to relinquish his rights (l).

Another question connected with the rights and responsibilities of the managers or governors of voluntary schools is that of local rates. Prior to 1944, non-provided elementary schools were exempted from rates but all secondary schools, not provided by a local education authority, and all schools provided by a local education authority, were rated. Section 64 of the Education Act, 1944, exempted all voluntary schools from the payment of rates but this section was repealed by the Rating and Valuation Act,1961. The rating authority has, however, under this Act, power to reduce or remit the payment of rates on schools; since the payment of rates is part of the cost of maintaining a school, such payments are a charge on the local education authority, and whether the rates are remitted or reduced is a matter for settlement between the rating authority and the local education authority.

(e) Education Act 1944, s. 99 (1).
(f) *Ibid.*, s. 68.
(g) *Ibid.*, s. 67 (1).
(h) Proposals approved under Education Act 1944, ss. 13 and 16.
(i) *Ibid.*, s. 33.
(k) Education Act 1973, s. 1.
(l) *Ibid.*, s. 2.

MANAGERS AND GOVERNORS

Managers of primary schools.—Prior to the 1944 Act all elementary schools not provided by a Local Education Authority were required to have a body of managers, but a local authority was not obliged to establish a body of managers for the schools it provided. This difference between provided and non-provided schools was abolished by the 1944 Act, and all primary schools, both county and voluntary, must have a body of managers.

A county primary school has a body of managers constituted by an instrument of management made by order of the local education authority (m). Membership of the managers is at the discretion of the authority except that where a school serves the area of a minor authority the instrument must provide for a body of managers not less than six in number of which two thirds are appointed by the Local Education Authority and the remainder by the minor authority (n).

A voluntary school must have a body of managers constituted by an instrument of management made by order of the Secretary of State (o). In the case of aided and controlled schools the number of managers must be not less than six of which for aided schools two thirds are foundation managers (p) and one third appointed by the Local Education Authority; for controlled schools the proportions are reversed. Where the school serves the area of a minor authority, between one third and one half of the non-foundation managers are appointed by the Local Education Authority and the reminder by the minor authority (q).

Every county and voluntary primary school must be conducted in accordance with the rules of management made by order of the local authority. In general, the rules of management determine the relationship between the local authority, the managers and the head teacher (r).

Governors. (a) Secondary schools.—Like elementary schools, secondary schools provided by a Local Education Authority were not required to have a body of governors prior to 1944; schools not so provided normally had governors set up under the Endowed Schools Acts or the Charitable Trusts Acts. The Education Act of 1944 unified the system of all secondary schools, county and voluntary, maintained by an authority.

Every county secondary school must have a body of governors constituted by an instrument of government made by order of the Local Education Authority (s). Membership is determined by the Authority; it was suggested that each body should contain a university representative and members associated with the commercial and industrial life of the area (t). During the last few years the composition and functions of governing bodies have been increasingly challenged; there have been demands for the inclusion of the head teacher, representatives of the teaching staff, of parents and pupils; some authorities had anticipated these demands, others have acceded to some of them. The question of membership by pupils has not been resolved since it is extremely doubtful whether a pupil under eighteen years of age can legally be a member of a governing body. Where pupils over this age have been appointed, the extent of their participation in the proceedings of the governors has been strictly prescribed. In 1975 the Secretary of State

(m) Education Act 1944, ss. 17, 18.
(n) *Ibid.* For definition of " minor Authority " see Local Government Act 1972, s. 192 (4).
(o) Education Act 1944, s. 17.
(p) Foundation managers and governors are managers and governors, not appointed by a local authority or minor authority, appointed for the purpose of securing that the character of the school as a voluntary school is developed and, in particular, that the school is conducted in accordance with any trust deed relating to the school (Education Act 1944, s. 114).
(q) Education Act 1944, s. 18.
(r) *Ibid.*, s. 17.
(s) *Ibid.*, ss. 17, 19.
(t) White Paper *Principles of Government in Maintained Secondary Schools*, Cmnd. 6523, 1944.

set up a committee to investigate, and make recommendations for, the functions and composition of governing bodies of secondary schools (u).

For every voluntary school the body of governors is established by an instrument of government made by order of the Secretary of State who determines the size of the membership (a). In the case of an aided or special agreement school, two thirds of the governors are foundation governors and one third appointed by the Local Education Authority. The proportions are reversed for a controlled school (b).

Schools are to be conducted in accordance with articles of government made in the case of county schools by order of the local authority with the approval of the Secretary of State and in the case of a voluntary schools by the Secretary of State. These articles determine the functions of the Local Education Authority, the governors and the head teacher and also provide for the procedure for the appointment and dismissal of the head teacher and the staff and for control, in aided schools, over secular instruction (c).

(b) Special schools.—Not until 1968 were maintained special schools required to have a body of governors. For such schools there must be an instrument of government constituting a body of governors for each school. The instrument is made by order of the local authority, and the body of governors, both as to size and composition, is at the discretion of the authority. Schools must be conducted in accordance with articles of government made by order of the local authority (d).

In the case of a non-maintained special school, a condition of recognition as a special school by the Secretary of State is that it must be under the direction of a body of managers composed of a sufficient number of suitably qualified persons; no member of staff may be a manager (e).

Grouping of schools under one management.—A Local Education Authority may constitute a single governing or managing body for any two or more county or maintained voluntary schools (in the latter case the consent of the managers or governors is necessary) and this arrangement may apply exclusively to primary schools, or to secondary schools or partly to primary and partly to secondary schools (f). Similarly two or more special schools maintained by an authority may be grouped under a single governing body (g).

Meetings of managers and governors.—The minutes of meetings of managers and governors must be open to inspection by the Local Education Authority; a quorum for meetings is not less than three or one third of the whole body of managers or governors, whichever is the greater; meetings must be held at least once a term (h).

(c) Other educational establishments.—Until 1968 colleges of education and establishments of further education maintained by local education authorities were not required to have bodies of governors although the majority had such bodies; in some cases these were, in fact, subcommittees of the education committee.

Discussion about the nature and purpose of governing bodies of establishments of higher and further education was initiated by the Robbins report (i);

(u) Taylor Committee. Its brief includes the management and government of all maintained schools.

(a) Education Act 1944, ss. 17, 19. It should be noted that at the time of writing the Secretary of State has refused to include parents or teachers as members of managing or governing bodies of voluntary schools.

(b) *Ibid.*, s. 19.

(c) *Ibid.*, ss. 17, 23.

(d) Education (No. 2) Act 1968, s. 2.

(e) Handicapped Pupils and Special Schools Regulations, S.I. 1959 No. 365.

(f) Education Act 1944, s. 20.

(g) Education (No. 2) Act 1968, s. 2.

(h) Education Act 1944, s. 21 and Sch. 4.

(i) Committee of Enquiry on Higher Education (1963).

shortly afterwards the Weaver report (k) was published. This sought to reconcile the view point of college governors and staff with that of the Local Education Authority. On the one hand the former wanted " to be able to take as many as possible of their decisions which have a significant bearing on the quality of their academic and corporate life ". On the other hand the local authorities felt themselves " in the last resort responsible for the college, for its general efficiency, for financing its expenditure, for its staff (who are appointed to the authority's service) and for its premises ". The recommendations of the Weaver report as to the structure of the government of colleges and the powers of governors were generally accepted and embodied in the Education (No. 2) Act 1968.

This Act compelled Local Education Authorities to constitute, by an instrument of government, a body of governors for all maintained colleges of education and establishments of further education (including polytechnics). For colleges of education the instrument is made by the authority with the approval of the Secretary of State and for establishments of further education by the local authority. The governors may consist of such persons appointed in such manner as the local authority decides but approval as to the size and composition of the body of governors for a college of education requires the approval of the Secretary of State.

Colleges of education and establishments of further education must be conducted in accordance with articles of government made by order of the local authority with the approval of the Secretary of State; these articles determine the functions to be exercised, respectively, by the Local Education Authority, the governors, the principal and the academic board (l). In addition they provide for procedures in matters, including discipline, relating to students.

As with schools, a local authority may, with the approval of the Secretary of State, establish a single body of governors for two or more institutions of further education maintained by the authority (m).

Voluntary colleges of education must also be conducted in accordance with articles of government approved by the Secretary of State; these articles must define the relationship between the body providing the college, the governors, the academic board and the principal (n).

Special Schools and Special Educational Treatment.—Prior to 1944 Local Education Authorities had a duty to provide special education for blind, deaf, physically defective, epileptic and mentally defective children, but there were difficulties, particularly outside the large towns and cities, in providing the necessary facilities and in insisting that parents made use of the provision for their handicapped children. Consequently a considerable number of children who would have benefited from special education attended the local school.

The duties of Local Education Authorities were extended by the Education Act 1944 which required them to have regard to the need for securing provision for children, in special schools or otherwise, who suffered from a disability of mind or body (o). For his part, the Secretary of State was required to make regulations defining the categories of pupils in need of special educational treatment and to lay down the requirements to be observed before a school (whether maintained by a local authority or a voluntary body) could be recognised as a special school (p).

Ten categories (blind, partially sighted, deaf, partially hearing, delicate, educationally subnormal, epileptic, maladjusted, physically handicapped and

(k) Study Group on the Government of Colleges of Education (1966).
(l) For guidance on articles of government see DES Administrative Memorandum 8/67 for polytechnics and DES Circular 7/72 for other establishments of further education.
(m) Education (No. 2) Act 1968, s. 1.
(n) The Further Education Regulations, S.I. 1975 No. 1054.
(o) Education Act 1944, s. 8 (c).
(p) *Ibid.*, s. 33.

those suffering from speech defects) are listed in regulations (q). For children in each category where the disability is serious the Local Education Authority must provide special treatment in special schools, but if this is impracticable or the disability is not serious, the authority may arrange for special educational treatment in any school maintained by an Authority or in a school not so maintained provided that the school has not been notified by the Secretary of State as unsuitable for this purpose (r). Local Education Authorities may establish special schools in hospitals and where the number of children in hospital (normally less than 25) does not justify the establishment of a school, education may be given under the provision (s) enabling an authority to provide education otherwise than at school. Exceptionally, when a handicapped child living at home is unable to attend school, individual tuition may be given under the same provision.

The types of handicap requiring special educational treatment have changed considerably since 1944; poliomyelitis and tuberculosis have virtually disappeared, the number of blind and delicate pupils has declined sharply whereas those suffering from spina bifida, multiple handicaps, educational subnormality and maladjustment have increased in number. At the same time other handicaps have been identified; in 1970 Local Education Authorities were required to provide in any school maintained or assisted by them special educational treatment for the deaf-blind, for children suffering from autism and other forms of early childhood psychosis and for those with acute dyslexia (t). From 1971 Local Education Authorities acquired additional duties by being made responsible for the education of severely subnormal children who, previously categorised as " unsuitable for education " at school, had been the responsibility of mental health committees of local authorities (u).

The rigidity of the categories has been criticised as also have been the regulations specifying the size of classes in schools for certain types of handicap and there is now a more flexible approach to the organisation of special treatment. The problems of children with multiple handicaps are being met by co-operation between authorities in planning new schools, by the admission of children from the areas of other authorities and by the use of schools provided by voluntary bodies; experiments are being made with special units attached to primary and secondary schools, e.g. for the partially hearing, the educationally subnormal and the maladjusted. The children in these units are normally integrated with those in the school for at least some of their activities. The Secretary of State no longer specifies the maximum size of classes in special schools or special units, but he has suggested staffing ratios appropriate for the various handicaps (a).

Where a handicapped child requires boarding education, whether because of home circumstances or the nature of the handicap, the Local Education Authority must accept the full cost of such education.

Local education authorities have developed child guidance and school psychological services during the last thirty years although there is no reference to such services in the Education Acts. These services local authorities have regarded as necessary to enable them to fulfil their duties towards children with behavioural, emotional or learning difficulties. Considerable variety of organisation and control of child guidance services has developed. Generally the Local Education Authority has provided the

---

(q) Handicapped Pupils and Special Schools Regulations, S.I. 1959 No. 365.
(r) Education Act 1944, s. 33; Education (Miscellaneous Provisions) Act 1953, s. 17 and First Schedule.
(s) Education Act 1944 s. 56; Education (Miscellaneous Provisions) Act 1948, s. 11 (1), Part I of First Schedule. See DES Circular 5/74.
(t) The Chronically Sick and Disabled Persons Act 1970, ss. 25–27. As to autistic children see DES Circular 6/71.
(u) Education (Handicapped Children) Act 1970, s. 1.
(a) DES Circular 4/73.

premises and the staff, paying the hospital boards for the services of psychiatrists: the clinics were normally the responsibility of the principal school medical officer but in some cases the clinics were established in hospitals and sometimes the non-medical staff were provided by the social service authorities. Consequent upon the transfer of the school health service to the area health authority and upon the expansion of the responsibility of social service authorities, the central government appreciated that this variety of pattern required a clearer definition of responsibility lest the interests of children with behavioural and emotional difficulties suffered. The new pattern of child guidance envisaged is a network of services collaborating to handle individual and general problems (b).

The school psychological service, on the other hand, is essentially an educational service, staffed by educational psychologists and remedial teachers, whose purpose is twofold; first, to help individual children with problems of personal adjustment or learning and secondly, to assist and advise teachers as well as parents in the handling of such children. The service is likely, therefore, to remain the responsibility of Local Education Authorities. The development of these services, particularly the child guidance service, has made possible a much more flexible approach to children in the category "maladjusted" although it remains a category difficult to define.

The Education Act 1944 imposes upon every Local Education Authority the duty to ascertain what children in their area require special educational treatment and prescribes formal procedures for discovering and placing handicapped pupils (c). The Authority may authorise any of their officers to serve notice in writing on the parent of any child over two years of age requiring him to submit the child for examination by a medical officer of the Authority (or of the regional or area health authority employed for this purpose), to obtain his advice as to whether the child is suffering from any disability of mind or body and as to its nature and extent. If a parent refuses to comply with such a notice without reasonable excuse, he will be liable to a fine not exceeding ten pounds. The parent of any child over two years of age may himself ask the Authority to arrange for the child to be examined. In either case the parent is entitled to be present at the examination. After considering the advice of the medical officer who conducted the examination and reports from teachers and other persons, if the Authority decides that the child requires special educational treatment, they must give notice to the parent of the decision and provide the treatment. If the Authority or the parent require it, a certificate in the prescribed form (d) will be issued to them. The certificate states whether the child is suffering from a disability requiring special educational treatment, its nature and extent. The certificate may be cancelled by the Secretary of State who has power to arrange for the child to be medically examined by one of his medical officers (e) or by the medical officer of the appropriate authority. If a certificate is cancelled, the Authority must cease providing special educational treatment.

The procedure as to certification or indeed any formal procedure is not, however, generally necessary. The ambiguity and formalities for ascertainment implied by the Act have recently been removed by the Secretary of State. The former emphasis on the role of medical opinion has been transferred to educational psychologists and special education advisers who are urged to secure the co-operation of teachers and parents as well as doctors and social workers before making a decision as to the type of special education appropriate to a child's handicap (f).

(b) See DES Circular 3/74. (c) Education Act 1944, s. 34.
(d) Handicapped Pupils (Certificate) Regulations, S.I. 1961 No. 476 amended by S.I. 1975 No. 328.
(e) Education Act 1944, s. 34. (f) See DES Circular 2/75.

Direct Grant schools.—Direct grant schools are first described as they were until the changes made in 1975; these changes and their effects are set out later in the section. Direct grant schools were schools which received grant from the Secretary of State under the Education Act 1944, s. 100 (1)(b); the majority were grammar schools. The most important condition of grant was for 25 per cent. of the places available at the age of eleven to be free places for children who had previously attended a maintained school for a period of at least two years between the ages of five and eleven. Preference was to be given in the admission of fee payers and free place holders to those children who by ability and aptitude were most likely to profit from the type of education provided (g).

A Local Education Authority had the power to take up free places in order to supplement their own provision of secondary education; in exercising this power they had to accept responsibility for the payment of fees of pupils filling these places (h). In addition, the local authority had the power to require a direct grant school to put at their disposal "reserved" places up to a maximum of 25 per cent. of the intake if these places were needed to increase the secondary provision in the area (i). The fees for these places were paid by the authority, but the provision as to previous attendance at a maintained school did not apply in filling these places. A school qualified for direct grant if the free places were offered and paid for by the governors of the school and not the authority. All direct grant schools had to operate a fee remission scheme, based on parental income and approved by the Secretary of State (k). The grant received from the Secretary of State consisted of a capitation grant for each pupil between the ages of 11 and 19, a sixth form grant and the difference between the normal fees and the remitted fees. There were, in May 1975, 174 direct grant grammar schools. Among their number were such famous day schools as Manchester Grammar School together with small schools in rural areas with a considerable boarding element. About one third of the schools were for Roman Catholics; these were often an essential part of the local provision for Roman Catholic children in the area, and in many cases virtually all the places were taken up by the Local Education Authority.

Since admission to direct grant grammar schools depended essentially on selection by ability, the future of these schools was under continuous discussion after 1965 when local authorities were first asked to prepare plans for reorganisation of secondary education on non-selective lines. The Donnison report (l) made recommendations with regard to these schools and as a result a number voluntarily renounced direct grant status and became independent. More recently several local authorities ceased taking up places at these schools.

The future of direct grant grammar schools is, however, no longer in doubt. In March 1975 the Secretary of State announced in Parliament that he proposed to phase them out, and in May he circulated a letter to the governors of the schools stating that new regulations were to be made. These regulations were made in July and came into operation in August 1975 (m). They exclude from grant all pupils who entered the school on or after 1st August, 1976 unless the governors have satisfied the Secretary of State that they intend the school to become a maintained comprehensive school within a local authority's pattern of secondary education and that they have notified the authority of their intention to make proposals for that purpose.

Where the governors propose to seek entry to the maintained system

(g) Direct Grant Schools Regulations 1959, S.I. 1959 No. 1832, Part II.
(h) Education (Miscellaneous Provisions) Act 1953, s. 6.
(i) Direct Grant Schools Regulations 1959 S.I. 1959 No. 1832, Part II.
(k) *Ibid.*
(l) Public Schools Commission, Second Report (1970).
(m) Direct Grant Grammar Schools (Cessation of Grant) Regulations 1975, S.I. 1975 No. 1198.

(and in doing so they must indicate their willingness to admit pupils without reference to their ability and aptitude), the Secretary of State may continue to make grants in respect of new entrants to the school in the year 1976–77 and in later school years provided he is satisfied with the progress made in discussions with a local authority and provided that the governors' proposals have not been rejected by him. It will be open to the governors to seek voluntary aided or controlled status; the regulations enable the Secretary of State to pay grants to the proprietors of schools which become county or voluntary schools to cover the balance of certain capital debts, 85% of certain expenditure on building undertaken after 10th March 1975 and expenses necessarily incurred in connection with the school becoming a maintained school.

Schools which decide not to enter the maintained system will receive grant only in respect of pupils who entered the school before 1st August, 1976. Unless the school closes it will become an independent school; many of the requirements in regulations relating to direct grant grammar schools remain in force as long as grant is payable to the school, but the governors are free to decide the fees and other charges in respect of pupils for whom no grant is payable. The school will be recognised as efficient, unless the governors are notified to the contrary, subject to review in the normal way for independent schools.

Local authorities may take up places at a school to which the direct grant arrangements no longer apply in the same way as they may at independent schools if they are satisfied that there is a shortage of places in maintained schools in their own area and in the area of neighbouring authorities (n). Again, as in the case of independent schools, local authorities may also pay, or assist with the payment of, fees of children attending schools to which direct grant arrangements no longer apply (o).

Independent Schools.—Independent schools are schools which receive no assistance from public funds. This category includes the major public schools and well known preparatory schools as well as small local schools often catering only for young children. They may be registered as charities or run by their proprietors for profit.

As far back as 1861 suggestions were made that such schools should be registered and open to inspection but it was not until 1944 that definite steps were taken to ensure that all independent schools were " sufficiently well found and staffed to fulfil the educational purposes they purport to do " (p). The proposals in the White Paper (q) formed the basis of Part III of the Education Act 1944 which came into operation in 1957.

From this date it became the duty of the Secretary of State to appoint one of his officers to be Registrar of Independent Schools to keep a register of all independent schools (r), whose proprietors make application in the prescribed manner (s). Six months after the commencement of this part of the Act it became an offence to conduct an independent school which is not registered or provisionally registered, or for the proprietor of a provisionally registered school to do any act calculated to lead to the belief that the school is a registered school. The penalty for such an offence is a fine not exceeding twenty pounds, or in the case of a second or subsequent offence a fine not exceeding fifty pounds or up to three months' imprison-

---

(n) Education (Miscellaneous Provisions) Act 1953, s. 6.

(o) Regulations for Scholarships and Other Benefits 1945, S.R. and O. 1945 No. 666.

(p) White Paper on *Educational Reconstruction* 1943, Cmnd. 6458.

(q) *Ibid.*

(r) By s. 114 (1) of the 1944 Act an independent school is any school at which full-time education is provided for five or more pupils of compulsory school age (whether or not such education is also provided for pupils under or over that age) not being a school maintained by a Local Education Authority or a school in respect of which grants are made by the Minister.

(s) Education Act 1944, s. 70 (1).

ment or both. The Minister made regulations (t) prescribing the particulars to be furnished to the Registrar by the proprietor (u) for the notification of any changes in the particulars, and as to the circumstances in which the Minister might order the name of the school to be deleted from the register if the Registrar were unable to obtain sufficient particulars. Independent schools must be open to inspection at all reasonable times, and until the school has been inspected on behalf of the Secretary of State (a) and notice has been given to the proprietor that the registration is final, the registration of a school will be regarded as provisional. No independent school may be registered if the proprietor is disqualified, or if the school premises are used for any purpose for which they are disqualified. If the Secretary of State is satisfied that he is in possession of sufficient information with respect to any independent school or class of independent schools (b) and that registration is unnecessary, he may exempt such schools from registration but the schools will be deemed to be registered.

If at any time the Secretary of State is satisfied that any registered or provisionally registered school is objectionable upon any of the following grounds: that the school premises or any part of them are unsuitable for a school, that the accommodation is unsuitable to the number, age or sex of the pupils, that efficient and suitable instruction is not being provided or that the proprietor or any teacher employed in the school is not a proper person, then the Secretary of State will serve on the proprietor a notice of complaint setting out full particulars of the matters complained of (c). Unless the matters complained of are, in the opinion of the Secretary of State, irremediable, the notice will specify the measures necessary to remedy them and the time, not being less than six months after the service of the notice, within which the measures specified must be taken. If it is alleged in the notice of complaint that a teacher is not a proper person to be employed in the school, that teacher must be named in the notice and a copy of it served on him.

Any person upon whom a notice or copy of a notice of complaint has been served, within the time limit stated in the notice, being not less than one month after the service of the notice, may appeal, in the manner laid down by rules, to the Independent Schools Tribunal (d), consisting of two impartial persons from an " educational panel " to be appointed by the Lord President of the Council and an impartial chairman from a " legal panel " to be appointed by the Lord Chancellor (e). The Independent Schools Tribunal will have power, after hearing all the evidence, to order that the complaint be annulled or that the school be struck off the register, or that it be struck off unless the requirements, subject to any modifications, are complied with, to disqualify the premises or any part of them for use as a school, or for pupils exceeding such a number or of such an age or sex as may be specified, or disqualify a proprietor or teacher complained of from being a proprietor or teacher. If the complaint is not referred to an Independent Schools Tribunal within the time limit, the Secretary of State will have

---

(t) Independent Schools Registration Regulations, 1957, S.I. 1957 No. 929. See also the Explanatory Memorandum issued by the Minister in 1956 and Admin. Memo. 557 (15.7.1957).

(u) This term means the person or body of persons responsible or proposing to be responsible for the management of a school (Education Act, 1944, s. 114 (1)).

(a) The Secretary of State has the duty under s. 77 to cause an inspection to be made of any educational establishment, including independent schools, at such intervals as appear to him to be appropriate and for this purpose inspectors may be appointed by Her Majesty on the recommendation of the Secretary of State. Penalties may be imposed on persons obstructing an inspector in the execution of his duty.

(b) By the Independent Schools (Exemption from Registration) Order 1957, he has exempted from registration those schools which he has " recognised as efficient ". For recognition as efficient, a school must satisfy the conditions laid down in Rules 16 as revised in December 1965. DES List 70 is a list of primary and secondary schools recognised as efficient.

(c) *Ibid.*, s. 71 (1).

(d) *Ibid.*, s. 72.

(e) Education Act 1944. Sixth Schedule, and Independent Schools Tribunal Rules 1958 N. 519.

power to make any order that the Tribunal could have made. The penalties to enforce any orders made by the Secretary of State or by an Independent Schools Tribunal are defined in s. 73. Anyone may apply to the Secretary of State to remove a disqualification owing to a change of circumstances, and if he is aggrieved by the refusal of the Secretary of State to remove the disqualification, he may appeal to the Independent Schools Tribunal (f).

5. THE DUTIES OF PARENTS

Parents have a duty to ensure that their children of compulsory school age receive full-time education suitable to their age, ability and aptitude either by regular attendance at school or otherwise (g). The term " parent " here includes a guardian and the person who has actual custody of the child (h). Compulsory school age is any age between five and sixteen (i). In order to avoid broken terms, no child need be admitted to school except at the beginning of a term unless he was prevented from entering then because of illness, change of residence or other causes beyond the parent's control (k). This, in effect, means that a child does not become of compulsory school age until the beginning of the term after that in which he attains the age of five. At the upper end of compulsory school age a child may leave school only at the end of the spring or on a specified date in the summer term depending on the incidence of his sixteenth birthday.

Section 76 of the Education Act 1944 requires the Secretary of State and Local Education Authorities to have regard to the general principle that children are to be educated in accordance with their parents' wishes; Schools Regulations (l) reinforce this principle by stating that a child may not be refused admission to, or excluded from, a school other than on reasonable grounds. The limitation placed on meeting parental wishes is the avoidance of unreasonable public expenditure; in a leading case when parental choice of school involved considerable cost, the court held that it did not override the need to avoid unreasonable public expenditure (m). This section has given rise to numerous appeals to the Secretary of State against decisions made by Local Authorities and to a number of court cases. The section was also used in an attempt to assert that in a particular area the wishes of parents generally, and not only those of individual parents, should be taken into account. This interpretation was not upheld by the courts (n).

Shortages of places and the reorganisation of secondary schools on comprehensive lines have increased the problems of local authorities in acceding to the general principle of parents' wishes. The pressure on accommodation at some schools, particularly in areas of growing population, has necessitated zoning schemes involving the refusal of admission to children living outside the zone in order to prevent overcrowding and to make full use of places available in other schools. The policy of some authorities of recruiting the full range of ability to comprehensive schools and the desire of others to establish neighbourhood schools have also reduced the element of choice for the parent in the selection of a school for his child, as has also the declining number of single sex schools.

With a view to the enforcement of regular attendance of children at school, the proprietor of every independent school and the managers or governors of county, voluntary and direct grant schools must arrange for a register to be kept of all pupils at the school (o); if any child of compulsory

(f) *Ibid.*, s. 74. (g) Education Act 1944, s. 36.
(h) *Ibid.*, s. 114 (1).
(i) The school leaving age was raised to sixteen in 1972–3. The dates on which a pupil ceases to be of compulsory school age are set out in Education Act 1962, s. 9 and Education Act 1976.
(k) Education (Miscellaneous Provisions) Act 1948, s. 4.
(l) S.I. 1959 No. 364. (m) See note to s. 76.
(n) *Wood* v. *Ealing London Borough*, [1966], 3 All E.R. 514; [1967] Ch. 364.
(o) Education Act 1944, s. 80 and Pupils' Registration Regulations, S.I. 1956 No. 357.

school age who is a registered pupil at a school fails to attend regularly, the parent is guilty of an offence (p). In practice, the headteacher is normally responsible for the maintenance of registers and for checking regular attendance while educational welfare officers employed by the local education authority investigate the reasons for irregular attendance. Their objective is to encourage, by advice and persuasion, parents to send their children to school regularly and most authorities have procedures for the informal interviewing of parents whose children fail to attend school regularly. Only as a last resort is a person prosecuted.

There are thus two duties imposed on parents, first, to cause their children to receive efficient education suitable to their age, ability and aptitude, and secondly, if they are registered pupils at a school, to cause them to attend regularly. In the first case, if it appears to the Local Education Authority that the parent is failing to perform the duty imposed on him, it is their duty to serve upon the parent a notice requiring him to satisfy them, before the date specified in the notice (which must not be less than fourteen days from the service of the notice), that the child is receiving efficient full time education suitable to his age, ability and aptitude either by regular attendance at school or otherwise (q). If the parent fails to satisfy the authority of this, then, if the authority is of opinion that the child should attend school, they must, if practicable, afford the parent an opportunity of selecting a school for the child. If he does not select a school within fourteen days then the authority will serve on him an order, in the form prescribed by the School Attendance Order Regulations (r) requiring him to cause the child to become a registered pupil at a school named in the order. If he does select a school then that school must be named in the order, unless the Secretary of State directs otherwise. If the Local Education Authority are of the opinion that the school selected by the parent is unsuitable to the age, ability and aptitude of the child, or that the attendance of the child at that school would involve the authority in unreasonable expense, they may, after giving the parent notice, apply to the Secretary of State for a direction as to which school should be named in the order. A school-attendance order will remain in force, subject to any amendment which may be made by the Local Education Authority, so long as the child is of compulsory school age, unless it is revoked by the authority, or the parent is acquitted in proceedings for failure to comply with it and the court directs that the order shall cease to be in force, though the authority may make a new order if there is any change of circumstances. The parent may, at any time while the order is in force, make application to the authority by whom it was made requesting that another school be substituted for that named in the order, or that it be revoked on the ground that arrangements have been made for the child to receive efficient full time education suitable to his age, ability and aptitude, otherwise than at school. On such application the authority must comply with the request unless they are of opinion that the proposed change of school is unreasonable or inexpedient in the interests of the child or that satisfactory arrangements have not been made for the education of the child otherwise than at school. If the parent is aggrieved by a refusal of the authority to comply with his request, he has the right to refer the question to the Secretary of State, who will give whatever direction he thinks fit (s). Failure to comply with the requirements of a school attendance order is an offence, unless the parent proves that he is causing the child to receive efficient full time education suitable to his age, ability and aptitude otherwise than at school. If a child is resident in the area of one authority and attends school

---

(p) *Ibid.*, s. 39.

(q) *Ibid.*, s. 37, as amended by the Education (Misc. Prov.) Act, 1953, s. 10.

(r) S.R. & O. 1944 No. 1470. See Adm. Memo 163 (6.6.1946). Circular 268 (17.8.1953) gives a model form of notice to parents.

(s) Education Act 1944, s. 37 (4).

in the area of another, it is the duty of the authority who made the order to enforce its observance (t).

Action by means of a school attendance order would be taken by a local education authority (*i*) in the case of a child not attending school and (*ii*) if the child is attending a school unsuitable to his age, ability and aptitude, for example a primary or secondary school instead of a special school if the medical officer has issued a certificate that the child is suffering from a serious disability of mind or body (u). The parent has the right of naming the school in the first instance and the authority has the duty of providing education in accordance with the parent's wishes (a) even to the extent of providing transport or paying the expenses of such transport (b) unless such expense would be unreasonable. This right and this duty are of special importance to safeguard, so far as is practicable, the parent's right to have his child educated in accordance with his religious opinions. But the parent's duty to cause his child to have suitable education, even in a school which does not normally provide religious instruction of the kind desired by the parent, is an overriding duty, though provision is made, so far as possible and in various ways, for the desired religious instruction to be given or for the child to be withdrawn from that given in the school (c). This duty may oblige the parent to allow his child to reside away from home, either in a boarding school or with another person, though here again, so far as is practicable, effect must be given to the wishes of the parent with regard to the religious denomination of the person with whom he will reside (d). Where, however, board and lodging is provided by a Local Education Authority on the ground that the pupil could not otherwise be provided with education suitable to his age, ability and aptitude, whether such board and lodging is provided at school (e) or not (f), then no charge may be made to the parent for the cost of such board and lodging. In extraordinary circumstances, and with the approval of the Secretary of State, education suitable to the child may be provided otherwise than at school (g). These provisions are of great importance in the case of children who require special educational treatment owing to some disability of body or mind, very many of whom might otherwise be deprived of suitable education through their parents' natural desire to keep them at home; but in these cases especially is it of importance for the parent to have the right of appeal to the Secretary of State against a decision of the Local Education Authority. The final decision as to which school should provide education suitable to a child's age, ability and aptitude rests with the Secretary of State, and if he gives a direction under section 37 (2), (3) or (4) of the Act as to which school shall be attended his decision is final, though he may vary or revoke it (h). If it is not obeyed the parent may be charged with the offence of non-compliance with the requirements of the school attendance order, and the only defence to this charge is that the child is receiving efficient full-time education suitable to his age, ability and aptitude otherwise than at school (i). It is not a defence that he is receiving it in another school not named in the

---

(t) Education (Misc. Prov.) Act, 1948, First Schedule.

(u) Education Act 1944, s. 34 (5).

(a) *Ibid.*, s. 76, but see the decision in *Watt* v. *Kesteven County Council*, [1955] 1 All E.R. 473 [1955] 1 Q.B. 408.

(b) *Ibid.*, s. 55. The child must, of course, live more than the statutory " walking distance " from the school, unless the Secretary of State has approved some lesser distance.

(c) *Ibid.*, s. 25 (4) and see Chapter 7 of this Introduction.

(d) *Ibid.*, s. 50 (2).

(e) *Ibid.*, s. 61 (2) (*a*) and Education (Misc. Prov.) Act, 1953, s. 6 (2) (*b*).

(f) *Ibid.*, s. 52 (1) (*a*).

(g) *Ibid.*, s. 56. The Minister's views on the arrangements to be made by Local Education Authorities in providing education otherwise than at school for handicapped pupils were set out in Manual of Guidance, Special Services No. 1 (Sept., 1950) and addendum (Aug., 1953). The Minister decided that education may be provided at home by an authority until the pupil attains the age of eighteen years.

(h) *Ibid.*, s. 111.

(i) *Ibid.*, s. 37 (5).

order. Another point to be noticed is that the authority may decide or the Secretary of State direct that the school named in the order should be an independent school, so that the force of the law may be used to require a child to attend an independent school.

The second duty of a parent is to secure that his child should attend regularly at the school at which he is registered (k). This duty is independent of the duty just discussed to comply with the directions in a school attendance order, and proceedings can be taken against a parent who fails to send his child regularly to the school at which he is registered, whether or not a school attendance order has been served upon him. A child will not be deemed to have failed to attend regularly at school by reason of his absence with leave granted by any person authorised by the managers, governors or proprietor of the school (l); nor if at any time he was prevented by sickness or any unavoidable cause, nor on a day exclusively set apart for religious observance by the religious body to which his parent belongs; nor if the school at which the child is registered is not within walking distance of the child's home, and the Local Education Authority have not made suitable arrangements either for his transport to and from school, or for boarding accommodation at or near the school or for enabling him to become a registered pupil at a school nearer his home. The expression "walking distance" means two miles in the case of a child under the age of eight and three miles in the case of a child over that age, the distance to be measured by the nearest available route. It has been decided that the distance and not the safety of the route is the determining test, and a parent cannot claim that the nearest available route is not safe (m). It is worth noticing the change from the word "road" in the corresponding clause in the Education Act, 1921, to the word "route" in the present law. Under the old law it has been held that "road" was not confined to highways or to roads constructed for the purpose of carrying every class of traffic, and that it meant simply a route from the residence of the child to the nearest school (n). The use of the word route now emphasises that this was the intention, and it would appear that any footpath, or any public or private way may be a "route" if in fact it is available for use; e.g., a track over the hills or a practicable way over fields in the parent's occupation. The distance of the home from the school will not be a defence in proceedings under this section if the Local Education Authority have provided suitable boarding accommodation at or near the school. If a child is a boarder at a school the child will be deemed to have failed to attend regularly if he is absent without leave (o) during any part of a school term at a time when he was not prevented by sickness or any avoidable cause. If a child is provided with boarding accommodation near the school, the person who has the actual custody of the child will have the duty of securing his regular attendance at the school.

If a child has no fixed abode, the provision with regard to the distance of home from school does not apply. If a parent proves that he is engaged in any trade or business which requires him to travel from place to place and that his child has attended the school at which he is a registered pupil as regularly as the nature of the parent's trade or business permits and in the case of a child over six has made at least 200 attendances during the previous twelve months, the parent must be acquitted of any offence relating to school attendance (p).

(k) *Ibid.*, s. 39 (1).

(l) Leave of absence may not be granted to enable a pupil to be employed during school hours or to enable a pupil to take holidays during term except in those cases mentioned in the Regulation 12 of the Schools Regulations, S.I. 1959 No. 364, as amended by S.I. 1969 No. 231.

(m) Education Act 1944, s. 39. See *Shaxted* v. *Ward*, [1954] 1 All E. R. 336.

(n) *Hares* v. *Curtin*, [1913] 2 K. B. 328 at p. 331. This turned on the construction of bye-laws which used the word "road" in the same context as s. 49 (*b*) of the Education Act, 1921.

(o) This meets in particular the case of a weekly boarder.

(p) Education Act 1944, s. 39 (3).

Under the Children and Young Persons Act 1969, only a Local Education Authority can take proceedings in a case where a child is not receiving efficient full-time education and appears in need of care and control which he is not likely to receive unless the court makes an order (q). In such a case the court requires to be satisfied, before making an order, that the child is already the subject of a school attendance order which has not been complied with; or that the child is a registered pupil at a school which he is not attending regularly; or that he is a child whom a person habitually wandering from place to place takes with him (r).

Any person found guilty either of failure to comply with an attendance order or of failure to secure the regular attendance of a child at the school where he is registered will be liable, on summary conviction, in the case of a first offence to a fine not exceeding ten pounds, in the case of a second offence to a fine not exceeding twenty pounds and in the case of a third offence to a fine not exceeding twenty pounds or to a term of imprisonment not exceeding one month or to both fine and imprisonment (s). It is the duty of the Local Education Authority to institute proceedings for such offences whenever in their opinion it is considered necessary; before instituting proceedings the Authority must consider whether it would be appropriate, instead of or as well as instituting the proceedings, to bring the child before a juvenile court (t).

There is a further point worth noticing. The parent is responsible for proving a child's age where this is disputed in school attendance proceedings, but anyone who requires to prove the age of a child (or of any person) for the purposes of the Act may obtain a birth certificate upon payment of a fee of 75p. (u). Considerable difficulties have arisen in proving the age of immigrant children for whom it is impossible to obtain a birth certificate; an affidavit, sworn by a child's relative, is the only, though unsatisfactory, solution to this problem.

The responsibility of local education authorities for the issue of licences for children to take part in entertainments must be mentioned. Such licences are given at present to children over the age of twelve under certain conditions prescribed in the Children and Young Persons Act, 1933. To these conditions was later added another (a), namely, that the licence shall specify the times, if any, during which a child may be absent from school for the purpose authorised by the licence and a child absent from school during these times shall be deemed to be absent with leave.

The law relating to children taking part in entertainments is now contained in the Children and Young Persons Act, 1963, and the Children (Performances) Regulations, 1968, which safeguards children appearing in television programmes as well as providing comprehensive safeguards for children taking part in performances of all kinds.

The employment of children.—Children under the age of thirteen may not be employed (b); children over that age but still of compulsory school age may only be employed under certain restrictions. These relate to the timing of such employment; in addition the Secretary of State has powers to make regulations prohibiting employment in specified occupations and prescribing conditions for other occupations and for employment in general (c).

(q) Children and Young Persons Act 1969, ss. 1 (2) (*e*), 2 (8) (*a*).
(r) *Ibid.*, s. 2 (8) (*b*) (i) (ii) (iii).
(s) Education Act 1944, s. 40 (2)–(4) amended by Children and Young Persons Act 1969, Sch. 5, para. 13.
(t) *Ibid.*
(u) Education Act 1944, s. 94 (1), and Education (Misc. Prov.) Act 1948, s. 9 (1).
(a) See Children and Young Persons Act 1963, s. 37.
(b) Employment of Children Act 1973, Sch. 1, Part II.
(c) *Ibid.*

Local education authorities have the duty to supervise the employment of children. They can require a child's parent, or the person appearing to employ the child, to provide particulars of the child's employment; if the Authority is of the opinion that the employment, while not unlawful, is unsuitable for the child owing to his age, state of health or to its being prejudicial to his education, they may prohibit the employment or impose conditions in the interests of the child (d). Failure to provide the required information or to comply with the conditions prescribed constitutes an offence (e).

Leave of absence may not be given to a pupil to undertake employment, paid or unpaid, during school hours except in accordance with arrangements approved by the Secretary of State permitting employment temporarily in the interests of the welfare of the community or in accordance with a licence granted under sections of the Children and Young Persons Acts (f).

6. TEACHERS

IN SCHOOLS

During the last forty years major changes affecting the teaching profession have taken place. One important factor has been fluctuation in the demand for supply of teachers. Immediately after the war ended, emergency training colleges were set up to compensate for the shortage of men teachers due to the cessation of training during the war and also to cope with the additional numbers of children in schools when the minimum school leaving age was raised in 1947 to fifteen. In the early fifties the temporary post-war " bulge " in the birth rate occasioned stresses in the successive stages of education and contrary to expectation the birth rate remained high. Consequently there was a general shortage of teachers complicated by their uneven distribution over the country. To meet the major problem of shortage which continued in the fifties and sixties and also to reduce the size of classes, the Government planned a very large expansion in teacher training provision which led to a change in the age structure of the profession, to the recruitment of part-time teachers, to the encouragement of married women to return to teaching and to arrangements for enabling mature men and women to enter the profession after experience in other fields. To meet the problem of uneven distribution and the special problem of industrial conurbations, the Secretary of State after consultation with local authorities and teachers' organisations introduced a rationing procedure, whereby a Local Education Authority could employ only a prescribed quota of teachers.

After continuing to rise each year between the mid-fifties and mid-sixties, the birth rate in England and Wales began to fall in 1965 and has continued to do so ever since (g). The Secretary of State was therefore forced to review his policies for the employment, recruitment and training of teachers.

Apart from the recruitment in some inner city areas and of teachers with certain specialist qualifications, there is no longer a shortage of teachers and the quota system now serves a different purpose: it is used by the Secretary of State to urge local authorities to appoint their full quota in order to prevent unemployment among teachers, particularly of those entering teaching for the first time. In consequence it is probable that the openings for part-time teachers and married women returning to teaching will decline.

In response to the demands of teachers for a higher professional status combined with their increasing responsibilities for curriculum development

---

(d) *Ibid.*, s. 2 (2) and (3).
(e) *Ibid.*, s. 2 (4).
(f) Schools Regulations, S.I. 1959 No. 364, amended by S.I. 1969 No. 231.
(g) The birth rate dropped from 876,000 in 1964 to 676,000 in 1973; see DES Report on Education No. 80, Dec. 1974.

and pastoral care, the initial training course was lengthened in 1961 from two to three years, a fourth year B.Ed. course was introduced in the sixties and compulsory professional training was required for all graduates (with certain exceptions) in the seventies.

Changes in the salary structure together with the increasing size of schools have resulted in a clearly defined career structure for teachers; their security of tenure, always considerable, has been increased by the various recent provisions affecting all employees. The last decade has also seen disruption of schools by the industrial action of various teachers' organisations; in most cases, the local authorities in which such action occurred were unable to resolve the teachers' grievances since these were the subject of national negotiation.

It is not too sweeping an assertion to say that the teaching profession in numbers, qualifications, responsibilities and in opportunities for promotion has changed out of all recognition since 1944. The various aspects of the profession briefly mentioned are discussed in greater detail in the following paragraphs.

Training.—The Secretary of State is required to ensure that there are sufficient facilities available for the training of teachers needed in schools, colleges and other educational establishments maintained by local education authorities and he is empowered to direct local authorities to provide, maintain and to assist such facilities (h). The majority of teacher training places, both before and after 1944, have been in colleges of education provided by Local Education Authorities; the remainder were in colleges provided by voluntary bodies and in university departments of education for graduates.

In surveying higher education, the Robbins Committee in 1963 considered teacher training but their recommendations in this field, apart from the introduction of a course leading to the B.Ed. degree, were not generally accepted (i). The James Committee, reporting in 1972, suggested radical changes in the approach to teacher training both at the initial and post-experience stages. These suggestions were to a certain extent modified in the policy statement contained in the 1972 White Paper *Education—A Framework for Expansion* (k) which proposed (1) three-year courses leading to a B.Ed. degree and qualified teacher status for students possessing the normal entry requirement for admission to a university. For the student uncommitted to teaching on entry to higher education the degree and training could be related to an initial two-year course leading to the Diploma in Higher Education; (2) the present three-year course leading to qualified status as a teacher should continue for those students without the minimum qualification for entry to a university; (3) the one-year training course for graduates should continue.

The James Committee had considered also the education of teachers after the completion of their college or university course. Their two major recommendations are set out in a somewhat different form in the White Paper. They are (1) that systematic help and support should be given to teachers in their first year of teaching (the probationary year) and, in particular, that they should have a lightened timetable and regular weekly release for in-service training; (2) that experienced teachers should be released at regular intervals for in-service education. Although both these innovations were widely endorsed by teachers and Local Education Authorities, it is probable that in the current economic climate progress in these directions will be slow.

The pattern of teacher training for the end of this decade and for the

(h) Education Act 1944, s. 62.
(i) See p. 50 in section on Further and Higher Education.
(k) Cmnd. 5174.

next will not emerge until reorganisation of higher education (l) is completed during the next two or three years; it is as yet impossible to assess how many students will choose each of the different routes to qualification as a teacher listed in the White Paper.

Qualifications.—A " qualified " teacher is a person who has completed a course of initial training for teachers; qualified status may also be obtained on completion of a comparable course or by possession of specialist qualifications provided they are approved by the Secretary of State. Every qualified teacher must have been accepted as such by the Secretary of State and must not subsequently have been disqualified by him (m).

Men and women who graduated before 1970 and 1974 receive qualified status on appointment to posts in primary and secondary schools respectively although they have received no professional training; graduates in science and mathematics may still be appointed to secondary schools as " qualified " teachers without professional training.

Teachers in special schools or units for the blind, the deaf and the partially hearing must hold additional qualifications prescribed by the Secretary of State.

Only qualified teachers may be employed as teachers in maintained schools, but there are certain other categories of staff who may be employed for work in the classroom. They are (1) student teachers: these may only be employed for limited periods and are either students who have failed to complete successfully an initial course of training but propose to retrieve their failure, or students with the necessary qualifications for entry to college who propose to enter teacher training; (2) instructors: these may be employed to give instruction in a specialist art or skill provided a qualified teacher is not available to give such instruction; (3) nursery assistants: these may be employed in nursery classes provided they have completed a course in the care of young children (n).

Salaries of teachers.—Prior to 1963 salaries of teachers were negotiated by the Burnham Committee which consisted of representatives of Local Education Authorities and teachers under an independent chairman (o). The duty of this Committee was to submit salary scales which they had agreed to the Secretary of State when they thought fit (which, in practice, was when the teachers' representatives gave notice of the termination of the current agreement and the Committee had negotiated a new agreement). The Secretary of State had no power to compel the Committee to reach agreement nor could he modify the scales recommended. The only alternatives open to him were acceptance or rejection of the scales recommended. Revised salary scales could not be operated by local authorities until the Secretary of State had made the necessary order nor could payment be back dated.

Approval to recommended scales was forthcoming until 1960 when deadlock was averted by the Committee altering their proposals to meet the wishes of the Secretary of State. In 1963 the Secretary of State refused to approve the proposed new scales because certain aspects of them were unacceptable to him. Compromise proved impossible, and for the first time new salary scales were determined by Act of Parliament (Remuneration of Teachers Act 1963). This Act was an interim measure pending further legislation to enable the Secretary of State to take an active part in future

---

(l) See p. **51** in section on Further and Higher Education.

(m) Schools Regulations 1959 No. 364, amended by S.I.s 1969 No. 1777, 1971 No. 342 and 1973 No. 2021. There are also certain other teachers who, under specific conditions, may be given qualified teacher status.

(n) For qualifications of teachers in detail, see Schools Regulations 1959 No. 364, amended by S.I.s 1968 No. 1281, 1969 No. 1777, 1971 No. 342, 1973 No. 2021; Handicapped Pupils and Special Schools Regulations 1959 No. 365, amended by S.I.s 1971 No. 342, 1973 No. 2021; see DES Circular 11/73.

(o) Education Act 1944, s. 89 repealed by Remuneration of Teachers Act 1965, s. 7 (6).

negotiations. The Remuneration of Teachers Act 1965, provides for the setting up of committees under an independent chairman to consider the salaries of teachers. The most important features of the Act are (1) the inclusion in the committees of representatives of the Secretary of State; (2) provision for arbitration in default of agreement by the committees; (3) provision for an order made under the Act to have retrospective effect. Recommendations made by the Pay Board as to the London weighting of salaries were unacceptable to teachers and the additional allowances for teaching in the Greater London area are based on a three-tier system—the highest weighting is given to the ILEA and certain outer London boroughs, the next to the remaining outer London boroughs and the lowest weighting to a limited number of areas in the Home Counties.

Following the recommendations of the Plowden report for positive discrimination in favour of schools with a large proportion of deprived children, Local Education Authorities were enabled to pay additional allowances to teachers working in these schools; during 1974 this scheme was considerably extended to include teachers in a large number of schools of " special difficulty ".

Dissatisfaction with the level of salaries has been a major cause of discontent among teachers for a number of years and their demands for an independent enquiry were eventually met by the establishment in 1974 of the Houghton Committee of Enquiry to review the remuneration of all teachers other than those in universities. The Committee reported in December of the same year, recommending substantial increases retrospective to May 1974, particularly for the more experienced teachers. These recommendations were accepted in their entirety by the Government.

Appointment and dismissal of teachers.—All teachers in maintained schools are paid by the Local Education Authority and the nationally negotiated conditions of service are similar for all teachers, but the procedure for the appointment and dismissal of teachers differs according to the type of school.

County schools.—In every county school, unless otherwise stated in the rules of management or articles of government, the appointment of teachers is under the control of the authority. No teachers may be dismissed except by the Authority; the procedure for dismissal is included in the conditions of service and, in some cases, in the rules of management or articles of government (p).

Controlled schools.—The above arrangements apply also to controlled schools (q) except that in the case of the appointment of a head teacher the Authority must inform the managers or governors as to the person they propose to appoint and consider any representations made by the managers or governors concerning the proposed appointment (r). The teaching staff of schools above a certain size must include a specified number of " reserved " teachers selected for their fitness to give religious instruction in accordance with the trust deed or the former practice of the school and specifically appointed to give such instruction. Where the Authority propose to appoint a person as a reserved teacher the foundation managers or governors must be consulted and satisfied that he or she is competent to give the necessary instruction. If the foundation managers or governors consider that a reserved teacher has failed to give religious instruction in an efficient manner they may require the authority to dismiss the teacher from employment as a reserved teacher (s). This, however, does not necessarily mean that he cannot continue as a teacher at the school.

(p) Education Act 1944, s. 24 (1).
(q) *Ibid.*
(r) *Ibid.*, s. 27 (3).
(s) *Ibid.*, s. 27 (4) (5).

Aided schools.—In aided schools the teachers are the employees of the managers or governors, and the rules of management or articles of government regulate the appointment and dismissal of teachers; the rules or articles must, however, make provision for the Authority (1) to determine the number of teachers employed; (2) to prohibit the dismissal of a teacher without the consent of the authority; (3) to require the dismissal of a teacher (t). There is one exception to this provision: where a teacher appointed to give religious instruction in accordance with the trust deed fails to do so efficiently he may be dismissed by the managers or governors of the school without the consent of the Authority (u).

Special agreement schools.—Appointment and dismissal of teachers in special agreement schools is the same as for county schools (a) except that where the special agreement provides for the employment of reserved teachers their appointment and dismissal is similar to that in controlled schools (b).

General.—Where a teacher's engagement is terminated, either by dismissal or resignation, owing to misconduct or conviction of a criminal offence, the facts must be reported to the Secretary of State; if the Secretary of State determines that the teacher is unsuitable for employment as a teacher he may not be employed as a teacher in any school, maintained or otherwise (c). The Secretary of State may also require, on educational or medical grounds, that a teacher's employment be suspended or terminated or made subject to conditions determined by him. In all such cases the Secretary of State gives the teacher the opportunity of making representations to him and considers any request for his disqualification to be removed (d).

Teachers, like other employees, are protected by the Redundancy Payments Act 1965, the Contract of Employments Act 1972 and the Trade Union and Labour Relations Act 1974. The number of cases arising out of the provisions of this legislation brought by teachers before industrial tribunals and the courts has increased significantly in recent years.

IN FURTHER AND HIGHER EDUCATION

There are no detailed provisions relating to teachers in institutions of further and higher education similar to those for schools. The regulations require only that the teachers should be sufficient in number and should have the qualifications necessary for adequate instruction in the courses provided (e). Conditions of service are nationally negotiated and the procedure for appointment and dismissal of staff are prescribed in the articles of government. It is usual for all but the most senior appointments to be made by the governors in consultation with the principal and heads of departments. A person who, on the grounds of misconduct or conviction of a criminal offence, is determined by the Secretary of State as unsuitable for employment as a teacher, may not be so employed; in addition, the Secretary of State may prohibit the employment of a teacher on medical grounds if he is satisfied that his employment as a teacher is undesirable (f).

As in the case of teachers in primary and secondary schools, salaries are negotiated by a committee set up under the Remuneration of Teachers Act

---

(t) *Ibid.*, s. 24 (2).
(u) *Ibid.*, s. 28 (2).
(a) *Ibid.*, s. 24 (1).
(b) *Ibid.*, s. 28 (3) (4).
(c) Schools Regulations 1959 No. 364, amended by S.I. 1964 No. 1311 (a list (List 99) of such teachers is circulated to employers of teachers). Teachers may be held to be unsuitable to teach in certain kinds of school though suitable in others. Some are excluded from schools but not from colleges.
(d) *Ibid.*
(e) Further Education Regulations 1975 No. 1054.
(f) *Ibid.* These regulations apply also to leaders of youth clubs, youth and community workers.

1965; a separate committee deals with salaries in farm institutes. The Houghton Report included recommendations, which were implemented in 1974, for the salaries of teachers in institutions of further and higher education.

7. RELIGIOUS EDUCATION

A contemporary student approaching the Education Act 1944, without some acquaintance with the history of English education could well be astonished at the detailed attention devoted in the Act to religion in schools. Now, in the second half of this century an aspect of education that arouses only occasional and minor public interest, it was for a hundred years a major political and educational issue. Like other social causes, popular education was first supplied by voluntary bodies—the churches; then the state gave financial support, and later as the demand and need grew beyond the ability and resources of voluntary bodies to control, the state was compelled to supplement and finally make direct provision for the service.

Briefly, the first provision of popular elementary education was undertaken by voluntary societies such as the National Society acting for the Church of England and by the British and Foreign Schools Society acting for the Free Churches. From 1833 these societies received direct grants from the Treasury: after 1847 Roman Catholic schools were eligible for grants. In the " British " schools, religious instruction was undenominational, but in other schools it was given in accordance with the doctrines of the providing churches. When in 1870 school boards were instituted by the state " to fill the gaps " left by religious bodies, their schools were forbidden to adopt a catechism or formulary distinctive of any denomination.

Aided by changed attitudes to religion (notably the decline of the " nonconformist conscience "), the promoters of the Education Act 1944 by skilful negotiation, ended the sectarian conflicts which had delayed educational developments for generations.

One aspect of the settlement achieved—the creation of a new school system of county schools and a threefold choice of status for voluntary schools—has already been discussed. Another aspect described below is the detailed approach adopted towards religious teaching in each of the four types of schools.

The significance of religion in education was recognised by an entirely new provision that in all schools, both county and voluntary, the school day must begin with collective worship on the part of all pupils at the school, subject, of course, to the right of the parent to withdraw his child from such worship (g). Collective worship on the part of the whole school is not, however, obligatory in cases where the Local Education Authority for county schools, and the managers or governors for voluntary schools, consider that the school premises make it impracticable to assemble all the pupils (h). Since the passing of the Act, alternative arrangements to a single act of worship have been increasingly approved by Local Education Authorities, governors and managers for various reasons, e.g. schools are sometimes located on two or more sites; the assembly hall may be too small to accommodate the whole school; changes in school organisation, particularly the growth of comprehensive schools and sixth form centres encourage groupings by house or age; the influx of commonwealth immigrants has led to separate assemblies to meet the needs of a multi-racial society.

The act of collective worship (i) must take place on the school premises, though on special occasion it may take place elsewhere in the case of aided

---

(g) Education Act 1944, s. 25 (4).
(h) *Ibid.*, s. 25 (1).
(i) This need not be Christian. It may be, for example, in appropriate cases, Jewish, Sikh or Hindu.

or special agreement schools (k). Religious instruction, also, must now be given in every county and voluntary school (l), but no pupil may be required to attend or abstain from attending any Sunday School or any place of religious worship, and if the parent of any pupil requests that he be excused from attendance at religious worship or instruction in the school, then the pupil must be excused from such attendance. If the parent of a pupil at any school who has been excused from attendance at religious worship or instruction, desires him to receive religious instruction of a kind not provided at the school, and the pupil cannot with reasonable convenience be sent to another county or voluntary school where such instruction is provided, the pupil may be withdrawn from the school to receive the instruction during school hours elsewhere, but only if the Local Education Authority are satisfied that this will not interfere with his attendance at school except at the beginning or end of the school session (m). A Local Education Authority may not give directions as to the secular instruction to be given to pupils at a voluntary school, so as to interfere with the provision of reasonable facilities for religious instruction during school hours. The foregoing provisions apply to all schools whether county or voluntary. Special provision is made to meet the different circumstances and histories of county, controlled, aided and special agreement schools.

In *county schools* neither the act of worship nor the religious instruction may be distinctive of any particular denomination, and the religious instruction must be given in accordance with an agreed syllabus (n). The preparation and nature of this syllabus are discussed below. If the school is a county secondary school it may be impossible to find suitable premises elsewhere for those parents who desire to withdraw their children from the religious instruction given in the school, in order that they may receive instruction in accordance with the tenets of a particular denomination. In such cases, if the Local Education Authority are satisfied that satisfactory arrangements have been made for the provision of denominational instruction in the school, and that the cost will not fall on the authority, they must provide facilities for this purpose, unless they are of the opinion that there are special circumstances which would make it unreasonable to do so (o). (No provision is made for children in primary schools to receive denominational instruction on the school premises.) Thus the " right of entry " to county schools, so frequently denied to the clergy, has now been granted in certain cases. Although the act of worship as has been stated, must be held in the school at the beginning of the day, there appears to be no objection to a service being held in a local church on a special occasion, even during school hours, in *addition* to the statutory act of worship at the beginning of the day. Due notice must, however, be given to the parents in order that they may withdraw their children if they so wish, and the attendance of teachers must be entirely voluntary.

In *controlled schools* there is nothing to prevent the collective act of worship from being distinctive of the denomination which originally provided the school, but the religious instruction must be in accordance with the agreed syllabus adopted by the authority (p), unless the parents of any pupils in attendance request that they may receive religious instruction in accordance with the provisions of the trust deed or the previous practice in the school. In that case the foundation managers, unless they are satisfied that it would be unreasonable to do so, must make arrangements for the denominational instruction to be provided during not more than two periods

(k) Education Act 1946, s. 7.
(l) Education Act 1944, s. 25 (2).
(m) *Ibid.*, s. 25 (5). In at least one instance there has been argument as to what is " reasonably convenient." Such disputes can be referred to the Secretary of State under s. 67.
(n) Education Act 1944, s. 26.
(o) Education Act 1944, s. 26, proviso.
(p) *Ibid.*, s. 27 (6).

a week (q). In order that this may be possible, the Local Education Authority must, if the number of the teaching staff exceeds two, appoint reserved teachers as to whose fitness and competence to give the required religious instruction the foundation managers or governors are satisfied. If it is not possible to appoint any reserved teachers owing to the limitations imposed by the Act, the foundation managers or governors still have the duty of arranging for the instruction required, but it may be given by anyone acceptable to them. Similar arrangements may be made for the holding of a service in a local church on a special occasion as have been suggested for county schools.

The agreed syllabus.—*The agreed syllabus* (r) for use in county and controlled schools must be drawn up by a conference, convened by the Local Education Authority, consisting of four committees. These committees must be representative of each of the following: (1) those religious denominations which the authority consider ought to be represented (Roman Catholics decline the invitation to take part); (2) the Church of England; (3) such associations of teachers as in the opinion of the authority ought to be represented; (4) the authority itself. The conference must be unanimous in recommending an agreed syllabus: the authority may accept or reject but not modify the syllabus. In case of failure in unanimous recommendations the Secretary of State must appoint a similarly representative body of persons experienced in religious education to prepare a syllabus (s).

In the thirty years which have elapsed since the passing of the Act, changes in educational ideas, the development of a multi-cultural society and increased secularism have led to demands for a new approach to religious education to be based on a much broader type of syllabus. Whereas the subject was generally taught by form or class teachers giving instruction in Bible study and promoting Christian doctrines and values, it is now largely influenced by specialist teachers who regard religious education " not as indoctrination but as a part of a total preparation for life ". Furthermore with the development of integrated studies, the parental right to withdraw a child from lessons in which religion is one element in social studies has become inappropriate. Even more important in producing a new climate of opinion has been the presence in many schools of a considerable proportion of immigrant children belonging to other faiths. Revision of the agreed syllabus to meet these new conditions proceeded without dissension in many areas until public controversy was aroused in Birmingham in 1973 when a duly constituted conference produced after four years' work an agreed syllabus and teachers' manual which included sections on world religions and on communism and humanism.

The proposed syllabus and manual were rejected by the county borough council and subsequently accepted by the Birmingham Metropolitan District Council in 1974. But issues had been raised that resulted in postponement. These issues were (1) should the syllabus be confined to Christianity? There is no such restriction in the Act; (2) should communism be regarded as part of religious education? The conference had been unanimous in accepting both these non-religious stances alongside religious studies; (3) the detailed work was set out in a 600 page manual whereas the actual syllabus consisted of one page so a query arose as to whether the latter constituted a syllabus. Advised by counsel that it did not, the Birmingham authority requested the conference to revise and amplify the syllabus. The new syllabus was accepted in 1975. During the debate a fundamental issue had emerged—should religious education cease to be a compulsory component of the curriculum? To make this possible ss. 25–29 of the Education Act, 1944, would need to be amended.

(q) *Ibid.*, s. 27 (1).
(r) *Ibid.*, s. 114 (1).
(s) *Ibid.*, s. 29 and Fifth Schedule.

In *aided* or *special agreement schools* the religious instruction given is under the control of the managers or governors, and must be in accordance with the provisions of the trust deed or the practice observed in the school before it became a voluntary school (t). If, however, the parents of any of the pupils desire them to receive religious instruction in accordance with an agreed syllabus, and they cannot with reasonable convenience cause them to attend a school at which that syllabus is in use, then the managers or governors must make arrangements for such instruction to be given during the times set apart for religious instruction, unless the authority consider it would be unreasonable to do so. If the managers or governors are unwilling to make such arrangements then the authority themselves must make the arrangements.

It will be noted that in cases where parents require religious instruction of a kind not given at the school attended by their children, the question arises as to the reasonable convenience of the children attending another school where the required instruction is given. In this connection the possibility of the provision of transport under s. 55 must be considered. Assurances were given to the various denominations that the Minister, in considering the proposals of a Local Education Authority in their Development Plan as regards transport, would have regard to the desirability of arrangements being made to facilitate the attendance of children at schools where religious instruction of a kind desired by the parents was given. Local Education Authorities must have regard to the general principle that, so far as is compatible with the provision of efficient instruction and training and the avoidance of unreasonable public expenditure, pupils are to be educated in accordance with the wishes of their parents (u). In *Watt* v. *Kesteven County Council*, [1955] 1 All E.R. 473; [1955] 1 Q.B. 408, it was held that this did not mean that there was a duty to provide education for the child of a particular parent in the particular way that the parent wished, but only to consider the wishes of parents in general terms, and, in any case, the duty, if any, could only be enforced by the Minister under ss. 68 and 99 (i) and not by the Courts. The Manual of Guidance, Schools No. 1, " Choice of Schools ", issued by the Ministry, gave the Minister's view on the principles which should be observed by the authorities in this matter.

As regards special schools, the regulations as to their conduct must secure that, so far as is practicable, every pupil in attendance at such schools will attend religious worship and religious instruction or will be withdrawn from attendance at such worship or instruction in accordance with the wishes of his parent (a). If a Local Education Authority consider that education suitable to a child can best be given at a particular school and it is therefore necessary that he should be provided with boarding accommodation, otherwise than at the school, they must arrange, so far as is practicable, to give effect to the wishes of the parent of the child, with respect to the religious denomination of the person with whom he will reside (b). As regards pupils in boarding schools, if a parent wishes his child to attend worship in accordance with the tenets of a particular religious denomination on a day exclusively set apart for religious observance, or to receive denominational religious instruction outside school hours, the managers or governors must afford reasonable opportunities for this, though not so as to entail expenditure by the Local Education Authority (c).

Religious instruction in accordance with an agreed syllabus, given in any school maintained by a Local Education Authority, may only be inspected

(t) *Ibid.*, s. 28 (1). In a special agreement school the religious instruction will be given by reserved teachers, the number of whom will be specified in the agreement.

(u) Education Act, 1944, s. 76.

(a) *Ibid.*, s. 33 (4) and Handicapped Pupils and Special Schools Regulations, Reg. 8, S.I. 1959 No. 365.

(b) Education Act 1944, s. 50 (2).

(c) *Ibid.*, s. 25 (7).

by one of Her Majesty's inspectors or by a person ordinarily employed to inspect secular instruction either by the Secretary of State or by the authority. Religious instruction in a voluntary school, other than that in accordance with an agreed syllabus, may be inspected under arrangements made by the managers or governors of the school. In controlled schools such arrangements may be made only by the foundation managers. Inspections so arranged by the managers or governors may not be held on more than two days in a year, and fourteen days notice of them must be given to the Local Education Authority (d).

Except for teachers employed in aided schools and reserved teachers in controlled or special agreement schools (who may not be penalised because of the fact that they give religious instruction or because of their religious opinions or because of their attending religious worship), no person may be disqualified by reason of his religious opinions, or of his attending or omitting to attend religious worship, from being a teacher in a county or voluntary school, or from being otherwise employed for the purposes of such a school (e.g., as a caretaker), and no teacher may be required to give religious instruction or be penalised in any way because he does or does not give religious instruction, or by reason of his religious opinions, or of his attending or omitting to attend religious worship. Similar protection is also given to teachers in special schools (e).

8. FURTHER and HIGHER EDUCATION

Further and higher education (f) is one of the major and most costly responsibilities of Local Education Authorities, but its current importance is not reflected in the 1944 Act; this is not surprising since the growth of this sector of the education service could not have been foreseen in 1944.

Prior to 1944 Local Education Authorities had the power to supply or aid the supply of education for students over compulsory school age otherwise than at school; under the 1944 Act this power became a duty and authorities were required to secure provision of further education in the form of (1) full-time and part-time education for persons over compulsory school age and (2) leisure time occupation for persons over compulsory school age who are able and willing to profit by the facilities provided (g). In addition it was intended that county colleges should be established for the compulsory part-time education of young persons during the period between leaving school and attaining the age of eighteen (h). No such colleges were established and this type of further education is no longer national policy. That the promoters of the Act attached great importance to the continued education of school leavers up to the age of eighteen is indicated by the four lengthy sections devoted to county colleges and enforcement of attendance at them. Despite developments in further education and the raising of the school-leaving age, the fact remains that the majority of young people, particularly young women, between the ages of sixteen and eighteen do not continue their education after leaving school.

Local Education Authorities were required to submit schemes of further education to the Secretary of State by the end of March 1948 (i); in preparing

(d) Education Act 1944, *Ibid.*, s. 77 (5).

(e) *Ibid.*, s. 30 and Handicapped Pupils and Special Schools Regulations, 1959, S.I. 1959 No. 365, Reg. 17 (2).

(f) The term "higher" education as currently used does not appear in the 1944 Act nor indeed in the Further Education Regulations. It is used to describe "advanced" courses leading to qualifications of higher standard than GCE advanced level or its equivalent. This is the sense in which the Committee of Enquiry on Higher Education (Robbins Committee, 1963) used the term; it includes the full- and part-time work of universities, colleges of education, polytechnics and other institutions concerned with advanced courses. Further education denotes the remainder of educational provision (vocational and recreational) for persons over compulsory school age not still in attendance at school.

(g) Education Act 1944, s. 41.

(h) *Ibid.*, ss. 43–46.

(i) *Ibid.*, s. 42.

their schemes they had to have regard to any facilities provided by other bodies and were required to consult such bodies as well as adjacent local authorities. The schemes submitted were, in general, less detailed than the development plans for schools; in any case they soon became irrelevant owing to the rapid expansion of further education and the need for planning of the more advanced work at regional and national level.

As far back as 1925 the growth of further education had led to unnecessary duplication of courses; a major step in rationalising the provision was taken in 1947 with the establishment of nine regional advisory councils (the Welsh Joint Education Committee acted as the regional advisory council in Wales) to cover the whole of England (k). Their purpose was to bring education and industry together in order first, to find out the needs of young people for further education and to advise on the necessary provision, and second, to secure reasonable economy of provision.

In 1956 the White Paper on Technical Education (l), in reviewing the contemporary position, remarked that " there never has been any uniform pattern of technical education throughout the country over the last sixty years. Technical colleges had grown up in response to local demand and their siting had been largely dictated by the location of industry. A remarkable variety of studies existed, from the preliminary courses for boys and girls of fifteen to postgraduate work. Courses at every level could be found in the same technical colleges ". In addition, there were also a number of national colleges financed in some cases by the then Ministry of Education and in others jointly by the Ministry and the industry concerned (m). Technical education is, of course, only part of further education which includes also courses in commerce and art, but it was this aspect which at the time concerned the Government most. The White Paper set out a five year plan for the development of technical education over the country as a whole. Systematisation by levels of work, recommended in the White Paper, was gradually established. There were local colleges engaged mainly in supplying education, full or part time, for students below the age of eighteen; area colleges providing more advanced courses as well as courses similar to those in local colleges; regional colleges concerned almost exclusively with more advanced courses including a substantial amount of full time study; finally, there were colleges of advanced technology whose courses led to a degree or postgraduate qualification. All these colleges were to be maintained by local education authorities but an exception to this pattern was made in 1957 when colleges of advanced technology (CATs) became institutions financed by a direct grant from the Secretary of State; the process of transfer from local authorities was not, however, completed until 1962 (n). In accordance with recommendations made by the Robbins Committee (n), these colleges later became universities, the first college receiving its charter in 1965. The other recommendation of the Committee implemented at about the same time was the establishment of the Council for National Academic Awards (CNAA); it took over the work of the National Council for Technological Awards which had previously been responsible for the award of Diplomas in Technology. The CNAA was empowered to grant pass, honours and postgraduate degrees in science, technology and other subjects on the successful completion of approved courses in regional and area colleges. The Council's work has now expanded considerably; it validates many of the courses in polytechnics, some degree courses in colleges of education and courses leading to the new Diploma in Higher Education (o).

(k) Regional advisory councils had, in fact, been established in Yorkshire in 1929 and in the West Midlands in 1935.
(l) Cmnd. 9703.
(m) e.g. National Leathersellers College, National College of Rubber Technology (now a department of the Northern Polytechnic).
(n) Committee of Enquiry on Higher Education (1963).
(o) See note (u), p. 51.

Concurrently with these developments opportunities for higher education were increased by the creation of new universities in addition to those established by the conversion of colleges of advanced technology into universities. The most recent development in university education was the establishment of the Open University in 1971.

In 1965 the Secretary of State outlined the Government's policy with regard to advanced further education (p); this policy accepted a dual system (later termed the " binary " system) based on two sectors represented by institutions of university status on the one hand and by leading technical colleges and colleges of education on the other. In the Government's view it was desirable that a substantial part of higher education should be " under social control and directly responsible to social needs ".

In the following year the White Paper *A Plan for Polytechnics and Other Colleges* (q) was issued announcing the intention of the Government to designate a limited number of large regional colleges as polytechnics and indicating that future planning would aim at building up advanced work—full and part time—in polytechnics rather than in other colleges. Polytechnics were to be thought of " as comprehensive institutions of higher education embracing full time, part time and sandwich students as well as bringing together in a single combined college, engineering, social studies commerce and art ". They were to continue to be administered by Local Education Authorities. The first polytechnics were designated in 1968 and by the end of 1969 schemes for 29 polytechnics had been approved by the Secretary of State. Polytechnics were in general, formed by the amalgamation of some or all of the existing colleges of art, commerce and technology maintained by the Local Education Authority; they have since diversified their work to provide courses in social work, teacher training, management studies and foreign languages, catering not only for the student seeking an initial qualification but also for the post-experience student from industry and commerce and for postgraduate students.

In order to appreciate the most recent changes in higher education it is necessary to look briefly at the provision for teacher training. Training colleges for teachers have traditionally been somewhat apart from the mainstream of further and higher education. Provided by Local Education Authorities and by voluntary bodies, they have always been subject to close supervision by the Board of Education and subsequently by the Department of Education and Science. Providing courses (of two years' duration, increased to three in 1961) only for intending teachers, colleges fitted in neither with universities nor further education. After 1944 links between colleges and universities were developed through area training organisations but not to the extent that the colleges had hoped; moreover, throughout the late fifties and early sixties the colleges and their providing bodies were preoccupied with the expansion needed to provide sufficient teachers for the growing school population and to reduce the size of classes.

Not until the training of teachers was included in the terms of reference of the Committee of Enquiry on Higher Education (r) had teacher training been regarded as an integral part of the system of higher education. The Committee recommended fundamental changes in the administration of training colleges, notably that local authorities should cease to maintain them and that they should be free from control by the Secretary of State; instead it was suggested that they should be financed by the universities by means of an earmarked grant from the University Grants Committee. This recommendation proved unacceptable to the Secretary of State and to local authorities so the colleges remained under the control of the local authorities and voluntary bodies in partnership with the Secretary of State. A recommendation that a fourth-year course leading to a university degree (B.Ed.)

(p) In a speech delivered on the occasion of the 75th anniversary of Woolwich Polytechnic 27.4.65.

(q) Cmd. 3006.

(r) Robbins Committee (1963).

as well as a professional qualification should be made available to suitably qualified students in the colleges was implemented as also was the suggestion that the colleges should be renamed " colleges of education ".

In 1972 a further review of teacher training was undertaken by the James Committee (s) whose report recommended radical changes which involved integrating the colleges of education fully into the pattern of higher education. These were, in general, acceptable and incorporated into the most recent policy decisions about the future of higher education announced in the White Paper *Education—A Framework for Expansion* (t).

The White Paper envisages that the major expansion up to 1981 in the provision of higher education will take place in polytechnics, colleges of further education and colleges of education rather than in universities. Local Education Authorities and governors of voluntary colleges of education were asked to consider the future of the colleges in relation to other institutions of higher education and to submit proposals to the Secretary of State. The pattern emerging is for the amalgamation of two or more colleges of education: for colleges to merge with a polytechnic or a college of further education; and for the enlargement of a number of big colleges and for the closure of some small and geographically isolated colleges. The colleges which remain will no longer be exclusively concerned with teacher training but will provide courses, among others, leading to the Diploma in Higher Education (u).

Parallel with the rationalisation of further education at the more advanced level, developments have taken place at the lower level. The White Paper *Better Opportunities in Technical Education* (a) of 1961 contained proposals for " a major reconstruction of the system of courses for technicians, craftsmen and operatives in technical colleges ". The proposed changes were intended to broaden the students' education, to increase the variety of courses available and to reduce the number of students who failed to complete the courses successfully. The proposals, particularly those relating to trainee technicians, were largely implemented during the sixties. Although they did not apply to courses at the same level in commerce and other non-technical fields, a similar reorganisation was taking place in the field of commerce on the lines recommended by the McMeeking Report (b); the resulting reorganisation during the sixties closely resembled that taking place in the technical field. At the same time changes were taking place in day release courses and as a result of the Industrial Training Act 1964. Under the Act, industrial training boards were established for each main industry; their principal duties are to provide, or secure the provision of, facilities for the training of persons employed or to be employed in the industry: to publish recommendations as to the nature and length of training and the further education to be associated with it: to apply or arrange for the application of tests of selection and attainment (c).

A further review of technical education at the lower level was undertaken in 1969 by a committee of the National Advisory Council on Education in Industry and Commerce (d). The committee, after an exhaustive review of the developments which had taken place in day release and further education for technicians, considered that the administrative machinery for a rapidly evolving system of further education at this level was too inflexible. They therefore recommended the establishment of a Technician Education

(s) Committee of Enquiry into Teacher Education and Training.
(t) Cmnd. 5174 (1972). See also DES Circulars 7/73 and 6/74.
(u) This qualification was first recommended by the James Committee and its scope expanded in the White Paper. It is obtained after a two-year course of study of post-A level standard, the normal minimum entry qualification being the same as for admission to a degree or comparable course. It is intended that the course should be offered by institutions in each of the main sectors of higher education.
(a) Cmnd. 1254.
(b) Report of the Advisory Committee on Further Education in Commerce (1959).
(c) These duties were continued by the Employment and Training Act 1973.
(d) Hazlegrave Report 1969.

Council " to plan, administer and keep under review the development of a unified national pattern of courses of technical education for technicians in industry; and in pursuance of this to devise or approve suitable courses, establish and assess standards of performance, and award certificates and diplomas as appropriate ". The Council was established in 1973. The committee also recommended that similarly a Business Education Council should be set up to perform analagous functions for commerce; this Council was also established in 1973.

It is clear that a national pattern is evolving in further and higher education at all levels to replace the provision of further education organised at local level in 1944 and to increase the supply of higher education which existed at that time only in universities. It will be noted that all these changes and developments have been initiated by central government, either following the publication of white papers or reports of committees of enquiry, and are not the result of legislation. The implementation of national policy, as set out in the various policy documents, has been closely controlled by the Secretary of State though, he has, of course, consulted the various interested bodies before making decisions. This control has, perhaps, been most obvious in his attitude to the proposals of Local Education Authorities relating to the future of colleges of education.

Non-vocational education.—Under s. 41 of the Education Act 1944 Local Education Authorities are required to provide or to assist in the provision of facilities for leisure time occupations—cultural and recreational—for both young people and adults. Although local authorities provide the majority of these facilities, " responsible bodies " supply a sizeable proportion as do a large number of local voluntary associations.

For young people local authorities organise a youth service in conjunction with local voluntary bodies, the service taking the form of youth clubs, courses of the outward bound type, local voluntary service groups, arrangements for foreign travel and exchange with foreign youth groups together with many other activities depending on local need and demand.

For other age groups there are classes in evening institutes, community centres and short courses in residential colleges maintained by local authorities. Authorities also assist with the provision of classes for such bodies as the Townswomen's Guild and Womens Institutes.

The most important " responsible bodies " are the Workers Educational Association and the university extra-mural departments both of which organise mainly cultural courses requiring a high degree of commitment on the part of the student to private reading and to a willingness to participate in discussion; they also organise short courses at summer schools. The current most popular subjects of study are social studies, archaeology, history, particularly local history, and English language and literature (e). These bodies work in close association with the Local Education Authority in order to avoid duplication; they receive financial aid both from the Authority and in the form of a direct grant from the Secretary of State (f). There are, in addition, six independent adult colleges which receive grants from the Secretary of State; they provide long courses and essentially offer " second chance " education to enable students to go on to professional or occupational training or to universities as mature students (g). Most of the students at these six colleges receive discretionary awards from Local Education Authorities.

As well as providing courses and classes, Local Education Authorities have the power to organise or assist with the organisation of concerts, exhibitions and plays.

(e) For an analysis of the subjects studied see *Adult Education—A Plan for Development* (Russell Report) (1973).

(f) Further Education Regulations, S.I. 1975 No. 1054.

(g) The colleges are Ruskin, Plater, Fircroft, Hillcroft, Harlech and the Cooperative College.

Non-vocational further education is essentially a service to meet local needs as local authorities see them but how far there is an unmet need is difficult for an authority to know. The Russell Committee (h) were asked to assess this need and " to make recommendations with a view to obtaining the most economical deployment of available resources to enable adult education to make its proper contribution to the national system of education conceived of as a process continuing through life ". The Committee suggested that there should be a planned quaternary stage of education which is identifiably *adult*; that the needs of various groups—for example, the disadvantaged, those taking up new responsibilities (as parents, elected representatives, shop stewards), the retired—must be taken into account in future planning. The Committee recommended the establishment of a Development Council for Adult Education with a local council in the area of each Education Authority together with sub-committees of the regional advisory councils for adult education. Such councils have not yet been set up.

In addition to their duties under s. 41 of the Act, Local Education Authorities have powers under s. 53. These include the power to establish, maintain and manage, or assist in doing so, camps, holiday classes, play centres and other places, such as playgrounds, gymnasia and swimming baths (not appropriated to any school or college) at which facilities for recreation and training are available for persons receiving primary, secondary or further education. Authorities may also organise games, expeditions and other activities for such persons and pay or assist in the payment of the expenses involved.

Grants to students.—Prior to 1944, assistance to students attending universities consisted of a limited number of state scholarships awarded by the Board of Education and scholarships or exhibitions given by Local Education Authorities. The latter varied in number and value from authority to authority but they rarely covered the full cost of maintenance and fees; some Authorities provided loans for students. After 1944 state scholarships continued as did the power of local authorities to give assistance (i). Not until the Education Act 1962 (k) did it become mandatory upon Local Education Authorities to make awards to all students with the necessary educational qualifications pursuing first degree or comparable courses (l). At the same time the Secretary of State ceased to award state scholarships to such students.

The regulations (m) issued by the Secretary of State under the Act define the qualifications and courses to which mandatory awards apply and specify the value of the award, taking into account parental income with exceptions to be made in the case of older students and students with dependents. Mandatory awards now also apply to students pursuing full-time courses leading to the Diploma in Higher Education and the Higher National Diploma (n) and to students undertaking initial training as teachers whether in colleges of education or in university departments of education (o). In special circumstances the Secretary of State may supplement mandatory awards (p).

The Education Act 1962 enables the Secretary of State to bestow awards on students pursuing postgraduate or comparable courses, on mature students undertaking first degree courses in certain subjects, on students

(h) Committee of Enquiry into Adult Education.

(i) Education Act 1944, s. 81 (c); Education Act 1962, s. 4 (4) amends the principal Act.

(k) This was based on the recommendations of the Anderson Report *Grants to Students* (1960).

(l) Education Act 1962, s. 1.

(m) The Local Education Authorities Awards Regulations 1975, S.I. 1975 No. 1207.

(n) Education Act 1975, s. 1.

(o) *Ibid.*

(p) Education Act 1973, s. 3. See also The Students Dependants' Regulations 1975, S.I. 1975 No. 1125.

taking first degree courses in initial studies and on students attending courses at adult education colleges (q).

Local Education Authorities have the power to make awards to students (not entitled to mandatory awards) undertaking full-time or part-time courses of further and higher education. These are generally known as "discretionary" awards; the criteria for, and number of, such awards is, as the name suggests, at the discretion of the local authority (r).

The provision of transport for students is referred to in s. 55 of the Education Act, 1944, under which local education authorities are required to make such arrangements for the provision of transport as they consider necessary or as the Secretary of State may direct for the purpose of facilitating the attendance of pupils (i.e., persons of any age for whom education is required to be provided under the Act) at any course or class provided under a scheme of further education, and no charge may be made for such transport. An authority may also pay the whole or part of the reasonable travelling expenses in the case of a pupil attending a course of further education for whom no transport has been arranged.

9. SPECIAL SERVICES

The powers and duties in relation to certain aspects of children's welfare were acquired by Local Education Authorities during the first half of the twentieth century. They ante-dated the statutory duties for the welfare of society as a whole which have now become an integral part of governmental responsibility. That welfare functions formed a part of the education service was wholly due to the need to ensure that children were in a position to benefit from the education provided.

From the beginning of compulsory attendance at school, it became obvious that many children were in poor health and lacked medical treatment, suffered malnutrition, were inadequately clothed and were compelled to leave school at the earliest possible moment owing to their families' inability to afford to let them remain at school.

The first welfare power acquired by Local Education Authorities was in 1906 when the Education (Provision of Meals) Act enabled them to assist voluntary organisations in feeding necessitous children attending elementary schools. On the ground that there might be children in schools who were unable by reason of lack of food to take full advantage of the education provided, the Act also empowered Local Education Authorities to provide meals, but the cost had to be recovered unless parents were unable to pay. During the Second World War, the provision of meals was greatly expanded, partly to ensure that children during a period of strict rationing were adequately fed and partly to enable mothers to work. Cheap milk was also provided during this period for all children at school.

Medical inspection was first introduced by the school boards of London and Bradford but not until 1907 did it become the duty of Local Education Authorities to arrange medical inspection for children in elementary schools; at the same time they acquired the power to attend to the health and physical condition of children in these schools. In 1921 the power to provide medical treatment became a duty for children in elementary schools; in secondary schools medical inspection but not medical treatment, was obligatory. In both types of schools the cost of medical treatment where provided had to be recovered if the parents could afford to pay.

No further welfare duties or powers were acquired until 1944 although voluntary organisations, with co-operation from the local education authority, often provided boots for necessitous children and authorities gave scholar-

---

(q) Education Act 1962, s. 3; Education Act 1975, s. 2; State Awards Regulations 1963, S.I. 1963 No. 1223, amended by S.I. 1969 No. 554.

(r) Education Act 1962, s. 2; Education Act 1975, Sch. Part 1.

ships and bursaries to pupils in secondary schools who remained at school beyond the age of compulsory attendance.

Evacuation of children from vulnerable areas during the Second World War revealed that, despite the powers and duties of Local Education Authorities, many children were undernourished, badly clothed and in poor physical condition, a fact that influenced the framing of the Education Act in 1944 and led to the inclusion in the Act of a number of provisions relating to the welfare of children. Under the Act the provision of milk and meals was put on a completely new footing; medical inspection and treatment (and from 1953 dental inspection and treatment) became obligatory and free in all maintained schools; Local Education Authorities acquired the power to ensure cleanliness among children, to provide clothing and to pay maintenance allowances to children at school over compulsory school age.

With the welfare services now provided for the community as a whole, the need for the Local Education Authority to provide welfare services especially for children at school has been questioned as also has the justification of such services being a charge upon the Local Education Authority. To a certain extent the latter question is academic since some at least of these services would have to be provided by the Local Authority and the charge merely transferred to another department of the Authority. On the other hand, it can be argued that it is the responsibility of the Secretary of State for Health and Social Services to secure, through his social security arrangements, that children are adequately clothed, adequately fed (i.e. that he should be responsible for providing clothing and the cost of free meals) and in receipt of maintenance allowances where these are necessary to retain children at school. The fact that expenditure on medical and on dental inspection and treatment has been transferred to the Secretary of State for Health and Social Services tends to reinforce this argument. A further point to be considered is the problem of means-tested benefits operated by different agencies, e.g. the provision of free meals, clothing and maintenance allowances is administered by the Local Education Authority while other benefits are a matter for the Department of Health and Social Services.

Provision of meals.—The 1944 Act placed a duty upon Local Education Authorities to provide a midday meal for all children in maintained schools whose parents wished them to have a meal (s). The original regulations issued under the Act required Local Education Authorities to establish a school meals service, to appoint an organiser of school meals and to employ suitable staff for the preparation, cooking, service and transport of meals. An Authority is, however, no longer required to appoint an organiser (t). The same regulations gave Local Education Authorities the power to require teachers to supervise meals. This regulation was a source of conflict between teachers and the Secretary of State, and since 1968 teachers have no longer been obliged to undertake supervision although they may do so voluntarily (u).

Until 1967 approved expenditure on the school meals service was reimbursed in full to Local Education Authorities by the Secretary of State, but since that date expenditure has become a charge upon the local authority (a).

Managers and governors of all maintained schools must offer such facilities in the school as are required by the authority for the school meals

---

(s) Education Act 1944, s. 49.

(t) Local Government Act 1972, s. 112 (3).

(u) Provision of Milk and Meals (Amendment No. 2) Regulations, S.I. 1968 No. 1251. These regulations were revoked and in the current regulations no reference is made to supervision by teachers. Although non-professional ancillary help is provided for the supervision of children, the position regarding the safety and well being of children during the dinner break is obscure. In practice, the headteacher normally undertakes this responsibility (see DES Circular 16/68, Appendix 1, para. 7) but whether it is reasonable that he should be expected to do so is a question that has not been determined.

(a) Local Government Act 1966, s. 14.

service. Any necessary expenditure in making alterations or additions in connection with the school meals service is a charge on the authority (b).

The original regulations provided that parents should be charged for dinners, a charge to cover approximately the cost of food, but that the charge should be remitted in cases of financial hardship in accordance with approved income scales drawn up by the Authority. Owing to the variation in the scales, local scales were replaced in 1964 by national scales. The scales are adjusted from time to time by regulation as also is the price of meals. The last increase took place on 1st April 1975 when the charge was raised from 12p to 15p; the Secretary of State has announced that increases are likely to be made annually (c).

Provision of milk.—The original regulations made under the Act stipulated that all children in maintained schools should be provided daily with free milk (d). In 1968 free milk for children in secondary schools and in middle schools deemed to be secondary schools was withdrawn (e); in 1970 free milk for children of primary school age in middle schools was restored (f). Finally, in 1971, free milk was withdrawn from all children over the age of seven other than those attending special schools and those of primary school age whom a medical officer had certified as in need of milk. Local Education Authorities may provide milk for other children but no cost may fall on the authority (g). Expenditure on milk was reimbursed by the Secretary of State to Local Authorities until 1967 when it became a charge on the authority (h).

Provision of clothing.—Local Education Authorities have the power to provide children with clothing (i). Where it appears to them that a pupil at a school maintained by them or at a special school whether maintained by them or not, is unable by reason of the inadequacy or unsuitability of his clothing to take full advantage of the education provided, they may provide him with such clothing as they consider necessary. Assistance with school uniform is not given under the provision of clothing regulations but by virtue of the regulations made under s. 81 of the Act (k).

Provision of transport.—Local Education Authorities are required to make arrangements for the provision of transport and otherwise (i.e. pay fares) as they consider necessary or as the Secretary of State may direct, to enable children to attend schools (l). Authorities may pay wholly or partly the reasonable travelling expenses for children attending schools and for students attending courses of further education (m).

Maintenance allowances.—Local Education Authorities have the power to make maintenance allowances to children over compulsory school age. There is no national scale for such allowances and each authority operates its own scale taking into account parental income (n).

School health service.—For thirty years after the passing of the Education Act 1944, Local Education Authorities were responsible for the

(b) Provision of Milk and Meals Regulations, S.I. 1969 No. 483.
(c) Provision of Milk and Meals Regulations, S.I. 1975 No. 311.
(d) Education Act 1944, s. 49.
(e) Public Expenditure and Receipts Act 1968, s. 3.
(f) The Education (School Milk) Act 1970.
(g) The Education (Milk) Act 1971.
(h) Public Expenditure and Receipts Act 1968, s. 3.
(i) Education Act 1948, s. 5; Education (Miscellaneous Provisions) Act 1953, s. 17 and Sch. 1.
(k) Regulations for Scholarships and Other Benefits S.R. and O. 1945 No. 666, amended by S.I. 1948 No. 2223.
(l) Education Act 1944, s. 55 (1). See p. 37 as to the definition of walking distance from home to school.
(m) Education Act 1944, s. 55 (2); Education (Miscellaneous Provisions) Act 1948, s. 11.
(n) Education Act 1944, s. 81.

school health service, i.e. for the medical and dental inspection and treatment of pupils in maintained schools. In 1973 this responsibility was removed from Local Education Authorities and transferred to the Secretary of State for Health and Social Services who is required to provide for the medical and dental inspection at regular intervals of children in maintained schools and for the treatment of such pupils (o). In addition he may, by arrangement with the Local Education Authority and with the agreement of the governors, provide for the medical and dental inspection and treatment of senior pupils attending any educational establishment other than a school which is maintained by an Authority and at which full-time further education is provided.

He may also make similar provision for a child who is receiving education otherwise than at a school and, by arrangement with the proprietor, for junior and senior pupils attending an educational establishment not maintained by an Authority. The latter arrangement may include payment by the proprietor (p).

In county schools Local Education Authorities, and in voluntary schools the managers or governors, must make available to the Secretary of State for Health and Social Services the accommodation required for the purpose of medical and dental inspection and treatment (q). It is also the duty of Local Education Authorities to make arrangements for encouraging and assisting pupils to take advantage of the medical and dental facilities provided, but if the parent notifies the authority that he objects to his child availing himself of the treatment provided, the child shall not be encouraged or assisted to do so (r).

In practice, the school health service has become the responsibility of the Area Health Authority which is co-terminous with the Education Authority; arrangements for the school health service are co-ordinated through local joint consultative committees which contain members and officers from the Local Education Authority as well as members and officers of the area health authority (s).

The power to ensure cleanliness.—A local education authority has also the power to secure that the person or clothing of any pupil in attendance at a school maintained by them is not infested with vermin or in a foul condition. They may for this purpose authorise a medical officer to cause examinations of the persons and clothing of pupils in attendance at any or all of the schools maintained by them, whenever in his opinion such examinations are necessary in the interests of cleanliness (t). The examination will be made by a person authorised by the authority, and if the person or clothing of a pupil is found to be infested with vermin or in a foul condition, any officer of the authority may serve on the parent of the pupil a notice requiring him to cause the person and clothing of the pupil to be cleansed within the time stated on the notice, not being less than twenty-four hours, otherwise the cleansing will be carried out by the authority. If an order is made by a medical officer or if the cleansing is requested by a parent, it is the duty of the authority to secure that the cleansing is carried out at suitable premises by suitable persons with suitable appliances, and the local education authority may require the council of any county district in their area who are entitled to the use of any such premises or appliances, to permit the education authority to use them on such terms as may be agreed or determined, in default of agreement, by the Minister of Health.

(o) National Health Service Reorganisation Act 1973, s. 3.
(p) *Ibid.*
(q) *Ibid.*
(r) Education Act 1944, s. 48 (4).
(s) See DHSS Circular HRC (74) 19.
(t) Education Act, 1944, s. 54 (1). Guidance on the administration of this section is given in Adm. Memo. 156 (27.5.46).

An order by a medical officer will be sufficient to authorise any officer of the authority to convey the pupil to the suitable premises, detain him there and cause his person and clothing to be cleansed. After the cleansing has been carried out, if the person or clothing of the pupil is again, owing to neglect, found to be infested with vermin or in a foul condition at any time while he is in attendance at a school maintained by a local education authority, the parent will be liable on summary conviction to a fine not exceeding one pound. If a medical officer suspects that the person or clothing of a pupil is verminous or in a foul condition, but action for the examination or cleansing cannot be taken immediately, he may, if he considers it necessary, either in the interests of the pupil or of the other pupils, direct that the pupil be excluded from attendance until such action is taken. Such a direction will be a defence in proceedings for failure to cause the pupil to attend school unless it is proved that the exclusion was necessitated by the wilful default of the pupil or his parent. No girl may be examined or cleansed except by a qualified medical practitioner or by a woman authorised for that purpose by a local education authority.

CAREERS SERVICE

The concern of Local Education Authorities with the employment of " juveniles " dates back to 1910 when Authorities acquired the power to set up juvenile employment bureaux whose work was supervised by the Board of Education. Subsequently those Local Education Authorities which had opted to use this power were enabled to provide a complete employment service for young people which after 1927 was controlled by the Minister of Labour.

The Ince Committee, reporting in 1945, recommended that Local Education Authorities should again be given the opportunity of providing a youth employment service. The recommendation was implemented by the Employment and Training Act 1948, and the majority of Local Education Authorities accepted responsibility for a comprehensive service for persons up to the age of eighteen. The service was under the supervision of the Minister of Labour who contributed to the cost of local authority schemes. The service was responsible not only for advice and placement of young people in jobs and assistance to employers in obtaining suitable employees but also for payment of unemployment benefit and national assistance grants to unemployed young people.

The Local Government Act 1972 (u) required Local Education Authorities responsible for the Youth Employment Service before 1st April 1974 to continue carrying out their responsibilities, but this section of the Act was repealed before it came into operation and radical changes in the approach to the employment service for young people were made by the Employment and Training Act 1973.

Local Education Authorities are now required to provide a careers service for persons attending either full- or part-time all educational institutions (except universities), i.e. schools, colleges of further education, colleges of education and polytechnics. The service must provide (1) advice on suitable employment and its availability together with information about any necessary training required; (2) assistance in obtaining employment and training; (3) assistance by collecting and providing information about persons seeking and offering employment and about persons providing facilities for training. Local Authorities must also arrange to make the service available to university students who seek to make use of it.

The Local Education Authority may (and must in so far as the Secretary of State for Employment directs it to do so) provide advice and assistance in a similar manner to those who are seeking different employment.

(u) Section 209 repealed by Employment and Training Act 1973, Sch. 4.

Two or more Local Education Authorities may act jointly in carrying out their careers service functions for the whole or parts of their areas, and one local authority may act on behalf of another. Local Authorities must consult and co-operate with one another as far as it is necessary to do so to provide an efficient service (a).

Authorities must record the vocational advice given and forward the record on request by another Authority where a student leaves an educational institution in the first Authority to attend such an institution in the area of the second. When a person leaves school the Authority must give him a summary of the advice given and, provided he is under eighteen, must comply with a request from the parent or guardian for a copy of the summary (b).

Supervision of the service is carried out by the Secretary of State for Employment (c). The new careers service is based at present on the Youth Employment Service which existed before 1974 since the necessary administrative machinery and officers were already available in most Local Education Authorities. Its scope has been widened to provide a service for all those leaving educational institutions, whether they are over or under eighteen. This is a welcome innovation particularly for the minority of students who for one reason or another fail to complete the course on which they have embarked. It is, however, not possible at this stage of development of the service to assess whether there will be duplication of effort if both the careers service and employment exchanges or "job centres" organised by the Department of Employment deal with young people seeking different employment. It may be that the ultimate intention of the Secretary of State for Employment is to restrict the work of Local Education Authorities to initial vocational advice and assistance with employment. While this development would not be welcomed by Local Education Authorities, it is a less important matter than the retention of close links between schools and the careers service in order to provide a basis for the best possible vocational advice to school leavers.

10. EDUCATIONAL FINANCE

From the time that the government became involved in assisting public elementary education, one principle has been firmly pursued, namely that public education should not be administered or wholly financed centrally since, if this principle was not adhered to, too much power would be placed in the hands of the government of the day. That a counter-balance to central control was considered desirable in 1870 is clearly demonstrated by the creation of local school boards to administer and partially to finance public elementary schools.

By 1944 the principle had evolved in such a way as to suggest that the best method of administering education was by means of a partnership between the central government and Local Education Authorities with the role of each partner being clearly defined by statute (d). For effective partnership, for responsible local government and for reasonable local autonomy it follows that local authorities must bear a substantial proportion of the cost of the joint enterprise. Owing to the high cost of education and the large proportion of total local authority expenditure which it requires, suggestions are made from time to time that some of or all educational expenditure should be transferred to the Exchequer. Mandatory awards have been so transferred but since Local Education Authorities have no discretion in the making of these awards their autonomy is not thereby reduced. A more recent and controversial suggestion is for the transfer of the

---

(a) Employment and Training Act 1973, s. 8.
(b) *Ibid.*, s. 9.
(c) *Ibid.*, s. 10.
(d) See p. 4.

cost of teachers' salaries to central government in order to reduce the pressure on local rates—a suggestion which, if carried out, could have far-reaching effects on the relationship between local and central government.

A Local Education Authority derives its income from a variety of sources: fees paid by students or their employers for further education; payments by parents for school meals; receipts from letting of educational premises; recoupment in respect of the cost of providing education for pupils and students living in the areas of other Local Education Authorities. The income from these sources is, however, small; the main income of a local authority is drawn from the rate levied and from government grants.

Before government grants are considered reference must be made to a major problem in connection with their allocation. It has long been recognised that if the standard of education available in one local authority is to be approximately similar to that in another local authority, the grant must take into account the needs of individual local authorities (e.g. as measured by the number of pupils per thousand of the population) and their resources (e.g. as measured by the product of a penny rate). The difficulty of finding a suitable formula which matches the resources (from rates and grants combined) to the needs of an authority has exercised central government and local authorities since the First World War and has not yet been satisfactorily resolved.

A further problem is that local authorities have little discretion in the volume of their expenditure on education. Salaries of teaching staff in all educational institutions and of the majority of non-teaching staff are negotiated nationally, loan charges must be paid and statutory obligations (e.g. provision of sufficient places for children of school age, of special educational treatment and of further education) must be fulfilled. When all these commitments have been met, the area for discretion in expenditure is a small proportion of the total educational budget and this area includes what are, in effect, essentials such as the maintenance of buildings, supply of equipment, books and stationery for schools and colleges.

Until 1959 grants in aid of the local education service were based on a relatively simple formula taking into account the number of children in school and the rateable value of the authority. The major part of the grant, however, was based on the actual educational expenditure of the local authority on which a percentage grant was paid. Specific grants were made for certain sectors of the service (e.g. 100 per cent. grant on the provision of milk and meals and 75 per cent. for the Youth Employment Service) and the cost of teacher training was " pooled " and shared between authorities.

As a result of the Local Government Act 1958 the basis on which grants were made was completely changed. Percentage grants were, in the main, abolished and the local authority received a general grant, none of it earmarked for any particular local service, towards the expenditure incurred by local authorities in running all their services.

General grants continued until the Local Government Act 1966 made yet another change whereby " rate support grants " became payable to local authorities. The grant is based on a " needs " element, a " resources " element and a " domestic " element (e). The " needs " element of the rate support grant as far as education is concerned takes into account the following factors: the number of primary and secondary school children for whose education the authority is responsible (the latter being divided into those under and over sixteen respectively); the number of students in establishments of further education (divided into full-time, part-time and evening students); the number of school meals provided (f). These factors are weighted in accordance with the formula set out in regulations made by the

---

(e) Section 1 (4) repealed by Local Government Act 1974, and re-enacted by *ibid.*, s. 2 and Sch. 2.

(f) Rate Support Grant (No. 2) Regulations 1974 No. 1987.

Secretary of State for the Environment. Arrangements for the pooling and sharing between local authorities of the cost of certain sectors of the educational service were continued but specific grants for the provision of milk and meals ceased (g).

As a means of compensating local authorities faced with expenditure beyond their control, percentage grants based on actual expenditure reappear from time to time. For example, the Local Government Act 1966 (h) made provision for local authorities with a substantial proportion of Commonwealth immigrant children on the school roll to receive a specific grant in respect of additional staff employed in connection with the education and welfare of immigrant pupils. The Local Government (Social Need) Act 1969 (i) extended the specific grant to cover expenditure incurred by certain local authorities containing urban areas of special social need. This latter grant was part of the Urban Aid Programme introduced in 1968–9; the specific grant was in both cases 75 per cent. of the approved expenditure incurred by the authorities involved.

The Local Government Act 1974 re-enacted and extended the provisions with regard to rate support grant and, in particular, made provision for the financial treatment of certain aspects of the education service. This may be briefly summarised as follows: (1) expenditure on mandatory awards are no longer included in a local authority's expenditure (k) for the calculation of rate support grant but attracts a specific grant of 90 per cent. of the cost to the authority (l). (2) expenditure on teacher training (including awards to students), on further and higher education of an advanced character, on providing primary, secondary and further education for pupils and students not belonging to the area of any authority and on the training of persons to pursue educational research or to become educational psychologists is aggregated for all local authorities and apportioned among them in accordance with regulations (m).

The total amount of rate support grant available for distribution is, of course, decided by the Government in relation to its current financial policy, though before making a final settlement the Secretary of State for the Environment is required to consult with associations of local authorities. When the local authority receives notification of the amount of rate support grant to which it is entitled, it is at the discretion of the authority to decide how their resources from rates and grants will be deployed. It was, therefore, an unusual step for the major government departments concerned with the work of local authorities to issue in 1974 detailed information concerning the increased expenditure provided for in the grant and to indicate the sectors of local government services where no improvements could be considered. These included a number of services provided by education committees (discretionary awards to students, maintenance allowances to pupils and assistance with clothing and footwear, expenditure on youth, recreation and community services among others). On the other hand it was pointed out that provision had been made in the grant calculations for a slight improvement in staffing standards in schools and for the employment of teachers up to the quotas notified to local authorities (n).

Like previous local government acts, the 1974 Act contains the sanction of a reduction of grant. Where the appropriate minister is satisfied that an authority has failed to achieve or maintain a reasonable standard in the discharge of any of its functions, he may make a report to Parliament proposing a reduction in grant and setting out the reasons for the proposal (o).

(g) Local Government Act 1966, s. 14.
(h) Section 11 (1).
(i) Section 1 (1).
(k) Local Government Act 1974, s. 1 (5) (*b*) amended by Education Act 1975, Sch., Part 1.
(l) *Ibid.*, s. 8 (2) (*a*). (s. 8 (2) (*b*) repealed by Education Act 1975, Sch., Part 1.
(m) *Ibid.*, Sch. 2, Part 1, para. 3 (2) (4).
(n) DES Circular 12/74; see also Circulars 10/75 and 15/75.
(o) Local Government Act 1974, s. 5.

11. LOCAL AUTHORITY SERVICES

The Local Authorities (Goods and Services) Act, 1970, which came into force at the end of May of that year, implemented the main recommendation of the joint review body for local authority purchasing—*viz.*, that local authorities should be able to co-operate with one another in bulk purchasing. Under the Act, authorities may do four things: (i) enter into agreements to supply goods or materials to other local authorities or to public bodies, and to purchase and store goods for that purpose; (ii) provide other local authorities or public bodies with administrative, professional or technical services; (iii) allow another authority or body the use of any vehicle, plant, or apparatus together with services in connection therewith; and (iv) carry out maintenance work (though not construction) on land or buildings for another authority or public body.

The public bodies referred to in the Act now include—governors or other body responsible for an aided or special agreement school, a special school not maintained by an education authority, a school or any other body (including a college of education) in receipt of grant under the Education Act 1944, s. 100 (1) (b) ; and also the managers or governors of an independent school not operating for profit, a college of further education for the disabled, the Workers Educational Association and its branches, a regional advisory council for further education and the Welsh Joint Education Committee (p).

12. EDUCATION IN WALES

The provisions of the Education Act 1944 and subsequent legislation apply to Wales and Monmouthshire as they do to England. As a result of the Local Government Act 1972 Monmouthshire has been incorporated into Wales, and the Local Education Authorities for Wales are now the eight non-metropolitan counties established under that Act (q). A minor authority (r) in Wales is the community council; in an area where there is no community council, the council of the district is the minor authority (s).

There are certain arrangements for the administration of education which apply only to Wales, namely:

(1) There is a separate Central Advisory Council which, like the Council for England, is at the time of writing in abeyance. Between 1950 and 1967 the Council issued a number of reports dealing with special aspects of the curriculum in Welsh schools; the last report, Primary Education in Wales (t), was the result of an enquiry similar to that carried out by the Council for England under the chairmanship of Lady Plowden.

(2) In convening the conference for the preparation of an agreed syllabus of religious instruction, the Local Education Authority is not required to include members of the Church of England (u).

(3) There is a Welsh Joint Education Committee which was first established in 1948. Its membership consists of representatives of Local Education Authorities, teachers, the University of Wales, chief education officers, industrial interests together with persons acquainted with educational conditions in Wales. The Committee has referred to it for consideration the coordination of the provision of special educational treatment, boarding facilities, further education, facilities for recreation and social and physical training, agricultural education, the curriculum of maintained schools, refresher courses for teachers, educational research and other matters

(p) The Local Authorities (Goods and Services) (Public Bodies) Order 1975, S.I. 1975 No. 193.
(q) Local Government Act 1972, s. 20, Sch. 4 (Monmouthshire is now Gwent).
(r) For the purpose of Education Act 1944, s. 18.
(s) Local Government Act 1972, s. 192 (4).
(t) Gittins Report 1967.
(u) Education Act 1944, Sch. 5, para. 2 (*b*).

of common interest. The Committee also acts as the Regional Examining Board for the Certificate of Secondary Education and as the Regional Advisory Council for Further Education.

A major change in administration occurred in 1970 when responsibility for primary and secondary education in Wales was transferred from the Secretary of State for Education and Science to the Secretary of State for Wales. The division of functions between the Secretary of State for Wales and the Secretary of State for Education and Science is as follows (a):—

To the Secretary of State for Wales: compilation of school building programmes; consideration and approval of individual school building projects; grants and loans to voluntary schools; consideration and approval of plans of secondary school reorganisation submitted by local education authorities in Wales; issues arising under s. 13 of the Education Act, 1944, on the establishment, closure, or change of character of schools; powers with regard to management and government of schools; issues affecting individual school pupils attending schools in Wales (choice of school, transport, school attendance); compulsory purchase orders and other land transactions involving school sites; registration of independent schools and recognition of schools as efficient; responsibilities in relation to School Health Service; special educational treatment for handicapped pupils; nursery education; responsibilities in relation to school meals and milk; charities relating to primary and secondary schools.

To the Secretary of State for Education and Science: further and higher education; youth service; grants to community centres/village halls and adult education; the supply, training, qualifications, remuneration and superannuation of teachers; teacher misconduct cases; appointment of HM Inspectorate.

13. THE SEX DISCRIMINATION ACT 1975

The provisions of the Act relating to the recruitment of employees apply to the appointment of teachers in both single sex and co-educational establishments. In addition, Part III of the Act applies specifically to such establishments whether in the public or private sectors. Sex discrimination in the admission of pupils and students to educational institutions and to specific courses within them is prohibited (b), though single sex institutions are exempt from this provision (c) as also are courses in physical education and courses designed for teachers of this subject (d). Discriminatory admissions are permitted when a single sex establishment is changing to a co-educational one; the body responsible may apply to the Secretary of State for a " transitional exemption order " (e).

Local authorities are prohibited in carrying out duties imposed on them by the Education Acts 1944–75 from taking any action, not falling under those specified in the Act, which constitutes discrimination (f).

The Act imposes a general duty upon Local Education Authorities and other designated establishments (g) to ensure that all the facilities they provide are offered without sex discrimination (h).

Sections 68 and 99 of the Education Act 1944 apply to the performance by these bodies of duties imposed by the Sex Discrimination Act (i). Complaints of discrimination in the public sector (i.e. in establishments maintained by a local authority and in designated establishments) must be made in the first instance to the Secretary of State (k).

(a) Circular 18/70.
(b) S. 22.
(c) S. 26.
(d) S. 28.
(e) S. 27.
(f) S. 23.
(g) S. 24 (1); S.I. 1975 No. 1902.
(h) S. 25.
(i) S. 25.
(k) S. 66 (5). For the effects of the Act on education generally see DES Circular 2/76.

PART II

STATUTES

DIVISION A

THE EDUCATION ACTS, 1944–1975

SUMMARY

KEY TO MEANINGS AND STATUTORY DEFINITIONS

Words followed by an asterisk

The aim of the authors of this work is to provide full annotations to the text of the Education Acts, 1944 to 1975. On the other hand there are certain expressions which are used so often in the Acts that to state their meaning or refer to their statutory definition in the notes to each section in which they occur would make those notes unduly long; furthermore, in the majority of cases the precise meaning of the expression defined is not in issue (*e.g.*, the question is not likely to be, Who are within the definition of "managers"? but rather, What are the powers and duties of the managers?).

In this Edition, therefore, it will be found that, except where for some particular reason a special note is called for, each of these expressions is followed by an asterisk the first time it appears in any section. At the end of the General Note to any section containing one or more asterisks there will be found a note introduced by an asterisk referring to this and the next-following page, where references are given to the statutory definitions of such of the expressions as are defined by statute and an indication is given of the meaning of those that are not so defined. Readers, therefore, who for some particular purpose require to know the precise meaning of a "starred" expression can trace this by means of the list which follows, but where such information is not required readers will be able to ignore the asterisk. A fuller list of definitions is also given under the heading WORDS AND PHRASES at the end of the Index.

When referring to any provisions of the Acts mentioned below as containing definitions reference should also be made to the notes thereto, as it is in the notes to the section in which an expression is defined that any necessary commentary, amplification or cross-reference will be found.

Administrative Memorandum.—Throughout this Volume, unless otherwise expressly stated, the term "Administrative Memorandum" refers to Department of Education and Science Administrative Memoranda (before 1st April, 1964, Ministry of Education Administrative Memoranda).

Agreed Syllabus.—Defined by the 1944 Act, section 114 (1). The definition, which refers to the 1944 Act, Fifth Schedule, is subject to the transitional provisions (now spent) in the 1944 Act, section 114 (4).

Aided School.—This means a voluntary school which falls into the second of the three categories into which voluntary schools are to be classified pursuant to the 1944 Act, section 15.

Alterations.—The definition now in section 114 (1) of the 1944 Act was substituted by section 1 (3) of the Education Act, 1968.

Articles of Government.—This is not defined in the Acts, but means an instrument to be made in accordance with the 1944 Act, section 17 (3) (*b*), regulating the conduct of a maintained secondary school and, in particular, determining the respective functions in relation thereto of the local education authority, the governors and the head teacher.

Assist.—Defined by the 1944 Act, section 114 (1) and (2).

Child.—Defined by the 1944 Act, section 114 (1).

Circular.—Throughout this Volume, unless otherwise expressly stated, the term "Circular" refers to Department of Education and Science Circulars (before 1st April, 1964, Ministry of Education Circulars).

Compulsory School Age.—Defined by the 1944 Act, section 114 (1), by reference to the 1944 Act, section 35. See also the 1962 Act, section 9, as to school-leaving dates in England and Wales.

Controlled School.—This means a voluntary school which falls into the first of the three categories into which voluntary schools are to be classified pursuant to the 1944 Act, section 15.

County.—See now, as to new local government areas in England and Wales, sections 1, 20 of the Local Government Act 1972. As to the application of the Education Acts to the Isles of Scilly as if they were a separate county, see the 1944 Act, section 118.

County College.—Defined by the 1944 Act, section 43.

County School.—Defined by the 1944 Act, section 9 (2).

Development Plan.—Defined by the 1944 Act, section 11 (1).

Enlargement.—Defined by section 114 (1) of the Act of 1944 (inserted by section 1 (3) of the Education Act, 1968).

Former Authority.—Defined by the 1944 Act, section 114 (1).

Foundation Governors.—Defined by the 1944 Act, section 114 (1). As to the number of foundation governors, see the 1944 Act, section 19 (2).

Foundation Managers.—Defined by the 1944 Act, section 114 (1). As to the number of foundation managers, see the 1944 Act, section 18 (3).

Further Education.—Defined by the 1944 Act, section 41, to which the 1944 Act, section 114 (1), refers.

Independent School.—Defined by the 1944 Act, section 114 (1).

Junior Pupil.—Defined by the 1944 Act, section 114 (1).

Local Education Authority.—Still defined by the 1944 Act, section 6 and First Schedule, Part I, and also by the 1944 Act, section 114 (1). But see section 192 of the Local Government Act 1972, 42 Halsbury's Statutes (3rd Edn.) 1020, by which the local education authority for each non-metropolitan county shall be the council of the county and the local education authority for each metropolitan district shall be the council of the district.

Local Education Order.—Defined by the 1944 Act, section 12.

Maintain.—Defined by the 1944 Act, section 114 (1) and (2). As to what is included in the duty to maintain a voluntary school, see the 1946 Act, First Schedule.

Managers or Governors.—This phrase is not defined in the Acts but refers to the managing and governing bodies required to be constituted by the 1944 Act, section 17. See, further, note (b) to that section.

Minister of Education.—Now the Secretary of State for Education and Science. See note (b) to section 1 of the 1944 Act, *post.*

Ministry of Education.—Now the Department of Education and Science. See note (b) to section 1 of the 1944 Act, *post.*

Minor Authority.—Defined by the 1944 Act, section 114 (1), as substituted by section 192(4) of the Local Government Act 1972.

Nursery Schools.—Defined by the 1944 Act, section 9 (4).

Parent.—Defined by the 1944 Act, section 114 (1).

Person.—By the Interpretation Act, 1889, section 19 (24 Halsbury's Statutes (2nd Edn.) 222) in every Act passed after the commencement of that Act this expression includes, unless the contrary intention appears, any body of persons incorporate or unincorporate.

Primary Education.—Defined by the 1944 Act, section 114 (1), by reference to the 1944 Act, section 8 (1) (*a*).

Primary School.—Defined by the 1944 Act, section 114 (1).

Premises.—Defined by the 1944 Act, section 114 (1).

Proprietor.—Defined by the 1944 Act, section 114 (1).

Pupil.—Where used without qualification, defined by the 1944 Act, section 114 (1).

Registered Pupil.—Defined by the 1944 Act, section 114 (1).

Registered School.—Defined by the 1944 Act, section 114 (1).

Rules of Management.—This is not defined in the Acts, but means an instrument made in accordance with the 1944 Act, section 17 (3) (*a*), regulating the conduct of a maintained primary school and, in particular, determining the respective functions in relation to the school of the local education authority, the managers and the head teacher.

School.—Defined by the 1944 Act, section 114 (1).

School Buildings.—Defined by the 1946 Act, section 4 (2).

Secondary Education.—Defined by the 1944 Act, section 114 (1) by reference to the 1944 Act, section 8 (1) (*b*).

Secondary School.—Defined by the 1944 Act, section 114 (1).

Secretary of State for Education and Science.—As from 1st April, 1964, assumed all functions, rights, liabilities, etc., of the former Minister of Education. See note (b) to Section 1 of the Act of 1944.

Senior Pupil.—Defined by the 1944 Act, section 114 (1).

Significant.—Defined by section 114 (1) of the Education Act, 1944 (inserted by section 1 (3) of the Education Act, 1968).

Site.—Defined by the 1946 Act, section 16.

Special Agreement School.—This expression refers to the third of the three categories into which voluntary schools are to be classified pursuant to the 1944 Act, section 15.

Special Educational Treatment.—Defined by the 1944 Act, section 114 (1) by reference to the 1944 Act, section 8 (2) (*c*).

Special School.—Defined by the 1944 Act, section 9 (5).

Trust Deed.—Defined by the 1944 Act, section 114 (1).

Voluntary School.—Defined by the 1944 Act, section 9 (2).

Young Person.—Defined by the 1944 Act, section 114 (1).

THE EDUCATION ACT, 1944

7 & 8 Geo. 6, c. 31

ARRANGEMENT OF SECTIONS

Part I

CENTRAL ADMINISTRATION

Part II

THE STATUTORY SYSTEM OF EDUCATION

Local Administration

The Three Stages of the System

Primary and Secondary Education

Provision and Maintenance of Primary and Secondary Schools

Management of Primary Schools and Government of Secondary Schools

Secular Instruction and Appointment and Dismissal of Teachers in County and Voluntary Schools

Religious Education in County and Voluntary Schools

PART III

INDEPENDENT SCHOOLS

PART IV

GENERAL

GENERAL PRINCIPLES TO BE OBSERVED BY SECRETARY OF STATE AND LOCAL EDUCATION AUTHORITIES

MISCELLANEOUS PROVISIONS

ADMINISTRATIVE PROVISIONS

FINANCIAL PROVISIONS

PART V

SUPPLEMENTAL

An Act to reform the law relating to education in England and Wales.
[3rd August, 1944.]

GENERAL NOTE

The title of this Act, which is " to reform the law relating to education in England and Wales " shows by its very brevity that there was envisaged a great change in the law relating to education. It made, in fact, the most sweeping changes in the educational law of England and Wales since the passing of the first Elementary Education Act in 1870, and replaced and reformed almost the whole of the former law relating to education. The Act was based upon a White Paper (Cmd. 6458) which was presented to Parliament by the President of the Board of Education in July, 1943, and was then published under the title of " Educational Reconstruction ", though the proposals contained in the White Paper were later modified and additions made in the light of public consideration of the White Paper and Parliamentary consideration of the Education Bill which was subsequently introduced into the House of Commons.

In an Act such as this, instituting such wide changes in the educational system of the country, mistakes were bound to occur and matters to be overlooked, many of which have since come to light. It has, therefore, been necessary to pass several amending Acts: the Education Act, 1946, p. 209, *post*, the Education (Miscellaneous Provisions) Act, 1948, p. 219, *post*, the Education (Miscellaneous Provisions) Act, 1953, p. 229, *post*, the Education Act, 1959, p. 239, *post*, the Education Act, 1962, p. 240, *post*, the Education Act, 1964, p. 251, *post*, the Remuneration of Teachers Act 1965, p. 253, *post*, the Education Act 1967, p. 258, *post*, the Education Act 1968, p. 261, *post*, the Education (No. 2) Act 1968, p. 267, *post*, the Education (Handicapped Children) Act 1970, p. 269, *post*, the Education (Milk) Act 1971, p. 272, *post*, the Education Act 1973, p. 274, *post*, the Education (Work Experience) Act 1973, p. 280, *post*, and the Education Act 1975, p. 281, *post*. These Acts may be collectively cited as the Education Acts 1944 to 1975, the amendments made whereby are incorporated in the text of the present Act, *infra*. The Education Act 1959, is only of limited scope, its effect being merely to enlarge the powers of the Secretary of State with respect to the financial assistance of certain categories of voluntary schools. As to the Remuneration of Teachers Act 1965, see the Introduction, p. 41, *ante*.

PART I

CENTRAL ADMINISTRATION

1. [**Promotion of education by Secretary of State for Education and Science** (a).]—(1) [It shall be the duty of the Secretary of State for Education and Science (b)] to promote the education of the people of England and Wales and the progressive development of institutions devoted to that purpose, and to secure the effective execution by local authorities (c), under his control and direction (d), of the national policy for providing a varied and comprehensive educational service in every area.

(2) [The Secretary of State for Education and Science shall for all purposes be a corporation sole (e) under the name of Secretary of State for Education and Science.]

* * * * *

NOTES

(a) The original heading (marginal note) to this section has been adapted to suit the amendments explained in note (b), *infra*.

(b) The first Minister of Education was appointed on 10th August, 1944; the last ceased to hold office as such on 1st April, 1964. On that date the Ministry of Education was dissolved, and all the functions of the Minister of Education (together with his rights, liabilities, etc.) were transferred to the newly-appointed Secretary of State for Education and Science by the Secretary of State for Education and Science Order, 1964, S.I. 1964 No. 490 (26th March, 1964), p. 373, *post*.

By this Order in Council, the following repeals and amendments to the Act of 1944 were made: (1) The words in square brackets in section 1 (1), *supra*, were substituted for the former power of appointment of a Minister; (2) a new section 1 (2) was substituted; (3) section 1 (3), (4) were repealed; (4) section 3 (1), (2), (3), *post*, were amended by the substitution of terms (e.g. " Secretary of State for Education and Science " instead of " Minister "), as indicated by square brackets in those subsections; and (5) section 3 (4), *post*, was repealed except in relation to documents issued before 1st April, 1964.

In addition to these repeals and amendments the Order in Council provided that any enactment or instrument in force at the coming into operation of the Order should have effect as if (*a*) for any reference to the Minister of Education there were substituted a reference to the Secretary of State; and (*b*) for any reference to the Ministry of Education or any officer of the Minister or Ministry there were substituted a reference to the Department of the Secretary of State (now officially known as the Department of Education and Science) or an officer thereof.

Throughout this work, therefore, the expressions " the Minister of Education ", " the Minister ", " the Ministry of Education ", and " the Ministry ", have been replaced in the texts of Acts, statutory instruments, etc., which were already in force on 1st April, 1964, by the expressions "the Secretary of State for Education and Science", " the Secretary of State ", " the Department of Education and Science " and " the Department ".

The functions of the Secretary of State for Education and Science in connection with primary and secondary education were, in matters only affecting Wales, transferred to the Secretary of State for Wales by the Transfer of Functions (Wales) Order 1970, S.I. 1970 No. 1536.

For the power of the Parliamentary Commissioner to investigate the administrative actions of the Department of Education and Science, see the Parliamentary Commissioner Act, 1967, s. 4 and Schedule 2.

(c) **" Local authorities ".**—It has been suggested that the word " education " has been inadvertently omitted from this term.

(d) **" Under his control and direction ".**—The Secretary of State is specifically given the duty of controlling and directing the execution by local authorities of the national policy of education. The Secretary of State's powers of direction and control are given in various provisions of the Act in relation to a variety of matters. The Secretary of State is, under this section, required to take active steps to ensure that every local education authority complies with Government policy. Local education authorities have found that the principle of their freedom of action within the statutory limits of the various enactments relating to education is to a greater or lesser extent subordinated to the carrying out of that policy. This has been noticeable within recent years as regards the controversy over comprehensive education, which has become as much a political as an educational issue. In particular, section 99, p. 173, *post*, enables the Secretary of State to enforce the discharge of any duties placed upon local education authorities or upon the managers or governors of county or voluntary schools by or under any provision of the Act. Section 68, p. 155, *post*, goes even further than this. It enables the Secretary of State, if he thinks that a local education authority or the managers or governors of a county or voluntary school have acted or propose to act unreasonably, not only in the performance of a duty under the Act, but even in the exercise of a power, to give such directions as he thinks fit. This constitutes a greater restriction upon the autonomy of local authorities than had been contained in any previous local government statute.

(e) **" Corporation sole ".**—Halsbury (Laws of England, 3rd Edition, vol. 9, p. 7), defines the term as:—

> " a body politic having perpetual succession, constituted in a single person, who, in right of some office or function, has a capacity to take, purchase, hold, and demise (and in some particular instances, under qualifications and restrictions introduced by statute, power to alienate) lands, tenements, and hereditaments, and now, it would seem, also to take and hold personal property, to him and his successors in such office for ever, the succession being perpetual, but not always uninterruptedly continuous; that is, there may be, and often are, periods in the duration of a corporation sole, occurring irregularly, in which there is a vacancy, or no one in existence in whom the corporation resides and is visibly represented."

2. Transfer of property and functions . . . and construction of Acts and documents.

NOTE

It has not been considered necessary to print this section, which transferred the property and functions of the former Board of Education to the Minister of Education.

All such property, functions, rights and liabilities have now been transferred to the Secretary of State for Education and Science. See note (b) to section 1, *ante*.

3. Seal and acts of Secretary of State.—(1) The [Secretary of State for Education and Science] shall have an official seal which shall be authenticated by the signature of the [Secretary of State for Education and Science] or of a secretary to the [Department of the Secretary of State] or of any person authorised by the [Secretary of State for Education and Science] to authenticate the seal.

(2) The seal of the [Secretary of State for Education and Science] shall be officially and judically noticed, and every document purporting to be an instrument made or issued by the [Secretary of State for Education and Science] and either to be sealed with the seal of the [Secretary of State for Education and Science] authenticated in the manner provided by this section, or to be signed by a secretary to the [Department of the Secretary of State] or by any other officer of the [Department of the Secretary of State] authorised to sign it, shall in any legal proceedings be deemed to be so made or issued without further proof, unless the contrary is shown.

(3) A certificate signed by the [Secretary of State for Education and Science] certifying that any instrument purporting to be made or issued by him was so made or issued shall be conclusive evidence of the fact certified.

(4) [*Repealed.*]

NOTES

The words in square brackets in sub-sections (1), (2) and (3) were substituted by the Secretary of State for Education and Science Order, 1964. See note (b) to section 1, *ante*.

Sub-section (4).—Repealed, except in relation to documents issued before 1st April, 1964, by the Secretary of State for Education and Science Order, 1964, p. 373, *post*. The effect of the subsection was that *prima facie* evidence of any order or regulation or of any document made or issued by the former Minister might be given in all courts of justice, and in all legal proceedings, by the production of a Queen's printer's copy thereof, of the *London Gazette* containing a copy thereof, or of a copy or extract purporting to be certified to be true by any of the persons deemed by the sub-section to be included in the second column of the Schedule to the Act of 1868. In the event, for example, of the loss of an original document issued by the former Minister it would be sufficient to produce in legal proceedings a copy of the document certified by one of the authorised officers of the former Ministry of Education.

4. Central Advisory Councils.—(1) There shall be two Central Advisory Councils for Education, one for England and the other for Wales and Monmouthshire, and it shall be the duty of those Councils to advise the Secretary of State (a) upon such matters connected with educational theory and practice as they think fit, and upon any questions referred to them by him.

(2) The members of each Council shall be appointed by the Secretary of State, and the Secretary of State shall appoint a member of each Council to be Chairman thereof and shall appoint an officer of the Department of Education and Science (b) to be secretary thereto.

(3) Each Council shall include persons who have had experience of the statutory system of public education as well as persons who have had experience of educational institutions not forming part of that system.

(4) The Secretary of State (a) shall by regulations (c) make provision as to the term of office and conditions of retirement of the members of each Council, and regulations made by the Secretary of State (a) for either Council may provide for periodical or other meetings of the Council and as to the procedure thereof, but, subject to the provisions of any such regulations the

meetings and procedure of each Council shall be such as may be determined by them.

NOTES

As to appointments of chairman or members of, or secretary to, the Central Advisory Council for Wales, see the Transfer of Functions (Wales) Order 1970, S.I. 1970 No. 1536, art. 4.

The two Central Advisory Councils appointed under the present section are not only required to advise the Secretary of State on questions which he refers to them, but are also in a position to advise him upon any matters connected with educational theory and practice as they think fit and, by section 5, *post*, he is bound to include in his annual report to Parliament details of the composition and proceedings of the Councils. The first report of the Council for England on "School and Life" was published in 1947; the Council then began, on its own initiative, to enquire into the educational needs of young workers, but had to postpone this enquiry as the then Minister requested it to carry out an immediate investigation into the leisure time interests of school children. The results of this investigation appear in the Council's second report entitled "Out of School", which was published in 1948. It has subsequently published reports entitled "Early Leaving" (1954); "15 to 18" (Vol. 1, 1959; Vol. 2, 1960); "Half our Future" (1963); "Children and their Primary Schools" (1967). The Council for Wales has made reports entitled "The Future of Secondary Education in Wales" (1947), "The County College in Wales" (1949), "The Place of Welsh and English in Schools in Wales" (1953, re-issued 1960), "Drama in the Schools in Wales" (1954), "Arts and Crafts in the Schools in Wales" (1955), and "Education in Rural Wales" (1958) and "Primary Education in Wales" (1967).

(a) **"Secretary of State".**—See note (b) to s. 1, *ante*.

(b) **"Department of Education and Science".**—See note (b) to s. 1, *ante*.

(c) **"Regulations".**—See the Central Advisory Councils for Education Regulations, 1945, S.R. & O. 1945 No. 152, and the Central Advisory Councils for Education Amending Regulations, 1951, S.I. 1951 No. 1742, Part III, *post*. Regulations made by the Secretary of State under this section must, by section 112, p. 182, *post*, be laid before Parliament and may within forty days be annulled by resolution of either House.

5. Annual Report to Parliament.—The Secretary of State (a) shall make to Parliament an annual report giving an account of the exercise and performance of the powers and duties conferred and imposed upon him by this Act and of the composition and proceedings of the Central Advisory Councils for Education.

NOTES

The Secretary of State has made a report under the present section each year, these reports, which are very full, being published as Command Papers. The report and statistics have been issued separately since 1961. See the Introduction, p. 6, *ante*.

(a) **"Secretary of State".**—See note (b) to s. 1, *ante*.

PART II
THE STATUTORY SYSTEM OF EDUCATION
LOCAL ADMINISTRATION

6. Local education authorities.—(1) Subject to the provisions of Part I of the First Schedule (a) to this Act, the local education authority (b) for each county (*) shall be the council of the county, and the local education authority for each county borough shall be the council of the county borough.

(2) The local administration of the statutory system of public education (c) shall be conducted in accordance with the provisions of Part II . . . of the said Schedule (d).

(3) All property (e) which immediately before the date of the commencement of this Part of this Act (f) was held (g) by the council of any county district (h) solely or mainly (i) for the purposes of any functions exercisable by them under the Education Acts, 1921 to 1939 (j), and all rights and liabilities (k), whether vested or contingent (l), to which any such council were entitled or subject immediately before the said date by reason of the exercise of such functions shall save as may be otherwise directed (m) by the Minister (n) under the powers conferred on him by this Act be transferred by virtue of this section to the local education authority for the county in which the county district is situated.

(4) All officers who immediately before the said date were employed by the council of any county district solely or mainly for the purposes of

any such functions as aforesaid shall by virtue of this section be transferred to and become officers of the local education authority for the county in which the county district is situated, and shall be employed by that authority upon the terms and conditions upon which they were employed by the council of the county district immediately before that date.

NOTES

This section, with the remainder of Part II of the Act, came into operation on 1st April, 1945. By section 108 (1) (now, however, spent), the Minister, as he then was, was enabled, without prejudice to any powers exercisable under section 37 of the Interpretation Act, 1889; 32 Halsbury's Statutes (3rd Edn.) 457, to exercise, and to authorise or require any local education authority (as defined in this section and section 114 (1), p. 184, *post*), former authority (as defined in section 114 (1), p. 183, *post*), or other person or body of persons to exercise, during the period between the passing of the Act and the date on which Part II came into operation (1st April, 1945), any functions which would, on or after that date, become exercisable by him or them under any provision of the Act, in so far as the exercise of those functions during that period was, in his opinion, necessary or expedient for securing that that Part might be brought into operation without delay or for preventing difficulties in the operation of that Part after the date aforesaid.

Specific education grant to local education authorities (except in respect of expenditure on the removal of defence works, see section 100 (1) as amended, p. 175, *post*), was discontinued by the Local Government Act, 1958.

The words omitted in subsection (2) were repealed by the Local Government Act 1972, s. 272 (1), Sch. 30. See also section 192 of the Act of 1972, as to local education authorities, p. 308, *post*.

(*) As to the statutory definition of " county ", see p. 68, *ante*.

(a) " **Part I of the First Schedule** ".—See p. 196, *post*, and notes. This Part provided for the establishment of a joint education board as the local education authority for the areas of two or more councils to which Part I of the Schedule applied where it appeared to the Minister (now Secretary of State) that this would tend to diminish expense or to increase efficiency, or would otherwise be of public advantage (First Schedule, Part I, para. 1).

(b) " **Local education authority** ".—Various provisions of the Act lay specific duties upon local education authorities, *e.g.*, with regard to the appointment of a chief education officer (section 88, p. 169, *post*), and the establishment of education committees (Part II of the First Schedule, p. 198, *post*).

Section 114 (1), p. 184, *post*, also contains what appears to be a quite unnecessary repetition of the definition of " local education authority ". As to the application of the Act to London and to the Isles of Scilly, see the London Government Act, 1963, and section 118 of the present Act respectively, pp. 289 and 193, *post*. See also section 192 of the Local Government Act 1972, 42 Halsbury's Statutes (3rd Edn.) 1020, under which the Local Education Authority for each non-metropolitan county shall be the council of the county, and the Local Education Authority for each metropolitan district shall be the council of the district.

The educational functions of former authorities were not the only functions transferred to the local education authorities under the Act. As a result of section 120 (1) (*d*) and (4), p. 194, *post*, the functions exercised by local authorities under the Children and Young Persons Acts, 1933 and 1938 (now 1933 to 1969); 12 Halsbury's Statutes (2nd Edn.) 974, 1072, in their capacities as local education authorities for elementary education, were also transferred to the local education authorities under this Act.

As from 1st April, 1965, any reference in the Education Acts, 1944 to 1970, or in any other Act, to the local education authority is to be construed in relation to any outer London borough as a reference to the council of that borough, and in relation to the remainder of Greater London as a reference to the Greater London Council acting by means of a special committee known as the Inner London Education Authority. See section 30 of the London Government Act, 1963, p. 289, *post*.

(c) " **The statutory system of public education** ".—The whole of Part II of the Act deals with the various aspects of statutory system of education in its reorganised form, but section 7, p. 78, *post*, indicates the three stages into which the statutory system of public education is to be organised and imposes a general duty upon the local education authority to exercise its powers to that end.

(d) " **Part II of the said Schedule** ".—Part II of the First Schedule, p. 198, *post*, provides for the establishment of education committees and joint education committees of local education authorities. Part III of the First Schedule, which formerly provided for the delegation of functions of Local Education Authorities to divisional executives and to the councils of excepted districts by means of schemes of divisional administration was repealed by the Local Government Act 1972, s. 272 (1), Sch. 30.

(e) " **Property** ".—The term is not defined in the Act though, in the Education Act, 1921, it was, by section 170, deemed to have the same meaning as in the Local Government Act, 1888, section 100, providing (*inter alia*):—

> " The expression ' property ' includes all property, real and personal, and all estates, interests, easements, and rights, whether equitable or legal, in, to, and out of property real and personal, including things in action, and registers, books, and documents ; and when used in relation to any . . . . . . authority, includes any property which on the ' appointed

day' belongs to, or is vested in, or held in trust for, or would but for this Act have, on or after that day, belonged to, or been vested in, or held in trust for, such . . . . . . authority "

As to what may be transferred, see *Oldham Corporation* v. *Bank of England*, [1904] 2 Ch. 716 (annuity).

(f) **" Immediately before the date of the commencement of this Part of this Act ".** Since Part II of the Act came into operation on 1st April, 1945, this phrase means the 31st March, 1945.

(g) **" Held ".**—This presumably covers not only property owned by the council of the county district, but property held by way of lease or tenancy or even by way of loan.

(h) **" County district ".**—This means, in the present section, a non-county borough or an urban district, since the council of a rural district was incapable under the Education Act, 1921, of possessing powers relating either to higher or to elementary education.

(i) **" Solely or mainly ".**—This term, which probably represents the best possible attempt to deal with all the various questions which may arise, has no doubt gave rise to a number of difficult problems. The intention of this provision was obviously to transfer only those buildings which would be required for educational purposes by the new local education authority and would no longer be required by the former authority.

(j) **" Education Acts, 1921 to 1939 ".**—These were:—

(*a*) the Education Act, 1921;
(*b*) the Education (Institution Children) Act, 1923;
(*c*) the Education (Local Authorities) Act, 1931;
(*d*) the Education (Necessity of Schools) Act, 1933;
(*e*) the Education Act, 1936;
(*f*) the Education (Deaf Children) Act, 1937; and
(*g*) the Education (Emergency) Act, 1939.

In addition, section 120 (4), p. 227, *post*, provides that where by virtue of this Act any functions ceased to be exercisable by the council of a county district under the Children and Young Persons Acts, 1933 and 1938; 12 Halsbury's Statutes (2nd Edn.) 974, 1072, sub-sections (3) and (4) of this section (*inter alia*) were to have effect as if they had been exercisable under the Education Acts, 1921 to 1939; this means that those provisions regarding transfer of property and officers applied also in the case of functions under the Children and Young Persons Acts, 1933 and 1938. See, however, note (b), p. 77, *ante*.

(k) **"Rights and liabilities ".**—These words are undefined by the Act though section 170 (16) of the Education Act, 1921, gave the terms " powers ", " duties " and " liabilities ", as used in that Act, the same meanings as in the Local Government Act, 1888. By section 100 of that Act:—

(*a*) " powers " includes (*inter alia*) rights; and
(*b*) " the expression 'liabilities' includes liability to any proceeding for enforcing any duty or for punishing the breach of any duty, and includes all debts and liabilities to which any authority are or would but for this Act be liable or subject to, whether accrued due at the date of the transfer or subsequently accruing, and includes any obligation to carry or apply any money to any sinking fund or to any particular purpose ".

(l) **" Vested or contingent ".**—As to what may or may not be a contingent liability, see *Morris* v. *Carnarvon County Council*, [1910] 1 K.B. 840 (dangerous door).

(m) **" Save as may be otherwise directed ".**—This saving refers to section 96 (1) (*repealed*) which enabled the then Minister, if he was satisfied with regard to certain types of trust property that this provision should not operate, to direct that the transfer should be deemed not to have taken place.

(n) **" Minister ".**—" The Minister " here means the former Minister of Education appointed under s. 1, *ante*, as originally enacted. The Secretary of State for Education and Science has now been substituted for the Minister of Education (see note (b) to s. 1, *ante*) but as the transfers by virtue of this section, and any exceptions to them under s. 96 (1), *post*, must have occurred before 1964, effect has not been given to that substitution here.

THE THREE STAGES OF THE SYSTEM

7. Stages and purposes of statutory system of education.— The statutory system of public education (a) shall be organised in three progressive stages (b) to be known as primary education (*), secondary education (*), and further education (*); and it shall be the duty (c) of the local education authority (*) for every area, so far as their powers extend, to contribute towards the spiritual, moral (d), mental, and physical (e) development of the community by securing that efficient education throughout those stages shall be available to meet the needs of the population of their area.

NOTES

By section 1 of the Education Act, 1964, power is given to local education authorities to establish new schools with special age limits, such power to be exercisable notwithstanding anything contained in the Education Acts, 1944 to 1962, and, in particular, in section 7, *supra*. See section 1 (3) (*a*) of the Act of 1964, p. 251, *post*.

(*) As to the meaning or statutory definition of " primary education ", " secondary education ", " further education " and " local education authority ", see pp. 68, 69, *ante*.

(a) **" Statutory system of public education ".**—The provisions of the Act which give effect to the statutory system created by this section are contained in the remaining sections of Part II of the Act, viz. sections 8–69 inclusive. The reorganisation of the educational system was carried out, so far as primary and secondary education is concerned, in the following stages:—

(1) under section 11, p. 85, *post*, the local education authority had to estimate the immediate and prospective needs of the area and, within one year or such extended period as the then Minister might allow, prepare and submit to the Minister for his approval a " development plan ";

(2) after the Minister had approved the development plan he was required by section 12, p. 88, *post*, to make a " local education order " giving effect to the development plan regulating the duties of the local education authority in relation to the matters covered by the order which may be amended by the Minister (now Secretary of State) whenever expedient.

In addition, section 41, p. 135, *post*, requires every local education authority to secure the provision of adequate facilities for further education, as defined therein, and section 42, p. 136, *post*, enables the Secretary of State to require the local education authority to prepare and submit to him schemes of further education, the implementation of which the Secretary of State may, after giving his approval, direct. See, generally, as to further education, the Introduction, pp. 44–54, *ante*.

(b) **" Three progressive stages ".**—The system by which public education was divided into the two separate fields of elementary and higher education administered in many areas by different local authorities and in other areas by different committees of the same authority has now been replaced by a single system under the control of one authority to be organised as a continuous process conducted in three progressive stages to be known as primary, secondary and further education, and a duty has been placed on every local education authority to contribute towards the mental, moral, physical and spiritual development of the community by securing the provision of efficient education throughout those stages for all persons in the area capable of benefiting thereby. For the fulfilment of the duties thus laid upon them, local education authorities were required by section 11, p. 85, *post*, to make a comprehensive survey of the existing position and the present and prospective needs of their areas and to prepare and submit to the then Minister development plans giving a complete picture of the proposed layout of primary and secondary schools. As to revised development plans for Greater London, see section 31 of the London Government Act, 1963, p. 291, *post*.

The parent's duty is no longer confined to causing his child to be efficiently instructed in the three R's; under section 36, p. 128, *post*, he is to cause his child to receive efficient full-time education suitable to the child's age, ability and aptitude.

As to compulsory school age, see section 35, p. 127, *post*.

(c) **" It shall be the duty ".**—As to the enforcement of this and other duties imposed by the Act, see section 99, p. 173, *post*. It may be argued, in view of the words " so far as their powers extend ", which appear later in the section, that the Secretary of State's powers of compulsion under section 99 extend even to cases where the terms of a particular provision in the Act are hereby permissive, if it can properly be said that the exercise of those powers is necessary for the purpose of " securing that efficient education throughout those stages shall be available to meet the needs of the population " of an authority's area. In fact, section 68, p. 155, *post*, makes this even clearer by enabling the Secretary of State to give directions to the local education authority whenever he is of opinion that the authority has acted or proposes to act, unreasonably, not only in connection with the performance of a duty imposed by or under the Act, but even in relation to the exercise of a power.

(d) **" Moral ".**—The duty to contribute towards the moral development of the community in the way required by the section implies that the duties of the local education authority will be regarded as including the provision of sex education.

(e) **" Physical ".**—See section 53, p. 144, *post*, which deals (*inter alia*) with the provision of facilities for recreation and physical training.

PRIMARY AND SECONDARY EDUCATION

Provision and Maintenance of Primary and Secondary Schools

8. Duty of local education authorities to secure provision of primary and secondary schools.—(1) It shall be the duty (a) of every local education authority (*) to secure that there shall be available for their area (b) sufficient schools (c)—

(*a*) for providing primary education (d), that is to say, full-time education (e) suitable to the requirements of junior pupils (*) [who have not attained the age of ten years and six months, and full-time education suitable to the requirements of junior pupils who have attained that age and whom it is expedient to educate together with junior pupils who have not attained that age]; and (*b*) for providing secondary education (g), that is to say, full-time education suitable to the requirements of senior pupils (*), other than such full-time education as may be provided for senior pupils in pursuance of a scheme made under the provisions of this Act relating to further education (*), [and full-time education for junior pupils who have attained the age of ten years and six months and whom it is expedient to educate together with senior pupils.];

and the schools available for an area shall not be deemed to be sufficient unless they are sufficient in number, character, and equipment (i) to afford for all pupils opportunities for education offering such variety of instruction and training as may be desirable in view of their different ages, abilities, and aptitudes (k), and of the different periods for which they may be expected to remain at school, including practical instruction and training appropriate to their respective needs.

(2) In fulfilling their duties under this section a local education authority shall, in particular, have regard—

(*a*) to the need for securing that primary and secondary education are provided in separate schools (l) ;

(*b*) to the need for securing that provision is made for pupils who have not attained the age of five years by the provision of nursery schools (*) or, where the authority consider the provision of such schools to be inexpedient, by the provision of nursery classes (m) in other schools ;

(*c*) to the need for securing that provision is made for pupils who suffer from any disability of mind or body by providing, either in special schools or otherwise (n), special educational treatment (o), that is to say, education by special methods appropriate for persons suffering from that disability; and

(*d*) to the expediency of securing the provision of boarding accommodation (p), either in boarding schools or otherwise, for pupils for whom education as boarders is considered by their parents and by the authority to be desirable :

Provided that paragraph (*a*) of this sub-section shall not have effect with respect to special schools.

NOTES

(*) As to the meaning or statutory definition of "local education authority", "junior pupil", "senior pupil", "further education" and "nursery schools", see pp. 68, 69, *ante*.

(a) **"It shall be the duty".**—The general duty to secure that sufficient schools for the area are available is qualified by sub-section (2), section 12, p. 88, *post.* and section 4 (2) of the Education (Miscellaneous Provisions) Act, 1948, p. 220, *post.* It should be noted that the local education authority is not itself required to provide all the schools required, but to secure that they are available, and section 6 (1) of the Education (Miscellaneous Provisions) Act, 1953, p. 231, *post*, expressly provides that a local education authority has power, for the purpose of fulfilling its duties under the present Act, to make arrangements for the primary or secondary education of pupils at schools not maintained by a local education authority. As Denning, L. J. said in *Watt* v. *Kesteven County Council*, [1955] 1 All E.R. 473, at p. 475; [1955] 1 Q.B. 408, at p. 422; C.A. See also *Cumings* v. *Birkenhead Corporation*, [1970] 3 All E.R. 302; *affirmed*, [1971] 2 All E.R. 881; [1972] Ch. 12. "They may, for instance, make a grant to aid a school and in return, get a right to a number of free places. Or they may make arrangements with some particular independent school to take the boys, in which case the authority must pay the fees". As to the powers of the Secretary of State in the event of default by the local education authority, see section 99, p. 173, *post*, which affords the only remedy available, since no action at law will lie for a breach of the duty to make schools available (*Watt* v. *Kesteven County Council, supra*). The exercise and performance of all powers and duties conferred and imposed on the Secretary of State and upon local education authorities by the Act are subject to the guiding principle imposed by section 76, p. 162, *post*, that so far as is compatible with the provision of efficient instruction and training and the avoidance of unreasonable public expenditure, pupils are to be educated in accordance with the wishes of their parents, but where the local education authority has fulfilled its duty to provide sufficient schools either by maintaining schools itself or by making arrangements with certain other schools there is no more which they are bound to do. If a father wishes his child to go to yet another school of his own choice with which the county council have no arrangements, then he cannot claim as of right that the county council shall pay the fees (*Watt* v. *Kesteven County Council, supra, per* Denning, L.J., at pp. 475 and 422, respectively). See also *Wood* v. *Ealing London Borough*, [1966] 3 All E.R. 514; [1967] Ch. 364.

(b) "**Available for their area**".—The duties of a local education authority do not require the authority to secure the provision of schools for children or young persons from outside the area of the authority, even though it may be convenient for a child or young person to attend a school in an area other than that in which he lives. Section 6 of the Education (Miscellaneous Provisions) Act, 1948, p. 222, *post*, however, provides that where this does happen the local education authority is to be entitled, by making a claim within the prescribed period, to recover the cost thereof from the authority to whose area the child or young person belongs; see the Local Education Authorities (Recoupment) Regulations, 1953, S.I. 1953 No. 507 as amended by Amending Regulations, S.I. 1954 No. 991, S.I. 1959 No. 448, etc., p. 333, *post*. Before a child from outside the area is admitted, care should be taken to ascertain whether there is a sufficient reason therefor (1948 Act, section 6, sub-section (1), proviso). Disputes arising under the section are to be determined by the Secretary of State (sub-section (4)).

(c) "**Sufficient schools**".—See the definition of the term "school" in section 114 (1) p. 185, *post*. If in spite of compliance with this duty a child or young person is by reason or extraordinary circumstances unable to attend school for the purpose of receiving primary or secondary education, the local education authority may, with the approval of the Secretary of State, make special arrangements for him to receive such education otherwise than at school (section 56, p. 148, *post*). Subject to certain exceptions there is no obligation to admit a child as a registered pupil during the currency of a school term. See section 4 (2) of the Education (Miscellaneous Provisions) Act, 1948, p. 220, *post*. As to the position of schools which by reason of war damage or for other reasons connected with the war have ceased to be used as schools, see section 114 (7), p. 186, *post*.

(d) "**Primary education**".—The words in square brackets which were inserted by section 3 of the Education (Miscellaneous Provisions) Act, 1948, legalise the existing practice under which children are transferred from junior schools to secondary schools between the ages of ten and a half and twelve years according to their progress and abilities and the dates when their birthdays fall. See also section 4 (1) of the 1948 Act, p. 220, *post*. By section 35 of this Act, p. 127, *post*, the lower limit of "compulsory school age" continues to be five years, but no lower limit of age is imposed by the Act upon voluntary school attendance though in Circular 313 (18th September, 1956) local education authorities were required to restrict the admission to maintained primary schools of children under five. On the other hand, sub-section (2) (*b*) of the present section requires every local education authority, in fulfilling its duty under the section of securing that there are sufficient primary schools in the area, to have regard to the need for securing that provision is made for pupils under five by the provision of nursery schools or nursery classes, nursery schools being defined by section 9 (4), p. 83, *post*, as primary schools which are used mainly for the purpose of providing education for children who have attained the age of two years but have not attained the age of five years.

Primary education has been considerably affected by the recent establishment of middle schools, as to which see the Introduction, p. 15, *ante*.

(e) "**Full-time education**".—This term is nowhere defined in the Act, but section 23 (3), p. 111, *post*, provides that the power to control the secular instruction in schools given by sub-sections (1) and (2) of that section includes power (*inter alia*) to determine the times at which the school session is to begin and end on any day, to determine the times at which the school terms are to begin and end and to determine the school holidays. The minimum length of school sessions, the maximum number of school terms and their minimum aggregate length in the case of maintained schools are prescribed by Regulations 10–12 of the Schools Regulations, 1959, S.I. 1959 No. 364, pp. 350, 351, *post*.

(g) "**Secondary education**".—The words in square brackets which were inserted by section 3 of the Education (Miscellaneous Provisions) Act, 1948, legalise the existing practice under which children are transferred from junior schools to senior schools between the ages of ten and a half and twelve years. See also section 4 (1) of the 1948 Act, p. 220, *post*. Though the system of public education is to be a single continuous system, section 8 (2) (*a*), p. 80, *ante*, requires every local education authority, in securing the provision of sufficient schools, to have regard to the need for securing that primary and secondary education are provided in separate schools. Under section 35, p. 127, *post*, the upper limit of "compulsory school age" is sixteen. Thus secondary education may include, by virtue of the definition of "senior pupil" in section 114 (1), *post*, the education of persons who have passed the age at which they are compelled to attend school. It should be noted that the term "secondary education" does not include full-time education which is provided for senior pupils over compulsory school age under a scheme relating to further education made under section 42 of the Act (*see* p. 136 *post*).

For the recent developments in secondary education, including the establishment of comprehensive schools and the withdrawal of financial aid from direct grant grammar schools, see the Introduction, pp. 31, 32, *ante*.

(i) "**Equipment**".—The Act makes no attempt to limit the scope of this term. By the Health Services and Public Health Act, 1968, s. 67 (1) (*e*), the Secretary of State for Social Services may purchase and store and, on such terms as may be agreed between him and them, supply to local education authorities any goods or materials required by them for the discharge of their functions under this section.

(k) "**In view of their different ages, abilities and aptitudes**".—Section 36, p. 128, *post*, imposes a duty upon the parent of every child of compulsory school age to cause him to receive efficient full-time education suitable to his age, ability and aptitude. In order that children may be educated in accordance with their abilities and aptitudes at various ages the keeping of individual records is essential. See Circular 151 (July 18, 1947).

(l) "**Separate schools**".—Nothing in the definition of "school" in section 114 (1), p. 185, *post*, gives any assistance in determining what physically constitutes a school, *e.g.*, it is not specifically stated whether separate junior and senior departments constitute separate schools or not, though some assistance is given by section 114 (3), p. 186, *post*, which deals with the position existing before reorganisation of primary and secondary education was completed.

The proviso to this subsection states that where primary education in a school providing both primary and secondary education is provided in a separate junior or preparatory department the Minister (now Secretary of State) may direct that the school shall for the purposes of the Act be deemed to be a secondary school. In this case the use of the word " school " as covering both departments might be regarded as some evidence that such departments are not separate schools. Similarly, the component " sides " in a multi-lateral or bi-lateral school are clearly not separate schools. In the definition of " elementary school " in section 170 (1) of the Education Act, 1921, the expression covered a " school or department of a school ". Furthermore, in section 15 of the Education Act, 1936, " school " was defined as including a separate department of a school. Since these definitions were dropped in the present Act it could have been argued with some weight that the separation of primary and secondary education in separate departments would not be a sufficient compliance with the requirement to secure that they are provided in separate schools. Section 1 of the Education Act, 1964 (as amended by s. 2 of the Education Act, 1968), p. 251, *post*, enables new schools to be established in England and Wales to provide education for both junior and senior pupils. Proposals may specify lower age limits below 10 years and 6 months and upper age limits above 12. See generally, the Introduction, p. 18, *ante*.

Section 2 of the Education Act, 1946, p. 210, *post*, enables the Secretary of State, at the request of the local education authority in the case of a county school, or at the request of the managers or governors in the case of an aided or controlled school, to make an order dividing a school which is organised in two or more separate departments under a separate head teacher (section 16 of that Act, p. 215, *post*), into two or more separate schools. The power does not extend to special agreement schools, which are in a special category.

(m) **" Nursery classes ".**—This term is not defined in the Act but see regulation 3 (1) of the Schools Regulations, 1959, S.I. 1959 No. 364, p. 350, *post*. Whilst a nursery school cannot be a county school or a voluntary school (see section 9, *infra*) either may contain one or more nursery classes, so long as the school is not used mainly for children between two and five years of age and itself does not thereby become a nursery school. As used in section 21 of the Education Act, 1921, the expression " nursery schools " included nursery classes. Children are not accepted in nursery classes until they reach the age of three years unless special circumstances require it, see regulation 7 (2) of the Schools Regulations, 1959, S.I. 1959 No. 364, p. 350, *post*. See also the Standards for School Premises Regulations 1972, S.I. 1972, No. 2051, *post*.

Nursery classes are exempt from registration under the Nurseries and Child-Minders Regulation Act 1948; see section 8 (2) of that Act; 17 Halsbury's Statutes (3rd Edn.) 589. See also note (e), p. 83, *post*.

For the present position with regard to nursery education, see the Introduction, p. 14, *ante*.

(n) **" Or otherwise ".**—This term relates to the provision of special educational treatment otherwise than in a special school, whether or not the local education authority has itself provided a special school. Except, however, where section 56, p. 148, *post*, is applicable, by which the local education authority is enabled to make special arrangements in respect of a child who is unable to attend a suitable school, this term covers the giving of education, where education in a special school is impracticable, or where the disability is not serious, in any school maintained or assisted by a local education authority (section 33 (2), p. 122, *post*).

(o) **" Special educational treatment ".**—See generally the Introduction, pp. 28–30, *ante*.

(p) **" Provision of boarding accommodation ".**—Prior to the present Act the provision of boarding accommodation by local education authorities was limited largely to special schools for defective children and to normal children unable for special reasons to attend day schools, and the present provision which makes boarding education available for normal children for whom in the opinion of their parents and the local education committee this form of education is desirable is new.

Where boarding education is provided at a non-maintained boarding school pursuant to arrangements made by the local education authority and the authority is satisfied that education suitable to the age, ability and aptitude of the pupil cannot be provided by them for him unless board and lodging are also provided for him, the authority is under a positive duty to pay the whole of the boarding fees. See Education (Miscellaneous Provisions) Act, 1953, section 6, p. 231, *post*.

9. County schools, voluntary schools, nursery schools, and special schools.—(1) For the purpose of fulfilling their duties under this Act a local education authority (*) shall have power to establish (a) primary (*) and secondary (*) schools (*), to maintain (*) such schools whether established by them or otherwise (b), and, so far as may be authorised by arrangements approved by the Secretary of State (c), to assist (d) any such school which is not maintained by them.

(2) Primary and secondary schools maintained by a local education authority, not being nursery schools (e) or special schools (f), shall, if established by a local education authority or by a former authority (*) be known as county schools and, if established otherwise than by such an authority be known as voluntary schools (g).:

Provided that any school which by virtue of any enactment repealed by this Act (h) was to be deemed to be, or was to be treated as, a school provided by a former authority shall, notwithstanding that it was not in fact established by such an authority as aforesaid, be a county school.

(3) Subject to the provisions hereinafter contained (j) as to the discontinuance of voluntary schools, every school which immediately before the commencement of this Part of this Act (k) was, within the meaning of the enactments repealed by this Act, a public elementary school provided otherwise than by a former authority shall if it was then maintained (m) by a former authority (*) be maintained as a voluntary school by the local education authority for the area in which the school is situated.

(4) Primary schools which are used mainly (n) for the purpose of providing education for children who have attained the age of two years but have not attained the age of five years shall be known as nursery schools.

(5) Schools which are especially organised for the purpose of providing special educational treatment (*) for pupils (*) requiring such treatment and are approved by the Secretary of State (c) for that purpose shall be known as special schools.

(6) The powers conferred by subsection (1) of this section on local education authorities shall be construed as including power to establish maintain and assist schools outside as well as inside their areas.

NOTES

This section specifies the general types of primary and secondary schools under the new system which the Act creates. Under the system superseded by the Act public elementary schools were either " provided ", that is, schools provided by the local education authority (Education Act, 1921, section 28, or " non-provided ", that is, schools provided by a denominational or other voluntary body (*ibid.*, section 29).

As to the maintenance of county and voluntary schools in Greater London as from 1st April, 1965, see section 31 of the London Government Act, 1963, *post.*

(*) As to the meaning or statutory definition of " local education authority ", " primary school ", " secondary school ", " special educational treatment " and " pupil ", see pp. 68, 69, *ante.*

(a) **" Shall have power to establish ".**—This in most cases involved the acquisition of land and Part VII of the Local Government Act 1933 (repealed; see now, as to land transactions by principal and other councils, sections 120–131 of the Local Government Act 1972, 42 Halsbury's Statutes (3rd Edn.) 949 *et seq.*).

(b) **" Whether established by them or otherwise ".**—The local education authority's general power to establish primary and secondary schools is given by this section. Voluntary schools, which, by sub-section (2), are primary or secondary schools (other than nursery or special schools) maintained but not established by a local education authority or a former authority, may be any one of three types (section 15, p. 95, *post*). Schools which before 1st April, 1945, were " non-provided " public elementary schools maintained by a former authority (*i.e.*, any local education authority under an Act repealed by this Act) automatically became voluntary schools under the Act and the duty of maintenance was transferred from the former authority to the local education authority (sub-section (3) of this section). Apart from the provisions of this section other schools, whether or not they existed before 1st April, 1945, may become voluntary schools under section 13, p. 90, *post*, if the proprietor so desires and complies with the provisions of that section.

(c) **" Secretary of State ".**—See note (b) to s. 1, *ante.* As to the power of the Secretary of State to direct a local inquiry, see s. 93, p. 171, *post.*

(d) **" Assist ".**—Section 114 (1), p. 183, *post*, provides that this term, in relation to a school, shall have the meaning given to it by section 114 (2), p. 185, *post.*

Prior to the passing of the Education (Miscellaneous Provisions) Act, 1953, section 6, p. 231, *post*, which authorises a local education authority to take up places in direct grant and independent schools and to pay the whole of the tuition fees, and in certain cases the boarding fees, where their maintained school or special school provision is inadequate or does not offer education of the kind needed by the particular pupil, the only means by which an authority could pay the fees of pupils for whom it took up places in non-maintained schools was by " assisting " the schools under the present section. Cf. Manual of Guidance, Special Services, No. 1.

In Circular 350 (24th March, 1959) the Minister (now Secretary of State) announced that while in view of the wording of the present section his approval must be sought to arrangements for assisting schools made thereunder local education authorities may assume that such approval will be forthcoming.

(e) **" Nursery schools ".**—Nursery schools are defined by sub-section (4). See also regulation 7 (2) of the Schools Regulations, 1959, S.I. 1959 No. 364. Section 21 of the Education Act, 1921, enabled local authorities for elementary education to provide nursery schools, but section 8 (2) (*b*), p. 80, *ante*, imposes a duty upon local education authorities to " have regard " to the need for providing nursery schools or nursery classes though, since attendance at school below the age of five is not compulsory, accommodation in such schools is only " needed " for those children below compulsory school age whose parents desire to make use of it. The provision of new nursery schools has been regarded as less urgent than the provision of more and better primary and secondary schools, since few teachers could be spared for nursery schools who would otherwise work with children of compulsory school age. See also the Introduction, pp. 14–17, *ante.*

For recent developments, and the present position regarding nursery education, see the Introduction, p. 14, *ante*.

(f) **" Special schools ".**—Special schools are defined by sub-section (5) of this section. The present section imposes a duty upon local education authorities to secure the provision, for children suffering from any disability of mind or body, of special educational treatment, either in special schools or otherwise. It should be noted that there is no direct obligation upon the local education authority itself to provide a special school or schools, if that provision can be secured in any other way and in fact of 810 special schools existing on 1st January, 1959, only 679 were maintained by local education authorities and the remaining 131 were not so maintained. If, however, the arrangements mentioned in the development plan which were made and proposed to be made by the authority for meeting the needs of pupils who required special educational treatment (section 11 (2) (*e*), p. 86, *post*) did not satisfy the Minister (as he then was) he could, in pursuance of the power given by section 11 (4), p. 86, *post*, to modify the plan, require the authority to do so. Although the power of modification relates only to the purpose of securing that proper provision is made with respect to primary and secondary schools, special educational treatment is within the scope of primary and secondary education, and it is only the obligation to make provision for primary and secondary education in separate schools which is relaxed in the case of special schools by the proviso to section 8 (2), *ante*.

Over 9,000 children were receiving education in hospital schools in January, 1974 (Department of Education and Science Annual Report, 1974),

As to the conditions to be fulfilled by special schools maintained by local education authorities, see Handicapped Pupils and Special Schools Regulations, 1959, S.I. 1959 No. 365, p. 356 *post*; as to the conditions of grant in respect of special schools not so maintained, see the Special Schools and Establishments (Grant) Regulations 1959, S.I. 1959 No. 366, p. 361.

See also the Introduction, p. 28, *ante*.

(g) **" Voluntary schools ".**—Voluntary schools are primary and secondary schools maintained by a local education authority (not being nursery schools) but established otherwise than by a local education authority or a former authority. The term " school " is defined in section 114 (1), p. 185, *post*.

(h) **" Any enactment repealed by this Act ".**—This refers to sections 38 and 73 of the Education Act, 1921, and section 10 of the Education Act, 1936.

(j) **" Provisions hereinafter contained ".**—See sections 13, 14 and 16, pp. 90, 93 and 99, *post*.

(k) **" The commencement of this part of this Act ".**—By section 119, Part II came into operation on 1st April, 1945.

(m) **" If it was then maintained ".**—The object of these words is to exclude from the operation of the sub-section certain non-local orphanage or charitable schools which were called public elementary schools, the maintenance of which, but for these words, would have been placed upon local education authorities as from 1st April, 1945. The local education authority could, of course, if it thought fit, put any schools, even those to which these words apply, into or leave them out of a development plan.

(n) **" Mainly ".**—A school does not cease to be a nursery school because it provides education for children who have attained the age of five years. The definition of nursery school in this sub-section is in fact framed to enable children to remain at the school beyond the age of five but by regulation 7 (2) of the Schools Regulations, 1959, S.I. 1959 No. 364, p. 350, *post*, no child may be retained in a maintained nursery school after the end of the term in which he attains five years except in special circumstances.

10. Requirements as to school premises.—(1) The Secretary of State (a) shall make regulations (b) prescribing the standards to which the premises (*) of schools (c) maintained (*) by local education authorities (*) are to conform, and such regulations may prescribe different standards for such descriptions of schools as may be specified in the regulations.

(2) Subject as hereinafter provided, it shall be the duty (d) of a local education authority to secure that the premises of every school maintained by them conform to the standards prescribed (e) for schools of the description to which the school belongs:

Provided that, if the Secretary of State (a) is satisfied with respect to any school—

(*a*) that having regard to the nature of the existing site or to any existing buildings thereon or to other special circumstances affecting the school premises it would be unreasonable to require conformity with a requirement of the regulations as to any matter, or

(*b*) where the school is to have an additional or new site (f) that, having regard to shortage of suitable sites it would be unreasonable to require conformity with a requirement of the regulations relating to sites, or

(*c*) where the school is to have additional buildings or is to be transferred to a new site, and existing buildings not theretofore part of the school premises, or temporary buildings, are to be used for that purpose, that [having regard to the need to control public expenditure in the interests of the national economy] it would be unreasonable to require conformity with a requirement of the regulations relating to buildings,

he may give a direction (g) that, notwithstanding that that requirement is not satisfied, the school premises shall, whilst the direction remains in force, be deemed to conform to the prescribed standards as respects matters with which the direction deals if such conditions, if any, as may be specified in the direction as respects those matters are observed.

NOTES

This section enables the Secretary of State to require not only that all new schools shall conform to the prescribed standards, but also that all existing schools shall be brought up to those standards, though he is given, by the proviso to subsection (2), a power of dispensation in suitable circumstances. Furthermore, the regulations themselves may be varied from time to time by the making of new regulations to suit changed circumstances. No definition is given of the word " standards ", which is sufficiently wide to cover a variety of matters, including the materials to be used, accommodation to be provided and so on. " Premises " includes playing fields.

The proviso to sub-s. (2) was substituted by s. 7 (1) of the Education (Miscellaneous Provisions) Act, 1948, *post*, the substitution being deemed to have had effect from 1st April, 1945; and the words in square brackets were substituted by s. 3 (3) of the Education Act, 1968. The present proviso, which relates only to existing schools, is both wider and more precise than that for which it was substituted; it enables the Secretary of State to accept a lower standard in cases where site difficulties or reasons of economy make it impossible to insist on complete conformity with the prescribed standard. Similar powers to relax standards in relation to new schools are conferred by s. 7 (2) of the 1948 Act, *post*.

(*) As to the meaning or statutory definition of " premises ", " school ", " maintain " and " local education authority ", see p. 68, *ante*.

(a) **" Secretary of State ".**—See note (b) to s. 1, *ante*.

(b) **" Regulations ".**—See the Standards for School Premises Regulations 1972, S.I. 1972 No. 2051, p. 392, *post*.

(c) **" Schools ".**—See the definition of " school " in section 114 (1), p. 185, *post*, which is, however, qualified by the following words of this section.

(d) **" It shall be the duty ".**—As to the enforcement of this duty, see section 99, p. 173, *post*.

(e) **" Conform to the standards prescribed ".**—*See Reffell* v. *Surrey County Council*, [1964] 1 All E.R. 743, under which it was held that there is an absolute statutory duty to conform with the prescribed standards, the test for breach being objective.

(f) **" Additional or new site ".**—See the definition of the term " site " in s. 16 (1) of the Education Act, 1946, p. 215, *post*. A new or additional site for an existing voluntary school must in all cases be provided by the local education authority. See paragraph 1 of the First Schedule to the Education Act, 1946, p. 216, *post*. As to the transfer of county or voluntary schools to new sites, see section 16, thereof.

(g) **" Direction ".**—As to the revocation or variation of any such direction, see s. 111, p. 181, *post*.

11. Development plans as to primary and secondary schools.—(1) As soon as may be after the date of the commencement of this Part of this Act (a), every local education authority (*) shall estimate the immediate and prospective needs of their area, having regard to the provisions of this Act (b) and of any regulations (c) made thereunder and to the functions relating to primary and secondary education thereby conferred on them (d), and shall within one year after that date or within such extended period as the Secretary of State (e) may in any particular case allow, prepare and submit to the Secretary of State (e) a plan (in this Act referred to as a " development plan ") in such form as the Secretary of State (e) may direct (f), showing the action which the authority propose should be taken for securing that there shall be sufficient primary (*) and secondary schools (*) available for their area and the successive measures by which it is proposed to accomplish that purpose.

(2) A local education authority, before submitting to the Secretary of State (e) the development plan for their area, shall take into consideration all schools available for providing primary (*) and secondary education (*) for pupils (*) in the area (g), and the development plan for the area shall:—

(*a*) specify which of the said schools the authority propose should be county primary schools, county secondary schools (h), voluntary primary schools, and voluntary secondary schools (i) respectively, and, in relation to every such school, give particulars of the proposals of the authority as to the nature of the education to be provided in the school and as to the ages of the pupils to be taught therein ;

(*b*) specify what alterations (*) are, by reason of the provisions of this Act or of any regulations (j) made thereunder, required in the premises (*) of any school proposed to be either a county school or a voluntary school, and furnish estimates of the cost of those alterations ;

(*c*) specify what additional county schools and voluntary schools (k), if any, will be required for their area ;

(*d*) include information as to any arrangements proposed to be made with respect to schools not to be maintained by the authority, for the purpose of helping to secure that there shall be sufficient primary and secondary schools available for their area ;

(*e*) give particulars of the arrangements made and proposed to be made by the authority for meeting the needs of pupils who have not attained the age of five years (l) and of pupils who require special educational treatment (m) ;

(*f*) give particulars of the arrangements made and proposed to be made by the authority for the provision of boarding schools (n) ;

(*g*) include information as to any other measures which the authority propose to take in fulfilment of their duty to secure the provision of schools for providing primary and secondary education, such as the making of general arrangements for the transport of pupils to and from school ; and

(*h*) contain such other particulars (o) of the proposals of the authority with respect to schools for providing primary and secondary education for their area as the authority think necessary, or as the Secretary of State (e) may require:

Provided that (p), if the local education authority are satisfied that any county school or voluntary school which is for the time being organised for the provision of both primary and secondary education ought to continue to be so organised, the development plan may make provision for its continuing to be so organised during such period as they think necessary.

(3) A local education authority shall, before submitting their development plan to the Secretary of State (e) consult the managers or governors (q), or persons representing the managers or governors (r), of all schools other than county schools, whether within or without the area of the authority, which would in the opinion of the authority be affected by the execution of the plan, and shall, after submitting the plan to the Secretary of State (e), forthwith furnish to the managers or governors of every such school such particulars relating to the plan as are sufficient to show the manner in which the school would be affected by the execution thereof.

Where a development plan has been submitted to the Secretary of State (e) under this section, the Secretary of State (e) shall, if he is of opinion that no particulars or insufficient particulars of the plan have been furnished to any person (s) who, in his opinion, would be affected by the execution of the plan, give such directions (t) as he considers expedient for securing that sufficient particulars are so furnished.

(4) After considering any objections to a development plan made to him within the period of two months after the date on which he is satisfied that all necessary particulars have been furnished in accordance with the last foregoing subsection, and after making in the plan such modifications, if any, as after consultation with the local education authority he considers necessary or expedient for the purpose of securing that the plan makes proper provision for the immediate and prospective needs of the area with

respect to primary and secondary schools, the Secretary of State (e) shall approve (u) the plan, and shall give such directions to the local education authority as he considers desirable for the purpose of giving to the managers or governors of every voluntary school affected by the plan notice of the approval thereof, and otherwise for giving publicity to the plan as approved by him.

(5) The approval of the development plan submitted by a local education authority shall not, of itself, affect the duties of the authority, but in so far as the Secretary of State (e) considers it expedient to impose duties upon the authority for the purpose of securing that effect will be given to the plan as approved by him, those duties shall be imposed by the local education order (*) for the area made under the next following section.

NOTES

As to the continued operation and revision of development plans under this section in force immediately before 1st April, 1965 and relating to areas in Greater London, see section 31 of the London Government Act, 1963, p. 349, *post*.

(*) As to the meaning or statutory definition of " local education authority ", " primary school ", " secondary school ", " primary education ", " secondary education ", " alterations " and " local education authority ", see pp. 67–69, *ante*.

(a) **" The commencement of this Part of this Act ".**—By section 119, Part II of the Act came into operation on 1st April, 1945.

(b) **" Provisions of this Act ".**—As to the enforcement of the duty imposed by this section, see section 99 (1), p. 173, *post*.

(c) **" Regulations ".**—See, in particular, sections 10, p. 84, *ante*, 33, p. 122, *post*, 49, p. 141, *post*, 100, p. 175, *post*, etc. In addition to the various direct powers to make regulations contained in the Act, section 114 (1), p. 185, *post*, provides that wherever the word " prescribed " appears in the Act it means prescribed by regulations made by the Secretary of State.

(d) **" Functions relating to primary and secondary education thereby conferred upon them ".**—Section 7, p. 78, *ante*, imposes a general duty upon local education authorities to secure efficient education through the stages of primary and secondary education, whilst section 8, p. 79, *ante*, more specifically states the duty of the authority to secure sufficient schools for the purpose of providing education throughout those stages, which are reviewed at some length in notes (d) and (g) to that section.

(e) **" Secretary of State ".**—See note (b) to s. 1, *ante*.

(f) **" May direct ".**—As to revocation and variation of directions, see section 111, p. 181, *post*.

(g) **" In the area ".**—The phrase " in the area " relates to the word " pupils " and not to the earlier word " schools " in the same sentence, though this may not have been the intention of the draftsman, since sub-paragraph (*a*) requires the authority to specify which of " the said schools ", *i.e.*, the schools available, should be county primary schools, etc., and a particular available school might in fact have been established or be maintained or assisted by another authority or might be an independent school.

(h) **" County primary schools, county secondary schools ".**—For the definitions of these terms, see sections 114 (1) and (3), pp. 185, 186, *post* (primary schools, secondary schools) and 9 (2), p. 82, *ante* (county schools). Note that the term " county primary schools " does not include nursery schools nor does either term include special schools. In considering these requirements the authority was required to regard in particular to the requirements of section 8 (2), p. 80, *ante*.

(i) **" Voluntary primary schools, voluntary secondary schools ".**—For the definitions of these terms, see sections 114 (1) and (3), pp. 185, 186, *post*, and 9 (2), p. 82, *ante*, and the last preceding note.

(j) **" Regulations ".**—E.g., regulations made under section 10, p. 84, *ante*.

(k) **" Additional county schools and voluntary schools ".**—As to the provision of sites for new voluntary schools, see the First Schedule to the Education Act, 1946, p. 216, *post*, and section 10 of the Education (Miscellaneous Provisions) Act, 1948, p. 226, *post*.

(l) **" Pupils who have not attained the age of five years ".**—The duties of the authority in connection with nursery schools and nursery classes are set out in sections 8 (2) (*b*) and 9 (4), pp. 80 and 83, *ante*, and the notes thereto.

(m) **" Pupils who require special educational treatment ".**—The duties of the authority in relation to the provision of special educational treatment are set out in sections 8 (2) (*c*) and 9 (5), pp. 80 and 83, *ante*, and sections 33, 34, and 35, pp. 122, 125 and 127, *post* and the notes thereto.

(n) **" Boarding schools ".**—A duty to have regard to the expediency of securing the provision of boarding accommodation, either in boarding schools or otherwise, for pupils for whom education as boarders is considered by their parents and by the authority to be desirable is imposed by section 8 (2) (*d*), p. 80, *ante*. Power to provide board and lodging otherwise than at boarding schools or colleges is given by section 50, p. 142, *post*, and as to the recovery of the cost of such provision by section 52, p. 143, *post*. Fees in respect of board and lodging at maintained boarding schools and county colleges are provided for in section 61, p. 149, *post*. As to boarding fees where education is provided by the local education authority in a non-maintained school, see section 6 of the Education (Miscellaneous Provisions) Act, 1953, p. 231

(o) **" Such other particulars ".**—This is a general provision, designed to include any matter not specifically covered by the previous sub-paragraphs.

(p) **" Provided that ".**—Notwithstanding the duty of the authority to have regard to the need for securing that primary and secondary education are provided in separate schools (section 8 (2) (*a*), p. 80, *ante*), provision might be made for a school for the time being organised for the provision of both primary and secondary education to be continued as such during such period as the authority thinks necessary. Although unlimited discretion is apparently given to the authoritv with regard to the period during which it is to continue to be so organised, the fact that provision for this had to be made in the development plan gives the Secretary of State adequate power of control, and even where such a provision is contained in the local education order made by the Secretary of State under section 12, *infra*, his power of variation or revocation under section 111, p. 181, *post*, is a further safeguard.

(q) **" Managers or governors ".**—Before the coming into operation of the development plan and afterwards until the question whether a voluntary school was to be a controlled school, an aided school or a special agreement school was determined (section 15, p. 95, *post*), the body of managers or governors of the school remained constituted as it was immediately before 1st April, 1945

(r) **" Persons representing the managers or governors ".**—The inclusion of this phrase enabled the local education authority to consult with the diocesan education committees set up under the Diocesan Education Committees Measures, 1943 and 1951; 11 Halsbury's Statutes (3rd Edn.) 370; 30 Halsbury's Statutes (2nd Edn.) 67, with whom, under the Measure, the managers of church schools are also bound to consult before making any arrangement with the Secretary of State or the local education authority with regard to the school.

(s) **" Any person ".**—This phrase is considerably wider than that used earlier in this sub-section, for it is at least arguable that the parent of every child in attendance at or likely to attend a school in the authority's area would be affected by the plan.

(t) **" Directions ".**—Any such directions may be varied or revoked under section 111, p. 213, *post*. It was held in *Wood* v. *Ealing London Borough*, [1966] 3 All E.R. 514; [1967] Ch. 364, that this section negatived any general right of parents to be consulted as to the revision of a development plan.

(u) **" Approve ".**—Before approving a plan, the Secretary of State may, under section 93, p. 171, *post*, direct a local inquiry to be held. As provided in subsection (5), the Secretary of State's approval to the development plan does not of itself impose any obligation upon the authority, this being carried out by means of a local education order made under s. 12, *infra*.

12. Local education orders with respect to primary and secondary education.—(1) As soon as may be after approving the development plan (*) for the area of any local education authority (*), the Secretary of State (a) shall make an order to be called the local education order (b) for the area specifying the county schools (*) and voluntary schools (*) which it is the duty of the authority to maintain (*), and the order shall, to such extent as the Secretary of State (a) considers desirable, define the duties of the authority with respect to the measures to be taken by the authority for securing that there shall be sufficient (c) primary (*) and secondary schools (*) available for their area (d), and shall make provision as to which of the schools maintained or assisted (*) by the authority for providing primary (*) and secondary education (*) shall be primary schools and secondary schools respectively and as to which of them, if any, shall, for the time being, be organised for the provision of both primary and secondary education (e).

(2) The local education order for every area shall continue to regulate the duties of the local education authority (f) in respect of the matters therein mentioned and shall be amended (g) by the Secretary of State (a) whenever, in his opinion, the amendment thereof is expedient by reason of any change or proposed change of circumstances:

Provided that, before amending the local education order for any area in such manner as to vary the duties of a local education authority in any respect not either provided for by the development plan approved for the area or by proposals approved by him or occasioned by the discontinuance of a voluntary school (h) under the provisions hereinafter contained relating to those matters respectively, the Secretary of State (a) shall give to the local education authority, and to the managers, governors or other proprietor (*) of any school which, in his opinion, would be affected by the amendment, notice (i) of the amendment proposed to be made and shall consider any objections made to him by the authority or by such managers, governors or proprietor within two months after the service of the notice.

(3) If a local education authority inform the Secretary of State (a) that they are aggrieved by an order or by an amendment of an order made under this section the order or amendment shall be laid before Parliament as soon as may be thereafter and if either House of Parliament within the period of forty days beginning with the day on which any such order or amendment is laid before it resolves that the order or amendment be annulled the order or amendment shall cease to have effect but without prejudice to anything previously done thereunder or to the making of any new order or amendment.

In reckoning any such period of forty days no account shall be taken of any time during which Parliament is dissolved or prorogued or during which both Houses are adjourned for more than four days.

NOTES

After the preparation and approval of the development plan for the area under section 11, p. 85, *ante*, the Minister (as he then was) was required by this section to make an order to be called the local education order for the area for the following purposes:—

(1) specifying the county schools and voluntary schools which the authority is to maintain;

(2) defining the measures to be taken by the authority, to such extent as the Minister thought desirable, for securing that there shall be sufficient primary and secondary schools available for their area;

(3) providing which of the schools maintained or assisted by the authority shall be primary and secondary schools respectively, and which, if any, are for the time being to be organised for the provision of both primary and secondary education.

(*) As to the meaning or statutory definition of " development plan ", " local education authority ", " county school ", " voluntary school ", " primary school ", " secondary school ", " primary education ", " secondary education " and " proprietor ", see pp. 67–69, *ante*.

(a) **" Secretary of State "**— See note (b) to s. 1, *ante*.

(b) **" Local education order ".**—An order under this section must be regarded somewhat differently from other orders which the Secretary of State is empowered to make under the Act for, in their case, only section 111, p. 181, *post*, applies to their subsequent revocation or variation, whereas the amendment of a local education order is subject to the conditions referred to in subsection (2) and (3) of this section. The object of the order is to specify and define the duties of the local education authority in connection with the provision of proper educational facilities for the area. The Secretary of State is, by section 99, p. 173, *post*, given special powers to enforce the execution by a local education authority of its duties in the event of default. See also section 68, p. 155, *post*, which defines the powers of the Secretary of State to prevent the unreasonable exercise by a local education authority of its functions under the Act.

(c) **" Sufficient ".**—As to the meaning of this term, see the latter part of section 8 (1), p. 79, *ante*.

(d) **" Available for their area ".**—As to the availability of schools for the area of a local education authority, see note (g) to section 11, p. 87, *ante*.

(e) **" Both primary and secondary education ".**—See the proviso to section 11 (2), p. 86, *ante*, and section 114 (3), p. 186, *post*.

(f) **" The duties of the local education authority ".**—As to the enforcement of these duties, see section 99, p. 173, *post*, and note (b), *supra*. The duties imposed by the order must be strictly " *intra vires* " the provisions of the Act and the order must not impose any requirement or obligation upon a local education authority which is in any way outside the terms of the Act. Its purpose is in fact to define the duties of the authority " with respect to the measures to be taken by the authority for securing that there shall be sufficient primary and secondary schools available for their area " (subsection (1) of this section), *i.e.*, within the limits of the obligation imposed by section 8 (1), p. 79, *ante*.

(g) **" Shall be amended ".**—See also section 111, p. 181, *post*.

(h) **" Discontinuance of voluntary school ".**—See section 14, p. 93, *post*.

(i) **" Notice ".**—In this case the section specifies that the notice is to be *served*; in consequence there is no doubt that section 113, p. 182, *post*, applies.

13. Establishment and discontinuance of county and voluntary schools.—(1) Where a local education authority (*) intend—

(*a*) to establish (a) a new county school (*);
(*b*) to maintain (b) as a county school any school (c) which at the time being is not such a school; or
(*c*) to cease to maintain (d) any county school or, save as provided by the next following section of this Act, any voluntary school (*);

[or where a local education authority intend to make any significant change in the character, or significant enlargement of the premises, of a county school,] they shall submit proposals for that purpose to the Secretary of State (e).

(2) Where any persons propose (f) that any school established by them or by persons whom they represent which at the time being is not a voluntary school, or any school proposed to be so established, should be maintained by a local education authority as a voluntary school, [or where the managers or governors of a school maintained by a local education authority as a voluntary school intend to make any significant change in the character, or significant enlargement of the premises, of the school] they shall after consultation with the authority (g) submit proposals for that purpose to the Secretary of State. (e).

(3) After any proposals have been submitted to the Secretary of State (e) under this section the authority of persons by whom the proposals were submitted shall forthwith give public notice of the proposals in the prescribed manner (h), and the managers or governors (*) of any voluntary school affected by the proposals or any ten or more local government electors (i) for the area and any local education authority concerned, may within [two months] after the first publication of the notice submit to the Secretary of State (e) objections to the proposals;

Provided that this subsection shall not have effect in the case of proposals for the maintenance as a voluntary school of a school which is at the time being a school in respect of which grants are made (j) by the Secretary of State (e), if the proposals are made with the concurrence of the authority and of the proprietor (*) of the school and of any trustees in whom is vested any interest in the school premises (*).

(4) Any proposals submitted to the Secretary of State (e) under this section may be approved by him (k) after making such modifications therein, if any, as appear to him to be desirable:

Provided that the Secretary of State (e) shall not approve proposals for the maintenance as a county school of any school which, at the time being, is a voluntary school, unless he has, in accordance with the provisions of the Second Schedule to this Act, approved an agreement made under the powers conferred by that Schedule between the authority and the managers or governors of the school for the transfer to the authority of all necessary interests in the school premises.

(5) A local education authority shall not, without the leave of the Secretary of State (e), do or undertake to do anything (whether or not provided for by this development plan (*) for the area) for which proposals are required by this section to be submitted to the Secretary of State (e) until such proposals have been approved by him.

(6) After proposals for the establishment of a new school have been approved by the Secretary of State (e) under this section the authority or persons by whom the proposed school is to be established [shall unless they do not intend to give effect to the proposals submit] to him in such form and in such manner as he may direct (l) specifications and plans of the school premises [if the premises are new premises (that is to say, if the premises do not comprise buildings used for a school at the time when the proposals are approved) or if the Secretary of State (e) so directs], and the Secretary of State (e), on being satisfied that the school premises

will conform to the prescribed standards (m), may approve the specifications and plans:

Provided that, before submitting specifications and plans in respect of a school which is to be maintained as a voluntary school, the persons by whom the school is to be established shall consult the local education authority.

(7) When the proposals specifications and plans for a new school have been approved by the Secretary of State (e) under this section [or, in a case where specifications and plans are not required, when the proposals have been so approved and the Secretary of State (e) has notified the authority or persons by whom the proposed scheme is to be established that specifications and plans will not be required,] it shall be the duty (n) of the authority or persons by whom the proposed school is to be established to give effect to the proposals in accordance with the specifications and plans so approved, [if any,] except that in the case of proposals submitted under subsection (2) of this section the duty of providing playing fields (o) and any buildings [which are to form part of the school premises but are not to be school buildings (p)] shall be the duty of the local education authority.

(8) When proposals for the maintenance of any school have been approved by the Secretary of State (e) under this section, it shall be the duty of the local education authority to maintain it; and an authority shall not be under any duty to maintain a school after proposals that the authority shall cease to maintain it have been approved by the Secretary of State (e) under this section.

(9) Where proposals are made under this section for the enlargement of school premises, subsections (6) and (7) shall apply, with the necessary adaptations, as they apply in the case of proposals for the establishment of a new school (any reference to the persons by whom the proposed school is to be established being read as a reference to the managers or governors).

(10) References in this section to a change in the character of a school include in particular changes in character resulting from education beginning or ceasing to be provided for pupils above or below a particular age, for boys as well as for girls, or for girls as well as for boys, or from the making or alteration of arrangements for the admission of pupils by reference to ability or aptitude.

NOTES

This section states the powers of a local education authority in connection with the provision of new county schools, the transfer of schools other than county schools to the authority and the discontinuance of the maintenance of county or voluntary schools. The section is printed as amended, the various amendments being as follows:

(1) The words in square brackets in sub-s. (1) were inserted by s. 1 (2) (*a*) of the Education Act, 1968.

(2) The words in square brackets in sub-s. (2) were inserted by s. 1 (2) (*b*) of the Education Act, 1968.

(3) The words in square brackets in sub-s. (3) were substituted by s. 16 of the Education (Miscellaneous Provisions) Act, 1953.

4) The words in the first square brackets in sub-s. (6) were substituted by s. 17 of, and Sch. 1 to, the Education (Miscellaneous Provisions) Act, 1953; those in the second set of square brackets were inserted by s. 3 (1) (*a*) of the Education Act, 1968.

(5) The words in square brackets in sub-s. (7) were inserted by s. 3 (1) (*b*) of the Education Act, 1968.

(6) Sub-sections (9) and (10) were added by s. 1 (2) of the Education Act, 1968.

The reasons for the amendments made by the Act of 1968 were to enable the government then in power to press forward with its policy of establishing comprehensive schools despite the considerable opposition which had been aroused to such schemes. See, more fully, the general note to the Act of 1968, p. 261, *post*.

Sub-section (7) must be read subject to the overriding provisions of section 7 (2) of the Education (Miscellaneous Provisions) Act, 1948, *post*. See note (m), *infra*.

Compliance with the requirements of the section is necessary even where the proposal has already been included in the local education order made by the Secretary of State under section 12, p. 88, *ante*. The provision of new schools, whether county or voluntary, requires the issue of public notices. Public notices are also necessary if the local education authority proposes that an existing school should be closed. In either case the Secretary of State's approval must be obtained before the proposal can be put into effect and a period of two months is allowed for objections to the proposal to be submitted to the Secretary of State. The Committee on School Sites and Buildings Procedure suggest that there may be a saving of time in the area of a large authority in the simultaneous issue of a group of notices for a number of new schools with which it is intended to proceed in the ensuing year or so.

It is further provided, by section 1 of the Education Act, 1964, that new schools may be established with special age limits, a local education authority being thereby empowered to submit proposals for the establishment of a new county school (or for the maintenance of a new voluntary school) which specify an age below ten years and six months and an age above the age of twelve years, and which provide that the school shall be established for providing full-time education suitable to the requirements of pupils whose ages are between the ages so specified. See section 1 of the Act of 1964 and the notes thereto at p. 251, *post*. For the usual age-limits applicable to primary and secondary schools, see section 8 (1) of the Act of 1944 (as amended by section 3 of the Education (Miscellaneous Provisions) Act, 1948), at p. 79, *ante*.

On the approval of any such proposals the Secretary of State is to direct whether the school concerned is to be deemed a primary school or a secondary school (Act of 1964 section 1 (2), p. 251, *post*).

As to the approval of proposals under this section with respect to a school which is, or is to be, situated in the City of London or an inner London borough, see section 31 of the London Government Act, 1963, p. 291, *post*.

Where the Secretary of State approves a proposal, or makes an order, under this section he may by order make such consequential modifications of any trust deed as, after consultation, appear to him to be requisite: Education Act 1973, s. 1 (2), p. 274, *post*.

(*) As to the meaning or statutory definition of " local education authority ", " county school ", " voluntary school ", " managers or governors ", " proprietor ", " premises ", and " development plan ", see pp. 67–69, *ante*.

(a) **" Establish ".**—Power to establish primary and secondary schools is given by section 9 (1), p. 82, *ante*. The development plan which the authority prepared under section 11, p. 85, *ante*, will, unless the school was not in contemplation at that time, have specified that it was proposed to establish the school (section 11 (2) (*c*), p. 86, *ante*), and the duty of providing it will have been imposed by the local education order made by the Secretary of State under section 12, p. 88, *ante*, or, in the case of a school not referred to in the original order, by an amendment to the order under section 12 (2), *ibid*.

(b) **" Maintain ".**—As to the meaning of this term, see section 114 (1) and (2), pp. 184, 185, *post*, and see the First Schedule to the Education Act, 1946, p. 216, *post*. Power to maintain a school in the circumstances referred to is given by section 9 (1), p. 82, *ante*. A proposal under this provision may or may not have been made in the development plan prepared by the authority under section 11, p. 85, *ante* (see sub-section 2 (*a*), *ibid*.), or included in the local education order or an amendment thereof made under section 12, p. 88, *ante*.

(c) **" School ".**—The word " school " is defined as an institution for providing primary or secondary education or both primary and secondary education, being a school maintained by a local education authority, an independent school, or a school in respect of which grants are made by the Secretary of State to the proprietor of the school. Schools which are not for the time being maintained as county schools may be—

(*a*) nursery schools (see section 9 (4), p. 83, *ante*) ;
(*b*) special schools (see section 9 (5), p. 83, *ante*) ;
(*c*) voluntary schools (see sections 9 (2), p. 82, *ante*, and 15, p. 95, *post*);
(*d*) independent schools (see definition in section 114 (1), p. 183, *post*, and also Part III of the Act, p. 156, *post*) ;
(*e*) schools in respect of which grant is payable by the Secretary of State (section 100 (1) (*b*), *post*).

Of these nursery schools and special schools cannot become county schools unless their character is so changed that they cease to be nursery schools or special schools as the case may be.

(d) **" Cease to maintain ".**—The discontinuance of provided elementary schools was formerly covered by section 17 (4) of the Education Act, 1921. Section 19 of the Education Act, 1921, as amended by the Education (Necessity of Schools) Act, 1933, which dealt with the determination as to whether a school was necessary or not, is not re-enacted, since the closer supervision by the Department of Education and Science of the exercise by the local education authority of its functions renders the provision unnecessary (see the general note to this section). Section 14, p. 93, *post*, however, imposes certain restrictions upon the discontinuance of voluntary schools by managers or governors. The transfer of county and voluntary schools to new sites, and the substitution of new voluntary schools for old ones, is dealt with in section 16, p. 99, *post*. See *Legg* v. *Inner London Education Authority*, [1972] 3 All E.R. 177.

(e) **" Secretary of State ".**—See note (b) to s. 1, *ante*.

(f) **" Where any persons propose ".**—This subsection applies not only to the establishment of new denominational schools, but to cases where the proprietor (as defined in s. 114 (1), p. 185, *post*) of a direct grant school or an independent school thinks it would be desirable to take advantage of the financial and other facilities offered to the managers or governors of voluntary schools. In the case of direct grant schools, some relaxation of the requirements of the section is given by the proviso to sub-s. (3). Where the Secretary of State has approved proposals under this section for the establishment of an aided school or special agreement school for the accommodation of " displaced pupils " or as a substituted school, he may make to the managers or governors a grant towards the cost of providing the site and buildings; the maximum amount of the grant where proposals are approved now being 85 per cent. (Education Act, 1944, s. 103 (1), as amended by s. 3 of the Education Act, 1975). Where proposals are approved under the section for the establishment of a new aided secondary school which the Secretary of State is satisfied is needed wholly or mainly for children from certain aided or special agreement primary schools the Secretary of State may likewise make a grant of up to 85 per cent. of the cost of providing the site and buildings (Education Act, 1967, s. 1 (2), *post*). Where proposals are made under the section for the establishment of a new controlled school and the proposers and the local education authority satisfy the Secretary of State that it is required for the accommodation of pupils from some other voluntary school or schools no longer available for them the Secretary of State may direct the local education authority to pay the whole or part of the cost of establishment (Education (Miscellaneous Provisions) Act, 1953, s. 2, p. 229, *post*). As to the purchase of land by agreement by a local education authority for the purposes of a voluntary school, see s. 90, p. 169, *post*, and s. 10 of the Education (Miscellaneous Provisions) Act, 1948, p. 226, *post*.

(g) **" After consultation with the authority ".**—Where a new voluntary school is proposed to be established then if, as will commonly be the case, it is a major project (*i.e.*, of a gross cost exceeding £20,000) eligible for grant the result of such consultation must be that the local education authority agrees to include the project in its annual building programme for submission to the Secretary of State.

(h) **" In the prescribed manner ".**—The term " prescribed " means prescribed by regulations made by the Secretary of State (section 114 (1), p. 185, *post*), as to which see section 112, p. 182, *post*. See the County and Voluntary Schools (Notices) Regulations, 1968, S.I. 1968 No. 615, p. 381, *post*, which prescribe the manner in which public notice is to be given. Copies of an appropriate form of notice will be sent to the promoters by the Department of Education and Science after the project has been included in a building programme. The promoters will also be asked to submit an application for an order under section 15 (2), *post*, determining the status of the school, and, if the application is in respect of an aided or special agreement school, evidence that the managers or governors will be able and willing to meet the expenses which fall to be met under section 15 (3), *post*.

(i) **" Any ten or more local government electors ".**—This phrase takes the place of " any ten ratepayers " and thus substantially increases the number of those entitled to object. Most parents are local government electors though rarely are the mothers of schoolchildren themselves ratepayers. See the definition of " local government elector " in section 114 (1), p. 184, *post*.

(j) **" A school in respect of which grants are made ".**—See section 100 (1) (*b*), p. 175, *post*.

(k) **" May be approved by him ".**—In Circular 9/59 (21st August, 1959), it was stated that the Minister (now Secretary of State) desired to draw attention to the assurances he gave during the passage of the Bill for the Education Act, 1959 that " in considering proposals for new aided schools to which there are objections, he will need full information about the accessibility of the nearest county or controlled school. In all cases he will need to be satisfied that the proposal is compatible with an efficient and economical organisation of schools in the area. The diocesan bodies concerned are asked to consult local education authorities at a very early stage, if they contemplate any revision of their plans for providing secondary education in aided or special agreement schools ". As to the power of the Secretary of State to hold a local inquiry, see section 93, p. 171, *post*. The Secretary of State's approval will be given by an official letter which will normally indicate also whether the Secretary of State will be prepared to accord aided or special agreement status.

(l) **" As he may direct ".**—As to the revocation or variation of such directions, see section 111, p. 181, *post*.

(m) **" On being satisfied that the school premises will conform to the prescribed standards ".**—By section 114 (1), p. 185, *post*, " prescribed " means prescribed by regulations made by the Secretary of State. The regulations in question are the Standards for School Premises Regulations 1972, S.I. 1972 No. 2051, p. 392, *post*, made under section 10, p. 84, *ante*. See that section and the notes thereto and the regulations themselves, Part III, *post*.

Section 7 (2) of the Education (Miscellaneous Provisions) Act, 1948, p. 225, *post*, authorises the Secretary of State to approve specifications and plans for a new school which do not comply with the regulations as to sites or, where existing or temporary buildings are to be used, with those as to buildings if owing to the shortage of sites in the one case or of labour and materials in the other, it would be unreasonable to require conformity with the regulations.

(n) **" It shall be the duty ".**—As to the enforcement of this duty, see section 99 (1), p. 173, *post*.

(o) **" The duty of providing playing fields ".**—As to the provision of facilities for recreation and social and physical training (including playing fields), see section 53, p. 144, *post*. The proviso to paragraph 5 of the Third Schedule, *post*, makes it clear that the cost of providing new playing fields for special agreement schools is to be borne by the local education authority. It will be noted that under section 15 (3), p. 96, *post*, the managers or governors of a voluntary school are not responsible for repairs to the school playground or playing fields.

(p) **" School buildings ".**—The words in square brackets were substituted for the words " required only for affording facilities for medical inspection or treatment or for providing milk, meals or other refreshment ", by section 14 of and the Second Schedule to the Education Act, 1946. The new words are consequential upon the wording of other provisions of the Act of 1944 and refer to buildings which do not form part of the school buildings themselves. The point is important in relation to voluntary schools where the duty to provide the buildings which are not " school buildings " rests upon the local education authority. As to special agreement schools, see the proviso to paragraph 5 of the Third Schedule, p. 201, *post*.

14. Restrictions on discontinuance of voluntary schools by managers and governors.—(1) Subject to the provisions of this section (a), the managers or governors (*) of a voluntary school (*) shall not discontinue (b) the school except after serving on the Secretary of State (c) and on the local ecucation authority (*) by whom the school is maintained (*) not less than two years' notice (d) of their intention to do so:

[Provided that, except by leave of the Secretary of State (c), no such notice as aforesaid shall be served by the managers or governors of any voluntary school in respect of the premises (*) of which expenditure has been incurred (e) otherwise than in connection with repairs by the Secretary of State (c) or by any local education authority or former authority (*).]

If the Secretary of State (c) grants such leave, he may impose such requirements as he thinks just—

(*a*) in regard to the repayment of the whole or any part of the amount of the expenditure so incurred by the Secretary oi State (c);

(*b*) where the Secretary of State (c) is satisfied that the local education authority will require, for any purpose connected with education, any premises which are for the time being used for the purposes of the school in regard to the conveyance of those premises to the authority;

(*c*) in regard to the payment by the local education authority of such part of the value of any premises so conveyed as is just having regard to the extent to which those premises were provided otherwise than at the expense of the authority or a former authority;

(*d*) where any premises for the time being used for the purposes of the school are not to be so conveyed, in regard to the payment to the authority by the managers or governors of the school of such part of the value of those premises as is just having regard to the extent to which they were provided at the expense of the authority or a former authority.]

(2) No such notice as aforesaid shall be withdrawn (f) except with the consent of the local education authority.

(3) If, while any such notice as aforesaid is in force with respect to a voluntary school, the managers or governors of the school inform the local education authority that they are unable or unwilling to carry on the school until the expiration of the notice, the authority may conduct (h) the school during the whole or any part of the unexpired period of the notice as if it were a county school (i), and shall be entitled to the use of the school premises free of charge, for that purpose.

(4) While any school is being conducted by a local education authority as a county school under the last foregoing subsection, the authority shall keep the school premises in good repair (j), and for all purposes relating to the condition of the school premises, the occupation and use thereof, and the making of alterations thereto, any interest (k) in the said premises which is held for the purposes of the school shall be deemed to be vested in the authority:

Provided that the managers or governors of the school shall be entitled to the use of the school premises (l) or any part thereof when not required for the purposes of the school to the like extent as if they had continued to carry on the school during the unexpired period of the notice.

(5) Where any school is discontinued in accordance with the provisions of this section the duty of the local education authority (m) to maintain the school as a voluntary school shall be extinguished.

NOTES

This section places restrictions upon the closure of voluntary schools. It applies not only to closures which may take place as a result of reorganisation provided for by the development plan or the establishment of new schools pursuant to the development plan but also to any discontinuance which is contemplated during the life of the Act. The objects of the section are to avoid the difficulties which might arise were the managers or governors suddenly to discontinue a school without giving the local education authority a reasonable opportunity to provide alternative accommodation and to prevent a change of mind on the part of the managers or governors after the local education authority have made arrangements to provide such alternative accommodation.

The proviso to sub-section (1) was substituted by section 14 of and Part II of the Second Schedule to the Education Act, 1946, *post*, and is deemed to have had effect since 1st April, 1945. The proviso enables the Secretary of State to impose conditions as to the disposition of the premises in the event of the closure of a voluntary school, and should be a useful provision. It may be that many old village schools would still, for some time, perform a useful purpose, for example, as a village community centre and the proviso will enable the Secretary of State to assist in securing this end. Similarly the Secretary of State will be able to secure that the managers or governors of a voluntary school which, by circumstances beyond their control, is forced to close, are not saddled with the empty and possibly unmarketable premises.

In 1974 the number of schools discontinued was 244, including 84 voluntary schools (Department of Education and Science Annual Report, 1974).

The section is applied by the London Government Act, 1963, section 31 (5), p. 292, *post*.

(*) As to the meaning or statutory definition of "managers or governors" "voluntary school", "local education authority", "maintain" and "premises", see pp. 67–69, *ante*.

(a) **"Subject to the provisions of this section".**—This refers to sub-section (3), under which the local education authority may carry on the school during the currency of the notice if the managers or governors are unable or unwilling to do so.

(b) **"Shall not discontinue".**—The word "discontinue" in this sub-section takes the place of "close" in the Education Act, 1921, section 40. Normally in the case of voluntary schools the premises are held by the managers or by a body of trustees on trust for the purposes of carrying on a school or of allowing a school to be carried on and the Secretary of State has power to modify the trust deed of premises held on general trusts which include educational trusts so as to secure that they shall not be diverted from educational use so long as they are required as maintained schools (Education (Miscellaneous Provisions) Act, 1953, section 14, *post*). Failure to comply with this section would generally constitute also a breach of trust. Before determining any question under this section the Secretary of State may direct a local inquiry (section 93, p. 171, *post*).

(c) **"Secretary of State".**—See note (b) to s. 1, *ante*.

(d) **"Notice".**—As to the service of notices, see section 113, p. 182, *post*.

(e) **"Expenditure has been incurred".**—Expenditure of this nature may have been incurred by a local education authority in the case of special agreement schools (section 15, *infra*), and by the Secretary of State in the case of aided schools and special agreement schools under sections 103 and 105, pp. 177 *et seq.*, *post*.

(f) **"Shall be withdrawn".**—As stated in the general note, *supra*, this sub-section prevents the managers or governors from withdrawing their notice of discontinuance once given and thus avoids the difficulty which would arise had the local education authority made alternative arrangements as a result of receiving the notice.

(h) **"May conduct".**—No obligation is placed upon the local education authority to conduct the school in the place of the managers or governors, for the authority may be in a position to accept the pupils concerned into another school or there may be some other reason why they should not do so.

(i) **"County school".**—See section 9, p. 82, *ante*. The effect of the sub-section is that in the circumstances mentioned the local education authority may carry on the school exactly as if it was a school established by the authority. See, however, note (k), *infra*.

(j) **"In good repair".**—This re-enacts the obligation of the authority under the Education Act, 1921, section 40 (2), with the addition of the word "good", so far as the repair of the school premises is concerned. The former provision, however, imposed an obligation upon the authority to pay "any outgoings in respect" of the schoolhouse. Since the authority was to be allowed the use of the schoolhouse "free of charge" the meaning of this obligation is obscure, though it may possibly have referred to outgoings imposed by some other statute (see, for example, *Foulger* v. *Arding*, [1902] 1 K.B. 700; *Greaves* v. *Whitmarsh, Watson & Co., Ltd.*, [1906] 2 K.B. 340; *Henman* v. *Berliner*, [1918] 2 K.B. 236. The obligation does not reappear in the present Act.

(k) **"Any interest".**—This will enable the authority to take such action in relation to repairs, etc. as the managers or governors could have taken under the provisions of the instrument by which the school was previously carried on. It may, however, be argued that this provision limits, to some extent, the general power of the authority to conduct the school as if it were a county school, since the authority will presumably be compelled to comply with the terms of any trust deed applying to the school, so far as they are not inconsistent with this section.

(l) **"The use of the school premises".**—See section 22, p. 110, *post*.

(m) **"The duty of the local education authority".**—The powers of the Secretary of State until the duty is extinguished under this section, in the case of default by the local education authority, are contained in section 99 (3), p. 174, *post*.

15. Classification of voluntary schools as controlled schools, aided schools, or special agreement schools.—(1) Voluntary schools (*) shall be of three categories, that is to say, controlled schools (a), aided schools (b), and special agreement schools (c), and in schools of those several categories the management of the school (d), the secular instruction (e) and religious education (f), and the appointment and dismissal of teachers (g), shall be regulated in accordance with the provisions hereinafter contained relating to those matters in controlled schools, aided schools, and special agreement schools respectively.

(2) Upon application being duly made to him with respect to any voluntary school, the Secretary of State (h) may by order direct (i) that the school shall be a controlled school, an aided school or a special agreement school, and where he is satisfied that the managers of governors (*) of the school will be able and willing, with the assistance of the maintenance contribution (j) payable by the Secretary of State (h) under this Act, to defray the expenses which would fall to be borne by them under paragraph (*a*) of the next following subsection, the order shall direct that the school shall be an aided school, or, in the case of a school with respect to which a special agreement has been made under the Third Schedule to this Act (k), a special agreement school:

Provided that, subject to the provisions of this section, any application for an order (l) directing that a school shall be an aided school or a special agreement school must be made, in the case of a school which became a voluntary school by virtue of subsection (3) of section nine of this Act (m) not later than six months after the date on which the managers or governors of the school received notice (n) of the approval of the development plan (o) for the area, and in any other case not later than the submission to the Secretary of State (h) of the proposals (p) that the school should be maintained by the local education authority as a voluntary school; and, subject to the transitional provisions of this Act as to the management and maintenance of voluntary schools, a voluntary school with respect to which no order is in force under this section directing that it shall be an aided school or a special agreement school shall be a controlled school.

(3) The managers or governors of a controlled school shall not be responsible for any of the expenses of maintaining (q) the school, but the following provisions shall have effect with respect to the maintenance of aided schools and special agreement schools:

(*a*) the following expenses shall be payable by the managers or governors of the school, that is to say, the expenses of discharging any liability incurred (r) by them or on their behalf or by or on behalf of any former managers or governors of the school or any trustees thereof [in connection with the provision of premises or equipment for the purposes of the school] any expenses incurred in effecting such alterations (*) to the school buildings as may be required by the local education authority for the purpose of securing that the school premises (*) should conform to the prescribed standards (s), and any expenses incurred in effecting repairs to the [school buildings (*)] not being repairs which are excluded from their responsibility by the following paragraph:

[(*b*) the managers or governors of the school shall not be responsible for repairs to the interior of the school buildings, or for repairs to those buildings necessary in consequence of the use of the school premises, in pursuance of any direction (t) or requirement of the authority, for purposes other than those of the school.]

(4) If at any time the managers or governors of an aided school or a special agreement school are unable or unwilling to carry out their obligations under paragraph (*a*) of the last foregoing subsection it shall be their duty (u) to apply to the Secretary of State (h) for an order revoking the order by virtue of which the school is an aided school or a special agreement school, and upon such an application being made to him the Secretary of State (h) shall revoke the order (v).

(5) If at any time the Secretary of State (h) is satisfied that the grant made in respect of a special agreement school in pursuance of the special agreement made with respect to the school under this Act has been repaid to the local education authority (*) by which the school is maintained, the Secretary of State (h) shall, upon application being made to him for that

purpose by the managers or governors of the school, by order revoke the order by virtue of which the school is a special agreement school and, if satisfied that the managers or governors of the school will be able and willing, with the assistance of the maintenance contribution payable by the Secretary of State (h) under this Act, to defray the expenses which would fall to be borne by them under paragraph (*a*) of subsection (3) of this section, shall by order direct that the school shall be an aided school.

(6) [*Repealed.*]

NOTES

(a) **" Controlled schools ".**—Unless the managers or governors of a voluntary school could satisfy the Minister (now Secretary of State) within the period mentioned in the proviso to subsection (2) that they are able and willing to meet with the assistance of the maintenance contribution (now amounting to 85 per cent.) payable under section 102, as amended, p. 176, *post*, and in the case of capital expenditure of a loan under section 105, as amended, p. 179, *post*, the cost of the alterations and improvements needed to bring the buildings up to standard, and of the continuing external repair of the fabric or if they cease thereafter to be so able and willing (sub-section (4)) the school must become a controlled school (subsection (2)) and all financial obligations pass to the local education authority (subsection (3)), who may execute any necessary works themselves (1946 Act, section 6, p. 212, *post*). With these obligations there also pass to the authority the power of appointing and dismissing teachers (section 24 (1), p. 112, *post*), subject to the right of the managers or governors to be consulted as to the appointment of the head teacher (section 27 (3), p. 118, *post*), and to the right of the foundation managers to be satisfied as to the appointment of reserved teachers (section 27 (2), (4), p. 118, *post*). These teachers will give denominational instruction for not more than two periods a week to those children whose parents desire it (section 27 (1), p. 118, *post*). Apart from this, the religious instruction will be in accordance with an agreed syllabus (section 27 (6), p. 119, *post*). The school premises will be occupied and used in accordance with the directions of the local education authority, except on Saturdays and Sundays (section 22 (1), p. 110, *post*). The appointment and dismissal of caretakers will also be a matter for the local education authority (section 22 (4), p. 110, *post*). The constitution of the managers will be altered (section 18 (3), p. 105, *post*).

(b) **" Aided schools ".**—If the managers or governors of a voluntary school could satisfy the Minister (now Secretary of State) within the period mentioned in the proviso to subsection (2) that they are able and willing to meet with the assistance of the maintenance contribution (now amounting to 85 per cent.) payable under section 102 as amended, p. 176, *post*, and in the case of capital expenditure of a loan under section 105 as amended, *post*, the cost of alterations, improvements and external repairs, the school, unless a special agreement has been made under the Third Schedule, p. 201, *post*, is an aided school (subsection (2)). The powers and duties of managers in regard to the appointment and dismissal of teachers (section 24 (2), p. 112, *post*), and the giving of denominational religious instruction (section 28, p. 119, *post*), remain substantially unaltered, and denominational religious instruction may be given as formerly, subject to the right of parents who so desire to have their children given religious instruction in accordance with an agreed syllabus (proviso to section 28 (1), p. 119, *post*).

Each application under section 15 (2), for an order directing that a denominational school shall be an aided school is considered in the light of the estimated liabilities of the managers under section 15 (3) (*a*), the assets they have in hand or promised, any evidence furnished of their past experience in raising money and the measure of financial support undertaken by the diocesan authorities or other bodies. Managers are not required to have in hand at the date of their application any fixed percentage of the cost of reconstruction. They must provide evidence on Form 18 Schools of ability and willingness to meet their liabilities under section 15 (3).

Church of England aided schools may receive financial assistance under the Church Schools (Assistance by Church Commissioners) Measure, 1958; 10 Halsbury's Statutes (3rd Edn.) 1405.

(c) **" Special agreement schools ".**—This section and the Third Schedule, p. 201, *post*, in effect revive the provisions of the Education Act, 1936 (and corresponding provisions of the Senior Public Elementary Schools (Liverpool) Act, 1939), which enabled local education authorities for a limited period to pay not less than 50 per cent. nor more than 75 per cent. of the cost of providing new non-provided school buildings for senior children. By virtue of these provisions a local education authority may enter into agreements, or resuscitate agreements already made, to make grants, of between 50 and 75 per cent. of the cost of any of the projects for which proposals were submitted by the managers within the time limit prescribed by sections 8 and 15 of the Education Act, 1936. The Third Schedule, permits the revision of any such proposals where rendered necessary or desirable as a result of war damage or new planning or new educational requirements. Schools already built under the 1936 Act and schools built under these provisions are known as special agreement schools. The religious instruction is in accordance with the trust deed (section 28, p. 119, *post*), and under the control of the managers. " Agreed syllabus " instruction must be available for those children whose parents wish them to receive such instruction and cannot with reasonable convenience send them to a school where it is ordinarily given (proviso to section 28 (1)).

Church of England special agreement schools may receive financial assistance under the Church Schools (Assistance by Church Commissioners) Measure, 1958; 10 Halsbury's Statutes (3rd Edn.) 1405.

(d) **" The management of the school ".**—See sections 17–22 inclusive, pp. 100 *et seq.*, *post*.

(e) **" The secular instruction ".**—See section 23, p. 111, *post*.

(f) **" Religious education ".**—See generally, sections 25–30 inclusive, pp. 115 *et seq.*, *post*, and, in particular, as to controlled schools, section 27, p. 118, *post*, and as to aided schools and special agreement schools, section 28, p. 119, *post*, and for additional provisions as to all schools, see section 7 of the Education Act, 1946, p. 213, *post*.

(g) **"The appointment and dismissal of teachers".**—See generally, section 24, p. 118, *post*, and as to reserved teachers, section 27 (2), (4) and (5), p. 112, *post*, and as to the head teacher of a controlled school, section 27 (3). Special provision for the dismissal, on religious grounds, of a teacher in an aided school by the managers or governors is made by section 28 (2), p. 120, *post*, and as to the employment of reserved teachers in special agreement schools, see section 28 (3), (4), p. 120, *post*, and the Third Schedule, p. 201, *post*. Subject to the provisions referred to, section 30, p. 137, *post*, safeguards the religious freedom of teachers.

(h) **"Secretary of State".**—See note (b) to s. 1, *ante*.

(i) **"May by order direct".**—As to the variation or revocation of such an order, see section 111, p. 181, *post*, and sub-sections (3) and (4) of this section. If on an application for an order directing that a school shall become an aided school or a special agreement school it appears to the Secretary of State that the area served by the school is a "single-school area", then, unless he is satisfied that the expenses to be borne by the managers or governors under sub-section (3) (*a*) of this section can be defrayed without the assistance of a loan under section 105, p. 179, *post*, the Secretary of State must consult such persons or bodies of persons as appear to him to be representative of any religious denomination likely to be concerned, and must, unless he thinks it unnecessary, hold a local inquiry under section 93, p. 171, *post* (section 105 (3), p. 179, *post*). He may, in any event, hold a local inquiry if he thinks fit (section 93).

(j) **"Maintenance contribution".**—See section 114 (1), p. 184, *post*.

(k) **"The Third Schedule to this Act".**—See p. 201, *post*.

(l) **"Any application for an order".**—In the case of an aided or special agreement school the application must be accompanied by a statement of evidence on Form 18 Schools that the managers or governors will be able and willing to meet the expenses which will fall to be met by them under subsection (3) of this section.

At the beginning of 1974 there were 8,657 voluntary schools; of these 4,923 were aided 131 special agreement and 3,603 controlled.

As to the application of the transitional provisions to new voluntary schools resulting, from the sub-division of an existing school, see section 2 of the Education Act, 1946, p. 251, *post*.

(m) **"Sub-section (3) of section nine of this Act".**—See p. 83, *ante*.

(n) **"Notice".**—As to the service of notices, see section 113, p. 182, *post*.

(o) **"Approval of the development plan".**—See section 11, p. 85, *ante*, and see the general note, *supra*.

(p) **"Proposals".**—See section 13 (2), p. 90, *ante*.

(q) **"Expenses of maintaining".**—See the definition of "maintain" in section 114 (1) and (2), pp. 184, 185, *post*. For the purposes of this Act, the expenses of maintaining a voluntary school include the payment of rates.

(r) **"Expenses of discharging any liability incurred".**—As stated in the general note to this section, the discharge of such expenses will continue to be the liability of the managers or governors where the school becomes an aided school or a special agreement school, but will pass to the local education authority where the school becomes a controlled school.

(s) **"Prescribed standards".**—"Prescribed" is defined by section 114 (1), p. 185, *post*, as meaning prescribed by regulations made by the Secretary of State. Under section 10 (1), p. 84, *ante*, the Secretary of State is required to make regulations requiring local education authorities to secure that the school premises of every school maintained by them conform to such standards as may be prescribed. See the Standards for School Premises Regulations 1972, S.I. 1972 No. 2051, p. 392, *post*.

(t) **"Direction".**—See sections 22 (2), p. 110, *post*, and 111, p. 181, *post*.

(u) **"It shall be their duty".**—As to the enforcement of this duty, see section 99 (1) p. 173, *post*.

(v) **"Shall revoke the order".**—In the event of the Secretary of State revoking the order under this sub-section the school will become a controlled school. As to the application of this sub-section to an aided school constituted by a direction under section 2 (1) of the Education Act, 1946, p. 210, *post*, dividing a single school into two or more schools, see *ibid.*, section 2 (5). Special provision to enable a special agreement school to become an aided school is contained in sub-section (5) of the present section.

16. Transfer of county and voluntary schools to new sites, and substitution of new voluntary schools for old ones.—(1) Where the Secretary of State (a) is satisfied that it is expedient that any county school (*) or any voluntary school (*) should be transferred to a new site either because it is not reasonably practicable to make to the existing premises (*) of the school (*) the alterations (*) necessary for securing that they should conform to the prescribed standards (b), or in consequence of any movement of population or of any action taken or proposed to be taken under the enactments relating to housing (c) or to town and country planning (d), the Secretary of State (a) may by order authorise (e) the transfer of the school to the new site; and [a voluntary school shall not be transferred to a new site without the authority of an order under this sub-section (f)].

(2) Where in connection with any proposals submitted to the Secretary of State (a) under subsection (2) of section thirteen of this Act (g) it is claimed that any school or schools thereby proposed to be established should be maintained (*) by the local education authority (*) as a voluntary school in substitution for another school at the time being maintained by a local education authority as a voluntary school or for two or more such schools which is or are to be discontinued, then, if the Secretary of State (a) is satisfied that the school or schools proposed to be established will be so maintained, he may, if he approves the proposals with or without modifications, by order direct (h) that the school or schools to be established shall be established in substitution for the school or schools to be discontinued, and where such an order is made the provisions of this Act relating to the discontinuance of voluntary schools shall not apply with respect to the discontinuance of the school or schools to be discontinued.

(3) Before making any order under this section the Secretary of State (a) shall consult any local education authority which will, in his opinion, be affected by the making of the order, and the managers or governors (*) of any voluntary school which in his opinion will be so affected; and any such order may impose such conditions on any such local education authority or managers or governors and may contain such incidental and consequential provisions as the Secretary of State (a) thinks fit.

NOTES

This section applies to two separate sets of circumstances (1) to the transfer of a county or voluntary school to a new site because the existing school premises cannot reasonably be brought up to the prescribed standards or where the transfer is dictated by a movement of population, or by action taken or proposed to be taken relating to housing or town and country planning, and (2) where a denominational body seeks to establish a new voluntary school in substitution for one or more voluntary schools which are to be closed.

For the purposes of section 1 (2) of the Education Act 1959, *post*, a school replaces another if the Secretary of State by order under this section directs that it be established in substitution for another.

A new site for an existing school must in all cases be provided by the local education authority (para. 1 of the First Schedule to the Education Act, 1946, p. 216, *post*), who must bear the cost of any necessary preparation and clearance (*ibid.*, para. 3), and convey the same to the trustees of the school (*ibid.*, para. 6). Where an aided school or special agreement school is transferred to a new site the cost of the new school buildings (as defined by section 4 of the Education Act, 1946, p. 211, *post*) must be defrayed by the managers or governors with the assistance of grant under section 103 of the present Act, p. 177, *post*, which may be given where an existing building is purchased and adapted for school purposes as well as where a building is specially constructed, see section 8 (1) of the Education (Miscellaneous Provisions) Act, 1953, p. 234, *post*. If the managers or governors are unable to satisfy the Secretary of State of their ability and willingness to defray this cost the school will become a controlled school (para. 2 of the First Schedule to the Education Act, 1946, p. 216, *post*).

Where the Secretary of State approves a proposal, or makes an order, under this section he may by order make such consequential modifications of any trust deed or other instrument as, after consultation, appear to him to be requisite: Education Act 1973, s. 1 (2), p. 274, *post*.

As to the application of the proceeds of sale of the old site, see *ibid.*, paras. 7 and 8, p. 261, *post*.

(*) As to the meaning or statutory definition of " county school ", " voluntary school ", " premises ", " school ", " alterations ", " maintain ", " local education authority ", " managers or governors ", see pp. 67–69, *ante*.

(a) **" Secretary of State ".**—See note (b) to s. 1, *ante*.

(b) **" Prescribed standards ".**—See the Standards for School Premises Regulations, 1972, S.I. 1972 No. 2051, p. 392, *post*.

(c) " **Enactments relating to housing** ".—See the title HOUSING, 16 Halsbury's Statutes (3rd Edn.), and Continuation Volumes.

(d) " **Town and country planning** ".—The law of town and country planning is now largely consolidated in the Town and Country Planning Act, 1971.

(e) " **May by order authorise** ".—Application for an order should be made when proposals are first submitted. As to the variation or revocation of such an order, see section 111, p. 181, *post*. Before making an order the Secretary of State may, if he thinks fit, hold a local inquiry (section 93, p. 171, *post*). As to the powers of the Secretary of State, in certain circumstances, to make grants or loans to the managers or governors of aided or special agreement schools in the circumstances arising under this section, see section 105, p. 179, *post*, s. 8 (3) of the Education (Miscellaneous Provisions) Act 1953, p. 234, *post*, and s. 1 of the Education Act 1967, p. 258, *post*.

(f) The words in square brackets were substituted by s. 1, Sch. 1, of the Education Act, 1968.

(g) " **Sub-section (2) of section thirteen of this Act** ".—See p. 90, *ante*. Application for an order under sub-section (2) of the present section should be made at the time when proposals under section 13 (2) are first submitted. In the case of an aided school the managers or governors are responsible for the provision of the school buildings and the site. The proportion of the expenditure on which grant is assessed is calculated by reference to the extent to which the new premises replace the provision previously made for pupils in the discontinued school or schools. See *ibid.*, para. 27.

(h) "**May by order direct**".—By para. 2 of the First Schedule to the Education Act, 1946, p. 216, *post*, the Secretary of State is not to direct that the transferred school shall be an aided school or special agreement school unless he is satisfied that the managers or governors are able and willing to provide the new school buildings.

Management of Primary Schools and Government of Secondary Schools

17. Constitution of managers and governors and conduct of county schools and voluntary schools.—(1) For every county school (*) and for every voluntary school (*) there shall be an instrument (a) providing for the constitution of the body of managers or governors (b) of the school (*) in accordance with the provisions of this Act (c), and the instrument providing for the constitution of the body of managers of a primary school (*) is in this Act referred to as an instrument of management (d), and the instrument providing for the constitution of the body of governors of a secondary school (*) is in this Act referred to as an instrument of government (e).

(2) The instrument of management or the instrument of government, as the case may be, shall be made in the case of a county school by an order (f) of the local education authority (*) and in the case of a voluntary school by an order of the Secretary of State (g).

(3) Subject to the provisions of this Act (h) and of any trust deed (i) relating to the school :—

(*a*) every county primary school and every voluntary primary school shall be conducted (j) in accordance with rules of management (k) made by an order of the local education authority ; and

(*b*) every county secondary school and every voluntary secondary school shall be conducted in accordance with articles of government (l) made in the case of a county school by an order of the local education authority and approved by the Secretary of State (g), and in the case of a voluntary school by an order of the Secretary of State (g); and such articles shall in particular determine the functions to be exercised in relation to the school by the local education authority, the body of governors, and the head teacher respectively.

(4) Where it appears to the Secretary of State (g) that any provision included or proposed to be included in the instrument of management, rules of management, instrument of government, or articles of government, for a county school or a voluntary school is in any respect inconsistent with the provisions of any trust deed relating to the school, and that it is expedient in the interests of the school that the provisions of the trust deed should be modified for the purpose of removing the inconsistency, he may by order

make such modifications in the provisions of the trust deed as appear to him to be just and expedient for that purpose.

(5) Before making any order under this section in respect of any school, the Secretary of State (g) shall afford to the local education authority and to any other persons appearing to him to be concerned with the management or government of the school an opportunity of making representations to him with respect thereto, and in making any such order the Secretary of State (g) shall have regard to all the circumstances of the school, and in particular to the question whether the school is, or is to be, a primary or secondary school, and, in the case of an existing school, shall have regard to the manner in which the school has been conducted theretofore.

[(6) Where proposals for a significant change in the character of a voluntary school are approved under section 13 of this Act, then, without prejudice to the power to vary orders conferred by section 111, the Secretary of State may by order make such variations of the articles of government (if the school is a secondary school) . . . (m) as appear to him to be required in consequence of the proposed change in the character of the school; and so much of sub-section (5) of this section as relates to the making of representations with respect to orders under this section shall not apply to an order made in pursuance only of the power conferred by this subsection (n).

NOTES

Sections 17–20 provide for the continuance, in the case of primary schools, of arrangements for management by bodies of managers similar to those which formerly existed for public elementary schools, except that, in the case of controlled schools, which are conducted entirely at public expense, the proportion of foundation managers has been changed from two-thirds to one-third, the remaining managers being appointed by the local authorities concerned (sections 18 (3) (*a*) and 19 (2) (*a*), pp. 105,and 107, *post*).

Special provision is made to meet the case of secondary schools for which, with the exception of schools which were formerly senior elementary schools, there was no statutory provision relating to management prior to the coming into operation of this section. The Act provides for all secondary schools to be conducted under instruments and articles of government, of which the first is to prescribe the constitution of the governing body and the second is to define the functions to be exercised by the local education authority, the governors and the head teacher respectively (sub-sections (1) and (3) (*b*) of this section). These instruments and articles of government must be made, in the case of county secondary schools, by an order made by the local education authority and approved by the Secretary of State and, in the case of voluntary schools, by an order of the Secretary of State (sub-section (3) (*b*), *ibid.*). These provisions should be read with section 67, p. 154, *post*.

Under section 20 (1), p. 108, *post*, arrangements may be made for the constitution of a single governing body for two or more county or voluntary schools, whether primary or secondary, but no such arrangement which embraces a voluntary school may be made without the consent of the managers or governors.

As to the continued operation, in the case of any school maintained immediately before 1st April, 1965 by a local education authority who will not continue to maintain it after that date, of any instrument or rules of management or instrument or articles of agreement made by an order under this section, see section 31 (7) of the London Government Act, 1963, p. 292, *post*. See also the Introduction, p. 26, *ante*.

(*) As to the meaning or statutory definition of " county school ", " voluntary school ", " school ", " primary school ", " secondary school " and " local education authority ", see pp. 67–69, *ante*.

(a) **" There shall be an instrument ".**—As to the enforcement of a local education authority's duties in this connection, see section 9, p. 82, *ante*.

(b) **" Managers or governors ".**—In addition to this section, see sections 18–20, pp. 105 *et seq.*, *post*. It will be noted that the Act provides for the constitution of a body of managers for every primary school whether it is a county school or a voluntary school. Formerly a local education authority which was a council of a borough or urban district had a discretion to appoint a body of managers or not as it thought fit. As to the relationship of the managers of a non-provided school with the local education authority, see the remarks of Lord Haldane, L.C., in *Gillow* v. *Durham County Council*, [1913] A.C. 54, at p. 65.

As to the resignation or removal of a manager or governor, and as to the inspection of the minutes of proceedings of managers or governors, see sub-sections (1) and (3) respectively of section 21, p. 109, *post*, and as to their meetings and proceedings see section 21 (2), *ibid.*, and the Fourth Schedule, p. 203, *post*.

(c) **" The provisions of this Act ".**—See sub-sections (2) to (5) of this section, and sections 18 and 19, pp. 105, 106, *post*.

(d) **" Instrument of management ".**—See section 18, p. 105, *post*, and the general note to this section. As to the making of the instrument, see sub-section (2) of this section.

(e) **" Instrument of government ".**—See section 19, p. 106, *post*, and the general note to this section. As to the making of the instrument, see sub-section (2) of this section. The White

Paper (Cmd. 6523 of 1944) on the Principles of Government in Maintained Secondary Schools, which is quoted below (see note (l), *infra*) gave general guidance in connection with the preparation of instruments, as well as articles, of government.

(f) **"Order".**—As to the revocation and variation of such an order, see section 111, p. 181, *post*. As to the duty of the Secretary of State in cases where the order is to be made by him, see sub-section (5) of this section.

(g) **"Secretary of State".**—See note (b) to s. 1, *ante*.

(h) **"Subject to the provisions of this Act."**—See in particular sections 23 and 24, pp. 111, and 112, *post*.

(i) **"Trust deed".**—By section 114 (1), p. 185, *post*, this term, in relation to any voluntary school, includes any instrument (not being an instrument of management, instrument of government, rules of management, or articles of government, made under this Act) regulating the maintenance, management or conduct of the school or the constitution of the body of managers or governors thereof. As to the modification of a trust deed with which the instrument of management or of government or rules of management or articles of government are inconsistent, see sub-section (4) of this section.

(j) **"Shall be conducted".**—As to the powers of the Secretary of State in relation to the enforcement of the duties of the managers and governors, see section 99, p. 173, *post*; and as to the determination of disputes, see section 67, p. 154, *post*. Section 68, p. 155, *post*, gives the Secretary of State wide powers to prevent the managers or governors of a school from exercising their functions unreasonably.

(k) **"Rules of management".**—In connection with the rules of management, regard should be had to the terms of section 23, p. 111, *post*, which specifies the relationship between the managers of the various types of schools and the local education authority in relation to the control of secular instruction and indicates what is included within the scope of the power to control secular instruction.

(l) **"Articles of government".**—Regard should be had to the terms of section 23, p. 111, *post*, which specifies the relationship between the governors of the various types of schools and the local education authority in relation to the control of secular instruction and indicates what is included within the scope of the power to control secular instruction. In particular, the governors of aided secondary schools are, by section 23 (2), placed in a specially favourable position.

On 4th May, 1944, the Board of Education presented to Parliament, in accordance with a promise given during the Committee stage of the Bill, a White Paper (Cmd. 6523 of 1944) on the principles of government in maintained secondary schools.

The White Paper set out the principles upon which broad agreement was reached in the discussions between the Board of Education and the various interests concerned and serves as a general guide to the preparation of instruments and articles of government. In view of its importance the White Paper, with the exception of certain introductory paragraphs, is quoted in full, *infra*, making only such alterations (which are italicised) as are necessary to adapt the references to clauses of the Bill to the appropriate sections of the Act or amending Acts and to add such other references as appear desirable.

(m) The omitted words were repealed by the Education Act 1973, Sch. 2, Part II. The repeal (which dealt with the Secretary of State's powers to modify certain trust deeds), is not to effect any order previously made thereunder: *ibid.*, Sch. 1, p. 279, *post*. See now section 1 (2) of the Act of 1973.

(n) Sub-s. (6) was added by the Education Act 1968, s. 1 and Sch. 1.

PRINCIPLES OF GOVERNMENT IN MAINTAINED SECONDARY SCHOOLS

* * * * *

II. GOVERNING BODIES

10. *Constitution* :—All secondary schools are to be governed by governing bodies specially constituted for the purpose (*section* 19, p. 106, *post*). In the case of county schools the governing body is to consist of such number of persons appointed in such manner as the local education authority may determine (*section* 19 (1), *ibid.*) ; in the case of *voluntary* schools the governing body is to consist of such number of persons as the Secretary of State may determine, subject to compliance with the prescribed proportions of foundation governors and of governors appointed by the local education authority (*section* 18 (2), p. 105, *post*).

11. *Composition* :—In all schools it may be assumed that the governing body will include :—

(i) adequate representation of the local education authority (†) ;

(ii) other persons whose qualifications are such as to enable them to play a useful part in the government of a secondary school.

The practice of allowing a limited number of co-opted members nominated by the governing body has proved of advantage and might be continued in appropriate cases.

In the case of girls' and mixed secondary schools a proportion of women should be included on the governing bodies.

Among the persons referred to under (ii) above it would be appropriate to appoint a representative of a university or university college—particularly of the local university where one exists ; and the inclusion of one or more persons associated with the commercial and industrial life of the district is desirable.

(†) The authority's representatives will not necessarily be in all cases members of the authority.

There is general agreement that the interests of the teaching staff of the school or schools, as well as of parents and old scholars, should be reflected in the composition of the governing body. The majority of bodies consulted hold that this can be secured without the staff or parents' and old scholars' associations having the right to nominate governors for the purpose.

One section holds that governors should be specially nominated by the teaching staff and by parents' and old scholars' associations.

12. *Size* :—No precise guidance as to the size of the governing body can be given. In the past governing bodies have sometimes tended to be too large and in consequence their transactions have in some cases been formal and stereotyped. The governing body should be large enough to ensure that the various interests are adequately represented, but small enough for the effective conduct of business in such a way that all members can play an active part.

13. *Grouping* :—(*Section* 20, p. 108, *post*) provides for the grouping of schools under a single governing body and there can be no doubt that, with the great increase in the number of secondary schools, such grouping will frequently be necessary. In some cases the schools of a particular foundation or of a particular denominational character will most conveniently be grouped together, and it should be noted that *a voluntary* school cannot be grouped with another school without the consent of the governors (*proviso to section* 20 (1), *ibid.*). Usually, however, there will be solid advantage in grouping schools on a geographical or regional basis, schools of all types finding a place in an individual group. In this way experience will be brought to bear on the problems of self-government in the newer types of secondary schools, while community of interests, sharing of teaching staffs and transfer of pupils between the various types will be facilitated. Some fear has been expressed that under such an arrangement the individual character of each type of school might tend to be blurred, and the suggestion has been made that a nucleus of governors might be formed for the group with one or two additional members for each separate type of school, who would attend only when the affairs of their particular schools were being considered.

III. FINANCE

14. The practice will no doubt generally obtain by which governors prepare estimates covering a suitable period and submit them to the local education authority. Within the broad headings of the approved estimate the governors should have latitude to exercise reasonable discretion. It may be desirable that a small margin for contingencies should be allowed, particularly under the heading of " books, apparatus and stationery " ; in any case the allowance under this heading, which is commonly calculated on a capitation basis, should not be too rigidly defined and a school should be entitled to present a case for a higher rate to meet special difficulties and developments. There is general agreement that the school library, the special needs of which have often been overlooked in the past, should be given a separate allowance.

IV. APPOINTMENT AND DISMISSAL OF STAFF

15. *Teaching Staff* :—Under the provisions of the Act the appointment of teachers in county, controlled or special agreement schools is, with certain reservations, placed under the control of the local education authority (*section* 24, p. 112, *post*). In a controlled school the authority are obliged before making an appointment of a head teacher, to inform the governors as to the person proposed to be appointed and to consider any representations made by them (*section* 27 (3), p. 118, *post*). The dismissal of teachers rests with the local education authority (*section* 24 (1), p. 112, *post*). In aided schools the functions of the authority and the governors in regard to the appointment and dismissal of teachers are to be regulated by the articles of government, subject to certain mandatory or discretionary rights reserved to the authority and governors (*section* 24 (2), p. 112, *post*).

16. The appointment and dismissal of teachers, other than reserved teachers, may be conveniently considered separately for head masters or head mistresses and assistants :—

(*a*) *Appointment of head master or head mistress* :—In schools provided by local education authorities the practice has in the past varied very considerably. In some areas the appointment has been made by the governing body subject to confirmation by the authority; in others the authority has appointed in consultation with the governors. It is desirable that, so far as possible, some uniform practice should obtain and there is a wide measure of agreement in favour of associating the governors and the authority both at the stage of drawing up the short list and also of making the final appointment. The following two alternative methods appear to command acceptance :—

(i) Under the first method the governors consider the applications, a representative of the authority being present, and submit three names to the authority. The appropriate committee of the authority then makes the final appointment, a member of the governing body being present ;

(ii) Under the second method, the merits of which are being increasingly recognised, a joint committee is set up of an equal number of members of the governing body and the authority, under the chairmanship of a person nominated by the authority, to draw up the short list and, at a second meeting, to make the appointment.

One or other of these two methods would be suitable for county, controlled or special agreement schools and, with modifications, might be appropriate also in the case of aided schools. In the case of aided schools the proportions of members on a joint committee would no doubt be varied and the nomination of chairman be given to the governors at one or both stages of the appointment.

(*b*) *Dismissal of head master or head mistress* :—The normal procedure in the case of dismissal would be as follows :—

(i) The resolution would be taken by the governing body who would also have power to suspend in the case of misconduct or for other urgent causes :

(ii) The resolution would be passed at two meetings, held at an interval of not less than fourteen days, by not less than two-thirds of the governing body present and voting;

(iii) The resolution could not take effect (except as otherwise provided in the *Act*), until it had been accepted by the local education authority in the case of county, controlled or special agreement schools, or the consent of the authority had been obtained in the case of aided schools (*section* 24, p. 112, *post*).

It would be usual to provide that the head master or head mistress should have the right of appeal to the local education authority in cases where the authority's approval or consent was required;

(iv) The local education authority should have the power of dismissal on their own motion (except as otherwise provided in the *Act*) in county, controlled and special agreement schools, and to require dismissal in aided schools;

(v) It would be usual to provide that the head master or head mistress should be entitled to appear accompanied by a friend at any meeting of the governing body or the local education authority, at which his or her dismissal was to be considered, and should be given full notice of such meetings;

(vi) Except in cases of misconduct or other urgent cause dismissal would be subject to notice under the terms of appointment.

(*c*) *Appointment of assistant masters or mistresses*:—The appointment of assistant masters and mistresses in county, controlled or special agreement schools is to be under the control of the local education authority (*section* 24 (1), p. 112, *post*); in aided schools it is to be made by the governors, with the consent of the authority where so provided (*section* 24 (2), *ibid*). The usual practice will be for appointments to be made within the financial limits of the approved estimates, by the governors in full consultation with the head master or head mistress subject to confirmation by the local education authority. Vacancies should generally be notified in the first instance to the local education authority, in order that a multiplicity of advertisements may be avoided. The local education authority should be in a position to secure interchangeability of staff and appointment from a pool, particularly in the case of junior posts.

(*d*) *Dismissal of assistant masters or mistresses*:—The procedure would be generally similar to that in the case of the head master or head mistress (*but see sections* 27 (5) *and* 28 (2), pp. 118 *and* 120, *post*). It need not, however, necessarily be so elaborate provided that opportunity is given for the assistant to appear before a meeting of the governors accompanied by a friend and to appeal to the local education authority.

17. *Non-teaching staff*:—The appointment and dismissal of staff other than teachers fall under two headings—(*a*) caretakers and maintenance staff and (*b*) clerks to governing bodies.

(*a*) *Caretakers and maintenance staff*:—In county, controlled or special agreement schools appointments and dismissals are to be made by the local education authority; in the case of aided schools the authority may give directions to the governors (*as regards voluntary schools see section* 22 (3), p. 110, *post*). In practice the actual selection of persons to be appointed would no doubt rest with the governors on the advice of the head master or head mistress, subject to the approved estimates not being exceeded and the conditions of appointment being in accordance with the usual conditions for the area as regards wages and other matters. The authority should be in a position to require, at any rate in the case of county, controlled or special agreement schools, that the appointment be made from a pool.

(*b*) *Clerks*:—In county, controlled or special agreement schools it would be usual for the chief education officer (*see section* 88, p. 169, *post*) or his representative to be the clerk to the governing body, and, in view of the growing complexity of school business and the need for close co-operation with the authority, there are advantages in following the same practice in aided schools, particularly where the circumstances do not justify the appointment of a full-time clerk. The governors would, however, appoint their own clerk for foundation work and in some cases it may be found desirable, as at present, for the foundation and school work to be entrusted to the same person.

V. INTERNAL ORGANISATION AND CURRICULUM

18. *Division of functions*:—The local education authority would have the right, in framing the development plan for the area (*see section* 11, p. 85, *ante*) and subsequently, to settle the general educational character of the school and its place in the local system. Subject to this general responsibility the governors would have general direction of the conduct and curriculum of the school. The head master or head mistress would control the internal organisation, management and discipline of the school, and would also have the power of suspending pupils subject to a report being made forthwith to the governors and the local education authority.

19. *Relations of governing body, head master or head mistress and chief education officer*:—A particular aspect of this problem concerns the relations which are to exist between the head master or head mistress, the governing body and the chief education officer. The general lines should be as follows:—

(i) There should be free consultation at all times between the head master or head mistress and the chairman of the governing body;

(ii) All proposals and reports affecting the conduct and curriculum of the school should be submitted formally to the governing body, which should meet at reasonably frequent intervals. The chief education officer or his representative should be informed as long as possible beforehand and furnished with a copy of the proposals or report;

(iii) Decisions by the chairman of the governing body should be limited to urgent matters and should be reported without delay to the governing body;

(iv) The head master or head mistress should be entitled to attend throughout all meetings of the governing body, except on such occasions and for such times as the governing body might for good cause decide otherwise;

(v) Free consultation and co-operation should exist between the head master or head mistress and the chief education officer on matters affecting the welfare of the school;

(vi) Suitable arrangements should be made for enabling the teaching staff to submit their views or proposals to the governing body through the head master or head mistress.

20. *School holidays* :—The fixing of school holidays (*see section* 23, p. 111, *post*) is a matter of some importance, particularly in view of the provision that pupils who attain any age during the term of the school are deemed not to have attained that age until the end of term. In order to secure the necessary uniformity it will no doubt be necessary that the local education authority should fix the school terms, but the governors should be empowered to grant a limited number of occasional holidays at their discretion.

VI. ADMISSION OF PUPILS

21. *Procedure* :—The abolition of tuition fees in all maintained schools (*section* 61 (1), p. 149, *post*) will call for re-examination of the method adopted for deciding the type of secondary education which individual pupils are to receive. It is important that the wishes of parents should continue to be taken into account and effect given to them, in so far as is compatible with the attainments and promise of their children and with the claims of other children. The local education authority alone will have all the data on which to reach a decision on these matters and the ultimate responsibility for deciding which type of secondary education an individual pupil should follow must therefore rest with them. It is, however, generally agreed that the governors and the head master or head mistress should play an essential part in the selection of all pupils for their particular school. While it is not possible at present to dogmatise on methods of procedure, in regard to which a variety of views have been expressed, it is possible to indicate two solutions upon one or other of two lines according to the nature of the area concerned.

In the more compact type of area the local education authority might undertake centrally the task of deciding the broad type of education for which individual children are suited. Account would have to be taken of school records, teachers' reports, and parents' expressed wishes. When a decision on this question has been reached, parents should be free within reasonable limits to choose the particular school of the appropriate type, which they desire their children to attend, and governors should be given an opportunity of expressing any views they might have as to the admission of pupils desiring to enter their schools.

Alternatively, in the more scattered areas the local education authority might refer pupils on leaving the primary schools to a district board consisting of the heads of primary and secondary schools of the various types, assisted by one or more representatives of the local education authority. This board, on the basis of school records and other available information (including the parents' wishes), would advise the authority both on the general type of education most suitable for the child and on the particular school to which, subject to any views expressed by the governors, he or she should be admitted.

22. *Extra-district pupils* :—Special arrangements may well be necessary to meet the case of pupils who may desire admission to a school within the area of another authority. There are within the county and municipal systems certain schools which have built up a tradition of boarding education for pupils drawn from a wide area of the country. In view of the importance of meeting the reasonable wishes of parents and of preserving so far as possible the traditions of particular schools, local education authorities will no doubt be ready to co-operate in facilitating the admission of extra-district pupils, whether as day pupils or boarders, and to make the necessary financial adjustments, for which provision is made in section 6 of the Education (Miscellaneous Provisions) Act, 1948, p. 222, *post*.

VII. INTERPRETATION

23. The chief object of articles of government will be, as has already been stated, to determine the respective functions of the local education authority, the governing body and the head teacher in relation to the school. But, however, carefully the determination is made, disputes are liable to arise and this raises the question of interpretation. It has been customary in the past to include in articles of government a clause dealing with questions arising under the articles. In view of the provisions of section 67 of the Act relating to disputes between local education authorities and governors this clause will no longer be appropriate. It is, however, to be hoped that, given the co-operation which is essential to any successful scheme of school government, disputes on the determination of functions will be of rare occurrence ".

18. Managers of primary schools.—(1) The instrument of management (a) for every county primary school (b) serving an area in which there is a minor authority (c) shall provide for the constitution of a body of managers (d) consisting of such number of persons, not being less than six, as the local education authority (*) may determine:

Provided that two-thirds of the managers shall be appointed by the local education authority and one-third shall be appointed by the minor authority.

(2) The instrument of management for every county primary school serving an area in which there is no minor authority (f) shall provide for the constitution of a body of managers constituted in such manner as the local education authority may determine (g).

(3) The instrument of management for every voluntary primary school (h) shall provide for the constitution of a body of managers consisting of such number of persons not being less than six as the Secretary of State (i) may, after consultation with the local education authority, determine:

Provided that—

(*a*) if the school is an aided school (*) or a special agreement school (*) two-thirds of the managers shall be foundation managers (k), and, if the school is a controlled school (*), one-third of the managers shall be foundation managers ;

(b) where the school serves an area in which there is a minor authority (l), then of the managers who are not foundation managers not less than one-third nor more than one-half shall be appointed by the minor authority and the remainder shall be appointed by the local education authority ; and

(c) where the school serves an area in which there is no minor authority, all the managers who are not foundation managers shall be appointed by the local education authority.

NOTES

(*) As to the meaning or statutory definition of " local education authority ", " aided school " and " controlled school ", see pp. 67–69, *ante*.

(a) **" Instrument of management ".**—The requirement that there shall be an instrument of management providing for the constitution of a body of managers for every county primary school and voluntary primary school is imposed by section 17 (1), p. 100, *ante*. As to the manner in which the instrument of management is to be made, see section 17 (2), *ibid*. See also section 17 (4), *ibid*., as to the modification of the provisions of any trust deed with which the instrument of management is inconsistent.

The instrument of management only deals with the constitution of the body of managers. The conduct of the school itself (whether a county school or a voluntary school) must be controlled by rules of management made by an order of the local education authority under section 17 (3) (*a*), p. 100, *ante*.

Under section 20, p. 108, *post*, the local education authority may constitute a single governing body for two or more schools, in which case the constitution of the body may differ from those referred to in this section.

Special powers are given to the Secretary of State by section 99 (2), p. 173, *post*, where it appears to him that by reason of the default of any person there is no properly constituted body of managers or governors of any county school or voluntary school.

(b) **" County primary school ".**—As to the meaning of this term, see section 9 (2), p. 82, *ante*.

(c) **" Minor authority ".**—This sub-section applies only where the local education authority is the council of a county. " Minor authority " is defined by section 114 (1), p. 184, *post*. If the authorities concerned in the joint appointment of managers are unable to agree the Secretary of State may act in default; see section 99 (2), p. 173, *post*.

(d) **" Body of managers ".**—See section 17, p. 100, *ante*.

(f) **" An area in which there is no minor authority ".**—See note (c), *supra*. This sub-section applies to areas where the local education authority is the council of a county borough.

(g) **" May determine ".**—Though the local education authority appears to have an absolute discretion as to the constitution of a body of managers, there must be an instrument of management and there must be a body of managers. The duty so imposed upon the local education authority may be enforced by the Secretary of State under section 99, p. 173, *post*. It is questionable whether the local education authority may, if it so wishes, constitute its education committee or one of its education committees appointed under Part II of the First Schedule, p. 198, *post*, as the body of managers under this sub-section. If an authority should purport so to act and the Secretary of State is of opinion that this would not be a properly constituted body under the sub-section, he may take steps under section 99 (2), p. 173, *post*, to remedy the position.

Alternatively, the Secretary of State might regard such action in particular circumstances as an unreasonable exercise of the authority's functions, and take such steps as he might think desirable under section 68, p. 155, *post*.

(h) **" Voluntary primary school ".**—As to the meaning of this term, see section 9 (2), p. 82, *ante*.

(i) **" Secretary of State ".**—See note (b) to s. 1, *ante*.

(k) **" Foundation managers ".**—By section 114 (1), p. 183, *post*, the term means, in relation to any voluntary school, managers appointed otherwise than by a local education authority or a minor authority for the purpose of securing, so far as is practicable, that the character of the school as a voluntary school is preserved and developed, and, in particular, that the school is conducted in accordance with the provisions of any trust deed relating thereto. Unless the context otherwise requires, any references in the Act to " managers " must, in relation to any functions thereby conferred or imposed exclusively on foundation managers, be construed as references to such managers.

(l) **" Minor authority ".**—For the definition of " minor authority " see s. 114 (1), *post*.

19. Governors of secondary schools.—(1) The instrument of government (a) for every county secondary school (b) shall provide for the constitution of a body of governors (c) consisting of such number of persons appointed in such manner as the local education authority (*) may determine (d).

(2) The instrument of government for every voluntary secondary school (e) shall provide for the constitution of a body of governors of the school consisting of such number of persons (f) as the Secretary of State (g) may after consultation with the local education authority determine:

Provided that—

(*a*) where the school is a controlled school (*), one-third of the governors shall be foundation governors (h) and two-thirds of the governors shall be appointed by the local education authority;

(*b*) where the school is an aided school (*) or a special agreement school (*), two-thirds of the governors shall be foundation governors and one-third of the governors shall be appointed by the local education authority.

NOTES

The general note to section 17, p. 101, *ante*, summarises the changes made by the Act in the law applying to the management and government of both primary and secondary schools.

(*) As to the meaning or statutory definition of " local education authority ", " controlled school ", " aided school " and " special agreement school ", see pp. 67–69, *ante*.

(a) " **Instrument of government** ".—The requirement that there shall be an instrument of government providing for the constitution of a body of governors for every county secondary school and voluntary secondary school is imposed by section 17 (1), p. 100, *ante*. As to the manner in which the instrument of government must be made, see section 17 (2). See also section 17 (4) as to the modification of the provisions of any trust deed with which the instrument of government is inconsistent.

The instrument of government only deals with the constitution of the body of governors. By section 17 (3) (*b*), p. 100, *ante*, the conduct of the school itself (whether a county school or a voluntary school) is to be controlled by articles of government made—

(*a*) in the case of a county school by an order of the local education authority approved by the Secretary of State; and

(*b*) in the case of a voluntary school by an order of the Secretary of State.

The articles of government (see note (l) to section 17, p. 102, *ante*) must in particular determine the functions to be exercised in relation to the school by the local education authority, the body of governors and the head teacher respectively.

Under section 20, *infra*, the local education authority may constitute a single governing body for two or more schools, in which case the constitution of the body may differ from those referred to in this section.

Special powers are given to the Secretary of State by section 99 (2), p. 173, *post*, where it appears to him that by reason of the default of any person there is no properly constituted body of managers or governors of any county school or voluntary school. The Secretary of State may also take such steps as he thinks desirable if he thinks that the local education authority has acted, or proposes to act, unreasonably (see section 68, p. 155, *post*).

(b) " **County secondary school** ".—As to the meaning of this term, see section 9 (2) p. 82, *ante*.

(c) " **Body of governors** ".—See note (b) to section 17, p. 101, *ante*.

(d) " **May determine** ".—Though, as in the case of a body of managers appointed under section 18 (2), p. 105, *ante*, the local education authority appears to have an absolute discretion as to the number and manner of appointment of a body of governors of a county secondary school, there must be an instrument of government and there must be a body of governors. The duty so imposed upon the local education authority may be regulated by the Secretary of State under sections 68 and 99, pp. 155 and 173, *post*.

It will be noted that in the case of county secondary schools in county areas the Act does not provide, as it does in the case of county primary schools, for the appointment of a proportion of the managers by the minor authority, through there is no reason why, in the exercise of its discretion, the local education authority should not so provide.

(e) " **Voluntary secondary school** ".—As to the meaning of this term, see section 9 (2), p. 82, *ante*.

(f) " **Such number of persons** ".—In the case of voluntary secondary schools the instrument of government is to be made by the Secretary of State, but before making the order he is to consult with the local education authority. As to the proportion of foundation managers to managers appointed by the local education authority, similar provision is made as in the case of voluntary primary schools except that no provision is made for the appointment of governors by minor authorities in county areas, nor in fact, is any discretion left to the Secretary of State, as in the case of county secondary schools. See, however, note (b) to section 20, p. 109, *post*.

(g) " **Secretary of State** ".—See note (b) to s. 1, *ante*.

(h) " **Foundation governors** ".—By section 114 (1), p. 183, *post*, the term means, in relation to any voluntary school, governors appointed otherwise than by the local education authority (or if, in the case of a county secondary school in a county area, the local education authority provides for the appointment of governors by the minor authority, otherwise than by the minor authority) for the purpose of securing, so far as is practicable, that the character of the school as a voluntary school is preserved and developed, and, in particular, that the school is conducted in accordance with the provisions of any trust deed relating thereto. Unless the context so requires, any references in the Act to " managers " must, in relation to any functions thereby conferred or imposed exclusively on foundation managers, be construed as references to such managers.

20. Grouping of schools under one management.—(1) A local education authority (*) may make an arrangement for the constitution of a single governing body (a) for any two or more county schools (*) or voluntary schools (*) maintained (*) by them, and any such arrangement may relate exclusively to primary schools (*), or exclusively to secondary schools (*) or partly to primary schools and partly to secondary schools:

Provided that an authority shall not make any such arrangement with respect to a voluntary school except with the consent of the managers or governors (*) thereof.

(2) The governing body constituted in pursuance of any such arrangement as aforesaid shall, if all the schools to which the arrangement relates are county schools, consist of such number of persons appointed in such manner as the local education authority may determine (b).

(3) Where all or any of the schools to which any such arrangement relates are voluntary schools, the governing body constituted in pursuance of the arrangement shall consist of such number of persons appointed in such manner as may be determined by agreement (c) between the local education authority and the managers or governors of those schools, or, in default of such agreement, by the Secretary of State (d).

(4) The local education authority, in making any such arrangement as aforesaid which relates to a primary school serving an area in which there is a minor authority (e), shall make provision for securing that the minor authority is adequately represented (f) upon the governing body constituted in pursuance of the arrangement.

(5) Every arrangement made under this section may, if it does not relate to any voluntary school, be terminated (g) at any time by the local education authority by which it was made, and any such arrangement which relates to such a school may be terminated by agreement (h) between the local education authority and the governing body constituted in pursuance of the arrangement, or, in default of such agreement, by one year's notice (i) served by the local education authority on the said governing body or by one year's notice served by the said governing body on the local education authority.

(6) While an arrangement under this section is in force with respect to any schools, the provisions of the last three foregoing sections as to the constitution of the body of managers or governors shall not apply (j) to the school, and for the purposes of any enactment (k) the governing body constituted in accordance with the arrangement shall be deemed to be the body of managers or governors of each of those schools, and references to a manager or governor in any enactment shall, in relation to every such school, be construed accordingly.

NOTES

As to the continued operation, in the case of any school maintained immediately before 1st April, 1965 by a local education authority who will not continue to maintain it on or after that date, of any arrangement made under this section, see section 31 (7) of the London Government Act, 1963, p. 292, *post*.

Where a grouping arrangement is in force under this section, sections 17–19 inclusive, pp. 100 *et seq.*, *ante*, so far as they relate to the constitution of the body of managers or governors, do not apply.

In spite of possessing a wide discretion in the matter a local education authority must not act unreasonably or the Secretary of State may exercise his power under section 68, p. 155, *post*.

(*) As to the meaning or statutory definition of "local education authority", "county school", "voluntary school", "maintain", "primary school", "secondary school" and "managers or governors", see pp. 67–69, *ante*.

(a) **"Single governing body".**—The use of this term as applying to a group of schools which may all be primary schools, all secondary, or a combination of both, is not altogether happy in view of the fact that elsewhere in the Act great care has been taken to distinguish between the managers, instrument of management and rules of management of a primary school on the one hand and the governors, instrument of government and articles of government of a secondary school on the other, but it is difficult to suggest a better. Moreover, the section carefully avoids giving a name to the members of the single governing body. Presumably they will continue to be known as managers and governors respectively in the case of separate groups of primary and of secondary schools, but it is difficult to name the members of the governing body of a mixed group of primary and secondary schools. In such a case it has been suggested that it would perhaps be as well to take a lead from this term and to give them at least the nominal status of " governors ".

It should be noted that wherever grouping takes place under this section, sections 17-19 inclusive, pp. 100 *et seq.*, *ante*, so far as they relate to the constitution of the body of governors or body of managers, cease to apply.

(b) **" May determine ".**—See note (g) to section 18, p. 106, *ante*, and note (b) to section 17, p. 101, *ante*. The present section, however, does not specifically state that there shall be an instrument of management or of government and, since section 17 (1), p. 100, *ante*, does not apply (sub-section (5)), it must be presumed that this is not necessary.

(c) **" As may be determined by agreement ".**—For the reason stated in the previous note, it appears that where the managers or governors of a voluntary school consent (under sub-section (1)) to a grouping arrangement and agreement is reached under this sub-section the jurisdiction of the Secretary of State in relation to the making of the instrument of management or government is ousted, even where the arrangement relates solely to voluntary schools. Even if agreement is not reached under this sub-section the Secretary of State's jurisdiction is limited to determining the number of persons and the manner of their appointment and cannot affect, for example, the number of schools to be included in the group, though he retains his power of intervention under section 68, p. 155, *post*.

(d) **" Secretary of State ".**—See note (b) to s. 1, *ante*.

(e) **" Minor authority ".**—See note (c) to section 18, p. 106, *ante*.

(f) **" Adequately represented ".**—No indication is given of the meaning of this term, but it presumably means that, as far as possible, the proportionate representation of the minor authority upon bodies of managers of single schools under section 18, p. 105, *ante*, should be maintained. For example, where all the schools in the group are county schools the representation of the minor authority should be one-third of the total. Where, however, one or more or all, the schools in the group are voluntary schools the position is more complicated, especially if there is more than one voluntary school, one being a controlled school and another an aided school or a special agreement school. In such circumstances the securing of adequate representation for the minor authority might give rise to acute difficulty and the Secretary of State's intervention might well be necessary. Although this sub-section refers only to primary schools, the arrangement proposed might provide for the grouping of a primary school with a secondary school, and this appears to be the only case where a minor authority has a right to representation upon a governing body which controls a secondary school. As to the enforcement of this duty by the Secretary of State, see section 99, p. 173, *post*.

(g) **" Be terminated ".**—Since section 17, p. 100, *ante*, does not apply to an arrangement under this section, so far as the constitution of the governing body is concerned, section 111, p. 181, *post*, as to the revocation or variation of orders and directions, does not apply.

(h) **" Terminated by agreement ".**—The agreement should specify a date for the termination of the arrangement and, before the termination takes effect, whether by agreement or not, care should be taken to ensure that the provisions of sections 17–19, pp. 100 *et seq.*, *ante*, as to the constitution of separate bodies of managers or governors for each school concerned, are complied with.

(i) **" One year's notice ".**—As to the service of notices, see section 113, p. 182, *post*. Such a notice may be given to expire at any time and if no date is specified in the notice it will take effect at the expiry of one year from the date of service.

(j) **" Shall not apply ".**—It is only the provisions of sections 17–19, pp. 100, *et seq.*, *ante*, which relate to the constitution of the governing body which do not apply, and consequently section 17 (2), p. 100 *ante*, which relates to rules of management and articles of government, and so much of sub-sections (4) and (5), *ibid.*, as relates to those matters, continues in force.

(k) **" Any enactment ".**—This will include any relevant provision of this Act.

21. Proceedings of managers and governors of county and voluntary schools.—(1) Any manager or governor (*) of a county school (*) or of a voluntary school (*), may resign his office, and any such manager or governor appointed by a local education authority (*) or by a minor authority (*) shall be removable (a) by the authority by whom he was appointed.

(2) The provisions of the Fourth Schedule to this Act (b) shall have effect with respect to the meetings and proceedings of the managers or governors of any county school (c) or voluntary school.

(3) The minutes of the proceedings of the managers or governors of any county school or voluntary school shall be open to inspection by the local education authority (d).

NOTES

(*) As to the meaning or statutory definition of " managers or governors ", " county school ", " voluntary school ", " local education authority " and " minor authority ", see pp. 67–69, *ante*.

(a) **" Shall be removable ".**—Normally the period of office of a manager or governer will be fixed by the instrument of management or government referred to in sections 17–19, pp. 100 *et seq.*, *ante*, or in the case of a grouping arrangement will be determined under section 20

(2) or (3), p. 108, *ante*, but if not a manager or governor will presumably continue to hold office until he is removed or resigns.

(b) **" Fourth Schedule to this Act ".**—See p. 203, *post*.

(c) For the purposes of this section a special school maintained by a local education authority shall be treated as if it were a county school. See s. 2 (5) of the Education (No. 2) Act, 1968, p. 268, *post*.

(d) **" Inspection by the local education authority ".**—Since the local education authority is a corporate body, inspection by the authority itself is physically impossible and the intervention of an agent is necessary. Although no specific reference is made, it is reasonable to assume that the managers or governors have the right, if they think it necessary to request the production of some proof of authority from any person purporting to act as agent of a local education authority.

22. Powers of local education authority as to use and care of premises of voluntary schools.—(1) The managers or governors (*) of a controlled school (*) shall be entitled to determine the use to which the school premises (*) or any part thereof shall be put on Saturdays, except when required to be used on Saturdays for the purposes of the school or for any purpose connected with education or with the welfare of the young for which the local education authority (*) desire to provide accommodation on the premises or on that part thereof, and the foundation managers (*) or foundation governors (*) shall be entitled to determine the use to which the school premises or any part thereof shall be put on Sundays, but save as aforesaid the local education authority may give such directions (a) as to the occupation and use of the school premises of a controlled school as they think fit.

(2) If the local education authority desire to provide accommodation for any purpose connected with education or with the welfare of the young and are satisfied that there is no suitable alternative accommodation in their area for that purpose, they may direct the managers or governors of any aided school (*) or special agreement school (*) to provide free of charge (b) accommodation for that purpose on the school premises or any part thereof on any week-day when not required for the purposes of the school, so, however, that the managers or governors shall not be directed to provide such accommodation on more than three days in any week.

(3) Subject to any directions given by a local education authority under the foregoing provisions of this section and to the requirements of any enactment other than this Act or the regulations made thereunder, the occupation and use of the school premises of any voluntary school (*) shall be under the control of the managers or governors thereof.

(4) At any controlled school or special agreement school the persons employed for the purposes of the care and maintenance of the school premises shall be appointed and dismissed by the local education authority, and the local education authority may give directions to the managers or governors of an aided school as to the number and conditions of service of persons employed at the school for such purposes.

(5) In relation to any school with respect to which the trust deed (*) provides for any person other than the managers or governors of the school being entitled to control the occupation and use of the school premises, this section shall have effect as if for the references to the managers or governors there were substituted references to that person.

NOTES

Under sub-section (1) of section 4 of the Education Act, 1946, p. 211, *post*, all sums received by the managers, governors or trustees of a voluntary school in respect of the letting or hiring of any part of the school premises, other than the school buildings (as defined by *ibid.*, sub-section (2)), are to be paid over to the local education authority.

As to the continued operation, in the case of any school maintained immediately before 1st April, 1965 by a local education authority who will not continue to maintain it on and after that date, of any direction of the local education authority under this section, see section 31 (7) of the London Government Act, 1963, p. 292, *post*.

(*) As to the meaning or statutory definition of " managers or governors ", " controlled school ", " premises ", " local education authority ", " foundation managers ", " foundation governors ", " aided school ", " special agreement school ", " voluntary school " and " trust deed ", see pp. 67–69, *ante*.

(a) "**Directions**".—As to the revocation or variation of such directions, see section 111, p. 181, *post*, and as to the enforcement thereof, see sections 68 and 99, pp. 155 and 173, *post*.

(b) "**Free of charge**".—The right of the authority in this connection is limited to the provision, free of charge, of accommodation. Nothing in the section requires the managers or governors to provide lighting, heating, etc.

Secular Instruction and Appointment and Dismissal of Teachers in County and Voluntary Schools

23. Secular instruction in county schools and in voluntary schools.—(1) In every county school (*) and, subject to the provisions hereinafter contained as to religious education (a), in every voluntary school (*) except an aided secondary school (b), the secular instruction (c) to be given to the pupils (*) shall, save in so far as may be otherwise provided by the rules of management (*) or articles of government (*) for the school (*), be under the control of the local education authority (*).

(2) Subject to the provisions hereinafter contained as to religious education, the secular instruction to be given to the pupils in every aided secondary school shall, save in so far as may be otherwise provided by the articles of government for the school, be under the control of the governors (d) of the school.

(3) Save in so far as may be otherwise provided by the rules of management or articles of government for the school, the power to control the secular instruction (e) provided in any county school or voluntary school shall include power to determine the times at which the school session (f) shall begin and end on any day, to determine the times at which the school terms (g) shall begin and end, to determine the school holidays (h), and to require that pupils in attendance at the school shall attend any class not conducted on the school premises for the purpose of receiving instruction or training included in the secular curriculum of the school.

NOTES

Subject to the provisions of the rules of management or articles of government which may apply in any particular case, this section specifies the relationship between the managers or governors of county and voluntary schools, primary and secondary, and the local education authority in relation to the control of secular instruction, and also indicates the extent of the power of either body to control such instruction.

The guiding principle of section 76, p. 162, *post*, that, so far as is compatible with the provision of efficient instruction and training and the avoidance of unreasonable public expenditure, pupils are to be educated in accordance with the wishes of their parents has especial importance in relation to this section.

(*) As to the meaning or statutory definition of "county school", "voluntary school", "pupil", "rules of management", "articles of government", "school" and "local education authority", see pp. 67–69, *ante*.

(a) "**Religious education**".—The provisions of the Act relating to religious education are contained in sections 25–30 inclusive, pp. 115 *et seq.*, *post*.

(b) "**Aided secondary school**".—This means a secondary school, *i.e.*, a school for providing secondary education (as to which see section 8 (1), p. 79, *ante*), which is also an aided school (see section 15, p. 95, *ante*).

(c) "**Secular instruction**".—Under the previous law it was held that the control of secular education might interfere with the managers' control of religious instruction—see, for instance, *Blencowe* v. *Northamptonshire County Council*, [1907] 1 Ch. 504. Now, however, see section 25 (6), p. 115, *post*. Generally the term would cover such matters as the time-table of the school session, the curriculum and the school books to be used; but see subsection (3), which provides that the power to control secular instruction shall include the additional matters there mentioned. In secondary schools the curriculum is largely influenced by the examination system in force, as to which see note (g) to section 8, *ante*.

There is no longer any requirement that all secular instruction in maintained schools is to be given on the school premises, unless the consent of H.M. Inspector to its being given elsewhere has first been obtained. Activities such as school visits may, therefore, be arranged without the necessity for consulting the Inspector. The place of any instruction regularly given elsewhere than on the school premises must be shown on the school time-table; see regulation 14 of the Schools Regulations, 1959, S.I. 1959 No. 364, p. 352, *post*.

(d) "**Governors**".—See sections 17 and 19, pp. 100 and 106, *ante*.

(e) "**The power to control the secular instruction**".—This sub-section replaces and extends section 29 (8) of the Education Act, 1921, which gave statutory form in general terms to the decision in *Bunt* v. *Kent*, [1914] 1 K.B. 207, that a child who ordinarily attended at one elementary school could properly be required by the local education authority to attend a cooking class held at another school. The words of the sub-section merely state that the power of control shall include the matters mentioned. They do not exclude other matters—see note (c), *supra.*

(f) **" School session ".**—As to the hours of secular instruction to be comprised in each session, see Regulation 10 of the Schools Regulations, 1959, S.I. 1959 No. 364, p. 350, *post.*

(g) **" School terms ".**—See Regulation 11 of the Schools Regulations, 1959, S.I. 1959 No. 364, p. 351, *post,* which prescribes the number of sessions to be held in any year.

(h) **Holidays.**—See the regulation referred to in note (g), *supra.*

24. Appointment and dismissal of teachers in county schools and in voluntary schools.—(1) In every county school (a) and, subject to the provisions hereinafter contained as to religious education (b), in every controlled school (*) and special agreement school (*), the appointment (c) of teachers shall, save in so far as may be otherwise provided by the rules of management (*) or articles of government (*) for the school, be under the control (d) of the local education authority (*), and no teacher shall be dismissed (e) except by the authority.

(2) In every aided school (*) the respective functions of the local education authority and of the managers or governors (*) of the school with respect to the appointment of teachers, and, subject to the provisions hereinafter contained as to religious education, with respect to the dismissal of teachers, shall be regulated by the rules of management or articles of government for the school:

Provided that the rules of management or articles of government for every aided school—

(*a*) shall make provision for the appointment (f) of the teachers by the managers or governors (g) of the school, for enabling the local education authority to determine the number of teachers to be employed, and for enabling the authority, except for reasons for which the managers or governors are expressly empowered by this Act to dismiss teachers (h) without such consent, to prohibit the dismissal of teachers without the consent of the authority (i) and to require the dismissal of any teacher (j); and

(*b*) may make such provision as may be agreed between the local education authority and the managers or governors of the school, or in default of such agreement as may be determined (k) by the Secretary of State (l), for enabling the authority to prohibit the appointment, without the consent of the authority, of teachers to be employed for giving secular instruction (m), and for enabling the authority to give directions (n) as to the educational qualifications (o) of the teachers to be so employed.

(3) [Repealed.]

NOTES

Though the main provisions of the Act relating to the appointment and dismissal of teachers in county schools and voluntary schools are contained in this section, certain matters, largely related to the appointment and dismissal of teachers on religious grounds, are contained in sections 27, 28 and 29, pp. 118 *et seq., post.*

It should be noted also that sub-section (2) of this section is affected by the Trade Union and Labour Relations Act 1974. See note (e), *infra.*

Section 62, p. 151, *post,* sets out the respective duties of the Secretary of State and of local education authorities in relation to the training of teachers. As regards teachers in independent schools, see sections 71–74, pp. 158 *et seq., post.*

The present position as to the appointment and dismissal of teachers (which applies equally to primary and secondary schools) may be summarised as follows:—

(1) *Generally:* No woman is to be disqualified for appointment as a teacher in any county school or voluntary school or dismissed by reason only of marriage (sub-section (3) of this section);

(2) *County Schools:* The appointment of teachers is under the control of the local education authority, except as may be otherwise provided by the rules of management or articles of government. Suggestions with regard to the content in this connection of the articles of government of maintained secondary schools are contained in the White Paper on the Principles of Government in Maintained Secondary Schools (Cmd. 6523 of 1944) (see pp. 102–105, *ante*). No teacher is to be dismissed except by the authority (sub-section (1) of this section);

(3) *Voluntary Schools :*

(*a*) *Aided Schools :* The respective functions of the local education authority and the managers or governors as to the appointment and dismissal of teachers are to be regulated by the rules of management or articles of government, subject to the following reservations (sub-section (2) of this section) :—

(i) The functions of the authority and managers or governors respectively relating to the dismissal of teachers are subject to the provisions of the Act as to religious education, *infra* (*ibid.*) ;

(ii) The rules of management or articles of government must provide for the appointment of teachers by the managers or governors, must enable the local education authority to determine the number of teachers to be employed at the school, and must enable the authority, except for reasons for which the managers or governors are expressly empowered by the Act to dismiss teachers without such consent, to prohibit the dismissal of teachers without its consent and to require the dismissal of any teacher (*ibid.*) ;

(iii) The rules of management or articles of government may enable the authority (if agreed between the authority and the managers or governors or, in default of agreement, determined by the Secretary of State) to prohibit the appointment, without consent, of teachers to be employed for giving secular instruction, and to give directions as to the educational qualifications of the teachers to be so employed (*ibid*);

(iv) The consent of the local education authority is not required to the dismissal by the managers or governors of a teacher appointed to give religious instruction other than instruction in accordance with an agreed syllabus for failure to give that instruction efficiently and suitably (section 28 (2), p. 120, *post*).

(*b*) *Controlled Schools :* Subject to the provisions referred to below as to religious education, and except as may be otherwise provided by the rules of management or articles of government, the appointment of teachers is to be under the control of the local education authority. Suggestions with regard to the content in this connection of articles of government are contained in the White Paper on the Principles of Government in Maintained Secondary Schools (Cmd. 6523 of 1944) (see pp. 102–105, *ante*). No teacher is to be dismissed except by the authority (sub-section (1) of this section).

Where the staff at a school exceeds two it must include persons (referred to as " reserved teachers ") selected for their fitness and competence to give such religious instruction in accordance with the trust deed or the practice observed before the school became a controlled school (section 27 (2), p. 118, *post*). The local education authority must consult the foundation managers or foundation governors before appointing a reserved teacher and may not make the appointment unless the managers or governors are satisfied as to his fitness and competence to give such religious instruction (section 27 (4), p. 118, *post*).

The foundation managers or foundation governors may require the authority to dismiss a reserved teacher from employment as a reserved teacher in the school if they are of opinion that he has failed to give such religious instruction efficiently and suitably (section 27 (5), p. 118, *post*).

The head teacher of a controlled school is not to be a reserved teacher, but before appointing a head teacher the authority must consult the managers or governors with regard to the person proposed to be appointed (section 27 (3), p. 118, *post*).

(*c*) *Special Agreement Schools :* Except as regards the provisions relating to religious education, the appointment and dismissal of teachers in special agreement schools is the same as in controlled schools (see the first paragraph of the note on *Controlled Schools, supra*) (sub-section (1) of this section).

Where the special agreement provides for the employment of reserved teachers, similar provisions apply in respect of the appointment and dismissal of such reserved teachers as apply to reserved teachers in controlled schools (section 28 (3) and (4), p. 120, *post*).

(4) *Saving provision* : Subject to the following exceptions, no person is to be disqualified by reason of his religious opinions, or of his attending or omitting to attend religious worship, from being a teacher in any county school or voluntary school, or from being otherwise employed for the purposes of the school, nor required to give religious instruction or receive any less emolument or be deprived of, or disqualified for, any promotion or other advantage by reason of the fact that he does or does not give religious instruction (section 30, p. 122, *post*). These provisions, however, do not apply to teachers in aided schools, or to reserved teachers in controlled schools or special agreement schools, except that such teachers are not to receive any less emolument or be deprived of, or disqualified for, any promotion or other advantage by reason of the fact that he gives religious instruction, of his religious opinions, or of his attending religious worship (proviso to section 30, p. 122, *post*).

(*) As to the meaning or statutory definition of " county school ", " controlled school ", " special agreement school ", " rules of management ", " articles of government ", " local education authority " and " managers or governors ", see pp. 67–69, *ante*.

(a) For the purposes of this section a special school maintained by a local education authority is to be treated as if it were a county school. See s. 2 (5) of the Education (No. 2) Act, 1968, p. 268, *post*.

(b) **" Religious education ".**—The provisions of the Act relating to religious education are contained in sections 25–30 inclusive, pp. 115 *et seq.*, *post*. See also the general note, *supra*.

(c) **" Appointment ".**—See the case of *Powell* v. *Lee* (1908), 72 J.P. 353, with respect to the method of communication of an appointment to a teacher and the result of failure to communicate it in the proper manner.

(d) **" Under the control ".**—This phrase would appear to mean that, subject to the rules of management or articles of government and to the special provisions regarding religious education, it is for the local education authority to determine whether appointments shall be made by the authority, by the managers or governors, by both in consultation, by the managers or governors with consent or by some other method. If the authority authorises the governors to make appointments it would appear that the governors act either as agents or as a body to which power to appoint has been delegated, according to the circumstances. Reference is made in note (e), *infra*, to the cases of *Young* v. *Cuthbert*, [1906] 1 Ch. 451, and *Crocker* v. *Plymouth Corporation*, [1906] 1 K.B. 494. It would seem that in such circumstances as have been mentioned those cases no longer apply and that there is privity of contract between the teacher and the local education authority, even where the appointment is made by the managers or governors. It is doubtful, however, whether these remarks apply to the appointment of teachers in aided schools, in view of the first words in proviso (*a*) to sub-section (2) of this section.

(e) **" Dismissed ".**—In cases where under this Act there is a transfer of responsibility for dismissal to the local education authority a case similar to that arising in *Jones* v. *Hughes*, [1905] 1 Ch. 180, might arise. There the managers gave notice to the plaintiff before the Education Act, 1902, came into operation, which did not expire until afterwards. The notice was held to be good and not to require the consent of the authority.

It was held in *Young* v. *Cuthbert*, [1906] 1 Ch. 451, that the requirements of section 7 of the Education Act, 1902, as to the consent of the authority to dismissal by the managers were only operative as between the managers and the local education authority and gave no right to the teacher, and in *Crocker* v. *Plymouth Corporation*, [1906] 1 K.B. 494, that that section did not make a personal contract between the local education authority and the teacher so that the teacher could sue the authority for salary, even though it was paid direct. It would appear that these cases are superseded so far as they relate to the dismissal of the teachers in that there must be such a degree of privity of contract between the authority and the teacher as is necessary to enable the dismissal to be made by the authority.

It is provided by Sch. 1, para. 27, to the Trade Union and Labour Relations Act 1974, that where a teacher in an aided school is dismissed by the governors or managers of the school in pursuance of a requirement of the local education authority, the parts of the 1974 Act relating to unfair dismissal and the jurisdiction of tribunals (Parts II and III of Sch. 1) shall have effect in relation to the dismissal as if (*a*) the local education authority had at all material times been the teacher's employers and (*b*) the local education authority had dismissed him, and the reason or principle reason for which they did so had been the reason or principal reason for which they required his dismissal.

(f) **" Appointment ".**—As to the manner of making an appointment, in the case of managers or governors, see *Meyers* v. *Hennell*, [1912] 2 Ch. 256.

(g) **" Appointment of the teachers by the managers or governors ".**—See note (d), *supra*.

(h) **" Expressly empowered by this Act to dismiss teachers ".**—The managers or governors of an aided school may, without consent, dismiss a teacher appointed to give religious instruction other than in accordance with an agreed syllabus on the ground that he has failed to give such instruction efficiently and suitably (section 28 (2), p. 120, *post*).

(i) **" Without the consent of the authority ".**—See the cases referred to in note (b), *supra*. In *Smith* v. *Macnally*, [1912] 1 Ch. 816, a teacher was dismissed by the managers, who alleged dissatisfaction with the religious instruction given by her, though in fact the ground was that she had ceased to be a member of the Church of England and had become a Wesleyan. It was held that the true ground of dismissal was not connected with the giving of religious instruction in the school and that the consent of the authority was, therefore, necessary; and, furthermore, that she had a statutory right under the Act until the requirements of the Act (then the Act of 1902) had been complied with.

(j) **" To require the dismissal of any teacher ".**—It appears that the authority has power to require the dismissal of a teacher under this provision on any ground other than that mentioned in section 28 (2), p. 120, *post*, and that the power will not be limited, as it was in section 29 (2) (*a*) of the Education Act, 1921, to dismissal " on education grounds ". In consequence the cases on the meaning of these words in previous legislation, e.g., *Martin* v. *Eccles Corporation*, [1919] 1 Ch. 387; *Hanson* v. *Radcliffe Urban District Council*, [1922] 2 Ch. 490; [1922] All E.R. Rep. 160, and *Dyson* v. *Sheffield Corporation*, *Sadler* v. *Sheffield Corporation*, [1924] 1 Ch. 483, are superseded.

(k) **" As may be determined ".**—In the case of an aided primary school it will be necessary for one of the parties, in the event of failure to agree, to seek the aid of the Secretary of State, since the rules of management must be made by order of the local education authority. In the case of an aided secondary school the articles of government must be made by order of the Secretary of State, who will presumably approach the authority and the governors and endeavour to secure agreement on the contents of the articles in relation to the matters specified before imposing his will upon them. In addition to this reference to the Secretary of State, section 67 (1), p. 154, *post*, makes provision for the settlement by the Secretary of State of disputes between the local education authority and the managers or governors of a school.

(l) **" Secretary of State ".**—See note (b) to s. 1, *ante*.

(m) **" Secular instruction ".**—As to the meaning of this term, see note (c) to section 23, p. 111, *ante*.

(n) **" Directions ".**—As to the revocation or variation of directions given by a local education authority, see section **111**, **p.** 181, *post*.

(o) **" Educational qualifications ".**—The power of the local education authority to control the educational qualifications of teachers in an aided school is not necessarily as strong as it was under section 29 (2) (*a*) of the Education Act, 1921, where the managers were required

to carry out *any* directions of the authority with respect to the educational qualifications of the teachers to be employed at the school.

(p) Section (3) was repealed by the Sex Discrimination Act 1975.

Religious Education in County and Voluntary Schools

25. General provisions as to religious education in county and in voluntary schools.—(1) Subject to the provisions of this section, the school day (a) in every county school (*) and in every voluntary school (*) shall begin (b) with collective worship (c), on the part of all pupils (*) in attendance at the school (*), and the arrangements made therefor shall provide for a single act of worship attended by all such pupils unless, in the opinion of (d) the local education authority (*) or, in the case of a voluntary school, of the managers or governors (*) thereof, the school premises (*) are such as to make it impracticable to assemble them for that purpose.

(2) Subject to the provisions of this section, religious instruction (e) shall be given in every county school and in every voluntary school.

(3) It shall not be required, as a condition of any pupil attending any county school or any voluntary school, that he shall attend or abstain from attending any Sunday school or any place of religious worship.

(4) If the parent (*) of any pupil in attendance at any county school or any voluntary school requests (f) that he be wholly or partly excused from attendance at religious worship in the school, or from attendance at religious instruction in the school, or from attendance at both religious worship and religious instruction in the school, then, until the request is withdrawn, the pupil shall be excused (g) from such attendance accordingly.

(5) Where any pupil has been wholly or partly excused from attendance at religious worship or instruction in any school in accordance with the provisions of this section, and the local education authority are satisfied :—

(*a*) that the parent of the pupil desires him to receive religious instruction of a kind which is not provided in the school during the periods during which he is excused from such attendance ;

(*b*) that the pupil cannot with reasonable convenience be sent to another county or voluntary school where religious instruction of the kind desired by the parent is provided ; and

(*c*) that arrangements have been made for him to receive religious instruction during school hours elsewhere,

the pupil may be withdrawn from the school during such periods as are reasonably necessary for the purpose of enabling him to receive religious instruction in accordance with the arrangements :

Provided that the pupil shall not be so withdrawn unless the local education authority are satisfied that the arrangements are such as will not interfere with the attendance of the pupil at school on any day except at the beginning or end of the school session on that day.

(6) No directions (h) shall be given by the local education authority as to the secular instruction (i) to be given to pupils in attendance at a voluntary school so as to interfere with the provision of reasonable facilities for religious instruction in the school during school hours ; and no such direction shall be given so as to prevent a pupil from receiving religious instruction in accordance with the provisions of this section during the hours normally set apart (k) for that purpose, unless arrangements are made whereby the pupil shall receive such instruction in the school at some other time.

(7) Where the parent of any pupil who is a boarder at a county school or at a voluntary school requests that the pupil be permitted to attend worship in accordance with the tenets of a particular religious denomination on Sundays or other days exclusively set apart for religious observance by

the religious body to which his parent belongs, or to receive religious instruction in accordance with such tenets outside school hours (l), the managers or governors of the school shall make arrangements for affording to the pupil reasonable opportunities for so doing and such arrangements may provide for affording facilities for such worship or instruction on the school premises, so however, that such arrangements shall not entail expenditure by the local education authority.

NOTES

This and the four following sections deal with the provision of religious education in both county and voluntary schools. The following note outlines the various provisions contained in these sections. See also the Introduction, pp. 44–48, *ante*.

In order to emphasise the importance of the subject provision has been made, in subsection (1) of this section, for the school day in all primary and secondary schools to begin with collective worship. Except where the nature of the school premises makes it impracticable there must be a single act of worship attended by all pupils. Sub-section (1) of section 7 of the Education Act, 1946, p. 213, *post*, emphasises that the collective act of worship must take place on the school premises but sub-section (2), *ibid.*, provides that in the case of aided schools and special agreement schools it may take place elsewhere, *e.g.* in church, on special occasions. Statutory provision is made, in sub-section (2), of the present section, for the giving of religious instruction in all primary and secondary schools. This instruction may be given at any time.

The obligation in sub-sections (1) and (2) to provide for collective worship and for the giving of religious instruction does not mean that all children are required to participate in the corporate act of worship or in religious instruction.

The religious instruction to be given in county schools is to be in accordance with an agreed syllabus (section 26, p. 117, *post*), drawn up by representatives of the Established Church (except in Wales) and other religious denominations, the teachers and the local education authority, under the procedure described in the Fifth Schedule, p. 204, *post*. Neither the corporate act of worship nor the religious instruction required to be given may include any catechism or formulary distinctive of any particular religious denomination (section 26, *post*). See also, with regard to the adoption of an agreed syllabus, section 29, p. 121, *post*, which also enables the local education authority to set up a standing advisory council on religious education.

As regards withdrawal, parents may not only withdraw their children entirely from religious observance and instruction (sub-section (4) of this section) but, if they wish their children to receive some form of denominational instruction and it is not reasonably convenient to send them to another school where religious instruction of the kind desired by the parents is provided, may withdraw them for that purpose also (sub-section (5), *ibid.*). This right of withdrawal does not justify a local education authority in refusing to convey a child to a school of the denomination concerned or to make an extra-district payment under section 6 of the Education (Miscellaneous Provisions) Act, 1948, p. 222, *post*, where that can be done compatibly with the conditions laid down in section 76 of this Act, p. 162, *post*. In the case of some county secondary schools, situated in the open country in order to serve the needs of a number of villages, there may be no building reasonably accessible to which the children can be withdrawn for denominational instruction. In such cases the local education authority is required by the proviso to section 26, p. 117, *post*, unless there are special circumstances which would make it unreasonable to do so, to provide facilities for the denominational instruction to be given on the school premises. It is for the denomination concerned to provide the teacher and to meet the cost of the instruction.

In controlled schools the religious instruction is to be in accordance with an agreed syllabus (section 27 (6), p. 119, *post*), but the parents of any pupils attending the school may request that their children shall receive religious instruction in accordance with the persuasion to which the school adhered before it became a controlled school and, unless owing to special circumstances it would be unreasonable to do so, the foundation managers or foundation governors must make arrangements for such denominational instruction to be given at the school to the pupils concerned for not more than two periods a week (section 27 (1), p. 118, *post*). Without prejudice to this duty, but for the purpose of facilitating its execution, where the number of teaching staff exceeds two the teaching staff is to include persons (referred to as "reserved teachers") selected for their fitness and competence to give such religious instruction and the reserved teachers are to be specifically appointed to do so (section 27 (2), p. 118, *post*); see also the general note to section 24, p. 128, *ante*. Where the staff does not exceed two and reserved teachers may not be appointed the religious instruction may be given by persons who are acceptable to the foundation managers, *e.g.*, local clergy or lay workers. Furthermore, there is no reason why members of the ordinary teaching staff should not give the instruction, if they volunteer to do so (Explanatory Memorandum to the Bill, Cmd. 6492 of 1943, p. 7). They may not, however, be required to do so (section 30, p. 122, *post*). Even where reserved teachers have been appointed the instruction may be given by the clergy, lay workers, or non-reserved teachers if invited by the foundation managers and willing to give it.

In aided schools and special agreement schools the religious instruction is to be in accordance with the provisions of the trust deed or, if there is no trust deed, with the practice in operation before the school became a voluntary school (section 28 (1), p. 119, *post*). Anxiety was felt during the passing of the Bill regarding children in single school areas who might be compelled by force of circumstances to attend a school at which denominational instruction was given of a kind which certain parents might not desire their children to receive. By the proviso to section 28 (1), *ibid.*, if parents of children attending an aided or special agreement school wish them to receive religious instruction in accordance with an agreed syllabus, and the children cannot reasonably attend a school where that instruction is ordinarily given, provision at the school must be made accordingly, unless owing to special circumstances the local education authority is satisfied that it would be unreasonable to do so. The arrangements are to be made by the managers or governors, but if they are unwilling to do so the local education authority is required to make the arrangements in their place.

Provision is also made (by subsection (7) of the present section) to enable pupils at boarding schools to attend religious worship and to receive religious instruction in accordance with the wishes of the parents.

(*) As to the meaning or statutory definition of " county school ", " voluntary school ", " pupil ", " school ", " local education authority ", " managers or governors " and " parent ", see pp. 67–69, *ante*.

(a) **" School day ".**—As to the power to determine the times on which the school day shall begin and end, see section 23 (3), p. 111, *ante*, and see Regulation 10 of the Schools Regulations, 1959, S.I. 1959 No. 364, p. 350, *post*.

(b) **" Shall begin ".**—As to the enforcement of this requirement, see section 99, p. 173, *post*.

(c) **" Collective worship ".**—The requirement to provide an act of collective worship at the beginning of each school day was new as a statutory obligation, though prior to the Act the great majority of schools provided such an opportunity in the past. All pupils attending the school are required to attend, unless—

(*a*) the school premises are such as to make it impracticable to assemble them for the purpose (sub-section (1));

(*b*) the parent of any pupils requests that he be wholly or partly excused from attendance at religious worship in the school (sub-section (2)).

The section does not specify that the request must be in writing, but it is desirable, for obvious reasons, that a written request should be obtained wherever possible. If a request has not been received but the pupil refuses or fails to attend, enquiry should be made without delay as to the parent's wishes. As to the collective act of worship in county schools, see section 26, *infra*.

(d) **" Unless in the opinion of ".**—It will be noticed that the sub-section imposes a positive duty upon the local education authority, or the managers or governors, as the case may be *unless in their opinion* it is impracticable. Section 68, p. 155, *post*, enables the Secretary of State to take steps to prevent the unreasonable exercise by a local education authority, or by the managers or governors of any county or voluntary school, of any of their functions under the Act.

(e) **" Religious instruction ".**—As to the position prior to the present Act, see *A. G.* v. *West Riding of Yorkshire County Council*, [1907] A.C. 29. See also the general note to this section. As to the provisions of this Act relating to the inspection of religious instruction, see section 77, p. 163, *post*.

(f) **" Requests ".**—As to the form of such a request, see note (c), *supra*.

(g) **" The pupil shall be excused ".**—Excuse from attendance at religious worship and for religious instruction does not excuse entire absence from school during the period of such worship or instruction, except as is provided in sub-section (5) of this section. The pupil remains subject to the provisions relating to compulsory school attendance—see sections 35–40 inclusive, pp. 127 *et seq.*, *post*.

(h) **" Directions ".**—As to the revocation or variation of directions given by a local education authority, see section 111, p. 181, *post*.

(i) **" Secular instruction ".**—See section 23, p. 111, *ante*, and, in particular, note (c) to that section.

(k) **" The hours normally set apart ".**—Under the present Act no restriction is placed upon the times at which religious instruction shall be given, as was the case under the previous law.

(l) **" School hours ".**—See section 23 (3), p. 111, *ante*.

26. Special provisions as to religious education in county schools.—Subject as hereinafter provided, the collective worship (a) required by subsection (1) of the last foregoing section shall not (b), in any county school (*), be distinctive of any particular religious denomination, and the religious instruction given to any pupils (*) in attendance at a county school in conformity with the requirements of subsection (2) of the said section shall be given in accordance with an agreed syllabus (*) adopted for the school or for those pupils and shall not include any catechism or formulary which is distinctive of any particular religious denomination (c):

Provided that, where a county secondary school is so situated that arrangements cannot conveniently be made for the withdrawal of pupils (d) from the school in accordance with the provisions of this Act to receive religious instruction elsewhere, then, if the local education authority are satisfied:—

(*a*) that the parents of pupils in attendance at the school desire them to receive religious instruction in the school in accordance with the tenets of a particular religious denomination; and

(*b*) that satisfactory arrangements have been made for the provision of such instruction to those pupils in the school, and for securing that the cost of providing such instruction to those pupils in the school will not fall upon the authority;

the authority shall, unless they are satisfied that owing to any special circumstances it would be unreasonable so to do, provide facilities for the carrying out of those arrangements.

NOTES

The provisions of sections 25–30 inclusive, pp. 115 *et seq.*, *post*, are considered in the general note to section 25.

(*) As to the meaning or statutory definition of " county school ", " pupil " and " agreed syllabus ", see pp. 67–69, *ante*.

(a) **" Collective worship ".**—See note (c) to section 25, p. 117, *ante*. In the case of county schools the collective act of worship must always take place on the school premises. See section 7 of the Education Act, 1946, p. 213, *post*.

(b) **" Shall not ".**—As to the enforcement of this requirement, see section 99, p. 173, *post*.

(c) **" Distinctive of any particular religious denomination ".**—The requirement that the religious instruction to be given in county schools must not include any distinctive catechism or formulary is a re-enactment of section 28 of the Education Act, 1921, which itself originated in section 14 of the Elementary Education Act, 1870 (the " Cowper-Temple " clause).

(d) **" Withdrawal of pupils ".**—See section 25 (5), p. 115, *ante*, and the general note to that section.

27. Special provisions as to religious education in controlled schools.—(1) Where the parents (*) of any pupils (*) in attendance at a controlled school (*) request (a) that they may receive religious instruction in accordance with the provisions of the trust deed (*) relating to the school (b), or where provision for that purpose is not made by such a deed in accordance with the practice observed in the school before it became a controlled school (c), the foundation managers (*) or foundation governors (*) shall, unless they are satisfied (d) that owing to special circumstances it would be unreasonable so to do, make arrangements for securing that such religious instruction is given to those pupils at the school during not more than two periods in each week.

(2) Without prejudice to the duty to make such arrangements as aforesaid whatever the number of the teaching staff of the school, where the number of the teaching staff of a controlled school exceeds two the teaching staff shall include (e) persons (hereinafter referred to as " reserved teachers ") (f) selected for their fitness and competence to give such religious instruction as is required to be given under such arrangements and specifically appointed to do so :

Provided that the number of reserved teachers in any controlled school shall not exceed one-fifth of the number of the teaching staff of the school including the head teacher, so, however, that where the number of the teaching staff is not a multiple of five it shall be treated for the purposes of this subsection as if it were the next higher multiple thereof.

(3) The head teacher of a controlled school shall not while holding that position be a reserved teacher, but before appointing any person to be the head teacher of such a school the local education authority shall inform the managers or governors (*) of the school as to the person whom they propose to appoint and shall consider any representations made by the managers or governors with respect to the proposed appointment.

(4) Where the local education authority propose to appoint any person to be a reserved teacher in a controlled school, the authority shall consult the foundation managers or foundation governors of the school, and, unless the said managers or governors are satisfied as to that person's fitness and competence to give such religious instruction as is required in pursuance of such arrangements as aforesaid the authority shall not appoint that person to be a reserved teacher.

(5) If the foundation managers or foundation governors of a controlled school are of opinion that any reserved teacher has failed to give such religious instruction as aforesaid efficiently and suitably they may require the authority to dismiss (g) him from employment as a reserved teacher in the school.

(6) Subject to any arrangements made under subsection (1) of this section, the religious instruction given to the pupils in attendance at a controlled school shall be given in accordance with an agreed syllabus (*) adopted for the school or for those pupils.

NOTES

The provisions of sections 25–30 inclusive, as they relate to religious education, are considered in the general note to section 25, p. 116, *ante*. The appointment and dismissal of reserved teachers and consultation between the managers or governors and the local education authority regarding the appointment of the head teacher of a controlled school are considered in the general note to section 24, p. 112, *ante*. The position of controlled schools under the Act is discussed in note (a) to section 15, p. 97, *ante*. The collective act of worship in a controlled school must always take place on the school premises. See section 7 of the Education Act, 1946, p. 213, *post*.

As to the determination of disputes as to whether the religious instruction given in a voluntary school is in accordance with the trust deed, see section 67, p. 154, *post*.

(*) As to the meaning or statutory definition of " parent ", " pupil ", " controlled school ", " trust deed ", " foundation managers ", " foundation governors ", " managers or governors ", and " agreed syllabus ", see pp. 67–69, *ante*.

(a) **" Request ".**—As to the form of such a request, see note (c) to section 25, p. 117, *ante*.

(b) **" School ".**—The term is defined in section 114 (1), p. 185, *post*, but is, of course, to be understood subject to the qualification introduced by this section.

(c) **" Before it became a controlled school ".**—As to the time at which and the manner in which a school becomes a controlled school, see section 15, p. 95, *ante*.

(d) **" Shall, unless they are satisfied ".**—As to the power of the Secretary of State to prevent the unreasonable exercise of this function, see section 68, p. 155, *post*.

(e) **" The teachers shall include ".**—As to the enforcement of this and other requirements in the section, see section 99 (1), p. 173, *post*.

(f) **" Reserved teachers ".**—As to the appointment and dismissal of reserved teachers in relation to teachers generally, see the general note to section 24, p. 112, *ante*. The term " reserved teacher " first appeared in the Education Act, 1936, in relation to teachers appointed for a similar purpose in schools in respect of which a grant was made by the local education authority under section 8 of that Act (now special agreement schools—see section 28 (3) and (4), *infra*), and has been adopted in relation also to controlled schools which are created under this Act. It will be noted that though the subsection refers to " persons " the effect of the proviso to the subsection is such that there will be only one reserved teacher for any school having a total teaching staff of three, four or five. It should be noted that section 30, p. 122, *post*, has only a limited application to reserved teachers. The head teacher of a controlled school cannot be a reserved teacher (subsection (3) of this section) whilst holding that position.

(g) **" Dismiss ".**—The power given to the foundation managers or foundation governors by this subsection only enables them to require the local education authority to dismiss a reserved teacher from employment as a reserved teacher in that particular school. There is, therefore, no reason why the teacher should not continue to be employed if the authority thinks fit (subject to subsection (4) of this section or section 28 (3), *infra*), as a reserved teacher in any other controlled school or in a special agreement school, or even as one of the teachers who are not reserved teachers in the same school.

28. Special provisions as to religious education in aided schools and in special agreement schools.—(1) The religious instruction given to the pupils (*) in attendance at an aided school (*) or at a special agreement school (*) shall be under the control of the managers or governors (*) of the school (*) and shall be in accordance with any provisions of the trust deed (*) relating to the school, or, where provision for that purpose is not made by such a deed, in accordance with the practice observed in the school before it became a voluntary school (*) :

Provided that where the parents (*) of pupils in attendance at the school desire them to receive religious instruction in accordance with any agreed syllabus (*) adopted by the local education authority (*) and cannot with reasonable convenience cause those pupils to attend any school at which that syllabus is in use, then, unless the authority are satisfied that owing to any special circumstances it would be unreasonable so to do, arrangements shall be made (a) for religious instruction in accordance with that syllabus to be given to those pupils in the school during the times set apart (b) for the giving of religious instruction therein, and such arrangements shall be made by the managers or governors of the school, so, however, that if the local education authority are satisfied that the managers or governors are unwilling to make such arrangements the arrangements shall be made by the authority.

(2) If a teacher appointed to give in an aided school religious instruction other than instruction in accordance with an agreed syllabus fails to give

such instruction efficiently and suitably, he may be dismissed (c) on that ground by the managers or governors of the school without the consent of the local education authority.

(3) Where the special agreement (d) made with respect to any special agreement school provides for the employment of reserved teachers (e), the local education authority shall, when they propose to appoint any person to be such a teacher in the school, consult the foundation managers (*) or foundation governors (*) of the school, and unless the said managers or governors are satisfied as to that person's fitness and competence to give such religious instruction as aforesaid, the authority shall not appoint that person to be such a teacher.

(4) If the foundation managers or foundation governors of a special agreement school are of opinion that any such reserved teacher as aforesaid has failed to give, efficiently and suitably, such religious instruction as he was appointed to give, they may require the authority to dismiss (f) him from employment as a reserved teacher in the school.

NOTES

The provisions of sections 25–30 inclusive, as they relate to religious education, are considered in the general note to section 25, p. 116, *ante*. The appointment and dismissal of reserved teachers in special agreement schools and controlled schools, and of teachers in aided schools, are considered in the general note to section 24, p. 112, *ante*. The collective act of worship in aided schools and special agreement schools may, on special occasions, take place elsewhere than on the school premises. See section 7 (2) of the Education Act, 1946, p. 213, *post*.

(*) As to the meaning or statutory definition of " pupil ", " aided school ", " special agreement school ", " managers or governors ", " school ", " trust deed ", " voluntary school ", " parent ", " agreed syllabus ", " local education authority ", " foundation managers " and " foundation governors ", see pp. 67–69, *ante*.

(a) **" Arrangements shall be made ".**—As to the power of the Secretary of State to prevent the unreasonable exercise of this function, see section 68, p. 155, *post*.

(b) **" During the times set apart ".**—Under the present Act no restriction is placed upon the times at which religious instruction shall be given, as was the case under the previous law. Furthermore, section 25 (6), p. 115, *ante*, now prohibits the local education authority from giving directions regarding secular instruction so as to interfere with the reasonable facilities for religious instruction in the school during school hours, or so as to prevent a pupil from receiving such instruction during the hours normally set apart for that purpose, unless arrangements are made for the pupil to receive such instruction in the school at some other time. Consequently under this section the managers or governors may fix the times for the giving of religious instruction in the school and, if ultimately the duty falls upon the local education authority to make arrangements for the provision of agreed syllabus instruction, the instruction must be given at the times fixed by the managers or governors.

(c) **" Dismissed ".**—In aided schools, unlike other voluntary schools, the teachers are to be appointed by the managers or governors, but may not be dismissed without the consent of the local education authority, except in pursuance of this subsection (proviso (a) to section 24 (2), p. 112, *ante*). The power given by this subsection may be compared with the power of the managers or governors in controlled schools and special agreement schools, not to dismiss, but to require the dismissal of reserved teachers in such schools (section 27 (5), p. 118, *ante*, and subsection (4) of this section). See also the general remarks regarding dismissal of teachers in the general note to section 24, p. 112, *ante*.

(d) **" Special agreement ".**—See section 15, p. 95, *ante*, and the Third Schedule, p. 201, *post*. Section 114 (1), p. 185, *post*, defines the term as an agreement made under the provisions of the Third Schedule to the Act.

(e) **" Reserved teachers ".**—Paragraph 7 of the Third Schedule, p. 202, *post*, provides that a special agreement may provide for the giving of religious instruction in the school in accordance with the provisions of the trust deed relating to the school, or, where provision for that purpose is not made by such a deed, in accordance with the practice observed in the school before it became a voluntary school and for the employment in the school, for the purpose of giving such religious instruction, of a specified number of reserved teachers. Neither this section nor the Third Schedule, p. 201, *post*, defines the term " reserved teachers " so that, though section 27, p. 118, *ante*, refers only to controlled schools, it is necessary to have regard to that section (subsection (2)) in order to discover that it means " persons selected for their fitness and competence to give such religious instruction as is required to be given " under the arrangements referred to in paragraph 7 of the Third Schedule, p. 202, *post* " and specifically appointed to do so."

(f) **" Dismiss ".**—The power given to the foundation managers or foundation governors by this subsection only enables them to require the local education authority to dismiss a reserved teacher from employment as a reserved teacher in that particular school. There is, therefore, no reason why the teacher should not continue to be employed, if the authority thinks fit (subject to section 27 (4), p. 118, *ante*, and subsection (3) of this section) as a reserved teacher in any other special agreement school or in a controlled school, or even as one of the teachers who are not reserved teachers in the same school.

29. Provisions as to religious instruction in accordance with agreed syllabus.—(1) The provisions of the Fifth Schedule to this Act (a) shall have effect with respect to the preparation, adoption and reconsideration of an agreed syllabus (*) of religious instruction.

(2) A local education authority (*) shall have power to constitute a standing advisory council on religious matters connected with the religious instruction (b) to be given in accordance with an agreed syllabus and, in particular, as to methods of teaching, the choice of books, and the provision of lectures for teachers.

(3) The method of appointment of the members of any council constituted under the last foregoing subsection and the term of office and conditions of retirement of the members thereof shall be such as may be determined (c) by the local education authority.

(4) A local education authority shall have regard (d) to any unanimous recommendations which may be made to them by any conference convened in accordance with the provisions of the said Fifth Schedule with respect to the expediency of constituting such an advisory council as aforesaid or with respect to the method by which or the terms and conditions upon which members of any such council shall be appointed.

NOTES

Subsection (1) of this section links the Fifth Schedule, p. 204, *post*, with those provisions of the Act which require or enable religious instruction to be given in various classes of schools in accordance with an agreed syllabus. See also the Introduction, p. 44, *ante*.

Subsections (2) to (4) enables the local education authority to constitute a standing advisory committee on religious education to advise the authority upon matters connected with religious instruction to be given in accordance with an agreed syllabus and in particular as to methods of teaching, the choice of books and the provision of lectures for teachers.

The terms of reference of the first conference convened under the Fifth Schedule, were confined to the making of a unanimous recommendation or recommendations regarding the adoption of an agreed syllabus (or syllabuses) for the authority's area for, under paragraph 12 of the Schedule, the constitution of a further conference will be necessary if the preparation of further syllabuses is required subsequently. This section, however, fills the important need of providing a continuing committee to make suggestions for the improvement of the syllabus and analogous subjects and should be of great value. There is no legal reason why a local education authority should not have appointed the members of the first conference constituted under the Fifth Schedule, as the original members of the standing advisory council under this section.

(*) As to the meaning or statutory definition of " agreed syllabus " and " local education authority ", see pp. 67–69, *ante*.

(a) **" The Fifth Schedule to this Act ".**—See p. 204, *post*.

(b) **" Religious instruction ".**—The circumstances in which an agreed syllabus must or may be used in schools maintained by a local education authority are as follows :

(1) **County schools.**—Subject to the parent's power of withdrawal under section 25 p. 115, *ante*, and in the case of county secondary schools to the provision, in certain circumstances, of facilities for the giving of other forms of religious instruction, religious instruction must be given in accordance with an agreed syllabus ;

(2) **Controlled schools.**—Subject to the parent's right of withdrawal under section 25, and to the provision, where the parents of pupils at the school so request, for not more than two periods in each week, of religious instruction in accordance with the trust deed or the practice observed before the school became a controlled school, religious instruction must be given in accordance with an agreed syllabus.

(3) **Aided and Special Agreement Schools.**—Though religious instruction is normally to be given in accordance with the trust deed or previous practice, arrangements are to be made for the provision of agreed syllabus instruction for pupils whose parents so desire and cannot reasonably cause them to attend school where the syllabus is in use.

(c) **" Shall be such as may be determined ".**—This gives the local education authority a wide discretion as to the constitution of such a council, subject to regard being had to the unanimous recommendation of any conference constituted under the Fifth Schedule, p. 204, *post*.

(d) **" Shall have regard ".**—The extent of this requirement is not entirely clear. On the one hand it may be argued that the subsection has been complied with if the local education authority considers such a recommendation but decides not to accept it ; on the other hand it may well be argued that the subsection requires the authority to accept any such recommendation which might, as stated in the general note to this section, put forward the members of the conference as a suitable body for appointment. Probably the true meaning is that the authority is required to give consideration to the resolution but not necessarily to adopt it. In the event of refusal to adopt such a recommendation, the Secretary of State's powers under section 68, p. 155, *post*, are sufficient to enable him to require the authority to do so, if he thinks its refusal unreasonable.

30. Saving as to position of teachers.—Subject as hereinafter provided, no person shall be disqualified (a) by reason of his religious opinions, or of his attending or omitting to attend religious worship, from being a teacher in a county (*) or in a voluntary school (*), or from being otherwise employed (b) for the purposes of such a school ; and no teacher in any such school shall be required to give religious instruction or receive any less emolument or be deprived of, or disqualified for, any promotion or other advantage by reason of the fact that he does or does not give religious instruction or by reason of his religious opinions or of his attending or omitting to attend religious worship :

Provided that, save in so far as they require that a teacher shall not receive any less emolument or be deprived of, or disqualified for, any promotion or other advantage by reason of the fact that he gives religious instruction or by reason of his religious opinions or of his attending religious worship, the provisions of this section shall not apply with respect to a teacher in an aided school (*) or with respect to a reserved teacher (d) in any controlled school (*) or special agreement school (*).

NOTES

The appointment and dismissal of teachers generally is considered in the general note to section 24, p. 112, *ante*. The present section, as a statutory exposition of the law, is new, but regard may be had to the case of *Smith* v. *Macnally*, [1912] 1 Ch. 816.

The application of the section to teachers in aided schools or to reserved teachers in controlled schools or special agreement schools is limited by the proviso to the section.

There are no longer any restrictions on the employment as teachers of ministers of religion.

As to religious freedom of teachers in special schools, see regulation 17 (2) of the Handicapped Pupils and Special Schools Regulations, 1959, S.I. 1959 No. 365, p. 359, *post*.

(*) As to the meaning or statutory definition of " county school ", " voluntary school ", " aided school ", " controlled school " and " special agreement school ", see pp. 67–69, *ante*.

(a) **" No person shall be disqualified ".**—Presumably the provisions of section 99, p. 173, *post*, apply with respect to the enforcement of the duties imposed by this section as they do in a case of other provisions of the Act which impose duties upon either the local education authority or the managers or governors of a school. It would appear, however, to be somewhat more difficult to apply these enforcement provisions since it would be simple for an authority, or the managers or governors of a school, to refrain from offering an appointment, or promotion, whilst refraining from stating a reason.

(b) **" Or from being otherwise employed ".**—It is not entirely clear what this phrase includes. If the phrase " a teacher in a school " implies full-time employment, it would include visiting teachers and teachers employed in other premises (*e.g.*, a domestic science centre) to which pupils are sent from a number of schools. In any case it would include caretaking and other staff whose work is not connected with teaching.

(c) **" Reserved teacher ".**—See note (f) to section 27, *ante*, and note (e) to section 28, *ante*.

Transitional Provisions as to County and Voluntary Schools

31. Transitional provisions as to the separation of primary and secondary schools.—[*Spent.*]

32. Transitional provisions as to the management and maintenance of voluntary schools.—[*Spent*].

Primary and Secondary Education of pupils requiring Special Educational Treatment

33. Education of pupils requiring special educational treatment.—(1) The Secretary of State (a) shall make regulations (b) defining the several categories of pupils (c) requiring special educational treatment (d) and making provision as to the special methods appropriate for the education of pupils of each category (e).

(2) The arrangements made by a local education authority (*) for the special educational treatment of pupils of any such category shall, so far as is practicable, provide for the education of pupils in whose case the disability is serious in special schools (f) appropriate for that category (g), but where that is impracticable, or where the disability is not serious, the arrangements may provide for the giving of such education in any school

maintained (*) by a local education authority (h) or [in any school not so maintained (i) other than one notified by the Secretary of State (a) to the local authority to be, in his opinion, unsuitable for the purpose (j)].

(3) The Secretary of State (a) may by regulations make provision as to the requirements to be complied with by any school (k) as a condition of approval of the school as a special school, and as to the withdrawal of approval from any school which fails to comply with requirements so prescribed (l) and, notwithstanding that the provisions of this Act requiring local education authorities to have regard to the need for securing that primary (*) and secondary education (*) are provided in separate schools (m) do not apply with respect to special schools, such regulations may impose requirements as to the organisation of any special school as a primary school (*) or as a secondary school (*).

(4) The regulations made under this section with respect to special schools shall be such as to secure that, so far as practicable, every pupil in attendance at any such school will attend religious worship and religious instruction (m) or will be withdrawn from attendance (o) at such worship or instruction in accordance with the wishes of his parent (p).

NOTES

This and the next succeeding section, in the words of the Explanatory Memorandum issued with the Bill (Cmd. 6492 of 1943, p. 8), " open the way to fuller and better provision for children handicapped by physical or mental disabilities . . . they replace in general the provisions of Part V of the Education Act, 1921, and with certain other (sections in the Act) modify some of its provisions which have been found to hamper development in the past ".

The two sections extend the duty of ascertainment, previously confined to defective and epileptic children, to all types of children needing special educational treatment. Under section 34, p. 125, *post*, it is the duty of every local education authority to ascertain what children in its area require special educational treatment. By section 114 (1), p. 185, *post*, " special educational treatment " is given the meaning assigned to it by section 8 (2) (*c*), p. 80, *ante*, namely, education in special schools or otherwise, by special methods appropriate for persons suffering from any disability of mind or body. The duty thus imposed upon local education authorities ensures that no child suffering from any disability of mind or body shall go unprovided for, and makes special provision for maladjusted children. See also the Introduction, pp. 28–30, *ante*.

Local education authorities are obliged under subsection (2) of this section to provide special educational treatment for the less severely handicapped children within the ordinary schools and for the more severely handicapped in special schools.

No distinction is made in the limits of compulsory school age between normal children and children requiring special educational treatment (see sections 35 and 36, pp. 127, 128, *post*). Furthermore, the duty of ascertaining what children require special educational treatment is not limited to children of five and over but, by reason of the definition of " child " in section 114 (1), p. 183, *post*, extends to all children not over compulsory school age. For the purpose of fulfilling this duty the parent of any child who has attained the age of two years may be required to submit him for examination by a medical officer of the local education authority for advice as to whether he is suffering from any disability of mind or body (section 34 (1), p. 125, *post*). The parent of any child who has attained the age of two years may also request the local education authority to arrange for the child to be similarly examined (section 34 (2), *ibid.*).

If, after considering the advice of a medical officer as a result of such a medical examination and any reports or other information available to the local education authority, the authority decides that the child requires special educational treatment, notice of the decision must be given to the parent and the authority is required to provide the treatment unless the parent makes suitable arrangements for the child to receive such treatment otherwise than by the authority (section 34 (4), p. 125, *post*).

As to the qualifications of teachers in special schools, see regulations 15 and 16 of the Handicapped Pupils and Special Schools Regulations, 1959, S.I. 1959 No. 365, p. 358, *post*.

The words in square brackets in subsection (2) were substituted for the words " in any school maintained or assisted by a local education authority " by section 17 of and the First Schedule to the Education (Miscellaneous Provisions) Act, 1953. The effect of the last part of subsection (2) as it now stands is that where there is no place available for a child in a special school or his disability is not sufficiently serious to justify his taking up a place in a special school the local education authority may arrange for him to receive special educational treatment either in a school maintained by the education authority themselves or by some other authority or in an independent school. As to contributions between local education authorities where one authority provides education for a child belonging to the area of another authority, see section 6 of the Education (Miscellaneous Provisions) Act 1948, p. 222, *post*.

(*) As to the meaning or statutory definition of " local education authority ", " maintain " " primary education ", " secondary education ", " primary school " and " secondary school " see pp. 67–69, *ante*.

(a) **" Secretary of State "**—See note (b) to s. 1, *ante*.

(b) **" Regulations ".**—See the Handicapped Pupils and Special Schools Regulations, 1959, S.I. 1959 No. 365, as amended by the Handicapped Pupils and Special Schools Amending Regulations 1962, S.I. 1962 No. 2073, p. 356, *post*, the Handicapped Pupils and Special Schools Amending Regulations 1966, S.I. 1966 No. 1576, and the Qualified Teachers and Teachers in Special Schools Regulations 1971, S.I. 1971, No. 342, p. 390, *post*, and the Handicapped Pupils and Special Schools (Size of Classes) Regulations 1973, S.I. 1973 No. 340. See also the regulations made under the Education (Handicapped Children) Act 1970, p. 269, *post*.

(c) **" Pupils ".**—Section 114 (1), p. 185, *post*, defines " pupil ", where used without qualification, as a person of any age for whom education is required to be provided under the Act. In addition to the general duty of providing education for children of compulsory school age (sections 35 and 38, pp. 127 and 131, *post*) the local education authority is required by sections 8 (2) (*b*), p. 80, *ante*, and 9 (4), p. 83, *ante*, to secure that provision is made for pupils between two and five years of age. Though section 8 (2) (*b*), refers to the provision of, nursery schools and nursery classes this is a form of education which is required to be provided under the Act and the regulations must therefore cover children from two years of age upwards.

(d) **" Special educational treatment ".**—Section 114 (1), p. 185, *post*, gives this term the meaning assigned to it by section 8 (2) (*c*), p. 80, *ante*, namely, education by special methods appropriate for persons suffering from any disability of mind or body.

(e) **" Pupils of each category ".**—By Regulation 4 of the Handicapped Pupils and Special Schools Regulations, 1959, S.I. 1959 No. 365, as amended by S.I. 1962 No. 2073, p. 356, *post*, the several categories are defined as blind, partially sighted, deaf, partially hearing, educationally sub-normal, epileptic, maladjusted, physically handicapped pupils, pupils suffering from speech defect and delicate pupils. Boarding homes not maintained by local authorities no longer require the Secretary of State's approval, but a limited number continue to be shown in List 42, cf., Part VII of the 1963 Edition.

(f) **" Special schools ".**—Section 9 (5), p. 83, *ante*, defines " special schools " as schools which are especially organised for the purpose of providing special educational treatment for pupils requiring such treatment and are approved by the Secretary of State for that purpose. Paragraph (*a*) of section 8 (2), p. 80, *ante*, which requires the local education authority, in fulfilling its duties under the section, to have regard to the need for securing that primary and secondary education are provided in separate schools does not apply to special schools (proviso to section 8 (2), p. 80, *ante*), but the regulations which the Secretary of State may make under sub-section (3) of this section may impose requirements as to the organisation of any special school as a primary school or as a secondary school. The existing regulations, the Handicapped Pupils and Special Schools Regulations, 1959, S.I. 1959 No. 365 (see note (*b*), *supra*), do not directly impose any such requirements, but regulation 6 provides that each school shall be organised for the purpose of providing special educational treatment for handicapped pupils of such age, category and sex as the Secretary of State may approve.

(g) **" Appropriate for that category ".**—The Act does not specifically require that special educational treatment for different categories of children shall be given in separate special schools though, before approving any particular school, the Secretary of State will consider whether it should provide for one or more categories, see regulation 6 of the Handicapped Pupils and Special Schools Regulations, 1959, S.I. 1959 No. 365, as amended, p. 357, *post*.

(h) **" In any school maintained by a local authority ".**—If it is not practicable or desirable to provide the special educational treatment in special schools, the arrangements made by the local education authority may provide for the treatment to be given in any school maintained by the authority or by some other local education authority or in an independent school other than one which the Secretary of State has declared to be unsuitable. Where special educational treatment is provided for any child in an ordinary school, regulation 20 of the Schools Regulations, 1959, S.I. No. 364, p. 354, *post*, must be complied with. Where the authority is satisfied that it is expedient in the interests of the child that special educational treatment shall be provided in a non-maintained school they must pay the whole of the tuition fees and, in the case of a boarding school, must, if satisfied that suitable education cannot be provided unless board and lodging are also provided, pay the whole of the boarding fees. See s. 6 of the Education (Miscellaneous Provisions) Act, 1953, *post*. As from 1st January, 1964, such a school has also (subject to exceptions in particular cases) had to be recognised as efficient under Rule 16. See Circular 4/61 (27th March, 1961), p. 461, *post*.

As to the conditions which a non-maintained special school must fulfil in order to be eligible for grant, see the Special Schools and Establishments (Grant) Regulations, 1959, S.I. 1959 No. 366 (as amended by the Special Schools and Establishments (Grant) (Amendment) Regulations 1969, S.I. 1969 No. 410), p. 361, *post*. Provision is made by section 56, p. 148, *post*, for very special cases in which by reason of extraordinary circumstances a child or young person is unable to attend a suitable primary or secondary school, by enabling the local education authority, with the approval of the Secretary of State, to make arrangements for him to receive such education otherwise than at school.

(i) **Any school not so maintained.**—See the last preceding note.

(j) **" Notified . . . to be . . . unsuitable for the purpose ".**—By Circular 4/61 (27th March, 1961), *post*, local education authorities were notified, under this section, that as from 1st January, 1964, the Secretary of State will regard an independent school which is not recognised as efficient under Rules 16 as unsuitable for providing special educational treatment unless, upon receipt of an application from an authority, he decides to make an exception in the case of a particular school either generally or for a particular pupil or category of pupils. Circular 4/61 is set out in full at p. 461, *post*.

(k) **Requirements to be complied with by any school.**—See the Handicapped Pupils and Special Schools Regulations 1959, S.I. 1959 No. 365 (as amended; see note (b), *supra*.).

(l) **" Prescribed ".**—By section 114 (1), p. 185, *post*, this means prescribed by regulations made by the Secretary of State.

(m) " **Separate schools** ".—See note (1) to section 8, p. 81, *ante*.

(n) " **Religious worship and religious instruction** ".—Since, by section 9 (2), p. 82, *ante*, special schools cannot be either county schools or voluntary schools the provisions of the Act relating to religious education in such schools (sections 25–30 inclusive, pp. 115 *et seq.*, *ante*) do not apply. The Secretary of State is, however, empowered to make regulations to secure that, so far as practicable, the pupil and the parent shall have similar opportunities to those available to pupils, and parents of pupils attending county and voluntary schools.

See regulation 8 of the Handicapped Pupils and Special Schools Regulations, 1959, S.I. 1959 No. 365, p. 357, *post*.

The religious freedom of teachers in special schools is safeguarded by regulation 17 of the above-mentioned Regulations.

(o) " **Withdrawn from attendance** ".—See note (n), *supra*, and compare this provision with the provisions applicable to withdrawal contained in section 25 (4), (5) and (7), p. 115, *ante*.

(p) " **In accordance with the wishes of his parent** ".—See the definition of " parent " in section 114 (1), p. 216, *post*. This phrase governs not only withdrawal from attendance at religious worship and instruction but also attendance thereat, so that the authority may be required, if the regulations so state, to make arrangements for the giving of various types of religious instruction. The Cowper-Temple clause, as re-enacted in section 26, p. 117, *ante*, does not apply to special schools established and maintained by a local education authority.

34. Duty of local education authorities to ascertain what children require special educational treatment.—(1) It shall be the duty (a) of every local education authority (*) to ascertain (b) what children (c) in their area require special educational treatment (d) and for the purpose of fulfilling that duty any officer of a local education authority authorised in that behalf (e) by the authority may by notice (f) in writing served upon the parent (*) of any child who has attained the age of two years require him to submit the child for examination (g) by a medical officer of the authority (h) for advice as to whether the child is suffering from any disability of mind or body (i) and as to the nature and extent of any such disability (k) ; and if a parent upon whom such a notice is served fails without reasonable excuse to comply with the requirement thereof he shall be liable on summary conviction (l) to a fine not exceeding [ten] pounds.

(2) If the parent of any child who has attained the age of two years requests the local education authority for the area to cause the child to be so medically examined as aforesaid, the authority shall comply with the request unless in their opinion the request is unreasonable (m).

(3) Before any child is so medically examined as aforesaid, the authority shall cause notice to be given to the parent of the time and place at which the examination will be held, and the parent shall be entitled to be present at the examination if he so desires.

(4) If after considering the advice given with respect to any child by a medical officer in consequence of any such medical examination as aforesaid and any reports or information which the local education authority are able to obtain from teachers or other persons with respect to the ability and aptitude (n) of the child, the authority decide that the child requires special educational treatment, they shall give to the parent notice of their decision and shall provide such treatment for the child [unless the parent makes suitable (o) arrangements for the provision of such treatment for the child otherwise than by the authority].

(5) The advice given with respect to any child by a medical officer in consequence of any such medical examination as aforesaid shall be communicated to the parent of the child and to the local education authority, and the medical officer by whom the examination was made shall if required by the parent or by the authority so to do, issue to the authority and to the parent a certificate in the prescribed form (p) showing whether the child is suffering from any such disability as aforesaid and if so the nature and extent thereof :

Provided that a local education authority shall not require the issue of such a certificate in respect of any child unless the certificate is, in their opinion, necessary for the purpose of securing the attendance of the child at a special school in accordance with the provisions of this Act relating to compulsory attendance (q) at primary (*) and secondary schools (*).

(6) Any certificate issued under the last foregoing subsection may be cancelled (r) by the Secretary of State (s) or by a medical officer of the local education authority and upon the cancellation of such a certificate the local education authority shall [if they are providing] special educational treatment for the child with respect to whom the certificate was issued [shall cease to provide such treatment for the child] and shall notify the parent accordingly.

NOTES

The general note to section 33, p. 123, *ante*, refers not only to the provisions of that section but to this also, and should be read in relation to this section.

The words in square brackets in subsections (4) and (6) were inserted by section 14 of, and Part II of the Second Schedule to, the Education Act, 1946, pp. 214 and 218, *post*, the words in the first set of square brackets in subsection (6) being substituted for the words " cease to provide ". The effect of the amendment of subsection (4) is to give the parent of a handicapped child the alternative of allowing it to receive special educational treatment provided by the local educational authority or of making proper arrangements for the child to receive such treatment in an independent school or from a tutor or governess. The amendments of subsection (6) are consequential only. The amendments, both of subsection (4) and subsection (6) are to be deemed to have been made as from 1st April, 1945.

The fine in subsection (1) is increased to £10 by virtue of the Criminal Justice Act 1967, section 93 and Sch. 3.

(*) As to the meaning or statutory definition of " local education authority ", " parent ", " primary school ", " secondary school ", see pp. 67–69, *ante*.

(a) **" It shall be the duty ".**—As to the enforcement of this and other duties imposed by the section, see section 99, p. 173, *post*. In addition, section 68, p. 155, *post*, enables the Secretary of State to prevent a local education authority from exercising its powers or duties unreasonably.

(b) **" To ascertain ".**—The section does not specify how the local education authority is to comply generally with the duty to ascertain what children in its area require special educational treatment, other than by requiring individual children to be submitted to medical examination. Presumably, however, the authority will as a normal practice obtain school records and reports from teachers and/or inspectors and from medical officers, school nurses, etc., upon children who do not appear to be suitable for instruction by normal educational methods. The section does not, however, only apply to children of school age—see note (c), *infra*. Children who are merely backward should not be " ascertained " under this section. See Circular 2/75.

(c) **" Children ".**—Section 114 (1), p. 183, *post*, defines " child " as a person who is not over compulsory school age, so that the duty of ascertainment under the section applies to children from birth.

(d) **" Special educational treatment ".**—See note (d) to section 33, p. 124, *ante*.

(e) **" Authorised in that behalf ".**—The authorisation may be general or may relate to a specific child.

(f) **" Notice ".**—As to the service of notices, see section 113, p. 182, *post*.

(g) **" Examination ".**—By section 69 (2) p. 156, *post*, the Secretary of State is empowered in certain circumstances to have a pupil examined by a qualified medical practitioner. See now as to medical and dental treatment for pupils, section 3 of the National Health Service Reorganisation Act 1973, p. 310, *post*, and Circular 1/74, *post*.

(h) **" A medical officer of the authority ".**—By section 114 (1), p. 184, *post*, " medical officer " means, in relation to any local education authority, a duly qualified medical practitioner employed or engaged, whether regularly or for the purposes of any particular case, by that authority. As to his qualifications, see the National Health Service (Medical Examinations—Educationally Sub-normal Children) Regulations 1974, S.I. 1974 No. 183.

(i) **" Any disability of mind or body ".**—The duty is imposed on the authority by section 8 (2) (*c*), p. 80, *ante*, to secure that special educational treatment is provided for pupils who suffer from any disability of mind or body.

(k) **" Nature and extent of any such disability ".**—Upon the nature and extent of the disability depends the decision of the authority as to whether the special educational treatment is to be provided in a special school, if practicable, and if so whether in a boarding school, or in any school maintained or assisted by the authority (s. 33 (2), p. 122, *ante*).

(l) **" On summary conviction ".**—See note (b) to s.134, *post*.

(m) **" Unreasonable ".**—If the local education authority considers that the request is unreasonable the parent may refer the matter to the Secretary of State who, under section 68, p. 155, *post*, may require the authority to comply with the request if he thinks fit.

(n) **" Ability and aptitude ".**—Under section 8, p. 79, *ante*, the local education authority is required to secure that there shall be available sufficient schools for providing primary and secondary education to afford for all pupils opportunities for education offering such variety of instruction and training as may be desirable in view of their different ages, abilities and aptitudes, etc., and the parent of every child of compulsory school age is required by section 36, p. 128, *post*, to cause him to receive efficient full-time education suitable to his age, ability, and aptitude, either by regular attendance at school or otherwise. This section imposes additional duties upon the parents of children requiring special educational treatment, in that the treatment is to be provided by the authority (unless the parent makes other suitable arrangements for the child's education) and the authority may require any child of two years or more to receive such treatment. The method of securing that advantage is taken of the special educational treatment provided may be found in sections 37–40 inclusive, pp. 129 *et seq.*, *post*.

(o) " **Suitable** ".—This word is not defined, but it clearly means suitable having regard to the degree of disability from which the child is suffering, the intention being that a handicapped child for whom other arrangements are made shall receive at least as efficient education as though he were receiving special educational treatment provided by the local education authority.

(p) " **Prescribed form** ".—See the Handicapped Pupils (Certificate) Regulations, 1961, S.I. 1961 No. 476, as amended by the Handicapped Pupils' (Certificate) (Amendment) Regulations 1975, S.I. 1975 No. 328, p. 369, *post*. A certificate under the subsection is only given where the parent demands it or the local education authority requires it for the purpose of enforcing attendance at a special school.

(q) " **Compulsory attendance** ".—See sections 35–40 inclusive, *infra*.

(r) " **Cancelled** ".—The manner of cancellation is not specified but it should presumably be in writing.

(s) " **Secretary of State** ".—See note (b) to s. 1, *ante*.

Compulsory Attendance at Primary and Secondary Schools

35. Compulsory school age.—In this Act the expression " compulsory school age " (a) means any age between five years and [sixteen] years, and accordingly a person shall be deemed to be of compulsory school age if he has attained the age of five years (b) and has not attained the age of [sixteen] years and a person shall be deemed to be over compulsory school age as soon as he has attained the age of [sixteen] years (c). . . .

NOTES

The law applying to compulsory attendance at primary and secondary schools is now contained in this and the next five sections, s. 4 (2) of the Education (Miscellaneous Provisions) Act, 1948, p. 220, *post* and ss. 1, 2 of the Children and Young Persons Act, 1969. The number of school leaving dates in the year was reduced from three to two by s. 9 of the Education Act, 1962, p. 246, *post*.

The present section provided for the raising of the school leaving age from fifteen years to sixteen years by Order in Council as soon as the Secretary of State was satisfied that this was practicable. Such an Order in Council was made with effect from 1st September, 1972, viz., the Raising of the School Leaving Age Order 1972, S.I. 1972 No. 444, p. 391, *post*.

The proviso allowing for the raising of the age to sixteen, as originally enacted in the section, has accordingly been omitted.

Notwithstanding the raising of the school leaving age, the minimum age at which it is lawful for a child to be employed remains the age of thirteen years: Children Act 1972, s. 1, p. 306, *post*.

It is the duty of the parent of every child of compulsory school age to cause him to receive efficient full-time education suitable to his age, ability and aptitude either by regular attendance at school or otherwise, though the parent is absolved from this duty by section 4 (2) of the Education (Miscellaneous Provisions) Act, 1948, p. 220, *post*, during any period in which it is not practicable to arrange for the child to become a registered pupil at a school by reason of the preceding provisions of that subsection which enable the proprietors of schools to refuse to admit children as registered pupils during the currency of a school term except in certain specified cases.

Section 80, p. 165, *post*, requires the proprietor of every school (in the case of a county school or voluntary school the managers or governors), to cause to be kept in accordance with regulations made by the Secretary of State a register containing the prescribed particulars of all persons who are pupils at the school. Section 39, p. 132, *post*, requires the parent of every child of compulsory school age who is a registered pupil at a school to cause the child to attend regularly. Where a parent fails to satisfy the local education authority that he is discharging the duty imposed on him by section 36, *infra*, and referred to above, the authority must serve upon him a school attendance order requiring him to send his child to a specified school (section 37, p. 129, *post*). The parent is to be allowed fourteen days in which to select the school to be named in the order and may at any time apply for the order to be revoked because other arrangements have been made for the child to receive the necessary instruction, or for another school to be substituted for the school named in the order (section 37 (4), p. 130, *post*). If the authority is of opinion that the parent's choice of school is unsuitable, the Secretary of State is to determine the matter (section 37 (3), p. 129, *post*).

Penalties are imposed by section 40 (1), p. 134, *post*, for non-compliance with a school attendance order or for failure to send a child regularly to the school at which he is registered and a persistent truant child may be brought directly before the juvenile court as an alternative to, as well as in addition to, bringing the parents before the magistrates' court.

By s. 2 of the Children and Young Persons Act, 1969, local education authorities may bring care proceedings in juvenile courts. If such a court is satisfied that a child or young person is (*inter alia*) of compulsory school age and is not receiving efficient full time education suitable to his age, ability and aptitude, and *also* that he is in need of care or control, the court may make one of various types of order, e.g., a supervision order, a care order, a guardianship order, etc.

For the court to be satisfied, it must be proved that the relevant infant is of compulsory school age and that either:

(i) he is the subject of a school attendance order which has not been complied with; or

(ii) he is a registered pupil at a school which he is not attending regularly; or

(iii) he is a person whom another person habitually wandering from place to place takes with him,

unless it is also proved that he is in fact receiving proper education (*ibid.*, s. 2 (8)).

So long as a school attendance order is in force the inherent jurisdiction of the Chancery Division over wards of court is restricted so that no directions that the child should receive education otherwise than in accordance with the order can be given (*Re Baker* (*Infants*), [1961] 2 All E.R. 250).

(a) **" Compulsory school age ".**—By section 114 (1), p. 183, *post*, " compulsory school age " has the meaning assigned to it by this section.

In addition to the special provision made in section 38, p. 131, *post*, as regards persons who are registered pupils at special schools, this section now has effect subject to the following provisions—

(*a*) By section 8 (3) of the Education Act, 1946, p. 213, *post*, for the purposes of the Act a person required to attend any county college who attains the age of 18 years during a term is to be deemed not to have attained that age, until the end of the term (no county colleges have in fact been established). Sub-sections (1), (2) of section 8 of the Act of 1946 were repealed by section 13, Schedule II, Education Act, 1962, which reduces the number of school leaving dates in the year from three to two. By section 9 of the Act of 1962, if a child reaches the school leaving age in the five months September to January inclusive, he must stay at school until the following Easter holidays; if he reaches it in February to August inclusive, he must stay until the summer holidays in the same year.

(*b*) By section 114 (6), p. 186, *post*, any person who ceases to be of compulsory school age shall not, on any subsequent change in the upper limit of the compulsory school age being made, again become a person of compulsory school age.

The meaning of " compulsory school age " is applied for the purposes of Part I of the Children Act, 1958, by *ibid.*, section 17 (17 Halsbury's Statutes (3rd Edn.) 53); and for the purposes of the Adoption Act, 1958, by *ibid.*, section 57 (1) (17 Halsbury's Statutes (3rd Edn.) 679).

(b) **" If he has attained the age of five years ".**—Though a child does not become of compulsory school age until he attains the age of five years, the local education authority is required, in the course of securing that sufficient schools are available for providing primary and secondary education, to have regard to the need for securing that provision is made for pupils who have not attained the age of five years, in nursery schools or nursery classes (section 8 (2) (*b*), p. 80, *ante*). The lower age limit for which provision is to be made is two years (section 9 (4), p. 83, *ante*). Where a child attains the age of five years during the currency of a school term there is no obligation on the parent to cause him to receive full-time education until the commencement of the next term where it is not practicable for the parent to arrange for him to become a registered pupil at a school before the commencement of that term. See section 4 (2) of the Education (Miscellaneous Provisions) Act, 1948, p. 220, *post*.

(c) **" As soon as he has attained the age of [sixteen] years ".**—As to the attainment of any particular age, see s. 9 of the Education Act, 1962, and the notes thereto. See also note (a), *supra*. As to the provision of further education for persons over compulsory school age, see ss. 41–47 of the present Act, pp. 135 *et seq*.

36. Duty of parents to secure the education of their children.— It shall be the duty (a) of the parent (*) of every child (*) of compulsory school age (*) to cause him to receive efficient full-time education (b) suitable to his age, ability, and aptitude, either by regular attendance (c) at school (d) or otherwise (e).

NOTES

The general note to section 35, p. 127, *ante*, refers to the previous and the present law regarding school attendance.

(*) As to the meaning of " parent ", " child ", and " compulsory school age ", see pp. 67–69, *ante*.

(a) **" Duty ".**—As to the action which is to be taken by the local education authority if it appears that the parent is failing to perform this duty, see section 37, *infra*. The parent is relieved from this duty during any period in which it is not practicable for him to arrange for the child to become a registered pupil at a school owing to the proprietor relying on his right to refuse to admit the child as a registered pupil otherwise than at the commencement of a term; see section 4 (2) of the Education (Miscellaneous Provisions) Act, 1948, p. 220, *post*. The proprietor of a school may not refuse to admit during the currency of a term a child who was prevented from entering the school at the beginning of the term by his own illness or other circumstances beyond his parent's control or by his parent's having been resident at a place whence the school was not accessible with reasonable facility. It seems, therefore, that the most usual, if not the only, period during which a parent will be relieved from the duty to cause the child to receive full-time education as a consequence of the exercise of the right to refuse to admit new registered pupils during the course of the term is the period between the fifth birthday of a child who attains the age of five during a term and the beginning of the next following term.

(b) **" Full-time education ".**—This term is not defined in the Act.

(c) **" By regular attendance ".**—See section 39 (2), p. 132, *post*, and particularly note (a) to that section. The only specific indication as to what may in particular circumstances constitute regular attendance is contained in the proviso to section 39 (3), *ibid.*, which only applies to certain children having no fixed abode.

(d) **" At school ".**—The term " school " is defined in section 114 (1), p. 185, *post*, as an institution for providing primary or secondary education or both primary and secondary education being a school maintained by a local education authority, an independent school, or a school in respect of which grants are made by the Secretary or State to the proprietor of the school; and the expression, where used without qualification, includes any such school or all such schools as the context may require. By reason of his powers and duties under the Act the

Secretary of State is able to ensure that efficient and suitable education is provided at schools maintained by the local education authority and at schools in respect of which he makes grants to the proprietor. As to the grant regulations now in force, see the notes to s. 100, pp. 175, 176, *post*. In the event of the education provided at an independent school being inefficient or unsuitable, having regard to the age and sex of the child, it is the duty of the Secretary of State to take action under section 71, p. 158, *post* (see note (c) to that section). In addition if the local education authority is not satisfied that a child is receiving *efficient* full-time education suitable to his age, ability and aptitude, the authority may serve a notice under section 37 (1), p. 129, *post*. In Administrative Memorandum No. 557 (15th July, 1957), p. 454, *post*, the then Minister emphasized that the introduction of Part III of the Act " neither intensifies nor lessens the responsibility of local education authorities in regard to sections 36 and 37 ".

(e) **" Or otherwise ".**—It is necessary for the local education authority to examine more closely cases where a parent attempts to fulfil his duty before the Act by providing efficient full-time education otherwise than at school—see section 37, p. 129, *post*. The following cases decided under the previous law may still be of value:—

(1) *R.* v. *Walton, etc., Justices, Ex parte Dutton* (1911), 75 J.P. 558 (admissibility of evidence as to the state of child's education);

(2) *Bevan* v. *Shears*, [1911] 2 K.B. 936 (efficiency of education provided);

(3) *R.* v. *West Riding of Yorks. Justices, Ex parte Broadbent*, [1910] 2 K.B. 192 (efficiency of alternative education);

(4) *Osborne* v. *Martin* (1927), 91 J.P. 197 (withdrawal from school for piano lessons).

For a case under the present law see *Baker* v. *Earl* (1960), *Times*, 6th February, (parent disapproved of schools and occupied, but did not educate the children at home). See also Administrative Memorandum No. 557 (15th July, 1957), p. 454, *post*, where it is pointed out that a local education authority should not *ipso facto* conclude that a child is not receiving efficient full-time education suitable for his age and aptitude because he is attending an institution which is not required to submit particulars to the Registrar of Independent Schools.

If by reason of extraordinary circumstances a child or young person is unable to attend a suitable primary or secondary school, the local education authority may, with the approval of the Secretary of State, make special arrangements for him to receive such education otherwise than at school (section 56, *post*).

37. School attendance orders.—(1) If it appears to a local education authority (*) that the parent (*) of any child (*) of compulsory school age (a) in their area is failing to perform the duty imposed on him by the last foregoing section (b), it shall be the duty (c) of the authority to serve upon the parent a notice (d) requiring him, within such time as may be specified in the notice not being less than fourteen days from the service thereof, to satisfy the authority that the child is receiving efficient full-time education (e) suitable to his age, ability, and aptitude either by regular attendance (g) at school (h) or otherwise (i).

(2) If after such a notice has been served upon a parent by a local education authority the parent fails to satisfy the authority in accordance with the requirements of the notice that the child to whom the notice relates is receiving efficient full-time education suitable to his age, ability, and aptitude, then, if in the opinion of the authority it is expedient that he should attend school, the authority shall serve (k) upon the parent an order (l) in the prescribed form (m) (hereinafter referred to as a " school attendance order ") requiring him to cause the child to become a registered pupil (n) at a school named in the order:

[Provided that—

(*a*) no such order shall be served by the authority upon the parent until the expiration of the period of fourteen days beginning with the day next following that on which they have served upon him a written notice of their intention to serve the order stating that if, before the expiration of that period, he selects a school (o) at which he desires the child to become a registered pupil, that school will, unless the Secretary of State (p) otherwise directs (q), be named in the order: and

(*b*) if, before the expiration of that period, the parent selects such a school as aforesaid, that school shall, unless the Secretary of State (p) otherwise directs, be so named.]

(3) If the local education authority are of opinion that the school selected by the parent as the school to be named in a school attendance order is unsuitable to the age, ability or aptitude of the child with respect to whom the order is to be made, or that the attendance of the child at the

school so selected would involve unreasonable expense to the authority, the authority may, after giving to the parent notice of their intention to do so, apply to the Secretary of State (p) for a direction determining what school is to be named in the order.

(4) If at any time while a school attendance order is in force with respect to any child the parent of the child makes application to the local education authority by whom the order was made requesting that another school be substituted for that named in the order, or requesting that the order be revoked on the ground that arrangements have been made for the child to receive efficient full-time education suitable to his age, ability, and aptitude otherwise than at school, the authority shall amend or revoke the order in compliance with the request unless they are of opinion that the proposed change of school is unreasonable or inexpedient in the interests of the child, or that no satisfactory arrangements have been made for the education of the child otherwise than at school, as the case may be; and if a parent is aggrieved by a refusal of the authority to comply with any such request, he may refer the question to the Secretary of State (p) who shall give such direction thereon as he thinks fit.

(5) If any person upon whom a school attendance order is served fails to comply with the requirements of the order he shall be guilty of an offence against this section (r) unless he proves (s) that he is causing the child to receive efficient full-time education suitable to his age, ability, and aptitude otherwise than at school.

(6) If in proceedings against any person for a failure to comply with a school attendance order that person is acquitted, the court may direct that the school attendance order shall cease to be in force, but without prejudice to the duty of the local education authority to take further action under this section (t) if at any time the authority are of opinion that having regard to any change of circumstances it is expedient so to do.

(7) Save as provided by the last foregoing subsection, a school attendance order made with respect to any child shall, subject to any amendment thereof (u) which may be made by the local education authority, continue in force so long as he is of compulsory school age unless revoked by that authority.

NOTES

This section is printed as amended by section 10 of the Education (Miscellaneous Provisions) Act, 1953, *post*, which substituted the proviso to sub-section (2), which is printed in square brackets, for the original proviso which was in the following terms namely: " Provided that before serving such an order upon a parent the authority shall where practicable afford him an opportunity of selecting the school to be named in the order, and, if a school is selected by him that school shall, unless the Minister otherwise directs, be the school named in the order." The object of the substitution is to speed up the procedure for making school attendance orders by setting a time limit of fourteen days to the parent's right of selecting the school to be named in the order.

The notice to be served under sub-paragraph (a) of the new proviso provides a suitable opportunity for reminding the parent of his rights and duties which the Secretary of State desires shall be taken, and in order to assist local education authorities a model form of notice has been prepared.

In connection with the present section, see *Surrey County Council* v. *Ministry of Education*, [1953] 1 All E.R. 705; *Spiers* v. *Warrington Corporation*, [1953] 2 All E.R. 1052; and *Chapman* v. *Essex County Council* (1957), 55 L.G.R. 28; and *Re Baker* (*Infants*), [1961] 3 All E.R. 276, C.A.

For the effect of the Children and Young Persons Act 1969, see notes to s. 35, *ante*.

(*) As to the meaning or statutory definition of " local education authority ", " parent " and " child ", see pp. 67–69, *ante*.

(a) **" Compulsory school age ".**—See sections 35, p. 127, *ante*, and 38, p. 131, *post*, and particularly note (a) to the former section. For the purposes of a prosecution of a parent for an offence against the present section the onus of proof that the child was not of compulsory school age at the material time lies on the parent. See section 9 of the Education (Miscellaneous Provisions) Act, 1948, p. 226, *post*.

(b) **" Duty imposed on him by the last foregoing section ".**—See section 36, p. 128, *ante*, and the notes thereto.

(c) **" It shall be the duty ".**—Under section 68, p. 155, *post*, the Secretary of State may take steps to prevent the unreasonable exercise of this duty.

(d) **" Notice ".**—As to the service of notices, see section 113, p. 182, *post*.

(e) **" Full-time education ".**—This term is nowhere defined in the Act.

(g) " **By regular attendance** ".—See note (c) to section 36, p. 128, *ante*, and note (a) to section 39, p. 133, *post*.

(h) " **At school** ".—See note (d) to section 36, p. 128, *ante*.

(i) " **Or otherwise** ".—See note (e) to section 36, p. 129, *ante*.

(k) " **The authority shall serve** ".—Although the duty envisaged by this sub-section is contingent upon the opinion of the authority, if the Secretary of State considers the circumstances require the service of a school attendance order he may compel the authority accordingly (section 68, p. 155, *post*). As to service, see section 113, as amended by section 14 of and the Second Schedule to the Education Act, 1946, p. 182, *post*.

(l) " **An order** ".—As to the revocation or variation of such an order, see section 111, p. 181, *post*; but see also subsection (4) of this section. If not previously revoked the order will cease to have effect when the child ceases to be of compulsory school age (sub-section (7) of this section).

(m) " **In the prescribed form** ".—By section 114 (1), p. 185, *post*, " prescribed " means prescribed by regulations made by the Secretary of State. See the School Attendance Order Regulations, 1944, S.R. & O. 1944 No. 1470, p. 325, *post*, which prescribe the form of school attendance order.

(n) " **Registered pupil** ".—By section 114 (1), p. 185, *post*, the term means in relation to any school a pupil registered as such in the register kept in accordance with the requirements of the Act. As to the registration of pupils at schools, see section 80, p. 165, *post*, and the Pupils' Registration Regulations, 1956, S.I. 1956 No. 339, p. 389, *post*.

(o) **Selects a school.**—The parent's right of selection is in accordance with the general principle laid down in section 76, p. 162, *post*, that pupils are to be educated in accordance with the wishes of their parents, but it is to be noted that under that section the exercise of the parent's choice is contingent on its being compatible with the provision of efficient education and avoidance of undue expenditure, and the acceptance of the parent's choice under the present section is subject to the same two conditions.
Schools No. 1, p. 500, *post*.

(p) " **Secretary of State** ".—See note (b) to s. 1, *ante*.

(q) " **Otherwise directs** ".—As to the revocation or variation of such a direction, see section 111, p. 181, *post*. If a choice of schools is " practicable " but for any reason the authority thinks the parent's choice should not be accepted, the authority should refer the matter to the Secretary of State for his direction (sub-section (3) of this section). As to directions by the Secretary of State under sub-sections (3) and (4) of this section regarding the attendance of children at a special school, see section 38 (3), *infra*.

(r) " **An offence against this section** ".—As to proceedings and penalties in respect of such an offence, see section 40, p. 134, *post*. Proceedings under the present section can only be instituted by the local education authority by whom the school attendance order was made

(s) " **Unless he proves** ".—It would appear that, if the school attendance order was duly made and served, it is no defence to prove that the child is receiving efficient full-time education at some school other than that named in the order. The child will be presumed to be of compulsory school age at the material time unless the parent proves the contrary. See section 9 of the Education (Miscellaneous Provisions) Act, 1948, p. 226, *post*.

(t) " **Further action under this section** ".—It would appear from this sub-section that, even though the opinion of the authority may differ from the decision of the court, a direction under this sub-section absolves the authority from the duty to take any further action unless there is a change of circumstances.

(u) " **Subject to any amendment thereof** ".—An amendment of a school attendance order may become necessary not only as a result of a request made by the parent under sub-section (4), but because, for example, the child reaches an age at which it becomes necessary to transfer him to another school, or because of reorganisation or the establishment of a new school

38. Additional provisions as to compulsory attendance at special schools.—[(1) *While the upper limit of the compulsory school age* (*) *is, in relation to other children* (a), *less than sixteen, a person who is a registered pupil* (*) *at a special school* (*) *shall nevertheless be deemed to be of compulsory school age until he attains the age of sixteen* (b) *and shall not be deemed to be over compulsory school age until he has attained that age.*]

(2) A child who has under arrangements made by a local education authority (*) become a registered pupil at a special school shall not be withdrawn from the school without the consent of that authority (c); but if the parent (*) of any such child is aggrieved by a refusal of the authority to comply with an application made by the parent requesting such consent, he may refer the question to the Secretary of State (d) who shall give such direction (e) thereon as he thinks fit.

(3) No direction given by the Secretary of State (d) under the last foregoing subsection or under subsection (3) or subsection (4) of the last foregoing section shall be such as to require a pupil (*) to be a registered pupil at a special school unless either the parent consents (f) to his attending such a school or there is in force a certificate (g) issued by a medical officer (h) of the

local education authority showing that the child is suffering from some disability of mind or body of such a nature and extent that, in the opinion of the Secretary of State (d), it is expedient that the child should attend a special school (i).

NOTES

The provisions of the Act relating to compulsory school attendance are discussed in the general note to section **35**, p. 127, *ante*, and the education of pupils requiring special educational treatment in the general note to section 33, p. 123, *ante*.

By section 2 of the Education Act, 1964, p. 252, *post*, regulations may be made to empower local education authorities to grant maintenance allowances in respect of persons who (*a*) being registered pupils at special schools, are deemed by virtue of section 38 (1), *supra*, to be of compulsory school age, but (*b*) apart from the subsection, *supra*, would be over compulsory school age. See the Regulations for Scholarships and Other Benefits, 1945, reg. 2 (*g*), as inserted by the Scholarships and Other Benefits Amending Regulations, 1964, at p. 328, *post*.

(*) As to the meaning or statutory definition of " compulsory school age ", " registered pupil ", " special school ", " local education authority ", " parent " and " pupil ", see pp. 67–69, *ante*.

(a) **" Other children ".**—By section 114 (1), p. 183, *post*, " child " means a person who is not over compulsory school age so that the phrase " other children " means here " children of compulsory school age who are not registered pupils at special schools ".

(b) **" Attains the age of sixteen years ".**—The compulsory school-leaving age is now sixteen: see section 35, *ante*. Subsection (1) of this section was repealed by the Education (School-Leaving Dates) Act 1976.

(c) **" Without the consent of that authority ".**—It should be noted that this section does not authorise a local education authority to allow a pupil who is " handicapped " to leave a special school before he reaches sixteen. It contemplates cases where (*a*) the parent wants to change the special school, or (*b*) contends that his child is no longer handicapped. See Administrative Memorandum No. 163 (6th June, 1946).

(d) **" Secretary of State ".**—See note (b) to s. 1, *ante*.

(e) **" Direction ".**—As to the revocation or variation of such a direction, see section **111** p. 181, *post*.

(f) **" Unless . . . the parent consents ".**—No form or method of consent is specified by the section but it is, for obvious reasons, desirable that any such consents should be in writing.

(g) **" A certificate ".**—See section 34 (5), p. 123, *ante*.

(h) **" A medical officer ".**—See note (h) to section 34, p. 126, *ante*.

(i) **" The child should attend a special school ".**—See section 33 (1), p. 122, *ante*, and the regulations made by the Secretary of State under sub-section (1) of that section.

39. Duty of parents to secure regular attendance of registered pupils.—(1) If any child (*) of compulsory school age (*) who is a registered pupil (*) at a school (*) fails to attend regularly (a) thereat the parent (*) of the child shall be guilty of an offence against this section (b).

(2) In any proceedings for an offence against this section in respect of a child who is not a boarder (c) at the school at which he is a registered pupil, the child shall not be deemed to have failed (d) to attend regularly at the school by reason of his absence therefrom with leave (e) or—

(*a*) at any time when he was prevented from attending by reason of sickness or any unavoidable cause (f) ;

(*b*) on any day exclusively set apart for religious observance (g) by the religious body to which his parent belongs ;

(*c*) if the parent proves that the school at which the child is a registered pupil is not within walking distance of the child's home, and that no suitable arrangements (h) have been made by the local education authority for his transport (i) to and from the school or for boarding accommodation (k) for him at or near the school or for enabling him to become a registered pupil at a school nearer to his home.

(3) Where in any proceedings for an offence against this section it is proved that the child has no fixed abode, paragraph (*c*) of the last foregoing subsection shall not apply, but if the parent proves that he is engaged in any trade or business of such a nature as to require him to travel from place to place and that the child has attended at a school at which he was a registered pupil as regularly as the nature of the trade or business of the parent permits, the parent shall be acquitted :

Provided that, in the case of a child who has attained the age of six years the parent shall not be entitled to be acquitted under this subsection unless he proves that the child has made at least two hundred attendances during the period of twelve months ending with the date on which the proceedings were instituted.

(4) In any proceedings for an offence against this section in respect of a child who is a boarder at the school at which he is a registered pupil, the child shall be deemed to have failed to attend regularly at the school if he is absent therefrom without leave during any part of the school term at a time when he was not prevented from being present by reason of sickness or any unavoidable cause.

(5) In this section the expression " leave " in relation to any school means leave granted by any person authorised in that behalf by the managers, governors of proprietor (l) of the school, and the expression " walking distance " means, in relation to a child who has not attained the age of eight years two miles, and in the case of any other child three miles, measured by the nearest available route (m).

NOTES

As to compulsory school attendance generally, see the general note to section 35, p. 127, *ante*.

(*) As to the meaning or statutory definition of " child ", " compulsory school age ", " registered pupil ", " school " and " parent ", see pp. 67–69, *ante*.

(a) **" Fails to attend regularly ".**—The question as to what constitutes regular attendance is, subject to the excuses mentioned in sub-section (2) of this section, one of fact for the justices to decide, though in the case of certain children a qualification is introduced by sub-section (3) of this section. In *Hinchley* v. *Rankin*, [1961] 1 All E.R. 692 it was held that the regular attendance required by the present section is regular attendance for the times prescribed by the local education authority charged with the duty of providing education, and that there may be failure to attend regularly where the child frequently arrives after the attendance register is closed.

The meaning of " attend regularly " is applied by the Children and Young Persons Act 1969, s. 2 (8) (*b*) (ii), 40 Halsbury's Statutes (3rd Edn.) 852.

A child who is sent to school dressed in such a way that it is known that the head teacher will, as a matter of discipline, refuse him admission, fails to attend school regularly, see *Spiers* v. *Warrington Corporation*, [1953] 2 All E.R. 1052; [1954] 1 Q.B. 61 (girl dressed in trousers).

An additional defence to those enumerated in this section is given by section 54, p. 145, *post*, in certain circumstances to pupils who have been excluded from school under that section.

(b) **" An offence against this section ".**—As to proceedings and penalties in respect of such an offence, see section 40, *infra*.

(c) **" A boarder ".**—As to the duty of securing the provision of boarding accommodation, see sections 8 (2) (*d*), p. 80, *ante*, and 50, p. 142, *post*. A child for whom boarding accommodation is provided under section 50, is presumably not a boarder under this sub-section.

(d) **" Shall not be deemed to have failed ".**—The defences open to the parent are limited to those specified in paragraphs (*a*) to (*c*) of the present section. The reasonableness or otherwise of the parent's conduct is irrelevant.

(e) **" With leave ".**—As to the meaning of " leave ", see sub-section (5) of this section.

(f) **" Unavoidable cause ".**—This means a cause affecting the child (*Jenkins* v. *Howells*, [1949] 1 All E.R. 942; [1949] 2 K.B. 218).

(g) **" Exclusively set apart for religious observance ".**—In *Marshall* v. *Graham*, [1907] 2 K.B. 112, a Divisional Court held that Ascension Day is a day so set apart by the Church of England. The Schools Council of the Church of England Board of Education in their handbook for foundation managers and governors, trustees and head teachers of Church of England controlled schools state, that it is only on an Ascension Day, if an occasional holiday is not given by the managers, that children should stay away all day.

(h) **" Suitable arrangements ".**—See *Surrey County Council* v. *Ministry of Education*, [1953] 1 All E.R. 705.

(i) **" Transport ".**—As to the provision of transport and other facilities by a local education authority, see section 55, p. 147, *post*.

(k) **" Boarding accommodation ".**—See note (c), *supra*.

(l) **" Managers, governors or proprietor ".**—As to the meaning of " managers " and " governors ", see note (b) to section 17, p. 101, *ante*. " Proprietor ", in relation to a school, is defined in section 114 (1), p. 185, *post*.

(m) **" Nearest available route ".**—Distance not safety is the test for ascertaining the nearest available route. If there is a route along which children can walk and which is not more than the stipulated length it is within walking distance even if the parents think it is unsafe for unescorted children (*Shaxted* v. *Ward*, [1954] 1 All E.R. 336. If the route were flooded that might be a reasonable excuse for not using it on a particular day (*ibid*.).

It seems that the route need not be along a road of any particular class (*Hares* v. *Curtin*, [1913] 2 K.B. 328 (cart track); *Shaxted* v. *Ward*, *supra*).

40. Enforcement of school attendance.—(1) Subject to the provisions of this section, any person guilty of an offence against section thirty-seven or section thirty-nine of this Act (a) shall be liable on summary conviction (b), in the case of a first offence against that section to a fine not exceeding [ten pounds], in the case of a second offence against that section to a fine not exceeding [twenty pounds], and in the case of a third or subsequent offence against that section to a fine not exceeding [twenty pounds] or to imprisonment for a term not exceeding one month or to both such fine and such imprisonment.

[(2) Proceedings for such offences as aforesaid shall not be instituted except by a local education authority; and before instituting such proceedings the authority shall consider whether it would be appropriate, instead of or as well as instituting the proceedings, to bring the child in question before a juvenile court under section 1 of the Children and Young Persons Act 1969 (c).

(3) The court by which a person is convicted of an offence against section 37 (d) of this Act or before which a person is charged with an offence against section 39 (e) of this Act may if it thinks fit direct the authority who instituted the proceedings to bring the child to whom the proceedings relate before a juvenile court under the said section 1; and it shall be the duty of the authority to comply with the direction.

(4) Where a child in respect of whom a school attendance order is in force is brought before a juvenile court by a local education authority under the said section 1 and the court finds that the condition set out in subsection (2) (*e*) of that section (f) is not satisfied with respect to him, the court may direct that the order shall cease to be in force.]

NOTES

Subsections (2)–(4) of this section were substituted by the Children and Young Persons Act 1969, Sch. 5, para. 13, as to which, see Circular 19/70, *post*. The fines were increased, as shown in square brackets, by the Criminal Justice Act 1967.

(a) **" Offence against section thirty-seven or section thirty-nine of this Act ".**—Section 37, p. 129, *ante*, relates to school attendance orders, and section 39, p. 132, *ante*, to the duty of parents to secure the regular attendance at school of registered pupils.

An attempt to enforce a school attendance order otherwise than under the present section failed in *Re Baker* (*Infants*), [1961] 2 All E.R. 250.

(b) **" On summary conviction ".**—See now the Magistrates' Courts Act, 1952; 21 Halsbury's Statutes (3rd Edn.) 181, as to summary trial, and see section 104, thereof; 21 Halsbury's Statutes (3rd Edn.) 273. For the jurisdiction of justices acting for petty sessional divisions in the County of London to hear proceedings under section 37, p. 129, *ante*, and section 39, p. 132, *ante*.

(c) **S. 1 of the Children and Young Persons Act, 1969.**—This section provides that any local authority, constable or authorised person who reasonably believes that there are grounds for making an order under the section in respect of a child or young person may bring him before a juvenile court. If the court is then of opinion that (*inter alia*) the child or young person is of compulsory school age and is not receiving full-time education suitable to his age, ability and aptitude, and also that he is in need of care and control, then it may make one of various types of order, e.g., an order requiring parental control, a supervision order, a care order, etc. As to a school attendance order which has not been complied with, see s. 2 (8) of the Act of 1969.

(d) **S. 37 of this Act.**—This section empowers a local education authority to serve school attendance orders. See p. 129, *ante*.

(e) **S. 39 of this Act.**—This section imposes a duty upon parents to secure regular attendance of registered pupils. See p. 132, *ante*.

(f) **Sub-s. 2 (e) of section 1.**—This is the sub-section which deals with the child or young person of compulsory school age not receiving proper education; see note (c), *supra*.

40A. [*Repealed.*]

NOTE

This section, which dealt with the school attendance of vagrant children, was repealed by the Children and Young Persons Act, 1969, Sch. 6. Under s. 2 (8) (*b*) (iii) of the latter Act, care proceedings in a juvenile court can now be taken by a local education authority where it is proved that a child of compulsory school age is a person whom another person habitually wandering from place to place takes with him and who is not receiving education. See Circular 19/70, *post*.

FURTHER EDUCATION

41. General duties of local education authorities with respect to further education.—Subject as hereinafter provided (a), it shall be the duty of every local education authority (*) to secure the provision for their area of adequate facilities (b) for further education (c), that is to say :—

(*a*) full-time and part-time education (d) for persons over compulsory school age (*) ; and

(*b*) leisure-time occupation, in such organized cultural training and recreative activities as are suited to their requirements, for any persons over compulsory school age who are able and willing to profit by the facilities provided for that purpose :

Provided that the provisions of this section shall not empower or require local education authorities to secure the provision of facilities for further education otherwise than in accordance with schemes of further education or at county colleges (*).

NOTES

(*) As to the meaning or statutory definition of " local education authority ", " compulsory school age " and " county college ", see pp. 67–69, *ante*.

(a) **" Subject as hereinafter provided ".**—This refers, in the first place, to the proviso to this section, and secondly to varying dates on which different provisions relating to further education came into operation. This section, with section 42, p. 136, *post*, and section 43 (other than subsection (1), p. 136, *post*), came into operation on 1st April, 1945. In the case of this section, however, April 1, 1945, was no more than a theoretically operative date, since the proviso limits the duty imposed by it to facilities secured in accordance with schemes of further education (under section 42, p. 136, *post*) or at county colleges (under section 43, p. 136, *post*), and neither of those sections automatically came into operation on that date. In the case of section 42 the duty to prepare and submit schemes of further education did not arise until 19th March, 1947, when by Circular No. 133, the then Minister issued a direction, that schemes be submitted by 31st March, 1948. After a scheme has been approved the Secretary of State may from time to time direct the local education authority to take measures for giving effect to it.

The general duty imposed by this section is subject to the more specific duties imposed or which may be imposed under the following sections with regard to the preparation and submission of schemes and plans and as to the provision of facilities for further education and the establishment of county colleges.

Power to enforce the execution of the local education authority's functions with respect to further education is given to the Secretary of State by section 99, p. 173, *post*.

(b) **" Adequate facilities ".**—Except as regards county colleges (section 43, p. 136, *post*), the section does not stipulate that the adequate facilities here referred to shall be provided by the local education authority, but that the authority must secure the provision of facilities. This may take several forms, *e.g.*, the stimulation of private efforts, the provision of assistance (as defined in section 114 (1) and (2), pp. 183 and 185, *post*), the maintenance of schools, colleges, and other institutions not established by the authority, and the grant of scholarships, etc., under section 81, p. 166, *post*, as well as the establishment and maintenance of schools, colleges and institutions by the local education authority. In fact by far the greater burden of liberal adult education is shouldered by " responsible bodies " (see the Report issued in 1954 of the committee under the chairmanship of Dr. Eric Ashby on the Organisation and Finance of Adult Education). Provision for the payment by the Secretary of State of grants to any organisation in respect of expenditure incurred by them in the provision of recreation and leisure-time activities is made by the Further Education Regulations 1975, S.I. 1975 No. 1054, p. 411, *post*.

By section 53, p. 144, *post*, every local education authority must secure that the facilities for further education provided for its area include adequate facilities for recreation and social and physical training.

There is no definition of " adequate facilities " in the Act but it seems that a wide meaning is intended to be attributed thereto, cf., the statement in Circular No. 302 (3rd May, 1956) that " under their general powers for the provision of facilities for further education, local education authorities may also provide milk for drinking to students under the age of 18 attending grant-aided, full-time courses of further education. " The duty to secure the provision of " adequate facilities " may be enforced by the Secretary of State under section 99, p. 173, *post*, if necessary by *mandamus*, so that the Secretary of State is in a position to determine whether or not the duty has been fulfilled.

(c) **" Further education ".**—By section 114 (1), p. 183, *post*, the term has the meaning assigned to it by this section so that reference is necessary for a definition to paragraphs (*a*) and (*b*) hereof. The definition is wide enough to include not only the advanced education of normal persons but also the training of the disabled. See regulations 7 and 8 of the Special Schools and Establishments (Grant) Regulations, 1959, S.I. 1959 No. 366, p. 362, *post*.

(d) **" Full-time and part-time education ".**—" Full-time " education is not defined in the Act. Part-time education presumably means anything less than full-time.

42. Schemes of further education.—(1) Every local education authority (*) shall, at such times and in such form as the Secretary of State (a) may direct (b), prepare and submit to the Secretary of State schemes of further education (c) for their area, giving particulars of the provision which the authority propose to make for fulfilling such of their duties with respect to further education, other than duties with respect to county colleges (d), as may be specified in the direction.

(2) Where a scheme of further education has been submitted to the Secretary of State (a) by a local education authority, the Secretary of State (a) may, after making in the scheme such modifications if any as after consultation with the authority he thinks expedient, approve (e) the scheme, and thereupon it shall be the duty of the local education authority to take such measures as the Secretary of State (a) may from time to time, after consultation with the authority, direct for the purpose of giving effect to the scheme.

(3) A scheme of further education approved by the Secretary of State (a) in accordance with the provisions of this section may be modified supplemented or replaced by a further scheme prepared submitted and approved in accordance with those provisions, and the Secretary of State (a) may give directions revoking any scheme of further education, or any provision contained in such a scheme, as from such dates as may be specified in the directions, but without prejudice to the preparation submission and approval of further schemes.

(4) A local education authority shall, when preparing any scheme of further education, have regard to any facilities for further education provided for their area by universities, educational associations, and other bodies, and shall consult (f) any such bodies as aforesaid and the local education authorities for adjacent areas; and the scheme, as approved by the Secretary of State (a) may include such provisions as to the co-operation of any such bodies or authorities as may have been agreed between them and the authority by whom the scheme was submitted.

NOTES

As to the continued operation and restatement of schemes under this section in force immediately before 1st April 1965, and relating to areas in Greater London, see section 31 (1) (*c*), (4) of the London Government Act, 1963, pp. 291, *post*.

(*) As to the statutory definition of " local education authority ", see p. 68, *ante*.

(a) **" Secretary of State ".**—See note (b) to s. 1, *ante*.

(b) **" May direct ".**—By Circular No. 133 (19th March, 1947), local education authorities were directed to prepare schemes of further education and to submit them not later than 31st March, 1948, unless, having regard to the special difficulties of individual authorities, the Minister (as he then was) should approve submission of their schemes at a later date.

(c) **" Schemes of further education ".**—By section 114 (1), p. 183, *post*, " further education " has the definition given to it by section 41, p. 135, *ante* (see paragraphs (*a*) and (*b*) thereof). As to the revocation, modification, supplementation or replacement of a scheme of further education, see sub-section (3) of this section. See, as to provisions for the government of institutions providing full-time further education under this section, s. 1 (1) of the Education (No. 2) Act, 1968.

(d) **" County colleges ".**—See sections 43, *infra*, and 44–46, p. 136 *et seq.*, *post*.

(e) **" Approve ".**—In the case of schemes submitted under this section, the duty to carry them out is imposed, in theory at any rate, immediately approval is given by the Secretary of State, but in the case of development plans submitted under section 11, p. 85, *ante*, by local education orders made by the Secretary of State under section 12, p. 88, *ante*. The reasons for these differences of procedure are not apparent. As to the enforcement of the duty, see sections 99 (1), p. 173, *post*.

(f) **" Consult ".**—In Circular No. 133, it was suggested that the necessary consultations could most conveniently be carried out through the Regional Councils for further education where these exist.

43. County colleges.—(1) *On and after such date as His Majesty may by Order in Council determine, not later than three years after the date of the commencement of this Part of this Act*, it shall be the duty of every local education authority to establish and maintain county colleges, that is to say, centres, approved by the Secretary of State for providing for young persons who are not in full-time attendance at any school or other educational institution such further education, including physical, practical and vocational training, as will enable them to develop their various aptitudes and capacities and will prepare them for the responsibilities of citizenship.

(2) As soon after the date of the commencement of this Part of this Act as the Secretary of State considers it practicable so to do, he shall direct (k) every local education authority to estimate the immediate and prospective needs of their area with respect to county colleges having regard to the provisions of this Act, and to prepare and submit to him within such time and in such form as may be specified in the direction a plan (l) showing the provision which the authority propose to make for such colleges for their area, and the plan shall contain such particulars as to the colleges proposed to be established as may be specified in the direction.

(3) The Secretary of State shall, after considering the plan submitted by a local education authority and after consultation with them, make an order for the area of the authority specifying the county colleges which it is the duty of the authority to maintain, and the order shall require the authority to make such provision for boarding accommodation (n) at county colleges as the Secretary of State considers to be expedient: the order so made for any area shall continue to regulate the duties of the local education authority in respect of the matters therein mentioned and shall be amended by the Secretary of State, after consultation with the authority, whenever, in his opinion, the amendment thereof is expedient by reason of any change or proposed change of circumstances.

(4) The Secretary of State may make regulations as to the maintenance government and conduct of county colleges and as to the further education to be given therein.

NOTES

This section, together with sections 41, 42 and 44–46, pp. 135 and 136, *ante*, and 137 *et seq.*, *post*, is discussed in the general note to section 41. The words in italics at the beginning of this section were repealed by the Statute Law Revision Act 1950; 32 Halsbury's Statutes (3rd Edn.) 695. The repeal was consequent on the words being spent, April 1, 1947, having been determined by the County Colleges Order, 1947, S.R. & O. 1947 No. 527, to be the day on which the duty to establish and maintain county colleges arose, though this duty is not yet enforced since no orders have been made under sub-section (3) of this section. There is in fact little likelihood of any such orders being made. See the Introduction, p. 48, *ante*.

44. Duty to attend county colleges in accordance with college attendance notices.—(1) This section shall come into operation (a) on such date as soon as practicable after the date determined by Order in Council under the last foregoing section as the Secretary of State (b) may by order direct.

(2) It shall be the duty of the local education authority (*) to serve upon every young person residing in their area who is not exempt from compulsory attendance for further education a notice (hereinafter referred to as a " college attendance notice ") directing him to attend at a county college, and it shall be the duty of every young person upon whom such a notice is served to attend at the county college named in the notice in accordance with the requirements specified therein.

(3) Subject to the provisions of the next following subsection, the requirements specified in a college attendance notice shall be such as to secure the attendance of the person upon whom it is served at a county college—

(*a*) for one whole day, or two half-days, in each of forty-four weeks in every year while he remains a young person ; or

(*b*) where the authority are satisfied that continuous attendance would be more suitable in the case of that young person, for one continuous period of eight weeks, or two continuous periods of four weeks each, in every such year ;

and in this section the expression " year " means, in relation to any young person, in the case of the first year the period of twelve months beginning with the first day on which he is required by a college attendance notice served on him to attend a county college, and in the case of every subsequent year the period of twelve months beginning immediately after the expiration of the last preceding year :

Provided that in respect of the year in which the young person attains the age of eighteen the requirements specified in the notice shall be reduced to such extent as the local education authority think expedient for securing that the attendances required of him until he attains that age shall be as nearly as may be proportionate to those which would have been required of him during a full period of twelve months.

(4) If, by reason of the nature of the employment of any young person or of other circumstances affecting him, the local education authority are satisfied that attendance in accordance with the provisions of the last foregoing subsection would not be suitable in his case, a college attendance notice may, with the consent of the young person (n), require his attendance in accordance with such other arrangements as may be specified in the notice may, with the consent of the young person, require his attendance ance with such arrangements as aforesaid shall be such as to secure the attendance of the young person for periods amounting in the aggregate to three hundred and thirty hours in each year, or in the case of the year in which he attains the age of eighteen, to the proportionately reduced number of hours.

(5) Except where continuous attendance is required, no college attendance notice shall require a young person to attend a county college on a Sunday or on any day or part of a day exclusively set apart for religious observance by the religious body to which he belongs, or during any holiday or half-holiday to which by any enactment regulating his employment or by agreement he is entitled, or, so far as practicable, during any holiday or half-holiday which is allowed in accordance with any custom of his employment, or between the hours of six in the evening and half past eight in the morning:

Provided that the Secretary of State may, on the application of any local education authority, direct that in relation to young persons in their area or in any part thereof employed at night or otherwise employed at abnormal times this subsection shall have effect as if for the reference to the hours of six in the evening and half past eight in the morning there were substituted a reference to such other times as may be specified in the direction.

(6) The place, days, times, and periods, of attendance required of a young person, and the period for which the notice is to be in force, shall be specified in any college attendance notice served on him ; and the requirements of any such notice in force in the case of a young person may be amended as occasion may require either by the authority by whom it was served on him or by any other local education authority in whose area he may for the time being reside, so, however, that the provisions of every such notice shall be such as to secure that the requirements imposed on the young person during each year while he remains a young person shall comply with the provisions of the last three foregoing subsections.

(7) In determining what requirements shall be imposed upon a young person by a college attendance notice or by any amendments to such a notice, the local education authority shall have regard, so far as practicable, to any preference which he, and in the case of a young person under the age of sixteen years his parent, may express, to the circumstances of his employment or prospective employment, and to any representations that may be made to the authority by his employer or any person proposing to employ him.

(8) The following persons shall be exempt from compulsory attendance for further education, that is to say—

(*a*) any person who is in full time attendance at any school or other educational institution (not being a county college);

(*b*) any person who is shown to the satisfaction of the local education authority to be receiving suitable and efficient instruction either full time or for such times as in the opinion of the authority are equivalent to not less than three hundred and thirty hours instruction in a period of twelve months;

(*c*) any person who having been exempt under either of the last two foregoing paragraphs did not cease to be so exempt until after he had attained the age of seventeen years and eight months;

(*d*) any person who is undergoing a course of training for the mercantile marine or the sea fishing industry approved by the Secretary of State or who, having completed such a course, is engaged in the mercantile marine or in the said industry;

(*e*) any person to whom, by reason of section one hundred and fifteen or section one hundred and sixteen of this Act, the duties of local education authorities do not relate;

(*f*) any person who attained the age of fifteen years before the date on which this section comes into operation, not being a person who immediately before that date was required to attend a continuation school under the provisions of the Education Act, 1921.

If any person is aggrieved by a decision of a local education authority given under paragraph (*b*) of this subsection, he may refer the question to the Secretary of State, who shall give such direction thereon as he thinks fit.

(9) If any young person upon whom a college attendance notice has been served fails to comply with any requirement of the notice, he shall be guilty of an offence against this section (y) unless he proves (z) either—

(*a*) that he was at the material time exempt from compulsory attendance for further education; or

(*b*) that he was prevented from complying with the requirement by reason of sickness or any unavoidable cause; or

(*c*) that the requirement does not comply with the provisions of this section.

NOTES

This section, together with sections 41–43, pp. 135, 136, *ante*, and 45–46, pp. 139 *et seq.*, *post*, is discussed in the general note to section 41. There is little likelihood of any orders being made to establish county colleges.

45. Administrative provisions for securing attendance at county colleges.—(1) For the purpose of facilitating the execution by local education authorities of their functions under the last foregoing section, the following provisions shall, on and after the date on which that section comes into operation, have effect, that is to say:—

(*a*) every young person who is not exempt from compulsory attendance for further education shall at all times keep the local education authority in whose area he resides informed of his proper address;

(*b*) any person by whom such a young person as aforesaid is employed otherwise than by way of casual employment shall notify the local education authority for the area in which the young person resides when the young person enters his employment and again when he ceases to be employed by him, and shall also notify the authority of any change of address of the employer, and, if known to him, of the young person, which occurs during the continuance of the employment;

and any person who fails to perform any duty imposed on him by the foregoing provisions of this section shall be guilty of an offence against this section.

(2) The local education authority by whom a college attendance notice is served upon any young person shall serve a copy thereof upon any person who notifies the authority that the young person is employed by him.

(3) The Secretary of State may by regulations make provision as to the form of college attendance notices, as to consultation and the exchange of information between different local education authorities, as to the issue of certificates of exemption in respect of young persons who are exempt from compulsory attendance for further eudcation, and generally for the purpose of facilitating the administration by local authorities of the provisions of this Part of this Act as to attendance at county colleges.

(4) The Secretary of State and the Minister of Labour shall issue instructions to local education authorities and to local offices of the Ministry of Labour respectively for ensuring due consultation and exchange of information between such authorities and offices.

(5) Any certificate of exemption in the prescribed form (l) purporting to be authenticated in the prescribed manner shall be received in evidence in any legal proceeding, and shall unless the contrary is proved, be sufficient evidence of the fact therein stated.

NOTE

This section, together with sections 41–44, pp. 135, 136, *ante*, and 46, *infra*, is discussed in the general note to section 41. It is now unlikely that county colleges will be established.

46. Enforcement of attendance at county colleges.—(1) Any person guilty of an offence against either of the last two foregoing sections shall be liable on summary conviction, in the case of a first offence against that section to a fine not exceeding one pound, in the case of a second offence against that section to a fine not exceeding five pounds, and in the case of a third or subsequent offence against that section to a fine not exceeding ten pounds or to imprisonment for a term not exceeding one month or to both such fine and such imprisonment.

(2) It shall be the duty of the local education authority in whose area the young person in question resides to institute proceedings for such offences as aforesaid wherever, in their opinion, the institution of such proceedings is expedient, and no such proceedings shall be instituted except by or on behalf of a local education authority.

(3) If, in furnishing any information for the purposes of either of the last two foregoing sections, any person makes any statement which he knows to be false in any material particular, or recklessly makes any statement which is false in any material particular, he shall be liable on summary conviction to a fine not exceeding twenty pounds or to imprisonment for a term not exceeding three months or to both such fine and such imprisonment.

(4) Without prejudice to the provisions of any enactment or rule of law relating to the aiding and abetting of offences, if the parent of a young person or any person by whom a young person is employed or the servant or agent of any such person has conduced to or connived at any offence committed by the young person against either of the last two foregoing sections, the person who has conduced to or connived at the offence shall,

whether or not any person is proceeded against or convicted in respect of the offence conduced to or connived at, be guilty of the like offence and punishable accordingly.

NOTE

This section, together with sections 41–45, pp. 135 *et seq.*, *ante*, is discussed in the general note to section 41. It is now unlikely that county colleges will be established. See Introduction, p. 48, *ante*.

47. Interim provisions as to further education.—[*Spent.*]

NOTE

See generally, as to further education, the Introduction, pp. 48–54, *ante*.

SUPPLEMENTARY PROVISIONS AS TO PRIMARY, SECONDARY AND FURTHER EDUCATION

Ancillary Services

48. Medical inspection and treatment of pupils.—(1)–(3) [*Repealed.*]

(4) It shall be the duty of every local education authority to make arrangements for encouraging and assisting pupils (a) to take advantage of [the provision for medical and dental inspection and treatment made for them in pursuance of section 3(1), or 3(2)(*a*)(i) of the National Health Service Reorganisation Act 1973 (b)]:

Provided that if the parent of any pupil gives to the authority notice (c) that he objects to the pupil availing himself of [the provision so made (b)] the pupil shall not be encouraged or assisted so to do.

(5) [*Repealed.*]

NOTES

Subsections (1)–(3), (5) were repealed by the National Health Service Reorganisation Act 1973, s. 57, Sch. 5.

The section as originally enacted imposed upon local education authorities the duty of providing for the medical and dental treatment of all children and young persons attending maintained schools and county colleges and of taking such steps as might be necessary to ensure that those found to be in need of medical treatment, other than domiciliary treatment, received it free of cost.

In addition, power was given to provide for the medical and dental inspection and medical treatment of senior pupils in attendance at any other educational establishment maintained by the local education authority.

See now section 3 of the National Health Service Reorganisation Act 1973, p. 310, *post*, and Circular 1/74, *post*.

(a) **" Arrangements for encouraging and assisting pupils ".**—Though the local education authority may require the submission of a pupil for medical and dental inspection, and has a duty to see that facilities for free medical and dental treatment are available, it is still no part of the national policy to require that a pupil shall take advantage of any free treatment offered in preference to any other treatment which the parent or the pupil may desire.

(b) The words in square brackets were substituted by the National Health Service Reorganisation Act 1973, section 57, Sch. 4.

(c) **" Notice ".**—As to the service of notices, see section 113, p. 182, *post*.

49. Provision of milk and meals.—Regulations (a) made by the Secretary of State (b) shall impose upon local education authorities (*) the duty of providing (c) milk (d) meals (e) and other refreshment for pupils (*) in attendance at schools (f) and county colleges (*) maintained (*) by them; and such regulations shall make provision as to the manner in which and the persons by whom the expense of providing such milk, meals or refreshment is to be defrayed, as to the facilities to be afforded (including any buildings or equipment to be provided) and as to the services to be rendered by managers, governors (*) and teachers (g) with respect to the provision of such milk, meals or refreshment, and as to such other consequential matters as the Secretary of State (b) considers expedient, so, however, that such regulations shall not impose upon teachers at any school or college duties upon days on which the school or college is not open for instruction, or duties in respect of meals (h) other than the supervision of pupils, and shall not require the managers of governors of a voluntary school (*) to incur expenditure.

NOTES

No imperative duty to provide school meals was imposed on local education authorities until regulations were made in 1945 pursuant to the present section. Those, and various amending regulations, were revoked and consolidated in the Provision of Milk and Meals Regulations 1969. These regulations have been amended from time to time. See the regulations, S.I. 1969 No. 483, as amended, at p. 383, *post*.

The present requirement is that on every school day one third of a pint of milk must be provided free for (*a*) every pupil in every special school; (*b*) every pupil in every primary school until the end of the summer term ending next after the date on which he attains the age of seven; (*c*) every other pupil in a primary school, and every junior pupil in an all-age school or a middle school, where his health requires it (as certified by medical certificate). There also may be provided milk for other pupils provided that they or their parents pay for it (Education (Milk) Act 1971, p. 272, *post*; Provision of Milk and Meals Regulations 1969, reg. 10, as amended, p. 384, *post.*).

Local education authorities no longer have power to require teachers to supervise pupils during school meals, but must make suitable arrangements for the supervision and social training of pupils during meals (regulation 9). In practice, many teachers still do supervision duties.

(*) As to the meaning or statutory definition of " local education authority ", " pupil ", " county college ", " maintained ", " managers or governors " and " voluntary school ", see pp. 67–69, *ante*.

(a) **" Regulations ".**—See the Provision of Milk and Meals Regulations, 1969, S.I. 1969 No. 483 (as amended by the Provision of Milk and Meals (Amendment) Regulations, 1970, S.I. 1970 No. 339, the Provision of Milk and Meals (Amendment No. 2) Regulations, 1970, S.I. 1970 No. 511, the Provision of Milk and Meals (Amendment No. 3) Regulations 1970, S.I. 1970 No. 1417, the Provision of Milk and Meals (Amendment) Regulations 1971, S.I. 1971 No. 169, the Provision of Milk and Meals (Amendment No. 2) 1971, S.I. 1971 No. 1368, the Provision of Milk and Meals (Amendment) Regulations 1972, S.I. 1972 No. 1098, the Provision of Milk and Meals (Amendment) Regulations 1973, S.I. 1973 No. 271, the Provision of Milk and Meals (Amendment No. 2) Regulations 1973, S.I. 1973 No. 1299, the Provision of Milk and Meals (Amendment) Regulations 1974, S.I. 1974 No. 1125, and the Provision of Milk and Meals (Amendment) Regulations 1975 No. 311), p. 383, *post*.

(b) **" Secretary of State ".**—See note (b) to s. 1, *ante*.

(c) **" The duty of providing ".**—As to the enforcement of this duty, see section 99, *post*.

(d) **" Milk ".**—By Regulation 4 (4) of the Provision of Milk and Meals Regulations 1969, as amended, *supra*, the source and quality of milk supplied for drinking is to be approved by the Medical Officer of Health for the area of the authority after such consultations as in the said regulation mentioned and by regulation 4 (5), where suitable liquid milk is not available the authority may provide full-cream dried milk prepared for drinking or milk tablets.

(e) **" Meals ".**—Regulation 5 of the Provision of Milk and Meals Regulations 1969 (*supra*) provides that on every school day there *shall* be provided, and on any other day there *may* be provided, a midday dinner for every pupil, suitable in all respects as the main meal of the day. Other meals and refreshment may be provided as the authority think appropriate.

Regulation 10 (3) provides that a charge (at present 15p) may be made for every mid-day meal provided in a county or voluntary school, and an " appropriate "'charge for any meal in a special school. The charge may be remitted in the case of any parent who satisfies the authority that he is unable to pay it without hardship. For this latter purpose a means test, according to size of family and not weekly income, is provided (see Schedule 1 to the Regulations of 1969).

Schedule 2 to the Regulations revoked all relevant regulations made prior to 1969.

(f) **" Schools ".**—By section 114 (1), p. 185, *post*, the term as here qualified means institutions for providing primary or secondary education or both primary and secondary education, being schools maintained by a local education authority. As regards schools not maintained by the authority, section 78 (2), p. 164, *post*, empowers the local education authority, with the consent of the proprietors of the schools, and upon such financial and other terms, if any, as may be agreed, to make similar arrangements to those contemplated by this section for the pupils in attendance at such schools, subject, however, to a proviso that, so far as practicable, the cost to the authority shall not exceed the cost of making similar provision for pupils at schools maintained by the authority.

(g) **" Teachers ".**—Local education authorities no longer have power to require teachers to supervise pupils during school meals. See general note, *supra*.

(h) **" Duties in respect of meals ".**—The collection of money for school meals is a duty in respect of meals other than the supervision of pupils and, therefore, cannot be imposed on teachers, and a resolution of the local education authority requiring teachers to collect such money is, accordingly, void (*Price* v. *Sunderland Corporation*, [1956] 3 All E.R. 153). See also *Gorse* v. *Durham County Council*, [1971] 2 All E.R. 666 (whether refusal to serve meals amounted to repudiation of contract of service).

50. Provision of board and lodging otherwise than at boarding schools or colleges.—(1) Where the local education authority (*) are satisfied with respect to any [pupil] (*) that primary (*) or secondary education (*) suitable to his age, ability and aptitude (a) can best be provided by them for him at any particular county school (*), voluntary school (*), or special school (b), or are satisfied with respect to any young person (*) that further education (*) should in his case be provided by requiring his continuous attendance (c) at a county college (*), but that such education cannot be so provided unless boarding accommodation (d) is provided for him otherwise than at the school or college, [and where the authority are satisfied with respect to a pupil requiring special educational treatment (*) that provision for him of board and lodging is necessary for enabling him to receive the required special educational treatment (e)] the authority may provide such board and lodging for him under such arrangements as they think fit.

(2) In making any arrangements under this section for any [pupil] or young person, a local education authority shall, so far as practicable, give effect to the wishes of the parent (*) of the [pupil] or to the wishes of the young person, as the case may be, with respect to the religious denomination of the person with whom he will reside.

NOTES

The word " pupil ", wherever it occurs, was substituted for the word " child " by section 14 of and Part I of the Second Schedule to the Education Act, 1946, pp. 214 and 218, *post*. The effect of the amendment is to enable the local authority to provide board and lodging for children who are still attending county, voluntary or special schools, although they are over compulsory school age.

The other words in square brackets were inserted by section 11 (1) of and Part I of the First Schedule to the Education (Miscellaneous Provisions) Act, 1948, p. 227, *post*, and make it clear that board and lodging may be provided for handicapped children receiving special educational treatment otherwise than in special schools.

The section not only enables a local educational authority to make special arrangements for the boarding of individual pupils but also to set up hostels for children of special classes, such as the children of canal boatmen.

As to the continuance of certain grants made before 1st April, 1965, under this section, see section 33 of the London Government Act, 1963, p. 294, *post*.

(*) As to the meaning or statutory definition of " local education authority ", " pupil ", " primary education ", " secondary education ", " county school ", " voluntary school ", " young person ", " further education ", " county college ", " special educational treatment " and " parent ", see pp. 67–69, *ante*.

(a) **" Suitable to his age, ability and aptitude ".**—See note (k) to section 8, p. 81, *ante*.

(b) **" Special school ".**—See sections 9 (5), p. 83, *ante*, and 33, p. 122, *ante*.

(c) **" Continuous attendance ".**—As to the circumstances in which and the extent to which continuous attendance may be required, see section 44 (3), p. 137, *ante*.

(d) **" Boarding accommodation ".**—As to the recovery of the cost of providing such board and lodging, see section 52, *infra*. The general duty of securing the provision of boarding accommodation in relation to primary and secondary schools, whether in boarding schools or otherwise, is imposed by section 8 (2) (*d*), p. 80, *ante*, whilst section 11 (2) (*f*), p. 86, *ante*, required the local education authority to give particulars in the development plan for the area of the arrangements made and proposed to be made by the authority for the provision of boarding schools, though not of other boarding accommodation contemplated by this section.

(e) **" Special educational treatment ".**—As to the requirements to be observed by local authorities in respect of board and lodging provided by them for handicapped pupils otherwise than at boarding special schools, see the Handicapped Pupils (Boarding) Regulations, 1959, S.I. 1959 No. 362, as amended, p. 348, *post*.

51. Provision of clothing at schools maintained by local educational authorities.—[*Repealed.*]

NOTE

This section was repealed by section 11 (2) of and the Second Schedule to the Education (Miscellaneous Provisions) Act, 1948. Power to provide clothing is now conferred on local education authorities by section 5 of the 1948 Act, p. 221, *post*.

52. Recovery of cost of boarding accommodation and of clothing.

—(1) Where a local education authority (*) have, under the powers conferred by the foregoing provisions of this Act (a), provided a pupil (*) with board and lodging (b) otherwise than at a boarding school or college, *or with clothing* (c), the authority shall require (d) the parent (*) to pay to the authority in respect thereof such sums, if any, as in the opinion of the authority he is able without financial hardship to pay:

Provided that—

(*a*) where the board and lodging provided for the pupil were so provided under arrangements made by the local education authority on the ground that in their opinion education suitable to his age ability and aptitude (e) could not otherwise be provided by the authority for him, no sum shall be recoverable in respect thereof under this section; and

(*b*) where the board and lodging have been so provided for a pupil in attendance at a county college (*), the authority, if satisfied that the pupil is in a financial position to pay the whole or any part of a sum recoverable from the parent under this section, may recover that sum or that part thereof from the pupil instead of from the parent.

(2) The sums recoverable under this section shall not exceed the cost to the local education authority of providing the board and lodging, ***or the cost of the clothing provided, as the case may be*** (f).

(3) Any sums payable by virtue of this section may be recovered summarily as a civil debt (g).

NOTES

(*) As to the meaning or statutory definition of "local education authority", "pupil". "parent" and "county college", see pp. 67–69, *ante*.

(a) **"The foregoing provisions of this Act".**—See section 50, p. 166, *ante*.

(b) **"Board and lodging".**—See note (d) to section 142, *supra*.

(c) **"Or with clothing".**—These words and the words printed in italics in subsection (2) were repealed by the Education (Miscellaneous Provisions) Act, 1948, section 11 (2) and Second Schedule. As to recovery by local education authorities of the cost of clothing provided by them, see now section 5 of the 1948 Act, p. 221, *post*.

(d) **"Shall require".**—Where, as here, the performance by the local education authority of a duty is made contingent upon the opinion of the authority, section 68, p. 155, *post*, enables the Secretary of State to give such directions as he thinks expedient to prevent the unreasonable exercise of the duty.

(e) **"Suitable to his age ability and aptitude".**—See note (k) to section 8, p. 81, *ante*. This provision means that wherever it is necessary for a pupil to be provided with boarding accommodation otherwise than at a school or college because suitable education cannot otherwise be provided, *e.g.* within a reasonable distance of his home, no fees may be charged for board and lodging. Section 61 (2), p. 150, *post*, contains a similar provision with regard to the remission of fees for board and lodging provided at boarding schools or colleges; see also section 6 (2) (*b*) of the Education (Miscellaneous Provisions) Act, 1953, p. 231, *post*, as to the duty of the local education authority to pay the fees for board and lodging for certain pupils for whom they provide primary or secondary education in non-maintained schools in cases where suitable education cannot be provided at any school unless board and lodging are also provided.

(f) **"Or the cost of the clothing provided, as the case may be".**—See note (c), *supra*.

(g) **"May be recovered summarily as a civil debt".**—By section 50 of the Magistrates Courts Act, 1952; 21 Halsbury's Statutes (3rd Edn.) 227; any sum (subject to certain exceptions) the payment of which may be ordered by a magistrates' court is recoverable summarily as a civil debt. For restrictions on committal for non-payment see *ibid.*, section 73; 21 Halsbury's Statutes (3rd Edn.) 246.

53. Provision of facilities for recreation and social and physical training.—(1) It shall be the duty (a) of every local education authority (*) to secure that the facilities for primary (*) secondary (*) and further education (*) provided for their area include adequate facilities for recreation and social and physical training, and for that purpose a local education authority, with the approval of the Secretary of State (b), may establish maintain (c) and manage, or assist (d) the establishment, maintenance, and management of camps (e), holiday classes, playing fields, play centres, and other places (including playgrounds, gymnasiums, and swimming baths not appropriated to any school or college), at which facilities for recreation and for such training as aforesaid are [available for persons receiving primary secondary or further education] (f), and may organise games expeditions and other activities for such persons, and may defray or contribute towards the expenses thereof (g).

(2) A local education authority, in making arrangements for the provision of facilities or the organisation of activities under the powers conferred on them by the last foregoing subsection shall, in particular, have regard to the expediency of cooperating with any voluntary societies or bodies whose objects include the provision of facilities or the organisation of activities of a similar character.

(3) [*Repealed* (h).]

(4) [*Repealed* (i).]

NOTES

(*) As to the meaning or statutory definition of " local education authority ", " primary education ", " secondary education " and " further education ", see p. 67–69, *ante*.

(a) **" It shall be the duty ".**—As to the enforcement of this duty, see section 99, *post*.

(b) **" Secretary of State ".**—See note (b) to s. 1, *ante*. In Circular 350 (24th March, 1959) the then Minister gave general approval to the exercise by local education authorities of the powers conferred on them by sub-s. (1) of this section in relation to the provision of and assistance in the provision of facilities for recreation and social and physical training.

(c) **" Maintain ".**—By section 114 (1), p. 184, *post*, this expression, in relation to any school or county college, is given the meaning assigned to it by subsection (2) of that section. By the same section, " premises ", in relation to a school, includes any detached playing fields, but it is not clear how far some of the matters referred to are part of or are related to a school or county college and in relation to such matters the application of the definition of " maintain " may be of some doubt.

(d) **" Assist ".**—By section 114 (1), p. 183, *post*, this expression, like " maintain " (see note (c), *supra*), in relation to any school, college or institution, also has the meaning assigned to it by subsection (2) of that section and the remarks in that note are equally applicable.

(e) **" Camps ".**—All functions of the Minister of Health under the Camps Act, 1939, were by the Camps Act, 1945 (11 Halsbury's Statutes (3rd Edn.) 406) transferred to the Secretary of State.

In his report for the years 1958 and 1959 the Chief Medical Officer of the Ministry of Education (now the Department of Education and Science) pointed out that under the present section local education authorities have power to contribute towards the cost of sending handicapped boys and girls to the various camps catering for them which are now run by certain voluntary societies.

(f) **" Persons receiving primary secondary or further education ".**—The words in square brackets were substituted by section 11 (1) of and Part I of the First Schedule to the Education (Miscellaneous Provisions) Act, 1948, *post*, for the much narrower words " available for persons for whom primary secondary or further education is provided by the authority ", the effect of the amendment being to enable a local education authority to provide the facilities mentioned in the section for persons receiving education whether or not this education is provided by the authority.

(g) **" Expenses ".**—The reasonable expenses (including travelling expenses) of individual children attending camps, expeditions or other activities organised under the present section may, with the Secretary of State's approval, be paid by the local education authority; see Circular 26 (March 13, 1945).

(h) **Sub-section (3).**—This subsection, which related to the provision of clothing for physical training, was repealed by section 11 (2) of and the Second Schedule to the Education (Miscellaneous Provisions) Act, 1948, *post*. All the powers of a local education authority as to the provision of clothing are now contained in section 5 of the 1948 Act, p. 221, *post*.

(i) **Sub-section (4).**—This subsection, which provided that sections 1 and 2 of the Physical Training and Recreation Act, 1937 (which related to National Advisory Councils and local committees and sub-committees for the promotion of physical training) and so much of section 3 thereof as related to the grants committee should cease to have effect, was repealed by the Statute Law Revision Act 1950; 32 Halsbury's Statutes (3rd Edn.) 695. These provisions of the Physical Training and Recreation Act, 1937, were also repealed, except so far as they extended to Scotland, by section 121, *post*, and Part I of the Ninth Schedule, *post*, so that subsection (3) of this section was always redundant.

Those provisions of the Physical Training and Recreation Act, 1937, which empower local euthorities in general to provide facilities for recreative physical training remain in force. The power of the Secretary of State to make capital grants to local authorities under the Act has been removed by section 1 of and Part I of the First Schedule to the Local Government Act, 1958; 19 Halsbury's Statutes (3rd Edn.) 771.

54. Power to ensure cleanliness.—(1) A local education authority (*) may, by directions in writing (a) issued with respect to all schools maintained by them (b) or with respect to any of such schools named in the directions, authorise a medical officer of the authority (c) to cause examinations of the persons and clothing (d) of pupils (e) in attendance at such schools to be made whenever in his opinion such examinations are necessary in the interests of cleanliness; and if a medical officer of a local education authority has reasonable cause to suspect (f) that the person or clothing of a pupil in attendance at any county college (*) is infested with vermin or in a foul condition, he may cause an examination thereof to be made.

(2) Any such examination as aforesaid shall be made by a person authorised by the local education authority to make such examinations, and if the person or clothing of any pupil is found upon such an examination to be infested with vermin or in a foul condition, any officer of the authority may serve upon the parent (*) of the pupil, or in the case of a pupil in attendance at a county college upon the pupil, a notice (g) requiring him to cause the person and clothing of the pupil to be cleansed.

(3) A notice served under the last foregoing subsection shall inform the person upon whom it is served that unless within the period limited by the notice, not being less than twenty-four hours after the service thereof, the person and clothing of the pupil to whom the notice relates are cleansed to the satisfaction of such person as may be specified in the notice the cleansing thereof will be carried out under arrangements made by the local education authority; and if, upon a report being made to him by that person at the expiration of that period, a medical officer of the authority is not satisfied that the person and clothing of the pupil have been properly cleansed, the medical officer may issue an order (h) directing that the person and clothing of the pupil be cleansed under such arrangements.

(4) It shall be the duty (i) of the local education authority to make arrangements for securing that any person or clothing required under this section to be cleansed may be cleansed (whether at the request of a parent or pupil or in pursuance of an order issued under this section) at suitable premises by suitable persons and with suitable appliances; and where the council of any county district (k) in the area of the authority are entitled to the use of any premises or appliances for cleansing the person or clothing of persons infested with vermin, the authority may require the council to permit the authority to use those premises or appliances for such purposes upon such terms as may be determined by agreement between the authority and the council or, in default of such agreement, by the Minister of Health.

(5) Where an order has been issued by a medical officer under this section directing that the person and clothing of a pupil be cleansed under arrangements made by a local education authority, the order shall be sufficient to authorise any officer of the authority to cause the person and clothing of the pupil named in the order to be cleansed in accordance with arrangements made under the last foregoing subsection, and for that purpose to convey him to, and detain him at, any premises provided in accordance with such arrangements.

(6) If, after the cleansing of the person or clothing of any pupil has been carried out under this section, his person or clothing is again found to be infested with vermin or in a foul condition at any time while he is in attendance at a school maintained by a local education authority or at a county college, and it is proved that the condition of his person or clothing is due to neglect on the part of his parent (l), or in the case of a pupil in attendance at a county college to his own neglect, the parent or the pupil, as the case may be, shall be liable on summary conviction (m) to a fine not exceeding [one pound].

(7) Where a medical officer of a local education authority suspects that the person or clothing of any pupil in attendance at a school maintained by the authority or at any county college is infested with vermin or in a foul condition, but action for the examination or cleansing thereof cannot immediately be taken, he may, if he considers it necessary so to do either in the interest of the pupil or of other pupils in attendance at the school or college, direct (n) that the pupil be excluded from the school or college until such action has been taken; and such a direction shall be a defence to any proceedings under this Act in respect of the failure of the pupil to attend school (o) or to comply with the requirements of a college attendance notice, as the case may be, on any day on which he is excluded in pursuance of the direction, unless it is proved that the issue of the direction was necessitated by the wilful default of the pupil or his parent.

(8) No girl shall be examined or cleansed under the powers conferred by this section except by a duly qualified medical practitioner or by a woman authorised for that purpose by a local education authority.

NOTES

(*) As to the meaning or statutory definition of "local education authority", "county college" and "parent", see pp. 67–69, *ante*.

(a) **" Directions in writing ".**—As to the variation or revocation of such directions, see section 111, p. 181, *post*.

(b) **" All schools maintained by them ".**—As here qualified, " schools " means, by section 114 (1), p. 185 *post*, institutions for providing primary or secondary education or both primary and secondary education, being schools maintained by the local education authority. The expression " maintain " is, by section 114 (1), given the meaning assigned to it by sub-section (2) of that section.

(c) **" A medical officer of the authority ".**—By section 114 (1), p. 184, *post*, " medical officer " means, in relation to any local education authority, a duly qualified medical practitioner employed or engaged, whether regularly or for the purposes of any particular case, by that authority.

(d) **" Clothing ".**—By section 114 (1), p. 183, *post*, clothing includes boots and other footwear.

(e) **" Pupils ".**—Where used without qualification, this word means persons of any age for whom education is required to be provided under the Act (section 114 (1), p. 185, *post*). Here the word refers to a pupil at a school maintained by the authority. See note (b), *supra*.

(f) **" Reasonable cause to suspect ".**—Where a medical officer of an authority suspects that a pupil or his clothing is infested with vermin or in a foul condition but an examination cannot immediately be made, the pupil may be excluded from school or college under subsection (7) of this section.

(g) **" Notice ".**—As to the service of notices, see section 113, p. 182, *post*.

(h) **" Order ".**—It is questionable whether the order here referred to is an order of a local education authority so as to render applicable the provisions of section 111, p. 181, *post*, as to the variation or revocation thereof.

(i) **" It shall be the duty ".**—As to the enforcement of this duty, see section 99, p. 173, *post*.

(k) **" County district ".**—This provision, which applies only in the case of the local education authority for a county, enables the authority to require the use of the premises of the council of a non-county borough or an urban or a rural district within the county. By section 32 (7) of the London Government Act, 1963, the present subsection, in its application to the Inner London Education Authority, is to have effect as if for the words " the council of any county district in the area of the authority " there were substituted the words " the council of any inner London borough or the Common Council of the City of London ".

Generally, as to the reorganisation of local government areas in England and Wales, see the Local Government Act 1972, Parts I and II (42 Halsbury's Statutes (3rd Edn.) 853 *et seq*.

(l) **" Neglect on the part of his parent ".**—If the condition of the child is due to the neglect of the mother she can be convicted even though living with the father (*Plunkett* v. *Alker*, [1954] 1 All E.R. 396.

(m) **" On summary conviction ".**—See note (b) to section 40, p. 134, *ante*.

(n) **" Direct ".**—See note (a), *supra*.

(o) **" Failure of the pupil to attend school ".**—See sections 39 and 40, pp. 132–134, *ante*.

55. Provision of transport and other facilities.—(1) A local education authority (*) shall make such arrangements (a) for the provision of transport and otherwise (b) as they consider necessary or as the Secretary of State (c) may direct (d) for the purpose of facilitating the attendance of pupils (e) at schools (*) or county colleges (*) or at any course or class provided in pursuance of a scheme of further education (f) in force for their area, and any transport provided in pursuance of such arrangements shall be provided free of charge.

(2) A local education authority [may pay the whole or any part, as the authority think fit, of the reasonable travelling expenses] of any pupil in attendance at any school or county college or at any such course or class as aforesaid for whose transport no arrangements are made under this section (g).

NOTES

The Department of Education and Science issued in 1973 a Working Party Report on School Transport, suggesting radical changes in the law. Up to the time of going to press no action had been taken, and is now unlikely because of the increased costs involved.

The words in square brackets were substituted by section 11 (1) of and Part I of the First Schedule to the Education (Miscellaneous Provisions) Act, 1948, p. 227, *post*, for words which while empowering the local education authority to pay reasonable travelling expenses did not expressly authorise the payment of a part only of such expenses.

Section 12 of the Education (Miscellaneous Provisions) Act, 1953, p. 235, *post*, empowers local education authorities to fill any vacant places in motor-vehicles provided for the free transport of pupils under subsection (1) of this section by taking up other pupils and charging them a reasonable fare.

(*) As to the meaning or statutory definition of " local education authority ", " school " and " county college ", see pp. 67–69, *ante*.

(a) **" Shall make such arrangements ".**—The duty imposed by this section is imposed in somewhat different terms from those generally adopted in other sections of the Act, and it appears that the duty may be enforced by directions of the Secretary of State issued under the section and, in suitable circumstances by the issue of directions under section 68, p. 155, *post.*

(b) **" And otherwise ".**—These words presumably enable the local education authority to provide not only the actual means of conveyance but also guides and other persons to take care of the pupils on their journey. As to the obligation of the authority to provide for the safety of pupils for whom transport is provided, see *Shrimpton* v. *Hertfordshire County Council* (1911), 75 J.P. 201.

(c) **" Secretary of State ".**—See note (b) to s. 1, *ante.*

(d) **" May direct ".**—See note (a), *supra.* As to the variation or revocation of such directions, see section 111, p. 181, *post.*

(e) **" Pupils ".**—Subject to the qualifications here used, section 114 (1), p. 185, *post,* provides that pupils mean persons of any age for whom education is required to be provided under the Act.

(f) **" Scheme of further education ".**—See section 42, p. 136, *ante.*

(g) **Subsection (2).**—Arrangements under the subsection must be " suitable " within the meaning of section 39 (2) (*c*), p. 132, *ante,* and if a child lives more than three miles from his school must provide for his transport for the full distance (*Surrey County Council* v. *Ministry of Education,* [1953] 1 All E.R. 705.

56. Power to provide primary and secondary education otherwise than at school.—If a local education authority (*) are satisfied that by reason of any extraordinary circumstances (a) a child (*) or young person (*) is unable to attend a suitable school (*) for the purpose of receiving primary (*) or secondary education (*), [they shall have power with the approval of the Secretary of State (b) to make special arrangements for him to receive education otherwise than at school being primary or secondary education, as the case may require, or, if the authority are satisfied that it is impracticable for him to receive full-time education and the Secretary of State (b) approves, education similar in other respects but less than full-time.]

NOTES

This section permits the local education authority in special cases to make arrangements for a child or young person to receive either primary or secondary education otherwise than at school.

The words in square brackets at the end of the section were substituted by section 11 (1) of and Part I of the First Schedule to the Education (Miscellaneous Provisions) Act, 1948, p. 227, *post,* for words which conferred power to provide full-time education but not part-time education otherwise than at school. In general education otherwise than at school is only provided under this section for handicapped pupils, and even in the case of such pupils there must be some " extraordinary circumstances " why they cannot attend an ordinary or special school, since the normal place for the education of a handicapped child is in a school.

(*) As to the meaning or statutory definition of " local education authority ", " child," " young person ", " school ", " primary education " and " secondary education ", see pp. 67–69, *ante.*

(a) **" By reason of any extraordinary circumstances ".**—Examples of " extraordinary circumstances " in the case of handicapped children are given in para. 15 of Manual of Guidance, Special Services No. 1. In the case of children who are not suffering from any disability of mind or body it is difficult to see what would amount to extraordinary circumstances within the meaning of the section. Mere distance from a suitable school would presumably not be sufficient, since such a case would be adequately covered by section 50, *ante.*

(b) **" Secretary of State ".**—See note (b) to s. 1, *ante.* In Circular 350 (24th March, 1959) the then Minister announced his intention that local education authorities should be free to make arrangements under this section at their discretion. They must seek his approval of new arrangements but may assume that it will be forthcoming.

57, 57A, 57B.—[*Repealed*].

NOTE

Sections 57, 57A, and 57B (which dealt with medical examination and classification of children unsuitable for education) were repealed by the Education (Handicapped Children) Act 1970. See p. 269, *post.*

Employment of Children and Young Persons

58. Adaptation of enactments relating to the employment of children or young persons.—For the purposes of any enactment (a) relating to the prohibition or regulation of the employment of children (*) or young persons (*), any person who is not for the purposes of this Act over compulsory school age (*) shall be deemed to be a child within the meaning of that enactment (b).

NOTES

This and section 60, *infra*, relate to the employment of children and young persons.

The purpose of the present section is to effect the necessary modifications of the various enactments relating to the employment of children which are necessitated by the raising of the school leaving age to sixteen years under section 35, p. 127, *ante*. Some of these Acts prohibit the employment of children under fourteen years of age and, in view of the raising of the school leaving age, it was obviously essential to take steps to avoid leaving in operation any enactments which permitted the whole-time employment of children below the statutory school leaving age.

(*) As to the meaning or statutory definition of " child ", " young person " and " compulsory school age ", see pp. 67–69, *ante*.

(a) **" For the purposes of any enactment ".**—The enactments here referred to include Part II (sections 18 to 30 inclusive) of the Children and Young Persons Act, 1933 (17 Halsbury's Statutes (3rd Edn.) 448–60) as amended by the Employment of Children Act 1973, p. 308, *post*; the Young Persons (Employment) Act, 1938 (17 Halsbury's Statutes (3rd Edn.) 526); Part II of the Children and Young Persons Act 1963; and the Employment of Children Act 1973 itself.

(b) **" Child within the meaning of that enactment ".**—The definition in, for example, the Children and Young Persons Act, 1933, section 107; 17 Halsbury's Statutes (3rd Edn.) 575 of the term " child " as " a person under the age of fourteen years " must now be read subject to the provisions of this section.

59. [*Repealed.*]

NOTE

This section, which empowered local authorities to prohibit or restrict the employment of children, was repealed by the Employment of Children Act 1973, section 3 (3), as from a date to be appointed.

60. Effect of college attendance notices on computation of working hours.—(1) Where a young person is employed in any employment with respect to which a limitation upon the number of working hours during which he may be employed in that employment otherwise than by way of overtime in any week is imposed by or under any enactment, any period of attendance at a county college required of him during that week by a college attendance notice served on him shall, for the purposes of the limitation, be deemed to be time during which he has been so employed in that week.

(2) Where a young person employed in any employment is entitled by or under the provisions of any enactment or of any agreement to overtime rates of pay in respect of any time during which he is employed in that employment on any day or in any week in excess of any specified number of hours or before or after any specified hour, any period of attendance at a county college required of him during that week or on that day by a college attendance notice served on him shall, for the purposes of those provisions, be deemed to be a period during which he was employed in that employment otherwise than in excess of the specified number of hours, or otherwise than before or after the specified hour, as the case may be.

NOTE

This section cannot take effect until the Secretary of State directs that section 44, p. 137, *ante*, is to come into operation (see subsection (1) of that section). It is now unlikely that county colleges will be established; see the Introduction, p. 48, *ante*.

Miscellaneous Provisions

61. Prohibition of fees in schools maintained by local education authorities and in county colleges.—(1) No fees shall be charged (a) in respect of admission to any school (*) maintained (*) by a local education authority (*), or to any county college (*), or in respect of the education provided in any such school or college.

(2) Subject as hereinafter provided (b), where any pupil (*) in attendance at any such school or college is provided at the school or college with board and lodging (c) at the expense of the local education authority, fees shall be payable (d) in respect of the board and lodging not exceeding such amounts as may be determined in accordance with scales approved by the Secretary of State (e):

Provided that—

(*a*) where the board and lodging provided for the pupil is so provided under arrangements made by the local education authority on the ground that, in their opinion, education suitable to his age ability and aptitude (f) cannot otherwise be provided by the authority for him, the authority shall remit (g) the whole of the fees payable under this subsection ; and

(*b*) where the local education authority are satisfied that payment of the full fees payable under this subsection would involve financial hardship to the person liable to pay them, the authority shall remit such part of the fees as they consider ought to be remitted in order to avoid such hardship, or if, in the opinion of the authority, such hardship cannot otherwise be avoided, shall remit the whole of the fees.

(3) Any sums payable under the last foregoing subsection in respect of a pupil shall be payable by his parent (*), so, however, that where the local education authority are satisfied in the case of any young person (*) in attendance at a county college that his financial circumstances are such that the sums so payable in respect of the board and lodging provided for him ought to be defrayed by him, those sums shall be payable by him instead (h) of by his parent; and any sums so payable shall be recoverable summarily as a civil debt (i).

NOTES

Subsection (1) of this section applies to primary (including nursery), secondary and special schools maintained by local education authorities a prohibition on the charging of admission and tuition fees. The subsection does not apply to schools not maintained by a local education authority, whether they are in receipt of grants or not. But in the case of all schools in receipt of grant from a local authority or the Secretary of State, the charging of fees is either prohibited or restricted as a condition of grant aid.

It was made a condition of direct grant recognition that a grammar school should offer annually free places numbering not less than twenty-five per cent. of the previous year's admissions to the upper school to pupils who had been for not less than two years at a primary school which was either maintained by a local authority or in receipt of grant out of Government Funds. Further, the local education authority might require the governors to put at their disposal such number of " reserved places " as they needed and the tuition fees for pupils occupying such reserved places had to be paid in full by the authority, see section 6 (2) (*a*) (*i*) of the Education (Miscellaneous Provisions) Act, 1953, *post*, but the total number of free and reserved places might not without the express agreement of the governors exceed one half of the previous year's admissions. The fees for education and boarding and other charges had to be approved by the Secretary of State and fees and charges payable in respect of day pupils in the upper school had to be wholly or partly remitted to parents unable to pay them in accordance with arrangements approved by the Secretary of State.

Direct grant grammar schools are now being phased out under the Direct Grant Grammar Schools (Cessation of Grant) Regulations 1975, S.I. 1975 No. 1198, p. 418, *post*.

In the case of direct-grant schools other than direct-grant grammar schools, the fees for education and boarding or other charges must be approved by the Secretary of State.

Further, a local education authority must pay the whole of the tuition fees of pupils for whom education is provided in independent schools because of a shortage of places in maintained schools or in non-maintained special schools because the special educational treatment needed cannot be provided in maintained special schools. See section 6 (2) (*a*) (*ii*) and (*iii*) of the Education (Miscellaneous Provisions) Act, 1953, *post*.

Subsection (2) of the present section provides that fees for boarding in maintained schools are to be charged in accordance with scales to be approved by the Secretary of State, but the Secretary of State announced in Circular No. 350 (24th March, 1959), that he no longer wished to determine fees or scales of fees thereunder. Authorities may, therefore, subject to provisos (*a*) and (*b*), and without seeking the Secretary of State's approval charge any fees which are necessary to cover the cost of board and lodging. In Circular 14/60 (27th September, 1960) it was pointed out that " authorities' arrangements for assisting with the cost of boarding education at maintained schools have never required the Secretary of State's approval by virtue of section 61 (2) (*b*) ". No such fees will, however, be payable where a child cannot be suitably educated except at a maintained boarding school and they may be reduced or remitted altogether, in cases of financial hardship. As to the provision, free of charge, of clothing for boarders in maintained schools, see section 5 of the Education (Miscellaneous Provisions) Act, 1948, *post*.

Under section 6 (2) (*b*) of the Education (Miscellaneous Provisions) Act, 1953, *post*, the local education authority must pay the whole of the boarding fees for any pupil for whom they provide education in a non-maintained school if suitable education cannot be provided unless board and lodging are also provided.

As to the continuance of certain grants made before 1st April, 1965, under this section, see section 33 of the London Government Act, 1963, *post*.

(*) As to the meaning or statutory definition of " school ", " maintain ", " local education authority ", " county college ", " parent ", " young person ", see pp. 67–69, *ante*.

(a) **" No fees shall be charged ".**—The duty hereby imposed may be enforced by the Secretary of State under section 99, p. 173, *post*.

(b) **" Subject as hereinafter provided ".**—This refers to the provision made for the remission of the whole or part of the fees under provisos (*a*) and (*b*) to this subsection.

(c) **" Board and lodging ".**—Section 8 (2), p. 80, *ante*, requires the local education, authority, in fulfilling its duties under that section, to have regard (*inter alia*) to the expediency of securing the provision of boarding accommodation, either in boarding schools or otherwise for pupils for whom education as boarders is considered by their parents and by the authority to be desirable. As to the provision of board and lodging otherwise than at boarding schools or colleges and as to the recovery of the cost thereof, see, respectively, sections 50 and 52, pp. 142, 143, *ante*.

(d) **" Fees shall be payable ".**—As to the recovery of fees, see the last part of subsection (3) of this section and note (i), *infra*.

(e) **" Secretary of State ".**—See note (b) to s. 1, *ante*.

(f) **" Education suitable to his age, ability and aptitude ".**—See note (k) to section 8, p. 81, *ante*. This provision means that wherever it is necessary for a pupil to be provided with boarding accommodation at a school or college because suitable education cannot otherwise be provided, *e.g.*, within a reasonable distance of his home, no fees may be charged for board and lodging. For instance, no fees for board and lodging will be chargeable where it is necessary for a pupil to attend a special school which is also a boarding school, and also where board and lodging has to be provided at a school or college because as a result of the area covered all the pupils cannot travel to school daily. *Cf.* section 6 of the Education (Miscellaneous Provisions) Act, 1953, p. 231, *post*.

(g) **" The authority shall remit ".**—The duty of remission in this proviso and in proviso (*b*) to the subsection, though contingent upon the opinion of the authority, may be enforced by the Secretary of State under section 68, p. 155, *post*.

(h) **" Shall be payable by him instead ".**—No indication is given as to the circumstances in which the local authority may be so satisfied, but it will obviously be prudent to have regard, in coming to a decision whether to effect recovery from the parent or the young person, to the probable attitude of the court.

(i) **" Shall be recoverable summarily as a civil debt ".**—See note (g) to section 52, p. 144, *ante*.

62. Duties of Secretary of State (a) and of local education authorities as to the training of teachers.—(1) In execution of the duties imposed on him by this Act (b), the Secretary of State (a) shall, in particular, make such arrangements as he considers expedient for securing that there shall be available sufficient facilities for the training of teachers for service in schools (*) colleges (c) and other establishments maintained (*) by local education authorities (*), and for that purpose the Secretary of State (a) may give to any local education authority such directions as he thinks necessary (d) requiring them to establish maintain or assist (e) any training college or other institution or to provide or assist the provision of any other facilities specified in the direction.

(2) Where by any direction given under this section a local education authority are required to perform any such functions as aforesaid, the Secretary of State (a) may give such directions to other local education authorities requiring them to contribute towards the expenses (f) incurred in performing those functions as he thinks just.

NOTES

Under this section the Secretary of State has a general responsibility for ensuring that adequate facilities are available for the training of teachers and may give any necessary directions to local education authorities for this purpose.

The training colleges have undergone great expansion partly on account of the introduction from September, 1960, of three year training, see Circular No. 325 (17th June, 1957); partly with a view to the training of an adequate number of specialist teachers of science in secondary modern schools and the lower forms in grammar schools, and also to enable the desired reduction in the size of classes to be made. In January, 1963, the then Minister of Education announced the government's acceptance of a recommendation by the National Advisory Council on the Training and Supply of Teachers that the student population of the training colleges should be built up to 80,000 by the academic year 1970/71. See Annual Report for 1963 (Commd. 2316). In fact, by the end of 1969, the total number of students in initial training courses, including those in the university departments of education, was over 115,000 (Annual Report for 1969).

It is now proposed that the number should be reduced to 60,000 places in 1981. See the Introduction, pp. 39 *et seq.*, *ante.*

See, as to general conditions of grant to voluntary establishments, the Further Education Regulations 1975, S.I. 1975 No. 1054, reg. 20, p. 415, *post.*

(*) **As to the meaning or statutory definition of " school ", " maintain " and " local education authority ", see pp. 67–69, *ante.***

(a) **" Secretary of State ".**—See note (b) to s. 1, *ante.*

(b) **" The duties imposed on him under this Act ".**—This refers in particular to the duty imposed on the Secretary of State by section 1, p. 73, *ante,* " to promote the education of the people of England and Wales and the progressive development of institutions devoted to that purpose, and to secure the effective execution by local authorities, under his control and direction, of the national policy for providing a varied and comprehensive educational service in every area ".

(c) **" Colleges ".**—This word refers mainly to county colleges, which are no longer part of national policy. See the Introduction, p. 48, *ante.*

(d) **" Such directions as he thinks necessary ".**—As to the enforcement of such directions, see section 99, *post,* and as to the variation or revocation of such directions, see section 111, *post.*

(e) **" Maintain or assist ".**—By section 114 (1), p. 216, *post,* the words " maintain " and " assist " have, in relation to any school or county college (or, in the case of " assist ", in relation to " any school, college or institution "), the meanings assigned to them by subsection (2) of that section. Since the same section provides that a school is an institution for providing primary or secondary education or both, and a county college is a special form of part-time educational establishment, the words " maintain " and " assist " as here used cannot in strictness have the above-mentioned definitions applied to them.

(f) **" Contribute towards the expenses ".**—The principle has been adopted that " provision made by local education authorities shall be treated as a common service, each authority bearing its proper share of such provision and no special burden falling on those authorities which themselves provide and maintain training colleges ". See now the Rate Support Grants (Pooling Arrangements) Regulations, 1967, S.I. 1967 No. 467, p. 378, *post.*

63. Exemption from building byelaws of buildings approved by the Secretary of State (a) (1) [*Repealed by the Health and Safety at Work, etc. Act, 1974.*]

(2) Where plans for any building required for the purposes of any school or other educational establishment are approved by the Secretary of State (a), he may by order direct (b) that any provision of any local Act or of any byelaw made under such an Act shall not apply in relation to the building or shall apply in relation thereto with such modifications as may be specified in the order.

NOTES

Detailed requirements as to the size, lay-out, etc., of maintained schools are contained in the Standards for School Premises Regulations 1972, S.I. 1972 No. 2051, p. 392, *post.*

(a) **" Secretary of State ".**—See note (b) to s. 1, *ante.*

(b) **" He may by order direct ".**—As to the revocation and variation of orders and directions, see section 111, *post,* and as to the enforcement thereof, see section 99, *post.*

64. [*Repealed.*]

NOTE

This section, which exempted voluntary schools from rates, was repealed as from 1st April, 1963 by the Rating and Valuation Act, 1961, sections 12 (2), 29 (2) and Schedule V, Part I. Section 12, however, further provided that no rates should be payable for 1963/64; and that as respects each of the next four succeeding years (i.e., 1964/65, 1965/66, 1966/67 and 1967/68) the amounts of rates payable in respect of any such hereditament should be one-fifth, two-fifths, three-fifths and four-fifths respectively of the amount that would otherwise be payable. Full payment was therefore not made until 1968/69.

The Act of 1961 has been, with some savings, repealed. See now the General Rate Act 1967, which provides that:

(1) the Secretary of State for Education and Science, in consultation with local authorities, may make regulations, providing that the gross value is calculated according to the regulations:—

(*a*) that the Secretary of State certifies in accordance with relevant factors, that the amount is " the average cost of providing a place for one pupil in a school of that class completed not less than one year before the coming into force of the valuation lists to which the regulations apply;

(*b*) providing for the determination for any school of that class of an amount equal to the product of—

(i) a standard gross value for each such place, being a prescribed percentage of the amount certified under paragraph (*a*) of this subsection; and

(ii) the number of places determined in accordance with the regulations to be available for pupils in that school; and

(c) providing for taking as the gross value of any such school the amount arrived at under paragraph (b) of this subsection as adjusted in the prescribed manner by reference to the age, layout and construction of the buildings, the facilities and amenities provided at the school " and any other relevant factors.

(2) Regulations may provide that land of any description forming part of a voluntary or county school, may be treated for rating purposes as a separate hereditament and not as forming part of the school.

65. Endowments for maintenance of voluntary schools.— Where any sums which accrue after the date of the commencement of this Part of this Act (a) in respect of the income of any endowment (b) are required by virtue of the provisions of any trust deed (*) to be applied towards the maintenance of a school (c) which a local education authority(*) are required to maintain (d) as a voluntary school (*), the said sums shall not be payable to the local education authority, but shall be applied by the managers or governors (*) of the school towards the discharge of their obligations, if any, with respect to the maintenance of the school (e), or in such other manner, if any, as may be determined by a scheme for the administration of the endowment made after the date of the commencement of this Part of this Act.

NOTES

Section 41 of the Education Act, 1921, provided that nothing in that Act was to affect any endowment or the discretion of any trustees in respect thereof. Where, however, under the trusts or other provisions affecting an endowment the income thereof was to be applied in whole or in part for purposes of a public elementary school for which provision was to be made by the local education authority, the whole or the part of the income, as the case might be, was to be paid to that authority. Such moneys were to be applied in relief of rates and, in counties, in aid of the rate levied in the parish or parishes served by the school, except in London.

The White Paper on Educational Reconstruction (Cmd. 6458 of 1943) indicated that it was proposed to alter the law, which was believed to be the only known case of the statutory diversion of charitable funds to the relief of rates, and was directly contrary to a long established rule of the Court of Chancery. In London, it was pointed out, the income of such endowments was not paid in relief of rates and the Board of Education had power to substitute new trusts by a scheme to be made on the application of the trustees or the local education authority. It was proposed to extend the London provisions to the rest of the country in respect of the endowment of both primary and secondary schools and this is the effect of the present section, after the obligations of the managers or governors, if any, in respect of the maintenance of the school premises have been met.

(*) As to the meaning or statutory definition of " trust deed ", " local education authority ", " voluntary school " and " managers or governors ", see pp. 67–69, *ante*.

(a) **" The date of the commencement of this Part of this Act ".**—Part II of the Act came into operation on 1st April, 1945.

(b) **" Endowment ".**—Endowments relating to schools were formerly subject to the provisions of the Endowed Schools Acts 1869 to 1948, now repealed. See now, as to general and special powers relating to educational trusts, sections 1, 2 of the Education Act 1973, pp. 274–277, *post*.

(c) **" School ".**—This word is defined by section 114 (1), p. 185, *post*, but must be read in relation to the qualifying words contained in this section.

(d) **" Are required to maintain ".**—By section 114 (1), p. 184, *post*, the word " maintain " has the meaning assigned to it by subsection (2) of that section, which provides (*inter alia*) that, for the purposes of the Act, the duty of a local education authority to maintain a school is to include the duty of defraying all the expenses of maintaining the school except, in the case of an aided school or a special agreement school (as to which see section 15, p. 95, *ante*), any expenses that by virtue of any provision of this Act or of any special agreement made thereunder are payable by the managers or governors of the school, and the expression " maintain " is to be construed accordingly. See also the First Schedule to the Education Act, 1946, p. 216, *post*, which clarifies the duties of local authorities as to the maintenance of voluntary schools.

(e) **" Their obligations, if any, with respect to the maintenance of the school ".**— In the case of a controlled school, the managers or governors have no obligations with respect to the maintenance of the school, but the managers or governors of aided and special agreement schools are responsible for the expenses referred to in paragraph (*a*) of section 15 (3), p. 96, *ante*. See also the First Schedule to the Education Act, 1946, p. 216, *post*.

66. Power of local education authorities to assist governors of aided secondary schools in respect of liabilities incurred before commencement of Part II.—[*Spent.*]

NOTE

This section, which is spent, enabled a local education authority, if it thought fit and the Secretary of State approved, to assist the governors of a school which became an aided secondary school under the Act to meet liabilities incurred before the date of the commencement of Part II.

67. Determination of disputes and questions.—(1) Save as otherwise expressly provided by this Act (a), any dispute (b) between a local education authority (*) and the managers or governors (*) of any school (c) with respect to the exercise of any power conferred or the performance of any duty (d) imposed by or under this Act, may, notwithstanding any enactment rendering the exercise of the power or the performance of the duty contingent upon the opinion of the authority or of the managers or governors, be referred to the Secretary of State (e); and any such dispute so referred shall be determined by him.

(2) Any dispute between two or more local education authorities as to which of them is responsible for the provision of education for any pupil (*), or whether contributions (f) in respect of the provision of education for any pupil are payable under this Act by one local education authority to another, shall be determined by the Secretary of State (e).

(3) Where any trust deed (*) relating to a voluntary school (*) makes provision whereby a bishop or any other ecclesiastical or denominational authority has power to decide whether the religious instruction given in the school (g) which purports to be in accordance with the provisions of the trust deed (h) does or does not accord with those provisions, that question shall be determined (i) in accordance with the provisions of the trust deed.

[(4) If in the case of a county or voluntary school a question arises whether a change in the character of the school or enlargement of the school premises would be a significant change or enlargement, that question shall be determined by the Secretary of State.]

NOTES

This section deals with four distinct matters:—

(1) disputes between a local education authority and the managers or governors of a school (subsection (1));

(2) disputes between two local education authorities as to the provision of education for a pupil or the payment of contributions by one authority to another (subsection (2));

(3) the question whether religious instruction given in a school is in accordance with the provisions of the trust deed (subsection (3)); and

(4) changes in the character of schools or enlargement of school premises (subsection (4)).

Subsection (1) relates to disputes in which the managers or governors of any school are concerned, and also to the exercise of any power or the performance of any duty imposed by or under the Act, unless any particular section expressly provides some other method of determining the dispute. Disputes arising under instruments of management or government, or under rules of management or articles of government, may be determined under this subsection. The subsection is applied in relation to colleges of education and other institutions providing further education, and to special schools, by s. 3 (3) (*a*) of the Education (No. 2) Act, 1968, p. 268, *post.*

Subsection (2) provides for the determination of disputes arising between two or more local education authorities as to the responsibility for the provision of primary or secondary education, under section 8, p. 79, *ante,* or further education, under section 41, p. 135, *ante,* for any pupil, or as to the payment of contributions under section 6 of the Education (Miscellaneous Provisions) Act, 1948, p. 222, *post,* or section 7 of the Education (Miscellaneous Provisions) Act, 1953, p. 232, *post.*

Subsection (4). Questions as to whether a change in the character of a school or an enlargement of school premises are significant changes are to be determined by the Secretary of State for Education and Science. This subsection was substituted by Sch. I to the Education Act 1968. See the General Note to that Act, at p. 261, *post.*

(*) As to the meaning or statutory definition of "local education authority", "managers or governors", "pupil", "trust deed", "voluntary school", "alterations", "premises" and "county school", see pp. 67–69, *ante.*

(a) "**Save as otherwise expressly provided by this Act**".—See, for instance, section 11, p. 85, *ante,* regarding objections to the development plan of the local education authority, section 13, p. 90, *ante,* regarding objections to proposals made under that section, section 20, p. 108, *ante,* as to failure to agree on the number of managers or governors of a group of schools and section 24, p. 112, *ante,* regarding the contents of the rules of management or articles of government of an aided school.

(b) "**Any dispute**".—The following cases decided under the previous law may have some relevance: *Blencowe* v. *Northamptonshire County Council,* [1907] 1 Ch. 504; *Wilford* v. *West Riding of Yorkshire County Council,* [1908] 1 K.B. 685 (a change of character of a non-provided school, against the managers' wishes, was not a matter for the Board's decision), *Board of Education* v. *Rice,* [1911] A.C. 179; *West Suffolk County Council* v. *Olorenshaw,* [1918] 2 K.B. 687 (the Courts have no jurisdiction over any matter coming within the scope of the enactment).

(c) "**Any school**".—Apparently this subsection applies to every school coming within the definition in section 114 (1), p. 185, *post,* namely, any institution for providing primary or secondary education or both primary and secondary education, being a school maintained by a local education authority, an independent school, or a school in respect of which grants are made by the Secretary of State to the proprietor of the school. However, the reference to " managers or governors " of any school casts some doubt upon this interpretation, since the phrase "managers or governors", as used in the Act, relates only to county and voluntary schools.

(d) **" The performance of any duty".**—As to the enforcement of duties imposed on local education authorities and upon managers or governors by or under the Act, see section 99, *post*.

(e) **" Secretary of State ".**—See note (b) to s. 1, *ante*.

(f) **" Contributions ".**—See section 6 of the Education (Miscellaneous Provisions) Act, 1948, *post*, and section 7 of the Education (Miscellaneous Provisions) Act, 1953, *post*.

(g) **" Religious instruction given in the school ".**—As to religious education in county and voluntary schools, see sections 25–30, pp. 115 *et seq.*, *ante*.

(h) **" In accordance with the provisions of the trust deed ".**—As to the giving of such religious instruction in controlled schools, see section 27, p. 118, *ante*, and in aided and special agreement schools, see section 28, p. 119, *ante*.

(i) **" That question shall be determined ".**—Where the trust deed makes no such provision, the question may have to be decided by reference to the Court or, where the dispute is between the local education authority and the managers or governors, by the Secretary of State under subsection (1) of this section.

68. Power of Secretary of State to prevent unreasonable exercise of functions.—If the Secretary of State (a) is satisfied (b) either on complaint by any person (c) or otherwise (d), that any local education authority (*) or the managers or governors (*) of any county* or voluntary school (*) have acted or are proposing to act unreasonably with respect to the exercise of any power conferred or the performance of any duty imposed by or under this Act, he may, notwithstanding any enactment rendering the exercise of the power or the performance of the duty contingent upon the opinion of the authority or of the managers or governors, give such directions (e) as to the exercise of the power or the performance of the duty as appear to him to be expedient.

[In this section references to a local education authority shall be construed as including references to any body of persons authorised in accordance with the First Schedule to this Act (f), to exercise functions of such an authority.]

NOTES

The purpose of this section is to ensure that the powers of local education authorities (including joint education boards), and their education committees, joint education committees, and of the managers or governors of county and voluntary schools are not exercised unreasonably. The words in square brackets at the end of the section were added by section 14 of and Part I of the Second Schedule to the Education Act 1946, p. 214, *post*, the addition being intended to remedy an omission discovered after the present Act was passed. The section is applied in relation to institutions providing further education, and to special schools, by s. 3 (3) (*b*) of the Education (No. 2) Act, 1968, p. 268, *post*.

The words omitted in the second paragraph were repealed by the Local Government Act 1972, s. 272 (1), Sch. 30.

In the case of duties imposed by or under the Act which are not made contingent upon the opinion of the authority or the managers or governors, the powers of the Secretary of State to enforce their performance, if necessary by *mandamus*, are contained in section 99, p. 173, *post*.

The above provisions apply in relation to the governing bodies of voluntary establishments: Further Education Regulations 1975, S.I. 1975 No. 1054, p. 411, *post*.

(*) As to the meaning or statutory definition of " local education authority ", " managers or governors ", " county school " and " voluntary school ", see pp. 67–69, *ante*."

(a) **" Secretary of State ".**—See note (b) to s. 1, *ante*.

(b) **" Satisfied ".**—The use of this word makes it clear that the Secretary of State, at least if acting in good faith, is to be the sole judge whether acts or proposed acts are unreasonable, see, *e.g.*, *Robinson* v. *Minister of Town and Country Planning*, [1947] 1 All E.R. 851; [1947] K.B. 702; *Re Beck and Pollitzer's Application*, [1948] 2 K.B. 339; and see also *Thorneloe and Clarkson Ltd.* v. *Board of Trade*, [1950] 2 All E.R. 245; *Smith* v. *East Elloe Rural District Council*, [1956] 1 All E.R. 855; [1956] A.C. 736, H.L., and 11 Halsbury's Laws of England (3rd Edn.) 53 *et seq.*

(c) **" Person ".**—By section 19 of the Interpretation Act, 1889; 32 Halsbury's Statutes (3rd Edn.) 449, in every Act passed after the commencement of that Act, unless the contrary intention appears, this expression includes any body of persons corporate or unincorporate.

(d) **" Or otherwise ".**—It is not necessary for the Secretary of State to wait for a complaint before taking action under this section, and he is free to act no matter how he received the information on which his subsequent actions are based.

(e) **" Directions ".**—As to the revocation or variation of any such directions, see section 111, *post*.

(f) **" First Schedule to this Act ".**—See p. 196, *post*.

69. Powers of Secretary of State as to medical examinations and inspections.—(1) [*Repealed.*]

(2) Where any question is referred to the Secretary of State (a) under this Part of this Act (b), then, if in the opinion of the Secretary of State (a) the examination of any pupil (*) by a duly qualified medical practitioner appointed for the purpose by him would assist the determination of the question referred to him, the Secretary of State (a) may by notice in writing (c) served on the parent (*) of that pupil, or if that pupil is in attendance at a county college (*) upon him, require the parent to submit him, or require him to submit himself, as the case may be, for examination by such a practitioner; and if any person on whom such a notice is served fails without reasonable excuse to comply with the requirements thereof, he shall be liable on summary conviction (d) to a fine not exceeding [ten] pounds.

NOTES

Subsection (1) was repealed by the National Health Service Reorganisation Act 1973, section 57, Sch. 5. See now, as to medical and dental service for pupils, section 3 of the Act of 1973, p. 310, *post*.

Subsection (2) enables the Secretary of State to require any pupil to submit to a medical examination if a question is referred to the Secretary of State under Part II of the Act and the Secretary of State thinks that a medical examination would serve a useful purpose. The fine referred to in the subsection was increased to £10 by virtue of the Criminal Justice Act 1967, s. 93 and Sch. 3.

(*) As to the meaning or statutory definition of " pupil ", " parent " and " county college " see pp. 67–69, *ante*.

(a) **" Secretary of State ".**—See note (b) to s. 1, *ante*.

(b) **" Where any question is referred . . . under this Part of this Act ".**—See sections 38 (2), p. 131, *ante* (withdrawal of registered pupil from special school) and 44 (8), p. 139, *ante* (exemption from compulsory attendance for further education).

(c) **" Notice in writing ".**—As to the service of notices, see section 113, *post*.

(d) **" On summary conviction ".**—See note (b) to section 40, *ante*.

PART III

INDEPENDENT SCHOOLS

70. Registration of independent schools.—(1) The Secretary of State (a) shall appoint one of his officers to be Registrar of Independent Schools; and it shall be the duty of the Registrar of Independent Schools to keep a register of all independent schools (*), which shall be open to public inspection at all reasonable times, and, subject as hereinafter provided, to register therein any independent school of which the proprietor (*) makes application for the purpose in the prescribed manner (b) and furnishes the prescribed particulars:

Provided that—

(*a*) no independent school shall be registered if, by virtue of an order made under the provisions hereinafter contained (c), the proprietor is disqualified (d) from being the proprietor of an independent school or the school premises (*) are disqualified (d) from being used as a school, or if the school premises are used or proposed to be used for any purpose for which they are disqualified by virtue of any such order; and

(*b*) the registration of any school shall be provisional only (f) until the Secretary of State (a), after the school has been inspected on his behalf under the provisions of Part IV of this Act (g), gives notice (h) to the proprietor that the registration is final.

(2) If the Secretary of State (a) is satisfied that he is in possession of sufficient information with respect to any independent school or any class of independent schools, and that registration of that school or the schools comprised in that class is unnecessary, the Secretary of State (a) may by order exempt (i) that school or schools of that class from registration, and any school so exempted shall be deemed to be a registered school (*).

(3) If after the expiration of six months from the date of the commencement of this Part of this Act (j) any person (*)—

(*a*) conducts an independent school (whether established before or after the commencement of that Part) which is not a registered school or a provisionally registered school (*); or

(*b*) being the proprietor of an independent school does any act calculated to lead to the belief that the school is a registered school while it is a provisionally registered school;

he shall be liable on summary conviction (k) to a fine not exceeding twenty pounds or in the case of a second or subsequent conviction to a fine not exceeding fifty pounds or to imprisonment for a term not exceeding three months or to both such imprisonment and such fine.

(4) The Secretary of State (a) may make regulations (l) prescribing the particulars to be furnished to the Registrar of Independent Schools by the proprietors of such schools, and such regulations may provide for the notification to the Registrar of any changes in the particulars so furnished and as to the circumstances in which the Secretary of State (a) may order the name of any school to be deleted from the register in the event of theRegistrar being unable to obtain sufficient particulars thereof.

NOTES

Part III of the Act, *i.e.*, sections 70–75, came into operation on 30th September, 1957 by virtue of section 119, *post*, and the Education Act, 1944 (Commencement of Part III) Order, 1957, S.I. 1957 No. 96. See Administrative Memorandum No. 557 (15th July 1957), p. 454, *post*.

The six sections contained in Part III of the Act implement the proposals with regard to independent schools outlined in the White Paper on Educational Reconstruction (Cmd. 6458 of 1943). Subsection (1) of the present section provides for the establishment of a register of independent schools, and sections 71–73, *infra*, contain provisions enabling the Secretary of State to deal with schools where the premises are unsuitable, the accommodation inadequate, the instruction inefficient or the proprietor, or a member of the teaching staff, not a fit person to have the charge of children. Section 71 provides that such defects are to be brought to the notice of the person concerned by means of a notice of complaint served by the Secretary of State, whilst section 72, p. 158, *post*, gives the person upon whom such a notice is served the right of appeal to the Independent Schools Tribunal constituted in accordance with the Sixth Schedule, *post*. Section 74 (1), p. 161, *post*, makes provision for the removal of disqualifications where circumstances change.

(*) As to the meaning or statutory definition of "independent school", "proprietor", "premises", "registered school", "person" and "provisionally registered school", see pp. 67–69, *ante*.

(a) "**Secretary of State**".—See note (b) to s. 1, *ante*.

(b) "**In the prescribed manner**".—As used here and subsequently in this section the word "prescribed", by section 114 (1), p. 185, *post*, means prescribed by regulations made by the Secretary of State. The manner of making application for registration of an independent school and the particulars to be furnished are prescribed by Regulation 3 of and the Schedule to the Independent Schools Registration Regulations, 1957, S.I. 1957 No. 929, p. 343, *post*.

(c) "**An order made under the provisions hereinafter contained**".—This refers primarily to an order made by the Independent Schools Tribunal under section 72, p. 158, *post*, but may also relate to an order of the Secretary of State made under regulations which the Secretary of State is empowered to make by virtue of subsection (4) of this section.

(d) "**The proprietor is disqualified**".—See section 73 (3), p. 160, *post*.

(e) "**The school premises are disqualified**".—See section 73 (2), p. 160, *post*.

(f) "**Shall be provisional only**".—By the end of 1963 only 45 schools remained provisionally registered and 30 of these were new schools. See Annual Report for 1963 (Cmnd. 2316).

(g) "**After the school has been inspected on his behalf under the provisions of Part IV of this Act**".—Section 77, p. 163, *post*, imposes a duty upon the Secretary of State to cause inspections to be made of every educational establishment (as defined in subsection (1) of that section) at such intervals as appear to him to be appropriate. As to the penalty for obstructing an inspector, see subsection (4) of that section.

(h) "**Notice**".—As to the service of notices, see section 113, p. 182, *post*.

(i) "**May by order exempt**".—By the Independent Schools (Exemption from Registration) Order, 1957, S.I. 1957 No. 1173, p. 344, *post*, any school which has received a notification that the Secretary of State recognises it as efficient unless and until such notification is withdrawn is exempt from registration and the Royal Marines School of Music, Deal, and the Duke of York's Royal Military School, Dover, are also exempt from registration. Rules for the recognition of independent schools as efficient are stated in Rules 16 (Revised, December, 1965). At the end of 1974, 1,327 schools were recognised as efficient and the number of finally registered schools was 926 (Department of Education and Science Annual Report, 1974).

(j) "**The date of the commencement of this Part of this Act**".—30th September, 1957, see the general note to this section.

(k) "**On summary conviction**".—See note (b) to section 40, p. 134, *ante*.

(l) "**Regulations**".—See the Independent Schools Registration Regulations, 1957, S.I. 1957 No. 929, p. 342, *post*.

71. Complaints.—(1) If at any time the Secretary of State (a) is satisfied (b) that any registered (*) or provisionally registered school (*) is objectionable upon all or any of the following grounds—

(*a*) that the school premises (*) or any parts thereof are unsuitable for a school (*);

(*b*) that the accommodation provided at the school premises is inadequate or unsuitable having regard to the number, ages, and sex of the pupils (*) attending the school:

(*c*) that efficient and suitable instruction (c) is not being provided at the school having regard to the ages and sex of the pupils attending thereat;

(*d*) that the proprietor (*) of the school or any teacher employed therein is not a proper person to be the proprietor of an independent school or to be a teacher in any school, as the case may be;

the Secretary of State (a) shall serve upon the proprietor of the school a notice of complaint (d) stating the grounds of complaint together with full particulars of the matters complained of, and, unless any of such matters are stated in the notice to be in the opinion of the Secretary of State (a) irremediable, the notice shall specify the measures necessary in the opinion of the Secretary of State (a) to remedy the matters complained of, and shall specify the time, not being less than six months after the service of the notice, within which such measures are thereby required to be taken.

(2) If it is alleged by any notice of complaint served under this section that any person employed as a teacher at the school is not a proper person to be a teacher in any school, that person shall be named in the notice and the particulars contained in the notice shall specify the grounds of the allegation, and a copy of the notice shall be served upon him.

(3) Every notice of complaint served under this section and every copy of such a notice so served shall limit the time, not being less than one month after the service of the notice or copy, within which the complaint may be referred to an Independent Schools Tribunal (e) under the provisions hereinafter contained (f).

NOTES

As to the provisions of Part III of the Act generally, see the general note to section 70, p. 157, *ante*.

(*) As to the meaning or statutory definition of "registered school", "provisionally registered school", "premises", "school", "pupil" and "proprietor", see pp. 67–69, *ante*.

(a) "**Secretary of State**".—See note (b) to s. 1, *ante*.

(b) "**Satisfied**".—See note (b) to section 68, *ante*.

(c) "**Efficient and suitable instruction**".—Section 36, p. 128, *ante*, requires the parent of every child of compulsory school age to cause him to receive efficient full-time education suitable to his age, ability and aptitude, either by regular attendance at school or otherwise. In Administrative Memorandum No. 557 (15th July, 1957), p. 454, *post*, the point is made that the attendance of a child of compulsory school age at a registered independent school is not evidence that he is necessarily receiving efficient full-time education suitable to his age, ability and aptitude.

(d) "**A notice of complaint**".—As to the service of notices under this Act, see section 113, p. 182, *post*.

(e) "**Independent Schools Tribunal**".—See section 72 (1), *infra*, and the Sixth Schedule, *post*.

(f) "**Under the provisions hereinafter contained**".—See section 72, *infra*. If the complaint is not referred to an Independent Schools Tribunal under subsection (1) of that section within the time limited, the Secretary of State may, by subsection (3), *ibid*., make any order which such a tribunal would have had power to make (see subsection (2), *ibid*.) if the complaint had been so referred.

72. Determination of complaints.—(1) Any person (*) upon whom a notice of complaint or a copy of such a notice is served (a) under the last foregoing section may, within the time limited by the notice (b), appeal therefrom by referring the complaint, in such manner as may be provided by rules made under this Part of this Act (c), to an Independent Schools Tribunal constituted in accordance with the provisions of the Sixth Schedule to this Act (d).

(2) Upon a complaint being referred to an Independent Schools Tribunal the tribunal shall, after affording to all parties concerned an opportunity of being heard (e), and after considering such evidence as may be tendered by them or on their behalf, have power—

(*a*) to order (f) that the complaint be annulled:

(*b*) to order that the school (*) in respect of which the notice of complaint was served be struck off the register (g):

(*c*) to order that the school be so struck off unless the requirements of the notice, subject to such modifications, if any, as may be specified in the order are complied with to the satisfaction of the Secretary of State (h) before the expiration of such time as may be specified in the order:

(*d*) if satisfied that the premises (*) alleged by the notice of complaint to be unsuitable for use as a school or any part of such premises are in fact unsuitable for such use, by order to disqualify the premises or part from being so used, or, if satisfied that the accommodation provided at the school premises is inadequate or unsuitable having regard to the number, ages and sex of the pupils attending the school, by order to disqualify the premises from being used as a school for pupils exceeding such number or of such age or sex as may be specified in the order:

(*e*) if satisfied that any person alleged by the notice of complaint to be a person who is not proper to be the proprietor of an independent school or to be a teacher in any school is in fact such a person, by order to disqualify that person from being the proprietor of any independent school or from being a teacher in any school, as the case may be.

(3) Where a notice of complaint has been served under this Act on the proprietor of any school and the complaint is not referred by him to an Independent Schools Tribunal within the time limited in that behalf by the notice, the Secretary of State (h) shall have power to make any order (i) which such a tribunal would have had power to make if the complaint had been so referred:

Provided that, if it was alleged by the notice of complaint that any person employed as a teacher at the school is not a proper person to be a teacher in any school and that person has, within the time limited in that behalf by the copy of the notice served upon him, referred the complaint to an Independent Schools Tribunal, the Secretary of State (h) shall not have power to make an order requiring his dismissal or disqualifying him from being a teacher in any school.

(4) Where by virtue of an order made by an Independent Schools Tribunal or by the Secretary of State any person is disqualified either from being the proprietor of an independent school or from being a teacher in any school, then, unless the order otherwise directs, that person shall, by virtue of the order, be disqualified both from being the proprietor of an independent school and from being a teacher in any school.

NOTES

As to the provisions of Part III of the Act generally see the general note to section 70, p. 157, *ante*.

(*) As to the meaning or statutory definition of " person ", " school " and " premises ", see pp. 67–69, *ante*.

(a) **" Upon whom a notice of complaint or a copy of such a notice is served ".**— Provision is made for the service of notices of complaint upon the proprietors of schools and copies thereof upon teachers employed therein by section 71, p. 158, *ante*, in the circumstances mentioned in that section. As to the service of notices, see section 113, p. 182, *post*.

(b) **"Within the time limited by the notice".**—By section 71 (3), p. 158, *ante*, the time so limited is not to be less than one month after the service of the notice or copy thereof.

(c) **"Rules made under this Part of this Act".**—As to the making of such rules by the Lord Chancellor, with the concurrence of the Lord President of the Council, and the purposes for which they may be made (including the manner of making appeals), see section 75 (1), p. 161, *post*. The rules now in force are the Independent Schools Tribunal Rules, 1958, S.I. 1958 No. 519, amended by the Independent Schools Tribunal (Amendment) Rules 1968, S.I. 1968 No. 588, the Independent Schools Tribunal (Amendment) Rules 1972, S.I. 1972 No. 4, the Independent Schools Tribunal (Amendment) Rules 1974, S.I. 1974 No. 563, and the Independent Schools Tribunal (Amendment No. 3) Rules 1974, S.I. 1974 No. 1972). See p. 344, *post*. Rule 2 thereof prescribes the manner of instituting an appeal.

(d) **"An Independent Schools Tribunal constituted in accordance with the provisions of the Sixth Schedule to this Act".**—The Sixth Schedule, p. 206, *post*, provides for the appointment of two panels, a legal panel, appointed by the Lord Chancellor, of persons available to act when required as chairman of any Independent Schools Tribunal, and an educational panel, appointed by the Lord President of the Council, of persons available to act when required as members of any such Tribunal. Where any appeal under this section is required to be determined a tribunal, consisting of a chairman and two other members, is specially appointed from the two panels by the Lord Chancellor and the Lord President of the Council respectively, in accordance with para. 4 of the Sixth Schedule, *post*.

Independent Schools Tribunals are under the direct supervision of the Council on Tribunals, in accordance with the Tribunals and Inquiries Act, 1971.

(e) **"After affording to all parties concerned an opportunity of being heard".**—See rules 7–11 of the rules referred to in note (c), above.

(f) **"Order".**—This is not an order to which section 111, p. 181, *post*, applies, though that section will apply to a similar order made by the Secretary of State under subsection (3) of this section. See also section 74, p. 161, *post*, as to the removal of disqualifications imposed by such orders.

An appeal on a point of law against a decision of an Independent Schools Tribunal lies to the High Court by virtue of the Tribunals and Inquiries Act, 1971. For a case in which such an appeal was made but failed see *Gedge* v. *Independent Schools Tribunal* (1959), *Times*, 7th October.

(g) **"Struck off the register".**—As to the effect of an order (other than an order under paragraph (a) of this subsection) and the penalties for failure to comply therewith, see section 73, *infra*.

(h) **"Secretary of State".**—See note (b) to s. 1, *ante*.

(i) **"Power to make any order".**—See note (f), *supra*.

73. Enforcement.—(1) Where an order (a) is made by the Secretary of State (b) or by an Independent Schools Tribunal (c) directing that any school (*) be struck off the register (d), the Registrar of Independent Schools (e) shall as from the date on which the direction takes effect strike the school off the register.

(2) If any person (*) uses any premises (*) for purposes for which they are disqualified (f) by virtue of any order made under this Part of this Act, that person shall be liable on summary conviction (g) to a fine not exceeding twenty pounds or in the case of a second or subsequent conviction (whether in respect of the same or other premises) to a fine not exceeding fifty pounds, or to imprisonment for a term not exceeding three months or to both such imprisonment and such fine.

(3) If any person acts as the proprietor (*) of an independent school (*), or accepts or endeavours to obtain employment as a teacher in any school (h), while he is disqualified from so acting or from being so employed by virtue of any such order as aforesaid, he shall be liable on summary conviction to a fine not exceeding twenty pounds or in the case of a second or subsequent conviction to a fine not exceeding fifty pounds, or to imprisonment for a term not exceeding three months or to both such imprisonment and such fine.

(4) No proceedings shall be instituted for an offence against this Part of this Act except by or on behalf of the Secretary of State (b).

[(5) For the purposes of the provisions of this Part of this Act, a person who is disqualified by an order made under Part IV of the Education (Scotland) Act, 1945 (i), from being the proprietor of an independent school or from being a teacher in any school shall be deemed to be so disqualified by virtue of an order made under this Part of this Act.]

NOTES

As to the provisions of this Part of the Act generally, see the general note to section 70, p. 157, *ante.* Subsection (5) was added by section 14 of and Part I of the Second Schedule to the Education Act, 1946, p. 259, *post,* and is designed to prevent a person who has been disqualified under the corresponding Scottish Act from entering the teaching profession in England.

(*) As to the meaning or statutory definition of " school ", " person ", " premises ", " proprietor " and " independent school ", see pp. 67–69, *ante.*

(a) **" Order ".**—Where a complaint of which notice is given by the Secretary of State under section 71 (1), p. 158, *ante,* is referred to an Independent Schools Tribunal under section 72 (1), p. 158, *ante,* the Tribunal may make an order of any of the kinds mentioned in paragraphs (*a*) to (*e*) of subsection (2) of the latter section. Where the complaint is not so referred within the time limited by the notice, the Secretary of State may under subsection (3), *ibid.,* make a similar order. Section 111, p. 181, *post,* as to the revocation or variation of orders and directions, will apply to orders made by the Secretary of State but not to those made by the Independent Schools Tribunal, but see also section 74, *infra,* as to the removal of disqualifications imposed by such orders.

(b) **" Secretary of State ".**—See note (b) to s. 1, *ante.*

(c) **" Independent Schools Tribunal ".**—See note (d) to section 72, p. 160, *ante.*

(d) **" Struck off the register ".**—See paragraph (*b*) of section 72 (2), p. 159, *ante,* and note (g) to that section.

(e) **" The Registrar of Independent Schools ".**—*I.e.,* the officer appointed by the Secretary of State to fulfil that office pursuant to section 70 (1), *ante.*

(f) **" For purposes for which they are disqualified ".**—See paragraphs (*b*), (*c*) and (*d*) of section 72 (2), p. 159, *ante.*

(g) **" On summary conviction ".**—See note (b) to section 40, p. 134, *ante.*

(h) **" Any school ".**—Here the expression is not limited to independent schools and refers to schools of every type referred to in the definition thereof in section 114 (1), p. 185, *post.* Such a person is not, however, prohibited by the subsection from accepting or endeavouring to obtain employment in a county college or any other educational institution or establishment not coming within the definition of a school.

(i) **" Part IV of the Education (Scotland) Act, 1945 ".**—This Part of the Scottish Act corresponds to Part III of the present Act.

74. Removal of disqualifications.—(1) If on the application of any person (*) the Secretary of State (a) is satisfied that any disqualification imposed by an order made under this Part of this Act is, by reason of any change of circumstances, no longer necessary, the Secretary of State (a) may by order (b) remove the disqualification.

(2) Any person who is aggrieved by the refusal of the Secretary of State (a) to remove a disqualification so imposed may, within such time after the refusal has been communicated to him as may be limited by rules made under this Part of this Act (c), appeal to an Independent Schools Tribunal (d).

NOTES

As to the provisions of this Part of the Act generally, see the general note to section 70, p. 157, *ante.*

(*) As to the statutory definition of " person ", see p. 68, *ante.*

(a) **" Secretary of State ".**—See note (b) to s. 1, *ante.*

(b) **" Order ".**—As to the revocation or variation of such an order, see section 111, p. 181, *post.* It is doubtful whether the proviso to that section would operate so as to enable an appeal to be made under subsection (2) of this section against the revocation or variation of such an order, though it would be manifestly unjust that such an appeal should not be permissible.

(c) **" Rules made under this Part of this Act ".**—See section 75 (1), *infra.* The rules now in force are the Independent Schools Tribunal Rules 1958, S.I. 1958 No. 519, as amended. See note (c) to section 72, *ante.*

(d) **" Independent Schools Tribunal ".**—See section 72 (1), p. 158, *ante,* and the notes thereto.

75. Proceedings before Independent Schools Tribunals and matters relating thereto.—(1) The Lord Chancellor may, with the concurrence of the Lord President of the Council, make rules (a) as to the practice and procedure to be followed with respect to the constitution of Independent Schools Tribunals (b), as to the manner of making appeals to such tribunals, and as to proceedings before such tribunals (c) and matters incidental to or consequential on such proceedings, and, in particular, such rules may make provision requiring any such tribunal to sit at such places (d) as may be directed in accordance with the rules, and may make provision as to appearance before such tribunals by counsel or solicitor (e) and as to the payment to members of such tribunals, as part of the expenses of the Secretary of State (f) under this Act, of such remuneration and allowances (g) as may, with the consent of the Treasury, be provided for by the rules.

(2) The provisions of the Arbitration Acts, 1889 to 1934 (h) shall not apply to any proceedings before an Independent Schools Tribunal except so far as any provisions thereof may be applied thereto with or without modifications by rules made under this section.

(3) Every order of an Independent Schools Tribunal (i) shall be registered by the Registrar of Independent Schools (j) and shall be open to public inspection at all reasonable times.

NOTES

As to the provisions of this Part of the Act generally, see the general note to section 70, p. 157, *ante*.

(a) **" Rules ".**—See the Independent Schools Tribunal Rules, 1958, S.I. 1958 No. 519, as amended, p. 344, *post*.

(b) **" The constitution of Independent Schools Tribunals ".**—See rule 3 of the Rules above referred to.

(c) **" Appeals to such tribunals ".**—See section 72 (1) p. 158, *ante* and section 74 (2), *supra* and as to the manner of making such appeals see rule 2 of the Rules above referred to.

(d) **" Sit at such places ".**—See *ibid.*, rule 4.

(e) **" Appearance before such tribunals by counsel or solicitor ".**—See *ibid.*, rule 7.

(f) **" Secretary of State ".**—See note (b) to s. 1, *ante*.

(g) **" Remuneration and allowances ".**—See *ibid.*, rule 11.

(h) **" The Arbitration Acts, 1889 to 1934 ".**—These Acts have been repealed and are replaced by the Arbitration Act, 1950; 2 Halsbury's Statutes (3rd Edn.) 433; certain provisions whereof are applied to proceedings before an Independent Schools Tribunal by rule 10 of the Rules above referred to.

(i) **" Every order of an Independent Schools Tribunal ".**—*I.e.*, an order or an appeal under section 72, *ante*, or section 74 (2), *supra*. No provision is made, however, for the registration of similar orders made by the Secretary of State under subsection (3) of that section, or under section 74 (1), *supra*, removing disqualifications imposed under this Part of the Act, though the Registrar of Independent Schools, as an officer of the Secretary of State, will doubtless take cognisance of such orders.

(j) **" Registrar of Independent Schools ".**—*I.e.*, the officer appointed under section 70 (1), p. 156, *ante*, to be Registrar of Independent Schools.

PART IV
GENERAL

GENERAL PRINCIPLE TO BE OBSERVED BY SECRETARY OF STATE AND LOCAL EDUCATION AUTHORITIES

76. Pupils to be educated in accordance with wishes of parents.—In the exercise and performance of all powers and duties conferred and imposed on them by this Act the Secretary of State (a) and local education authorities (*) shall have regard (b) to the general principle (c) that, so far as is compatible with the provision of efficient instruction and training and the avoidance of unreasonable public expenditure, pupils (*) are to be educated in accordance with the wishes of their parents (*).

NOTES

The effect of this section is that there must be read into each provision of the Act conferring a power or imposing a duty or obligation in the exercise of that power or the performance of that duty to have regard to the " general principle " enunciated, as to which see below (*Watt* v. *Kesteven County Council*, [1955] 1 All E.R. 473; [1955] 1 Q.B. 408, C.A.

(*) As to the meaning or statutory definition of " local education authority ", " pupil " and " parent ", see pp. 67–69, *ante*.

(a) **" Secretary of State ".**—See note (b) to s. 1, *ante*.

(b) **" Shall have regard ".**—Any supposed failure to have regard to the principles of the section must be related either to the performance of a duty imposed specifically by some other provision of the Act or to the exercise of a power given and it may be that a breach of some of the obligations imposed by the Act would afford a right of action to a parent who had suffered damage, but where a duty under the Act can only be enforced by the Secretary of State under section 99, p. 173, *post*, a breach of the present section in the exercise of that duty can also only be enforced under section 99. (*Watt* v. *Kesteven County Council*, [1955] 1 All E.R. 473; [1955] 1 Q.B. 408, C.A. Therefore, though it would not be practicable to enforce the section directly, the Secretary of State must have regard to the principle enunciated in it in taking action under either section 99, or section 68, p. 155, *ante*. See also *Cumings* v. *Birkenhead Corporation*, [1971] 2 All E.R. 881.

(c) **" The general principle ".**—The section does not say that pupils must in all cases be educated in accordance with the wishes of their parents. It only lays down a general principle to which the local education authority must have regard. This leaves it open to the authority to have regard to other things as well, and also to make exceptions to the general principle if it thinks fit to do so (*Watt* v. *Kesteven County Council, supra*).

The obligation imposed by the section is to consult the wishes of particular parents in regard to their own children, not to consult parents generally. As regards education this obligation relates to such matters as the curriculum, or the inclusion of religious education, or whether education should be co-educational; but it does not relate to the size of the school or the conditions of entry (*Wood* v. *Ealing London Borough*, [1966] 3 All E.R. 514; [1967] Ch. 364).

MISCELLANEOUS PROVISIONS

77. Inspection of educational establishments.—(1) In this section the expression " educational establishment " means a school (*), a county college (*), any establishment which under a scheme of further education made and approved under this Act (a) is used for further education (*), and any training college or other institution (b) being a training college or other institution maintained (*) by a local education authority (*); and if the persons responsible for the management of any institution which is not an educational establishment within the foregoing definition request the Secretary of State (c) or any local education authority to cause an inspection of that institution to be made under the powers conferred by this section, the institution shall, for the purposes of that inspection, be deemed to be also included within that definition (d).

(2) It shall be the duty of the Secretary of State (c) to cause inspections to be made of every educational establishment at such intervals as appear to him to be appropriate, and to cause a special inspection of any such establishment to be made whenever he considers such an inspection to be desirable; and for the purpose of enabling such inspections to be made on behalf of the Secretary of State (c) inspectors may be appointed by [Her] Majesty on the recommendation of the Secretary of State (c), and persons may be authorised by the Secretary of State (c) to assist such inspectors and to act as additional inspectors:

Provided that the Secretary of State (c) shall not be required by virtue of this sub-section to cause inspections to be made of any educational establishment during any period during which he is satisfied that suitable arrangements are in force for the inspection of that establishment otherwise than in accordance with this subsection (e).

(3) Any local education authority may cause an inspection to be made of any educational establishment maintained by the authority, and such inspections shall be made by officers (f) appointed by the local education authority.

(4) If any person obstructs any person authorised to make an inspection in pursuance of the provisions of this section in the execution of his duty, he shall be liable on summary conviction (g) to a fine not exceeding twenty pounds, or, in the case of a second or subsequent conviction, to a fine not exceeding fifty pounds or to imprisonment for a term not exceeding three months or to both such imprisonment and such fine.

(5) Subject as hereinafter provided, the religious instruction given in any school maintained by a local education authority shall not be subject to inspection except by one of [Her] Majesty's Inspectors or by a person ordinarily employed for the purpose of inspecting secular instruction either as an additional inspector appointed by the Secretary of State (c) or as an officer in the whole-time employment of a local education authority:

Provided that the religious instruction given in a voluntary school (*) otherwise than in accordance with an agreed syllabus (h) shall not be subject to such inspection as aforesaid but may be inspected under arrangements made for that purpose by the managers or governors (*) of the school, or, in the case of a controlled school (*), by the foundation managers (*) or foundation governors (*) thereof so, however, that such inspections shall not be made on more than two days in any year and not less than fourteen days' notice (i) of the dates fixed therefor shall be given to the local education authority.

(6) No pupil (*) who has been excused from attendance at religious worship or instruction (j) in a voluntary school in accordance with the provisions of this Act shall be required to attend the school on a day fixed for an inspection by arrangements made under the proviso to the last foregoing subsection.

NOTES

Under this section: (1) It is the Secretary of State's duty to inspect every " educational establishment " as defined in the section; this covers every type of school, including independent schools, county colleges, any establishment used to provide further education under a scheme made and approved under the Act, and any training college or other institution maintained by a local education authority; and (2) inspectors, both of the Secretary of State and the local education authority, may inspect religious instruction given in accordance with an agreed syllabus.

The above provisions apply to voluntary establishments as they apply to maintained establishments: Further Education Regulations 1975, S.I. 1975 No. 1054, p. 411, *post*.

In the case of independent schools a copy of the inspector's report is normally sent to the proprietor of the school. A copy is also sent to the local education authority except where the school is recognised as efficient under Rules 16, p. 468, *post*. See Administrative Memorandum No. 557 (15th July, 1957), p. 454, *post*.

(*) As to the meaning or statutory definition of " school ", " county college ", " further education ", " maintain ", " local education authority ", " voluntary school ", " managers or governors ", " controlled school ", " foundation managers ", " foundation governors " and " pupil ", see pp. 67–69, *ante*.

(a) **" A scheme of further education made and approved under this Act ".**—See section 42, p. 136, *ante*.

(b) **" Any training college or other institution ".**—See section 62, p. 151, *ante*.

(c) **" Secretary of State ".**—See note (b) to s. 1, *ante*.

(d) **" Deemed to be also included within that definition ".**—If a request is made to the Secretary of State under this subsection it becomes the duty of the Secretary of State to cause inspections to be made at appropriate intervals. If, however, the request is made to the local education authority the authority is not compelled to cause inspections to be made (subsection (3) of this section).

(e) **" Otherwise than in accordance with this subsection ".**—See subsection (3) of this section.

(f) **" Such inspections shall be made by officers ".**—Formal inspections caused to be made by a local education authority must be made by officers appointed by the authority, though managers and governors of voluntary schools would generally be wise to provide reasonable facilities for visits from members of the local education authority also.

(g) **" On summary conviction ".**—See note (b) to section 40, p. 134, *ante*.

(h) **" Otherwise than in accordance with an agreed syllabus ".**—As to the provision of denominational instruction, see section 27 (1) (controlled schools) and 28 (1) (aided schools and special agreement schools), pp. 118, 119, *ante*. By section 114 (1), p. 183, *post*, " agreed syllabus " means (subject to subsection (4) of that section) an agreed syllabus of religious instruction prepared in accordance with the provisions of the Fifth Schedule, p. 204, *post*, and adopted or deemed to be adopted under that Schedule. As to the circumstances in which this form of instruction may or must be given, see sections 26 (county schools), 27 (6) (controlled schools) and 28 (1) (aided schools and special agreement schools), pp. 117–119, *ante*.

(i) **" Not less than fourteen days' notice ".**—As to the service of notices under the Act, see section 113, p. 182, *post*.

(j) **" Excused from attendance at religious worship or instruction ".**—See section 25 (4), p. 115, *ante*.

78. Provision of certain ancillary services for pupils not in attendance at schools maintained by local education authorities.—

(1) [*Repealed.*]

(2) A local education authority may, with the consent of the proprietor (*) of any school in their area which is not a school maintained by the authority (a), and upon such financial and other terms, if any, as may be determined by agreement between the authority and the proprietor of the school, make arrangements for securing—

(*a*) the provision of milk, meals and other refreshment (b) for pupils in attendance at the school;

(*b*) [*Repealed*],

. . . Provided that any arrangements made under this subsection shall be such as to secure, so far as is practicable (c), that the expense incurred by the authority in connection with the provision under the arrangements of any service or article shall not exceed the expense which would have been incurred by them in the provision thereof if the pupil had been a pupil at a school maintained by them.

NOTES

Subsection (1) of this section was repealed by the National Health Service Reorganisation Act 1973, section 57, Sch. 5.

Subsection (2) of this section was especially important in that it enabled the benefits of the school meals service to be extended to the pupils of direct grant and independent schools by agreement between the local education authority and the proprietor or responsible governing body. Adequate provision for the supply to day pupils of milk to drink and midday meals was made a condition of direct grant from the Secretary of State by the Direct Grant Schools Regulations 1959, S.I. 1959 No. 1832, as amended by the Direct Grant Schools (Amendment) Regulations 1968, S.I. 1968 No. 1148), p. 363, *post*, and the milk for drinking supplied to day pupils had to be supplied free of charge. The power to make such arrangements for the provision of milk to such schools does not, however, now apply to any pupil after the summer term ending next after the date on which he attains the age of seven, unless he is in attendance at a special school: see s. 1 (3) of the Education (Milk) Act 1971, p. 272, *post*.

As to the provision of milk and meals in maintained schools, see the Notes to s. 49, p. 142, *ante*.

Paragraph (*b*) of subsection (2), which related to the provision of clothing for pupils at non-maintained schools, was repealed by section 11 (2) of and the Second Schedule to the Education (Miscellaneous Provisions) Act, 1948. See now section 5 of that Act, p. 221, *post*.

The words omitted before the proviso to subsection (2) were repealed by the National Health Service Reorganisation Act, 1973, section 57, Sch. 5.

(*) As to the meaning or statutory definition of " proprietor ", see p. 185, *post*.

(a) **" Not a school maintained by the local education authority ".**—As a result of the definition of " school " in section 114 (1), p. 185, *post*, this phrase includes independent schools and schools in respect of which grants are made by the Secretary of State to the proprietor of the school.

(b) **" Milk, meals and other refreshment ".**—As to the provision of milk, meals and other refreshment, see s. 49, p. 141, *ante*.

(c) **" Shall be such as to secure, so far as is practicable ".**—These words impose a duty upon the authority which will be enforceable by the Secretary of State under section 99, p. 173, *post*.

79. [*Repealed.*]

NOTE

This section was repealed by the National Health Service Reorganisation Act 1973, section 57, Sch. 5.

80. Registration of pupils at schools.—(1) The proprietor (*) of every school (*) (that is to say in the case of a county school (*) or voluntary school (*) the managers or governors (*) thereof) shall cause to be kept (a) in accordance with regulations made by the Secretary of State (b) a register containing the prescribed particulars (c) with respect to all persons *of compulsory school age* (d) who are pupils (*) at the school, and such regulations may make provision for enabling such registers to be inspected, for enabling extracts therefrom to be taken for the purposes of this Act by persons duly authorised in that behalf under the regulations, and for requiring the persons by whom any such register is required to be kept to make to the Secretary of State (b), and to local education authorities (*), such periodical or other returns (e) as to the contents thereof as may be prescribed.

(2) If any person contravenes or fails to comply with any requirement imposed on him by regulations made under this section, he shall be liable on summary conviction (f) to a fine not exceeding ten pounds.

(3) [*Repealed* (g).]

NOTES

This section is printed as amended by the Education (Miscellaneous Provisions) Act, 1948 (see notes (d) and (f), *infra*.) Under section 37, p. 129, *ante*, any child with respect to whom the local education authority is not satisfied that he is receiving efficient full-time education suitable to his age, ability and aptitude may be required by means of a school attendance order to become a registered pupil at a school named in the order; but, by this section, every child who attends school will automatically become a registered pupil at that school.

(*) As to the meaning or statutory definition of " proprietor ", " school ", " county school ", "voluntary school ", " managers or governors ", " pupil " and " local education authority", see pp. 67–69, *ante*.

(a) **" Shall cause to be kept ".**—As to the enforcement of this duty, apart from the penalty imposed by subsection (2) of this section, see in the case of maintained schools, section 99, p. 173, *post*.

(b) **" Secretary of State ".**—See note (b) to s. 1, *ante*. As to regulations made by him, see the Pupils' Registration Regulations 1956, S.I. 1956 No. 357, p. 339, *post*, which prescribe both the matters which *may* be prescribed under sub-s. (1) of the present section and those relating to the deletion of names from a register which *must* be prescribed under s. 4 (6) of the Education (Miscellaneous Provisions) Act, 1948, *post*.

(c) **" Prescribed particulars ".**—By section 114 (1), p. 185, *post*, " prescribed " means prescribed by regulations made by the Secretary of State.

(d) **" Of compulsory school age ".**—These words were repealed by sections 4 (4) and 11 (2) of and the Second Schedule to the Education (Miscellaneous Provisions) Act, 1948. The result of the repeal is that only one admission register need now be kept in each school which will contain the prescribed particulars about all pupils at the school. Any person registered under this section becomes a registered pupil. See the definition of registered pupil in section 114 (1), p. 185, *post*.

(e) **" Periodical returns ".**—Regulation 7 of the Regulations referred to in note (b) above, provides that the proprietor of every school shall make to the local education authority for the area to which the pupil in question belongs, at such intervals as may be agreed with the authority, or, in default of agreement determined by the Secretary of State, a return giving the full name and address of every registered pupil who fails to attend school regularly or has been continuously absent for two weeks. On the introduction of Part III of the Act the attention of independent school proprietors was again drawn to their responsibilities under this Regulation, see Administrative Memorandum No. 557 (15th July, 1957), p. 454, *post*.

(f) **" On summary conviction ".**—See note (b) to section 40, *ante*.

(g) **Subsection (3).**—This subsection was repealed by sections 4 (5) and 11 (2) and the Second Schedule to the Education (Miscellaneous Provisions) Act, 1948, *post*, and is replaced by section 4 (6) of the 1948 Act, p. 220, *post*.

81. Power of local education authorities to give assistance by means of scholarships and otherwise.—Regulations (a) shall be made by the Secretary of State (b) empowering local education authorities (*), for the purpose of enabling pupils (*) to take advantage without hardship to themselves or their parents (*) of any educational facilities available to them—

(*a*) to defray such expenses of children (*) attending county schools (*), voluntary schools (*), or special schools (*), as may be necessary to enable them to take part in any school activities (c):

(*b*) to pay the whole or any part of the fees and expenses payable in respect of children attending schools at which fees are payable (d):

(*c*) to grant scholarships, exhibitions, bursaries, and other allowances (e) in respect of pupils over compulsory school age (*), including pupils undergoing training as teachers (f):

(*d*) to grant allowances in respect of any child in respect of whom any scholarship exhibition bursary or other allowance has been granted by a former authority (*) before the date of the commencement of this Part of this Act (g).

NOTES

This section enabled a local education authority (*inter alia*) to grant scholarships and maintenance allowances to pupils over compulsory school age, and still empowers a local education authority to pay the fees of children attending fee-charging schools including boarding schools. Similar powers are conferred on the Secretary of State by section 100 (1) (*c*), p. 175, *post*.

By section 4 (4) of the Education Act, 1962, *post*, sections 1, 2 of the Act of 1962 are to have effect in substitution for (*a*) the provisions of this section in so far as they require regulations to be made for the purpose of empowering local education authorities to grant scholarships, exhibitions, bursaries and other allowances in respect of pupils over compulsory school age in connection with their attendance at courses to which sections 1, 2 (1) of the 1962 Act apply, or in connection with their undergoing training as teachers; and (*b*) the provisions of any regulations made under this section, in so far as they provide for the granting of such scholarships, exhibitions, etc., and cease to have effect so far as they impose any such requirement or make any such provision as is mentioned above, subject to savings. See s. 4 of the Act of 1962, and the Notes thereto, at p. 245, *post*.

This section, and the Regulations for Scholarships and Other Benefits, 1945, S.R. & O. 1945 No. 666, p. 327, *post*, as amended, remain in force with respect to the payment of fees, allowances and other expenses of pupils attending schools. See Circular 4/62 (18th April, 1962), p. 462, *post*.

(*) As to the meaning or statutory definition of "local education authority", "pupil", "parent", "child", "county school", "voluntary school", "special school", "compulsory school age" and "former authority", see pp. 67–69, *ante*.

(a) "**Regulations**".—See the Regulations for Scholarships and Other Benefits, 1945, S.R. & O. 1945 No. 666, p. 327, *post*, which is printed as amended by Amending Regulations No. 1, 1948, S.I. 1948 No. 688, No. 2, 1948, S.I. 1948 No. 2223 and S.I. 1964 No. 1294.

Regulations under paragraph (*c*) of this section may include provision empowering local education authorities to grant maintenance allowances in respect of persons who (*a*) being registered pupils at special schools, are by virtue of section 38 (1) of the Act of 1944 deemed to be of compulsory school age, but (*b*) apart from section 38 (1) would be over compulsory school age. See section 2 of the Education Act, 1964, p. 252, *post*.

(b) "**Secretary of State**".—See note (b) to s. 1, *ante*.

(c) "**Any school activities**".—See Regulations 3 (*b*) of the Regulations for Scholarships and Other Benefits, 1945, as substituted by the Amending Regulations of 1948 (see note (a), *supra*), which provides that expenses to be defrayed by a local authority under this head shall not include expenditure on clothing which the authority are authorised to provide by section 5 of the Education (Miscellaneous Provisions) Act, 1948, p. 221, *post*.

(d) "**Schools at which fees are payable**".—See section 61, p. 149, *ante*, and the notes to that section. Arrangements for assistance with fees at maintained schools under the Regulations for Scholarships and Other Benefits, 1945, referred to in note (a), *supra*, no longer require the approval of the Secretary of State; see Circular No. 14/60 (27th September, 1960). Under Regulation 3 (c) of those Regulations the fees defrayed by a local authority may include the whole or part of any fees for board and lodging, but the power thereby conferred is now in effect superseded by the duty imposed by section 6 (2) (*b*) of the Education (Miscellaneous Provisions) Act, 1953, p. 231, *post*.

(e) "**Scholarships, exhibitions, bursaries and other allowances**".—See general note to this section, *supra*.

(f) "**Pupils undergoing training as teachers**".—Such grants are no longer payable by reason of section 4 (4) of the Education Act 1962, p. 245, *post*.

(g) "**The commencement of Part II of this Act**".—Like this Part of the Act, Part II came into operation on 1st April, 1945.

82. Powers of local education authorities as to educational research, etc.—A local education authority (*) may, with the approval of the Secretary of State (a) make such provision for conducting or assisting (b) the conduct of research as appears to the authority to be desirable for the purpose of improving the educational facilities provided for their area (c).

NOTES

This section enlarges the powers conferred on local education authorities to aid research which would improve the educational facilities of its area. So far as the Secretary of State is concerned, the general powers given by section 1 (1), p. 73, *ante*, enable him to foster educational research, whilst section 100 (1) (*b*), p. 175, *post*, specifically empowers him to make grants for the purpose to persons other than local education authorities. See the Educational Services and Research Grant Regulations, 1946, S.R. & O. 1946 No. 424, Part III, p. 329, *post*.

(*) As to the statutory definition of "local education authority", see p. 68, *ante*.

(a) "**Secretary of State**".—See note (b) to s. 1, *ante*. As to approval of the Secretary of State, note that in Circular No. 350 (24th March, 1959), the then Minister gave general approval to the exercise by local education authorities of their powers under this section.

(b) "**Assisting**".—The definition of "assist" in section 114 (1), p. 183, *post*, does not apply to the use of the word in this section.

(c) "**The purpose of improving the educational facilities provided for their area**".—Section 84, *infra*, in addition enables local education authorities, for the purpose of improving the facilities for further education available for its area, with the consent of the Secretary of State to provide financial assistance to any university or university college.

83. Powers of local education authorities as to educational conferences.—Subject to any regulations (a) made by the Secretary of State (b) a local education authority (*) may organise, or participate in the organisation of, conferences for the discussion of questions relating to education, and may expend such sums as may be reasonable in paying or contributing towards any expenditure incurred in connection with conferences for the discussion of such questions, including the expenses of any person authorised by them to attend any such conference.

NOTES

(*) As to the statutory definition of "local education authority", see p. 184, *post*.

(a) "**Subject to any regulations**".—No such regulations are now in force, and local education authorities may therefore exercise their powers under this section without supervision on the part of the Secretary of State.

(b) "**Secretary of State**".—See note (b) to s. 1, *ante*.

84. Power of local education authorities to make grants to universities and university colleges.—A local education authority (*) may with the consent of the Secretary of State (a) provide financial assistance to any university or university college for the purpose of improving the facilities for further education (b) available for their area.

NOTES

This section which had no counterpart in previous legislation gives facilities to local education authorities which are additional to those contained in section 82, p. 167, *ante*.

(*) As to the statutory definition of " local education authority ", see p. 184, *post*.

(a) **" Secretary of State ".**—See note (b) to s. 1, *ante*. The Secretary of State has given his general consent to the exercise by local education authorities of their powers under this section. See Circular No. 350 (24th March, 1959).

(b) **" The facilities for further education ".**—The term " further education " is defined in section 41, p. 135, *ante*. In preparing schemes of further education under section 42, p. 136, *ante*, a local education authority is, by subsection (4), *ibid.*, to have regard to any facilities for further education provided for its area by universities, educational associations and other bodies, and is required to consult them. The scheme, as approved by the Secretary of State, may include agreed provisions as to the co-operation of the authority and any such bodies. Generally, as to further education see the Introduction, p. 48, *ante*.

85. Power of local education authorities to accept gifts for educational purposes.—(1) Subject to the provisions of this section, a local education authority (*) shall have power, and any such authority or any former authority (*) shall be deemed always to have had power, to accept hold and administer any property upon trust for purposes connected with education (a).

(2) A local education authority shall not, on or after the date of the commencement of Part II of this Act (b), be constituted trustees of any school (*) providing primary (*) or secondary education (*) other than a nursery school (*) or a special school (*) except after the submission to the Secretary of State (c) of proposals for that purpose; and where proposals are so submitted to the Secretary of State (c) they shall be treated for the purposes of this Act as proposals (d) for the maintenance (*) as a county school(*) of a school which at the time being is not such a school, and the provisions of this Act relating to such proposals shall have effect accordingly.

(3) [Any school for providing primary or secondary education which, in pursuance of proposals in that behalf submitted under this section to the Secretary of State (d), is vested in a local education authority as trustees thereof, not being a nursery school or special school, shall be a county school.]

NOTES

This section is printed as amended by section 9 of the Education (Miscellaneous Provisions) Act, 1953, p. 235, *post*, which substituted a new subsection (3), the substitution being expressed to be retrospective to the commencement of Part II of this Act. The original subsection only differed from the substituted subsection in that it did not contain the words " in pursuance of proposals in that behalf submitted under this section to the Minister (now Secretary of State; see note (d), *infra*) ". The reason for the insertion of these words is to remove a doubt arising from the apparent contradiction between the original subsection and section 9 (2), *ante*, by making it clear that the present section applies only to schools vested in a local education authority after 1st April, 1945. In the case, therefore, where local education authorities became trustees of an endowed grammar school foundation upon trust " to carry on the school of the foundation ", as it is understood was done in about twenty cases before 1908, and the school would now be a voluntary school under section 9 (2), *ante*, there is nothing now in subsection (3) of this section which conflicts with this result.

(*) As to the meaning or statutory definition of " local education authority ", " former authority ", " school ", " primary education ", " secondary education ", " nursery school ", " special school ", " maintain " and " county school ", see pp. 67–69, *ante*.

(a) **" Upon trust for purposes connected with education ".**—As to the application of an endowment of an existing school transferred under this section, see the remarks of the Master of the Rolls in *Re Poplar and Blackwall Free School* (1878), 8 Ch.D. 543.

(b) **" The date of the commencement of Part II of this Act ".**—Part II of the Act came into operation on 1st April, 1945.

(c) **" Secretary of State ".**—See note (b) to s. 1, *ante*.

(d) **" Proposals ".**—As to proposals for the maintenance of a new county school, see section 13, p. 90, *ante*.

86. [*Repealed.*]

NOTE

This section, which provided for the extension of power to make schemes under the Endowed Schools Acts 1869 to 1908, was repealed by the Education Act 1973, Sch. 2, Part II. Of those Acts the Endowed Schools Acts 1869 and 1873 (the only ones of which any provisions were still in force) were also repealed by the same Schedule to the Act of 1973.

87. [*Repealed.*]

NOTE

This section, which exempted assurances of property for educational purposes from the Mortmain Acts, was repealed by the Charities Act 1960, section 48 (2) and Schedule VIII. The Mortmain Acts were themselves repealed by the Act of 1960.

ADMINISTRATIVE PROVISIONS

88. Appointment of chief education officers of local education authorities.—The duties of a local education authority (*) with respect to the appointment of officers under the provisions of the Local Government Act, 1933 (a), shall, without prejudice to the generality of those provisions, include the duty of appointing (b) a fit person to be the chief education officer of the authority.

NOTES

The object of the section which had no counterpart in previous legislation is to enable the Secretary of State to ensure that persons of real educational knowledge and experience are appointed as chief education officers. The words omitted at the end of the section were repealed by the Local Government Act 1972, s. 272 (1), Sch. 30.

Section 112 of the Act of 1972 (42 Halsbury's Statutes (3rd Edn.) 944) empowers local authorities to appoint staff, but the present section is specifically excluded therefrom, and chief education officers are still to be appointed hereunder.

The chief education officer of the Inner London Education Authority is appointed under section 30 (4) of the London Government Act 1963, 20 Halsbury's Statutes (3rd Edn.) 483.

(*) As to the statutory definition of " local education authority ", see p. 184, *post*.

(a) **" The appointment of officers under the provisions of the Local Government Act 1933 ".**—The Local Government Act 1933, was repealed by the Local Government Act 1972, s. 272 (1), Sch. 30. For local education authorities, see section 192 of the Act of 1972.

(b) **" The duty of appointing ".**—The Secretary of State may enforce compliance with the requirements of this section by virtue of section 99, p. 173, *post*.

89. [*Repealed.*]

This section, which dealt with the remuneration of teachers, was repealed by s. 7 (6) of the Renumeration of Teachers Act, 1965. See generally that Act, pp. 253, *post*, and the Introduction, pp. 41, *ante*.

90. Compulsory purchase of land and other dealings in land by local education authorities.—(1) A local education authority (*) may be authorised by the Secretary of State (a) to purchase compulsorily any land, whether situate within or without the area of the authority, which is required for the purposes of any school (b) or college (c) which is, or is to be, maintained by them (d) [or which they have power to assist (e)], or otherwise for the purposes of their functions under this Act; . . .

Provided that the Secretary of State (a) shall not [authorise] the purchase of any land required for the purposes of a voluntary school (*) unless he is satisfied that the arrangements made as to the vesting of the land to be purchased, and as to the appropriation thereof for those purposes, are such as to secure that the expenditure ultimately borne by the local education authority will not include any expenditure which, if the land had been purchased by the managers or governors (*) of the school, would have fallen to be borne by the managers or governors (f).

(2) Section one hundred and sixty-three of the Local Government Act, 1933 (which relates to the appropriation for purposes approved by the Minister of Health, of land belonging to local authorities and not required for the purposes for which it was acquired or has since been appropriated)

shall, in relation to any land for the time being vested in a local education authority for the purposes of any of their functions under this Act, and not required for the purposes of that function, have effect as if for the references therein to the Minister of Health there were substituted references to the Secretary of State (a).

(3) Sections one hundred and sixty-four and one hundred and sixty-five of the Local Government Act, 1933 (which relate to the sale letting and exchange of land vested in local authorities) shall, in relation to any land vested in a local education authority for the purposes of their functions under this Act, have effect as if for the references in those sections to the Minister of Health there were substituted references to the Secretary of State (a).

NOTES

In order to see clearly the changes made by this Act in relation to the compulsory acquisition of, and dealings in, land for educational purposes it is essential to consider, together with this section, the effect of what appears at first sight to be a very small amendment made by this Act in the Local Government Act 1933 (now repealed), which, however, substituted an entirely different series of provisions for those formerly contained in the Education Acts, relating to the acquisition of land, etc.

The previous law relating to the compulsory acquisition, appropriation and alienation of land was contained in Part IX (sections 109–117 inclusive) of the Education Act, 1921, and in the School Sites Acts, 1841, 1844, 1849, 1851 and 1852 (which, by the Short Titles Act, 1896, are known by the collective title of the School Sites Acts), the School Grants Act, 1855, and certain other minor provisions. The above-mentioned provisions of the Education Act, 1921, contained express powers of purchasing and dealing with land for educational purposes. No such specific powers to acquire or otherwise to deal in land for educational purposes are given by the present Act but as to the power of local education authorities to acquire land by agreement, see section 10 of the Education (Miscellaneous Provisions) Act, 1948, p. 226, *post*.

The provisions of Part VII (sections 156–179 inclusive; 19 Halsbury's Statutes (3rd Edn.) 486–501) of the Local Government Act 1933, applied to the acquisition of, and all forms of dealings in, land by local authorities generally. The Act of 1933 was repealed by the Local Government Act 1972, s. 272, Sch. 30. See now, as to the acquisition of land, either by enforcement or compulsorily, and the appropriation and disposal of land by principal councils, sections 120 *et seq.* of the Act of 1972, 42 Halsbury's Statutes (3rd Edn.) 949 *et seq.*

An incidental effect of bringing dealings in land for educational purposes into line with the provisions relating to local authorities generally is that now local education authorities are not able to acquire or deal in land under the School Sites Act, though these Acts continue to regulate the transactions of managers and governors of voluntary schools and of trustees, subject to the powers of acquisition of land for the purposes of voluntary schools under this section—as to which, see notes (d) and (e), *infra* and section 10 of the 1948 Act, p. 226, *post*.

The section is printed as amended by section 6 of and the Fourth Schedule to the Acquisition of Land (Authorisation Procedure) Act 1946; 6 Halsbury's Statutes (3rd Edn.) 160, 172, which substituted the words in the first set of square brackets for words rendered obsolete by section 1 of that Act and repealed further words which are omitted, and by section 10 (1) of the Education (Miscellaneous Provisions) Act, 1948, p. 272, *post*, which inserted the word in the second set of square brackets.

As to the power of a local education authority to acquire land by agreement, see section 10 of the Education (Miscellaneous Provisions) Act, 1948, p. 226, *post*, and notes thereto.

(*) As to the meaning or statutory definition of " local education authority ", " voluntary school " and " managers or governors ", see pp. 67–69, *ante*.

(a) **" Secretary of State ".**—See note (b) to s. 1, *ante*. As to authorisation procedure, see the First Schedule to the Acquisition of Land (Authorisation Procedure) Act, 1946; 3 Halsbury's Statutes (3rd Edn.) 163.

(b) **" School ".**—This term is defined in section 114 (1), p. 185, *post*, but the definition as there given is qualified by the following words of this subsection.

(c) **" College "**—This term covers any type of college which may be established, maintained or assisted by the local education authority under the Act, *e.g.*, any college provided under section 42, p. 136, *ante*, as part of a scheme of further education, or a teachers' training college established, maintained or assisted by an authority under section 62, p. 151, *ante*. The exact limitations of the word are not, however, important, in view of the later words of the subsection " or otherwise for the purposes of their functions under this Act ".

(d) **" Which is, or is to be, maintained by them ".**—These words enable the authority to acquire land compulsorily for the purpose of any school or college which is, or is to be, maintained by the authority. In the light of the definition of the term " maintain " in section 114 (1) and (2), pp. 184, 185, *post*, this power extends to the compulsory acquisition of land by the local education authority for the purposes of enlarging or providing playing fields for existing voluntary schools and even for proposed new voluntary schools.

(e) **" Or which they have power to assist ".**—These words were inserted by section 10 (1) of the Education (Miscellaneous Provisions) Act, 1948, p. 226, *post*. Power to assist a school not maintained by the local education authority is given by section 9 (1), p. 82, *ante*. As to the assistance of training colleges, see section 62, p. 151, *ante*. The word " assist " is defined by section 114 (1) and (2), pp. 183, 185, *post*.

(f) **" Would have fallen to be borne by the managers or governors ".**—It would appear from this proviso that the local education authority may, if it thinks fit, bear the costs involved in obtaining the compulsory purchase order, since compulsory powers of acquisition are not available to managers or governors, and, if the land had been purchased by them, no such costs could have arisen.

91. [*Repealed.*]

NOTE

This section, which dealt with the accounts of councils of county boroughs and their audit, was repealed by the Local Government Act 1972, s. 272 (1), Sch. 30.

92. Reports and returns.—Every local education authority (*) shall make to the Secretary of State (a) such reports and returns and give to him such information as he may require (b) for the purpose of the exercise of his functions under this Act.

NOTES

The above provision applies in relation to the governing bodies of voluntary establishments: Further Education Regulations 1975, S.I. 1975 No. 1054, p. 411, *post.*

(*) As to the statutory definition of " local education authority ", see p. 68, *ante.*

(a) " **Secretary of State** ".—See note (b) to s. 1, *ante.*

(b) " **As he may require** ".—In view of the general duty imposed upon the Secretary of State by section 1, p. 73, *ante*, and of his power under section 99, p. 173, *post*, to enforce the general duties of local education authorities under sections 8 and 41, pp. 79 and 152, *ante*, in addition to the various functions specifically conferred upon the Secretary of State throughout the Act, this section is sufficiently wide to enable the Secretary of State to call upon a local education authority to provide him with any information which he may wish to have relating to the exercise by a local education authority of any of its functions under the Act.

93. Power of Secretary of State to direct local inquiries.—The Secretary of State (a) may cause a local inquiry to be held for the purpose of the exercise of any of his functions under this Act (b); and the provisions of subsections (2) (3) (4) and (5) of section two hundred and ninety of the Local Government Act, 1933 (c), shall have effect with respect to any such inquiry as if the Secretary of State (a) were a department for the purposes of that section.

NOTES

As to London, see Part IV of the London Government Act, 1963, pp. 289 *et seq, post.*

(a) " **Secretary of State** ".—See note (b) to s. 1, *ante.*

(b) " **For the purpose of the exercise of any of his functions under this Act** ".—Since, apart from functions specifically given to the Secretary of State under the Act, section 1 (1), p. 83, *ante*, imposes on the Secretary of State a general duty to promote the education of the people of England and Wales and the progressive development of institutions devoted to that purpose, and to secure the effective execution by local authorities, under his control and direction, of the national policy for providing a varied and comprehensive educational service in every area, the functions of the Secretary of State cover the entire scope of the Act and he is therefore entitled to hold a local inquiry in connection with any matter arising under the Act.

(c) " **Subsections (2), (3), (4) and (5) of section two hundred and ninety of the Local Government Act 1933** ".—Repealed by the Local Government Act 1972, section 272 (1), Sch. 30. As to the power to direct inquiries, see now section 250 of the Act of 1972, 42 Halsbury's Statutes (3rd Edn.) 1074.

94. Certificates of birth and registrars' returns.—(1) Where the age of any person is required to be proved for the purposes of this Act (a) or of any enactment relating to the employment of children or young persons (b), the registrar (c) having the custody of the register of births and deaths (d) containing the entry relating to the birth of that person shall, upon being presented by any person with a written requisition in such form and containing such particulars as may be determined by regulations made by the Minister of Health (e) and upon payment of a fee of [two shillings (f)], supply that person with a copy of the entry certified under his hand.

Every registrar shall, upon being requested so to do, supply free of charge a form of requisition for the purposes of this subsection.

(2) Every registrar shall supply to a local education authority (*) such particulars of the entries contained in any register of births and deaths in his custody, and in such form, as, subject to any regulations made by the Minister of Health, the authority may from time to time require; and in respect of every entry in respect of which particulars are furnished by a registrar to a local education authority in compliance with any such requirement, the authority shall pay (g) to the registrar such fee not exceeding twopence as may be agreed between the authority and the registrar, or

in default of such agreement as may be determined by the Minister of Health.

(3) In this section, the expression "register of births and deaths" means a register of births and deaths kept in pursuance of the Births and Deaths Registration Acts, 1836 to 1929 (h), and the expression "registrar" (j) includes a registrar of births and deaths and a superintendent registrar.

NOTES

(*) As to the statutory definition of "local education authority", see p. 184, *post*.

(a) **"Is required to be proved for the purposes of this Act".**—Proof of age may, for example, be required for the purposes of sections 34–39 inclusive, pp. 125 *et seq.*, *ante*, and section 58, p. 148.

(b) **"Any enactment relating to the employment of children or young persons".**—See, for example, the Children and Young Persons Acts, 1933 to 1969; 17 Halsbury's Statutes (3rd Edn.) 435 *et seq.*, and the Young Persons (Employment) Act 1938; 17 Halsbury's Statutes (3rd Edn.) 529; Employment of Children Act 1973. The terms "child" and "young person" are respectively defined in section 114 (1), pp. 183, 185, *post*, as—

(1) a person who is not over compulsory school age; and
(2) a person over compulsory school age who has not attained the age of eighteen years.

"Compulsory school age" is also defined by section 114 (1) as having subject to the provisions of section 38, p. 131, *ante*, the meaning assigned to it by section 35, p. 127, *ante*.

(c) **"Registrar".**—By subsection (3) of this section this term includes a registrar of births and deaths and a superintendent registrar.

(d) **"Register of births and deaths".**—See sub-s. (3) of this section; and, generally, the Registration of Births, Deaths and Marriages Regulations, 1968, S.I. 1968 No. 2049.

(e) **"Regulations made by the Minister of Health".**—As to the making of regulations by the Minister of Health, see section 112, p. 182, *post*. By section 121, p. 228, *post*, any regulations in force under any enactment repealed by this Act is to continue in operation and have effect as if made under this Act and may be varied or revoked accordingly.

(f) The fee for obtaining a copy of an entry relating to a birth was raised to 75p. by the Registration of Births, Deaths and Marriages (Fees) Order 1975, S.I. 1975 No. 1291.

(g) **"The authority shall pay".**—As to the enforcement of this duty, see section 99, p. 173, *post*.

(h) **Births and Deaths Registration Acts, 1836 to 1929.**—See now the Births and Deaths Registration Act 1953; 27 Halsbury's Statutes (3rd Edn.) 1021.

(j) **Registrar.**—See sections 6 and 7 of the Registration Service Act, 1953; 27 Halsbury's Statutes (3rd Edn.) 1057, 1058.

95. Provisions as to evidence.—(1) Where in any proceedings under this Act (a) the person by whom the proceedings are brought alleges that any person whose age is material to the proceedings is under, of, or over, any age (b), and satisfies the court that having used all reasonable diligence to obtain evidence as to the age of that person (c) he has been unable to do so, then, unless the contrary is proved (d), the court may presume that person to be under, of, or over, the age alleged.

(2) In any legal proceedings any document purporting to be—

(*a*) a document issued by a local education authority (*), and to be signed by the clerk of that authority or by the chief education officer (e) of that authority or by any other officer of the authority authorised to sign it;

(*b*) an extract from the minutes of the proceedings (f) of the managers or governors (*) of any county school (*) or voluntary school (*), and to be signed by the chairman of the managers or governors or by their clerk;

(*c*) a certificate giving particulars of the attendance of (g) a child (*) or young person (*) at a school (*) or at a county college (*), and to be signed by the head teacher of the school or college; or

(*d*) a certificate issued by a medical officer (h) of a local education authority and to be signed by such an officer;

shall be received in evidence and shall, unless the contrary is proved, be deemed to be the document which it purports to be, and to have been signed by the person by whom it purports to have been signed, without proof of his identity, signature, or official capacity, and any such extract or certificate as is mentioned in paragraph (*b*) (*c*) or (*d*) of this sub-section shall be evidence of the matters therein stated.

NOTES

(*) As to the meaning or statutory definition of " local education authority ", " managers or governors ", " county school " " voluntary school ", " child ", " young person ", " school " and " county college ", see pp. 67–69, *ante*.

(a) **" In any proceedings under this Act ".**—See sections 34, 40, 46, 59 and 80, *ante*. In proceedings under section 37 or 39, *ante*, the child is to be presumed to be of compulsory school age at the material time unless the parent proves the contrary. See section 9 (2) of the Education (Miscellaneous Provisions) Act, 1948, *post*.

(b) **" Is under, of, or over, any age ".**—As to the time at which, for the purposes of the Act, a person in attendance at a county college attains the age of 18, see section 8 of the Education Act, 1946, p. 255, *post*. No county colleges have been established under the Act and it is unlikely that they now will be (see the Introduction, p. 48, *ante*).

As to school leaving dates, see section 9 of the Education Act, 1962, p. 246, *post*.

(c) **" Evidence as to the age of that person ".**—See, for example, section 94, p. 171, *ante*.

(d) **" Unless the contrary is proved ".**—Under the present section, before the onus of proof of age (of a child or young person) is placed upon the defendant, it is necessary for the person by whom the proceedings are brought first to show that he has used all reasonable diligence to obtain evidence as to the age of the person concerned and has been unable to do so.

Section 9 (2) of the Education (Miscellaneous Provisions) Act, 1948, p. 226, *post*, provides however, that in the case of proceeding to enforce attendance at school a child shall be presumed to be of compulsory school age unless the parent proves the contrary.

(e) **" Chief education officer ".**—As to the appointment of a chief education officer of a local education authority, see section 88, p. 169, *ante*.

(f) **" Minutes of the proceedings ".**—As to the proceedings of managers and governors of county and voluntary schools, see section 21, p. 109, *ante*.

(g) **" Particulars of the attendance."**—See *Hinchley* v. *Rankin*, [1961] 1 All E.R. 692.

(h) **" Medical officer ".**—By section 114 (1), p. 184, *post*, this expression, in relation to a local education authority, means a duly qualified medical practitioner employed, or engaged, whether regularly or for the purposes of any particular case, by that authority or whose services are made available to that authority by the Secretary of State.

96. Provisions consequential on cessation of functions of former authorities.—[*Spent.*]

97. [*Spent.*]

NOTE

The effect of this section was to transfer to the county councils the obligation imposed on the former Part III authorities by the Local Government Staffs (War Service) Act, 1939; 19 Halsbury's Statutes (3rd Edn.) 646, to reinstate their officers and teachers in non-provided public elementary schools, who undertook war service.

98. [*Spent.*]

NOTE

This section, which is now spent, provided for the compensation of officers of former Part III authorities and of councils exercising functions under s. 70 of the Education Act, 1921, and also of teachers who suffered direct pecuniary loss as a result of the passing of the Act.

99. Powers of Secretary of State in default of local education authorities or managers or governors.—(1) If the Secretary of State (a) is satisfied either upon complaint by any person interested or otherwise, that any local education authority (*), or the managers or governors (*) of any county school (*) or voluntary school (*), have failed to discharge any duty imposed upon them (b) by or for the purposes of this Act, the Secretary of State (a) may make an order (c) declaring the authority, or the managers or governors, as the case may be, to be in default in respect of that duty, and giving such directions for the purpose of enforcing the execution thereof as appear to the Minister (a) to be expedient; and any such directions shall be enforceable, on an application made on behalf of the Secretary of State (a), by mandamus (d).

(2) Where it appears to the Secretary of State (a) that by reason of the default of any person (*) there is no properly constituted body (e) of managers or governors of any county school or voluntary school, the Secretary of State (a) may make such appointments and give such directions as he thinks

desirable (f) for the purpose of securing that there is a properly constituted body of managers or governors thereof, and may give directions rendering valid any acts or proceedings (g) which in his opinion are invalid or otherwise defective by reason of the default.

(3) Where it appears to the Secretary of State (a) that a local education authority have made default in the discharge of their duties relating to the maintenance (*) of a voluntary school, the Secretary of State (a) may direct that any act done by or on behalf of the managers or governors of the school for the purpose of securing the proper maintenance thereof shall be deemed to have been done by or on behalf of the authority, and may reimburse to the managers or governors any sums which in his opinion they have properly expended for that purpose; and the amount of any sum so reimbursed shall be a debt due to the Crown (h) from the authority, and, without prejudice to any other method of recovery, the whole or any part of such a sum may be deducted from any sums payable to the authority by the Secretary of State (a) in pursuance of any regulations relating to the payment of grants (i).

NOTES

This section relates not only to local education authorities but also to the managers or governors of county and voluntary schools. It has also been applied in relation to colleges of education and other institutions providing further education, and to special schools, by s. 3 (3) (*c*) of the Education (No. 2) Act, 1968, p. 268, *post*. The Secretary of State is not bound to hold a public inquiry, though he may hold a local inquiry if he thinks fit under section 93, p. 171, *ante*, and would probably do so in relation to any matter of importance. By virtue of paragraph 16 (1) of the Eighth Schedule to the Local Government Act, 1958; 19 Halsbury's Statutes (3rd Edn.) 816, subsection (1) applies to a failure to discharge a duty imposed by regulations under section 4 (3) of that Act as it applies to a failure to discharge a duty imposed for the purposes of the Education Act, 1944. See also the terms of section 68, p. 155, *ante*, which is printed as amended by Part I of the Second Schedule to the Education Act, 1946, and as so amended enables the Secretary of State to give directions to a local education authority or the managers of a county or voluntary school regarding the exercise of any power or the performance of any duty where he is of opinion that the authority, or the managers or governors, have acted or are proposing to act unreasonably.

(*) As to the meaning or statutory definition of "local education authority", "managers or governors", "county school", "voluntary school", "person" and "maintain", see pp. 67–69, *ante*.

(a) **"Secretary of State".**—See note (b) to s. 1, *ante*.

(b) **"Any duty imposed on them".**—Specific duties are imposed both upon local education authorities and upon the managers and governors of county and voluntary schools by numerous sections of the Act. Duties may also be imposed upon either by the regulations which the Secretary of State for Education and Science and the Minister of Health are empowered to make under the Act and upon the managers and governors by the rules of management and articles of government which are to be made under section 17, p. 100, *ante*. Reference may be made to the cases of *Board of Education* v. *Rice*, [1911] A.C. 179 and *R.* v. *Poplar Borough Council* (*No.* 1), [1922] 1 K.B. 72; *R.* v. *Poplar Borough Council* (*No.* 2), [1922] 1 K.B. 95.

(c) **"Make an order".**—As to the revocation and variation of orders and directions, see section 111, p. 181, *post*. Before making such an order the Secretary of State may, but is not bound to, hold a local inquiry under section 93, p. 171, *ante*.

(d) **"Mandamus".**—The case of *R.* v. *Staines Union* (1893), 58 J.P. 182, affords an example of the issue of a *mandamus* at the instance of the Minister of Health. The court is bound to grant the order at the request of the Secretary of State, unless there has been some legal error or some omission to apply the ordinary legal procedure. In the event of failure to comply with a *mandamus*, members of the authority responsible for the failure may be liable to attachment (*R.* v. *Worcester Corporation* (1905), 69 J.P. 296.

(e) **"No properly constituted body".**—Section 17, p. 100, *ante*, provides for the constitution of a body of managers or governors for every county school and every voluntary school in the case of a primary school by means of an instrument of management (as to which see section 18, p. 105, *ante*), and in the case of a secondary school by means of an instrument of government (as to which see section 19, p. 106, *ante*). Section 20, p. 108, *ante*, enables two or more schools to be grouped under one management.

(f) **"Give such directions as he thinks desirable".**—See note (b), *supra*.

(g) **"Any acts or proceedings".**—As to the proceedings of managers and governors of county and voluntary schools, see section 21, p. 109, *ante*.

(h) **"A debt due to the Crown".**—Instead of taking proceedings to recover such debt, the Secretary of State will no doubt generally prefer the simpler alternative of deducting the sum due from any grants payable to the authority.

(i) **"Regulations relating to the payment of grants".**—See section 100, *infra*.

FINANCIAL PROVISIONS

100. Grants in aid of educational services.—(1) The Secretary of State (a) shall by regulations (b) make provision:—

(*a*) for the payment by him to local education authorities (*) of annual grants in respect of the expenditure incurred by such authorities

[(i), (ii) [*Spent.*]

(iii) in the removal of works constructed for the purpose of air-raid precautions or of temporary works (c) constructed for defence purposes by or on behalf of the Secretary of State, the Admiralty or the Minister of Home Security in pursuance of Regulation fifty or fifty-one of the Defence (General) Regulations, 1939, or by agreement, and in the reinstatement of premises so far as it is rendered necessary by any such removal.]

(*b*) for the payment by him to persons (*) other than local education authorities of grants in respect of expenditure incurred or to be incurred for the purposes of educational services (d) provided by them or on their behalf or under their management or for the purposes of educational research (e) ; and

(*c*) for the payment by him (f), for the purpose of enabling pupils to take advantage without hardship to themselves or their parents (*) of any educational facilities available to them, of the whole or any part of the fees and expenses payable in respect of children attending schools at which fees are payable (g) . . .

(2) [*Repealed.*]

(3) Any regulations made by the Secretary of State (a) . . . under this section may make provision whereby the making of payments by him in pursuance thereof is dependent upon the fulfilment of such conditions as may be determined by or in accordance with the regulations, and may also make provision for requiring (h) local education authorities and other persons to whom payments have been made in pursuance thereof to comply with such requirements as may be so determined.

(4) [*Repealed.*]

(5) Nothing in this section shall affect any grants in aid of university education (i) payable out of moneys provided by Parliament otherwise than in accordance with the provisions of this Act.

NOTES

This section is printed as amended by the Local Government Act, 1958, sections 62 and 67 and Eighth and Ninth Schedules; 19 Halsbury's Statutes (3rd Edn.) 802, 804, 816, 821, which substituted the words in square brackets in subsection (1) and repealed subsection (2) and the words omitted in sub-s. (3). The words omitted in sub-s. 1 (*c*) were repealed by s. 13 (1) of, and Schedule II to, the Education Act, 1962. Sub-s. (1) (*a*) (i) and (ii) are omitted as spent since grants thereunder (in connection with the provision of milk and meals) are no longer payable. See s. 14 of the Local Government Act 1966, and the Note to that Act at p. 298, *post*. Subsection (4) was repealed by the Education Act 1973, Sched. 2, Part II. The repeal is not to affect any order made by virture of the provisions repealed (which enabled the Secretary of State to modify the provisions of a trust deed or other instrument relating to the management of a school or institution), or the operation in relation to any such order of section 111 of the Act of 1944; *ibid.*, Sch. I.

(*) As to the meaning or statutory definition of " local education authority ", " person ", " parent " and " trust deed ", see pp. 67–69, *ante*.

(a) **" Secretary of State ".**—See note (b) to s. 1, *ante*. As to the making of regulations under the Act by the Secretary of State for Education and Science and the Minister of Health, see s. 112, p. 182, *post*. The following regulations have been made under this section.

(*b*) *Educational Research*—Educational Services and Research Grant Regulations, 1946 (S.R. & O. 1946 No. 424), p. 329, *post*.

State Scholarships.—State Scholarships Regulations 1954 (S.I. 1954 No. 657), amended by Amending Regulations No. 1, 1955 (S.I. 1955 No. 933) (revoked), No. 2, 1957 (S.I. 1957 No. 1303), No. 3, 1958 (S.I. 1958 No. 1143) (revoked); State Scholarships Amending Regulations, 1961 (S.I. 1961 No. 1621); and State Scholarships Amending Regulations, 1962 (S.I. 1962 No. 1868). These regulations, being virtually obsolete, are not printed in this volume.

Further Education.—Further Education Regulations 1975, S.I. 1975 No. 1054, p. 411, *post.*

Training of Teachers.—Further Education Regulations 1975, S.I. 1975 No. 1054, p. 411, *post.*

Special Schools and Establishments.—Special Schools and Establishments (Grant) Regulations, 1959 (S.I. 1959 No. 366), as amended by the Special Schools and Establishments (Grant) Amending Regulations, 1964 (S.I. 1964 No. 1083) and the Special Schools and Establishment (Grant) (Amendment) Regulations, 1969 (S.I. 1969 No. 410); see p. 361, *post.*

Direct Grant Schools.—Direct Grant Schools Regulations 1959 (S.I. 1959 No. 1832) (as amended by the Direct Grant Schools Amending Regulations 1963 (S.I. 1963 No. 1379), 1964 (S.I. 1964 No. 1312), 1968 (S.I. 1968 No. 1148) and 1973 (S.I. 1973 No. 1535). See p. 363, *post.* See also the Direct Grant Grammar Schools (Cessation of Grant) Regulations 1975, S.I. 1975 No. 1198, p. 418, *post.*

By virtue of section 121, p. 196, *post*, the Social and Physical Training Grant Regulations, 1939, p. 324, *post*, made by the Board of Education under the Education Act, 1921, section 118, have effect as if made under the present Act.

(c) **" Removal of works constructed for the purposes of air-raid precautions or of temporary walls constructed for defence purposes ".**—See the Removal of Defence Works Grant Regulations 1959 (S.I. 1959 No. 337), and the Removal of Defence Works (Grants) Regulations 1971 (S.I. 1971 No. 534).

(d) **" Educational services ".**—Under this heading grants are payable to approved establishments providing facilities for adult education (see the Further Education Regulations 1975, S.I. 1975 No. 1054, p. 000, *post*), to direct grant schools (see the Direct Grant Schools Regulations 1959, S.I. 1959 No. 1832, p. 411, *post*), and to institutions for the training of teachers not maintained by a local education authority, including university departments and voluntary training colleges (see the Further Education Regulations 1975, S.I. 1975 No. 1054, p. 411, *post*). Grants are also payable under this heading to the persons (not being a local education authority) who are responsible for the establishment or maintenance of a special school or institution for further education and training of disabled persons. See the Special Schools and Establishments (Grant) Regulations 1959, S.I. 1959 No. 366, as amended, note (b), *supra.*

(e) **" Educational research ".**—The Secretary of State is enabled to make grants in aid of educational research independently of any assistance which may be given by the local education authority under section 82, p. 167, *ante.* See the Educational Services and Research Grant Regulations, 1946, S.R. & O. 1946 No. 424, p. 329, *post*, providing for the payment by the Secretary of State to recognised persons of grants towards the cost of approved educational research; and see generally the Introduction, p. 6, *ante.*

(f) **" For the payment by him ".**—This power also is additional to and may be exercised independently of any assistance which may be given by the local education authority by virtue of Regulations made by the Secretary of State under section 81, p. 166, *ante.* In exercise thereof the Secretary of State has made the State Scholarships Regulations, 1954, S.I. 1954 No. 957, amended by Amending Regulations No. 1, 1955, S.I. 1955 No. 933, No. 2, 1957, S.I. 1957 No. 1303, and No. 3, 1958, S.I. 1958 No. 1143, also S.I. 1961 No. 1621 and S.I. 1962 No. 1868. As these regulations are virtually obsolete they are not printed.

(g) **" Schools at which fees are payable ".**—See the definition of " school " in section 114 (1), p. 185, *post.* Section 61 (1), p. 149, *ante*, prohibits the charging of fees in respect of admission to any school maintained by a local education authority or in respect of the education provided in any such school. See note (d) to section 81, p. 167, *ante.*

(h) **" May also make provision for requiring ".**—See, for example, regs. 4 (3) and 5 (3) of the Direct Grant Schools Regulations, 1959, S.I. 1959 No. 1832, p. 364, *post*, enabling grant to be withheld in whole or in part if the conditions thereof are not fulfilled.

(i) **" Grants in aid of university education ".**—This refers to grants made by the Treasury through the medium of the University Grants Committee.

101. [*Repealed.*]

NOTE

This section, which contained special provisions relating to Wales and Monmouthshire, was repealed by the Local Government Act, 1958, section 67 and Schedule IV, Part II.

102. Maintenance contributions payable by the Secretary of State in respect of aided schools and special agreement schools.— The Secretary of State shall pay to the managers or governors of every aided school and of every special agreement school maintenance contributions (a) equal to [85 per cent.] of any sums expended by them in carrying out their obligations under paragraph (*a*) of subsection (3) of section fifteen of this Act (b) in respect of alterations and repairs to the school buildings (c) [and may pay the managers or governors of any aided school or special agreement school maintenance contributions not exceeding 85 per cent. of any sums expended by them on the provision of a site or of school buildings in pursuance of proposals approved under section 13 of this Act for a significant enlargement of the school premises]:

Provided that no maintenance contribution shall be payable under this section in respect of any expenditure incurred by the managers or governors of a special agreement school in the execution of repairs or alterations for the execution of which provision is made by the special agreement relating to the school (d) [nor shall a maintenance contribution be payable under this section in respect of any expenditure incurred by the managers or governors of a special agreement school in pursuance of proposals for a significant enlargement of the school premises, being proposals to which the special agreement for the school relates].

NOTES

This and the next following section provide for the payment of grants by the Secretary of State in respect of aided schools and special agreement schools to which reference has been made in the notes to s. 15, p. 97, *ante*. As amended by s. 1 of the Education Act, 1967, p. 258, *post*, by Sch. 1 to the Education Act 1968, p. 266, *post*, and by s. 3 of the Education Act 1975, p. 282, *post*, this section, in particular, provides that the managers and governors of aided and special agreement schools shall receive a grant of 85 per cent. towards the cost of any alterations and repairs which may be required to the school buildings, the words " 85 per cent. " in the first set of square brackets having been substituted by s. 3 of the Education Act 1975. The words in the second and third sets of square brackets were amendments by the Education Act 1968, Sch. I, p. 266, *post*, except that " 85 per cent. " where it occurs for the second time, was also substituted by the Act of 1975. The next section provides for the payment of grant towards the cost of transferred schools under s. 16, p. 99, *ante*. The rate of this grant also has been increased to 85 per cent. by the Education Act 1967, s. (1) 1, as amended by the Act of 1975, but in this case again the amendment is not retrospective.

As to the respective duties of the local education authority and the managers or governors as to the maintenance of voluntary schools, see also the First Schedule to the Education Act, 1946, *post*.

As to the application of the Act to London, see Part IV of the London Government Act, 1963, p. 289, *post*; and to the Isles of Scilly, see section 193, *post*.

(*) As to meaning or statutory definition of " managers or governors ", " aided school ", "special agreement school " and " alterations ", see pp. 67–69, *ante*.

(a) " **Maintenance contributions** ".—Section 114 (1), p. 184, *post*, provides that in relation to any voluntary school this expression means a contribution payable under this section.

(b) " **Obligations under paragraph (a) of subsection (3) of section fifteen of this Act** ".—Section 15 (3) (*a*) (as amended by the Second Schedule to the Education Act, 1946), p. 96, *ante*, imposes upon the managers or governors of aided schools and special agreement schools an obligation to pay any expenses incurred in effecting such alterations to the school buildings as may be required by the local education authority for the purpose of securing that the school premises conform to the prescribed standards, and any expenses incurred in effecting repairs to the school premises not being repairs which are excluded from their responsibility by the following paragraph.

Paragraph (*b*) of the same subsection provides that the managers or governors of such schools shall not be responsible for repairs to the interior of the school buildings or for repairs to those buildings necessary in consequence of the use of the school premises, in pursuance of any direction or requirement of the authority, for purposes other than those of the school.

(c) " **School buildings** ".—By section 4 (2) of the Education Act, 1946, p. 211, *post*, the term " school buildings " in the present Act is to be deemed always to have meant any building or part of a building forming part of the school premises other than a building or part of a building which is required (*a*) as a caretaker's dwelling; (*b*) for use in connection with playing fields; (*c*) for affording facilities for medical examination or treatment; or (*d*) for affording canteen facilities for pupils.

(d) " **The special agreement relating to the school** ".—Section 15 (2), p. 96, *ante*, provides (*inter alia*) that the Secretary of State may direct that any voluntary school with respect to which he is satisfied that the managers or governors of the school will be willing, with the assistance of the maintenance contribution payable by the Secretary of State under this section, to defray the expenses which would fall to be borne by them under subsection (3) (*a*) of that section shall if a special agreement has been made with respect to the school under the Third Schedule, p. 201, *post*, be a special agreement school. See particularly the general note to that section. Expenses to be incurred in pursuance of a special agreement are within the scope of the term " initial expenses " with respect to which the Secretary of State may make a loan to the managers or governors under section 105, p. 179, *post*.

103. Power of the Secretary of State to make grants in respect of aided schools and special agreement schools transferred to new sites . . .—(1) Where the Secretary of State (a) by an order made under section sixteen of this Act (b) authorises the transfer of any voluntary school (*) to a new site . . . then, if the school to be transferred . . . in pursuance of the order is to be maintained (*) as an aided school (*) or a special agreement school (*), the Secretary of State (a) may pay to the managers or governors (*) of the school in respect of any sums expended by them in the construction of the school (c) a grant not exceeding [85 per cent.] thereof:

Provided that no grant shall be payable under this section to the managers or governors of a special agreement school in respect of any sums expended by them in the execution of proposals to which the special agreement for the school relates (d).

(2) [*Repealed.*]

(3) Without prejudice to the general discretion of the Secretary of State (a) as to the making of any grant under this section and as to the amount of any such grant, the Secretary of State (a) shall, in determining the amount of any such grant, take into account any sums which may accrue to the managers governors or trustees of the school in respect of the disposal of the site (e) from which the school is to be transferred . . .

NOTES

This and the last preceding section provide for the payment of grants by the Secretary of State in respect of aided schools and special agreement schools to which reference has been made in the general notes to ss. 15 and 16, pp. 95 *et seq.*, *ante*. In particular, this section, subsection (2) whereof was repealed by s. 17 (2) of, and the Second Schedule to, the Education (Miscellaneous Provisions) Act, 1953, *post*, and which must now be read in conjunction with s. 8 (1) of that Act, *post*, enables the Secretary of State, if he thinks fit, to pay a grant of up to 85 per cent. of the cost of transferring a voluntary school to a new site. The maximum rate of grant is now 85 per cent., the words in square brackets having been substituted by s. 3 of the Education Act 1975.

The words omitted in sub-s. (1) were repealed by s. 1 (5) (*a*) of the Education Act, 1967, p. 259, *post*. The repealed provisions are superseded by s. 1 (2) of the Act of 1967.

Sub-s. (3), which makes provision for the exercise of the Secretary of State's discretion in determining the amount of grants under the section, is applied to grants under s. 1 (2) of the Education Act, 1967, p. 258, *post*. See also s. 1 (3) of the Act of 1967.

The omitted words at the end of sub-s. (3) were repealed by s. 1 (5) (*a*) of the Education Act, 1967.

As to the application of the Act to London, see Part IV of the London Government Act, 1963, *post*; and to the Isles of Scilly, see section 193, *post*.

(*) As to the meaning or statutory definition of "voluntary school", "maintain" "aided school", "special agreement school" and "managers or governors", see pp. 67–69, *ante*.

(a) "**Secretary of State**".—See note (b) to s. 1, *ante*.

(b) "**By an order made under section sixteen of this Act**".—Two forms of order are provided for under section 16, p. 99, *ante*, viz.:—

(1) Subsection (1) enables the Secretary of State by order to authorise the transfer of (*inter alia*) a voluntary school to a new site either because it is not reasonably practicable to make the necessary alterations to the existing school premises for securing that they conform to the prescribed standards, or in consequence of any movement of population or of any action taken or proposed to be taken under the enactments relating to housing or to town and country planning;

(2) Subsection (2) enables the Secretary of State by order to direct that a proposed new voluntary school shall be deemed to be in substitution for another voluntary school or schools which is or are to be discontinued.

As to the revocation or variation of orders and directions, see section 111, p. 181, *post*.

Section 16 should now be read in conjunction with para. 2 of the First Schedule to the Education Act, 1946, *post*.

(c) "**The construction of the school**".—The effect of section 8 (1) of the Education (Miscellaneous Provisions) Act, 1953, *post*, is that there must be substituted for this reference to the construction of the school in relation to a transferred school a reference to the provision, whether before or after July 14, 1953 (the date of passing of the 1953 Act), of the school buildings, and in relation to a substituted school a reference to the provision, whether before or after the said date, of a site for the school and the school buildings. The result is to make the purchase price and cost of adaptation of an existing building as eligible for grant as the cost of construction of a new building. As to the duty of the local education authority to provide the site for a transferred voluntary school, see para. 1 of the First Schedule to the Education Act, 1946, *post*.

(d) "**Proposals to which the special agreement for the school relates**".—See note (e) to section 102, p. 176, *ante*.

(e) "**Disposal of the site**".—As to the power of the trustees of the school to sell or exchange the site of the school, see section 14 of the School Sites Act 1841; 11 Halsbury's Statutes (3rd Edn.) 387, and as to the application of the proceeds of sale in certain cases, see para. 8 of the First Schedule to the Education Act 1946, *post*.

104. [*Superseded.*]

NOTES

This section dealt with the problem of providing help for new aided and special agreement schools which were established wholly or partially in order to accommodate children who were unable to attend some existing school, although that school had not ceased to exist.

The section has now been superseded by s. 1 of the Education Act, 1967, p. 258, *post*, under which extended powers are given to make contributions, grants and loans. Note, however, the saving in s. 1 (6) of the Act of 1967, which provides that nothing in s. 1 of the Act of 1967 shall extend to contributions or grants in respect of expenditure or work which (*a*) was begun before 4th July, 1966, or (*b*) was approved by the Secretary of State before that date under s. 13 (6) of the Education Act, 1944, or under any arrangements relating to work to which that section does not apply; or (*c*) was included in a programme notified to a local education authority as the main building programme approved by the Secretary of State for the twelve months beginning with April, 1966, or for any earlier period; or in respect of expenditure on the provision of the site on which or buildings to which any such work was done or proposed to be done.

105. Power of Secretary of State to make loans to aided schools and special agreement schools in respect of initial expenditure.—(1) If upon the application of the managers or governors (*) of any aided school (*) or special agreement school (*) the Secretary of State (a) is satisfied after consultation with persons representing them that their share of any initial expenses (c) required in connection with the school premises (*) will involve capital expenditure which, in his opinion having regard to all the circumstances of the case, ought properly to be met by borrowing, he may make to the managers or governors of the school for the purpose of helping them to meet that expenditure, a loan of such amount at such rate of interest and otherwise on such terms and conditions as may be specified in an agreement made between him and them with the consent of the Treasury.

(2) For the purposes of this section, the expression " initial expenses " means in relation to any school premises—

(*a*) expenses to be incurred in defraying the cost of any alterations (*) required by the development plan approved by (c) the Secretary of State (a) for the area;

(*b*) expenses to be incurred in pursuance of any special agreement (d);

[(*c*) (i) expenses to be incurred in providing a site or school buildings on a significant enlargement of the school premises, being expenses in respect of which a maintenance contribution may be paid;

(ii) expenses to be incurred in providing school buildings on a site to which the school is to be transferred under the authority of an order under section 16 (1) of this Act (e);

(iii) expenses to be incurred in providing a site or school buildings for a new school which by virtue of an order under section 16 (2) (f) of this Act is deemed to be in substitution for a discontinued school or schools.]

(*d*) expenses certified by the Secretary of State (a) under the last foregoing section (g) as being attributable to the provision of education for displaced pupils (h);

and the managers' or governors' share of any such initial expenses shall be taken to be so much thereof as remains to be borne by them after taking into account the amount of any maintenance contribution (j), grant under a special agreement (k), or grant under either of the last two foregoing sections (l) as may be paid or payable in respect of those expenses.

(3) If upon an application being made to him under subsection (2) of section fifteen of this Act (m) for an order directing that a school shall be an aided school or a special agreement school it appears to the Secretary of State (a) that the area served by the school will not be also served by any county school (*) or controlled school (*), then, unless he is satisfied that the managers or governors of the school will be able to defray the expenses which would fall to be borne by them under paragraph (*a*) of subsection (3) of that section (n) without the assistance of a loan under this section, the Secretary of State (a) shall consult such persons or bodies of persons as appear to him to be representative of any religious denomination which, in his opinion having regard to the circumstances of the area, is likely to be concerned;

and, unless after such consultation he is satisfied that the holding of a local inquiry (o) is unnecessary, shall cause such inquiry to be held before determining the application.

NOTES

This section, which is closely related to the foregoing sections (ss. 102 and 103, pp. 176 *et seq.*, *ante*), enables the Secretary of State to make loans to the managers or governors of aided and special agreement schools in respect of " initial expenses ", as defined in sub-s. (2) of the section. Such loans may be made in four differing circumstances:—

(1) to enable the managers or governors to carry out any alterations required by the development plan approved by the Secretary of State for a particular area or specified in the plan submitted to the Secretary of State and approved by the Secretary of State prior to the approval of the plan as a whole (this being a loan in respect of that half of the cost which is to be borne by the managers or governors, the other half being defrayed by means of the maintenance contribution to be paid under s. 102, *ante*);

(2) in the case of a special agreement school only, to enable the managers or governors to defray the costs of carrying out the special agreement for the school (s. 15, p. 107, *ante*, and the Third Schedule, p. 201, *post*. In relation to this matter see the proviso to s. 102, *ante*, and s. 103 (3), p. 178, *ante*;

(3) to enable the managers or governors to defray the cost of providing a site or school buildings or a significant enlargement of the school premises, on transfer to a new site, or in providing a new school;

(4) to enable the managers or governors to provide accommodation for displaced pupils (see note (*k*), *infra*).

The object of the loans which may be made under this section is to place the denominations and managers of voluntary schools in the same situation as local authorities find themselves in when borrowing to carry out public work.

The new paragraph (*c*) to sub-s. 2, shewn in square brackets, was substituted by the Education Act 1968, Sch. I.

As to the application of the Act to London see Part IV of the London Government Act, 1963, *post*; and to the Isles of Scilly, see section 118, p. 193, *post*.

(*) As to the meaning or statutory definition of " managers or governors ", " aided school ", " special agreement school ", " premises ", " alterations ", " county school " and " controlled school ", see pp. 67–69, *ante*.

(a) **" Secretary of State ".**—See note (b) to s. 1, *ante*.

(b) **" Initial expenses ".**—This expression is defined in subsection (2) of this section, but to the list of expenses therein referred to there must now, by virtue of section 1 (4) of the Education Act, 1959, *post*, be added a reference to any expenses in respect of which the Secretary of State may make a grant under section 1 (2) of that Act, *post*, which gives the Secretary of State power to pay grants towards the cost of providing sites and school buildings for certain new aided secondary schools.

(c) **" Required by the development plan ".**—The reference to alterations so required must now be read as including a reference to expenses, whether incurred before or after the passing of the 1953 Act, in defraying the cost of any alterations specified in the development plan as submitted to the Secretary of State " being alterations to the carrying out of which the Secretary of State has given approval before the approval by him of the plan ". See the Education (Miscellaneous Provisions) Act, 1953, section 8 (3) (*a*), *post*. Generally as to development plans, see section 11, *ante*.

(d) **" Special agreement ".**—See section 15, p. 95, *ante*, and the Third Schedule, p. 201, *post*.

(e) **" Section 16 (1) of this Act ".**—This subsection provides that the Secretary of State may by order authorise the transfer of a school to a new site, either because the old site cannot be made to conform to prescribed standards or in consequence of any movement of population, etc. See p. 99, *ante*.

(f) **" Section 16 (2) of this Act ".**—This subsection provides that the Secretary of State may by order direct that the normal provisions as to discontinuance of one or more voluntary schools shall not apply where a new voluntary school is to be established to take their place. See p. 99, *ante*.

(g) **" Under the last foregoing section ".**—S. 104, which enabled the Secretary of State to make grants in respect of aided schools and special agreement schools established for the accommodation of displaced pupils. Superseded by s. 1 of the Education Act 1967, p. 258, *post*.

(h) **" Displaced pupils ".**—This term was defined by s. 104 (superseded, see *supra*) thus: " The expression ' displaced pupils ' means, in relation to any such proposed school [aided schools and special agreement schools for displaced pupils] . . . pupils for whom education would, in the opinion of the [Secretary of State], have been provided in some other aided school or special agreement school if that school had not ceased to be available for them in consequence of its having ceased to be used for providing both primary and secondary education or in consequence of a substantial reduction in the number of pupils for whom education is to be provided in it ".

This definition was extended by s. 1 of the Education (Miscellaneous Provisions) Act, 1953 (now also superseded by the Act of 1967) as follows: " . . . the expression ' displaced pupils ' shall, in relation to a proposed school, include pupils who, in consequence of action taken or proposed to be taken under the enactments relating to housing or to town and country planning, have ceased to reside in the area served by some other aided school or special agreement school, being—

(*a*) pupils for whom education was being provided in that other school immediately before they cease to reside in the area served by it; or

(*b*) pupils, other than as aforesaid, for whom education would, in the opinion of the [Secretary of State], have been provided in that other school had they continued to reside in the area served by it."

(j) " **Maintenance contribution** ".—Section 114 (1), p. 184, *post*, provides that in relation to any voluntary school this expression means a contribution payable under section 102, p. 176, *ante*.

(k) " **Grant under special agreement** ".—See paragraphs (4) and (5) of the Third Schedule, p. 201, *post*.

(l) " **Grant under either of the last two foregoing sections** ".—Section 103, *ante*, enables the Secretary of State to make grants in respect of aided schools and special agreement schools which are transferred to new sites. S. 104 is superseded.

By virtue of the Education Act, 1959, section 1 (4), *post*, any grant paid or payable under *ibid.*, section 1 (2), *post*, which enables the Secretary of State to make grants in respect of the provision of sites or school buildings of certain new aided secondary schools, is to be taken into account in the same way as grants under s. 103.

(m) " **Subsection (2) of section fifteen of this Act** ".—Section 15 (2), p. 96, *ante*, enables the Secretary of State (*inter alia*), where he is satisfied that the managers or governors of a voluntary school with respect to which application is duly made to him will be able and willing, with the assistance of the maintenance contribution payable under section 102, p. 176, *ante*, to defray the expenses falling to be borne by them under section 15 (3) (*a*), p. 96, *ante*, by order to direct that the school shall be an aided school, or, if a special agreement has been made with respect to the school under the Third Schedule, p. 201, *post*, a special agreement school.

(n) " **Paragraph (a) of subsection (3) of that section** ".—Section 15 (3) (*a*), as amended by the Second Schedule to the Education Act, 1946, specifies the expenses for which the managers or governors of aided and special agreement schools are liable under the Act. See the notes to that section.

(o) " **Local inquiry** ".—As to the powers of the Secretary of State in relation to the holding of local inquiries, see section 93, p. 171, *ante*.

106. Contributions between local education authorities.—[*This section is superseded as regards the recovery of expenditure incurred after* 31*st March,* 1948, *by section* 6 *of the Education* (*Miscellaneous Provisions*) *Act,* 1948, post; *see subsection* (7) *thereof. As no expenditure is now recoverable under this section it is regarded as spent.*]

107. Expenses of Ministers.—Any expenses incurred by the Secretary of State (a) or by the Minister of Health in the exercise of their functions under this Act shall be defrayed out of monies provided by Parliament.

NOTE

This section must now be read in conjunction with section 15 of the Education Act, 1946 *post*, section 13 of the Education (Miscellaneous Provisions) Act, 1948, *post*, and section 19 of the Education (Miscellaneous Provisions) Act, 1953, *post*, which provide that any increased expenditure attributable to the provisions of those Acts shall also be defrayed out of moneys so provided. See also section 4 (c) of the Education Act, 1964, p. 252, *post*.

(a) " **Secretary of State** ".—See note (b) to section 1, *ante*.

PART V

SUPPLEMENTAL

108. [*Spent.*]

109. [*Spent.*]

NOTE

This section, which was substituted by s. 5 of the Education Act, 1946, enabled local education authorities to provide temporary accommodation for voluntary schools. The section is to be regarded as spent.

110. [*Spent.*]

111. Revocation and variation of orders and directions.—Any order made or directions given by the Secretary of State (a), the Minister of Health or a local education authority (*) under the provisions of this Act may be varied or revoked by a further order or further directions made or given by the Secretary of State (a), the Minister of Health, or that authority, as the case may be:

Provided that where the power to make or give any such order or directions is exercisable only upon the application or with the consent of any person (*) or body of persons, or after consultation with any person or body of persons or otherwise subject to any conditions, no order or directions made or given thereunder shall be varied or revoked except upon the like application, with the like consent, after the like consultation or subject to the like conditions, as the case may be.

NOTES

This section gives a general power to revoke or vary an order made or directions given under the Act by the Secretary of State for Education and Science or the Minister of Health or by local education authorities.

The repeals made in sections 17, 100, *ante*, by the Education Act 1973, Sch. 2, Part II, are not to affect any order made by virtue of the provision repealed, or the operation in relation to any such order of the above section: Education Act 1973, Sch. 1, para. 3.

(*) As to the statutory definition of "local education authority" and "person", see pp. 184, 185, *post.*

(a) **"Secretary of State".**—See note (b) to s. 1, *ante.*

112. Regulations to be laid before Parliament.—All regulations made under this Act shall be laid before Parliament as soon as may be after they are made, and if either House of Parliament, within the period of forty days beginning with the day on which any such regulations are laid before it, resolves that the regulations be annulled the regulations shall cease to have effect, but without prejudice to anything previously done thereunder or to the making of any new regulations.

In reckoning any such period of forty days no account shall be taken of any time during which Parliament is dissolved or prorogued or during which both Houses are adjourned for more than four days.

NOTES

The present section enables any regulations made under the Act (which are now made by statutory instrument, see section 1 (2) of the Statutory Instruments Act, 1946; 32 Halsbury's Statutes (3rd Edn.) 668) to be annulled by a positive resolution of either House of Parliament during the period when the regulations are laid before them.

As to regulations made for the purposes of the Education (Miscellaneous Provisions) Act, 1948, see section 12 thereof, *post*, and as to regulations made under powers conferred by the Education (Miscellaneous Provisions) Act, 1953, see section 18 of that Act, *post.*

It should also be noted that by section 121, p. 196, *post*, any regulation in force under any enactment repealed by the Act is to continue in operation and have effect as if made under this Act and may be varied or revoked accordingly.

113. Notices.—Any [order (a), notice or other document], required or authorised by this Act to be served upon any person (b) may be served by delivering it to that person, or by leaving it at his usual or last known place of residence (c), or by sending it in a pre-paid letter addressed to him at that place.

NOTES

The words in square brackets were substituted for the word "notice" by section 14 of the Education Act, 1946, p. 259, *post.* As originally enacted the section applied to school attendance notices under subsection (1) of section 37, p. 129, *ante*, but not to school attendance orders under subsection (2) thereof.

Reference may be made, in connection with this section, to section 26 of the Interpretation Act 1889; 32 Halsbury's Statutes (3rd Edn.) 452, which provides that where an Act passed after the commencement of that Act authorises or requires any document to be served by post, whether the expression "serve", or the expression "give" or "send", or any other expression is used, then, unless the contrary intention appears, the service shall be deemed to be effected by properly addressing, prepaying, and posting a letter containing the document, and unless the contrary is proved to have been effected at the time at which the letter would be delivered in the ordinary course of post.

It was decided in *Walthamstow Urban District Council* v. *Henwood*, [1897] 1 Ch. 41, that prepayment of the letter must be proved in order to prove service. It has also been held (*R.* v. *Westminster Unions Assessment Committee, Ex parte Woodward & Sons*, [1917] 1 K.B. 832) that the presumption that a notice has been received when properly addressed, prepaid and delivered to the post office is not merely a presumption of fact unless the contrary is shown, but is a presumption of law whether in fact the notice was received by the addressee or not.

The service of notices for various purposes is authorised or required by numerous provisions of the Act. The service of school attendance orders is required by section 37 (2), p. 129, *ante*.

(a) **" Order ".**—As to school attendance orders, see section 37, as amended by section 10 of the Education (Miscellaneous Provisions) Act, 1953, p. 129, *ante*.

(b) **" Any person ".**—Section 19 of the Interpretation Act, 1889; 32 Halsbury's Statutes (3rd Edn.) 449, provides that in any Act passed after the commencement of that Act the word " person ", unless the contrary expressly appears, includes any body of persons corporate or unincorporate. It therefore includes local education authorities but in this connection regard must also be had to section 231 of the Local Government Act 1972, 42 Halsbury's Statutes (3rd Edn.) 1059, which deals with the service of notices upon local authorities and upon parish meetings.

(c) **" Usual or last-known place of residence ".**—As to the meaning of the word " residence ", see *Blackwell* v. *England* (1857), 27 L.J. (Q.B.) 124; *R.* v. *Braithwaite*, [1918] 2 K.B. 319; and *R.* v. *Hastings Justices, Ex parte Mitchell* (1925), 89 J.P. Jo. 86.

114. Interpretation.—(1) In this Act, unless the context otherwise requires, the following expressions have the meanings hereby respectively assigned to them, that is to say :—

" Agreed syllabus " means, subject to the provisions of subsection (4) of this section, an agreed syllabus of religious instruction (a) prepared in accordance with the provisions of the Fifth Schedule to this Act (b) and adopted or deemed to be adopted (c) thereunder ;

[" Alterations ", in relation to any school premises, includes improvements, extensions and additions, but does not include any significant enlargement of the school premises (d).]

" Assist ", in relation to any school, college or institution, (e), has the meaning assigned to it by subsection (2) of this section ;

" Child " means a person who is not over compulsory school age (f);

" Clothing " (g) includes boots and other footwear;

" Compulsory school age " (f) has, [*subject to the provisions of section thirty-eight of this Act, the meaning assigned to it by section thirty-five of this Act* (h) ;]

" County " means an administrative county within the meaning of the Local Government Act, 1933 (i);

" Enlargement ", in relation to school premises, includes any modification of the existing premises which has the effect of increasing the number of pupils for whom accommodation can be provided, and " enlarge " shall be construed accordingly (k).

" Former authority " means any authority which was a local education authority within the meaning of any enactment repealed by this Act or any previous Act ;

" Foundation managers " and " foundation governors " (l) mean, in relation to any voluntary school (m), managers and governors (n) appointed otherwise than by a local education authority (o) or a minor authority (p) for the purpose of securing, so far as is practicable, that the character of the school as a voluntary school is preserved and developed, and, in particular, that the school is conducted in accordance with the provisions of any trust deed relating thereto (q) ; and, unless the context otherwise requires, references in this Act to " managers " or " governors " shall, in relation to any function thereby conferred or imposed exclusively (r) on foundation managers or foundation governors, be construed as references to such managers or governors ;

" Further education " (s) has the meaning assigned to it by section forty-one of this Act ;

" Independent school " (t) means any school (u) at which full-time education (v) is provided for five or more pupils (w) of compulsory school age (x) (whether or not such education is also provided for pupils under or over that age), not being a school maintained (y) by a local education authority (z) or a school in respect of which grants are made (a1) by the Secretary of State (b1) to the proprietor of the school;

" Junior pupil " means a child (c1) who has not attained the age of twelve years;

" Local education authority " (e1) means, in relation to any area for which a joint education board is constituted as the local education authority under the provisions of Part I of the First Schedule to this Act, the board so constituted, and, save as aforesaid, means, in relation to a county (f1), the council of the county, and, in relation to a county borough, the council of the county borough ;

" Local education order " (g1) means an order made by the Secretary of State (b1) under section twelve of this Act;

" Local government elector " has the meaning assigned to it by section three hundred and five of the Local Government Act, 1933 (h1) ; and in relation to the area of any joint education board constituted under Part I of the First Schedule to this Act (i1) a local government elector for the area of any council by whom members are appointed to the board shall be deemed to be a local government elector for the area of the authority ;

" Maintain " in relation to any school or county college (j1) has the meaning assigned to it by subsection (2) of this section ;

" Maintenance contribution ", in relation to any voluntary school (k1), means a contribution payable under section one hundred and two of this Act (l1) ;

" Medical officer " means, in relation to any local education authority, a duly qualified medical practitioner (m1) employed, or engaged, whether regularly or for the purposes of any particular case, by that authority [or whose services are made available to that authority by the Secretary of State]:

[" Minor authority " (n1) means, in relation to a school maintained by a local education authority (o1)—

(*a*) where the area which appears to the local education authority to be served by the school is a parish or community, the parish or community council, or, in the case of a parish which has no council, the parish meeting;

(*b*) where the said area is a community having no community council or is an area in England which is not within a parish and is not situated within a metropolitan county, the council for the district of the area concerned;

(*c*) where the said area comprises two or more of the following, a parish, a community or an area in England which is not within a parish and is not situated in a metropolitan county—

(i) the parish or community council or councils, if any;

(ii) in the case of a parish which has no council, the parish meeting;

(iii) in the case of an area which is a community having no community council or which is in England and is not within a parish, the council of the district concerned;

acting jointly.]

" Parent " (p1), in relation to any child or young person (q1), includes a guardian and every person who has the actual custody of the child or young person ;

"Premises" (r[1]), in relation to any school, includes any detached playing fields, but, except where otherwise expressly provided, does not include a teacher's dwelling-house;

"Prescribed" (a[2]) means prescribed by regulations made by the Secretary of State (b[1]);

"Primary education" (b[2]) has the meaning assigned to it by section eight of this Act;

"Primary school" (c[2]) means, subject to the provisions of subsection (3) of this section, a school for providing primary education;

"Proprietor" (d[2]), in relation to any school, means the person or body of persons responsible for the management of the school, and for the purposes of the provisions of this Act relating to applications for the registration of independent schools (e[2]), includes any person or body of persons proposing to be so responsible;

"Provisionally registered school" (f[2]) means an independent school registered in the register of independent schools, whereof the registration is provisional only;

"Pupil" (g[2]), where used without qualification, means a person of any age for whom education is required to be provided under this Act;

"Registered pupil" (h[2]) means, in relation to any school, a pupil registered as such in the register kept in accordance with the requirements of this Act, *but does not include any child who has been withdrawn from the school in the prescribed manner;*

"Registered school" (i[2]) means an independent school registered in the register of independent schools, whereof the registration is final;

"School" (j[2]) means an institution for providing primary or secondary education (k[2]) or both primary and secondary education (l[2]), being a school maintained by a local education authority (m[2]), an independent school (t), or a school in respect of which grants are made by the Secretary of State (b[1]) to the proprietor of the school (o[2]); and, the expression "school" where used without qualification includes any such school or all such schools as the context may require;

"Secondary education" (p[2]) has the meaning assigned to it by section eight of this Act;

"Secondary school" (q[2]) means, subject to the provisions ofsubsection (3) of this section, a school for providing secondary education,

"Senior pupil" (r[2]) means a person who has attained the age of twelve years but has not attained the age of nineteen years;

"Significant", in relation to a change in the character of a school or an enlargement of school premises, implies that there is a substantial change in the function or size of the school.

"Special agreement" (s[2]) means an agreement made under the provisions of the Third Schedule to this Act;

"Special educational treatment" (t[2]) has the meaning assigned to it by paragraph (*c*) of subsection (2) of section eight of this Act;

"Trust deed" (u[2]), in relation to any voluntary school (v[2]), includes any instrument (not being an instrument of management, instrument of government (w[2]), rules of management, or articles of government (x[2]), made under this Act) regulating the maintenance, management or conduct of the school or the constitution of the body of managers or governors (y[2]) thereof;

"Young person" (z[2]) means a person over compulsory school age who has not attained the age of eighteen years.

(2) For the purposes of this Act:—

(*a*) the duty of a local education authority (a[3]) to maintain a school or county college shall include the duty of defraying all the expenses of maintaining the school or college except, in the case of an aided school or a special agreement school (b[3]), any expenses that by virtue of any provision of this Act or of any special agreement (c[3]) made thereunder are payable by the managers or governors (d[3]) of the school, and the expression "maintain" shall be construed accordingly; and

(*b*) where a local education authority make to the proprietor of any school which is not maintained by the authority or to the persons responsible for the maintenance of any training college or other institution which is not so maintained, any grant in respect of the school college or institution or any payment in consideration of the provision of educational facilities thereat, the school college or institution shall be deemed to be assisted (e[3]) by the authority.

(3) So long as any county school or voluntary school is used for providing both primary and secondary education, references in this Act to primary schools (f[3]) shall be construed as including references to that school and references therein to secondary schools shall be construed as excluding any reference thereto:

Provided that where the primary education provided in any such school is provided in a separate junior or preparatory department, the Secretary of State (b[1]) may direct (g[3]) that the school shall be deemed for the purposes of this Act to be a secondary school and such references as aforesaid shall be construed accordingly.

(4) Where before the date of the commencement of Part II of this Act (h[3]) a syllabus of religious instruction had been adopted by a former authority (i[3]) for use in any school which after that date is a county school or a voluntary school or for any class or description of pupils, that syllabus shall be deemed to be the agreed syllabus (j[3]) for that school, or for that class or that description of pupils, as the case may be, until a syllabus in substitution therefor is prepared in accordance with the provisions of the Fifth Schedule to this Act (k[3]) and adopted or deemed to be adopted thereunder, or until the expiration of two years after the said date, whichever first occurs.

(5) [*Repealed.*]

(6) [*Any person who before the commencement of Part II of this Act had attained an age at which his parent had ceased to be under any obligation imposed under section forty-six of the Education Act, 1921* (*m*[3]), *shall be deemed to be over compulsory school age, and any person who after the said date ceases to be of compulsory school age* (*n*[3]) *shall not, in the event of any subsequent change in the upper limit of the compulsory school age, again become a person of compulsory school age.*[o3]]

(7) Where at any time before the date of the commencement of Part II of this Act the premises of any school which was for the time being a public elementary school within the meaning of the enactments repealed by this Act (p[3]) have ceased by reason of war damage (q[3]), or by reason of any action taken in contemplation or in consequence of war, to be used for the purposes of a school, then, for the purposes of this Act, the school, unless it has been closed in accordance with those enactments (r[3]), shall be deemed to have been a public elementary school within the meaning of those enactments immediately before that date and, if it was maintained by a former authority immediately before the premises ceased to be used for the purposes of a school, to have been maintained by such an authority immediately before that date.

(8) In this Act, unless the context otherwise requires, references to any enactment (s[3]) or any provision of any enactment shall be construed as references to that enactment or provision as amended by any subsequent enactment, including this Act.

NOTES

Subsection (5), which contained provisions for avoiding broken terms, was repealed and replaced by section 8 of the Education Act, 1946, itself repealed in part by section 9 of the Education Act, 1962, p. 246, *post*, which reduces the number of school leaving dates in England and Wales from three to two.

Generally as to the effect of an interpretation clause in a statute, see *R.* v. *Cambridgeshire Justices* (1838), 7 Ad. & El. 480; (remarks of Lord Denman, C.J., at p. 491); and *A.-G.* v. *Worcester Corporation* (1846), 15 L.J. (Ch.) 398; (remarks of Lord Cottenham, L.C., at p. 399). Pollock, C.B., in *Allsopp* v. *Day* (1861), 7 H. & N. 457, at p. 463; stated that an interpretation clause ought to be strictly construed. As to the application of definitions to incorporated enactments, see *Sale* v. *Phillips*, [1894] 1 Q.B. 349. Definitions of " medical inspection " and " medical treatment " formerly contained in subsection (1) were repealed by the National Health Service Reorganisation Act 1973, section 57, Sch. 5.

(a) **" Agreed syllabus of religious instruction ".**—Section 29 (1), p. 121, *ante*, provides that the provisions of the Fifth Schedule, p. 204, *post*, are to have effect with respect to the preparation, adoption, and reconsideration of an agreed syllabus of religious instruction. The remainder of that section enables a local education authority to constitute a standing advisory council on religious education to advise the authority upon matters connected with the religious instruction to be given in accordance with an agreed syllabus, including methods of teaching, choice of books and the provision of lectures for teachers. Section 26, p. 117, *ante*, provides that the religious instruction to be given in county schools is, subject to an exception in cases where arrangements cannot conveniently be made for withdrawal of pupils under the Act to receive religious instruction elsewhere, to be given in accordance with an agreed syllabus. Subject to the exceptions contained in section 27 (1), p. 118, *ante*, the religious instruction to be given in controlled schools is, by subsection (6) of that section, also to be in accordance with an agreed syllabus. In the case of aided and special agreement schools the religious instruction is normally to be under the control of the managers or governors and to be in accordance with the provisions of the trust deed or of previous practice, but even in those schools arrangements are to be made to enable pupils whose parents so desire and who cannot reasonably attend elsewhere to receive religious instruction in accordance with an agreed syllabus.

Subsection (4) of this section, which is now spent, provided for the temporary continuance of syllabuses adopted before 1st April, 1945, by a former authority as agreed syllabuses under this Act.

(b) **" Fifth Schedule to this Act ".**—See p. 204, *post*, for this Schedule, which details the procedure to be adopted in relation to the preparation and adoption of an agreed syllabus.

(c) **" Adopted or deemed to be adopted ".**—In order that a syllabus might be adopted it was necessary for the committees set up under paragraph 2 of the Fifth Schedule, p. 204, *post*, to reach unanimous agreement (paragraph 9, *ibid*). In the event of failure to reach unanimous agreement, or of failure by a local education authority to adopt a syllabus unanimously recommended to it, the Secretary of State was to appoint a body of persons to prepare a syllabus (paragraph 10, *ibid.*) which, as from a date directed by the Secretary of State, is deemed to be the agreed syllabus (paragraph 11, *ibid.*). See also paragraph 12, *ibid.*, as to the reconsideration of an agreed syllabus. A syllabus might also be deemed temporarily to be an agreed syllabus under subsection (4) of this section.

(d) The definition of " alterations " was substituted by Sch. I to the Education Act, 1968.

(e) **" School, college or institution ".**—The word " school " is defined by this section. The words " college or institution " will cover all types of educational institution referred to in the Act, including teachers' training colleges (section 62, p. 151, *ante*), except schools.

(f) **" Compulsory school age ".**—According to this section, this term has, subject to the provisions of section 38, p. 131, *ante*, the meaning assigned to it by section 35, p. 127, *ante*. It should be noted that the word " child " includes persons who are below the lower limit of compulsory school age and, indeed, this is essential in the circumstances in which the word is used in several sections of the Act, *e.g.*, sections 9 (4), p. 83, *ante* (definition of nursery schools), 34, p. 125, *ante* (ascertainment of children who require special educational treatment). As to the date on which a person ceases to be of compulsory school age, see subsection (6) of this section and section 9 of the Education Act, 1962, p. 246, *post*. As to the altered meaning of the word " child " when used in any enactment relating to the prohibition or regulation of the employment of children or young persons, see section 58, p. 148, *ante*.

(g) **" Clothing ".**—As to the provision of clothing by local education authorities, see section 5 of the Education (Miscellaneous Provisions) Act, 1948, p. 221, *post*.

(h) The words in italics were repealed by the Education (School-Leaving Dates) Act 1976.

(i) **" An administrative county within the meaning of the Local Government Act 1933 ".**—The Local Government Act 1933, was repealed by the Local Government Act 1972. See now, as to new local government areas in England and Wales, sections 1, 20 of the Act of 1972.

(k) The definitions of " enlargement " and " significant " were added by Sch. I to the Education Act, 1968.

(l) **" Foundation managers "; " foundation governors ".**—Foundation managers existed under the previous law, see section 31 (1) of the Education Act, 1921. Foundation governors are a creation of the present Act in consequence of the inclusion of secondary schools within the scope of the general system. Foundation managers and governors only exist in relation to voluntary schools and form only a proportion of the managers and governors of such schools (see sections 18 and 19, pp. 105, 106, *ante*).

(m) **" School ".**—See the definition of this word in this section.

(n) **" Managers and governors ".**—See note (b) to section 17, p. 101, *ante*.

(o) **" Local education authority ".**—See note (e^1), *infra*.

(p) **" Minor authority ".**—This term is defined in this section.

(q) **" Trust deed ".**—See the definition of this term elsewhere in this section. The previous words make it clear that the foundation managers or foundation governors may be appointed otherwise than in accordance with the trust deed. In fact, under section 17, p. 100, *ante*, the managers or governors (including the foundation managers or the foundation governors, in the case of a voluntary school) of a school are to be appointed by means of an instrument of management or instrument of government made by order of the Secretary of State, and the Secretary of State is, of course, able to vary the terms of a trust deed in various ways. By reason of this definition the Secretary of State is able to adjust the previously existing composition of the managers or governors to accord with modern conditions and to take advantage of the formation of parochial church councils, diocesan education committees and the like, which have come into existence since many existing trust deeds were executed.

(r) **" In relation to any functions thereby conferred or imposed exclusively ".**—The object of the latter part of the definition is to enable foundation managers or governors, who have, in respect of their limited functions (see, for example, sections 27 and 28, pp. 118, 119, *ante*), a dispute with the local education authority, to take that dispute to the Secretary of State under section 67, p. 154, *ante*. It also enables the Secretary of State to make use, where necessary, of his powers of enforcement under section 99, p. 173, *ante*, in relation to those functions of foundation managers and governors which are expressed to be duties, and also of his power to give directions under section 68, p. 155, *ante*, to prevent the unreasonable exercise, by foundation managers or governors, of any of their functions, whether expressed to be duties or not.

(s) **" Further education ".**—Section 41, p. 135, *ante*, defines this term as :—

(*a*) full-time and part-time education for persons over compulsory school age ; and

(*b*) leisure-time occupation, in such organised cultural training and recreative activities as are suited to their requirements, for any persons over compulsory school age who are able and willing to profit by the facilities provided for that purpose.

The same section imposes a duty upon local education authorities to secure the provision for their areas of adequate facilities for further education, as so defined, but neither empowers nor requires them to secure that provision otherwise than in accordance with schemes of further education (to be made under section 42, p. 136, *ante*) or at county colleges (to be provided under section 43, p. 136, *ante*). See the notes to those sections.

As to recoupment to a local education authority of the cost of providing further education for persons not belonging to their area, see section 7 of the Education (Miscellaneous Provisions) Act, 1953, p. 232, *post*.

(t) **" Independent school ".**—Part III of the Act (sections 70 to 75, pp. 156, *et seq*., *ante*) deals with the registration of independent schools.

(u) **" School ".**—Though this word is defined in this section, the meaning there given is here qualified by the latter part of this definition.

(v) **" Full-time education ".**—This expression is nowhere defined in the Act.

(w) **" Pupils ".**—The word " pupil " is defined elsewhere in this section.

(x) **" Compulsory school age ".**—See s. 35, p. 127, *ante* and, in particular, note (f), *ante*.

(y) **" Maintained ".**—By the definition contained in this section, the word " maintain ", in relation to any school or county college, has the meaning assigned to it by subsection (2) of this section. See also the First Schedule to the Education Act, 1946, p. 216, *post*.

(z) **" Local education authority ".**—See note (e[1]), *infra*.

(a[1]) **" School in respect of which grants are made ".**—See section 100, p. 175,

(b[1]) **" Secretary of State ".**—See note (b) to s. 1, *ante*.

(c[1]) **" Child ".**—See the definition of this term elsewhere in this section.

(e[1]) **" Local education authority ".**—See section 6, p. 76, *ante*, and the First Schedule, p. 198, *post*. As from 1st April, 1965, any reference in the Education Act, 1944 to 1962 or in any other Act to the local education authority is to be construed in relation to any outer London borough as a reference to the council of that borough, and in relation to the remainder of Greater London as a reference to the Greater London Council acting by means of a Special Committee known as the Inner London Education Authority. See section 30 of the London Government Act 1963, p. 289, *post*. As to the application of the Act to the Isles of Scilly, see section 118, p. 193, *post*. See also section 192 of the Local Government Act 1972, 42 Halsbury's Statutes (3rd Edn.) 1020, under which the local education authority for each non-metropolitan county is the council for the county and the local education authority for each metropolitan district is the council of the district.

(f[1]) **" County ".**—See the definition of this word in this section, and note (k), *ante*.

(g[1]) **" Local education order ".**—Section 12, p. 88, *ante*, requires the Secretary of State, as soon as may be after approving, under section 11, p. 85, *ante*, the development plan for the area of any local education authority, to make a local education order for the area of the authority making various provisions with regard to the various types and categories of schools established and to be established for the area and defining the duties of the authority in relation thereto.

(h[1]) **" Section three hundred and five of the Local Government Act 1933 ".**—Repealed by the Local Government Act 1972, s. 272 (1), Sch. 30. By section 270 (1) of the Act of 1972 the term " local government elector " is defined as a person registered as a local government elector in the register of electors in accordance with the provisions of the Representation of the People Acts. See now section 2 of the Representation of the People Act 1949; 11 Halsbury's Statutes (3rd Edn.) 545.

(i[1]) **" Part I of the First Schedule to this Act ".**—See p. 196, *post*.

(j[1]) **" School or county college ".**—See the respective definitions of these terms elsewhere in this section.

(k[1]) **" Voluntary school ".**—See section 9 (2), p. 82, *ante*, and, as to the classification of voluntary schools as controlled, aided and special agreement schools, section 15, p. 95, *ante*.

(l^1) **" Section one hundred and two of this Act ".**—Section 102, as amended, p. 176, *ante,* requires the Secretary of State to pay to the managers or governors of every aided school and of every special agreement school maintenance contributions equal to three-quarters of sums expended in carrying out their obligations under section 15 (3) (*a*), p. 96, *ante.* See the notes to both those sections.

(m^1) **" Duly qualified medical practitioner ".**—Section 69, p. 156, *ante,* enables the Secretary of State to notify a parent that his child, in certain circumstances, is required to submit to a medical examination. The words in square brackets in the definition of " medical officer " were added by the National Health Service Reorganisation Act 1973, section 57, Sch. 4.

(n^1) **" Minor authority ".**—This definition was substituted by section 192 (4) of the Local Government Act 1972. As to the functions of a minor authority under the present Act, see sections 18, 19 and 20, pp. 105 *et seq., ante,* with respect to the appointment of managers of primary schools and governors of secondary schools.

(o^1) **" School maintained by a local education authority ".**—See the definition of " school " elsewhere in this section.

(p^1) **" Parent ".**—Apart from including persons liable to maintain a child or young person as well as persons having the actual custody the definition of this word in section 170 (12) of the Education Act, 1921, was similar to that now contained in this section. The following cases refer to various persons who, for different purposes and under different statutes, have been regarded as the parent or as having the custody of another person; *Hance* v. *Burnett* (1880), 45 J.P. 54; *Hance* v. *Fairhurst* (1882), 51 L.J. (M.C.) 139; *London School Board* v. *Jackson* (1881), 7 Q.B.D. 502; *Southwark Union* v. *London County Council,* [1910] 2 K.B. 559; *Gateshead Union* v. *Durham County Council,* [1918] 1 Ch. 146; and *Woodward* v. *Oldfield,* [1928] 1 K.B. 204; [1927] All E.R. Rep. 645; *London County Council* v. *Stansell* (1935), 154 L.T. 241, but see now *Plunkett* v. *Alker,* [1954] 1 All E.R. 396; [1954] 1 Q.B. 420.

(q^1) **" Child or young person ".**—See the definitions of these terms elsewhere in this section.

(r^1) **" Premises" .**—This word usually appears in the Act in conjunction with the word " school "—also defined in this section—in the phrase " school premises ". In the Education Act, 1921, and other statutes comprising the Education Acts, 1921–1939, the phrase was not used. Instead, in comparable circumstances, it was usual to use the term " schoolhouse " which, by section 170 (6) of the Act of 1921, in relation to an elementary school included the teacher's dwelling-house and the playground (if any) and the offices and all premises belonging to or required for a school. The exclusion, in the present definition, of teachers' dwelling-houses, except where they are expressly included, prevents certain difficulties which arose under the previous law. As to the standards to which school premises are required to conform under the Act, see section 10, p. 84, *ante,* and as to the provision of playing fields, etc., see section 53, p. 144, *ante.*

(a^2) **" Prescribed ".**—This word appears in a number of places in the Act, sometimes in clear relation to an express power to make regulations and elsewhere by itself. As to the procedure to be adopted in making regulations under the Act, see section 112, p. 182, *ante.* The various regulations made under the Act which are now in force are referred to in the notes to the respective sections under which they were made. Section 121, p. 228, *post,* provides that any regulation in force under any enactment hereby repealed is to continue in operation and have effect as if made under the present Act and may be varied or revoked accordingly.

(b^2) **" Primary education ".**—Section 8 (1) (*a*), p. 79, *ante,* is printed as amended by section 3 of the Education (Miscellaneous Provisions) Act, 1948, p. 219, *post,* and defines primary education as full-time education suitable to the requirements of junior pupils, the term " junior pupils " being defined elsewhere in this section. See that definition and also notes (d) and (e) to section 8, *ante.*

(c^2) **" Primary school ".**—See, in addition to subsection (3) of this section, the definitions of " school " and " primary education " elsewhere in this section. It will be noted that " primary school " may include a nursery school (see section 9, p. 83, *ante*). As to financial assistance for primary schools which are Church of England aided schools and secondary schools which are Church of England aided schools or Church of England special agreement schools, see the Church Schools (Assistance by Church Commissioners) Measure, 1958 (No. 2) (10 Halsbury's Statutes (3rd Edn.) 1405).

(d^2) **" Proprietor ".**—At least in theory this term includes the managers or governors of a school maintained by the local education authority, but in relation to such schools the Act usually refers expressly to the managers or the governors as the case may be, and where used the term usually refers, therefore, to schools not so maintained. The terms " school " and " independent school ", used in the definition, are themselves defined in this section. The phrase " or body of persons " appears to be tautologous in view of section 19 of the Interpretation Act, 1889; 32 Halsbury's Statutes (3rd Edn.) 449.

(e^2) **" Applications for the registration of independent schools ".**—Part III of the Act (sections 70–75 inclusive, pp. 156, *et seq., ante*), deals with the registration of independent schools.

(f^2) **" Provisionally registered school ".**—Proviso (*b*) to section 70 (1), p. 156, *ante,* states that the registration of any independent school, for which application has been made under that subsection, is to be provisional only until the Secretary of State, after the school has been inspected under section 77, p. 163, *ante,* notifies the proprietor that the registration is final. The same subsection requires the Registrar of Independent Schools, appointed by the Secretary of State, to keep a register of all independent schools, to be open to public inspection at all times.

(g^2) **" Pupil ".**—This term was not used in the Education Act, 1921, so as to need definition in the interpretation. Instead the terms " child " and " young person " were used in appropriate circumstances. In this Act those terms are used in appropriate circumstances but the term " pupil " is also used, either to denote all persons for whom education must be provided, namely, from the time a child reaches the age of two years to the time when, as a young person, he attains the age of nineteen years, or in a qualified form. It should be noted that the requirement to provide education does not relate only to children of compulsory school age, but also to children below that age (see sections 8 (2) (*b*) and 9 (4), pp. 80 and 83, *ante*), and to young persons over compulsory school age (see the definitions of " secondary education " and " senior pupil " in section 8 (1) (*b*), p. 79, *ante*, and this section respectively), and even to adults (see the definition of " further education " in section 41, p. 135, *ante*). The term " pupil " is also used with the prefixes " junior ", " senior " and " registered ", in each of which cases the phrases are defined in this section.

(h²) **" Registered pupil ".**—The words in italics were repealed by section 11 (2) of and the Second Schedule to the Education (Miscellaneous Provisions) Act, 1948, the repeal being consequential on section 4 of that Act, p. 220, *post*. As to the meaning of the word " pupil " when used alone, see note (g²) to this section, *supra*. Section 36, p. 128, *ante*, imposes a duty upon the parent of every child of school age to cause him to receive education in accordance with that section either at school or otherwise. In the great majority of cases that duty is discharged by causing the child to attend school, and section 80, p. 165, *ante*, as amended by section 4 of the Education (Miscellaneous Provisions) Act, 1948, p. 220, *post*, requires the proprietor of every school to cause a register to be kept containing prescribed particulars of all persons who are pupils at the school. Any person so registered is a " registered pupil ", as here defined. The local education authority may require a parent who cannot satisfy the authority that he is fulfilling his duty under section 36, *ante*, to cause his child to become a registered pupil at a named school by serving upon him a school attendance order under section 37, p. 129, *ante*. A parent whose child of compulsory school age is a registered pupil at a school and fails to attend regularly is guilty of an offence under section 39, p. 132, *ante*.

The words " school ", " pupil ", " child " and " prescribed " which are used in this definition are each defined elsewhere in this section.

(i²) **" Registered school ".**—As to the meaning of the word " school " when unqualified, see note (j²) to this section, *infra*. Section 70, p. 156, *ante*, enables the proprietor of any independent school to apply for the registration of the school in the Register of Independent Schools to be kept under that section and, in fact, subsection (3) of that section makes it an offence for a person to conduct an independent school which is not either registered or provisionally registered. The meaning of the term " provisionally registered school " is given elsewhere in this section (see note (f²), *ante*), and a school does not, by virtue of proviso (*b*) to section 70 (1), p. 156, *ante*, cease to be a provisionally registered school and become a registered school until the Secretary of State gives notice to the proprietor that the registration is final, after the school has been inspected on his behalf under section 77, p. 163, *ante*. Subsection (2) of section 70, *ante*, enables the Secretary of State, however, to exempt any particular independent school or class of schools from registration, and any school so exempted will be deemed to be a registered school.

The term " independent school " is defined elsewhere in this section.

(j²) **" School ".**—This a generic term covering all types of schools and is used with many different qualifications throughout the Act, and even as a qualifying term itself.

Unless maintained by a local education authority or in receipt of direct grant from the Secretary of State, in which cases the point is hardly likely to arise, a school, to be a school, must have at least five pupils of compulsory school age (see the definition of " independent school " in this section).

(k²) **" An institution for providing primary or secondary education ".**—Definitions elsewhere in this section give to the terms " primary education " and " secondary education " the meanings assigned to them by section 8, p. 79, *ante* (see, respectively, paragraphs (*a*) and (*b*) of subsection (1) of that section, which are printed as amended by the Education (Miscellaneous Provisions) Act, 1948), whilst, subject to the provisions of subsection (3) of this section, schools for providing primary and secondary education are respectively called " primary schools " and " secondary schools ".

(l²) **" Both primary and secondary education ".**—Section 8 (2) (*a*), p. 80, *ante*, provides that in fulfilling their duties of securing that sufficient schools are available local education authorities are to have regard (*inter alia*) to the need for securing that primary and secondary education are provided in separate schools. By a proviso to the subsection this does not however, apply to special schools, though by regulations made under section 33 (3), p. 123, *ante*, the Secretary of State may impose requirements as to the organisation of any special school as a primary or secondary school. Since the reorganisation schemes of local education authorities in accordance with the Hadow Report had by no means been completed at the date of passing of the Act, and at that date there were many cases where senior pupils were not taught in separate schools or departments. Though much progress has been made recently it is still not possible to comply in all cases with the requirement of section 8 (2) (*a*), *ante*. The likelihood that this would take time was foreseen and provision was therefore made to enable the local education order which had to be made under section 12, p. 88, *ante*, to specify that individual schools for providing primary and secondary education which were maintained or assisted by the local education authority should, for the time being, be organised for the provision of both primary and secondary education. By subsection (3) of this section, schools so organised are to be regarded for the purposes of the Act as primary schools unless, in the case of schools in which the primary education is provided in a separate junior or preparatory department, the Secretary of State directs that, for the purposes of the Act, the school shall be deemed to be a secondary school. Under section 2 of the Education Act, 1946, p. 210, *post*, any county school, aided school or controlled school which is organised in two or more departments may be divided into two or more separate schools.

(m²) **" A school maintained by the local education authority ".**—Section 6, p. 76, *ante*, and the First Schedule, p. 196, *post*, specifies which authorities are to be local education authorities for the purposes of the Act, though section 118, p. 193, *post*, makes special provision in relation to the Isles of Scilly. As to London, see Part IV of the London Government Act, 1963, p. 289, *post*. The expression " maintain " is defined in subsection (2) of this section. Primary and secondary schools maintained by a local education authority may be:—

(1) **County schools,** which are schools of the type referred to established either by a local education authority or a former authority or, though not in fact established by a former

authority, deemed to be, or required to be treated as, schools provided by a former authority under an enactment repealed by the present Act (section 9 (2), p. 82, *ante*);

(2) **Voluntary schools,** which are primary or secondary schools so maintained but established otherwise than by a local education authority or a former authority (section 9 (2), *ante*), and may be of three categories, *i.e.*, controlled schools, aided schools and special agreement schools (see section 15, p. 95, *ante*);

(3) **Nursery schools,** which are neither county nor voluntary schools (nor necessarily in fact, maintained by a local education authority) but are defined by section 9 (4), p. 83, *ante*, as primary schools which are used mainly for the purpose of providing education for children who have attained the age of two years but have not attained the age of five years;

(4) **Special schools,** which also are neither county nor voluntary schools (nor necessarily maintained by a local education authority). They are defined by section 9 (5), p. 83, *ante*, as schools especially organised for the purpose of providing special educational treatment for pupils requiring such treatment and approved by the Secretary of State for that purpose. In addition section 33, p. 122, *ante*, enables the Secretary of State to make provision by regulations as to the requirements to be complied with by any school as a condition of such approval and as to the withdrawal of approval from a school which fails so to comply.

(o[2]) **" A school in respect of which grants are made . . . to the proprietor of the school ".**—These schools are commonly referred to as " direct grant " schools. Provision was made by the Act for the continuance of this type of school, and section 100, p. 175, *ante*, authorises the payment of such grants as are here referred to. As to the grant regulations now in force, see the notes to that section.

(p[2]) **" Secondary education ".**—See the definition in section 8 (1) (*b*), as amended by the Education (Miscellaneous Provisions) Act, 1948, p. 79, *ante*, and also notes (e) and (g) to section 8, *ante*.

(q[2]) **" Secondary school ".**—See, in addition to subsection (3) of this section, the definitions of " school " and " secondary education " elsewhere in this section.

(r[2]) **" Senior pupil ".**—As to the meaning of the word " pupil " when used alone, see the definition elsewhere in this section. As to the attainment of any particular age, see subsection (5) of this section. It will be noted that the term includes persons who are over, as well as persons who are of, compulsory school age, and the duties of securing sufficient schools for providing secondary education, imposed on local education authorities by section 8, p. 79, *ante*, extend by reason of this definition to require the provision of facilities for pupils up to the age of nineteen years if they or their parents desire such facilities.

(s[2]) **" Special agreement ".**—The Third Schedule, p. 201, *post*, relates to special agreements in respect of certain voluntary schools which are to be known as special agreement schools. See section 15, p. 95, *ante*, and the notes to that section.

(t[2]) **" Special educational treatment ".**—Section 8 (2) (*c*), p. 80, *ante*, defines this term as education by special methods appropriate for persons suffering from any disability of mind or body, either in special schools or otherwise. See notes (n) and (o) to that section, and sections 9 (5) and 33, pp. 83 and 122, *ante*.

(u[2]) **" Trust deed ".**—By section 170 (17) of the Education Act, 1921, this expression included any instrument regulating the trusts or management of a school or college, and therefore included not only trust deeds in the usual sense in which the term is used, but also Orders of the Chancery Division of the High Court, Orders of a county court under the Charitable Trusts Acts, orders and schemes of the Charity Commissioners and the Board of Education under the same Acts and schemes made under the Endowed Schools Acts, as well as certain other schemes or instruments. The present definition also covers all such instruments but is necessarily more specific owing to the creation under this Act of the various instruments, etc., referred to in the definition.

Information as to the instruments regulating the constitution of many of the older voluntary schools will be found in the " Return of the schools in England and Wales recognised on the 1st day of January, 1906, as non-provided Public Elementary Schools, showing as far as practicable the tenure of the premises of such schools and the character of the trusts, if any, to which the premises are subject under any trust deeds or instruments or otherwise "; House of Commons Paper 178, ordered to be printed on May 21, 1906.

(v[2]) **" Voluntary school ".**—See section 9 (2), p. 82, *ante*, and as to the classification of voluntary schools as controlled, aided and special agreement schools, section 15, p. 95, *ante*.

(w[2]) **" Instrument of management, instrument of government ".**—See sections 17, 18 and 19, pp. 100 *et seq.*, *ante*.

(x[2]) **" Rules of management, or articles of government ".**—As to the making of such rules and articles, see section 17 (3), p. 100, *ante*.

(y[2]) **" Managers or governors ".**—See note (b) to section 17, p. 101, *ante*.

(z[2]) **" Young person ".**—This expression was formerly defined by section 170 (14) of the Education Act, 1921, as a person under eighteen years of age who was no longer a child. Until a person reaches the upper limit of compulsory school age (now sixteen) he is called a child for the purposes of the Act. That term also is defined by this section. As to the attainment of any particular age by a person whose brithday falls during the term of a school at which he is a registered pupil or of a county college which he is for the time being required to attend by a college attendance notice, see section 8 of the Education Act 1946, *post*. It should be noted that the term " senior pupil ", as defined elsewhere in this section, includes persons who have ceased to be young persons.

(a[3]) **" The duty of a local education authority ".**—As to the duties of local education authorities in relation to the maintenance of primary and secondary schools, including county schools, nursery schools, special schools and voluntary schools, see sections 9 and 15, pp. 82, 95, *ante*, and the notes to those sections.

(b[3]) **" An aided school or a special agreement school ".**—As to the classification of voluntary schools as controlled, aided and special agreement schools, see section 15, p. 95, *ante*.

(c[3]) **" Special agreement ".**—See the definition of this term elsewhere in this section, and, for the provisions relating to special agreements, the Third Schedule, p. 201, *post*.

(d[3]) **" Managers or governors ".**—See note (b) to section 17, p. 101, *ante*.

(e[3]) **" Assisted ".**—Power to assist a school not maintained by the local education authority is given by section 9 (1), p. 82, *ante*. Other powers of assistance are given by sections 62, p. 151, *ante* (training of teachers), 81, p. 166, *ante* (assistance by means of scholarships and otherwise), and 82, p. 167, *ante* (educational research).

(f[3]) **" References in this Act to primary schools ".**—The meaning of this subsection is discussed in note (l) to section 8, p. 81, *ante*, and in the notes on the definition of " school " elsewhere in this section.

(g[3]) **" May direct ".**—As to the revocation or variation of orders and directions, see section 111, p. 181, *ante*.

(h[3]) **" The commencement of Part II of this Act ".**—Part II of the Act came into operation on 1st April, 1945.

(i[3]) **" Former authority ".**—See the definition of this term elsewhere in this section.

(j[3]) **" Agreed syllabus ".**—See the definition of this term elsewhere in this section.

(k[3]) **" Fifth Schedule to this Act ".**—See p. 204, *post*.

(l[3]) **" Sub-section (5) ".**—This subsection has been repealed and replaced by section 8 of the Education Act, 1946, p. 213, *post*, itself now repealed in part by the Education Act, 1962, section 13 and Schedule II.

(m[3]) **" Section forty-six of the Education Act, 1921 ".**—This section (*inter alia*) required every local education authority to make byelaws requiring the parents of children between the age of five years and such age not being less than fourteen nor more than fifteen as might be fixed by the byelaws to cause those children (unless there was some reasonable excuse) to attend school at such times as might be determined by the byelaws.

(n[3]) **" Deemed to be over compulsory school age ".**—This is a normal provision to include in an Act which raises the school-leaving age. It has a temporary effect, and means that a child who has left school before the age is raised cannot be required to return to school.

(o[3]) Subsection (6) was repealed by the Education (School-Leaving Dates) Act 1976.

(p[3]) **" A public elementary school within the meaning of the enactments repealed by this Act ".**—Section 27 of the Education Act, 1921, provided that every elementary school (as defined in section 170 (1), *ibid.*) which was conducted in accordance with the regulations therein contained should be a public elementary school within the meaning of that Act. There was one exception: by the second paragraph of section 18 (5), *ibid.*, schools provided by the local education authority for blind, deaf, epileptic or defective children, and any other schools which, in the opinion of the Board of Education, were not of a local character, should not be treated for the purposes of that subsection, which dealt with the provision of sites for new public elementary schools in London, as public elementary schools.

(q[3]) **" War damage ".**—This term is not defined in the Act. See, however, the definition of the term in section 2 of the War Damage Act 1943; 38 Halsbury's Statutes (3rd Edn.) 542).

(r[3]) **" Closed in accordance with those enactments ".**—See sections 19, 40 and 57 of the Education Act, 1921.

(s[3]) **" References to any enactment ".**—This subsection follows the lines of section 16 (3) of the Education Act, 1936, and is a usual provision in modern legislation.

115. Saving as to persons in the service of the Crown.—No power or duty conferred or imposed by this Act on the Secretary of State (a), on local education authorities (*), or on parents (*), shall be construed as relating to any person who is employed by or under the Crown in any service or capacity with respect to which the Secretary of State (a) certifies that, by reason of arrangements made for the education of children (*) and young persons (*) employed therein, the exercise and performance of those powers and duties with respect to such children and young persons is unnecessary.

NOTES

This section exempts from the provisions of the Act all children and young persons who are employed by or under the Crown in any service or capacity if the Secretary of State certifies that the arrangements made for their education render the application of the Act unnecessary. The only persons of compulsory school age now enlisted in the Armed Forces are boy musicians in the Royal Marines, and the Secretary of State has given a certificate under the present section that the exercise, with regard to children or young persons employed by the Crown in these capacities, of the powers and duties conferred or imposed on local education authorities by the Act is unnecessary. See Administrative Memorandum No. 278 (Revised) (19th December, 1952).

(*) As to the statutory definition of " local education authority ", " parent ", " child " and " young person ", see pp. 67–69, *ante*.

(a) **" Secretary of State ".**—See note (b) to s. 1, *ante*.

116. Saving as to persons of unsound mind and persons detained by a court.—No power or duty conferred or imposed by this Act on the Secretary of State (a), on local education authorities (*), or on parents (*) shall be construed as relating . . . to any person who is detained in pursuance of an order made by any court [or of an order to recall made by the Prison Commissioners, but a local education authority shall have power to make arrangements for a person who is detained in pursuance of an order made by a court, or of such an order of recall to receive the benefit of educational facilities provided by the authority. Where a child or young person is being educated as a boarder at a school, the fact that he is required to be at the school by virtue of an order made by a court under the Children and Young Persons Act, 1933, or by virtue of anything done under such an order, or by virtue of a requirement of a probation order or by virtue of anything done under such a requirement, shall not render him a person detained in pursuance of an order made by a court within the meaning of those words in this section].

NOTES

This section places outside the scope of the Act children and young persons detained by order of the court. No powers or duties under the Act are exercisable or enforceable in relation to such children or young persons while parents who are detained by order of the court are relieved against penalties to which they would otherwise have been liable. The words in square brackets were substituted by the Education (Miscellaneous Provisions) Act, 1948.

The words omitted were repealed by the Education (Handicapped Children) Act, 1970, p. 269, *post*. The section enables local education authorities to provide educational facilities for persons who are in prison or have been released from prison on licence. The expenses of a local education authority in providing education for persons in prison are met by the Prison Commissioners.

(*) As to the statutory definition of " child ", " local education authority ", and " parent ", see pp. 67–69, *ante*.

(a) **" Secretary of State ".**—See note (b) to s. 1, *ante*.

117. [*Repealed.*]

NOTE

This section, which applied the provisions of the Act to the special circumstances which arose as a result of the differences between the structure of local government in London and elsewhere, was repealed as from 1st April, 1965, by the London Government Act, 1963, Schedule 18, Part II.

118. Application to Isles of Scilly.—The Secretary of State (a) shall by order (b) provide for the application of this Act to the Isles of Scilly as if those isles were a separate county (c), and any such order may provide for the application of this Act to those isles subject to such modifications as may be specified in the order.

NOTES

This section requires the Secretary of State to provide by order for the application of the Act to the Isles of Scilly as if the islands were a separate county and had therefore a separate local education authority under section 6, p. 76, *ante*, and the First Schedule, p. 196, *post*. Pursuant to the section the then Minister of Education made the Isles of Scilly (Local Education Authority) Order, 1945, S.R. & O. 1945 No. 360, which provides that the Act, except section 88, p. 169, *ante*, shall apply to the isles as if they were a separate county and that the Council of the Isles of Scilly shall be the local education authority for the islands.

The Council of the Isles of Scilly is a council which was constituted by provisional order under section 49 of the Local Government Act, 1888, and confirmed by the Local Government Board Provisional Orders Confirmation (No. 6) Act, 1890.

(a) **" Secretary of State ".**—See note (b) to s. 1, *ante*.

(b) **" Order ".**—As to the revocation or variation of such an order, see section 111, *ante*.

(c) **" County ".**—See the definition of this term in section 114 (1), *ante*.

119. [*Repealed.*]

NOTE

This section, which dealt with the commencement of various parts of the Act, was repealed as spent by the Education Act 1973, Sch. 2, Part I.

120. Amendment of enactments.—(1) On and after the date of the commencement of Part II of this Act (a) any enactment passed before that date shall, unless the context otherwise requires, be construed as if :—

(*a*) for references therein to an elementary school or to a public elementary school (whether or not any reference is made therein to the payment of parliamentary grants in respect of the school) there were substituted references to a county school (*) or voluntary school (*) as the context may require ;

(*b*) for references therein to a school certified by the Board of Education, in accordance with the provisions of Part V of the Education Act, 1921, as suitable for providing education for blind, deaf, defective or epileptic children, there were substituted references to a special school (*) ;

(*c*) for references therein to the managers of a school there were substituted, in relation to a county secondary school or a voluntary secondary school (*), references to the governors (b) of the school ;

(*d*) for references therein to elementary education or to higher education there were substituted references to such education as may be provided by a local education authority (*) in the exercise of their functions under Part II of this Act ;

(*e*) for references therein to a local education authority, to a local education authority for elementary education, or to a local education authority for higher education, there were substituted references to a local education authority within the meaning of this Act.

(2) In relation to any young person (*) punishable under this Act or under section seventy-eight of the Unemployment Insurance Act, 1935, . . . and section fifty-four of the Children and Young Persons Act, 1933 (c) (which relate to the substitution of other punishments for imprisonment), shall have effect as if references therein to a young person included references to any person who has not attained the age of eighteen years.

(3) The enactments mentioned in the first column of the Eighth Schedule to this Act (d) shall, except in so far as any of them extend to Scotland (e) have effect subject to the amendments specified in the second column of that Schedule :

Provided that Part I of the said Schedule shall come into operation on the date of the commencement of Part II of this Act, and Part II of the said Schedule shall come into operation on the date on which section forty-four of this Act (f) comes into operation.

(4) Where by virtue of this Act any functions cease to be exercisable by the council of a county district under the Children and Young Persons Acts, 1933 and 1938 (g), the following provisions of this Act, that is to say:—

(*a*) subsections (3) and (4) of section six (h): and

(*b*) section ninety-seven (i);

shall have effect as if those functions had been exercisable under the Education Acts, 1921 and 1939 (k) ; and, in relation to any such functions, the provisions of section ninety-six and of subsection (3) of section ninety-eight of this Act (l) shall have effect as if for the references therein to the Minister of Education (m) there were substituted references to the Secretary of State.

(5) For the purposes of any bye-laws under Part II of the Children and Young Persons Act, 1933 (n), the expression "child" shall have the same meaning as it has for the purposes of the said Part II ; and any bye-laws made by the council of a county district under the said Part II which are in force immediately before the date of the commencement of Part II of this Act shall, in relation to the area to which they extend, continue in operation on and after that date as if they had been made by the local

education authority for the area in which the county district is situated, and may be varied or revoked accordingly.

NOTES

The Act includes in this and the next following section separate provisions dealing with amendments and repeals respectively.

The main reason for the inclusion of the present section may lie in the fact that the present Act is an Act to reform the law of education and is not a consolidating Act. It is, therefore, necessary to provide in numerous other statutes for references to educational matters in those statutes to be brought into line with the new system of education which was created by this Act.

The omitted words in sub-s. (2) of this section were repealed by the Criminal Justice Act, 1948, s. 83 and Tenth Schedule, as from December 27th, 1948 (S.I. 1948 No. 2349), in consequence of the repeal of s. 52 (3) of the Children and Young Persons Act, 1933, by the aforementioned Act.

(*) As to the meaning or statutory definition of " county school ", " voluntary school ", " special school ", " secondary school ", " local education authority " and " young persons ", see pp. 67–69, *ante.*

(a) **" The commencement of Part II of this Act ".**—Part II of the Act came into operation on 1st April, 1945.

(b) **" Governors ".**—See note (b) to section 17, p. 101, *ante.*

(c) **" Section fifty-four of the Children and Young Persons Act, 1933 ".**—Repealed by the Children and Young Persons Act 1969 (40 Halsbury's Statutes (3rd Edn.) 929, 959).

(d) **" Eighth Schedule to this Act ".**—See p. 206, *post.*

(e) **" Scotland ".**—By section 122 (2), p. 196, *post,* the Act does not extend to Scotland or Northern Ireland.

(f) **" Section forty-four of this Act ".**—By section 44 (1), p. 137, *ante,* that section is to come into operation on such date as soon as practicable after the date determined by Order in Council under section 43, p. 136, *ante,* as the Secretary of State may by order direct. Section 43 deals with the establishment of county colleges, and the date on which the duty of establishing and maintaining them was imposed on local education authorities was fixed by the County Colleges Order 1947, S.R. & O. 1947, as April 1, 1947; see the general note to section 43. It now seems unlikely that the establishment of county colleges will be proceeded with. See the Introduction, p. 48, *ante.*

(g) **" The Children and Young Persons Acts 1933 and 1938 ".**—By section 96 (1) of the Children and Young Persons Act, 1933; 17 Halsbury's Statutes (3rd Edn.) 508, the functions of local authorities under that Act were (subject, as regards the City of London, to section 97, *ibid.*), as respects children, to be functions of local education authorities for elementary education and, as respects other persons, functions of councils of counties and county boroughs. This meant that together with the transfer of educational functions from the former " Part III " authorities to local education authorities under section 6, p. 76, *ante,* there were also transferred the functions of those authorities under the Cbildren and Young Persons Acts.

Section 96 of the 1933 Act has, however, been amended by section 60 of, and the Third Schedule to, the Children Act, 1948, so as to provide that local education authorities shall be local authorities for the purposes of Part II only of the 1933 Act Section 38 of the 1948 Act provides that county councils and county borough councils shall be local authorities for the purposes of Parts III and IV of the 1933 Act, and section 39 requires every such local authority, unless exeused (section 40 (1)), or concurring in the appointment of a joint committee (section 40 (4)) to appoint a special children's committee for the purpose of dealing with all matters relating to the discharge of the authority's functions under Parts III and IV of the 1933 Act and under certain other enactments. Since except where a joint education board is established (see Part I of the First Schedule, p. 196, *post*) the local education authority is, under section 6, p. 76, *ante,* the county council or county borough council, as the case may be, which by virtue of section 38 of the 1948 Act is also the local authority for the purposes of Parts III and IV of the Children Act, 1933, the actual effect of the amendment of section 96 of the last-mentioned Act is only to transfer preliminary consideration of matters falling within the scope of Parts III and IV from the authority's education committee (as to which see Part II of the First Schedule, p. 198, *post*) to its children's committee.

The earlier Children and Young Persons Acts and the Children and Young Persons Act, 1969, may now be cited as the Children and Young Persons Acts, 1933 to 1969.

(h) **" Subsections (3) and (4) of section six ".**—Section 6 (3) and (4), p. 76, *ante,* deals with the transfer to local education authorities under this Act of property and officers of authorities whose educational powers are transfered which were held or who were employee solely or mainly in connection with educational functions.

(i) **" Section ninety-seven ".**—This section (repealed) dealt with the application of the Local Government Staffs (War Service) Act, 1939; 19 Halsbury's Statutes (3rd Edn.) 646, to persons who, before undertaking war service, were employed on educational matters by an authority whose functions were transferred by the Act.

(k) **" Education Acts, 1921 to 1939 ".**—See note (j) to section 6, p. 78, *ante.*

(l) **" Section ninety-six and of subsection (3) of section ninety-eight of this Act ".**—Section 96 is repealed and section 98 is spent.

(m) **" Minister of Education ".**—Now Secretary of State for Education and Science. See note (b) to section 1, *ante.*

(n) **" Bye-laws under Part II of the Children and Young Persons Act, 1933 ".**—Bye-laws may be made under the following sections of Part II of the Children and Young Persons Act, 1933 :—

(1) **Section 18** (17 Halsbury's Statutes (3rd Edn.) 448) (now amended by sections 84 and 64 (1), Schedule III, paragraph 4, of the Children and Young Persons Act, 1963 (17 Halsbury's Statutes (3rd Edn.) 739)), with respect to the employment of children (further amended by the Employment of Children Act 1973);

(2) **Section 20,** *ibid.*, 990 (as amended by section 35 of the Children and Young Persons Act, 1963 (17 Halsbury's Statutes (3rd Edn.) 722)), regulating or prohibiting street trading by persons under the age of seventeen years.

121. Repeal of enactments.—. . . Any regulation (a) Order in Council order (b) or other instrument in force under any enactment hereby repealed shall continue in operation and have effect as if made under this Act and may be varied or revoked accordingly . . .

NOTES

The omitted parts of this section were repealed as spent by the Education Act 1973, Sch. 2, Part I.

(a) **" Regulation ".**—As to the making of regulations under this Act, see section 112, p. 182, *ante.*

(b) **" Order ".**—As to the revocation and variation of orders made under this Act, see section 111, p. 181, *ante.*

122. Short title and extent.—(1) This Act may be cited as the Education Act, 1944.

(2) This Act shall not extend to Scotland or to Northern Ireland.

SCHEDULES

Section 6

FIRST SCHEDULE
LOCAL ADMINISTRATION

GENERAL NOTE

The First Schedule to the Act is complementary to section 6, p. 76, *ante*, and supplements the simplification of the local system of educational administration for which that section makes provision by—

(1) recognising the necessity of making a few exceptions by the creation, in suitable instances, of joint education boards;

(2) re-enacting, in a revised form, the provisions of the previous law relating to education committees ; and

(3) creating, for the dual purposes of softening the blow to the former " Part III " authorities caused by the transfer of their educational functions to the county councils and of stimulating interest in education in local government circles which had had no concern with educational administration, bodies called divisional executives to which some of the functions of the local education authority were to be delegated under schemes of divisional administration.

Detailed notes relating to the matters dealt with in this Schedule follow the respective Parts of the Schedule, *post.*

PART I

JOINT EDUCATION BOARDS

1. Where it appears to the Secretary of State (a) that the establishment of a joint board as the local education authority (b) for the areas of two or more councils to whom this Part of this Schedule applies (c) would tend to diminish expense or to increase efficiency or would otherwise be of public advantage, the Secretary of State (a) may by order (d) constitute a joint board (in this Act referred to as a " joint education board "), consisting of members appointed by those councils, and direct that the board shall be the local education authority for the areas of those councils:

Provided that the Secretary of State (a) shall not make such an order except after a local inquiry (e), unless all the councils for the areas of which the board is to be the local education authority have consented to the making of the order.

2. A joint education board so constituted shall be a body corporate with perpetual succession and a common seal . . .

3. An order constituting a joint education board :—

(*a*) may, without prejudice to the provisions of section two hundred and ninety-three of the Local Government Act, 1933 (f) (which authorises the application of provisions of that Act to joint boards) provide for regulating the appointment and term of office of members of the board, for regulating the meetings and proceedings of the board, and for determining the manner in which the expenses of the board are to be defrayed ;

(*b*) may contain such other provisions (including provision for the transfer of officers, property, and liabilities (g), and for the adjustment of accounts and apportionment of liabilities (h)) as appear to the Secretary of State (a) to be expedient for enabling the board to exercise their functions;

(*c*) may provide for securing that where in consequence of the establishment of the board as the local education authority for the area of any council any person who was an officer of that council immediately before the date on which the board became the local education authority for the area thereof suffers direct pecuniary loss by reason of the determination of his appointment or the diminution of his emoluments, he shall, unless provision for his compensation for that loss is made by or under any other enactment for the time being in force, be entitled to receive compensation therefore from the board, and for securing that the provisions of subsections (2) and (3) of section one hundred and fifty of the Local Government Act, 1933, and of the Fourth Schedule to that Act (m) shall have effect for the purposes of any claim for such compensation and for the purposes of the determination and payment of the compensation, subject to such modifications and adaptations as appear to the Secretary of State (a) to be necessary; and

(*d*) may, with the consent of the council of any county or county borough for the area for which the board is to be the local education authority, provide for the transfer to the board of any functions exercisable by that council under the Children and Young Persons Acts, 1933 and 1938 (n), otherwise than as a local education authority.

4. An order constituting a joint education board shall be laid before Parliament (o) as soon as may be after it is made.

5. This Part of this Schedule applies to the council of any county (p), to the council of any county borough, and to the council of any other borough of which the population was not less than half of the population of the county in which the borough is situated, according to the last census before the passing of this Act.

NOTES

The provisions of Part I of this Schedule were new to the law of education, though the Education Act, 1921, contained several sections under which co-operation could take place between local education authorities for various purposes by combination or otherwise. The words omitted in paragraph 2 were repealed by the Charities Act, 1960, section 48 (1), and Seventh Schedule, this repeal being consequential on the repeal by section 38 of that Act of the law of mortmain.

When the present Act was passed it was thought that, in the absence of a comprehensive scheme for the reform of local government, a simplification of the administrative system such as that carried out by section 6, p. 76, *ante*, might, as a result of the widely differing sizes and circumstances of counties and county boroughs and for other reasons, lead to anomalies. Provision was therefore made to enable the former Minister of Education, if he should think it desirable for any of the reasons specified in paragraph 1, to establish a joint board as the local education authority for the areas concerned, but suggestions for the constitution of such boards were not well received, and the only joint board in fact established pursuant to this Part of the Schedule is that for the Soke and City of Peterborough, constituted by S.R. & O. 1946 No. 1509. Power to vary the constitution, functions or area of or to dissolve a joint board established under this Part of this Schedule were conferred on the Secretary of State as " the appropriate Minister " as defined by section 66 of the Local Government Act 1958; 19 Halsbury's Statutes (3rd Edn.) 803, by *ibid.*, sections 26 (4), 27, 32; 19 Halsbury's Statutes (3rd Edn.) 783, 734, 735.

A new power to establish joint boards for the whole or part of a " special review area ", as defined by *ibid.*, section 17 and Third Schedule; 28 Halsbury's Statutes (2nd Edn.) 628, 669, and any adjoining areas was conferred by *ibid.*, section 26 and Sixth Schedule; 38 Halsbury's Statutes (2nd Edn.) 635, 671, and to vary the constitution, etc., of or to dissolve any such board was conferred by *ibid.*, section 27.

(a) **" Secretary of State ".**—See note (b) to s. 1, *ante*.

(b) **" Local education authority ".**—See section 6, p. 76, *ante*. As regards London, see section 30 of the London Government Act, 1963, p. 289, *post*; and as regards the Isles of Scilly, section 118, p. 193, *ante*.

(c) **" Councils to whom this Part of this Schedule applies ".**—See paragraph 5 of this Part.

(d) **" Order ".**—As to the revocation and variation of Orders and directions, see section 111, p. 181, *ante*.

(e) **" Local inquiry ".**—As to the power of the Secretary of State to direct local inquiries, see section 93, p. 171, *ante*.

(f) **" Section two hundred and ninety-three of the Local Government Act, 1933 ".**—Repealed by the Local Government Act 1972, s. 272 (1), Sch. 30.

(g) **" The transfer of officers, property and liabilities ".**—See subsections (3) and (4) of section 6, p. 76, *ante*, and the notes thereto regarding the above-mentioned terms.

(h) **" Adjustment of accounts and apportionment of liabilities ".**—See and compare section 90, p. 169, *ante*, and the notes thereto.

(m) **" Subsections (2) and (3) of section one hundred and fifty of the Local Government Act 1933, and the Fourth Schedule to that Act ".**—The Local Government Act 1933, was repealed by the Local Government Act 1972, s. 272 (1), Sch. 30.

(n) **" Children and Young Persons Acts, 1933 to 1938 ".**—See note (h) to section 120, p. 195, *ante*. These and subsequent Acts may now be cited as the Children and Young Persons Acts, 1933 to 1969.

(o) **" Laid before Parliament ".**—Compare this requirement with the requirements of section 112, p. 182, *ante*, regarding regulations made under the Act.

(p) **" Council of any county ".**—As to local government areas see now the Local Government Act 1972, Parts I and II (42 Halsbury's Statutes (3rd Edn.) 853).

PART II

EDUCATION COMMITTEES

1. Every local education authority (a) shall, in accordance with arrangements approved by the Secretary of State (b), establish such education committees as they think it expedient to establish for the efficient discharge of their functions with respect to education.

2. . . . (c).

3. Where it appears to the Secretary of State (b) to be expedient that two or more local education authorities should combine for the purpose of exercising some but not all of their functions with respect to education and that those authorities should establish a joint committee for that purpose, the Secretary of State (b) may after consultation with the authorities by order (d) establish a joint education committee of those authorities and provide for the reference to the committee of such questions relating to those functions as in the opinion of the Secretary of State (b) should be so referred; and any such order may provide for authorising the joint education committee to exercise any of those functions on behalf of the authorities concerned, and may include such incidental and consquential provisions, including provisions with respect to the appointment and functions of sub-committees, as the Secretary of State (b) thinks desirable.

4. In the following provisions of this Part of this Schedule the expression " education committee " includes a joint education committee.

5. Every education committee of a local education authority shall include persons of experience in education and persons acquainted with the educational conditions prevailing in the area for which the committee acts.

6. At least a majority (f) of every education committee of a local education authority shall be members of the authority ;

Provided that in the case of a joint education committee, the provisions of this paragraph shall be deemed to have been complied with if the committee consists, as to more than one half of the members thereof, of persons who are members of any of the authorities for which the committee is established.

7. Every local education authority shall consider a report (g) from an education committee of the authority before exercising any of their functions with respect to education :

Provided that an authority may dispense with such a report if, in their opinion, the matter is urgent . . .

8. A local education authority may authorise (h) an education committee of the authority to exercise on their behalf any of their functions with respect to education except the power to borrow money or to raise a rate.

9. The minutes of proceedings (i) of an education committee of the local education authority shall be open to the inspection of any local government elector (k) for the area on payment of a fee not exceeding one shilling and any such local government elector may make a copy thereof or an extract therefrom.

10. Every education committee of a local education authority may, subject to any restrictions imposed by the local education authority or the order of the Secretary of State (b) by which the committee was established:—

(a) appoint such sub-committees constituted in such manner as the committee may determine; and

(b) authorise any such sub-committees (l) to exercise any of the functions of the committee on their behalf.

11. Nothing in this Part of this Schedule shall require the reference to any education committee of a local education authority, or to any sub-committee of such a committee, of any matter which under any enactment for the time being in force is referred to any committee of the authority other than an education committee.

NOTES

Education committees are not constituted by means of schemes (as they were under the previous law) though joint education committees may be established by order of the Secretary of State under paragraph 3, and the Secretary of State's approval to the establishment of education committees is required by paragraphs 1 and 2.

As to the payment of allowances to members of local authorities and other bodies, see sections 173 *et seq.* of the Local Government Act 1972 (42 Halsbury's Statutes (3rd Edn.) 995 *et seq.*)

Education committees (including joint education committees) constituted under this Part of this Schedule are bodies to which the Public Bodies (Admission to Meetings) Act, 1960, applies; see section 2 thereof and the Schedule thereto.

See, further, section 101 of the Local Government Act 1972, and also Circulars 1/73 and 8/73, *post.*

(a) **" Local education authority ".**—See section 6, p. 76, *ante*, and this Schedule. As to the application of the Act to London, see Part IV of the London Government Act, 1963; and as to the Isles of Scilly, see section 118, p. 193, *ante*. A joint education board established under Part I of this Schedule, p. 196, *ante*, is a local education authority for all the purposes of the Act including the provisions of this Part of this Schedule with regard to the establishment, etc., of education committees.

(b) **" Secretary of State ".**—See note (b) to s. 1, *ante*.

(c) Paragraph 2 was repealed by the Local Government Act 1972, s. 272 (2), Sch. 30, as were the omitted words in the proviso to paragraph 7.

(d) **" Order ".**—As to the revocation or variation of such an order, see section 111, p. 181, *ante*. See *e.g.* the Welsh Joint Education Committee Order 1973, S.I. 1973 No. 1010.

(f) **" At least a majority ".**—This paragraph replaces and in general re-enacts paragraph, (1) (*a*) of Part I of the First Schedule to the Education Act, 1921, whilst the proviso re-enacts part of paragraph (2), *ibid.* Paragraph (1) (*c*), *ibid.*, also provided for the inclusion of women as well as men upon education committees. This requirement is not repeated but the Secretary of State may require their appointment as a condition of his approval of any proposals.

(g) **" Shall consider a report ".**—The proviso to this paragraph enables a local education authority to discuss an educational matter in certain circumstances, even if the education committee has not reported upon it. It does not, however, enable the authority to act, except as a matter of urgency, where the subject has only been discussed by a committee or sub-committee of the divisional executive. In its application to the Inner London Education Area, this Part of the Schedule has effect subject to the omission from paragraph 7 of the words in square brackets, the omission of paragraph 11, and a modification of paragraph 8. See section 30 (5) of the London Government Act, 1963, p. 290, *post.*

(h) **" May authorise ".**—As to the revocation of delegated powers and the exercise of such powers without revoking the delegation, see *Huth* v. *Clarke* (1890), 25 Q.B.D. 391. As to the ratification by a local authority of powers exercised without express delegation, see *Firth* v. *Staines*, [1897] 2 Q.B. 70; *Hussey* v. *Exeter Corporation* (1918), 87 L.J. (Ch.) 443; and *R.* v. *Chapman, Ex parte Arlidge*, [1918] 2 K.B. 298. As to the extent of the power of delegation, see *Richardson* v. *Abertillery U.D.C.*, *Thomas* v. *Abertillery U.D.C.* (1928), 92 J.P. 59.

As to the Inner London Education Authority, see note (g), *supra.*

(i) **" Minutes of proceedings ".**—This paragraph applies to education committees the obligation imposed regarding local authorities in general by section 228 (1) of the Local Government Act 1972, 42 Halsbury's Statutes (3rd Edn.) 1056. As to what may be inspected, see *Williams* v. *Manchester Corporation* (1897), 45 W.R. 412. See also Part VI of Sch. 12 to the Local Government Act 1972, 42 Halsbury's Statutes (3rd Edn.) 1157, which regulates the meetings and proceedings of local authorities in general.

As to the admission of the public to meetings of education committees, see the Public Bodies (Admission to Meetings) Act 1960.

(k) **"Local government elector ".**—See the definition of this term in section 114 (1), p. 184, *ante*. There have been various cases relating to the extent of the right to inspect minutes, *e.g.*, *Stevens v. Berwick-on-Tweed Corporation* (1835), 4 Dowl, 277; *R.* v. *Wimbledon U.D.C., Ex parte Hatton* (1897), 62 J.P. 84; *R.* v. *Bradford-on-Avon R.D.C., Ex parte Thornton* (1908), 72 J.P. 348; and *R.* v. *Godstone Rural Council* [1911] 2 K.B. 465. As to the production of the minute book in the absence of the clerk see *R.* v. *Andover R.D.C., Ex parte Thornhill* (1913), 77 J.P. 296.

(l) **" Authorise any such sub-committees ".**—This power overrides the general rule " *delegatus non potest delegare*". No restriction is specifically placed on the membership of such sub-committees, but local education authorities commonly ensure, by exercising their powers of imposing suitable restrictions, that there is a majority of members of the authority upon any such sub-committees which may incur liability to expenditure.

PART III

[*Repealed by the Local Government Act* 1972 *s.* 272 (2) *Sch.* 30.]

Section 13.

SECOND SCHEDULE

TRANSFER TO A LOCAL EDUCATION AUTHORITY OF AN INTEREST IN THE PREMISES OF A VOLUNTARY SCHOOL

1. A local education authority (a) and the managers or governors (b) of any voluntary school (c) maintained (d) by the authority may, subject to and in accordance with the provisions of this Schedule, make an agreement (e) for the transfer to the authority of any interest in the school premises (f) held by any persons for the purposes of any trust deed (g) relating to the school.

2. No such agreement shall take effect unless it has been approved by the Secretary of State (h).

3. The Secretary of State (h) shall not approve any such agreement unless he is satisfied—

(*a*) that due notice of the agreement has been given (i) to any persons other than the managers or governors of the school who, by virtue of any trust deed relating to the school, have an interest therein and to any other persons who appear to the Secretary of State (h) to be concerned; and

(*b*) that the execution of the agreement will effect the transfer of all interests necessary for the purpose of enabling the authority to maintain the school as a county school.

4. Before approving any such agreement, the Secretary of State (h) shall consider any representations made to him by or on behalf of any persons appearing to the Secretary of State (h) to be concerned with the proposed transfer.

5. An agreement under this Schedule may provide for the transfer to the authority, subject to such conditions, reservations and restrictions, if any, as may be specified in the agreement, of the whole of the interest in the premises held by any persons for the purposes of any trust deed relating to the school, or of any less interest in the premises, and may include such other provisions, whether relating to the consideration for the said transfer or otherwise, as may be agreed upon between the authority and the managers or governors of the school.

6. Where any agreement made under this Schedule has been approved by the Secretary of State (h), the managers or governors of the school may, whether or not the interest to be transferred to the authority by virtue of the agreement is vested in them, convey that interest to the authority.

7. Where any person other than the managers or governors of the school has a right to the occupation or use (j) of the school premises or any part thereof for any particular purpose, no provision of any agreement made under this Schedule shall affect that right unless he has consented thereto.

8. In this Schedule, the expression " premises " (k) includes a teacher's dwelling-house.

NOTES

This Schedule arises out of subsections (1) (*b*) and (4) of section 13, p. 90, *ante* (see the notes to that section).

Any school transferred under this Schedule must thereafter be maintained as a county school (subsections (1) (*b*) and (5) of section 13, *ante*).

There were a number of cases decided upon the construction of or otherwise relating to the provisions replaced by this Schedule or earlier equivalent provisions which may still have some relevance ; see, for example, *Re Burnham National Schools* (1873), L.R. 17 Eq. 241 ; *London School Board* v. *Faulconer* (1878), 8 Ch.D. 571; *National Society* v. *London School Board, A.-G.* v. *English* (1874), L.R. 18 Eq. 608; and *Llanbadarnfawr School Board* v. *Charitable Funds (Official Trustees)*, [1901] 1 K.B. 430.

(a) **" Local education authority ".**—See sections 6 and the First Schedule, pp. 76 and 196, *ante*. As to the application of the Act to London, see Part IV of the London Government Act, 1963, p. 289, *post*; and to the Isles of Scilly, see section 118, p. 193, *ante*.

(b) **" Managers or governors ".**—See note (b) to section 17, p. 101, *ante*. It will be noted that the persons who may enter into the arrangement are the managers or governors of the school, and not the foundation managers or governors (as defined in section 114 (1), p. 183, *ante*), or the persons holding the legal estate in the school premises. In the case of controlled schools it will often happen (see sections 18 and 19, pp. 105 and 106, *ante*) that a majority of the managers or governors is appointed by the local education authority, which might, by making suitable appointments, find a simple method of effecting a transfer of such controlled schools to the authority. The Secretary of State will no doubt exercise his powers under this Schedule to ensure that no unfair advantage of this opportunity is taken by local education authorities.

(c) **" Voluntary school ".**—See section 9 (2), p. 82, *ante*, and, as to the classification of voluntary schools as controlled, aided and special agreement schools, section 15, p. 95, *ante*.

(d) **" Maintained ".**—By section 114 (1), p. 184, *ante*, " maintain " in relation to a school has the meaning assigned to it by subsection (2) of that section, p. 185, *ante*.

(e) "**Make an agreement**".—Presumably, if an authority proposes to maintain a voluntary school as a county school under section 13 (1) (*b*), p. 90, *ante*, and is unable to reach agreement with the managers or governors, the matter may be referred to the Secretary of State as a dispute under section 67 (1), p. 154, *ante*.

(f) "**School premises**".—By section 114 (1), p. 185, *ante*, the word "premises" in relation to any school includes any detached playing fields, but, except where otherwise expressly provided, does not include a teacher's dwelling-house. By paragraph 8, however, the word as used in this Schedule does include a teacher's dwelling-house.

(g) "**Trust deed**".—Section 114 (1), p. 185, *ante*, provides that this term in relation to any voluntary school includes any instrument (not being an instrument of management, instrument of government, rules of management, or articles of government, made under this Act) regulating the maintenance, management or conduct of the school or the constitution of the body of managers or governors thereof.

(h) "**Secretary of State**".—See note (b) to s. 1, *ante*.

(i) "**Due notice of the agreement has been given**".—As to the service of notices, see section 113, p. 182, *ante*.

(j) "**A right to the occupation or use**".—See section 22, p. 110, *ante*.

(k) "**Premises**".—See note (f), *supra*.

THIRD SCHEDULE

Section 15.

SPECIAL AGREEMENTS IN RESPECT OF CERTAIN VOLUNTARY SCHOOLS

1. Where proposals for the establishment of a school or for the alteration (a) of the premises (b) of a school have been submitted to a former authority (c), within the time limited by subsection (2) of section eight of the Education Act, 1936 (d), with a view to the making of an agreement under that section, but the said proposals have not been carried out before the date of the commencement of Part II of this Act (e) a local education authority (f) shall have power to make an agreement in accordance with the provisions of this Schedule in respect of those proposals or in respect of any revised proposals submitted to the authority in accordance with those provisions :

Provided that no such agreement shall have effect unless it is approved by the Secretary of State (g), and no such agreement shall be made or approved unless the authority and the Secretary of State (g) are satisfied that the performance thereof will facilitate the execution of provisions relating to school accommodation for senior pupils (h) contained or proposed to be contained in the development plan (i) for the area.

2. If upon the application of any persons interested in any such proposals the Secretary of State (g) is satisfied that by reason of the passing of this Act or the making of any regulations thereunder, or by reason of movement of population or of any action taken or proposed to be taken under the enactments relating to housing or to town and country planning (j), or by reason of war damage (k) it is desirable that the proposals should be revised, the Secretary of State (g) may give directions (l) authorising a local education authority, in lieu of making an agreement in accordance with the provisions of this Schedule with respect to those proposals, to make such an agreement with respect to any revised proposals submitted to the authority before the expiration of such period as may be specified in the directions, being proposals which appear to the authority to serve substantially the same purpose as the proposals originally submitted.

3. No agreement shall be made under this Schedule after the expiration of six months or such extended period as the Secretary of State (g) may in any particular case allow from the date upon which the local education order (m) for the area of the local education authority first comes into force.

4. Any such agreement shall provide for the making of a grant by the local education authority to persons specified in the agreement in consideration of the execution by those persons of the proposals to which the agreement relates.

5. The amount of the grant to be made in pursuance of any such agreement shall not be less than one half or more than three quarters of the cost of executing the proposals to which the agreement relates.

[Provided that, where the proposals include proposals for establishing a playing field or any buildings of a kind which it is, under subsection (7) of section thirteen of this Act, the duty of the local education authority to provide (n),—

(*a*) if the proposals as respects the playing field or buildings are to be executed by the persons specified in the agreement, the amount of the grant so far as attributable to the cost thereof, shall be equal to the whole of that cost; and

(*b*) if the proposals as respects the playing field or buildings are to be executed by the local education authority, the cost thereof shall be borne by them and excluded in computing the amount of the grant.]

6. Where the agreement relates to proposals for the establishment of a school submitted to the local education authority for the County Borough of Liverpool, the authority may, if the agreement so provides, discharge their liabilities under the agreement by providing premises for the school and executing a lease of those premises to such persons as may be specified in the agreement for the purpose of enabling a voluntary school (o) to be conducted thereon.

Any such lease shall provide for the reservation of a yearly rent of an amount not less than one nor more than two per cent. of the cost incurred by the authority in providing the premises for the school.

7. Any agreement made under this Schedule may provide for the giving of religious instruction (p) in the school in accordance with the provisions of the trust deed (q) relating to the school, or, where provision for that purpose is not made by such a deed, in accordance with the practice observed in the school before it became a voluntary school, and for the employment in the school, for the purpose of giving such religious instruction, of such number of reserved teachers (r) as may be specified in the agreement.

8. Any agreement made by a local education authority under this Schedule may be varied by a further agreement between the authority and the managers or governors of the school to which the agreement relates, or in such other manner, if any, as may be specified in the agreement.

9. Where a grant has been made in respect of any school in pursuance of an agreement made under this Schedule, the managers or governors of the school may, at any time while the school is a special agreement school, repay the grant to the local education authority by which the school is maintained.

10. Where an agreement has been made under this Schedule in relation to any school, then, until the proposals to which the agreement relates have been carried out, the provisions of this Act (s) relating to the respective obligations of the managers or governors of voluntary schools and the local education authority in respect of repairs and alterations to the premises of the school shall not have effect in relation to that school, but the respective obligations of the managers or governors of the school and the local education authority in relation to those matters shall be such as may be determined by agreement between the managers or governors and the authority, or in default of such agreement, by the Secretary of State (g).

11. Where any local authority have, before the date of the commencement of Part II of this Act, made an agreement under the powers conferred by section eight of the Education Act, 1936 with respect to proposals submitted to the authority within the time limited by subsection (2) of that section, then :—

(*a*) if the said proposals have been carried out before that date the agreement shall be deemed to have been made under this Schedule, and the provisions of this Act relating to special agreements shall have effect accordingly ;

(*b*) if the said proposals have not been carried out before that date, the agreement shall cease to have effect, but without prejudice to the making of a further agreement, under this Schedule, with respect to those proposals or with respect to any revised proposals submitted to the authority in accordance with the provisions of this Schedule.

NOTES

This Schedule is printed as amended by section 11 (1) of and Part I of the Schedule to the Education (Miscellaneous Provisions) Act, 1948, *post*, which added the proviso to paragraph 5. In Circular No. 9/59 (21st August, 1959), which was issued shortly after the passing of the Education Act, 1959, it is stated as follows:

> " While it is likely that many proposals which fall within the Third Schedule to the Education Act, 1944, will now be eligible for 75 per cent. grant from the Exchequer, some will not. The latter include all proposals in the 1959/60 and earlier building programmes, and also proposals for new secondary schools in later programmes if their pupils will not be draw wholly or mainly from aided (as distinct from controlled) primary schools. Special agreements will continue to be needed to cover such schools; and it is of course open to local education authorities and promoters, if they wish, to make an agreement under the Third Schedule in other cases. The promoters should tell the Ministry [now the Department of Education and Science], when they submit a proposal, whether the school is to be an aided or a special agreement school ".

This schedule replaces the provisions of sections 8 and 9 of the Education Act, 1936. Special agreement schools, which are a limited class of school and were first created under the Act of 1936, form one of the three categories of voluntary schools referred to in section 15 (1), p. 95, *ante*, and as to which, see further the notes to that section, *ante*. Subsection (2) of that section (*inter alia*) enables the Secretary of State, upon application being duly made to him under the section, to direct that a voluntary school shall be a special agreement school, provided that—

(*a*) he is satisfied that the managers or governors of the school are able and willing with the assistance of the maintenance contribution payable by the Secretary of State under section 102, p. 176, *ante*, to defray the expenses falling to be borne by them under section 15 (3) (*a*), *ante*; and

(*b*) a special agreement has been made with respect to the school under this Schedule.

(a) **" Alteration ".**—By section 114 (1), p. 183, *ante*, as amended by Part II of the Second Schedule to the Education Act, 1946, " alterations ", in relation to any school premises, includes any improvements, enlargements or additions which do not amount to the establishment of a new school.

(b) **" Premises ".**—By section 114 (1), p. 185, *ante*, this term, in relation to any school, includes any detached playing fields, but, except where otherwise expressly provided, does not include a teacher's dwelling-house.

(c) **" Former authority ".**—Section 114 (1), p. 183, *ante*, provides that this term means any authority which was a local authority within the meaning of any enactment repealed by this Act or any previous Act, in this instance the Education Act, 1936.

(d) " **Subsection (2) of section eight of the Education Act, 1936** ".—The subsection required proposals under that section to be submitted to the local education committee at least eighteen months before the appointed day (by section 15 (1), *ibid.*, the appointed day was the 1st September, 1939) or before such later date, being not less than twelve months before the appointed day, as the authority might allow in a particular case. The Board of Education might, however, permit new proposals to be entertained at a later date if it was satisfied that proposals entertained by a local education authority (whether or not an agreement had been entered into) had become impracticable or undesirable owing to any decision made or action taken before the appointed day by any planning or housing authority.

(e) " **Date of the commencement of Part II of this Act** ".—Part II of the Act came into operation on 1st April, 1945. As to the position where the proposals had been carried out before that date, or an agreement had been entered into but the proposals had not been carried out, see paragraph 11.

(f) " **Local education authority** ".—See section 6 and the First Schedule, pp. 76 and 196, *ante*. As to the application of the Act to London, see Part IV of the London Government Act, 1963, p. 289, *post*; and as to the Isles of Scilly, see section 118, p. 193, *ante*.

(g) " **Secretary of State** ".—See note (b) to s. 1, *ante*.

(h) " **Senior pupils** ".—By section 114 (1), p. 185, *ante*, " senior pupil " means a person who has attained the age of twelve years but has not attained the age of nineteen years.

(i) " **Development plan** ".—As to the preparation of development plans, see section 11, p. 85, *ante*, and section 31 of the London Government Act, 1963, p. 291, *post*.

(j) " **Enactments relating to housing or to town and country planning** ".—See notes (c) and (d) to section 16, p. 114, *ante*.

(k) " **By reason of war damage** ".—See section 114 (7), p. 186, *ante*, and note (p[2]) to that section.

(l) " **Give directions** ".—As to the revocation or variation of such directions, see section 111, p. 181, *ante*.

(m) " **Local education order** ".—As to the making of local education orders, see section 12, p. 88, *ante*.

(n) " **Playing field or any buildings . . . which it is the duty of the local education authority to provide** ".—Under s. 13 (7), p. 91, *ante*, when proposals, specifications and plans for a new voluntary school have been approved by the Secretary of State it becomes the duty of the local education authority to provide playing fields and any buildings which are to form part of the school premises but not to be school buildings. The proviso to paragraph 7 of the present Schedule makes it clear that so far as the provision of playing fields and buildings other than school buildings is concerned, special agreement schools are to be on the same footing as other voluntary schools.

(o) " **Voluntary school** ".—See section 9 (2), p. 82, *ante*, and, as to the classification of voluntary schools as controlled, aided and special agreement schools, section 15, p. 95, *ante*.

(p) " **Religious instruction** ".—Special provision is made in section 28, p. 119, *ante*, with regard to religious education in (*inter alia*) special agreement schools. See also section 7 of the Education Act, 1946, p. 213, *post*, which permits the collective worship of pupils in special agreement schools to take place elsewhere than on the school premises on special occasions.

(q) " **Trust deed** ".—By section 114 (1), p. 185, *ante*, this term, in relation to any voluntary school, includes any instrument (not being an instrument of management, instrument of government, rules of management, or articles of government, made under this Act) regulating the maintenance, management or conduct of the school or the constitution of the body of managers or governors thereof. See also section 67 (3), p. 154, *ante*.

(r) " **Reserved teachers** ".—See section 28 (3), p. 120, *ante*, and particularly note (e) to that section.

(s) " **The provisions of this Act** ".—The reference is to section 15 (3), p. 96, *ante*.

FOURTH SCHEDULE

Section 21.

MEETINGS AND PROCEEDINGS OF MANAGERS AND GOVERNORS

1. The quorum of the managers or governors (a) shall not be less than three, or one third of the whole number of managers or governors, whichever is the greater.

2. The proceedings of the managers or governors shall not be invalidated (b) by any vacancy in their number or by any defect in the election, appointment or qualification of any manager or governor.

3. Every question to be determined at a meeting of the managers or governors shall be determined by a majority of the votes of the managers or governors present and voting (c) on the question, and where there is an equal division of votes the chairman of the meeting shall have a second or casting vote.

4. The managers or governors shall hold a meeting [at least once in every term (d)].

5. A meeting of the managers or governors may be convened by any two of their number.

6. The minutes of the proceedings of the managers or governors shall be kept in a book provided for the purpose (e).

NOTES

Section 21 (2), p. 109, *ante*, applies the provisions of this Schedule to the meetings and proceedings of the managers or governors of county schools and voluntary schools—see that section and the notes thereto.

The words in square brackets in paragraph 4 were substituted for the words " at least once in every three months " by section 11 (1) of, and Part I of the First Schedule to, the Education (Miscellaneous Provisions) Act, 1948, *post*.

For the purposes of this Schedule a special school maintained by a local education authority shall be treated as if it were a county school. See s. 2 (5) of the Education (No. 2) Act, 1968, p. 268, *post*.

(a) **" Managers or governors."**—See note (b) to section 17, p. 101, *ante*.

(b) **" Shall not be invalidated ".**—The effect of a similar provision in earlier enactments was discussed in *Bradley* v. *Sylvester* (1871), 25 L.T. 459; *Meyers* v. *Hennell*, [1912] 2 Ch. 256; and *Harries* v. *Crawfurd*, [1918] 2 Ch. 158. See, however, section 99 (2), p. 173, *ante*, which enables the Secretary of State to take steps to secure that there is a properly constituted body of managers or governors in cases where, owing to the default of any person, there is no such constituted body, and also to render valid any acts or proceedings which appear by reason of the default to be invalid or defective.

(c) **" Present and voting ".**—As to the meaning of the words " and voting ", see *R.* v. *Griffiths* (1851), 17 Q.B. 164. As to what amounts to voting, see *Everett* v. *Griffiths*, [1924] 1 K.B. 941.

(d) **" School term ".**—See, as to yearly number of sessions, ref. 11 of the Schools Regulations, 1959, S.I. 1959 No. 364, p. 351, *post*.

(e) **" In a book provided for the purpose ".**—As to the proper form of minute books, see *Hearts of Oak Assurance Co., Ltd.* v. *Flower (James) & Sons*, [1936] Ch. 76; [1935] All E.R. Rep. 420.

Section 29.

FIFTH SCHEDULE

PROCEDURE FOR PREPARING AND BRINGING INTO OPERATION AN AGREED SYLLABUS OF RELIGIOUS INSTRUCTION

1. For the purpose of preparing any syllabus of religious instruction to be adopted by a local education authority (a), the authority shall (b) cause to be convened a conference constituted in accordance with the provisions of this Schedule.

2. For the purpose of constituting such a conference as aforesaid the local education authority shall appoint constituent bodies (hereinafter referred to as " committees ") consisting of persons representing respectively—

(*a*) such religious denominations as, in the opinion of the authority, ought, having regard to the circumstances of the area, to be represented ;

(*b*) except in the case of an area in Wales or Monmouthshire, the Church of England;

(*c*) such associations representing teachers as, in the opinion of the authority, ought, having regard to the circumstances of the area, to be represented ; and

(*d*) the authority :

Provided that where a committee is appointed consisting of persons representing the Church of England, the committee of persons appointed to represent other religious denominations shall not include persons appointed to represent that Church.

3. Before appointing a person to represent any denomination or associations as a member of any such committee a local education authority shall take all reasonable steps (c) to assure themselves that he is representative thereof, but no proceedings under this Schedule shall be invalidated on the ground that a member of such a committee did not represent the denomination or associations which he was appointed to represent unless it is shown that the local education authority failed to take such steps as aforesaid.

4. A person so appointed may resign his membership of any such committee or may be withdrawn therefrom by the local education authority if in the opinion of the authority he ceases to be representative of the religious denomination or associations which he was appointed to represent, or of the authority, as the case may be ; and where a vacancy occurs among the persons so appointed the authority shall fill the vacancy in like manner as they made the original appointment.

5. The conference shall consist of the committees aforesaid and it shall be the duty of the conference (d) to seek unanimous agreement upon a syllabus of religious instruction to be recommended for adoption by the local education authority.

6. Where the local education authority propose to adopt more than one syllabus of religious instruction for use in schools maintained (e) by them, the authority shall inform the conference as to the schools in which, or in the case of a syllabus intended to be used for certain pupils (f) only, the class or description of pupils for which, the syllabus to be prepared by the conference is to be used.

7. Any sub-committees appointed by the conference shall include at least one member of each of the committees constituting the conference.

8. Upon any question to be decided by the conference or by any sub-committee thereof one vote only (g) shall be given for each of the committees constituting the conference.

9. If the conference unanimously recommend any syallbus of religious instruction the authority may adopt it (h) for use in the schools for which, or for the class or description of pupils for which, it was prepared.

10. If the authority report to the Secretary of State (i) that the conference are unable to reach unanimous agreement as aforesaid, or if it appears to the Secretary of State (i) that an authority have failed to adopt any syllabus unanimously recommended

to them by the conference, the Secretary of State (i) shall appoint to prepare a syllabus of religious instruction a body of persons having experience in religious instruction, which shall, so far as is practicable, be of the like representative character as is required by paragraph 2 of this Schedule in the case of a conference.

11. The body of persons so appointed :—

(*a*) shall give to the authority, the conference, and every committee constituting the conference, an opportunity of making representations to it, but, save as aforesaid, may conduct the proceedings in such manner as it thinks fit ;

(*b*) shall, after considering any such representations made to it, prepare a syllabus of religious instruction ;

(*c*) shall transmit a copy of the said syllabus to the authority and to the Secretary of State (i),

and as from such date as the Secretary of State (i) may direct (j), the syllabus so prepared shall be deemed to be the agreed syllabus adopted for use in the schools for which, or for the class or description of pupils for which, it was prepared until a further syllabus is prepared for use in those schools, or for pupils of that class or description, in accordance with the provisions of this Schedule.

12. Whenever a local education authority are of opinion (whether upon representations made to them or otherwise) that any agreed syllabus for the time being adopted by them ought to be reconsidered, the authority shall cause to be convened for that purpose a conference constituted in accordance with the provisions of this Schedule. If the conference convened for the reconsideration of any syllabus unanimously recommend that the existing syllabus should continue to be the agreed syllabus or that a new syllabus should be adopted in substitution therefor, the authority may give effect to the recommendation of the conference, but if the authority report to the Secretary of State (i) that the conference are unable to reach unanimous agreement, or if it appears to the Secretary of State (i) that the authority have failed to give effect to the unanimous recommendation of the conference, the Secretary of State (i) shall proceed in accordance with the provisions of paragraph 10 of this Schedule, and paragraph 11 thereof shall apply accordingly.

NOTES

By section 114 (1), p. 183, *ante*, an agreed syllabus is defined as an agreed syllabus of religious instruction prepared in accordance with the provisions of the Fifth Schedule to the Act and adopted or deemed to be adopted thereunder.

As to the requirements of the Act in relation to the giving of religious instruction in accordance with an agreed syllabus in county schools, controlled schools, and aided and special agreement schools, see sections 26, 27 and 28 respectively, pp. 117, *et seq.*, *ante*. As to religious education generally, see the general note to section 25, p. 116, *ante*. The agreed syllabus arises from the " Cowper-Temple " clause (originally section 14 of the Elementary Education Act, 1870), which, until replaced by section 26, p. 117, *ante*, appeared in section 28 (2) of the Education Act, 1921), which prohibited the use in provided schools of any religious catechism or religious formulary distinctive of any particular denomination. Formerly, however, so long as the religious instruction given in provided public elementary schools and, under sections 9 and 12 of the Education Act, 1936, in certain circumstances in non-provided schools, did not contravene the Cowper-Temple clause, the local education authority might adopt any particular syllabus which it pleased or might even leave the matter to the discretion of individual teachers. Now, however, the adoption of an agreed syllabus under this Schedule is obligatory.

(a) **" Local education authority ".**—See section 6 and the First Schedule, pp. 76 and 196, *ante*. As to the application of the Act to London, see Part IV of the London Government Act, 1963, p. 289, *post*; and as to the Isles of Scilly, see section 118, p. 193, *ante*.

(b) **" The authority shall ".**—The obligations imposed here and in later paragraphs of the Schedule may be enforced by the Secretary of State under section 99, p. 173, *ante*. The Secretary of State may also take steps under section 68, p. 155, *ante*, to prevent the unreasonable exercise by a local education authority of any of its functions under the Act.

(c) **" Shall take all reasonable steps ".**—The steps referred to are not specified, but it would no doubt be regarded as reasonable to accept the views of the denominations and associations concerned.

(d) **" It shall be the duty of the conference ".**—Unlike the duties imposed upon local education authorities, this duty cannot be enforced. As to the procedure to be adopted if the conference fails to reach unanimous agreement, see paragraphs 10 and 11 of the Schedule.

(e) **" Maintained ".**—The term " maintain ", in relation to a school, is by section 114 (1), p. 184, *ante*, assigned the meaning given to it by subsection (2) of that section, p. 185, *ante*.

(f) **" Pupils ".**—Subject to the qualification that the pupils referred to are pupils at schools maintained by the local education authority, this expression is defined by section 114 (1), p. 185, *ante*, as persons of any age for whom education is required to be provided under the Act.

(g) **" One vote only ".**—The requirement imposed by the Schedule is that the conference shall unanimously recommend ; since each of the committees has one vote only this presumably means, not that there shall be unanimity within each committee, but that there shall be unanimity of the committees as a whole, regarding each for that purpose as a single person or unit.

(h) **" The authority may adopt it ".**—The local education authority is not bound to adopt a syllabus unanimously recommended but, in the event of failure to do so, the procedure of paragraphs 10 and 11 of the Schedule will be followed and any syllabus so prepared will be deemed to have been adopted from such date as the Secretary of State may direct.

(i) **" Secretary of State ".**—See note (b) to s. 1, *ante*.

(j) "**May direct**".—As to the revocation or variation of such a direction, see section 111, p. 181, *ante*. Once adopted or deemed to be adopted the giving of religious instruction in accordance with the syllabus may be enforced by the Secretary of State under section 99, p. 173, *ante*, since, under section 26, p. 117, *ante*, and in certain circumstances under sections 27 and 28, pp. 118 *et seq.*, *ante*, the duty of giving instruction in accordance with an agreed syllabus is imposed.

Section 72.

SIXTH SCHEDULE

CONSTITUTION OF INDEPENDENT SCHOOLS TRIBUNALS

1. For the purpose of enabling Independent Schools Tribunals to be constituted as occasion may require there shall be appointed two panels, that is to say—

(*a*) a panel (hereinafter referred to as the "legal panel") appointed by the Lord Chancellor, of persons who will be available to act when required as chairman of any such tribunal; and

(*b*) a panel (hereinafter referred to as the "educational panel") appointed by the Lord President of the Council, of persons who will be available to act when required as members of any such tribunal.

2. No person shall be qualified to be appointed to the legal panel unless he possesses such legal qualifications as the Lord Chancellor considers suitable, and no person shall be qualified to be appointed to the educational panel unless he had had such experience in teaching or in the conduct management or administration of schools as the Lord President of the Council considers suitable. An officer of any government department and a person employed by a local education authority (a) otherwise than as a teacher shall be disqualified from being appointed to either of the said panels.

3. Any person appointed to be a member of either of the said panels shall hold office as such subject to such conditions as to the period of his membership and otherwise as may be determined by the Lord Chancellor or the Lord President of the Council, as the case may be.

4. Where any appeal (b) is required to be determined by an Independent Schools Tribunal the tribunal shall consist of a chairman being a member of the legal panel and two other members being members of the educational panel, and the chairman and other members of the tribunal shall be impartial persons appointed from those panels by the Lord Chancellor and the Lord President of the Council respectively.

NOTES

Section 72 (1), p. 158, *ante*, enables a person aggrieved by the service of a notice of complaint or a copy thereof, under section 71, p. 158, *ante*, to refer the matter to an Independent Schools Tribunal constituted in accordance with the provisions of this Schedule.

Section 75 (1), p. 161, *ante*, enables the Lord Chancellor, with the concurrence of the Lord President of the Council, to make rules as to (*inter alia*) the practice and procedure to be followed with respect to the constitution of Independent Schools Tribunals, and, with the consent of the Treasury, as to the payment of remuneration and allowances to members of such Tribunals. Pursuant to this section the Lord Chancellor has made the Independent Schools Tribunal Rules, 1958, S.I. 1958 No. 519, as amended by the Independent Schools Tribunal (Amendment) Rules 1968, S.I. 1968 No. 588, *post*. All members of an Independent Schools Tribunal are disqualified for membership of the House of Commons by the House of Commons Disqualification Act, 1957, s. 1 (1) (*f*), Schedule I, Part I; 24 Halsbury's Statutes (3rd Edn.) 426, 435. Independent Schools Tribunals are under the direct supervision of the Council on Tribunals, see the notes to s. 72, *ante*.

(a) "**Local education authority**".—See section 6 and the First Schedule, pp. 76 and 196, *ante*. As to the application of the Act to London, see Part IV of the London Government Act, 1963, p. 289, *post*; and as to the Isles of Scilly, see section 118, p. 193, *ante*.

(b) "**Any appeal**".—This refers not only to appeals under section 72 (1), p. 158, *ante*, but also to appeals under section 74 (2), p. 161, *ante*, against refusals of the Secretary of State to remove disqualifications imposed under Part III of the Act.

Section 110.

SEVENTH SCHEDULE

ADJUSTMENT OF VARIATIONS OF RATES CONSEQUENT UPON COMMENCEMENT OF PART II OF THIS ACT

[*Spent.*]

Section 120.

EIGHTH SCHEDULE

AMENDMENT OF ENACTMENTS

PART I

ENACTMENTS AMENDED FROM DATE OF COMMENCEMENT OF PART II OF THIS ACT

Enactment to be amended.	Amendment.
The Mental Deficiency Act, 1913.	
Section two	[*Entry repealed.*]
Section thirty-one	The section shall cease to have effect.
The Ministry of Agriculture and Fisheries Act, 1919.	
Section seven	In subsection (2), for the words "under the Education Act, 1902, stand referred to the education committee," there shall be substituted the words "relate to the functions of local education authorities."

Enactment to be amended.	Amendment.
The Children and Young Persons Act, 1933.	
Section ten	In subsection (1), after the word " years " there shall be inserted the words " or any young person who has not attained the age at which under the enactments relating to education children cease to be of compulsory school age ", and for the words from " is totally exempted " to the end of the subsection there shall be substituted the words " or young person is not, by being so taken with him, prevented from receiving efficient full-time education suitable to his age ability and aptitude, be liable on summary conviction to a fine not exceeding twenty shillings " ; in subsection (2) after the word " child " in both places where that word occurs, there shall be inserted the words " or young person " ; for subsection (3) there shall be substituted the following subsection :— " (3) Where in any proceedings for an offence against this section it is proved that the parent or guardian of the child or young person is engaged in any trade or business of such a nature as to require him to travel from place to place, the person against whom the proceedings were brought shall be acquitted if it is proved that the child or young person has attended a school at which he was a registered pupil as regularly as the nature of the trade or business of the parent or guardian permits : Provided that in the case of a child or young person who has attained the age of six years the person against whom the proceedings were brought shall not be entitled to be acquitted under this subsection unless it is proved that the child or young person has made at least two hundred attendances during the period of twelve months ending with the date on which the proceedings were instituted."
Section eighteen	[*Repealed by the Children Act* 1972.]
Sections twenty-two and sixty-one	[*Repealed by the Children and Young Persons Act,* 1963.]
Section ninety-six	In subsection (1), the words " as respects children " and the words from " for elementary education " (where those words first occur) to the end of the subsection shall be omitted ; subsection (2) shall be omitted ; in subsection (3) for the words from " for elementary education " to the end of the subsection there shall be substituted the words " shall be defrayed as expenses under the enactments relating to education " ; in subsection (4), for the word " under " (where that word secondly occurs) there shall be substituted the words " in accordance with ", and the words " as expenses of elementary education under the Education Act, 1921 " shall be omitted.
The Local Government Act 1933	[*Repealed by the Local Government Act* 1972.]
The Factories Act 1937 ..	[*Repealed; see Factories Act* 1961.]
The London Government Act, 1939.	[*Repealed as from* 1*st April,* 1965, *by the London Government Act,* 1963, *Sched.* 18, *Part II*].

PART II

ENACTMENTS AMENDED FROM DATE ON WHICH SECTION FORTY-FOUR OF THIS ACT COMES INTO OPERATION

Enactment to be amended.	Amendment.
The Unemployment Insurance Act, 1935.	
Section seventy-eight	For the word " Minister " (wherever that word occurs) there shall be substituted the words "Minister of Education " (a); in subsection (2) for paragraph (*a*) there shall be substituted the following paragraph:—

Enactment to be amended.	Amendment.
	" (*a*) in England or Wales he shall be liable on summary conviction, in the case of a first offence to a fine not exceeding one pound, in the case of a second offence to a fine not exceeding five pounds, and in the case of a third or subsequent offence to a fine not exceeding ten pounds or to imprisonment for a term not exceeding one month or to both such fine and such imprisonment so, however, that no proceedings for such an offence shall be taken except by or on behalf of the Minister of Education " (a); for subsection (4) there shall be substituted the following subsection :— " (4) The regulations made by the Minister of Education (a) under this section shall make provision as to the functions to be performed by local education authorities with respect to persons required under this section to attend at authorised courses, and, in particular, shall direct such authorities to make in any college attendance notice served on any such person such modifications as may be provided by the regulations, and shall make provision as to the circumstances in which and the extent to which attendances in pursuance of requirements under this section may be reckoned as attendances in pursuance of the requirements of college attendance notices."
. . .	
Section one hundred and four	In subsection (1) after the word " Act ", where that word first occurs, there shall be inserted the words " except under section seventy-eight thereof "
Section one hundred and thirteen	In subsection (1) for the definition of " Authorised course " there shall be substituted the following definition :— " Authorised course means a county college established under the enactments relating to education or a training course provided under section seventy-seven of this Act and includes, in relation to insured contributors who have attained the age of eighteen years, any training course provided by the Assistance Board under the Unemployment Act, 1934 ".

NOTES

This Schedule has reference to section 120, p. 194, *ante*. The repealed entry relating to the Mental Deficiency Act, 1913, was repealed by the Mental Health Act 1959, section 149 (2), Sched. VIII, Part I: 25 Halsbury's Statutes (3rd Edn.) 164, 186. The italicised entry relating to section 18 of the Children and Young Persons Act, 1933, although not expressly repealed, has ceased to have effect since a new paragraph (*a*) of that section was substituted by section 11 (2) of, and Part II of the First Schedule to, the Education (Miscellaneous Provisions) Act, 1948. The repealed entry relating to section 94 of the Local Government Act, 1933, was repealed by section 10 of the Education Act, 1946, *post*.

(a) **" Minister of Education ".**—Now Secretary of State for Education and Science, See note (b) to section 1, *ante*.

NINTH SCHEDULE

Section 121.

[*This Schedule, which dealt with enactments repealed as from the date of commencement of Part II of the Act, was itself repealed as spent by the Education Act* 1973, *Sched.* 2, *Part I.*]

THE EDUCATION ACT, 1946

9 & 10 Geo. 6, c. 50.

ARRANGEMENT OF SECTIONS

An Act to amend and supplement the law relating to education, and to amend the law relating to the execution of the Public Libraries Acts, 1892 *to* 1919.

[22nd May, 1946.]

GENERAL NOTE

The provisions of this Act, which were drafted after consultation with local education authorities, teachers and representatives of religious denominations, fall into two main categories. Of these the first gives to local education authorities certain additional powers which they were anxious to obtain, and the second makes minor adjustments in the Education Act, 1944, and clarifies it in certain respects. The Public Libraries Acts, 1892 to 1919, have been repealed. See note (d) to s. 14, *post*.

1. Enlargement of controlled schools.—(1) If upon the application of a local education authority (*) and the managers or governors (*) of a controlled school (*) maintained (*) by the authority the Secretary of State for Education and Science (a) (hereinafter referred to as "the Secretary of State") is satisfied—

(*a*) that there should be a significant enlargement of the school premises (b); and

[(*b*) either

(i)] that the enlargement is wholly or mainly required for the purpose of providing accommodation for pupils (*) for whom accommodation would have been provided in some other voluntary school (*) if that other school had not been discontinued (c) or had not otherwise ceased to be available for the purpose (d);

[or

(ii) that the enlargement is desirable for the better provision of primary or secondary education at the premises to be enlarged or for securing that there is available for the area of the authority a sufficiency of suitable primary or secondary schools or for both those reasons;]

then, if proposals for carrying out the enlargement are thereafter approved under section thirteen of the Education Act, 1944 (e) (hereinafter referred to as "the principal Act"), the Secretary of State (a) may by order direct that the expense of giving effect to those proposals shall be paid by the local education authority.

(2) [*Repealed.*]

NOTES

The effect of this section, which is printed as variously amended, is to enable a local education authority in certain circumstances and subject to certain conditions to pay the expenses of an enlargement of a controlled school. Thus, in order that use may be made of the powers conferred by the section there must be a nucleus school to which additions are to be made. Under the section as originally enacted the additions had to be wholly or mainly required for the purpose of accommodating displaced pupils from other voluntary schools. The effect of the insertion by s. 3 of the Education (Miscellaneous Provisions) Act, 1953, of the words in square brackets was to relax the requirement that the enlargement must be conditional on a reduction in voluntary school accommodation elsewhere. The Secretary of State now may require the local education authority to pay the cost of such an enlargement of a controlled school if he is satisfied that there should be a significant enlargement of the school premises, and that either of the further requirements of the subsection exist.

Subsequent amendments have been as follows:—

(*a*) A new paragraph (*a*) to sub-s. (1) was substituted by Sch. 1 to the Education Act, 1968;

(*b*) The words "primary or" were inserted before the word secondary, in both places where it occurs, by s. 2 of the Education Act, 1967;

(*c*) Subsection (2) (which defined "enlargement") was repealed by the Education Act, 1968, s. 1 (3) and Sch. 2. For definitions of "significant" and "enlargement", see now s. 114 (1) of the Education Act, 1944.

(*) As to the meaning or statutory definition of "local education authority", "managers or governors", "controlled school", "maintain", "premises", "pupil", "voluntary school", see pp. 67–69, *ante*.

(a) **"Secretary of State for Education and Science".**—See note (b) to s. 1 of the Act of 1944, *ante*.

(b) Paragraph (*a*) was substituted by Sch. 1 to the Education Act, 1968.

(c) **"Discontinued".**—As to the discontinuance of voluntary schools, see sections 13 and 14 of the 1944 Act, *ante*.

(d) **"Ceased to be available for the purpose".**—An example of a voluntary school ceasing to be available for pupils who would formerly have been accommodated there, even though it is not discontinued, is where a former all-age school becomes either a primary or secondary school pursuant to the local education order for the area.

(e) **"Section thirteen of the Education Act, 1944".**—See p. 90, *ante*. The public notice required by subsection (3) thereof must be given in the manner prescribed by the County and Voluntary Schools (Notices) Regulations 1968, S.I. 1968 No. 615, p. 381, *post*.

2. Division of a single school into two or more schools.—(1) Where a county school, an aided school or a controlled school is organised in two or more separate departments, and proposals are submitted to the Secretary of State—

(*a*) in the case of a county school by the local education authority; and

(*b*) in the case of an aided school or a controlled school, by the managers or governors of the school after consultation with the local education authority;

that the school should be divided into two or more separate schools, the Secretary of State may by order direct—

(i) if the school is a county school, that the school shall be divided into two or more separate county schools; and

(ii) if the school is an aided school or a controlled school, that the school shall be divided into two or more separate voluntary schools;

and when any such order comes into operation it shall become the duty of the local education authority to maintain each of the separate schools constituted by the order as a county school or as a voluntary school, as the case may be.

(2) The constitution of a separate school in pursuance of any such order shall not, for the purpose of section thirteen of the principal Act, be deemed to amount to the establishment of a new school.

(3) Where any such order is made upon proposals submitted by the managers or governors of a controlled school, the order shall direct that

each of the schools constituted in pursuance of the order shall be a controlled school.

(4) Where any such order is made upon proposals submitted by the managers or governors of an aided school, the order shall direct that each of the schools constituted in pursuance of the order shall be an aided school:

Provided that if the managers or governors of the original school have requested the Secretary of State to direct that all or any of the schools constituted in pursuance of the order shall be controlled schools, the order shall direct accordingly.

(5) Subsection (4) of section fifteen of the principal Act (which relates to the circumstances in which an order directing that a school is to be an aided school is to be revoked) shall have effect as if the references therein to an order by virtue of which a school is an aided school included references to a direction that a school shall be an aided school under this section.

(6) Where an order is made under this section upon proposals submitted by the managers or governors of a voluntary school which is being conducted in accordance with the transitional provisions contained in section thirty-two of the principal Act, the provisions of that section shall continue to have effect with respect to each of the schools constituted in pursuance of the order until the question whether that school shall be a controlled school, an aided school or a special agreement school is determined by an order made under subsection (2) of section fifteen of the principal Act.

(7) Any order made under this section shall come into operation upon such date as may be specified in the order and may contain such incidental, consequential and supplemental provisions as appear to the Secretary of State to be expedient, and, without prejudice to the generality of the preceding provisions of this subsection, may in particular provide for defining the premises of each of the separate schools to be constituted in pursuance of the order.

(8) No order shall be made under this section for the division of any school with respect to which a special agreement is in force.

NOTES

This section enables an existing school which was originally organised in two or more separate departments to be divided into two or more separate schools without the issue of public notices as required by section 13 of the Education Act 1944, *ante*. Under the section, 34 orders were made during 1974 (Department of Education and Science Annual Report, 1974).

3. Maintenance of voluntary schools.—(1) In relation to the maintenance of voluntary schools, the duties of local education authorities and of the managers and governors of such schools shall be performed in accordance with the provisions of the First Schedule to this Act.

(2) This section and the said First Schedule shall be deemed to have come into operation on the first day of April, nineteen hundred and forty-five (a).

NOTES

This section gives effect to the First Schedule, p. 216, *post*, which clarifies certain provisions of the Education Act, 1944, relating to the maintenance of voluntary schools.

(a) **"The first day of April, nineteen hundred and forty-five".**—This was the date when Part II of the Education Act, 1944, came into force.

4. Letting or hiring of school premises other than school buildings and definition of "school buildings".—(1) Any sum received after the passing of this Act by the managers, governors (a) or trustees (b) of a voluntary school (*), so far as it is paid in respect of the letting or hiring of any part of the school premises (*) other than school buildings (c), shall be paid over to the local education authority (*).

(2) In this Act the expression "school buildings", in relation to any school, means any building or part of a building forming part of the school

premises, except that it does not include any building or part of a building required only—

(*a*) as a caretaker's dwelling (d);

(*b*) for use in connection with playing fields (e);

(*c*) for affording facilities for enabling the [Secretary of State to carry out the functions conferred on him by section 3 of the National Health Service Reorganisation Act 1973 (*f*)]; or

(*d*) for affording facilities for providing milk, meals or other refreshment (g) for pupils in attendance at the school;

and in the principal Act the said expression shall be deemed always to have had the meaning assigned to it by this section.

NOTES

Subsection (1) of this section requires the managers, governors or trustees of a voluntary school to pay over to the local education authority any proceeds from the letting or hiring of any part of the school premises other than the school buildings; subsection (2) defines the expression "school buildings" not only for the purposes of subsection (1) but also for the purposes of the Education Act, 1944, and since by section 16 (2) of the present Act, p. 215, *post*, the two Acts are to be construed as one, for the purposes of other provisions of the present Act.

In the case of a controlled school the local education authority is responsible for providing and maintaining the whole of the school premises; in the case of an aided school or a special agreement school the managers or governors are responsible for providing the school buildings and for external repairs thereto other than repairs necessitated by the use of the premises at the direction or request of the local education authority for purposes other than that of a school and the local education authority is responsible for providing the site and all other buildings and for all maintenance expenses except those expressly thrown on the managers or governors. See section 15 (3) of the Education Act, 1944, as amended by the present Act, p. 96, *ante*, and the First Schedule to the present Act, p. 216, *post*. Since the provision and maintenance of the school premises, other than the school buildings, is in all cases the responsibility of the local education authority, it is only fair that the authority should receive the proceeds of all lettings thereof.

(*) As to the meaning or statutory definition of "voluntary school", "premises" and "local education authority", see pp. 67–69, *ante*.

(a) **"Managers, governors".**—See note (b) to section 17 of the Education Act, 1944, p. 101, *ante*.

(b) **"Trustees".**—This expression is not defined in the Education Act, 1944, or the present Act. It must, however, mean the trustees in whom the school premises are vested, *cf*. paragraph 6 of the First Schedule to the present Act, p. 216, *post*. See also section 22 (5) of the 1944 Act, p. 110, *ante*.

(c) **"School buildings".**—See the definition in subsection (2) of the present section.

(d) **"Caretaker's dwelling".**—As to the appointment of caretakers, see section 22 (4) of the Education Act, 1944, p. 110, *ante*.

(e) **"Playing fields".**—As to the duty to provide playing fields, see section 53 (1) of the Education Act, 1944, p. 144, *ante*. Even though they are quite detached from the school playing fields form part of the school premises; see the definition of premises in section 114 (1) of the Education Act, 1944, p. 185, *ante*.

(f) The words in square brackets in subsection (2) (*c*) were substituted by the National Health Service Reorganisation Act 1973, section 57, Sch. 4.

(g) **"Milk, meals or other refreshment".**—See section 49 of the Education Act, 1944, *ante*, and the notes thereto.

5. [*Spent.*]

NOTE

This section substituted a new s. 199 of the Education Act, 1944. That section is, however, now spent.

6. Power of local education authorities to execute work for the purposes of controlled schools.—Where a local education authority (*) are liable to pay the expense of carrying out any building work, repair work or work of a similar character (a) which is required for the purposes of a controlled school (*), that work shall, if the local authority so determine, be carried out by persons employed by the authority; and it shall be the duty of the managers or governors (*) of the school and of any trustees thereof (b) to provide the authority and any such persons with all such facilities as they may reasonably require for the purpose of securing that any such work is properly executed.

NOTES

This section makes it clear that in carrying out their duties with regard to the maintenance of controlled schools, as to which see section 15 (3) of the Education Act, 1944, as amended by the present Act, p. 108, *ante*, section 114 (2) of the Education Act, 1944, p. 185, *ante*, and the First Schedule to the present Act, p. 216, *post*, local authorities may execute any necessary works by their own workmen.

(*) As to the meaning or statutory definition of "local education authority", "controlled school" and "managers or governors", see pp. 67–69, *ante*.

(a) **"Building work, repair work or work of a similar character".**—As to the local education authority's obligations with regard to controlled schools which may involve the doing of such work see sections 9, 15 (3) and 114 (2) of the Education Act, 1944, pp. 82, 96, and 185, *ante*, and the First Schedule to the present Act, p. 216, *post*.

(b) **"Trustees".**—See note (b) to section 4 of the present Act, *supra*.

7. Additional provisions relating to religious worship.—(1) Subject to the provisions of this section, the collective worship (a) with which the school day in county schools (*) and voluntary schools (*) is required to begin shall take place on the school premises (*).

(2) If the managers or governors (*) of an aided school (*) or a special agreement school (*) are of opinion that it is desirable that a school day should, on any special occasion, begin with collective worship elsewhere than on the school premises, they may make such arrangements for that purpose as they think appropriate:

Provided that the powers of managers and governors under this subsection shall not be so exercised as to derogate from the rule that, in every aided school and special agreement school, the collective worship with which the school day is required to begin must normally take place on the school premises.

(3) Any reference in the principal Act to religious worship in any school shall be construed as including a reference to religious worship which, under the provisions of the last preceding subsection, takes place otherwise than on the school premises.

NOTES

Sub-section (1) makes it clear that the collective act of worship with which the school day must begin in county and voluntary schools must take place on the school premises.

In aided and special agreement schools, however, the collective act of worship may under subsection (2) take place elsewhere, *e.g.*, in church, on special occasions. Parents should be given adequate notice of any proposal to hold the collective act of worship off the school premises in case they should wish their children to be excused from attending under section 25 (4) of the 1944 Act.

(*) As to the meaning or statutory definition of "county school", "voluntary school" "premises", "managers or governors", "aided school" and "special agreement school", see pp. 67–69, *ante*.

(a) **"Collective worship".**—See section 25 of the Education Act, 1944, p. 115, *ante*, and note (c) thereto, and in the case of county schools see also section 26 of the Education Act, 1944, p. 117, *ante*.

8. Provisions for avoiding broken terms.

* * * * *

(3) Where a person attains the age of eighteen years during the term of any county college (*) which, when he attains that age, he is for the time being required to attend by a college attendance notice, he shall, for the purposes of the provisions of the principal Act relating to the period during which a person remains a young person (*), be deemed not to have attained that age until the end of the term, and the attendance required of him by any such notice may extend until the end of the term in which he has attained or will attain that age.

(4) Subsection (5) of section one hundred and fourteen of the principal Act is hereby repealed.

NOTES

This section repealed the former sub-s. (5) of s. 114 of the Act of 1944, which it replaced in more explicit terms.

The effect of subsections (1) and (2) of this section was to require pupils who reached the school leaving age in term time to remain at school until the end of the term during which they attained such age, and the effect of subsection (3) is to require young persons who reach the age of eighteen during the term of a county college which they are required to attend to continue to attend the college until the end of the term during which they attain such age. Establishment of county colleges is now unlikely.

Subsections (1) and (2) were repealed by the Education Act 1962, and provisions as to school leaving dates in England and Wales are now contained in section 9 of the Act of 1962, p. 246, *post*; the number of dates in the school year at which a sixteen-year-old may leave having been reduced thereby from three to two.

Provisions for avoiding a broken term when a child reaches the lower limit of compulsory school age are contained in section 4 of the Education (Miscellaneous Provisions) Act, 1948, *post.*

(*) As to the meaning or statutory definition of " county college " and " young person ", see pp. 67–69, *ante.*

9. [*Repealed.*]

NOTE

This section, which gave additional powers to provide clothing, was repealed by the Education (Miscellaneous Provisions) Act, 1948. All powers of local education authorities as to the provision of clothing are now consolidated in s. 5 of the Education (Miscellaneous Provisions) Act 1948, *post.*

10. [*Repealed.*]

NOTE

This section, which dealt with the qualification of teachers for membership of local authorities, was repealed by the Local Government Act 1972, s. 272 (1), Sch. 30. See now sections 80, 81 of the Act of 1972, 42 Halsbury's Statutes (3rd Edn.) 917–920.

11. [*Repealed.*]

NOTE

This section, which dealt with travelling expenses allowable to members of local authorities, was repealed by the Local Government Act 1948, itself partly repealed. See now ss. 173 *et seq.*, of the Local Government Act 1972 (42 Halsbury's Statutes (3rd Edn.) 995 *et seq.*).

12. [*Repealed.*]

NOTE

This section, which dealt with compensation for certain officers of county councils, was repealed by the Local Government Act 1972, s. 272 (1), Sch. 30.

13. Additional provisions relating to local administration.—(1) In any legal proceedings any document purporting to be a document issued by a divisional executive (a) and to be signed by a person authorised by the executive to sign it shall be received in evidence and shall, unless the contrary is proved, be deemed to be the document which it purports to be and to be signed by the person by whom it purports to have been signed without proof of his identity, signature or official capacity.

(2) . . .

NOTES

Subsection (1) provides that in any legal proceedings there shall be a rebuttable presumption that any document tendered in evidence purporting to be issued by a divisional executive, which not being a corporation, has no common seal, is the document it purports to be and was in fact signed by the person whose name appears as signatory.

Subsection (2) was repealed by the Local Government Act 1972, s. 272 (1), Sch. 30.

(*) As to the statutory definition of " local education authority ", see p. 68, *ante.*

(a) **" Divisional executive ".**—This term is defined in section 16 (1) of the present Act.

14. Miscellaneous amendments of enactments.—(1) The provisions of the principal Act specified in the first column of the Second Schedule to this Act shall have effect subject to the amendments specified in the second column of that Schedule, and the said amendments, so far as they are contained in Part II of the said Schedule, shall be deemed to have had effect since the commencement of Part II of the principal Act (a).

(2) [*Repealed* (b).]

(3) [*Repealed* (c)].

NOTES

This section gave effect to the Second Schedule now repealed; see p. 263, *post*.

(a) **" The commencement of Part II of the principal Act ".**—*I.e.*, 1st April, 1945.

(b) Subsection (2) was repealed by the Local Government Act 1972, s. 272 (1), Sch. 30.

(c) Under the Public Libraries Act, 1919, county councils were empowered to be the library authorities for the whole or any part of their counties (except parts which were already library authorities under existing legislation), and if a county council adopted these powers they were to be exercised by the education committee. Existing local authorities which were also local education authorities were also empowered to delegate their libraries to their education committees, although not many of them did so.

The repealed sub-s. (3), *supra*, amended section 6 of the Act of 1919, but that Act was repealed by the Public Libraries and Museums Act 1964, which also, by s. 26 and Sched. III thereof, repealed the consequential amendment which had been made by sub-s. (3), *supra*.

15. Expenses.—Any increase attributable to the passing of this Act in the expenditure of the Secretary of State (a) under the enactments relating to education shall be defrayed out of monies provided by Parliament.

NOTES

As stated in the Explanatory Memorandum issued with the Bill which became the present Act, the present Act only involves an additional charge on public funds in so far as it enlarges the existing powers of local education authorities, as it does in section 1, p. 209, *ante*, and s. 9 (now repealed, see p. 214, *ante*), or gives them new powers, as it did in section 11 (now repealed, see p. 214, *ante*). The net increased charge on the Exchequer is therefore comparatively small.

Section 13 of the Education (Miscellaneous Provisions) Act, 1948, p. 227, *post*, and section 19 of the Education (Miscellaneous Provisions) Act, 1953, p. 238, *post*, each contain a similar, though differently worded, provision as to the payment of the increase in expenses due to the passing of that Act.

(a) **" Secretary of State ".**—See note (b) to s. 1 of the Act of 1944.

16. Interpretation, etc.—(1) In this Act, unless the context otherwise requiries, the following expressions have the meanings hereby respectively assigned to them, that is to say :—

" department " (a) means such part, if any, of a school as is organised under a separate head teacher; . . . (b)

" site ", in relation to any school (*), does not include playing fields, but, save as aforesaid, includes any site which is to form part of the school premises (*).

(2) This Act shall be construed as one with the principal Act.

NOTES

(*) As to the statutory definition of " school " and " premises ", see p. 68, *ante*.

(a) **" Department ".**—Section 15 (1) of the Education Act, 1936, defined " school " for the purposes of that Act as including a separate department of a school, and in the definition of section 170 (1) of the Education Act, 1921, " elementary school " was defined as including a separate department.

For the purposes of the Education Act, 1944, and the present Act it seems clear that a separate department is not to be regarded as a separate school, see sections 8 (2) and 114 (3) of the Education Act, 1944, pp. 80 and 186, *ante*, and section 2 of the present Act, p. 210, *ante*. The test of what is a separate department appears to be the degree of independence of the head teacher, that is to say a preparatory division, however much separated from the rest of the school would not be a " department " within the meaning of the definition in the present section if the teacher in charge was responsible to, and required to act under, the orders of another teacher.

(b) The words omitted (definitions of " divisional executive " and " scheme of divisional administration ") were repealed by the Local Government Act 1972, s. 272 (1), Sch. 30.

17. Short title, citation and extent.—(1) This Act may be cited as the Education Act, 1946.

(2) This Act and the Education Act, 1944, may be cited together as the Education Acts, 1944 and 1946.

(3) This Act shall not extend to Scotland or to Northern Ireland.

SCHEDULES

Section 3.

FIRST SCHEDULE

MAINTENANCE OF VOLUNTARY SCHOOLS

1. The duty of a local education authority (a) to maintain (b) a voluntary school (c) under the principal Act (d) shall include the duty (e) of providing any site (f) which is to be provided for the school in addition to, or instead of, the whole or any part of the existing site of the school (f), and shall, in the case of a controlled school (g), include the duty of providing any buildings (h) which are to form part of the school premises (i):

Provided that nothing in this paragraph shall require a local education authority:—

(*a*) to perform any duties which, under section thirteen of the principal Act (k) (which includes provisions relating to the establishment of new schools and to the procedure by which a school which is not a voluntary school may become such a school) are required to be performed by any persons other than the authority; or

(*b*) to execute any proposals which are required to be executed under a special agreement made under the Third Schedule to the principal Act (l).

2. Where under subsection (1) of section sixteen of the principal Act the Secretary of State (m) has made an order authorising the transfer to a new site of an aided school (n) or a special agreement school (o), the duties of the managers or governors (p) of the school shall include the duty of defraying, with the assistance of any grant which may be made in accordance with section one hundred and three of the principal Act (q), the expenses of providing any school buildings (r) to be provided on the new site, and accordingly—

(a) the Secretary of State (m) shall not direct that a school shall be an aided school or a special agreement school unless he is satisfied that the managers or governors of the school will be able and willing to defray any such expenses;

(*b*) the duty of the local education authority to maintain an aided school or a special agreement school shall not include the duty of defraying any such expenses; and

(*c*) if at any time the managers or governors of an aided school or a special agreement school are unable or unwilling to carry out their obligations under this paragraph, it shall be their duty (s) to apply to the Secretary of State (m) for an order revoking the order or direction by virtue of which the school is an aided school or a special agreement school, and upon such an application being made to him the Secretary of State (m) shall revoke the order (t) or direction.

3. If when a local education authority provide a site for an aided school or a special agreement school in accordance with paragraph 1 of this Schedule, any work is required to be done to the site for the purpose of clearing it or making it suitable for building purposes, the authority and the managers or governors of the school may by agreement provide for the making of such payments, or of such other adjustments of their respective rights and liabilities, as will secure that the cost of that work is borne by the local education authority.

4. If when a local education authority provide a site for an aided school or a special agreement school in accordance with paragraph 1 of this Schedule there are, on the site so provided, any buildings which are of value for the purposes of the school, the authority and the managers or governors of the school may by agreement provide for the making of such payments, or of such other adjustments of their respective rights and liabilities, as appear to be desirable having regard to the duties of the managers or governors with respect to the school buildings.

5. Where it appears to the Secretary of State (m) that provision for any payment or other adjustment ought to have been made under either of the last two preceding paragraphs, but that such provision has not been made, he may by directions provide for the making of such payment or other adjustment as he thinks proper in the circumstances.

6. Where a local education authority provide a site for a school in accordance with the preceding provisions of this Schedule, it shall be the duty of the authority (u) to convey their interest (w) in the site and in any buildings on the site which are to form part of the school premises to the trustees of the school to be held on trust for the purposes of the school.

If any doubt or dispute arises as to the persons to whom a local education authority are required to make a conveyance under this paragraph, the conveyance shall be made to such persons as the Secretary of State (m) thinks proper.

7. Where an interest in any premises which are to be used for the purposes of a controlled school is conveyed in accordance with the last preceding paragraph to any persons who possess, or are or may become entitled to, any sum representing proceeds of the sale (x) of other premises which have been used for the purposes of the school, those persons or their successors shall pay to the local education authority so much of that sum as the Secretary of State (m) may determine to be just having regard to the value of the interest so conveyed; and any sum so paid shall be deemed for the purposes of section fourteen of the School Sites Act, 1841 (y) (which relates to the sale or exchange of land held on trust for the purposes of a school) to be a sum applied in the purchase of a site for the school.

In this paragraph the expression " sale " includes the creation or disposition of any kind of interest.

8. Where in accordance with paragraph 6 of this Schedule a local education authority convey premises (z) to be held on trust for the purposes of any voluntary school, and any person thereafter acquires the premises or any part thereof from the trustees, whether compulsorily or otherwise, the Secretary of State (m) may require the trustees or their successors to pay to the authority so much of the compensation or purchase money paid in respect of the acquisition as he thinks just having regard to—

(*a*) the value of the premises conveyed by the authority in accordance with the said paragraph 6; and

(*b*) any sums which have been received by the authority in respect of the premises under the preceding provisions of this Schedule.

In this paragraph the expression " premises " includes any interest in premises.

NOTES

This Schedule, which by section 3 (2), p. 211, *ante*, is deemed to have come into operation on 1st April, 1945, clarifies certain provisions of the 1944 Act relating to the maintenance of voluntary schools. It is not applicable in relation to temporary accommodation; see s. 3 (4) of the Education Act, 1968, p. 265, *post*.

The effect of the principal provisions of the Schedule was stated in the Explanatory Memorandum issued with the Bill which became the present Act in the following terms :—

> " Paragraph 1 makes clear that the responsibility for providing any additional site which may be needed for an existing voluntary school, or a new site to which a voluntary school is transferred under section 16 of the Act of 1944, rests with the Local Education Authority. The Local Education Authority are also responsible, in the case of a controlled school, for providing any buildings which are to form part of the school premises.
>
> Paragraph 2 makes it clear that where an aided or special agreement school is transferred to a new site the cost of the school buildings to be erected thereon will fall on the Managers or Governors, with the assistance of a contribution from the Minister [now Secretary of State] under section 103 (1).
>
> Paragraph 6 places a duty on Local Education Authorities where they extend the site of an existing voluntary school or provide a new site for a transferred voluntary school to convey the land to the Trustees of the school.
>
> Paragraph 7 places a duty on the Trustees of a controlled voluntary school which has been provided with an additional site, or transferred to a new site (see note on paragraph 1), to pay to the Local Education Authority, out of any proceeds of the sale of old premises such sum as the Minister [now Secretary of State] may consider just, as a contribution towards the cost of the buildings ".

As to the acquisition by agreement by a local authority of land for the purposes of a voluntary school, see section 10 of the Education (Miscellaneous Provisions) Act, 1948, p. 226, *post*.

(a) **" Local education authority ".**—See section 6 of and the First Schedule to the Education Act, 1944, pp. 76 and 196, *ante*. As to London, see Part IV of the London Government Act, 1963, p. 289, *post*; and as to the Isles of Scilly, see section 118 of the Act of 1944, p. 193, *ante*.

(b) **" Maintain ".** By section 114 (1) of the Education Act, 1944, p. 184, *ante*, this term in relation to any school is to have the meaning given to it by section 114 (2), p. 185, *ante*. In relation to voluntary schools the definition must now be read in conjunction with the more explicit provisions of the present Schedule.

(c) **" Voluntary school ".**—See sections 9 (2) and 15 of the Education Act 1944, *ante*.

(d) **" The principal Act ".**—*I.e.*, the Education Act, 1944, see section 1, p. 73, *ante*, which is to be construed as one with the present Act, see section 16 (2), p. 215, *ante*.

(e) **" Shall include the duty ".**—This is merely declaratory of the existing law. As explained by the then Minister of Education (Mr. R. A. Butler) in the course of the second reading of the Bill which became the present Act

> " Section 15 (3) (*a*) of the original Act had to be read with Section 114 (2) (*a*) if anybody wanted to understand the full meaning of Section 16 (1). . . . In fact, it was necessary to look at the interpretation Section to understand these two other vital sections of the Act itself. In the circumstances I think this Schedule makes it a great deal clearer, and does bring out, painfully perhaps but clearly, the duty of the authority to provide the site ".

(f) **" Site ".**—See the definition of this term in section 16 (1) of the present Act, *ante*.

(g) **" Controlled school ".**—See section 15 of the Education Act, 1944, p. 95, *ante*.

(h) **" Buildings ".**—This expression, when used alone, is not defined in the Education Act, 1944, or the present Act. As used here it clearly refers to all buildings on the school premises and not only those which are " school buildings " within the definition contained in section 4 (2) of the present Act, *ante*.

(i) **" School premises ".**—See the definition of " premises " in section 114 (1) of the Education Act, 1944, p. 185, *ante*.

(k) **" Section thirteen of the principal Act ".**—*I.e.*, section 13 of the Education Act, 1944, *ante*, see in particular subsections (2) and (7) thereof.

(l) **" The Third Schedule to the principal Act ".**—*I.e.*, the Third Schedule to the Education Act, 1944, p. 201, *ante*. Generally as to special agreement schools, see section 15 of the Education Act, 1944, *ante*, and the general note thereto.

(m) **" Secretary of State ".**—See note (b) to s. 1 of the Act of 1944, *ante*.

(n) **" Aided school ".**—See section 15 of the Education Act 1944, *ante*.

(o) **" Special agreement school ".**—See section 15 of the Education Act 1944, *ante*.

(p) **" Managers or governors ".**—See note (b) to section 17 of the Education Act 1944, *ante*.

(q) **" Section one hundred and three of the principal Act ".**—*I.e.*, section 103 of the Education Act, 1944, p. 177, *ante*, which authorises the Secretary of State to make grants in respect of transferred and substituted aided and special agreement schools.

(r) **" School buildings ".**—See the definition in section 4 (2) of the present Act, *ante*.

(s) **" It shall be their duty ".**—As to the enforcement of this duty, see section 99 (1) of the Education Act, 1944, *ante*.

(t) **" Shall revoke the order ".**—See note (w) to section 15 of the Education Act, 1944, *ante*.

(u) **" The duty of the authority ".**—As to the enforcement of this duty, see section 99 (1) of the Education Act, 1944, *ante*.

(w) **" Convey their interest ".**—With regard to this provision the then Minister of Education (Miss Ellen Wilkinson) made the following statement when moving the Second Reading of the Bill which became the present Act:

> " The Schedule does, however, break new ground in the fact that it requires that any land which is provided by the local education authority in those circumstances [*i.e.*, for a voluntary school] should be conveyed to the trustees of the school. This may, at first sight, appear to be rather unfair, but we find, as managers or governors have often to erect buildings on those sites out of charitable funds, they are up against the difficulty that many charitable funds do not allow the legatees—the owners and managers of the trust—to erect buildings on land which they do not own. Therefore, if the local authority does not actually convey ownership in the land to the governing body of the trust, the trust would be prevented by law from building the school, which was the purpose of the whole transaction. Therefore, we have to make it clear that the local education authority must convey ownership in the site to the governors or managers ".

(x) **" Sale ".**—See the definition in the proviso to the present paragraph.

(y) **" Section fourteen of the School Sites Act, 1841 ".**—See 11 Halsbury's Statutes (3rd Edn.) 387.

(z) **" Premises ".**—See the definition at the end of this paragraph.

SECOND SCHEDULE

Section 14.

[*This Schedule, which made miscellaneous amendments to the Education Act* 1944, *was repealed as spent by the Local Government Act* 1972, *s.* 272 (1), *Sch.* 30.]

THE EDUCATION (MISCELLANEOUS PROVISIONS) ACT, 1948

11 & 12 Geo. 6, c. 40

ARRANGEMENT OF SECTIONS

An Act to amend the Education Acts, 1944 *and* 1946, *the Endowed Schools Acts,* 1869 *to* 1908, *the provisions of the Mental Deficiency Act,* 1913, *as to children incapable of receiving education, and the provision of the Children and Young Persons Act,* 1933, *as to the minimum age of employment.*

[30th June, 1948.]

GENERAL NOTE

Like the Education Act, 1946, *ante*, this is an amending Act designed to make minor adjustments in the Education Act, 1944, which experience in the working of that Act have shown to be desirable. The various provisions of the present Act are for the most part unconnected, and their operation and effect are explained in the notes to the individual sections, *infra*.

1. [*Repealed.*]

NOTE

This section, which made provisions as to the transfer of powers conferred by the Charitable Trusts Acts, etc., was repealed by the Charities Act, 1960.

2. [*Repealed.*]

NOTE

This section, which extended the scope of the Endowed Schools Acts 1869 to 1908, was repealed by the Education Act 1973, Sched. 2, Part II. Of those Acts. the Endowed Schools Acts 1869 and 1873 (the only ones of which any provisions remained in force) were also repealed by Sch. 2 to the Act of 1973.

3. Allocation between primary and secondary education of children between ten and a half and twelve years old.—[*This section amends the definitions of primary and secondary education in subsection* (1) *of section* 8 *of the Education Act,* 1944, *which is printed as amended on p.* 89, *ante. The purpose of the amendments is to legalise the practice of transferring children from primary to secondary schools between the ages of ten and a half and twelve. See also section* 4 (1), *infra.*]

NOTE

Reference should also now be made to s. 1 of the Education Act 1964 (as amended by s. 2 of the Education Act 1968), p. 251, *post*, which deals with new schools with special age limits. As to recent developments in secondary education, see the Introduction, pp. 15–17, *ante*.

4. Provisions as to pupils becoming registered pupils at, and being withdrawn from, schools.—(1) A local education authority (*) shall have power to make arrangements with respect to a primary school (*) maintained (*) by them, not being a school which is for the time being organised for the provision of both primary (*) and secondary education (*), under which any junior pupils (*) who have attained the age of ten years and six months and who are registered pupils (*) at the school may be required to be withdrawn therefrom for the purpose of receiving secondary education.

(2) The provision of section eight of the principal Act (a) which renders it the duty of every local education authority to secure that there shall be available for their area sufficient schools for providing primary and secondary education shall not be construed as imposing any obligation on proprietors (*) of schools to admit children as registered pupils otherwise than at the beginning of a school term, except as regards admission at a school during the currency of a school term of a child who was prevented from entering the school at the beginning of the term—

(*a*) by his being ill or by other circumstances beyond his parent's (*) control; or

(*b*) by his parent's having been then resident at a place whence the school was not accessible with reasonable facility;

and, notwithstanding anything in section thirty-six of the principal Act (b), the parent of a child shall not be under any duty to cause him to receive full-time education during any period during which, having regard to the preceding provisions of this subsection, it is not practicable for the parent to arrange for him to become a registered pupil at a school.

(3) In cases not falling within the exception mentioned in the last preceding subsection, the managers or governors (*) of schools maintained by a local education authority shall comply, as respects the time of admission of children as registered pupils, with any general directions given by the authority in that behalf.

(4)–(5) [*These subsections amend section* 80 *of the Education Act,* 1944, *which is printed as amended on p.* 192, *ante.*]

(6) The regulations made under the said section eighty (c) shall prescribe the grounds on which names are to be deleted from a register kept thereunder, and the name of a person entered in such a register as a registered pupil shall be deleted therefrom when occasion arises on some one or other of the prescribed grounds and shall not be deleted therefrom on any other ground.

NOTES

The amendments of law made by this section are of a somewhat miscellaneous nature but all relate to the admission of pupils to schools, their registration in school registers and their withdrawal from schools.

Subsection (1) regularises the existing practice of requiring the transfer of pupils from primary to secondary schools at a mean age of eleven plus. Cf. the definitions of "primary education" and "secondary education" in section 8 of the Education Act, 1944, printed as amended by section 3 of the present Act on p. 79, *ante*. It should be noted that a local authority is not empowered to require the transfer of pupils from an all-age school.

Subsection (2) enables the admission of children to school to be deferred until the beginning of the term after they attain the age of five years.

Subsection (3) makes it clear that in the case of maintained schools the discretion as to whether children shall be admitted before the beginning of the term after they attain the age of five years is the local authority's, but that each local authority must adopt a settled practice in regard thereto.

Subsections (4) and (5) make amendments to section 80 of the Education Act, 1944, p. 165, *ante*, which relates to the registration of pupils and withdrawal of registered pupils from schools.

Subsection (6) makes an amendment as to the contents of regulations under section 80 of the 1944 Act, *supra*.

(*) As to the meaning or statutory definition of "local education authority", "primary school", "maintain", "primary education", "secondary education", "junior pupil", "registered pupil", "proprietor", "parent", "managers or governors", see pp. 67–69, *ante*.

(a) **"Section eight of the principal Act".**—See p. 79, *ante*.

(b) **"Section thirty-six of the principal Act".**—See p. 128, *ante*.

(c) **"Regulations under the said section eighty".**—See the Pupils' Registration Regulations, 1956, S.I. 1956 No. 357, p. 339, *post*.

5. Amendment and consolidation of enactments as to provision of clothing.—(1) A local education authority (*) may provide clothing (a)

(*a*) for any pupil (*) who is a boarder at any educational institution maintained (*) by the authority;

(*b*) for any pupil at a nursery school (*) so maintained; or

(*c*) for any pupil in a nursery class (b) at any school so maintained.

[and they may also provide clothing for a pupil for whom they are providing board and lodging elsewhere than at an educational institution so maintained, being a pupil receiving special educational treatment provided by them or by another authority or person in pursuance of arrangements made by them]

(2) Where it appears to a local education authority that—

(*a*) a pupil not falling within the preceding subsection at a school maintained by them, or

(*b*) a pupil not falling within the preceding subsection at a special school (*), whether maintained by them or not,

is unable by reason of the inadequacy or unsuitability of his clothing to take full advantage of the education provided at the school, the authority may provide him with such clothing as in the opinion of the authority is necessary for the purpose of ensuring that he is sufficiently and suitably clad while he remains a pupil at the school.

(3) The Secretary of State (c) may make regulations (d) empowering a local education authority to provide—

(*a*) for pupils at a school maintained by them, or at a county college (*) or other establishment for further education (e) so maintained, and

(*b*) for persons who make use of facilities for physical training made available for them by the authority under subsection (1) of section fifty-three of the principal Act (f),

such articles of clothing as may be prescribed suitable for the physical training provided at the school, college or other establishment, or under the facilities so made available.

(4) A local education authority may, with the consent of the proprietor (*) of a school not maintained by the authority other than a special school, and upon such financial and other terms, if any, as may be determined by agreement between the authority and the proprietor of the school, make arrangements for securing, for any pupil at the school who is unable by reason of the inadequacy or unsuitability of his clothing to take full advantage of the education provided at the school, the provision of such clothing as is necessary for the purpose of ensuring that he is sufficiently and suitably clad while he remains a pupil at the school:

Provided that any arrangements made under this subsection shall be such as to secure, so far as is practicable, that the expense incurred by the authority in connection with the provision of any article under the arrangements shall not exceed the expense which would have been incurred by them in the provision thereof if the pupil had been a pupil at a school maintained by them.

(5) Provision of clothing under any of the powers conferred by this section may be made in such way as to confer either a right of property in the clothing or a right of user only (g), at the option of the providing authority except in any circumstances for which the adoption of one or other way of making such provision is prescribed (h).

(6) Where a local education authority have, under the powers conferred by this section, provided a person with clothing, then, in such circumstances respectively as may be prescribed—

(*a*) the authority shall be under obligation to require the parent (*) to pay to them in respect thereof such sum, if any, as in the opinion of the authority he is able without financial hardship to pay, not exceeding the cost to the authority of the provision;

(*b*) the authority shall have power to require the parent to pay to them in respect thereof such sums as aforesaid or any less sums; or

(*c*) the parent shall not be required to pay any sum in respect thereof.

Any sum which a parent is duly required to pay by virtue of paragraph (*a*) or (*b*) of this subsection may be recovered summarily as a civil debt (i).

(7) The preceding provisions of this section shall be in substitution for the provisions of the Education Acts, 1944 and 1946, relating to the provision of clothing.

NOTES

This section (which is printed as amended by section 17 of and the First Schedule to the Education (Miscellaneous Provisions) Act, 1953, p. 238, *post*, whereby the words in square brackets were inserted in subsection (1)) replaces section 51 and part of section 52 of the Education Act, 1944, and section 9 of the Education Act, 1946. These enactments were repealed by section 11 (2) and the Second Schedule, of the present Act, themselves now repealed by the Statute Law Revision Act, 1950.

As to expenditure under section 81 of the 1944 Act, p. 166, *ante*, on distinctive school clothing for pupils attending maintained and transitionally assisted primary and secondary schools, see Circular No. 26 (13th March, 1945).

(*) As to the meaning or statutory definition of "local education authority", "pupil", "maintain", "nursery school", "special school", "county college", "proprietor" and "parent", see pp. 67–69, *ante*.

(a) **"Clothing".**—This includes boots and shoes. See section 114 (1) of the Education Act, 1944, p. 183, *ante*.

(b) **"Nursery class".**—See note (m) to section 8 of the Education Act, 1944, p. 82, *ante*.

(c) **"Secretary of State".**—See note (b) to s. 1 of the 1944 Act.

(d) **"Regulations".**—See the Provision of Clothing Regulations, 1948, S.I. 1948 No. 2222, as amended by the Provision of Clothing Amending Regulations, 1956, S.I. 1956 No. 559, p. 330, *post*. The amendment made by the amending regulations is consequential on the amendment to the present section made by the 1953 Act.

(e) **"Further educational establishment".**—This phrase is not defined in the present Act or in the Acts of 1944 or 1946.

(f) **"Section fifty-three of the principal Act".**—See p. 144, *ante*.

(g) **"A right of property or a right of user only".**—The Provision of Clothing Regulations, 1948, S.I. 1948 No. 2222, as amended by the Provision of Clothing Amending Regulations, 1956, S.I. 1956 No. 559, p. 330, *post*, prescribe certain conditions in which these respective rights are to be conferred.

(h) **"Prescribed".**—*I.e.*, by regulations. See section 114 (1) of the Education Act, 1944, *ante*.

(i) **"May be recoverable summarily as a civil debt".**—See note (b) to section 40 of the Education Act, 1944, p. 134, *ante*.

6. Recoupment to local education authority of cost of providing education for persons not belonging to their area.—(1) Where any provision for primary (*) or secondary education (*) is made by a local education authority (*) in respect of a pupil (*) who does not belong to their area, they shall be entitled to recoupment of an amount equal to the cost to them of the provision—

(*a*) if the pupil belongs to the area of another such authority, from that authority, the amount in that case being determined by agreement between the authorities, or, in default of agreement, by the Secretary of State (a), or

(*b*) if the pupil is one not belonging to the area of any local education authority, in accordance with regulations (b) to be made by the Secretary of State (a) for securing that the cost of such provision in such cases is apportioned amongst all local education authorities, the amount in that case being determined in accordance with the regulations,

subject in either case to the providing authority's making a claim in that behalf within the prescribed period:

Provided that in a case falling within paragraph (*a*) of this subsection, if the Secretary of State (a) is satisfied that the other authority ought not to be required to make recoupment in respect of the provision having regard to availability of provision of the kind in question under arrangements made by them and to all other circumstances of the case, he may, on their application, direct that the providing authority shall not be entitled to recoupment in respect thereof.

(2) For the purposes of this Act, a pupil shall be treated as belonging to the area of a particular local education authority, or as not belonging to the area of any such authority, in accordance with the following rule, namely—

(*a*) in the normal case, that is to say, where there is a person ordinarily resident in England or Wales with whom the pupil habitually resides, either both during terms and during holidays or, if he is being educated as a boarder, during holidays, being a person who has the actual charge of him whilst he is resident with that person, the pupil shall be treated as belonging to the area of the local education authority in whose area that person ordinarily resides; and

(*b*) in a case in which there is no such person, the pupil shall be treated as not belonging to the area of any local education authority;

subject however to the provisions of the next succeeding subsection.

(3) The general rule specified in the last preceding subsection shall be subject to the following exceptions, that is to say,—

(*a*) a pupil for whom a local education authority is for the time being appointed as a fit person under the Children and Young Persons Act, 1933, shall be treated as belonging to the area of that authority;

(*b*) a pupil for whom a person other than a local education authority is for the time being appointed as a fit person as aforesaid, or for whom a guardian is for the time being appointed (c) under the Guardianship (Refugee Children) Act, 1944, shall be treated as belonging to the area of such local education authority as may be prescribed, or, if none is prescribed, as not belonging to the area of any such authority;

(*c*) where immediately before the date of the commencement of Part II of the principal Act (d) a former authority had been required under the Education (Institution Children) Act, 1923 (e), to make payments in respect of a pupil to another former authority and were liable to make such payments, then, so long as the first-mentioned former authority would have remained so liable if the said Act of 1923 had not been repealed, the pupil shall be treated as belonging to the area of the local education authority responsible for the liabilities of the first-mentioned former authority; and

(*d*) in such other cases as may be prescribed a pupil shall be treated in accordance with the regulations either as belonging to the area of a prescribed local education authority or as not belonging to the area of any such authority.

(4) Any question whether a pupil ought to be treated as belonging to the area of any particular local education authority, or as not belonging to the area of any such authority, shall, in case of dispute, be determined by the Secretary of State (a).

(5) A local education authority may make a payment by way of recoupment to another such authority of cost incurred by the other authority in making any provision—

(*a*) for primary or secondary education in respect of a pupil belonging to the area of the paying authority, or

(*b*) for further education (f) in respect of a person ordinarily resident in the area of the paying authority,

notwithstanding that the paying authority are not under a legal obligation to make the payment.

(6) References in this section to provision for education include references to provision of any benefits or services for which provision is made by or under the enactments relating to education.

(7) This section shall have effect, as respects any provision for education, in substitution for section one hundred and six of the principal Act, in so far as the cost of the provision is attributable to any period after the thirty-first day of March, nineteen hundred and forty-eight, and regulations for the purposes of this section may accordingly be made so as to extend to any such provision made before the coming into operation of the regulations in so far as the cost of the provision is attributable to any such period.

NOTES

This section replaces section 106 of the Education Act, 1944, in regard to expenditure attributable to a period after March 31, 1948 (subsection (7), *supra*) incurred by local education authorities in providing education for children whose parents do not live in their area.

The section distinguishes between those extra-district pupils who belong to the area of another local education authority and those who do not belong to the area of any local education authority. Under subsection (2) a pupil is normally treated as belonging to the area of a particular local education authority if there is in that area a person ordinarily resident in England and Wales with whom he habitually resides and in whose charge he is, during both term time and holiday, either both during terms and during holidays, or, if he is being educated as a boarder, during holidays only.

In the case of such a pupil the educating authority is entitled to be recouped by the authority of origin if it makes the necessary claim within the prescribed period, unless, on application being made to him by the authority of origin under the proviso to subsection (1), the Secretary of State is satisfied that that authority should not be required to recoup the educating authority and gives a direction accordingly.

Where, however, the pupil does not belong to the area of any local education authority, the section provides that the cost of provision shall be apportioned among all local education authorities in accordance with regulations made by the Secretary of State.

Where boarding school education was clearly necessary for a child (daughter of a missionary in Jamaica) who did not belong to the area of any local education authority, the legal branch of the Ministry of Education (now Department of Education and Science) advised that such education should be provided by the local education authority for the area where the child would spend her holidays, which authority would be entitled to recoupment under subsection (1) (*b*).

Subsections (2)–(4) are applied by the London Government Act, 1963, section 33 (2), p. 294, *post*.

As to the recoupment to a local education authority of the cost of providing further education for persons not belonging to their area, see section 7 of the Education (Miscellaneous Provisions) Act, 1953, p. 232, *post*.

(*) As to the meaning or statutory definition of " primary education ", " secondary education ", " local education authority " and " pupil ", see p. 68, *ante*.

(a) **" Secretary of State ".**—See note (b) to s. 1 of the Act of 1944.

(b) **" Regulations ".**—See the Local Education Authorities (Recoupment) Regulations, 1953, S.I. 1953 No. 507 (as amended by the Local Education Authorities (Recoupment) Amending Regulations 1954, S.I. 1954 No. 199, the Local Education Authorities Recoupment (Primary, Secondary and Further Education) Amending Regulations 1959, S.I. 1959 No. 448, and the Local Education Authorities (Recoupment) (Amendment) Regulations 1973, S.I. 1973 No. 1676), *post*.

(c) " **Guardian is for the time being appointed** ".—As to guardians, see now the Guardianship of Minors Act 1971 (41 Halsbury's Statutes (3rd Edn.) 762).

(d) " **Commencement of Part II of the principal Act** ".—1st April, 1945.

(e) " **Education (Institution Children) Act, 1923** ".—This Act was repealed as from 1st April, 1945, by the Education Act, 1944, section 121 and Ninth Schedule, Part I, *ante*.

(f) " **Further education** ".—So far as this subsection relates to further education it is now superseded by section 7 of the Education (Miscellaneous Provisions) Act, 1953, p. 232, *post*; see subsection (7) thereof.

7. Amendments as to modifying the requirement of conformity to prescribed standards as to premises of schools.—(1) [*Substitutes new proviso to section* 10 (2) *of the Education Act,* 1944. *See that section, printed as hereby amended, at p.* 84, *ante*].

(2) Where it is proposed to establish a new school (a) to be maintained (*) by a local education authority (*), if the Secretary of State (b) is satisfied, on the submission to him of the specifications and plans of the school premises, either—

(*a*) with respect to the site (*) of the school, as to the matters mentioned in paragraph (*b*) set out in the preceding subsection, or

(*b*) with respect to buildings where the school is to be established in premises comprising existing buildings or temporary buildings, as to the matters mentioned in paragraph (*c*) set out in the preceding subsection,

[or if the Secretary of State is satisfied, on the submission to him of the specification and plans of the school premises where the premises are to comprise the existing site or buildings of another school, as to the matters set out in paragraph (*a*) of the preceding subsection] he may (notwithstanding the provisions of section thirteen of the principal Act as to conformity to the prescribed standards) approve the specifications and plans, and may undertake to give a direction as to the school under the proviso to subsection (2) of section ten of the principal Act on the school's being established.

[(2A) Notwithstanding the provisions of section 13 of the principal Act as to conformity to the prescribed standards, the Secretary of State may approve specifications and plans submitted to him under that section in connection with proposals for a significant enlargement of school premises in any case where he could under subsection (2) of this section do so if they were specifications and plans of the school premises of a new school proposed to be established.]

(3) This section [except subsection (2A)] shall be deemed to have had effect since the commencement of Part II of the principal Act (c).

NOTES

The object of this section, which has retrospective operation from April 1, 1945, is, first, to make more precise the Secretary of State's power to modify the application of the statutory building regulations to existing schools (subsection (1)), which is effected by substituting a new proviso to section 10 (2) of the Education Act, 1944, p. 84, *ante*, and secondly, to give him a similar power with regard to new schools. The section confines the Secretary of State's exercise of these powers to specific circumstances, *e.g.*, where siting difficulty, labour shortage or lack of materials makes it impracticable to have complete conformity with the building regulations; see 155 H. of L. Official Report 703.

The words in square brackets in sub-s. (2) were inserted by s. 3 (2) of the Education Act, 1968.

Subsection (2A) was added by the Education Act, 1968, Sch. I.

The words in square brackets in sub-s. (3) were also added by the Education Act, 1968, Sch. I.

(*) As to the meaning or statutory definition of " maintain ", " local education authority " and " site ", see pp. 67–69, *ante*.

(a) " **Establish a new school** ".—See section 13 of the Education Act, 1944, p. 90, *ante*, and the notes thereto.

(b) " **Secretary of State** ".—See note (b) to s. 1 of the Act of 1944.

(c) " **Commencement of Part II of the principal Act** ".—April 1, 1945.

8. [*Repealed.*]

NOTE

This section, which dealt with cancellation of reports on incapable children, was repealed by the Mental Health Act, 1959, section 149 (2) and Schedule VIII, Part I.

9. Presumption of age in proceedings to enforce attendance at school.—(1) For the purposes of a prosecution of the parent (*) of a child (*) for an offence against section thirty-seven or section thirty-nine of the principal Act (a) (which relate respectively to failure to comply with a school attendance order and to failure of a child to attend regularly at school), in so far as the child's having been of compulsory school age (*) at any time is material, the child shall be presumed to have been of compulsory school age at that time unless the parent proves the contrary.

(2) An obligation under the preceding subsection to presume a child to have been of compulsory school age at any time shall be in substitution, so far as regards the purposes for which that presumption is required to be made, for the power conferred on the court by subsection (1) of section ninety-five of the principal Act (b) (which is a power to presume a person to be under, of, or over, an age alleged by the person by whom any proceedings under the principal Act are brought on his satisfying the court that, having used all reasonable diligence to obtain evidence as to the age of that person, he has been unable to do so).

NOTES

This section places on the parent of a child whose age is disputed in school attendance proceedings the burden of proving that the child was not of compulsory school age at the material time. As a necessary corollary the general power conferred on the court by section 95 of the Education Act, 1944, p. 172, *ante*, to presume a person to be over or under a particular age is excluded in school attendance proceedings.

(*) As to the meaning or statutory definition of " parent ", " child " and " compulsory school age ", see pp. 67–69, *ante*.

(a) **" Section thirty-seven or section thirty-nine of the principal Act ".**—See pp. 129 and 132, *ante*.

(b) **" Subsection (1) of section ninety-five of the principal Act ".**—See p. 172, *ante*.

10. Provisions as to power of local education authorities to acquire land by agreement.—(1) [*This subsection amends section* 90 *of the Education Act*, 1944, *which is printed as amended on p.* 198, *ante.*]

(2) For the removal of doubt it is hereby declared that the rendering available of land for the purposes of a school, college or other institution which is, or is to be, maintained (*) by a local education authority, or which they have power to assist (*), is a function of the authority within the meaning of section one hundred and fifty-seven of the Local Government Act, 1933 (a), . . . (which relate to the acquisition by a local authority by agreement of land for the purpose of any of their functions), notwithstanding that the land will not be held by the authority.

(3) A local education authority shall not acquire by agreement any land required for the purposes of a voluntary school unless they are satisfied that the arrangements made as to the vesting of the land to be acquired, and as to the appropriation thereof for those purposes, are such as to secure that the expenditure ultimately borne by them will not include any expenditure which, if the land had been acquired by the managers or governors of the school, would have fallen to be borne by the managers or governors (b).

NOTES

Subsection (2) gives local education authorities express power to purchase land by agreement for both maintained and assisted schools. Under subsection (3) it is the duty of the managers or governors of a voluntary school to recoup the expenditure of a local education authority in buying land by agreement for the school if under the Acts of 1944 and 1946 it is the managers' or governors' duty to provide the land.

The words deleted in subsection (2) were repealed, as from 1st April, 1965, by the London Government Act, 1963, Schedule 18, Part II.

The section should be read in connection with Circular No. 2/60 (1st March, 1960), p. 455, *post*.

(*) As to the statutory definition of " maintain " and " assist ", see pp. 67–69, *ante*.

(a) **" Section one hundred and fifty-seven of the Local Government Act, 1933 ".**—Repealed by the Local Government Act 1972, s. 272 (1), Sch. 30. See now, as to the acquisition of land by principal councils, sections 120 *et seq.* of the Act of 1972, 42 Halsbury's Statutes (3rd Edn.) 949 *et seq.*

(b) **Subsection (2).**—Compare the proviso to section 90 (1) of the Education Act, 1944, p. 169, *ante*, and see the notes thereto.

11. Miscellaneous amendments and repeals.—(1) The provisions of the principal Act specified in the first column of Part I of the First Schedule to this Act . . . shall have effect subject to the amendments specified in the second column of that Schedule (being amendments which relate to minor matters and consequential amendments.)

(2) [*Repealed.*]

NOTES

The words omitted in subsection (1) were repealed by the Education Act 1973, Sch. 2, Part II.

Subsection (2), which provided for the repeal of the enactments specified in the Second Schedule to this Act, was, with that Schedule, repealed by the Statute Law Revision Act, 1950; 32 Halsbury's Statutes (3rd Edn.) 695.

12. Provisions as to regulations.—Regulations made for any of the purposes of this Act, save in so far as they are subject to corresponding provision by virtue of their being made under a power conferred by the principal Act, shall be made by statutory instrument (a) and shall be subject to annulment (b) in pursuance of resolution of either House of Parliament.

NOTES

(a) **" Made by statutory instrument ".**—See section 1 of the Statutory Instruments Act 1946; 32 Halsbury's Statutes (3rd Edn.) 668, the main provisions of which came into operation on 1st January, 1948; see S.I. 1948 No. 3.

(b) **" Subject to annulment, etc.".**—For the effect of this provision and the procedure to be followed, see section 5 (1) of the Statutory Instruments Act, 1946; 32 Halsbury's Statutes (3rd Edn.) 672.

13. Expenses.—Any increase attributable to the provisions of this Act (a) in the expenses to be defrayed out of moneys provided by Parliament under section one hundred and seven of the principal Act (b) shall be defrayed out of monies so provided.

NOTES

(a) **" Any increase attributable to the provisions of this Act ".**—The Act involves an increased charge on public funds only in so far as it enlarges the existing powers of local education authorities, as it does in section 5, p. 221, *ante*, as in the case of the power to provide clothing; see the Explanatory and Financial Memorandum attached to the Bill, which became the present Act.

(b) **" Section one hundred and seven of the principal Act ".**—This section, p. 181, *ante*, provides for the expenses of the Secretary of State for Education and Science and the Minister of Health in the exercise of their functions under that Act to be defrayed out of public funds.

14. Short title, citation, construction and extent.—(1) This Act may be cited as the Education (Miscellaneous Provisions) Act, 1948.

(2) This Act . . . and the Education Acts 1944 and 1946 (b), may be cited together as the Education Acts 1944 to 1948 . . .

(3) This Act . . . shall be construed as one (c) with the Education Acts 1944 and 1946.

(4) References in this Act to any other enactment shall, except so far as the context otherwise requires, be construed as references to that enactment as amended by or under any other enactment, including this Act.

(5) This Act shall not extend to Scotland or Northern Ireland.

NOTES

The omitted words were repealed by the Education Act 1973, Sch. 2, Part II, consequent upon the repeal, by the same Act and Schedule, of the Endowed Schools Acts 1869 and 1873.

(b) **" Education Acts, 1944 and 1946 ".**—Section 17 (2) of the Education Act, 1946, p. 215, *ante*, provides that that Act and the Education Act, 1944, referred to in the present Act as " the principal Act " may be cited together under this collective title.

(c) **" Shall be construed as one ".**—Accordingly, the relevant parts of this Act are to be construed as if they were contained in the earlier legislation referred to unless there is any manifest discrepancy showing that this Act has modified something to be found in the earlier Acts (*Canada Southern Rail. Co.* v. *International Bridge Co.* (1883), 8 App. Cas. 723, at p. 727; *Hart* v. *Hudson Brothers, Ltd.*, [1928] 2 K.B. 629, at p. 634; [1928] All E.R. Rep. 95; *Phillips* v. *Parnaby*, [1934] 2 K.B. 299, at p. 302; [1934] All E.R. Rep. 267). Thus words defined in the earlier Acts bear the like meaning in the relevant parts of this Act, unless it is clear from the context that their construction in this Act is different.

SCHEDULES

FIRST SCHEDULE

PART I

[*Repealed by the Children and Young Persons Act* 1969, *Sch.* 6.]

PART II

[*Repealed by the Education Act* 1973, *Sch.* 2, *Part II*.]

SECOND SCHEDULE

[*Repealed by the Statute Law Revision Act*, 1950.]

THE EDUCATION (MISCELLANEOUS PROVISIONS) ACT, 1953

1 & 2 Eliz. 2, c. 33

ARRANGEMENT OF SECTIONS

An Act to amend the law relating to education in England and Wales; and to make further provision with respect to the duties of education authorities in Scotland as to dental treatment. [14th July, 1953.]

GENERAL NOTE

This Act represents the third attempt to improve and clarify the Education Act, 1944. In particular the present Act provides additional financial relief to denominational bodies in connection with the establishment of new voluntary schools and, in a more limited class of cases, with the enlargement of existing voluntary schools, gives effect to certain suggestions made by the Local Government Manpower Committee and contains provisions simplifying administration and removing doubts as to some intentions of the principal Act.

1. [*Superseded.*]

NOTE

This section, which extended the definition of " displaced pupil " for the purposes of the principal Act, has been superseded by s. 1 of the Education Act, 1967, and has ceased to have effect. See, as to the meaning of " displaced pupil ", note (k) to s. 105 of the Act of 1944, p. 180, *ante*.

2. Power of Secretary of State, in certain circumstances, to require local education authority to defray expenses of establishing a controlled school.—Where—

(*a*) any persons submit, under subsection (2) of section thirteen of the principal Act (b), to the Secretary of State (a) proposals for the establishment by them, or by persons whom they represent, of a new school (*) . . . (c) and for its maintenance (*) by the local education authority (*) as a voluntary school (*); and

(*b*) the persons who submit the proposals and the local education authority show to the satisfaction of the Secretary of State (a) that the establishment of the school is required for the purpose of providing accommodation for pupils for whom [or for a substantial proportion of whom (d)] accommodation would have been provided in some other voluntary school (e) if that other school had not been discontinued or had not otherwise ceased to be available for the purpose (f); and

(*c*) no application is made under subsection (2) of section fifteen of the principal Act (g) to the Secretary of State (a) for an order directing that the school shall be an aided school (*) or a special agreement school (*);

the Secretary of State (a) may by order direct that the whole, or a special part, of so much of the cost incurred in the establishment of the school as would, apart from the order, fall to be defrayed by the persons who establish it shall be defrayed by the local education authority.

NOTES

This section makes it possible for a local education authority to pay the whole, or such part as the Secretary of State may direct, of the cost of a new controlled school if it is required for the accommodation of pupils from one or more other voluntary schools which have been closed or, for other reasons, ceased to be available for them.

Under section 1 (1) (*b*) (i) of the Education Act, 1946, *ante*, the Secretary of State may direct a local education authority to defray the cost of enlarging an existing controlled school where he is satisfied that there should be a significant enlargement of the school premises (see p. 209, *ante*). It may be, however, that there is no suitable nucleus school which can be enlarged and that what is wanted is a new school altogether, in a new situation, which will take the place of one or more existing voluntary schools. The present section enables public money to be spent on such a school provided that the promoters of the school and the local education authority agree and the Secretary of State approves.

As to the purchase of land by a local education authority for a new voluntary school, see section 90 of the Education Act, 1944, *ante*.

(*) As to meaning or statutory definition of "school", "maintain", "local education authority", "voluntary school", "aided school" and "special agreement school", see pp. 67–69, *ante*.

(a) **"Secretary of State".**—See note (b) to s. 1 of the Act of 1944.

"Subsection (2) of section thirteen of the principal Act".—Under that subsection, *ante*, the promoters of any new school which they propose shall be maintained by the local education authority as a voluntary school are required to submit proposals for that purpose to the Secretary of State. Public notice must be given of such proposals (subsection (3)), and, after considering any objections, the Secretary of State may approve the proposals with or without modification.

(c) The words omitted in para. (*a*) were repealed by Sch. 2 to the Education Act, 1968.

(d) The words "or for a substantial proportion of whom" are to be added to para. (*b*) of s. 2 (see s. 3 of the Education Act, 1967, as amended by s. 2 of the Education Act, 1968, p. 260, *post*) in cases where persons other than a local education authority submit proposals for the establishment of a new middle school and its maintenance as a voluntary school.

(e) **"Accommodation for pupils for whom accommodation would have been provided in some other voluntary school".**—Note that the power under this section can only be exercised where the new school is required for the accommodation of such pupils whereas under section 1 of the Education Act, 1946, *ante*, the cost of enlargement may be defrayed where it is required "wholly or mainly" for the accommodation of such pupils. The present section, therefore, requires a closer relationship than does section 1 of the 1946 Act between the accommodation to be provided in the new school and the accommodation to be given up elsewhere.

(f) **"Ceased to be available for the purpose".**—See note (d) to s. 1 of the 1946 Act, p. 210, *ante*.

(g) **"Subsection (2) of section 15 of the principal Act".**—Since the only categories of voluntary schools are controlled schools, aided schools and special agreement schools, the result of the exclusion of proposed schools in respect of which an application has been made under section 15 (2) of the Education Act, 1944, *ante*, for directions that they shall be aided or special agreement schools is to make this section applicable to new controlled schools only.

3. Extension of power . . . to require local education authority to pay for enlargement of a controlled school.—[*This section amends section* 1 (1) *of the Education Act,* 1946, *which is printed as amended on p.* 250, ante. *The effect of the amendment is to relax, in relation to secondary schools and subject to certain conditions, the requirement that any enlargement* *of a controlled school under that section must be conditional upon a reduction of voluntary school accommodation elsewhere.*]

4. [*Repealed.*]

NOTE

This section, which imposed duties on local education authorities as to dental treatment, was repealed by the National Health Service Reorganisation Act 1973, section 57, Sch. 5.

5. [*Applies to Scotland only.*]

6. Provision of education at non-maintained schools and payment of tuition and boarding fees for pupils attending thereat.—(1) For the purpose of fulfilling their duties under the principal Act (a), a local education authority (*) shall have, and be deemed always to have had, power to make, with the approval of the Secretary of State (b), arrangements for the provision of primary (*) and secondary education (*) for pupils (*) at a school (*) not maintained (*) by them or another local education authority.

(2) Where, in pursuance of arrangements made by a local education authority by virtue of the foregoing subsection or section thirty-three of the principal Act (c), primary or secondary education is provided for a pupil at a school not maintained by them or another local education authority, the authority by whom the arrangements are made—

(*a*) shall, in the following cases, that is to say—

(i) where the pupil fills a place in the school which the proprietors (*) of the school have put at the disposal of the authority and the school is one in respect of which grants are made by the Secretary of State (b) under paragraph (*b*) of subsection (1) of section one hundred of the principal Act (d),

(ii) where the authority are satisfied that, by reason of a shortage of places in schools maintained by them and schools maintained by other local education authorities, being schools to which the pupil could be sent with reasonable convenience (e), education suitable to the age, ability and aptitude of the pupil cannot be provided by them for him except at a school not maintained by them or another local education authority,

(iii) where, in a case not falling within either of the two foregoing sub-paragraphs, the authority are satisfied that the pupil requires special educational treatment (*) and that it is expedient in his interests that such treatment should be provided for him at a special school (*) not maintained by them or another local education authority,

pay the whole of the fees payable in respect of the education provided in pursuance of the arrangements;

(*b*) shall, where board and lodging are provided for the pupil at the school and the authority are satisfied that education suitable to his age, ability and aptitude (f) cannot be provided by them for him at any school unless board and lodging are also provided for him (either at school or elsewhere), pay the whole of the fees payable in respect of the board and lodging (g).

(3) The powers conferred on a local education authority by subsection (1) of this section shall be in addition to and not in derogation of the powers conferred on them by the principal Act.

NOTES

This section imposes on local education authorities a duty in certain circumstances, to take up places in direct-grant and independent schools, and, for handicapped pupils, in non-maintained special schools. Previously local education authorities found it necessary to do this, and to pay the tuition fees in full, without applying an income scale, because their maintained school or special school provision was inadequate or did not offer education of the kind needed by a particular pupil. The section provides more specific legal authority for this practice and makes the conditions and limits more precise.

Subsection (2) (*b*) requires the authority to pay the boarding fee as well as the tuition fee in cases where suitable education for a pupil cannot be provided otherwise than by boarding.

Where an authority has fulfilled its duty under section 8 of the 1944 Act, p. 79, *ante*, to secure that sufficient schools are available for its area by making arrangements for the payment of full tuition fees at an independent school there is no obligation on it to pay the whole tuition fees at some other independent school chosen by a parent (*Watt* v. *Kesteven County Council*, [1955] 1 All E.R. 473; [1955] 1 Q.B. 408, C.A.).

As to the continuance of certain grants made before 1st April, 1965, see section 33 of the London Government Act, 1963, *post*.

(*) As to the meaning or statutory definition of "local education authority", "primary education", "secondary education", "pupil", "school", "maintain", "proprietor", "special educational treatment", "special school", see pp. 67–69, *ante*.

(a) **"Their duties under the principal Act".**—See in particular the following sections of the 1944 Act, namely: section 8, *ante* (duty to secure provision of primary and secondary schools), section 33, *ante* (duty to provide special educational treatment), section 76, *ante* (duty to have regard to the wishes of parents).

(b) **"Secretary of State".**—See note (b) to s. 1 of the Act of 1944.

(c) **"Section thirty-three of the principal Act".**—See p. 122, *ante*, where that section is printed as amended by section 17 (1) of and the First Schedule to the present Act, *post*.

(d) **"Paragraph (b) of subsection (1) of section one hundred of the principal Act".**—Under this paragraph, *ante*, grants are payable to the schools which satisfy the conditions applicable to direct-grant schools contained in the Direct Grant Schools Regulations, 1959, S.I. 1959 No. 1832, p. 363, *post*.

(e) **With reasonable convenience.**—It would seem that for a pupil to be sent to a maintained school "with reasonable convenience" the school must be within reasonable distance of his home.

(f) **Suitable to the age, ability and aptitude of the pupil.**—See section 36 of the Education Act, 1944, *ante*, and notes thereto, and *cf.* proviso (*a*) to section 61 (2) of the Education Act, 1944.

(g) **"Fees payable in respect of the board and lodging".**—This provision for the payment of the fees in respect of board and lodging where suitable education cannot otherwise be provided is in line with proviso (*a*) to section 52 (1) of the Education Act, 1944, p. 143, *ante*, proviso (*a*) to section 61 (2) of the 1944 Act, p. 150, *ante*, and regulation 3 (*c*) (i) of the Regulations for Scholarships and Other Benefits, 1945, S.R. & O. 1945 No. 666, p. 328, *post*, the principle underlying all these provisions being that where the local education authority cannot fulfil its statutory duty to provide suitable education without providing board and lodging it must provide such board and lodging free of charge to the parent, whatever the parent's means may be.

7. Recoupment to local education authority of cost of providing further education for persons not belonging to their area.—(1) Where any provision for further education is made by a local education authority (*) in respect of a pupil (*) who belongs to the area of another such authority (a), and that other authority have consented to the making of the provision, the providing authority shall, upon making a claim in that behalf within the prescribed (b) period, be entitled to recoupment from the other authority of the prescribed fraction, or (if it is so prescribed) the whole, of the amount of the cost to the providing authority of the provision, the amount being determined by agreement between the authorities or, in default of agreement, by the Secretary of State (c).

(2) Where any provision for further education is made by a local education authority in respect of a pupil who does not belong to the area of any such authority, the providing authority shall, upon making a claim in that behalf within the prescribed period, be entitled to recoupment of the prescribed fraction, or (if it is so prescribed) the whole, of the amount aforesaid, in accordance with regulations (d) to be made by the Secretary of State (c) for securing that the cost of such provision in such cases is apportioned amongst all local education authorities, the amount in that case being determined in accordance with the regulations.

(3) A local education authority may make a payment by way of recoupment to another such authority of the cost incurred by the other authority in making any provision for further education in respect of a pupil belonging to the area of the paying authority notwithstanding that the paying authority are not under a legal obligation to make the payment.

(4) Subsection (2) of section six of the Education (Miscellaneous Provisions) Act, 1948 (e) (which lays down a rule for determining, for the purposes of the enactments relating to education, whether a pupil shall be treated as belonging to the area of a particular local education authority or as not belonging to the area of any such authority) and sub-section (3) of that section (which contains exceptions from the rule) shall not apply for the purposes of this section; but for the purposes of this section a pupil shall be treated as belonging to the area of a particular local education authority or as not belonging to the area of any such authority in accordance with the following rule, namely:—

(*a*) if the pupil is ordinarily resident (f) within the area of a local education authority, he shall be treated as belonging to the area of that authority; and

(*b*) if the pupil is not so resident, he shall be treated as not belonging to the area of any local education authority;

but that rule shall be subject to the exception that, in such cases as may be prescribed, a pupil shall be treated for the purposes of this section in accordance with the regulations either as belonging to the area of a prescribed local education authority or as not belonging to the area of any such authority.

(5) Any question whether a pupil ought to be treated as belonging to the area of any particular local education authority, or as not belonging to the area of any such authority, shall, in case of dispute, be determined by the Secretary of State (c).

(6) References in this section to provision for education include references to the provision of any benefits or services (g) for which provision is made by or under the enactments relating to education.

(7) This section shall have effect as respects provision for further education only in so far as the cost of the provision is attributable to any period after the passing of this Act (h) and, so far as relating to voluntary payments (i), shall so have effect in substitution for subsection (5) of section six of the Education (Miscellaneous Provisions) Act, 1948, so far as that subsection relates to further education.

NOTES

This section extends, with modifications, the right of local education authorities to recoupment of expenditure by them in relation to pupils for whom they are not responsible to expenditure on further education. Under section 6 of the Education (Miscellaneous Provisions) Act, 1948, *ante*, a local education authority is entitled to recoupment of an amount equal to the whole cost to the authority of the provision of primary or secondary education for a pupil who does not belong to their area, but has no such right to recoupment in respect of the cost of further education, though voluntary payments by way of recoupment of expenditure on further education could be made under subsection (5) of that section.

The present section applies in two separate sets of circumstances: (*a*) where a pupil from the area of one local education authority attends, with that authority's consent, an establishment for further education in the area of another local authority, in which case recoupment of the prescribed fraction, or the whole, of the cost can be claimed from the authority from whose area the pupil comes; and (*b*) where the pupil cannot be regarded as belonging to the area of any local education authority in which case the cost of providing further education for him is to be spread over all local education authorities.

(*) As to the meaning or statutory definition of " further education ", " local education authority " and " pupil ", see p. 68, *ante*.

(a) " **Belongs to the area of another such authority** ".—See subsection (4) of this section, and, as to the determination of disputes as to whether a pupil ought to be treated as belonging to the area of a particular authority, see subsection (5) of this section.

(b) " **Prescribed** ".—This means prescribed by regulations made by the Secretary of State, see section 114 (1) of the Education Act, 1944, *ante*.

(c) " **Secretary of State** ".—See note (b) to s. 1 of the Act of 1944.

(d) " **Regulations** ".—See the Local Education Authorities Recoupment (Further Education) Regulations 1954, S.I. 1954 No. 815 (as amended by Local Education Authorities Recoupment (Further Education) Amending Regulations S.I. 1955 No. 222, S.I. 1956 No. 588, S.I. 1965 No. 512, and S.I. 1971 Nos. 701 and 1821; also by the Local Education Authorities Recoupment (Primary, Secondary and Further Education) Amending Regulations 1959, S.I. 1959 No. 488), p. 336, *post*. The providing authority may now recoup the whole of the amount of the cost of providing further education for a pupil from another area.

(e) **Subsection (2) of section six of the Education (Miscellaneous Provisions) Act, 1948.**—See p. 223, *ante*.

(f) **" Ordinarily resident ".**—As to the meaning of residence, see *Blackwell* v. *England* (1857), 8 E. & B. 541; *R.* v. *Braithwaite*, [1918] 2 K.B. 319; *R.* v. *Hastings Justices, Ex parte Mitchell* (1925), 89 J.P. Jo. 86. A person under the age of twenty-one is not necessarily " ordinarily resident " where his father ordinarily resides (*Sawyer* v. *Kropp* (1916), 85 L.J. (K.B.) 1446.

As to " ordinary residence " for the purpose of local education authority awards for first degree university courses and other comparable courses in the United Kingdom, see Schedule I to the Education Act, 1962, p. 249, *post*.

(g) **" Benefits or services ".**—See, for example, sections 48, 49 and 50 of the Education Act, 1944, pp. 141, *et seq.*, *ante*.

(h) **" The passing of this Act ".**—*I.e.*, 14th July, 1953.

(i) **" Voluntary payments ".**—Such payments will now be made under subsection (3) of this section instead of under section 6 (5) of the Education (Miscellaneous Provisions) Act, 1953, *ante*.

8. Amendments of ss. 103 to 105 of principal Act as to matters in respect of which Secretary of State may make grants and loans.—(1) Subsection (1) of section one hundred and three of the principal Act (b) (which empowers the Secretary of State (a) to pay to the managers or governors (*) of a voluntary school (*) proposed to be transferred to a new site or established in substitution for any discontinued school or schools and to be maintained (*) as an aided school (*) or a special agreement school (*) a grant not exceeding one-half of any sums expended by them in the construction of the school) shall—

(*a*) in relation to a school of which the transfer has been authorised by the Secretary of State (a), have effect as if, for the reference therein to the construction of the school, there were substituted a reference to the provision (whether before or after the passing of this Act (c)) of the school buildings (*), and

(*b*) . . . (d)

(2) . . . (e)

(3) Section one hundred and five of the principal Act (f) (which empowers the Secretary of State (a) to make to the managers or governors of an aided school or a special agreement school a loan for the purpose of helping them to meet capital expenditure involved in defraying their share of the initial expenses relating to the school specified in subsection (2) of that section) shall have effect—

(*a*) as if the reference in paragraph (*a*) of that subsection to expenses to be incurred in defraying the cost of any alterations (*) required by the development plan (g) approved by the Secretary of State (a) for the area included a reference to expenses incurred before the passing of this Act or to be incurred thereafter in defraying the cost of any alterations specified in that plan as submitted to the Secretary of State (a), being alterations to the carrying out of which the Secretary of State (a) has given approval before the approval by him of the plan.

(*b*) [*Repealed* (h) .]

NOTES

Subsections (1) and (2) of this section amend sections 103 and 104 of the Education Act, 1944, *ante*, which enable the Secretary of State to pay grants in respect of aided and special agreement schools which are transferred to new sites, or established in substitution for former schools, or which are established for the accommodation of displaced pupils. Under these sections as originally enacted grant could only be paid if the new buildings were literally " constructed ", that is to say by the placing of one brick on top of another, though paragraph 4 of the First Schedule to the Education Act, 1946, *ante*, contemplates the utilisation of existing buildings on the site for a transferred school. The denominational bodies found, however, that it is frequently more economical to acquire and adapt existing mansions or other buildings rather than to build new schools from the foundations up. To enable them to take this course in appropriate cases provision is made by this section for grant to be related to the cost of the " provision " of the school and not of its " construction ". In the case of a transferred school the site must be provided by the local education authority, see paragraph 1 of the First Schedule to the Education Act, 1946, *ante*, so that grant is only given in respect of the school buildings. In the case of a substituted school or a school established for the accommodation of displaced pupils grant is given in respect of the site as well as of the school buildings. This accounts for the difference in wording between paragraph (*a*) of subsection (1) on the one hand and paragraph (*b*) of that subsection and subsection (2) on the other.

Subsection (3) amends section 105 of the 1944 Act, *ante*, as to the power of the Secretary of State to make loans to aided schools in respect of initial expenses. Subsection (2) of that section defines " initial expenses " as meaning, *inter alia*, " expenses to be incurred in defraying the cost of any alterations required by the development plan approved by the Minister [now Secretary of State] for the area ". In fact the development plans took much longer to work out than was thought likely in 1944, with the result that the managers and governors of aided and special agreement schools were in many cases unable to obtain loans for necessary alterations because these have not been " required " by an approved development plan. To meet this difficulty power was given to the Secretary of State by paragraph (*a*) of subsection (3) of the present section to make loans in respect of approved alterations to aided and special agreement schools specified in a development plan submitted to him even though he had not approved the plan as a whole. The amendment effected by paragraph (*b*) of the subsection makes it possible for loans to be paid in connection with the purchase and adaptation of existing buildings instead of their being confined as formerly to new construction. As in the case of the amendment to section 103 effected by subsection (1) of this section a distinction is drawn between transferred schools where loans are only required in connection with the provision of school buildings, and substituted schools where loans may be required for the provision of both site and buildings.

It should be noted that all the amendments made by the section are retrospective in that they enable grants and loans to be paid in respect of expenditure incurred before, as well as after, the passing of the Act.

(*) As to meaning or statutory definition of " managers or governors ", " voluntary school ", " maintain ", " aided school ", " special agreement school ", " school buildings " and " alterations ", see pp. 67–69, *ante*.

(a) **" Secretary of State ".**—See note (b) to s. 1 of the Act of 1944.

(b) **" Subsection (1) of section one hundred and three of the principal Act ".**—See p. 177, *ante*.

(c) **" The passing of this Act ".**—The Act was passed on 14th July, 1953.

(d) This paragraph has ceased to have effect, being superseded by s. 1 of the Education Act, 1967, *post*.

(e) Subsection (2), being also superseded by s. 1 of the Education Act, 1967, has similarly ceased to have effect.

(f) **" Section one hundred and five of the principal Act ".**—See p. 179, *ante*.

(g) **" Development plan ".**—As to the preparation, submission and approval of development plans, see section 11 of the Education Act, 1944, *ante*, and section 31 of the London Government Act, 1963, *ante*.

(h) This paragraph was repealed by Sch. 2 to the Education Act, 1968, *post*.

9. Amendment of s. 85 of principal Act.—(1) [*This subsection amends, by the substitution of a new subsection* (3), *section* 85 *of the Education Act*, 1944, *which is printed as amended on p.* 168, ante.]

(2) This section shall be deemed to have had effect as from the commencement of Part II of the principal Act.

NOTE

Part II of the Education Act, 1944, came into force on 1st April, 1945, see section 119 thereof, *ante*.

10. Amendment of procedure for making school attendance orders.—[*This section amends section* 37 (2) *of the Education Act*, 1944, *which is printed as amended on p.* 129, ante. *The purpose of the amendment is to limit to fourteen days the time during which a parent has the right to select a school to be named in a school attendance order*].

11. [*Repealed.*]

NOTE

This section, which made amendments to the principal Act with respect to the enforcement of school attendance, was repealed by the Children and Young Persons Act 1969, Sch. 6. See Circular 19/70, p. 492, *post*.

12. Provisions with respect to transport of certain pupils.—(1) Subject to the provisions of this section, a local education authority (*) shall have power, for the purpose of facilitating the attendance at any school (*) or county college (*) or at any course or class provided in pursuance of a scheme of further education (a) in force for their area of pupils (*) for whose transport free of charge (b) no arrangements are made by the authority under subsection (1) of section fifty-five of the principal Act (c), to permit such pupils, in consideration of the payment to the authority of fares of such amounts as appear to them to be reasonable, to be carried in a motor vehicle used for providing transport in pursuance of arrangements made under that subsection:

Provided that—

(*a*) the powers conferred by this subsection on a local education authority shall not be exercisable by them in respect of any part of the route on which a vehicle runs in pursuance of any such arrangements, being a part outside the special area (d), except with the written consent of the licensing authority for public service vehicles (e) in whose area that part of the route is situate, and shall not be exercisable by them in respect of any part of such a route, being a part within the special area, except with the written consent both of the licensing authority for public service vehicles for that area and of the [London Transport Board] (f); and

(*b*) the licensing authority for public service vehicles for any area shall not give their consent to an exercise by a local education authority of the powers conferred on them by this section unless they are satisfied that there are no other transport facilities which meet the reasonable needs of the pupils (g) proposed to be carried in exercise of those powers.

(2) [*This subsection was repealed by Road Traffic Act,* 1960.]

(3) [*Repealed* (h).]

NOTES

The purpose of this section, subsection (2) whereof was repealed by section 267 of and Part I of the Eighteenth Schedule to the Road Traffic Act, 1960, is to empower local education authorities to fill vacant seats in an omnibus which is provided for the free transport of pupils by taking up other pupils and charging them a reasonable fare. Section 118 (4) of the Road Traffic Act, 1960, provides that:

"a motor vehicle used for providing transport in pursuance of arrangements made under subsection (1) of section fifty-five of the Education Act, 1944—

(*a*) if belonging to a local education authority, shall not for the purposes of this Part of this Act be treated as carrying passengers for hire or reward;

(*b*) if not belonging to a local education authority, shall not for those purposes be treated as carrying passengers at separate fares;

by reason only of the carriage therein of a person who is charged a fare by virtue of subsection (1) of section twelve of the Education (Miscellaneous Provisions) Act, 1953."

Special provision to this effect is necessary since otherwise a local education authority would have had to obtain a road service licence under section 134 of the Road Traffic Act, 1960, before they could charge fares in an omnibus which they had hired, whilst if they owned and operated the omnibus themselves they would also have had to obtain a public service vehicle licence under section 127 of the Road Traffic Act, 1960, and every driver and conductor would have required a licence under section 144 of that Act. The procedure for obtaining road service licences and public service vehicle licences is lengthy and elaborate and it is obviously undesirable that a local education authority seeking to provide a convenience for a limited number of pupils who are not entitled to free transport should be required to embark upon it.

Under the present section a local education authority must, however, before they begin to carry fare-paying pupils in a school omnibus obtain the written consent of the proper licensing authority and, where any part of the route is in Greater London, that of the London Transport Board also. The interests of commercial operators are safeguarded by proviso (*b*) to subsection (1) which provides that the licensing authority shall not give its consent unless it is satisfied that there is no form of public transport available to meet the reasonable needs of the fare-paying pupils whom it is proposed to carry. In connection with this section, see Administrative Memorandum No. 455 (8th September, 1953), Part IV, *post*.

(*) As to the meaning or statutory definition of "local education authority", "school", "county college" and "pupil", see p. 68, *ante*.

(a) **"Scheme of further education".**—See section 42 of the 1944 Act, *ante*.

(b) **"Transport free of charge".**—Free transport must be provided in the case of a child who has not obtained the age of eight years where the distance from his home to the school at which he is a registered pupil exceeds two miles and in the case of any other child where such distance exceeds three miles, see section 39 (1) and (5) of the 1944 Act, *ante*.

(c) **"Arrangements . . . under subsection (1) of section 55 of the principal Act".**—Section 55 (1) of the 1944 Act, *ante*, requires a local education authority to make such arrangements for the provision of transport and otherwise as they may think necessary or as the Secretary of State may direct for the purpose of facilitating the attendance of pupils at schools or county colleges or at courses provided in pursuance of a scheme of further education and any transport provided in pursuance of such arrangements is to be provided free of charge.

(d) " **Special area** ".—This expression is defined in subsection (3) of this section.

(e) " **The licensing authority for public service vehicles** ".—References in any enactment to a licensing authority for public service vehicles are to be construed as references to the traffic commissioners for a traffic area constituted for the purposes of Part III of the Road Traffic Act, 1960; *ibid.*, section 265 (2).

(f) " **London Transport Board** ".—Substituted by the Transport Act, 1962, section 32 (1), Schedule II, Part I (26 Halsbury's Statutes (3rd Edn.) 954, 1010). The functions of the London Transport Board were transferred to the London Transport Executive, established under the Transport (London) Act 1969, s. 4.

(g) " **Other transport facilities which meet the reasonable needs of the pupils** ".—Presumably other forms of public transport would not be considered to meet the reasonable needs of the pupils unless they were convenient both geographically, *i.e.*, not involving a long walk at either end, and as to times of service.

(h) Sub-section (3) was repealed by the Transport (London) Act 1969, s. 47 (2) and Sch. 6, as from 1st January, 1970 under s. 47 (5) thereof, and by s. 17 (1) of, and Sch. 3, para. 11 to, that Act, for any reference in sub-s. (1) proviso (*a*) to the " special area " is substituted a reference to Greater London.

13. Removal of disqualification of persons employed in schools, &c., for appointment to children's committees.—(1) Section ninety-four of the Local Government Act 1933, shall have effect as if, in the provison thereto (which provides that a person shall not, by reason of his being a teacher in, or being otherwise employed in, an educational institution maintained or assisted by a local education authority, be disqualified for being a member of a committee or sub-committee of a local authority . . . appointed for the purposes mentioned in that proviso), the word " or " were omitted at the end of paragraph (*b*) and the following words were inserted at the end of paragraph (*c*), namely:—

" or

(*d*) appointed for the purposes of their functions under the enactments mentioned in subsection (1) of section thirty-nine of the Children Act, 1948 (a) ".

(2) [*Repealed.*]

NOTES

This section amended the proviso to section 94 of the Local Government Act 1933 (repealed by the Local Government Act 1972) to permit teachers and others employed in educational establishments maintained or assisted by local education authorities to serve on children's committees set up under the Children Act 1948. The words omitted in subsection (1), and the whole of subsection (2), were repealed by the London Government Act 1963, Sch. VIII, Part II.

(a) " **Subsection (1) of section thirty-nine of the Children Act, 1948** ".—By this subsection; 17 Halsbury's Statutes (3rd Edn.) 567, every local authority is required to establish a children's committee for the purposes of its functions under that and certain other Acts.

14. [*Repealed.*]

NOTE

This section, which empowered the Secretary of State to modify certain trusts, was repealed as spent by the Education Act 1973, Sch. 2, Part I.

15. [*Repealed.*]

NOTE

This section, which relaxed the obligation of the Secretary of State to send assurances of property for educational purposes, was repealed by the Charities Act, 1960, section 48 (2) and Schedule VII.

16. Reduction of period for objection to proposals for establishment, maintenance or discontinuance of schools.—[*This section amends section* 13 (3) *of the Education Act,* 1944, *which is printed as amended on p.* 90, ante. *The effect of the amendment is to reduce from three months to two months the period during which objections may be made to proposals for the establishment, maintenance or discontinuance of schools.*]

17. Miscellaneous amendments and repeals.—(1) The provisions of the principal Act (a) and the Education (Miscellaneous Provisions) Act, 1948, specified in the first column of the First Schedule to this Act shall have effect subject to the amendments specified in the second column of that Schedule (being amendments relating to minor matters and amendments consequential on the provisions of this Act).

(2) [*Repealed.*]

NOTE

Sub-section (2) was repealed as spent by the Education Act 1973, Sch. 2, Part I.

(a) The Education Act, 1944, *ante*, as amended by the Education Act, 1946, *ante*, and the Education (Miscellaneous Provisions) Act, 1948, *ante*, and references to it in the present Act are to be construed as references to it as so amended; see section 20 (4), *post*.

18. Provisions as to regulations.—Any power conferred by this Act on the Secretary of State (a) to make regulations shall be exercisable by statutory instrument (b) which shall be subject to annulment (c) in pursuance of a resolution of either House of Parliament.

NOTES

(a) **" Secretary of State ".**—See note (b) to s. 1 of the 1944 Act.

(b) **" Made by statutory instrument ".**—See section 1 of the Statutory Instruments Act 1946; 32 Halsbury's Statutes (3rd Edn.) 668.

(c) **" Subject to annulment ".**—See section 5 (1) of the Statutory Instruments Act, 1946; 32 Halsbury's Statutes (3rd Edn.) 672. See also the Laying of Documents before Parliament (Interpretation) Act 1940; 32 Halsbury's Statutes (3rd Edn.) 677.

19. Expenses.—Any increase attributable to the provisions of this Act in the sums which under any enactment are defrayed out of moneys provided by Parliament, shall be defrayed out of moneys so provided.

20. Short title, citation, construction and extent.—(1) This Act may be cited as the Education (Miscellaneous Provisions) Act, 1953.

(2) This Act, except section five thereof, and the Education Acts, 1944 to 1948 (a), may be cited together as the Education Acts, 1944 to 1953.

(3) This Act, except as aforesaid, shall be construed as one (b) with the Education Acts, 1944 to 1948.

(4) References in this Act to any other enactment shall, except so far as the context otherwise requires, be construed as references to that enactment as amended by or under any other enactment, including this Act.

(5) This Act, except sections five and nineteen thereof, shall not extend to Scotland.

(6) This Act shall not extend to Northern Ireland.

NOTES

(a) **" Education Acts, 1944 to 1948 ".**—See section 14 (2) of the Education (Miscellaneous Provisions) Act, 1948, *ante*.

(b) **" Construed as one ".**—See note (c) to section 14 of the Education (Miscellaneous Provisions) Act, 1948, *ante*.

SCHEDULES

FIRST SCHEDULE

MINOR AND CONSEQUENTIAL AMENDMENTS

[*The amendments effected by this Schedule have been incorporated in the text of the Education Act*, 1944, *and the Education* (*Miscellaneous Provisions*) *Act*, 1948, ante.]

SECOND SCHEDULE

[*Repealed as spent by the Education Act* 1973, *Sch.* 2, *Part II.*]

THE EDUCATION ACT, 1959

7 & 8 Eliz. 2, c. 60

An Act to enlarge the powers of the Secretary of State for Education and Science (b) *to make contributions, grants and loans in respect of aided schools and special agreement schools, and for purposes connected therewith.*

[29th July, 1959.]

1. Extended powers to make contributions, etc. [*Subsections* (1)–(3) *superseded.*]

(4) For the purposes of section one hundred and five of the Education Act, 1944 (a) (which authorises the Secretary of State for Education and Science (b) to make loans to the managers or governors of aided schools and special agreement schools for certain initial expenses involving capital expenditure), any expenses in respect of which the Secretary of State (b) may make a grant under subsection (2) of this section (c) shall be included in the expression " initial expenses ", and in determining the governors' share of any initial expenses the amount of any such grant paid or payable in respect of them shall be taken into account in the same way as grants under sections one hundred and three and one hundred and four (d) of that Act.

[*Subsections* (5)–(8) *superseded.*]

NOTES

(a) **" Section one hundred and five of the Education Act, 1944 ".**—See p. 179. *ante.* " Initial expenses " are defined for the purpose of that section by subsection (2) thereof which provides that the managers' or governors' share of the initial expenses so defined shall be taken to be so much as remains to be borne by them after taking into account the amount of any maintenance contribution, grant under a special agreement or grant under section 103 of the 1944 Act, *ante*, as may be paid or payable in respect of those expenses.

(b) **" Secretary of State for Education and Science ".**—See note (b) to section 1 of the Act of 1944.

(c) **" Subsection (2) of this section ".**—This subsection provided that the Secretary of State might, in certain circumstances, pay to the governors of a proposed school, in respect of any sums expended by them on the provision of a site for a school or the school buildings, a grant not exceeding three-quarters of such sums.

The whole of s. 1, *supra*, with the exception of sub-s. (4), has been superseded by s. 1 of the Education Act, 1967, and has ceased to have effect. Under the Act of 1967, as amended, 85 per cent. grants are payable. See p. 258, *post.*

(d) **" Sections one hundred and three and one hundred and four ".**—For s. 103, see p. 177, *ante.* Section 104 has been superseded by s. 1 of the Education Act 1967, p. 258, *post.*

2. Short title, citation and extent.—(1) This Act may be cited as the Education Act, 1959, and this Act and the Education Acts, 1944 to 1953, may be cited together as the Education Acts, 1944 to 1959.

(2) This Act does not extend to Scotland or to Northern Ireland.

THE EDUCATION ACT, 1962

10 & 11 Eliz. 2 c. 12

ARRANGEMENT OF SECTIONS

Awards and grants by local education authorities and Secretary of State for Education and Science in England and Wales

* * * * *

An Act to make further provision with respect to awards and grants by local education authorities and the Secretary of State for Education and Science in England and Wales, and by education authorities and the Secretary of State in Scotland . . .; to make further provision as to school leaving dates; and for purposes connected with the matters aforesaid. [29th March, 1962]

GENERAL NOTE

This Act, as to which see also Circular 4/62, p. 462, *post*, had two purposes. First, it gave statutory authority for the reforms announced following the Report of the Anderson Committee in 1960 on the system of awards from public funds to students attending first degree courses at universities and comparable courses at other institutions. Second, it reduced the number of school-leaving dates in the year from three to two, as recommended by the Central Advisory Council for England in the Crowther Report.

The majority of the Anderson Committee recommended that no parental contribution should be required in respect of first degree courses at universities, etc.; a minority recommended that parental contributions should be continued, but that the income scales should be made more generous.

The then Minister of Education (Sir David Eccles) accepted the latter recommendation. On the second reading of the Bill in the House of Commons (Hansard, 13th November, 1961) he explained that the cost of the complete abolition of a means test for parental contributions would be prohibitive, but that the test would be retained "in a relaxed form". He added that the effect of the relaxation of the means test would be that 40 per cent. of students would now receive the maximum grant against 25 per cent. on the old criteria, and that about 10,000 more families would be relieved from all contributions and that those in the middle range of income would pay substantially less.

As regards awards to students, it should particularly be noted that under section 81 of the Education Act, 1944, p. 166, *ante*, local education authorities already had the power to grant scholarships and other allowances to pupils over compulsory school age, but they were not obliged to make an award in any particular case, even though the applicant for a grant had high academic qualifications and had been offered a place at a university. There was also a lack of uniformity as between local education authorities in their methods of administering their power to make grants. Under section 1 of the present Act, the local education authorities have no longer a mere power but are under a duty to make grants to applicants with the prescribed qualification and who (*a*) are ordinarily resident in the area of the authority and (*b*) possess the requisite educational qualifications, in respect of their attendance at full-time courses at universities, colleges, etc., in Great Britain and Northern Ireland as may be designated by regulations as being first degree courses or comparable to first degree courses. The Local Education Authorities Awards Regulations 1975, S.I. 1975 No. 1207, p. 420, *post*, lay down the requisite educational qualifications and prescribe the designated courses in respect of which the grants are payable.

Apart from the duty just explained, a local education authority also has power (as opposed to a duty) by section 1 (4) to bestow an award on any person attending a course to which the section applies even though he may not, in some respects, be otherwise eligible.

Section 1 has been extended by the provisions of the Education Act 1975, p. 281, *post*. For the effect of the Act of 1975, see the Notes to section 1 of this Act, *infra*.

Section 2 of the Act confers a further power (again, not a duty) on local education authorities, to bestow awards on persons over compulsory school age in respect of certain courses of full-time or part-time education to which section 1 of the Act does not apply, and to persons training as teachers. This section is also extended by section 1 (3) of the Education Act 1975, *post*.

The provisions of sections 1, 2 replace the corresponding provisions of section 81 of the Education Act, 1944, and the Regulations for Scholarships and Other Benefits, 1945, as amended, although those provisions still remain in force with respect to the payment of fees and other expenses of pupils still attending county, voluntary or special schools. The duty of local education authorities, under section 1, took effect in respect of awards for courses beginning on or after 1st September, 1962. Awards current at that date continued under the former arrangements.

Section 3 of the Act redefines the power of the Secretary of State to make awards and grants, and replaces the corresponding provisions of section 100 (1) (*c*) of the Education Act, 1944, which is partly repealed. The Secretary of State continues to offer state studentships for advanced postgraduate study in arts subjects, as well as state scholarships to selected older candidates for first degree courses; but other state scholarships (*i.e.*, those formerly classed as General Certificate of Education, Supplemental and Technical state scholarships) were awarded for the last time in 1962 (in some cases postponed for one year to the autumn of 1963), and have been discontinued. The Secretary of State may also bestow awards on students attending courses at designated long-term residential colleges of adult education: Education Act 1975, section 2.

The State Awards Regulations, 1963, S.I. 1963 No. 1223, were made under section 3 on 11th July, 1963 and came into operation on 1st September, 1963. They are printed, as amended by the State Awards (Amendment) Regulations, 1969, S.I. 1969 No. 554, at pp. 370, *et seq.*, *post*.

The position under the above three sections may therefore be summarised as follows:

(*a*) A university or other establishment of further education is free to admit any student, whether or not he or she has the requisite qualifications (*e.g.*, passes at " A " level in two G.C.E. subjects) specified in the Local Education Authorities Awards Regulations 1975, S.I. 1975 No. 1207, p. 420, *post*.

(*b*) Where a student is admitted, the local education authority within whose area he is ordinarily resident is under a *duty* to make an award (Act of 1962, section 1 (1) and Local Education Authorities Awards Regulations 1975, *supra*).

(*c*) Conversely, unless the student has been admitted to a place at a university or other establishment of further education, even though he has the other necessary qualifications he is not entitled to an award.

(*d*) Where an award is made, parental contributions may be payable under the Local Education Authorities Awards Regulations 1975, *supra*.

(*e*) Local education authorities also have power (but are under no duty) to make awards to students over compulsory school age in respect of certain other courses to which section 1 is not applicable, and to pay grants (in accordance with arrangements to be approved by the Secretary of State) to persons undergoing training as teachers (Act of 1962, section 2 and Local Education Authorities Awards Regulations 1975, *supra.*).

(*f*) State grants may be payable by the Secretary of State in cases prescribed by regulations (*ibid.*, section 3 and Local Education Authorities Awards Regulations 1975, *supra.*).

Before the passing of the Act of 1962, children who reached the school leaving age in term time were required to remain at school until the end of the term during which they reached that age. A child could thus leave at the end of any one of the three school terms.

Section 9 of the Act of 1962 alters the number of school leaving dates in the year from three to two. Under the section, if a child reaches the school leaving age at any time from the beginning of September to the end of January, he is deemed not to have reached that age until the end of the following spring term; and if he attains that age on or after the beginning of February and before the beginning of September, he is deemed to have attained that age at the end of the summer term in that year.

The section, which followed a recommendation of the Crowther Report, was explained by the then Minister of Education (Sir David Eccles) on the second reading of the Bill (Hansard, 13th November, 1961):

> " The object of the change is to help the schools to make a better job of the fourth year of the secondary course. With large numbers of children leaving at Christmas, it has been found difficult to plan the fourth year. . . . If the children are grouped according to their abilities and attainments, the loss of part of the group unsettles the others. If, on the other hand, they are grouped according to the dates they are likely to leave school, the teacher has to deal in the same class with children of widely different capacity, and that is no easy matter. Indeed, from the viewpoint of school organisation, the best plan would be to have one leaving date in the year, but that would mean that practically a whole age group was looking for jobs at the same time."

Section 9 came into effect in September, 1963. It does not affect children who have stayed on at school beyond the compulsory school age limit, who are free to leave at the end of a Christmas term if they wish.

Formerly, under the rule in *Re Shurey, Savory* v. *Shurey*, [1918] 1 Ch. 263, a person attained a given age at the beginning of the day *preceding* the anniversary of his birth. Now, however, the time at which a person attains a particular age expressed in years is the commencement of the relevant anniversary of the date of his birth. See s. 9 of the Family Law Reform Act, 1969.

Awards and grants by local education authorities and Secretary of State for Education and Science in England and Wales

1. Local education authority awards for first degree university courses and comparable courses in United Kingdom.—(1) It shall be the duty (a) of every local education authority, subject to and in accordance with regulations (b) made under this Act, to bestow awards on persons who—

(*a*) are ordinarily resident (c) in the area of the authority, and
(*b*) possess the requisite educational qualifications (d),

in respect of their attendance at courses to which this section applies (e).

(2) This section shall apply to such full-time courses at universities, colleges or other institutions in Great Britain and Northern Ireland as may for the time being be designated (f) by or under the regulations for the purposes of this section as being first degree courses or comparable (g) to first degree courses; and for the purposes of the preceding sub-section the requisite educational qualifications (d), in relation to any course, shall be such as may be prescribed by or under the regulations, either generally or with respect to that course or a class of courses which includes that course.

(3) Regulations made for the purposes of sub-section (1) of this section shall prescribe the conditions and exceptions (h) subject to which the duty imposed by that sub-section is to have effect, and the descriptions of payments (i) to be made in pursuance of awards bestowed thereunder, and, with respect to each description of payments, shall—

(*a*) prescribe the circumstances in which it is to be payable, and the amount of the payment or the scales or other provisions by reference to which that amount is to be determined, and
(*b*) indicate whether the payment is to be obligatory or is to be at the discretion of the authority bestowing the award;

and, subject to the exercise of any power conferred by the regulations to suspend or terminate awards (j), a local education authority by whom an award has been bestowed under sub-section (1) of this section shall be under a duty, or shall have power, as the case may be, to make such payments as they are required or authorised to make in accordance with the regulations.

(4) Without prejudice to the duty imposed by sub-section (1) of this section, a local education authority shall have power to bestow an award on any person in respect of his attendance at a course to which this section applies, where he is not eligible for an award (k) under sub-section (1) of this section in respect of that course.

(5) The provisions of sub-section (3) of this section and of the regulations made in accordance with that sub-section (except so much of those provisions as relates to the conditions and exceptions (h) subject to which the duty imposed by sub-section (1) of this section is to have effect) shall apply in relation to awards under the last preceding sub-section as they apply in relation to awards under sub-section (1) of this section.

(6) Notwithstanding anything in sub-section (1) of this section, that sub-section shall not have effect so as to require a local education authority—

(*a*) to bestow awards in respect of any period beginning before the first day of September, nineteen hundred and sixty-two, or
(*b*) to bestow an award on a person in respect of any course, if a scholarship, exhibition, bursary or other allowance granted to him in respect of that course is in force on that day by virtue of regulations made under paragraph (*c*) of section eighty-one of the Act of 1944 (l).

(7) The reference in sub-section (1) of this section to persons who are ordinarily resident in the area of a local education authority is a reference

to persons who, in accordance with the provisions of the First Schedule to this Act, are to be treated as being so resident (m).

NOTES

This section imposes a duty on local education authorities to bestow awards on persons who (*a*) are ordinarily resident in the area of the authority, (*b*) who possess the requisite educational qualifications, and (*c*) who are attending full-time courses at universities, colleges or other institutions in Great Britain and Northern Ireland, as designated by regulations as being first degree courses or comparable to first degree courses. This *duty* may be contrasted with the *power* to make grants under section 81 of the Education Act, 1944, p. 166, *ante*. That power, and the provisions of any Regulations made under that section, have now ceased to have effect in so far as they relate to the granting of scholarships, exhibitions, bursaries and other allowances in respect of pupils over compulsory school age (see section 4 (4) of the present Act, p. 245, *post*); but a local education authority has a new power (under section 1 (4) of the present Act, p. 242, *ante*), to bestow an award on any person in respect of his attendance at a course to which this section applies even though he may not in fact be eligible under section 1 (1), *supra*.

The following courses have been added to those in respect of which local education authorities have a duty to bestow awards: courses at universities, colleges or other institutions in Great Britain and Northern Ireland as may for the time being be designated by or under regulations as being (*a*) full-time courses for the diploma of higher education or the higher national diploma; or (*b*) courses for the initial training of teachers (Education Act 1975, section 1, *post*).

As to the continuance of certain grants made before 1st April, 1965, under this section or section 2, *infra*, see the London Government Act, 1963, section 33, p. 294, *post*.

As to the fees that may be charged by local education authorities for tuition, or for board and lodging, such authorities must comply with any direction given by the Secretary of State: Further Education Regulations 1975, S.I. 1975 No. 1054, *post*.

(a) **" Duty ".**—As opposed to the *power* formerly given by section 81 of the Education Act, 1944, p. 166, *ante*. The duty is in respect of awards for courses beginning on or after 1st September, 1962.

(b) **" Regulations made under this Act ".**—See the Local Education Authorities Awards Regulations 1975, S.I. 1975 No. 1207, p. 420, *post*.

(c) **" Ordinarily resident ".**—As to the meaning of this phrase, see sub-section (7), *supra*, and Schedule I to this Act, p. 249, *post*.

(d) **" Requisite educational qualifications ".**—These have been prescribed by Sch. 4 to the Local Education Authorities Awards Regulations 1975, S.I. 1975 No. 1207, *post*. The main qualification is: passes at advanced level in two subjects in the General Certificate of Education examination. With this or one of the other qualifications mentioned in the regulation, and the promise of a place at a university or comparable institution, a student is automatically entitled to a grant under the section.

(e) **" Courses to which this section applies ".**—See note (f), *infra*.

(f) **" Designated ".**—The courses designated for the purposes of this section are those named in regulation 6 of the Local Education Authorities Awards Regulations 1975, S.I. 1975 No. 1207, *post*.

(g) **" Comparable course ".**—In advising the Secretary of State, the Standing Advisory Committee on Grants to Students employed the following definition: " A comparable course is a course normally intended for students of eighteen years or over, which consists of at least three years full-time or sandwich study and leads directly to a qualification accepted as a graduate equivalent for the purposes of the Burnham Report. A course which does not lead directly to such a qualification may, however, in exceptional circumstances be designated by the Minister of Education [Secretary of State] as a comparable course, provided that the educational requirements for entry to the course are two passes at Advanced Level in the General Certificate of Education or equivalent and that it satisfies the foregoing requirements as to age of entry and length of course ".

(h) **" Conditions and exceptions ".**—The conditions and exceptions are prescribed by regulations 7–9 of the Local Education Authorities Awards Regulations 1975, S.I. 1975 No. 1207, *post*. The duty of an authority to bestow an award is made subject to the condition that application in writing is made to the authority in time; and an authority is excepted from the duty of making an award to (*a*) a person who has previously attended a designated course, or a course of initial training as a teacher, or any full-time course of further education of two years' duration or more whether in the United Kingdom or elsewhere; (*b*) a person without a three-year residence qualification (unless his parents, or one of them have been abroad); (*c*) a person who has shown himself by his conduct to be unfitted to receive an award.

(i) **" Description of payments ".**—See regulations 13 *et seq.* of the Local Education Authorities Awards Regulations 1975, S.I. 1975 No. 1207, *post*.

(j) **" Suspend or terminate awards ".**—Power to withhold or to reduce payments is given in regulations 13 *et seq.* of the Local Education Authorities Awards Regulations 1975, S.I. 1975 No. 1207, *post*. An authority may in its discretion withhold payments if any obligation as to statement of income is not complied with, or it may reduce the amount of payments during approved absence through illness, etc.

(k) **" Person . . . not eligible for an award ".**—Subsections (4) and (5) empower local education authorities to make awards in their discretion to students who attend courses to which the section applies but who are not entitled to awards under the provisions of the previous subsection, *e.g.* because they do not possess the requisite educational qualifications, apply (with the exception of regulations 4, 5, 6 and 7) to such awards.

(l) **" Section eighty-one of the Act of 1944 ".**—See p. 166, *ante*.

(m) **Subsection (7).**—This subsection, and Schedule I to this Act, p. 299, *post*, provide for the determination of questions of ordinary residence arising under this section, in accordance with the criteria used for the purposes of section 7 of the Education (Miscellaneous Provisions)

Act, 1953 (see p. 232, *ante*). Where, under these criteria, a student otherwise eligible for an award would fall to be regarded as not ordinarily resident in the area of any local education authority, the Secretary of State may direct that he be treated as ordinarily resident in the area of a specified authority. This procedure enables students of this kind, *e.g.* those whose parents are employed abroad but intend eventually to return to England or Wales, to know for certain to which education authority they should apply for an award. See now the Local Education Authorities Awards Regulations 1975, S.I. 1975 No. 1207, *post*.

2. Local education authority awards for other courses of further education, and grants for training of teachers.—(1) A local education authority shall have power (a) to bestow awards on persons over compulsory school age . . . in respect of their attendance at courses to which this sub-section applies, and to make such payments as are payable in pursuance of such awards.

(2) The preceding sub-section applies to any course of full-time or part-time education (whether held in Great Britain or elsewhere) which is not a course of primary or secondary education, or (in the case of a course held outside Great Britain) is not a course of education comparable to primary or secondary education in Great Britain, and is not a course to which section one of this Act applies.

(3) [*Repealed.*]

NOTES

This section empowers local education authorities to make awards to students attending courses which fall outside the scope of section 1, *e.g.* courses at further education institutions below the level comparable with degree courses, courses at adult residential institutions, courses of teacher training, postgraduate courses, and courses at universities abroad (see Circular 4/62 (18th April, 1962), pp. 462, *et seq.*, *post*). The section also applies to part-time courses so far as assistance to students to meet the educational expenses arising from these courses is justified (*ibid.*). By section 4 (4) of the present Act, p. 245, *post*, the provisions of this section and section 1 have effect in substitution for the corresponding provisions of section 81 of the Education Act, 1944 (see p. 166, *ante*) and the Regulations for Scholarships and Other Benefits, 1945, as amended (see p. 327, *post*); but that section and those regulations remain in force with respect to the payment of fees, allowances and other expenses of pupils attending schools (*ibid.*).

Section 2 (1) is extended to any course for the training of teachers by the Education Act 1975, s. 1 (3), *post*.

The words omitted in subsection (1), and subsection (3), were repealed by the Education Act 1975, Sch., Part I.

(a) **"Shall have power".**—The *powers* given by this section are discretionary, as contrasted with the *duties* imposed by section 1, *ante*.

(b) **"Training".**—As to the meaning of this word, see section 4 (6), *post*.

(c) **"Secretary of State".**—See note (b) to s. 1 of the Act of 1944.

3. State grants for training of teachers and awards for post-graduate courses and students over prescribed age.—Provision may be made by regulations (a) under this Act for authorising the Secretary of State (b)—

(*a*) to pay grants to or in respect of persons undergoing training (c) as teachers;

(*b*) to bestow awards on persons in respect of their attendance at such courses at universities, colleges or other institutions (whether in Great Britain or elsewhere) as may for the time being be designated by or under the regulations for the purposes of this section as being postgraduate courses or comparable to postgraduate courses;

(*c*) to bestow awards on persons who, at such time as may be prescribed by the regulations, have attained such age as may be so prescribed, being awards in respect of their attendance at such courses at universities, colleges or other institutions (whether in Great Britain or elsewhere) as may for the time being be designated by or under the regulations for the purposes of this section as being first degree courses or comparable to first degree courses;

[(*d*) to bestow awards on persons who, at such time as may be prescribed by the regulations, have attained such age as may be so prescribed, being awards in respect of their attendance at courses at any institution which—

(i) is in receipt of payments under section 100 of the Education Act 1944 or section 15 of the Education (Scotland) Act 1962; and

(ii) is designated by or under the regulations as a college providing long-term residential courses of full-time education for adults.]

and, [in the case of awards bestowed in accordance with paragraph (*b*), (*c*) or (*d*) of this section,] for authorising the Secretary of State (b) to make such payments as are payable in pursuance of the awards.

NOTES

This section redefines the power of the Secretary of State to make awards and grants, and replaces the corresponding provisions of section 100 (1) (*c*) of the Education Act, 1944, p. 175, *ante*, which is repealed in part by section 13 of, and Schedule II to, this Act.

The words in the first square brackets were inserted, and those in the second square brackets substituted, by the Education Act 1975, section 2.

(a) " **Regulations** ".—See the State Awards Regulations, 1963, S.I. 1963 No. 1223, as amended by S.I. 1969 No. 554, p. 370, *post* and S.I. 1975 No. 940, p. 410, *post*; the Students' Dependants' Allowance Regulations 1975, S.I. 1975 No. 1225, *post*.

(b) " **Secretary of State** ".—See note (b) to s. 1 of the Act of 1944.

(c) " **Training** ".—As to the meaning of this word, see section 4 (6), *post*.

4. Provisions supplementary to sections 1 to 3.—(1) For the purposes of the exercise of any power or the performance of any duty conferred or imposed by or under any of the provisions of sections one to three of this Act, it is immaterial—

(*a*) whether an award is designated by that name or as a scholarship, studentship, exhibition or bursary or by any similar description, or

(*b*) in what terms the bestowal of an award is expressed.

(2) Any enactment contained in those sections which requires or authorises the making of regulations (a) shall be construed as requiring or authorising regulations to be made by the Secretary of State (b); and regulations made for the purposes of any such enactment may make different provision for different cases to which that enactment is applicable.

(3) Any power to make regulations (a) under those sections shall be exercisable by statutory instrument; and any statutory instrument containing any such regulations shall be subject to annulment in pursuance of a resolution of either House of Parliament.

(4) Subject to the next following sub-section, sections one and two of this Act shall have effect in substitution for the following provisions, that is to say—

(*a*) the provisions of section eighty-one of the Act of 1944 (c) in so far as they require regulations (a) to be made for the purpose of empowering local education authorities to grant scholarships, exhibitions, bursaries and other allowances in respect of pupils over compulsory school age in connection with their attendance at courses to which section one or sub-section (1) of section two of this Act applies, or in connection with their undergoing training as teachers (d), and

(*b*) the provisions of any regulations (a) made under the said section eighty-one in so far as they provide for the granting of such scholarships, exhibitions, bursaries and other allowances,

and (subject to the next following sub-section) those provisions shall cease to have effect in so far as they impose any such requirement or make any such provision as is mentioned in paragraph (*a*) or paragraph (*b*) of this sub-section.

(5) Nothing in the last preceding sub-section shall affect or prevent—

(*a*) the making of any payment in respect of a period ending before the first day of September, nineteen hundred and sixty-two, or the granting of any scholarship, exhibition, bursary or other allowance at any time before that day, or the making of any payment (whether before or after that day) in pursuance of a scholarship, exhibition, bursary or other allowance so granted, or

(*b*) the revocation of any regulations (a) made under section eighty-one of the Act of 1944 (d), or

(*c*) the variation of any such regulations in so far as they relate to matters not falling within paragraphs (*a*) and (*b*) of the last preceding sub-section, or in so far as they relate to payments or grants falling within paragraph (*a*) of this sub-section.

(6) In sections two and three of this Act and in this section " training " (in relation to training as a teacher) includes further training, whether the person undergoing the further training is already qualified as a teacher or not; and any reference to a person undergoing training includes a person admitted or accepted by the appropriate university, college or other authorities for undergoing that training.

NOTES

This section, which makes provisions supplementary to the three preceding sections, is largely self-explanatory. Sub-section (1) makes it immaterial whether an " award " is so described or is called by some other name. Sub-sections (2), (3) contain general provisions as to the making of regulations under the Act. Sub-section (6) explains what is meant (in sections 2, 3) by " training " of teachers. As to sub-sections (4), (5), see the notes below.

(a) **" Regulations ".**—See the Regulations for Scholarships and Other Benefits, 1945, p. 327, *post*, as amended by the Scholarships and Other Benefits Amending Regulations No. 1, 1948, p. 330, *post*, and the Scholarships and Other Benefits Amending Regulations No. 2, 1948 p. 331, *post*.

(b) **" Secretary of State ".**—See note (b) to s. 1 of the 1944 Act.

(c) **" Section eighty-one of the Act of 1944 ".**—This section, p. 166, *ante*, enabled the Secretary of State to make regulations empowering local education authorities (*inter alia*) to grant scholarships, exhibitions, bursaries and other allowances to pupils over compulsory school age, including pupils undergoing training as teachers. In so far as it required such regulations to be made, the section now ceases to have effect (as do any regulations made thereunder) subject to the provisions of subsection (5); and sections 1, 2 of the present Act have effect in substitution for it.

(d) **" Training as teachers ".**—The duties of the Secretary of State and of local education authorities as to the training of teachers are laid down in section 62 of the Education Act, 1944, p. 151, *ante*. The former power to grant scholarships, bursaries, and other allowances in respect of pupils undergoing training as teachers was contained in section 81 (c) of the Act of 1944 (see note (c), *supra*), for which sections 1, 2 of the present Act now have effect in substitution (see section 4 (4) of the present Act, *supra*.). The power of the Secretary of State, by regulations, to grant state scholarships to pupils over compulsory school age, including pupils undergoing training as teachers, was contained in section 100 (1) (*c*) of the Act of 1944, p. 175, *ante*. This latter provision was repealed by section 13 of, and Schedule 2 to, the present Act.

Grants and other payments by education authorities and Secretary of State in Scotland

5, 6. [*Related to Scotland; now repealed.*]

7. [*Spent.*]

8. [*Related to Scotland; spent.*]

School leaving dates

9. School leaving dates in England and Wales.—(1) The provisions of sub-sections (2) to (4) of this section shall have effect in relation to any person who on a date when either—

(*a*) he is a registered pupil (a) at a school, or

(*b*) not being such a pupil, he has been a registered pupil at a school within the preceding period of twelve months.

attains an age (b) which (apart from this section) would in his case be the upper limit of the compulsory school age (c).

(2) If he attains that age on any date from the beginning of September to the end of January, he shall be deemed not to have attained that age until the end of the appropriate spring term (d) at his school.

[(3) If he attains that age after the end of January but before the next May school-leaving date, he shall be deemed not to have attained that age until that date.

(4) If he attains that age after the May school-leaving date and before the beginning of September next following that date, he shall be deemed to have attained that age on that date.(e)]

(5) The provisions of this section shall have effect for the purposes of the Act of 1944, and for the purposes of any enactment whereby the definition of compulsory school age in that Act is applied or incorporated (f); and for references in any enactment to section eight of the Education Act, 1946 (g), there shall, in relation to compulsory school age, be substituted references to this section:

Provided that for the purposes of any enactment relating to family allowances [national insurance and social security] the provisions of this section shall have effect as if subsection (4) *thereof were omitted.*

(6) *This section shall not apply where the date referred to in subsection* (1) *thereof is a date before the beginning of September, nineteen hundred and sixty-three* (h).

(7) In this section " the appropriate spring term ", in relation to a person, means the last term at his school which ends before the month of May next following the date on which he attains the age in question, *and " the appropriate summer term ", in relation to a person, means the last term at his school which ends before the month of September next following that date* (h); and any reference to a person's school is a reference to the last school at which he is a registered pupil for a term ending before the said month of May *or month of September* (*as the case may be*) (h) or for part of such a term.

[(8) In this section " the May school-leaving date " means the Friday before the last Monday in May. (i)]

NOTES

The effect of this section was to reduce the number of dates in the school year, at which a pupil might leave, from three to two. As the law formerly stood, a child might leave at the end of any term in which he reached the upper limit of compulsory school age.

Under the present section, as originally enacted, if a child reached the school leaving age (now sixteen) in the five months September to January, inclusive, he had to stay at school until the following Easter holidays; if he reached it in February to August, inclusive, he had to stay until the beginning of the summer holidays in the same year. The object was to ensure that no child had less than three years and two terms in a secondary school, and that most children would have four years (see Circular 4/62, p. 462, *post*).

As amended by the Education (School-Leaving Dates) Act 1976, a new school-leaving date is substituted for pupils at schools in England and Wales who attain the age of sixteen years at any time between the end of January and the beginning of September. This new date is the Friday before the last Monday in May, *i.e.* some weeks before the end of the summer term.

The section became effective on 1st September, 1963 (see sub-section (6), *supra*).

(a) **" Registered pupil ".**—This means, in relation to any school, a pupil registered as such in the register kept in accordance with the provisions of the Act of 1944: Education Act, 1944, section 114 (1), p. 185, *ante*.

(b) **" Attains an age ".**—See last paragraph of General Note to the Act, p. 241, *ante*.

(c) **" Compulsory school age ".**—See sections 35, 114 (1) of the Education Act, 1944, *ante*.

(d) **" Appropriate spring term ".**—See sub-section (7) of this section.

(e) The words in square brackets were substituted by the Education (School-Leaving Dates) Act 1976.

(f) **" Any enactment whereby the definition of compulsory school age in that Act is applied or incorporated ".**—See, *e.g.*, section 17 of the Children Act 1958 (17 Halsbury's

Statutes (3rd Edn.) 630) and section 57 (1) of the Adoption Act 1958 (17 Halsbury's Statutes (3rd Edn.) 679).

(g) **" Section eight of the Education Act, 1946 ".**—See p. 213, *ante*.

(h) The words in italic were repealed by the Education (School-Leaving Dates) Act 1976.

(i) The words in square brackets were added by the Education (School-Leaving Dates) Act 1976.

10. [*Relates to Scotland.*]

Supplementary provisions

11. Financial provisions.—There shall be paid out of moneys provided by Parliament—

(*a*) any expenditure incurred by the Secretary of State (a) in consequence of regulations made for the purposes of section three of this Act (b);

(*b*) any increase in the sums payable out of moneys provided by Parliament in respect of general grants (c), under the enactments relating to local government in England and Wales . . . being an increase arising—

(i) from the inclusion, in the expenditure relevant to the fixing of the aggregate amounts of those grants, of expenditure under section one or section two of this Act, or

* * * * *

(iii) from the provisions of section seven of this Act;

* * * * *

(*d*) any increase in the sums payable out of moneys provided by Parliament under any enactment not contained in this Act, being an increase attributable to the provisions of section nine . . . of this Act;

(*e*) any increase attributable to this Act in the sums payable out of moneys provided by Parliament by way of Rate-deficiency Grant or Exchequer Equalisation Grant under the enactments relating to local government in England and Wales. . . .

NOTES

This section contains supplementary financial provisions to deal with expenditure arising through the application of the Act. The omitted portions of the section relate to Scotland only.

(a) **" Secretary of State ".**—See note (b) to s. 1 of the Act of 1944, *ante*.

(b) **" Regulations made for the purposes of section three of this Act ".**—See the State Awards Regulations, 1963, S.I. 1963 No. 1223, p. 370, *post*. And see note (a) to s. 13, *infra*.

(c) **" General grants".**—See the note to the Local Government Act 1966, p. 298, *post*.

12. Interpretation.—(1) In this Act " the Act of 1944 " means the Education Act, 1944. . . .

(2) References in this Act to any enactment shall, except where the context otherwise requires, be construed as references to that enactment as amended by or under any other enactment.

NOTE

The words omitted in sub-section (1) relate only to Scotland.

13. Repeals, transitional provisions and savings.—(1) [*Repealed by the Statute Law* (*Repeals*) *Act* 1974.]

(2) Any regulations relating to the training of teachers (a), in so far as they were made by virtue of the repealed grant provisions (b), shall continue

to have effect notwithstanding the repeal, and may be revoked or varied as if this Act had not been passed.

(3) Any other regulations, in so far as they were made by virtue of the repealed grant provisions, shall continue to have effect notwithstanding the repeal in so far as—

(*a*) they authorise the making of any payment in respect of a period ending before the first day of September, nineteen hundred and sixty-two, or

(*b*) they enable scholarships, exhibitions, bursaries or other allowances to be awarded at any time before that day, or authorise the making of any payment (whether before or after that day) in pursuance of a scholarship, exhibition, bursary or other allowance so awarded;

and in so far as any regulations continue to have effect by virtue of this sub-section, they may be revoked, or (within the limits subject to which they continue so to have effect) may be varied, as if this Act had not been passed.

(4) Sub-section (1) of this section, in so far as it repeals any of the provisions of section eight of the Education Act, 1946 (c), shall have effect subject to the provisions of sub-sections (5) and (6) of section nine of this Act as if it were contained in the said section nine.

(5) In this section " the repealed grant provisions " (b) means so much of section one hundred of the Act of 1944 as is repealed by this Act.

NOTES

(a) **" Training of teachers ".**—See note (c) to s. 4, *ante*. See also the Training of Teachers Regulations, 1967, S.I. 1967 No. 792.

(b) **" Repealed grant provisions ".**—This refers to the partial repeal of section 100 (1) (*c*) of the Act of 1944.

(c) **" Section eight of the Education Act, 1946 ".**—See p. 213, *ante*.

14. Short title, citation, construction and extent.—(1) This Act may be cited as the Education Act, 1962.

(2) The Education Acts, 1944 to 1959 (a), and this Act (except sections five, six, eight and ten thereof) may be cited together as the Education Acts, 1944 to 1962.

(3) [*Relates to Scotland.*]

(4) This Act shall, in its application to England and Wales, be construed as one with the Education Acts, 1944 to 1953.

(5) Sections one to four and sections seven, nine and thirteen of this Act, and the Schedules to this Act, shall not extend to Scotland; and sections five, six, eight and ten of this Act shall not extend to England and Wales.

(6) This Act shall not extend to Northern Ireland.

NOTES

(a) **" The Education Acts, 1944 to 1959 ".**—These are the Education Act, 1944, p. 73, *ante*; the Education Act, 1946, p. 209, *ante*; the Education (Miscellaneous Provisions) Act, 1948 (with the exception of certain parts relating only to endowed schools), p. 219, *ante*; the Education (Miscellaneous Provisions) Act, 1953 (except section 5 thereof, which relates only to Scotland), p. 229, *ante*; and the Education Act, 1959, p. 239, *ante*.

SCHEDULES

FIRST SCHEDULE

Section 1

ORDINARY RESIDENCE (a)

1. The provisions of this Schedule shall have effect for the purposes of section one of this Act.

2. Subject to the following provisions of this Schedule, a person shall be treated for those purposes as ordinarily resident in the area of a local education authority if he would fall to be treated as belonging to that area for the purposes of section seven of the Education (Miscellaneous Provisions) Act, 1953 (b) (which provides for recouping

to a local education authority the cost of providing further education for persons not belonging to their area); and the provisions of sub-section (4) of the said section seven and any regulations made for the purposes of that section, and any determination of the Secretary of State (c) under sub-section (5) thereof, shall have effect accordingly.

3.—(1) Regulations made under this Act may modify the operation of the last preceding paragraph in relation to cases where a person applies for an award under section one of this Act in respect of a course, and, at any time within the period of twelve months ending with the date on which that course is due to begin, a change occurs or has occurred in the circumstances by reference to which (apart from this paragraph) his place of ordinary residence would fall to be determined.

(2) Sub-sections (1) to (3) of section four of this Act shall have effect in relation to this paragraph as they have effect in relation to section one of this Act.

4.—(1) Where in accordance with the provisions mentioned in paragraph 2 of this Schedule (including any determination of the Secretary of State (c) under those provisions) a person would fall to be treated for the purposes of section one of this Act as not being ordinarily resident in any area, the Secretary of State (c) may direct that he shall be treated for those purposes as being ordinarily resident in the area of such local education authority as may be specified in the direction.

(2) In the exercise of the power to give a direction in respect of any person under this paragraph, the Secretary of State (c) shall have regard to the nature and extent of that person's association with the area in question and to any other material considerations.

NOTES

The above Schedule is applied by the London Government Act, **1963**, section **33** (**2**), p. 294, *post.*

(b) **" Section seven of the Education (Miscellaneous Provisions) Act, 1953 ".**— See p. 232, *ante.*

(c) **" Secretary of State ".**—See note (b) to s. **1** of the Act of 1944.

SECOND SCHEDULE

[*Repealed by the Statute Law* (*Repeals*) *Act* 1974.]

THE EDUCATION ACT, 1964

1964 c. 82

ARRANGEMENT OF SECTIONS

Provisions relating to England and Wales

An Act to enable county schools and voluntary schools to be established for providing full-time education by reference to age-limits differing from those specified in the Education Act, 1944, *as amended by the Education (Miscellaneous Provisions) Act,* 1948; *to enable maintenance allowances to be granted in respect of pupils at special schools who would be over compulsory school age . . . but for section* 38 (1) *of the said Act of* 1944 *or section* 32 (4) *of the Education (Scotland) Act,* 1962; *and for purposes connected with the matters aforesaid* [31st July, 1964]

GENERAL NOTE

This Act, which received the Royal Assent on 31st July, 1964, had two purposes. First, it enabled new schools to be established in England and Wales which would provide education for both junior and senior pupils. Second, it removed an anomaly in the law relating to the payment of maintenance allowances by local education authorities as it affected handicapped pupils (Circular 12/64 (27th August, 1964)).

Provisions relating to England and Wales

1. New schools with special age-limits. (1) [Where proposals with respect to a school maintained or to be maintained by a local education authority are submitted] to the Secretary of State under section 13 of the Education Act, 1944 (a), the proposals may, if the authority or persons submitting the proposals think fit,—

(*a*) specify an age which is below the age of ten years and six months and an age which is above the age of twelve years, and

(*b*) provide that the school shall be [a school] for providing full-time education suitable to the requirements of pupils whose ages are between the ages so specified.

(2) If the Secretary of State approves (with or without modification) any such proposals which make provision as mentioned in the preceding subsection, he shall by order direct that for the purposes of the Education Acts, 1944 to 1962 (b) the school shall be deemed to be a primary school (*), or shall be deemed to be a secondary school (*) as may be specified in the order.

(3) The powers conferred by this section shall be exercisable—

(*a*) notwithstanding anything contained in the Education Acts, 1944 to 1962, and, in particular, in section 7 of the Education

Act, 1944 (c) (which relates to the stages in which the statutory system of public education is to be organised), but

(*b*) without prejudice to the exercise of any other power conferred by those Acts.

NOTES

This section provides that proposals with respect to a school maintained or to be maintained by a local education authority may specify both (*a*) a lower age limit for pupils which is below 10 years and 6 months, and (*b*) an upper age limit which is above 12, and indicates that the school shall be a school for providing full-time education suitable to the requirements of pupils between the specified ages.

The words in square brackets were substituted by s. 2 of the Education Act, 1968, p. 263, *post*.

(*) As to the meaning or statutory definition of " local education authority ", " primary school " and " secondary school ", see pp. 67–69, *ante*.

(a) **" Section 13 of the Education Act, 1944 ".**—This section makes provision for the establishment and discontinuance of county and voluntary schools, see p. 90, *ante*.

(b) **" Education Acts, 1944 to 1962 ".**—These are the Education Act, 1944; the Education Act, 1946; the Education (Miscellaneous Provisions) Act, 1948 (with the exception of certain parts relating only to endowed schools); the Education (Miscellaneous Provisions) Act, 1953 (except section 5); the Education Act, 1959; and the Education Act, 1962. All these statutes are printed in this Part of the Volume, *ante*. They may now be cited, with later Acts, as the Education Acts, 1944 to 1975.

(c) **" Section 7 of the Education Act, 1944 ".**—This section organises the statutory system of public education in three progressive stages, *viz.*, primary, secondary and further education. See p. 78, *ante*.

2. [**Maintenance allowances in respect of pupils at special schools in England and Wales.**—*Regulations made under section 81 (c) of the Education Act, 1944 (a) (which relates to the grant of certain allowances in respect of pupils over compulsory school age), may include provision empowering local education authorities to grant maintenance allowances in respect of persons who—*

(*a*) *being registered pupils at special schools, are by virture of section 38 (1) (b) of that Act deemed to be of compulsory school age, but*

(*b*) *apart from the said section 38 (1), would be over compulsory school age.*]

NOTE

Since the raising of the school-leaving age to sixteen (see s. 35 of the Act of 1944, *ante*) the above section has become of no practical effect, and it was repealed by the Education (School-Leaving Dates) Act 1976.

3. [*Relates to Scotland only.*]

Supplementary provisions

4. Financial provisions.—There shall be paid out of moneys provided by Parliament—

(*a*) any increase attributable to this Act in the sums payable out of moneys so provided by way of Rate-deficiency Grant or Exchequer Equalisation Grant under the enactments relating to local government in England and Wales or in Scotland;

(*b*) any increase in the sums payable out of moneys so provided under the said enactments in respect of general grants, being an increase arising from any increase in the expenditure relevant to the fixing of the aggregate amounts of those grants which is attributable to the provisions of this Act;

(*c*) any increase attributable to this Act in the sums payable out of moneys so provided under section 107 of the Education Act, 1944 (a) or under section 1 (2) of the Education Act, 1959 (b).

NOTE

This section was explained by Circular 12/64 (27th August, 1964) as follows: " Section 4 deals with finance. It provides that authorities' expenditure under section 1 may be taken into account in fixing the general grant and other exchequer grants, and that the new voluntary schools established under the Act will be eligible on the same terms as other new voluntary schools for grants and loans under sections 102–105 of the Education Act, 1944 (as amended) and section 1 (2) of the Education Act, 1959. In the case of a new voluntary school deemed to be a secondary school, promoters should bear in mind that claims for matching grant will need to be considered in relation to the actual number of pupils of secondary school age likely to attend the school. Promoters will no doubt seek early consultation with the Secretary of State about any such proposal ".

(a) **" Section 107 of the Education Act, 1944 ".**—This section provides for the expenses of the Secretary of State to be defrayed by Parliament. See p. 181, *ante*.

(b) **" Section 1 (2) of the Education Act, 1959 ".**—Superseded by s. 1 of the Education Act 1967, *post*.

5. Short title, citation, construction and extent.—(1) This Act may be cited as the Education Act, 1964.

(2) The Education Acts, 1944 to 1962 (a) and this Act (except section 3 thereof) may be cited together as the Education Acts, 1944 to 1964.

(3) [*Relates to Scotland only.*]

(4) This Act, in its application to England and Wales, shall be construed as one with the Education Acts, 1944 to 1953 (b).

(5) Except in so far as the context otherwise requires, any reference in this Act to an enactment shall be construed as a reference to that enactment as amended or extended by or under any other enactment.

(6) Sections 1 *and 2* (c) of this Act shall not extend to Scotland; and section 3 of this Act shall not extend to England and Wales.

(7) This Act shall not extend to Northern Ireland.

NOTES

(a) **" Education Acts 1944 to 1962 ".**—See note (b) to section 1 of the present Act, *ante*.

(b) **" Education Acts, 1944 to 1953 ".**—These are the Education Act, 1944; the Education Act, 1946; the Education (Miscellaneous Provisions) Act, 1948 (with the exception of certain provisions relating only to endowed schools); and the Education (Miscellaneous Provisions) Act, 1953 (except section 5). See the General Note to the Act of 1944, p. 73, *ante*.

(c) The words in italic were repealed by the Education (School-Leaving Dates) Act 1976.

THE REMUNERATION OF TEACHERS ACT, 1965

1965 c. 3

An Act to make new provision for determining the remuneration of teachers; and for purposes connected therewith. [23rd March 1965]

ARRANGEMENT OF SECTIONS

GENERAL NOTE

This Act repealed the Remuneration of Teachers Act, 1963, and gave power to set up new committees to consider teachers' remuneration.

1. Committees to consider remuneration of teachers.—(1) The Secretary of State shall secure that, for the purpose of considering the remuneration payable to teachers by local education authorities, there shall be one or more committees consisting of—

(*a*) a chairman appointed by the Secretary of State as being an independent person;

(*b*) one or more persons nominated from time to time by the Secretary of State to represent him, together with persons representing one or more bodies to which this paragraph applies;

(*c*) persons representing one or more bodies to which this paragraph applies.

(2) The bodies to which paragraph (*b*) of the preceding subsection applies are local education authorities, joint education committees, organisations appearing to the Secretary of State to represent local education authorities and organisations appearing to the Secretary of State to represent education committees; and the bodies to which paragraph (*c*) of that subsection applies are organisations appearing to the Secretary of State to represent teachers or particular descriptions of teachers.

(3) The Secretary of State shall determine which bodies to which paragraph (*b*) or paragraph (*c*) of subsection (1) of this section applies are to be represented on each committee constituted under this section, and the number of persons by whom any such body is to be so represented, and (subject to the following provisions of this section) may from time to time vary or revoke any such determination.

(4) A determination of the Secretary of State whereby a body which is for the time being represented on a committee constituted under this section will cease to be so represented (except in a case where that body will have ceased to exist before the time when the determination is to take effect) shall not have effect unless it is embodied in an order made by the Secretary of State.

(5) Any order under the last preceding subsection may be revoked by a subsequent order made by the Secretary of State.

(6) Any power to make orders under this section shall be exercisable by statutory instrument; and any statutory instrument containing an order under subsection (4) of this section shall be subject to annulment in pursuance of a resolution of either House of Parliament.

(7) Subject to any determination of the Secretary of State under this section, it shall be for each body to which any such determination relates to nominate from time to time the person or persons by whom it is to be represented on a committee constituted under this section.

(8) The Secretary of State, either at the time when a committee is constituted under this section or at any subsequent time, may give directions specifying the descriptions of teachers whose remuneration any such committee are to consider, or allocating, as between two or more such committees, the descriptions of remuneration which they are to consider respectively.

NOTE

The National Union of Teachers is no longer represented on the Burnham Further Education Committee. See the Remuneration of Teachers (Further Education Committee) Order, 1966, S.I. 1966 No. 964.

2. Review of remuneration by committees.—(1) It shall be the duty of each committee, whenever they think fit or are required by the Secretary of State to do so, to review the relevant remuneration of teachers as that remuneration exists (whether in pursuance of this Act or of any previous enactment or otherwise) at the time of the review.

(2) Where, in consequence of such a review, a committee agree on any recommendations with respect to the relevant remuneration of teachers, they shall transmit those recommendations to the Secretary of State.

(3) Subject to the following provisions of this section, on the receipt of any recommendations of a committee under the last preceding subsection the Secretary of State shall prepare a draft document, setting out the scales and other provisions required for determining the relevant remuneration of

teachers, in the form in which, in his opinion, those scales and provisions should be so as to give effect to the recommendations of the committee.

(4) Where the Secretary of State has prepared a draft document under the last preceding subsection, he shall consult the committee in question with respect to the draft and shall make such modifications of the draft as are requisite for giving effect to any representations made by the committee with respect thereto; and he shall then—

(*a*) arrange for a document setting out the requisite scales and other provisions in the form of the draft, or in that form as modified under this subsection, as the case may be, to be published by Her Majesty's Stationery Office, and

(*b*) make an order referring to that document and directing that the relevant remuneration of teachers shall be determined in accordance with the scales and other provisions set out in the document.

(5) If at the time when any recommendations of a committee are transmitted to the Secretary of State under subsection (2) of this section—

(*a*) an order made under the last preceding subsection is in force with respect to the relevant remuneration of teachers, and

(*b*) it appears to the Secretary of State that effect could more conveniently be given to those recommendations by amending the scales and other provisions set out in the document referred to in that order,

the Secretary of State, instead of preparing a new draft document under subsection (3) of this section, may prepare a draft order setting out the amendments of those scales and other provisions which, in his opinion, are requisite for giving effect to the recommendations.

(6) Where the Secretary of State has prepared a draft order under the last preceding subsection, he shall consult the committee in question with respect to the draft and shall make such modifications of the draft as are requisite for giving effect to any representations made by the committee with respect thereto; and the Secretary of State shall then make the order in the form of the draft, or in that form as modified under this subsection, as the case may be.

NOTE

Orders made under this section are now as follows: the Remuneration of Teachers (Primary and Secondary Schools) No. 2 Order 1975, S.I. 1975 No. 1558, *post*; the Remuneration of Teachers (Further Education) No. 2 Order 1975, S.I. 1975 No. 1226, *post*; and the Remuneration of Teachers (Farm Institutes) No. 2 Order 1975, S.I. 1975 No. 1227, *post*, and amendment orders.

3. **Provision for arbitration.**—(1) The Secretary of State shall make arrangements whereby, in such circumstances and subject to such exceptions as may be provided by the arrangements, matters in respect of which agreement has not been reached in a committee after they have been considered by the committee in accordance with the preceding provisions of this Act may be referred to arbitration in such manner as may be so provided.

(2) Before making any arrangements under the preceding subsection in relation to a committee, the Secretary of State shall consult the bodies which are to be represented on the committee in accordance with any determinations made by him under section 1 of this Act which are for the time being in force.

(3) Any such arrangements may include provision for the appointment of arbitrators by the Minister of Labour for the purposes of any reference under this section; and, where arbitrators are so appointed, that Minister may pay to the arbitrators such remuneration (whether by way of fees or otherwise) and such allowances as he may with the consent of the Treasury determine, and may provide accommodation or other facilities required for the purposes of any such reference.

(4) The Arbitration Act, 1950, shall not apply to any reference under this section.

4. Action on recommendations of arbitrators.—(1) Any recommendations of the arbitrators, on a reference under section 3 of this Act with respect to any matters considered by a committee, shall be transmitted to the Secretary of State; and, except where those recommendations do not propose any change in the relevant remuneration of teachers, the provisions of subsections (3) to (6) of section 2 of this Act shall (subject to the next following subsection) have effect in relation to the recommendations of the arbitrators as if they were recommendations of that committee.

(2) If, in any case where any recommendations of arbitrators have been transmitted to the Secretary of State under the preceding subsection, each House of Parliament resolves that national economic circumstances require that effect should not be given to the recommendations, the provisions of section 2 of this Act referred to in the preceding subsection shall not have effect as mentioned in that subsection.

(3) Where such a resolution has been passed by each House of Parliament, the Secretary of State, after consultation with the committee in question, shall determine what changes (if any) in the relevant remuneration of teachers are appropriate in the circumstances, and, unless he determines that no such changes are appropriate, shall (subject to the next following subsection) proceed in accordance with subsections (3) and (4) of section 2 of this Act, or (where applicable) in accordance with subsections (5) and (6) of that section, as if the changes determined by him had been recommended by that committee under subsection (2) of that section.

(4) Subsections (4) and (6) of section 2 of this Act, as applied by the last preceding subsection, shall each have effect with the substitution, for the words from " shall make " to " giving effect to ", of the words " may, if he thinks fit, modify the draft in consequence of ".

5. Effect of orders as to remuneration.—(1) Where any order made under subsection (4) of section 2 of this Act is for the time being in force, then, subject to the next following subsection, remuneration to which the order applies shall be determined, and shall be paid to teachers by local education authorities, in accordance with the scales and other provisions set out in the document referred to in that order.

(2) Where, at any time while an order under subsection (4) of section 2 of this Act (in this subsection referred to as "the principal order") is in force, an order under subsection (6) of that section relating to remuneration to which the principal order applies (in this subsection referred to as "the amending order") comes into force, then, at any time while the amending order is in force, remuneration to which the principal order applies shall be determined, and shall be paid to teachers by local education authorities, in accordance with the scales and other provisions set out in the document referred to in the principal order as amended by the amending order.

(3) In this section any reference to subsection (4) or subsection (6) of section 2 of this Act includes a reference to that subsection as applied by section 4 of this Act.

6. Financial provisions. There shall be paid out of moneys provided by Parliament—

(*a*) any increase attributable to this Act in the sums payable out of moneys so provided by way of Rate-deficiency Grant or Exchequer Equalisation Grant under the enactments relating to local government in England and Wales or in Scotland;

(*b*) any increase in the sums payable out of moneys so provided under the said enactments in respect of general grants, being an increase arising from any increase in the expenditure relevant to the fixing of the aggregate amounts of those grants which is attributable to the provisions of this Act;

(*c*) any increase attributable to this Act in the sums payable out of moneys so provided under section 107 of the Education Act, 1944 (a), in respect of administrative expenses incurred by the Secretary of State;

(*d*) any expenses of the Minister of Labour in pursuance of section 3 of this Act.

NOTE

(a) **" Section 107 of the Education Act, 1944 ".**—See p. 181, *ante*. The section deals with the expenses of Ministers.

7. Supplementary provisions as to orders relating to remuneration, and repeals.—(1) Any power to make orders under the provisions of sections 2 to 4 of this Act shall be exercisable by statutory instrument.

(2) Any order made under those provisions may be revoked by a subsequent order thereunder.

(3) Any order under those provisions may be made with retrospective effect to any date specified in the order, and the remuneration of teachers to whom the order applies shall be deemed to have been payable accordingly:

Provided that nothing in this subsection shall be construed as authorising the remuneration of any teacher to be reduced retrospectively.

(4) Any order made under those provisions may include provision for revoking any order made under the Remuneration of Teachers Act, 1963 (a), which is for the time being in force.

(5) Subject to the proviso to subsection (3) of this section, any order made under those provisions may contain such transitional, supplementary and incidental provisions as the Secretary of State may consider necessary or expedient.

(6) Without prejudice to the operation of any order made (whether before or after the passing of this Act) under the Remuneration of Teachers Act, 1963 (a), section 89 of the Education Act, 1944 (b), is hereby repealed.

(7) The Remuneration of Teachers Act, 1963 (a), is hereby repealed as from the earliest date on which no order made under that Act (whether before or after the passing of this Act) continues to have effect.

NOTES

(a) **" Remuneration of Teachers Act, 1963 ".**—Now repealed, as no orders under that Act are any longer in force.

(b) **" Section 89 of the Education Act, 1944 ".**—This section, now repealed by sub-s. (6), *supra*, formerly empowered the Minister of Education (as he then was) to appoint one or more committees to consider and make recommendations to him regarding the remuneration of teachers; and under it three such committees were constituted: (1) the Burnham Committee on Scales of Salaries for Teachers in Primary and Secondary Schools; (2) a similar committee on Scales of Salaries for Teachers in Establishments for Further Education; and (3) a committee on Scales of Salaries for the Teaching Staff of Farm Institutes and for Teachers of Agricultural Subjects. Such committees had the duty of submitting their proposals to the Minister for his approval.

In March 1963 the then Minister refused to approve the proposals of the committees and made counter-proposals of his own. This resulted in deadlock. The Remuneration of Teachers Act, 1963 (now repealed; see sub-s. (7), *supra*) was passed to enable the Minister to make provision with respect to the remuneration of teachers by Order.

The present Act sets up new committees (see s. 1, *supra*).

8. Interpretation.—(1) In section 1 of this Act "education committee" means an education committee established by a local education authority or a joint education committee established by two or more local education authorities.

(2) In sections 2 to 4 of this Act "committee" means a committee constituted under section 1 of this Act, and " the relevant remuneration of teachers ", in relation to such a committee, means the remuneration which, in accordance with any directions under section 1 (8) of this Act which are for the time being in force, that committee are required to consider.

(3) Except in so far as the context otherwise requires, any reference in this Act to an enactment shall be construed as a reference to that enactment as amended or extended by or under any other enactment.

9. Short title, citation, construction and extent.—(1) This Act may be cited as the Remuneration of Teachers Act, 1965.

(2) The Education Acts, 1944 to 1964 (a), and this Act may be cited together as the Education Acts, 1944 to 1965.

(3) This Act shall be construed as one with the Education Acts, 1944 to 1964.

(4) This Act, except section 6 thereof, shall not extend to Scotland.

(5) This Act shall not extend to Northern Ireland.

NOTE

(a) **"Education Acts, 1944 to 1964".**—These are the Acts set out in note (b) on p. 252, *ante,* together with the Education Act, 1964. With later Acts, they may be cited as the Education Acts, 1944 to 1970.

THE EDUCATION ACT, 1967

(1967 c. 3)

ARRANGEMENT OF SECTIONS

An Act to enlarge the powers of the Secretary of State to make contributions, grants and loans in respect of aided schools and special agreement schools and to direct local education authorities to pay the expenses of establishing or enlarging controlled schools; and to provide for loans for capital expenditure incurred for purposes of colleges of education by persons other than local education authorities.

[16th February, 1967]

GENERAL NOTE

This Act had three purposes. First, it increased the rate and scope of the Secretary of State's grant to voluntary aided and special agreement schools. Second, it widened the scope for the enlargement or establishment of controlled schools under specified conditions. Third, it gave power to the Secretary of State to make regulations enabling him to make loans to voluntary colleges of education for capital expenditure.

1. Extended powers to make contributions, grants and loans.—

(1) [*Repealed by the Education Act* 1975, *Sch. Part II.*]

(2) Where the Secretary of State—

(*a*) has approved proposals submitted to him under section 13 (2) of the Education Act 1944 (b) that a school proposed to be established should be maintained by a local education authority as a voluntary school and has directed that the proposed school shall be an aided school or special agreement school;

(*b*) (*Repealed* (c)).

he may, out of moneys provided by Parliament, pay to the managers or governors of the school, in respect of any sums expended by them on the provision of a site for the school or of the school buildings, a grant not exceeding [85 per cent.] of those sums; but no such grant shall be payable to the managers or governors of a special agreement school in respect of any sums expended by them in the execution of proposals to which the special agreement for the school relates.

(3) Sub-section (3) of section 103 of the Education Act 1944 (d) (which makes provision for the exercise of the Secretary of State's discretion in determining the amount of grants under that section) shall, with the necessary modifications, apply to grants under sub-section (2) of this section.

(4) For the purposes of section 105 of the Education Act 1944 (e) (which authorises the Secretary of State to make loans to the managers or governors of aided schools and special agreement schools for certain initial expenses involving capital expenditure) any expenses in respect of which the Secretary of State may make a grant under sub-section (2) of this section shall be included in the expression "initial expenses", and in determining the managers' or governors' share of any initial expenses the amount of any such grant paid or payable in respect of them shall be taken into account in the same way as grants under section 103 of that Act (d).

(5) The following provisions, being superseded by this section, shall cease to have effect (subject to sub-section (6) of this section), that is to say—

(*a*) in section 103 of the Education Act 1944, in sub-section (1) (d) the words from " or directs " to " discontinued " and the words " or any school to be established ", and in sub-section (3) (d) the words from " or of the sites " to the end;

(*b*) section 104 of that Act;

(*c*) section 1 of the Education (Miscellaneous Provisions) Act 1953 and, in section 8 of that Act (f), paragraph (*b*) of sub-section (1) and the word " and " preceding that paragraph, and sub-section (2); and

(*d*) section 1 of the Education Act 1959 (g), except sub-section (4) of that section.

(6) Nothing in this section shall extend to contributions or grants in respect of expenditure on work which—

(*a*) was begun before 4th July 1966; or

(*b*) was approved by the Secretary of State before that date under section 13 (6) of the Education Act 1944 (b) or under any arrangements relating to work to which that section does not apply; or

(*c*) was included in a programme notified to a local education authority as the main building programme approved by the Secretary of State for the twelve months beginning with April 1966 or for any earlier period;

or in respect of expenditure on the provision of the site on which or buildings to which any such work was done or proposed to be done.

NOTES

The words " 85 per cent. " in square brackets in subsection (2) were substituted by section 3 of the Education Act 1975, *post*.

(b) **" Section 13 of the Education Act, 1944 ".**—See p. 90, *ante*.

(c) See Education Act, 1968, s. 1 (3) and Sch. 2, pp. 263, 266, *post*.

(d) **" Section 103 of the Education Act, 1944 ".**—See p. 177.

(e) **" Section 105 ".**—See p. 179.

(f) **" Section 8 of the Education (Miscellaneous Provisions) Act, 1953 ".**—See p. 234,

(g) **" Section 1 of the Education Act, 1959 "**—See p. 239.

2. Enlargement of controlled schools.—In section 1 of the Education Act 1946 (a) (which, as amended by section 3 of the Education (Miscellaneous Provisions) Act 1953, enables the Secretary of State to direct that the expenses of giving effect to proposals for enlarging the premises of a controlled school shall be payable by the local education authority if the enlargement is in the interest of secondary education and is not likely to amount to the establishment of a school of a new character)—

(*a*) before the word " secondary ", in both places where it occurs, there shall be inserted the words " primary or "; and

(*b*) the words from " and is not likely " to " new character " shall be omitted.

NOTE

(a) **" Section 1 of the Education Act, 1946 ".**—See p. 209, *ante*.

3. Extension of power to require local education authority to defray expenses of establishing controlled middle school.—Where persons other than a local education authority submit proposals to the Secretary of State under section 13 of the Education Act 1944 (a) for the establishment of a new school and its maintenance by the local education authority as a voluntary school, and the proposals make provision as mentioned in section 1 (1) of the Education Act 1964 (b) (new schools with special age limits), section 2 of the Education (Miscellaneous Provisions) Act 1953 (c) (power to require local education authority to defray expenses of establishing controlled school) shall apply in relation to the school established in pursuance of the proposals as if in paragraph (*b*) of that section (which limits the power conferred by it to cases where the new school is required for pupils for whom accommodation in some other voluntary school has ceased to be available) after the words " for whom " there were inserted the words " or for a substantial proportion of whom ".

NOTES

(a) **" Section 13 of the Education Act, 1944 ".**—See p. 90, *ante*.

(b) **" Section 1 (1) of the Education Act, 1964 ".**—See p. 73, The subsection has been amended by s. 2 of the Education Act 1968, p. 263, *post*.

(c) **" Section 2 of the Education (Miscellaneous Provisions) Act, 1953 ".**—See p. 229, *ante*.

4. Loans for capital expenditure for purposes of colleges of education.—(1) The Secretary of State may by regulations (a) make provision for the making by him out of moneys provided by Parliament of loans to persons other than local education authorities for the purpose of helping them to meet capital expenditure incurred or to be incurred by them or on their behalf in connection with the provision, replacement, extension, improvement, furnishing or equipment of colleges for the training of teachers.

(2) Any loan made to any persons in pursuance of regulations under this section shall be made on such terms and conditions as may be specified in an agreement made between the Secretary of State and those persons with the consent of the Treasury.

(3) Regulations under this section may make the making of loans dependent on the fulfilment of such conditions as may be determined by or in accordance with the regulations, and may also make provision for requiring persons to whom loans have been made in pursuance of the regulations to comply with such requirements as may be so determined.

(4) Regulations under this section shall be made by statutory instrument, which shall be subject to annulment in pursuance of a resolution of either House of Parliament.

NOTE

(a) **" Regulations ".**—See Part III of the Further Education Regulations 1975, S.I. 1975 No. 1054, *post*.

5. Expenses.—There shall be defrayed out of moneys provided by Parliament any increase attributable to this Act in the sums so payable under any other enactment.

6. Short title, citation, construction and extent.—(1) This Act may be cited as the Education Act 1967 and this Act and the Education Acts 1944 to 1965 (a) may be cited together as the Education Acts 1944 to 1967.

(2) This Act shall be construed as one with the Education Acts 1944 to 1965 (a).

(3) This Act does not extend to Scotland or to Northern Ireland.

NOTE

(a) **" Education Acts, 1944 to 1965 ".**—These comprise the following Acts: The Education Act, 1944; the Education Act, 1946; the Education (Miscellaneous Provisions) Act, 1948 (except

s. 2 and certain provisions of the Schedules); the Education (Miscellaneous Provisions) Act, 1953 (except s. 5); the Education Act, 1959; the Education Act, 1962 (except ss. 5, 6, 8, and 10); the Education Act, 1964 (except s. 3); and the Remuneration of Teachers Act, 1965. With later Acts, they may now be cited as the Education Acts, 1944 to 1975.

THE EDUCATION ACT, 1968

(1968, c. 17)

ARRANGEMENT OF SECTIONS

An Act to amend the law as to the effect of and procedure for making changes in the character, size or situation of county schools or voluntary schools to enable special age limits to be adopted for existing as well as for new schools, and to make certain other amendments as to the approval or provision of school premises; and for purposes connected therewith. [10th April, 1968]

GENERAL NOTE

The main purpose of this Act, as to which see also Circular 6/70, p. 469, *post*, was to amend the law relating to changes in the character and premises of county and voluntary schools and the standards to which the premises of such schools are required to conform. This was considered necessary by the government of the time after their policy of comprehensivisation of schools had encountered difficulties due to parental opposition.

In order to understand the reason for the introduction and passing of this Act it is necessary to consider, in some detail, the case of *Bradbury* v. *Enfield London Borough*, [1967] 3 All E.R. 434, C.A.

The respondent council, as local education authority by virtue of s. 30 of the London Government Act 1963, was under a statutory duty under s. 31 (5) of that Act not to cease to maintain existing county or voluntary schools except in accordance with s. 13 or s. 14 of the Education Act, 1944.

By s. 13 (1) of the Act of 1944 a local education authority intending to cease to maintain a school, or to establish a new school, was bound to submit proposals to the Secretary of State for Education and Science. By s. 13 (3) of the Act the authority was bound to give public notice of such proposals. By s. 13 (5) the authority was prohibited from doing anything for which proposals were required until such proposals were approved by the Secretary of State.

Government policy at the time was to do away with the distinction between grammar schools and other secondary schools, and to eliminate selection of pupils by examination, by the introduction of so-called " comprehensive " schools. In accordance with this policy, proposals were prepared by the Enfield Borough Council in respect of the schools within their area.

In regard to eight of these schools, no public notice of the proposals was given as required by s. 13 (3). The proposals in regard to these eight schools involved the combination of schools, e.g. the premises of an existing school would in future be used exclusively for the younger age group or exclusively for the older age group of pupils of a comprehensive school combining two or more former schools. Similarly a girls school might be changed, under the proposals, into a mixed school. There was also evidence that in many cases (not confined to the eight schools) the school premises did not come up to the prescribed standards.

On an action for an injunction against the council it was held:

" (i) The proposals with regard to the eight schools involved a fundamental change in the character of the schools owing, e.g., to the changes in age groups, and thus showed an intention on the part of the council ' to cease to maintain ' the existing schools and to ' establish new schools ' for the purposes of s. 13 of the Education Act, 1944; accordingly the council, having failed to fulfil the statutory requirements of sub-s. (3) of s. 13 in regard to giving public notice, were by virtue of s. 13 (5) of the Act of 1944 and of s. 31 (5) of the Act of 1963, not at liberty to cease to maintain the eight schools until the statutory requirements were fulfilled,

(ii) as the council had not fulfilled the requirements of the statute with which they were bound to comply, an injunction against acting on the proposals with regard to the eight schools would be granted and

(iii) the remedy for any failure (which, per DIPLOCK, L.J., would be a failure of non-feasance not malfeasance) of a local education authority to secure that the premises of a proposed new school were up to the prescribed standard lay under s. 99 of the Education Act, 1944 only, not by way of injunction; accordingly no injunction would be granted in respect of schools other than the eight schools referred to in (ii) above."

Entirely different proceedings had been going on concurrently with the *Bradbury* case, concerned with Enfield Grammar School only, and on September 13th 1967 an injunction was granted to restrain the London Borough of Enfield and the school governors from replacing selective intake of pupils aged 11 with a " mixed entry " scheme as being contrary to the school's articles of government. See the report of *Lee* v. *Enfield London Borough* (1967), *Times*, 14th September.

Following this latter defeat, the school governors decided to alter the school's articles. The then Secretary of State for Education and Science allowed only five days for objections to be made to the proposed alterations, and the same plaintiffs as in the proceedings above successfully applied for a declaration that this was wholly unreasonable and amounted to a denial of statutory rights. See the report of *Lee* v. *Secretary of State for Education and Science* (1967), 111 Sol. Jo. 756.

The present Act was intended to remove some of the difficulties which the government had unexpectedly found in its way, and so to prepare for the further establishment of " comprehensive " schools.

Certain changes in the character of schools made since the Act of 1944, but without compliance with s. 13 of that Act, were retrospectively validated by s. 1 (1) and (4) of the present Act. Section 1 (1) provides that references to discontinuing a school or establishing a new one are not to apply to any changes in the age range or sex of pupils or any enlargement or alteration of the premises or transfer of the school to a new site and by s. 1 (4), s. 1 (1) is deemed to have had effect since the beginning of April 1945 (*i.e.* when the Act of 1944 came into effect), to the extent mentioned in sub-s. (4).

Section 1 (2), amends s. 13 of the Act of 1944 for the future by expressly extending it, from the end of the summer term 1968, to " any significant change in the character or significant enlargement of the premises ". The question whether a change is a significant one is to be one for the Secretary of State to determine; see para. 3 of Sch. 1. Changes in arrangements for the admission of pupils by reference to ability or aptitude will, by s. 1 (2), in future, change the character of a school. Establishing a middle school by changing an existing school is, by s. 2, brought within the Education Act, 1964, s. 1.

By s. 3 it will only be necessary to submit specifications and plans of school premises under s. 13 (6) of the Act of 1944 where the premises are new or the Secretary of State so directs. Regulations as to prescribed standards for school premises may now be relaxed in the light of the need to control public expenditure in the interests of the national economy instead of, as hitherto, the shortage of labour and materials.

1. Changes in character, size or situation of schools.—(1) For purposes of the Education Acts 1944 to 1967 (a) and any other enactment relating to the duties of a local education authority, references in whatever terms to discontinuing a school (and, in particular, those in section 13 of the Education Act 1944 (b) to a local authority ceasing to maintain a county school or a voluntary school), or to establishing a new school, shall not be read as applying by reason of any change which is made to an existing school—

(*a*) by education beginning or ceasing to be provided for pupils above or below a particular age; or

(*b*) by education beginning or ceasing to be provided for girls as well as boys, or for boys as well as girls; or

(*c*) by any enlargement or alteration of the school premises or transfer of the school to a new site;

and the school existing before an event mentioned in paragraph (*a*), (*b*) or (*c*) above shall be regarded as continuing despite that event and as being the same school before and after that event (unless it is to be regarded for other reasons as discontinued).

(2) In section 13 of the Education Act 1944 (b) (which regulates, among other things, the procedure to be followed where a local education authority intend to establish, maintain or cease to maintain a school as mentioned in sub-section (1), or where persons propose that a school should be maintained as a voluntary school as mentioned in sub-section (2)) sub-sections (1) and (2) shall be amended as follows:—

(*a*) in sub-section (1) there shall be inserted after paragraph (*c*) the words " or where a local education authority intend to make any significant change in the character, or significant enlargement of the premises, of a county school "; and (*b*) in sub-section (2) there shall be inserted after the words "as a voluntary school " the words " or where the managers or governors of a school maintained by a local education authority as a voluntary school intend to make any significant change in the character, or significant enlargement of the premises, of the school ";

and at the end of that section there shall be added as new sub-sections (9) and (10)—

" (9) Where proposals are made under this section for the enlargement of school premises, subsections (6) and (7) shall apply, with the necessary adaptations, as they apply in the case of proposals for the establishment of a new school (any reference to the persons by whom the proposed school is to be established being read as a reference to the managers or governors).

(10) References in this section to a change in the character of a school include in particular changes in character resulting from education beginning or ceasing to be provided for pupils above or below a particular age, for boys as well as for girls, or for girls as well as for boys, or from the making or alteration of arrangements for the admission of pupils by reference to ability or aptitude ".

(3) In the enactments mentioned in Schedule 1 to this Act there shall be made the amendments provided for by that Schedule, being amendments arising out of or related to the provisions in sub-sections (1) and (2) above; and the enactments mentioned in Schedule 2 to this Act are hereby repealed to the extent specified in column 3 of that Schedule.

(4) Sub-section (1) above shall be deemed to have had effect since the beginning of April 1945 in so far as the effect is—

(*a*) that a school is to be or have been regarded as being the same school before and after any such event as is there mentioned; or

(*b*) that anything may be or have been lawfully done without proposals being approved under section 13 of the Education Act 1944.

(5) Subject to sub-section (4) above, this section shall not apply in relation to things proposed to be done before the end of the summer term 1968, nor in relation to proposals approved before then under section 13 of the Education Act 1944 (b) or to anything done or to be done in pursuance of any such proposals; and for this purpose " summer term " means, in the case of any school, the term ending last before the month of September.

NOTES

The broad effects of this section, together with the First Schedule, are as follows:—

(1) To apply the procedure of s. 13 of the Education Act, 1944 (see p. 90, *ante*) to all significant changes in the character or size of county and voluntary schools;

(2) to give the Secretary of State the duty of determining in case of doubt whether a proposed change in the character of a school or a proposed enlargement of the school premises would be a significant change or enlargement;

(3) to validate changes of the kind described in sub-s. (1) of the present section, *supra*, which have been made in the past without proposals having been submitted to and approved by the Secretary of State under s. 13 of the Act of 1944.

(a) **" Education Acts, 1944 to 1967 ".**—These comprise the Acts mentioned in the Note to s. 6 of the Education Act, 1967, p. 260, *ante*, together with that Act.

(b) **" Section 13 of the Education Act, 1944 ".**—See p. 90, *ante*.

2. Schools with special age limits.—Section 1 of the Education Act 1964 (which enables new county or voluntary schools to be established to provide both primary and secondary education) shall apply where it is proposed that an existing school maintained or to be maintained by a local education authority should provide both primary and secondary education, and accordingly in sub-section (1) of that section—

(*a*) for the words from " Where a local education authority intend to establish a new county school " to " for that purpose " there shall be substituted the words "Where proposals with respect to a school maintained or to be maintained by a local education authority are submitted"; and

(*b*) for the word "established" in paragraph (*b*) there shall be substituted the words "a school".

NOTE

This section amends s. 1 of the Education Act, 1964 (p. 251).

3. Approval or provision of school premises (miscellaneous amendments).—(1) In section 13 of the Education Act 1944 (a)—

(*a*) in sub-section (6) (which requires submission to the Secretary of State of specifications and plans of the school premises of a proposed new county or voluntary school) after the words "specifications and plans of the school premises" there shall be inserted the words "if the premises are new premises (that is to say, if the premises do not comprise buildings used for a school at the time when the proposals are approved) or if the Secretary of State so directs"; and

(*b*) in sub-section (7) (which requires those concerned to give effect to proposals for a new school after the proposals, specifications and plans have been approved under the section) after the words "under this section" there shall be inserted the words "or, in a case where specifications and plans are not required, when the proposals have been so approved and the Secretary of State has notified the authority or persons by whom the proposed school is to be established that specifications and plans will not be required", and after the words "so approved" there shall be inserted the words "(if any)".

(2) In section 7 (2) of the Education (Miscellaneous Provisions) Act 1948 (b) (which enables the prescribed standards for school premises to be relaxed by the Secretary of State in approving specifications and plans of a new school under section 13 (6) of the Education Act 1944 (a) and does so by reference to the proviso to section 10 (2) of that Act (c) as set out in sub-section (1) of the said section (7) after paragraph (*b*) there shall be inserted the words "or if the Secretary of State is satisfied, on the submission to him of the specifications and plans of the school premises where the premises are to comprise the existing site or buildings of another school, as to the matters mentioned in paragraph (*a*) set out in the preceding sub-section".

(3) In the proviso to section 10 (2) of the Education Act 1944 (c) as set out in section 7 (1) of the Education (Miscellaneous Provisions) Act 1948 (b) (which proviso enables the Secretary of State in certain circumstances to permit school premises not to conform to the prescribed standards) for the words "having regard to shortage of labour or materials" in paragraph (*c*) there shall be substituted the words "having regard to the need to control public expenditure in the interests of the national economy".

(4) If upon representations made to him by a local education authority the Secretary of State is satisfied—

(*a*) that the managers or governors of a voluntary school propose to make a significant enlargement of the school premises or alterations to those premises, and that it is desirable for them to do so for the better provision of primary or secondary education at the premises, or for securing that there is available for the area of the authority a sufficiency of suitable primary or secondary schools, or for both those reasons; and

(*b*) that, having regard to the need to control public expenditure in the interests of the national economy, it is not reasonably practicable to effect the enlargement or alterations by providing permanent accommodation;

then, subject to proposals for any significant enlargement being approved under section 13 of the Education Act 1944 (a) the Secretary of State may authorise the authority to provide, or assist in providing, temporary accommodation in accordance with arrangements approved by him; and Schedule 1 to the Education Act 1946 (d) (which relates to the duties of the local education authority and the managers or governors with regard to the provision of sites and buildings for voluntary schools) shall not apply in relation to temporary accommodation provided by virtue of this subsection.

NOTES

This section amends the law relating to school premises to accord with the new provisions of s. 1 of the Act, and substitutes a reference to the " need to control public expenditure in the interests of national economy " for the previous reference to " shortage of labour and materials " in s. 10 (2) of the Education Act, 1944, p. 84, *ante*. It also replaces s. 109 of the 1944 Act, which must now be regarded as spent, with new provisions.

(a) **" Section 13 of the Education Act, 1944 ".**—See p. 90, *ante*.

(b) **" Section 7 of the Education (Miscellaneous Provisions) Act, 1948 ".**—See p. 225, *ante*.

(c) **" Section 10 (2) of the Education Act, 1944 ".**—See p. 84, *ante*.

(d) **" Schedule 1 to the Education Act, 1946 ".**—See p. 216, *ante*.

4. Expenses. There shall be paid out of moneys provided by Parliament any increase attributable to this Act in the sums so payable under the Education Acts 1944 to 1967 (a).

NOTE

(a) **" Education Acts, 1944 to 1967 ".**—See note (a) to s. 1, *ante*.

5. Text of certain provisions as amended by this Act.—(1) In accordance with the provisions of this Act (apart from the transitional provisions in section 1 (5)), the following sections, namely,—

section 13 of the Education Act 1944 (a);
section 1 of the Education Act 1946; (b) and
section 7 of the Education (Miscellaneous Provisions) Act 1948 (c);

are to have effect as set out in Schedule 3 to this Act with the amendments made by this Act, by the Secretary of State for Education and Science Order 1964 and by the provisions listed in subsection (2) below, but without prejudice to the operation of any enactment affecting the operation of those sections and not so listed.

(2) The provisions above referred to, as regards provisions by which section 13 of the Education Act 1944 is amended, are—

The Education Act 1946, section 14 and Part II of Schedule 2; and
The Education (Miscellaneous Provisions) Act 1953, section 16, and section 17 and Schedule 1;

and, as regards provisions by which section 1 of the Education Act 1946 is amended, are—

The Education (Miscellaneous Provisions) Act 1953, section 3; and
The Education Act 1967, section 2.

NOTES

(a) **" Section 13 of the Education Act, 1944 ".**—See p. 90, *ante*.
(b) **" Section 1 of the Education Act, 1946 ".**—See p. 209, *ante*.
(c) **" Section 7 of the Education (Miscellaneous Provisions) Act, 1948 ".**—See p. 225, *ante*.

6. Short title, citation, construction and extent.—(1) This Act may be cited as the Education Act 1968 and this Act and the Education Acts 1944 to 1967 (a) may be cited together as the Education Acts 1944 to 1968.

(2) This Act shall be construed as one with the Education Acts 1944 to 1967 (a).

(3) This Act does not extend to Scotland or to Northern Ireland.

NOTE

(a) **" Education Acts, 1944 to 1967 ".**—See note (a) to s. 1, *ante*.

SCHEDULES

Section 1.

SCHEDULE 1

ADDITIONAL AMENDMENTS AS TO CHANGES IN CHARACTER, SIZE, OR SITUATION OF SCHOOLS

[This Schedule amended ss. 16 (1), 17, 67 (4), 102, 105 (2) and 114 (1) of the Education Act 1944; s. 1 (1) of the Education Act 1946; s. 7 of the Education (Miscellaneous Provisions) Act 1948; and s. 31 (5) of the London Government Act 1963. The Schedule itself was amended by the Education Act 1973, Sch. 2, Part II. The various amendments have been incorporated in the relevant Acts, *ante*.]

SCHEDULE 2

Section 1.

REPEALS

Chapter	Short title	Extent of repeal
9 & 10 Geo. 6 c. 50	The Education Act 1946	Section 1 (2). In Part II of Schedule 2, the entry relating to section 114 of the Education Act 1944.
1 & 2 Eliz. 2 c. 33	The Education (Miscellaneous Provisions) Act 1953	In section 2 (*a*), the words " (otherwise than by way of enlargement of an existing school) ". Section 8 (3) (*b*), together with the word " and " at the end of section 8 (3) (*a*).
1967 c. 3	The Education Act 1967	Section 1 (2) (*b*), together with the word " or " at the end of section 1 (2) (*a*).

NOTES

" Education Act, 1946 ".—See pp. 209 *et seq.*
" Education (Miscellaneous Provisions) Act, 1953 ".—See pp. 229 *et seq.*
" Education Act, 1967 ".—See pp. 258 *et seq.*

SCHEDULE 3

Section 5.

ENACTMENTS REPRINTED WITH AMENDMENTS

[This Schedule reprints, with the amendments specified in s. 5, p. 265, *ante*, the following enactments:

(a) Education Act, 1944, s. 13. (See p. 90, *ante.*)
(b) Education Act, 1946, s. 1. (See p. 209, *ante.*)
(c) Education (Miscellaneous Provisions) Act, 1948, s. 7. (See p. 225, *ante.*)

THE EDUCATION (No. 2) ACT, 1968

(1968 c. 37)

ARRANGEMENT OF SECTIONS

An Act to make further provision for the government and conduct of colleges of education and other institutions of further education maintained by local education authorities, and of special schools so maintained. [3rd July, 1968.]

GENERAL NOTE

This Act provides, by s. 1, for the drawing up of instruments and articles of government in respect of colleges of education and other institutions providing full-time education. Similar provision is made, by s. 2, in respect of special schools. See generally the Introduction, pp. 27, 28, *ante*.

1. Government and conduct of colleges of education and other institutions providing further education.—(1) For every institution maintained by a local education authority, being either—

(*a*) a college for the training of teachers (in this section referred to as a college of education); or

(*b*) an institution, other than a college of education, providing full-time education pursuant to a scheme of further education approved under section 42 of the Education Act 1944 (a),

there shall be an instrument (to be known as an instrument of government) providing for the constitution of a body of governors of the institution.

(2) The instrument of government for any such institution shall be made, in the case of a college of education, by order of the local education authority with the approval of the Secretary of State, and in any other case by order of the local education authority, and the body of governors to be constituted thereunder shall consist of such number of persons, appointed in such manner as the local education authority or, in the case of a college of education, that authority with the approval of the Secretary of State may determine.

(3) Every such institution shall be conducted in accordance with articles of government, to be made by order of the local education authority with the approval of the Secretary of State; and those articles shall determine the functions to be exercised respectively, in relation to the institution, by the local education authority, the body of governors, the principal, and the academic board, if any.

(4) A local education authority may, with the approval of the Secretary of State, make an arrangement for the constitution of a single governing body for any two or more such institutions maintained by them as are mentioned in paragraph (*b*) of sub-section (1) of this section; and the governing body constituted in pursuance of any such arrangement shall consist of such number of persons, appointed in such manner, as the local education authority may determine.

NOTE

(a) **" Section 42 of the Education Act, 1944 ".**—See p. 136, *ante*.

2. Government and conduct of special schools.—(1) For every special school maintained by a local education authority there shall be an instrument (to be known as an instrument of government) providing for the constitution of a body of governors of the school.

(2) The instrument of government for any such school shall be made by order of the local education authority, and the body of governors to be constituted thereunder shall consist of such number of persons, appointed in such manner, as that authority may determine.

(3) Every such school shall be conducted in accordance with articles of government to be made by order of the local education authority.

(4) A local education authority may make an arrangement for the constitution of a single governing body for any two or more special schools maintained by them; and the governing body constituted in pursuance of any such arrangement shall consist of such number of persons, appointed in such manner, as the local education authority may determine.

(5) For the purposes of section 21 of the Education Act 1944 (a) and Schedule 4 (b) to that Act (proceedings of managers and governors of county and voluntary schools) and of section 24 (c) of that Act (appointment and dismissal of teachers in such schools) a special school maintained by a local education authority shall be treated as if it were a county school.

NOTES

(a) " **Section 21 of the Education Act, 1944** ".—See p. 109, *ante*.
(b) " **Schedule 4** ".—See p. 203, *ante*.
(c) " **Section 24** ".—See p. 112, *ante*.

3. Supplemental.—(1) The articles of government made under this Act for any establishment may regulate the constitution and functions of committees of the body of governors of or any academic board of that establishment, and of sub-committees of such committees.

(2) Every arrangement made under sub-section (4) of section 1 or sub-section (4) of section 2 of this Act may be terminated at any time by the local education authority by which it was made; and while such an arrangement is in force with respect to any establishments—

(*a*) the foregoing provisions of this Act as to the constitution of the body of governors shall not apply to those establishments; and

(*b*) for the purposes of any enactment the governing body constituted in accordance with the arrangement shall be deemed to be the body of governors of each of those establishments, and references to a governor in any enactment shall, in relation to each of those establishments, be construed accordingly.

(3) The following provisions of the Education Act 1944, that is to say—

(*a*) sub-section (1) of section 67 (a) (determination of disputes between local education authorities and managers or governors of schools);

(*b*) section 68 (b) (power to prevent unreasonable exercise of functions by local education authorities or by managers or governors of county or voluntary schools);

(*c*) section 99 (c) (powers of Secretary of State in default of local education authorities or managers or governors of county or voluntary schools),

shall apply in relation to establishments to which this Act applies and governors of those establishments as they apply in relation to county schools and governors of county schools.

(4) References in this Act to provisions of the Education Act 1944 are references thereto as amended by or under any subsequent enactment.

NOTES

(a) " **Section 67 (1) of the Education Act, 1944** ".—See p. 154, *ante*.
(b) " **Section 68** ".—See p. 155, *ante*.
(c) " **Section 99** ".—See p. 173, *ante*.

4. Commencement.—(1) This Act shall come into force on such day as the Secretary of State may by order made by statutory instrument appoint; and different days may be appointed under this section for the purposes of different classes of establishments (a).

(2) Without prejudice to section 37 of the Interpretation Act 1889 (b), any instrument of government or articles of government to be made under this Act for any establishment and any arrangement under this Act for the constitution of a single governing body for two or more establishments may be made so as to come into force before the date on which this Act comes into force in relation to establishments of that class, and any functions to be exercised under that instrument or arrangement or those articles may be exercised accordingly.

NOTES

(a) The day appointed for the coming into force of the Act for the purposes of colleges of education was 1st July 1969. See the Education (No. 2) Act, 1968 (Commencement No. 1) Order, 1969, S.I. 1969 No. 709 (c. 16).

The day appointed for the coming into force of the Act for the purposes of special schools was 1st October 1969. See the Education (No. 2) Act, 1968 (Commencement No. 2) Order, 1969, S.I. 1969 No. 1106 (c. 30).

The day appointed for the coming into force of the Act for the purposes of establishments of further education was 1st September, 1972. See the Education (No. 2) Act 1968 (Commencement No. 3) Order 1972, S.I. 1972 No. 212 (c. 3).

(b) **" Section 37 of the Interpretation Act 1889 ".**—See 32 Halsbury's Statutes (3rd Edn.) 457.

5. Short title, citation, construction and extent.—(1) This Act may be cited as the Education (No. 2) Act 1968, and shall be included among the Acts which may be cited together as the Education Acts 1944 to 1968 (a).

(2) This Act shall be construed as one with the Education Acts 1944 to 1968.

(3) This Act does not extend to Scotland or Northern Ireland.

NOTE

(a) **" Education Acts, 1944 to 1968 ".**—These comprise the Acts listed in the Note to s. 6 of the Education Act, 1967, p. 260, *ante*, together with that Act and the Education Act, 1968.

EDUCATION (HANDICAPPED CHILDREN) ACT, 1970

(1970 c. 52)

ARRANGEMENT OF SECTIONS

* * * * *

An Act to make provision, as respects England and Wales, for discontinuing the classification of handicapped children as unsuitable for education at school, and for purposes connected therewith. [23rd July 1970]

GENERAL NOTE

Under the former sections 57, 57A and 57B of the Education Act, 1944 (all of which were inserted by the Mental Health Act, 1959) a procedure was made available by which certain children could, upon medical examination, be classified as suffering from such disability of mind as to make them totally unsuitable for education in any local education authority school. The care and treatment of such children was then thrown onto the local health authority.

The present Act repeals sections 57–57B of the principal Act, thus discontinuing the procedure referred to above.

It remains the duty of local education authorities to ascertain what children require special educational treatment under s. 34 of the Act of 1944.

See, generally, Circular 5/74, p. 507, *post*.

1. Mentally handicapped children.—(1) As from such day (" the appointed day ") as the Secretary of State may appoint by order made by statutory instrument—

(*a*) no further use shall be made of the powers conferred by section 57 of the Education Act 1944 (that is to say the section having effect as section 57 by virtue of the Mental Health Act 1959) for classifying children suffering from a disability of mind as children unsuitable for education at school; and

(*b*) a local health authority shall not, under section 12 of the Health Services and Public Health Act 1968 (a) have the power or be subject to a duty to make arrangements for training children who suffer from a disability of mind and who are for purposes of the Education Act 1944 of compulsory school age;

and, where immediately before the appointed day a decision under section 57 of the Education Act 1944 was in force with respect to a child, section 34 (4) to (6) (b) of that Act shall apply as if the decision had been made, and the examination in consequence of which it was made had been carried out, under section 34.

(2) The Secretary of State shall by order make such provision as appears to him to be necessary or expedient in consequence of subsection (1) above—

(*a*) for the transfer to the employment of local education authorities of persons employed by local health authorities (not being also local education authorities) or by regional hospital boards; and

(*b*) for the protection of the interests of persons who before the appointed day have been employed for the purpose of functions of local health authorities (including those functions of authorities which are also local education authorities) or functions of regional hospital boards; and

(*c*) for the transfer to local education authorities of property, rights and liabilities of local health authorities or regional hospital boards.

(3) The provision to be made under subsection (2) (*b*) above shall include provision—

(*a*) for the payment by a Secretary of State, local health authority or local education authority, subject to such exceptions or conditions as may be prescribed by the order, of compensation to or in respect of any such persons as are referred to in subsection (2) (*b*) who suffer loss of employment or loss or diminution of emoluments which is attributable to the provisions of this section; and

(*b*) as respects any person so referred to who on the appointed day is in consequence of this section employed for the purpose of functions of a local education authority, for securing that, so long as he continues in that authority's employment for the purpose of those functions—

(i) he shall enjoy terms and conditions of employment not less favourable than those he enjoyed immediately before that date, except as regards the scale of his salary or remuneration if on that date or afterwards he ceases to be engaged in duties reasonably comparable to those in which he was engaged immediately before that date; and

(ii) in the event of his ceasing to be so engaged, the scale of his salary or remuneration shall also be not less favourable so long as he has not been served with a statement in writing of new terms and conditions of employment.

A written statement given in accordance with section 4 of the Contracts of Employment Act 1963 (c) shall not be regarded as a statement of new terms and conditions of employment for the purposes of paragraph (*b*) above unless the statement indicates that it is to be.

(4) An order under subsection (2) above may include provision—

(*a*) for the determination of questions arising under any such order and as to the manner in which and persons to whom claims for compensation are to be made;

(*b*) for applying, with or without modifications, any provision made by or under any enactment and relating to the transfer of staff between authorities;

and the provision made under subsection (2) (*b*) shall have effect notwithstanding, and may amend or repeal, any provision made by or under any enactment and relating to the remuneration of teachers or to superannuation.

(5) Any order under subsection (2) above may be varied or revoked by a subsequent order of the Secretary of State, and the power of the Secretary of State to make orders under that subsection shall be exercisable by statutory instrument which shall be subject to annulment in pursuance of a resolution of either House of Parliament.

(6) There shall be defrayed out of moneys provided by Parliament—

(*a*) any expenses incurred by a Secretary of State in the payment of compensation under any provision made in accordance with subsection (3) (*a*) above; and

(*b*) any increase attributable to this section in the sums payable out of moneys so provided by way of rate support grant.

NOTES

(a) " **Section 12 of the Health Services and Public Health Act 1968** ".—23 Halsbury's Statutes (3rd Edn.) 174.

(b) " **Section 34 (4) of the Education Act, 1944** ".—See p. 125, *ante*.

(c) " **Section 4 of the Contracts of Employment Act 1963** ".—See 12 Halsbury's Statutes (3rd Edn.) 206.

2. Citation, repeal and extent.—(1) This Act may be cited as the Education (Handicapped Children) Act 1970 . . . (a)

(2) As from the appointed day (e), the enactments mentioned in the Schedule to this Act are hereby repealed to the extent specified in the third column of that Schedule.

(3) Nothing in this Act extends to Scotland or to Northern Ireland.

NOTES

(a) The words omitted in subsection (1) were repealed by the Education (Milk) Act 1971, section 4 (3), *post*.

(b) " **Appointed day** ".—1st April, 1971. See the Education (Handicapped Children) Act, 1970 (Appointed Day) Order, 1971, S.I. 1971 No. 187.

SCHEDULE

Section 2

* * * * *

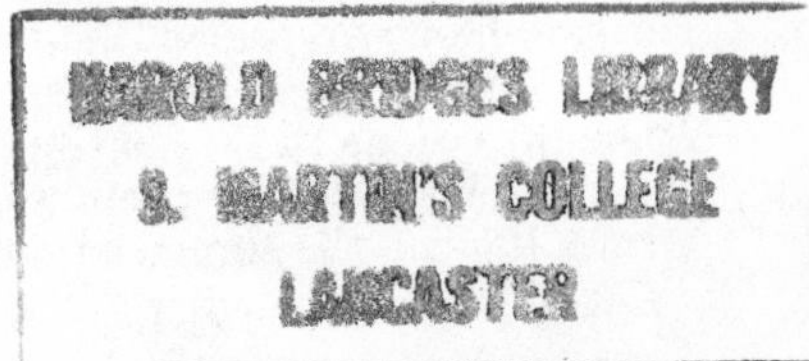

THE EDUCATION (MILK) ACT 1971

(1971 c. 74)

ARRANGEMENT OF SECTIONS

An Act to restrict the duty of education authorities to provide milk for pupils at educational establishments maintained by them or under their management and make further provision with respect to their power to do so; to restrict that power to secure provision of milk for pupils at other educational establishments; and for purposes connected therewith. [5th August 1971]

GENERAL NOTE

This Act, which does not apply to Northern Ireland, gives effect to a proposal to discontinue, in schools maintained by local education authorities in England and Wales, the supply of free milk to pupils at the end of the summer term after they reach the age of seven, unless they are attending special schools or, in the case of pupils under twelve, have a medical requirement. The Act confers power on authorities to provide milk on repayment for pupils in attendance at schools maintained by them. The Act also restricts the power of authorities to provide milk for pupils in attendance at schools not maintained by them.

1. School milk for pupils in England and Wales.—(1) Regulations made under section 49 of the Education Act 1944 (a) as to the provision of milk for pupils (*) shall not require a local education authority (*) to provide milk for a pupil after the summer term ending next after the date on which he attains the age of seven (b), unless—

(*a*) he is in attendance at a special school (c) or at a primary school (d) which is a school for providing primary education (e), or is a junior pupil (*) in attendance at a school which is deemed to be a primary school by virtue only of section 114 (3) of the Education Act 1944 or at a school which is deemed to be a primary or a secondary school by virtue of an order under section 1 (2) of the Education Act 1964 (a " middle school "); and

(*b*) (except in the case of a pupil in attendance at a special school) there is for the time being in force in respect of him a certificate given by a medical officer of the authority stating that his health requires that he should be provided with milk at school (*).

(2) Regulations made under section 49 may also confer power on local education authorities to provide milk for pupils in attendance at schools maintained by them, but any regulations so made by virtue of this subsection shall require the expense of providing milk in the exercise of the power to be defrayed by the pupils for whom it is provided or their parents (*).

(3) The power under section 78 (2) (*a*) of the Education Act 1944 (f) to make arrangements as to the provision of milk for pupils in attendance at schools not maintained by the local authority shall not apply to a pupil after the summer term ending next after the date on which he attains the age of seven unless he is in attendance at a special school.

(4) Section 3 of the Public Expenditure and Receipts Act 1968 (in so far as it applies to England and Wales) and the Education (School Milk) Act 1970 are hereby repealed; and any regulations or arrangements made before the coming into force of this section shall cease to have effect in so far as they make provisions to the contrary of subsection (1) or (3) above.

(5) This section, except subsection (2), shall not have effect until the term following the summer term 1971.

(6) In this section " summer term " means the term ending last before the month of September.

NOTES

(*) As to the meaning of " junior pupil ", " local education authority ", " maintain ", " parent ", " primary education ", " pupil " and " school ", see pp. 67–69, *ante.*
(a) **" Section 49 of the Education Act 1944 ".**—See p. 141, *ante.*
(b) **" Attains the age of seven ".**—As to the time at which a person attains a particular age, see s. 9 of the Family Law Reform Act 1969.
(c) **" Special school ".**—See s. 9 (5) of the Education Act 1944, *ante.*
(d) **" Primary school ".**—See s. 114 (1), (3) of the Education Act 1944, *ante,* and s. 1 (2) of the Education Act 1964, *ante.*
(e) **" Primary education ".**—See ss. 7, 8 of the Education Act 1944, *ante.*
(f) **" Section 78 (2) (a) of the Education Act 1944 ".**—See p. 165, *ante.*

2. (*Applies to Scotland.*)

3. Effect of sections 1 and 2 on rate support grant.—(1) The Secretary of State (a), in the exercise of his power, under section 3 (1) of the Local Government Act 1966 (b), to make an order varying, with respect to any year, a rate support grant order (c), may take into account any relief obtained or likely to be obtained, during the period covered by the rate support grant order by local authorities—

(*a*) which is attributable to the coming into operation of any provision of section 1 of this Act, and

(*b*) which was not taken into account in making the rate support grant order the variation of which is in question and has not since been taken into account by virtue of this subsection in making an order under section 3 (1) with respect to any other year comprised in that period.

The provisions of this subsection are without prejudice to section 3 (4) of the Local Government Act 1966 (under which an order under that section may vary the matters prescribed by a rate support grant order).

(2) (*Applies to Scotland.*)

NOTES

(a) **" Secretary of State ".**—This expression means " one of Her Majesty's Principal Secretaries of State for the time being ": see s. 12 (3) of the Interpretation Act 1889.
(b) **" Local Government Act 1966, ss. 3 (1), (4) ".**—Repealed by the Local Government Act 1966.
(c) **" Rate support grant order ".**—See sections 2–5 of the Local Government Act 1974.

4. Citation, construction, repeal and extent.—(1) This Act may be cited as the Education (Milk) Act 1971.

(2) The Education Acts 1944 to 1968 (a), the Education (Handicapped Children) Act 1970 (b), and this Act (in so far as it applies to England and Wales), may be cited together as the Education Acts 1944 to 1971.

(3) This Act, in its application to England and Wales, shall be construed as one (c) with the Education Acts 1944 to 1968, and, in its application to Scotland shall be construed as one with the Education (Scotland) Acts 1939 to 1971.

(4) In section 2 (1) of the Education (Handicapped Children) Act 1970 the words from " and " to the end of the subsection are hereby repealed.

(5) This Act does not extend to Northern Ireland.

NOTES

(a) **" Education Acts 1944 to 1968 ".**—See General Note to the Education Act 1944, p. 73, *ante.*
(b) **" Education (Handicapped Children) Act 1970 ".**—See p. 269, *ante.*
(c) **" Construed as one ".**—*I.e.,* the provisions in question are to be construed as if they were contained in one Act unless there is a manifest discrepancy; see, for example, *Phillips* v. *Parnaby,* [1934] 2 K.B. 299; [1934] All E.R. Rep. 267, at p. 302 and p. 269, respectively. It follows, in particular, that definitions applicable to the Education Act 1944 are, so far as applicable, relevant to the construction of this Act; cf. *Crowe* (*Valuation Officer*) v. *Lloyds British Testing Co., Ltd.,* [1960] 1 All E.R. 411; [1960] 1 Q.B. 592; and *Kirkness* v. *Hudson* (*John*) *& Co., Ltd.,* [1955] 2 All E.R. 345; [1955] A.C. 696.

THE EDUCATION ACT 1973

(1973 c. 16)

ARRANGEMENT OF SECTIONS

An Act to make provision for terminating and in part replacing the powers possessed by the Secretary of State for Education and Science and the Secretary of State for Wales under the Charities Act 1960 *concurrently with the Charity Commissioners or under the Endowed Schools Acts* 1869 *to* 1948, *and enlarging certain other powers of modifying educational trusts, and for supplementing awards under section* 1 *and restricting awards under section* 2 *of the Education Act* 1962, *and for purposes connected therewith.* [18th April 1973]

GENERAL NOTE

The first two sections of this Act contain general provisions as to educational trusts, and give special powers as to certain trusts for religious education. Section 2 of the Charities Act 1960 (under which the Secretary of State for Education and Science and the Secretary of State for Wales exercised powers over educational trusts concurrently with the Charity Commissioners) is repealed. So too are the Endowed Schools Acts 1869 to 1948, which formerly made provisions for the modernisation of educational trusts by schemes settled and approved in accordance with the Acts. The Secretary of State may, under the present Act, make modifications of any trust deed or other instrument (after consultations) as appear to him to be requisite under the provisions of ss. 13, 16, 33 or 100 of the Education Act 1944.

As to trusts for religious education, the Secretary of State is empowered, where premises have ceased to be used for a voluntary school, to make new provisions as to the use of endowments, where these have been held wholly or in part for the provision of religious education. An order may require or authorise the sale or other disposal of land.

Section 3 of this Act empowers the Secretary of State to make provision for supplementary awards to students in respect of any husband, wife or child (whether legitimate or illegitimate) so that students with such ties may continue their studies without hardship.

Section 4 of the Act enables the Secretary of State to exclude certain postgraduate courses from entitlement to grants.

Educational trusts

1. General provisions as to educational trusts.—(1) There shall cease to have effect—

(*a*) section 2 of the Charities Act 1960 (a) (by which, as originally enacted, the powers of the Charity Commissioners (b) were made exercisable concurrently by the Minister of Education (c)); and

(*b*) the Endowed Schools Acts 1869 to 1948 (d) (which made provision for the modernisation of educational trusts by schemes settled and approved in accordance with those Acts).

(2) The Secretary of State may by order—

(*a*) make such modifications of any trust deed or other instrument relating to a school (*) as, after consultation with the managers (*), governors or other proprietor of the school, appear to him to be requisite in consequence of any proposals approved or order made by him under section 13 or 16 of the Education Act 1944 (e) (which relate to the establishment of and changes affecting schools); and

(*b*) make such modifications of any trust deed (*) or other instrument relating to a school as, after consultation with the governors or other proprietor (*) of the school, appear to him to be requisite to enable the governors or proprietor to meet any requirement imposed by regulations under section 33 of the Education Act 1944 (f) (which relates in particular to the approval of schools as special schools (*)); and

(*c*) make such modifications of any trust deed or other instrument relating to or regulating any institution that provides or is concerned in the provision of educational services, or is concerned in educational research, as, after consultation with the persons responsible for the management of the institution, appear to him to be requisite to enable them to fulfil any condition or meet any requirement imposed by regulations under section 100 of the Education Act 1944 (g) (which authorises the making of grants in aid of educational services or research);

and any such modification made by an order under the subsection may be made to have permanent effect or to have effect for such period as may be specified in the order.

This subsection shall be construed, and the Education Acts 1944 to 1971 (h) shall have effect, as if this subsection were contained in the Education Act 1944.

(3) In connection with the operation of this section there shall have effect the transitional and other consequential or supplementary provisions contained in Schedule 1 to this Act.

(4) The enactments mentioned in Schedule 2 to this Act (which includes in Part I certain enactments already spent or otherwise no longer required apart from the foregoing provisions of this section) are hereby repealed to the extent specified in column 3 of the Schedule.

(5) Subsection (1) (*a*) above and Part III of Schedule 2 to this Act shall not come into force until such date as may be appointed by order (i) made by statutory instrument by the Secretary of State.

NOTES

This section repeals s. 2 of the Charities Act 1960, under which the Secretary of State for Education and Science had exercised powers over educational trusts concurrently with the Charity Commissioners. The Secretary of State retains the power to modify trust deeds or other instruments as seem to him requisite under certain sections of the principal Act. The section also repeals the Endowed Schools Acts 1869 to 1948, which had provided for the modernisation of educational trusts.

(*) As to the meaning or statutory definition of " school", " managers or governors ", "trust deed ", " proprietor " and " special school ", see pp. 67–69, *ante*.

(a) **" Section 2 of the Charities Act 1960 ".**—See 3 Halsbury's Statutes (3rd Edn.) 591. That section (hereby repealed) provided that any functions conferred on the Charity Commissioners should be functions equally of the Secretary of State for Education and Science, so that either could do anything necessary under or for the purposes of the trusts of a charity.

(b) **" Charity Commissioners ".**—See s. 1 of the Charities Act 1960 (3 Halsbury's Statutes (3rd Edn.) 590).

(c) **" Minister of Education ".**—Now Secretary of State for Education and Science. See note (b) to s. 1 of the Act of 1944.

(d) **" Endowed Schools Acts 1869 to 1948 ".**—These were the Endowed Schools Act 1869; the Endowed Schools Act 1873; three Acts previously repealed; and the Education (Miscellaneous Provisions) Act 1948, s. 2 and Sch. 1, Part II (see 11 Halsbury's Statutes (3rd Edn.) 346, 365, 372). They empowered the Secretary of State to make schemes as to educational endowments. See now his powers to modify trust deeds, etc., under the present section.

(e) **" Section 13 or 16 of the Education Act 1944 ".**—Section 13 (p. 90, *ante*) states the powers of a local education authority in connection with the provision of new county schools, the transfer of schools other than county schools to the authority and the discontinuance of maintenance of county or voluntary schools. Section 16 (p. 99, *ante*) applies (*a*) to the transfer of a county or voluntary school to a new site because the existing premises cannot reasonably be brought up to the prescribed standards, or for certain other reasons, and (*b*) in circumstances where a denominational body seeks to establish a new voluntary school in substitution for one or more voluntary schools which are to be closed.

(f) "**Section 33 of the Education Act 1944**".—This section (p. 122, *ante*) deals with the education of pupils requiring special educational treatment, and the approval of special schools.

(g) "**Section 100 of the Education Act 1944**".—This section (p. 175, *ante*) authorises the making of grants in aid of educational services or educational research.

(h) "**Education Acts 1944 to 1971**".—See General Note to the Education Act 1944, p. 73, *ante*.

(i) "**Date . . . appointed by order**".—Subsection (1) (*a*) and Part III of Sch. 2 came into force on 1st February, 1974: see the Education Act 1973 (Commencement) Order 1973, S.I. 1973 No. 1661, *post*.

2. Special powers as to certain trusts for religious education.—(1) Where the premises of a voluntary school (*) have ceased (before or after the coming into force of this section) to be used for a voluntary school, or in the opinion of the Secretary of State (a) it is likely they will cease to be so used, then subject to subsections (2) to (4) below he may by order made by statutory instrument make new provision as to the use of any endowment shown to his satisfaction to be or have been held wholly or partly for or in connection with the provision at the school of religious education in accordance with the tenets of a particular religious denomination; and for purposes of this section " endowment " includes property not subject to any restriction on the expenditure of capital.

(2) No order shall be made under subsection (1) above except on the application of the persons appearing to the Secretary of State to be the appropriate authority of the denomination concerned; and the Secretary of State shall, not less than one month before making an order under that subsection, give notice of the proposed order and of the right of persons interested to make representations on it, and shall take into account any representations that may be made to him by any person interested therein before the order is made; and the notice shall be given—

(*a*) by giving to any persons appearing to the Secretary of State to be trustees of an endowment affected by the proposed order a notice of the proposal to make it, together with a draft or summary of the provisions proposed to be included; and

(*b*) by publishing in such manner as the Secretary of State thinks sufficient for informing any other persons interested a notice of the proposal to make the order and of the place where any person interested may (during a period of not less than a month) inspect such a draft or summary, and by keeping a draft or summary available for inspection in accordance with the notice.

(3) An order under subsection (1) above may require or authorise the disposal by sale or otherwise of any land or other property forming part of an endowment affected by the order, including the premises of the school and any teacher's dwelling-house; and in the case of land liable to revert under the third proviso to section 2 of the School Sites Act 1841 (b) the Secretary of State may by order exclude the operation of that proviso, if he is satisfied either—

(*a*) that the person to whom the land would revert in accordance with the proviso cannot after due enquiry be found; or

(*b*) that, if that person can be found, he has consented to relinquish his rights in relation to the land under the proviso and that, if he has consented so to do in consideration of the payment of a sum of money to him, adequate provision can be made for the payment to him, of that sum out of the proceeds of disposal of the land.

(4) Subject to subsection (3) above and to any provision affecting the endowments of any public general Act of Parliament, an order under subsection (1) above shall establish and give effect, with a view to enabling the denomination concerned to participate more effectively in the administration of the statutory system of public education, to a scheme or schemes for the

endowments dealt with by the order to be used for appropriate educational purposes, either in connection with voluntary schools or partly in connection with voluntary schools and partly in other ways related to the locality served or formerly served by the voluntary school at the premises that have gone or are to go out of use for such a school; and for this purpose " use for appropriate educational purposes " means use for educational purposes in connection with the provision of religious education in accordance with the tenets of the denomination concerned.

(5) A scheme given effect under this section may provide for the retention of the capital of any endowment and application of the accruing income or may authorise the application or expenditure of capital to such extent and subject to such conditions as may be determined by or in accordance with the scheme; and any such scheme may provide for the endowments thereby dealt with or any part of them to be added to any existing endowment applicable for any such purpose as is authorised for the scheme by subsection (4) above.

(6) An order under subsection (1) above may include any such incidental or supplementary provisions as appear to the Secretary of State to be necessary or expedient either for the bringing into force or for the operation of any scheme thereby established, including in particular provisions for the appointment and powers of trustees of the property comprised in the scheme or, if the property is not all applicable for the same purposes, of any part of that property, and for the property or any part of it to vest by virtue of the scheme in the first trustees under the scheme or trustees of any endowment to which it is to be added or, if not so invested, to be transferred to them.

(7) Any order under this section shall have effect notwithstanding any Act of Parliament (not being a public general Act), letters patent or other instrument relating to, or trust affecting, the endowments dealt with by the order; but section 15 (3) of the Charities Act 1960 (c) (by virtue of which the court and the Charity Commissioners may exercise their jurisdiction in relation to charities mentioned in Schecule 4 to the Act (d) notwithstanding that the charities are governed by the Acts or statutory schemes there mentioned) shall have effect as if at the end of paragraph 1 (*b*) of Schedule 4 to the Act there were added the words " or by schemes given effect under section 2 of the Education Act 1973 ".

(8) This section shall apply where the premises of a non-provided public elementary school ceased before 1st April, 1945 to be used for such a school as it applies where the premises of a voluntary school have ceased to be used for a voluntary school.

(9) This section shall be construed, and the Education Acts 1944 to 1971 (e) shall have effect, as if this section were contained in the Education Act 1944.

NOTES

This section empowers the Secretary of State to make new provisions as to the use of endowments where the premises of a voluntary school have ceased, or are likely to cease, to be used for a voluntary school. Such endowment must have been held wholly or partly for, or in connection with, the provision at the school of religious education of a particular denomination. No order may be made without the application of the authority of the religious denomination concerned; and one month's notice must be given of any proposed order, before it is made. The order may require or authorise the disposal of land or other property.

(*) As to the meaning of " voluntary school ", see p. 79, *ante*.

(a) **" Secretary of State ".**—See note (b) to s. 1 of the Act of 1944.

(b) **" Section 2 of the School Sites Act 1841 ".**—This section (11 Halsbury's Statutes (3rd Edn.) 381) provides that land not exceeding one acre in extent may be conveyed for use as a site for a school, or for a residence for a school-master or school-mistress, provided that the person who would otherwise next be entitled joins in the grant. The third proviso, referred to above, provides that where land so granted ceases to be used for such purpose, it shall revert to and become part of the original estate or manor from which it originally came. In certain circumstances, by the present section, the operation of this proviso may be excluded, *e.g.*, where the person to whom the land would normally revert cannot be found.

(c) **" Section 15 (3) of the Charities Act 1960 ".**—See 3 Halsbury's Statutes (3rd Edn.) 609.

(d) **" Schedule 4 to the Act ".**—*I.e.*, to the Charities Act 1960. See 3 Halsbury's Statutes (3rd Edn.) 650.

(e) " **Education Acts 1944 to 1971** ".—See the General Note to the Education Act 1944, p. 73, *ante*.

Awards

3. Supplementation by Secretary of State, in special cases, of certain awards by local education authority.—(1) The Secretary of State (a) may by regulations (b) make provision for the payment by him to persons on whom awards have been bestowed by a local education authority (*) under section 1 of the Education Act 1962 (awards for first degree university courses and comparable courses in the United Kingdom), of an allowance in respect of a wife, husband or child for the purpose of enabling those persons to take advantage without hardship of their awards in cases where, in accordance with the regulations having effect under that section, account may not be taken of the wife, husband or child in determining the payments to be made by the authority in pursuance of the award.

(2) The amount of an allowance payable by virtue of this section to the holder of an award in respect of a wife, husband or child shall not exceed the amount by which the payments to be made by the local education authority in pursuance of the award would have been increased if the case had fallen within the provision made with respect to a wife, husband or child by the regulations having effect under section 1 of the Education Act 1962.

(3) Regulations under this section may make different provision for different cases; and the power of the Secretary of State to make regulations under this section shall be exercisable by statutory instrument which shall be subject to annulment on pursuance of a resolution of either House of Parliament.

(4) Any expenses incurred by the Secretary of State in the payment of allowances under this section shall be defrayed out of moneys provided by Parliament.

(5) In this section references to a person's child include that person's stepchild or illegitimate child and a child adopted by that person (alone or jointly with another) in pursuance of an order made by any court in the United Kingdom, the Isle of Man or the Channel Islands or by an adoption specified as an overseas adoption by order of the Secretary of State under section 4 of the Adoption Act 1968.

NOTES

This section provides for supplementary grants to be made where a student has a wife, husband or child (including a stepchild or illegitimate child).

(*) As to the meaning of " local education authority ", see p. 68, *ante*.

(a) " **Secretary of State** ".—See note (b) to s. 1 of the Act of 1944.

(b) " **Regulations** ".—See the Students' Dependants' Allowances Regulations 1975, S.I. 1975 No. 1225, *post*, which (excepting regulation 7) are to be construed as one with the Local Education Authorities Awards Regulations 1975, S.I. 1975 No. 1207, *post*.

4. Exclusion of postgraduate courses from grants under section 2 (1) of Education Act 1962.—(1) Section 2 (1) of the Education Act 1962 (a) (powers of local education authorities to bestow awards on persons over compulsory school age attending certain courses in Great Britain or elsewhere) shall not apply to such courses at universities, colleges or other institutions as may for the time being be designated by or under regulations (b) made by the Secretary of State for the purposes of this section as being postgraduate courses or comparable to postgraduate courses.

(2) The power of the Secretary of State to make regulations under this section shall be exercisable by statutory instrument, which shall be subject to annulment in pursuance of a resolution of either House of Parliament.

NOTES

(a) " **Section 2 (1) of the Education Act 1962** ".—See p. 244, *ante*.

(b) " **Regulations** ".—See the Postgraduate, etc., Courses (Exclusion from Discretionary Awards) Regulations 1973, S.I. 1973 No. 1232, *post*.

Supplementary

5. Citation and extent.—(1) This Act may be cited as the Education Act 1973, and the Education Acts 1944 to 1971 (a) and this Act may be cited together as the Education Acts 1944 to 1973.

(2) Nothing in this Act extends to Scotland or to Northern Ireland.

NOTE

(a) **" Education Acts 1944 to 1971 ".**—See the General Note to the Education Act 1944, p. 73, *ante*.

SCHEDULES

SCHEDULE 1

TRANSITIONAL AND SUPPLEMENTARY PROVISIONS AS TO CHARITIES ETC.

1.—(1) In section 43 of the Charities Act 1960, in its application to regulations made on or after the appointed day, there shall be substituted for subsection (1)—

> " (1) Save as otherwise provided by this Act, any power to make regulations which is conferred by this Act shall be exercisable by the Secretary of State ";

and in subsection (3) for the words (as originally enacted) " the Secretary of State or the Minister of Education " there shall be substituted the words " or the Secretary of State ".

(2) Section 210 (3) of the Local Government Act 1972 (which makes special provision for certain charitable property to vest in local education authorities, if it is held for purposes of a charity registered in a part of the charities register maintained by the Secretary of State by virtue of section 2 of the Charities Act 1960) shall have effect, unless the appointed day is later than the end of March 1974, as if the reference to a charity registered in a part of the register which is maintained by the Secretary of State were a reference to a charity so registered immediately before the appointed day.

(3) Any register, books and documents which on the appointed day are in the possession or custody of the Secretary of State for Education and Science, or of the Secretary of State for Wales, and which in his opinion he requires no longer by reason of the repeal of section 2 (1) of the Charities Act 1960, shall be transferred to the Charity Commissioners.

(4) The repeal by this Act of section 2 (1) of the Charities Act 1960 shall not affect the operation of section 2 (1)—

(*a*) in conferring on the Charity Commissioners functions belonging at the passing of that Act to the Minister of Education; or

(*b*) in extending to the Charity Commissioners references to the Secretary of State for Education and Science or the Secretary of State for Wales (or references having effect as if either of them were mentioned) so as to enable the Commissioners to discharge any such functions as aforesaid or to act under or for the purposes of the trusts of a charity;

but on the appointed day any functions so conferred and any reference so extended shall, subject to sub-paragraph (5) below, cease to be functions of or to extend to either Secretary of State.

(5) Where it appears to the Secretary of State for Education and Science or the Secretary of State for Wales that any reference which, in accordance with sub-paragraph (4) above would on the appointed day cease to extend to him, is not related (or not wholly related) to the functions ceasing to belong to him by the repeal of section 2 (1) of the Charities Act 1960, he may by order made at any time, whether before the appointed day or not, exclude the operation of that sub-paragraph in relation to the reference and make such modifications of the relevant instrument as appear to him approrpriate in the circumstances.

(6) The repeal of section 2 (1) of the Charities Act 1960 shall not effect the validity of anything done (or having effect as if done) before the appointed day by or in relation to the Secretary of State for Education and Science or the Secretary of State for Wales, and anything so done (or having effect as if so done) in so far as it could by virtue of section 2 (1) have been done by or in relation to the Charity Commissioners shall thereafter have effect as if done by or in relation to them.

(7) In this paragraph " appointed day " means the day appointed under section 1 (5) of this Act.

2.—(1) Where before the passing of this Act a scheme under the Endowed Schools Acts 1869 to 1948 has been published as required by section 13 of the Endowed Schools Act 1873, the scheme may be proceeded with as if section 1 of this Act had not been passed.

(2) Where before the passing of this Act a draft scheme under the Endowed Schools Acts 1869 to 1948 has been prepared in a case in which effect might be given to the scheme by order under section 2 of this Act, and the draft scheme has been published as required

by section 33 of the Endowed Schools Act 1869, the scheme may be proceeded with in pursuance of section 2 of this Act as if section 2 (2) (*a*) and (*b*) had been complied with on the date this Act is passed.

3. The repeals made by this Act in sections 17 and 100 of the Education Act 1944 shall not affect any order made by virtue of the provisions repealed, or the operation in relation to any such order of section 111 of that Act (which relates to the revocation and variation of orders).

SCHEDULE 2

REPEALS

(*Repeals of spent etc. enactments and other repeals.*)

THE EDUCATION (WORK EXPERIENCE) ACT 1973

(1973 c. 23)

An Act to enable education authorities to arrange for children under school-leaving age to have work experience, as part of their education.

[23rd May 1973]

This Act enables education authorities to arrange for children to have work experience, as part of their education, in the last year of compulsory schooling. The present compulsory school-leaving age is sixteen years: see s. 35 of the Education Act 1944, as amended, p. 127, *ante*. See, generally, Circular 7/74, *post*.

1. Work experience in last year of compulsory schooling.—(1) Subject to subsection (2) below, the enactments relating to the prohibition or regulation of the employment of children (a) shall not apply to the employment of a child in his last year of compulsory school (b) where the employment is in pursuance of arrangements made or approved by the local education authority with a view to providing him with work experience as part of his education.

(2) Subsection (1) above shall not be taken to permit the employment of any person in any way contrary to—

(*a*) an enactment which in terms applies to persons of less than, or not over, a specified age expressed as a number of years; or

(*b*) section 1 (2) of the Employment of Women, Young Persons and Children Act 1920 (c) or (when it comes into force) section 51 (1) of the Merchant Shipping Act 1970 (d) (prohibition of employment of children in ships;

(3) No arrangements shall be made under subsection (1) above for a child to be employed in any way which would be contrary to an enactment prohibiting or regulating the employment of young persons (e) if he were a young person (within the meaning of that enactment) and not a child; and where a child is employed in pursuance of arrangements so made, then so much of any enactment as regulates the employment of young persons (whether by excluding them from any description of work, or prescribing the conditions under which they may be permitted to do it, or otherwise howsoever) and would apply in relation to him if he were of an age to be treated as a young person for the purpose of that enactment shall apply in relation to him, in and in respect of the employment arranged for him, in all respects as if he were of an age to be so treated.

(4) In this Act—

"enactment" includes any byelaw, regulation or other provision having effect under an enactment;

other expressions which are also used in the Education Acts shall have the same meaning in this section as in those Acts; and

"the Education Acts" means in England and Wales the Education Acts 1944 to 1973 and, in Scotland, the Education (Scotland) Acts 1939 to 1971;

and for the purposes of subsection (1) above a child is in his last year of compulsory schooling at any time during the period of twelve months before he attains the upper limit of compulsory school age, or in Scotland, school age.

NOTES

(a) **"Enactments relating to the prohibition or regulation of the employment of children".**—See particularly the Employment of Children Act 1973 (43 Halsbury's Statutes (3rd Edn.) 637).

(b) **"Compulsory schooling".**—The compulsory school age is now sixteen: see s. 35 of the Education Act 1944, as amended, p. 127, *ante*.

(c) **"Employment of Women, Young Persons and Children Act 1920".**—12 Halsbury's Statutes (3rd Edn.) 58.

(d) **"Section 51 (1) of the Merchant Shipping Act 1970".**—31 Halsbury's Statutes (3rd Edn.) 770.

(e) **"Enactment prohibiting or regulating the employment of young persons".**—See, *e.g.*, the Children and Young Persons Acts 1933 to 1969 and the Young Persons (Employment) Act 1938. See also as to the meaning of "young person", s. 114 (1) of the Education Act 1944, p. 185, *ante*.

2.—(1) This Act may be cited as the Education (Work Experience) Act 1973; and—

(*a*) in relation to England and Wales, this Act shall be included among the Acts which may be cited together as the Education Acts 1944 to 1973 (a); and

(*b*) in relation to Scotland the Education Acts and this Act may be cited together as the Education (Scotland) Acts 1939 to 1973.

(2) Nothing in this Act extends to Northern Ireland.

NOTE

(a) **"Education Acts 1944 to 1973".**—These may, together with the Education Act 1975, be cited as the Education Acts 1944 to 1975.

THE EDUCATION ACT 1975

(1975 c. 2)

ARRANGEMENT OF SECTIONS

An Act to make further provision with respect to awards and grants by local education authorities; to enable the Secretary of State to bestow awards on students in respect of their attendance at adult education colleges; and to increase the proportion of the expenditure incurred in the maintenance or provision of aided and special agreement schools that can be met by contributions or grants from the Secretary of State. [25th February 1975]

GENERAL NOTE

This Act relates to awards and grants made by local education authorities and by the Secretary of State for Education and Science.

Section 1 (1) adds to the courses in respect of which the Education Act 1962, imposes a duty on local education authorities to bestow awards, while s. 1 (2) restricts the requirement of educational qualifications for an award to courses designated as comparable to first degree courses. Section 1 (3) extends s. 2 (1) of the Act of 1962 (discretionary powers of local education authorities to make awards for courses of further education not falling within s. 1 of that Act) to any course for the training of teachers.

Section 2 amends s. 3 of the Education Act 1962, enabling the Secretary of State to bestow awards on students attending courses at designated long-term residential colleges of adult education. Section 3 increases the rate at which contributions and grants may be made for aided and special agreement schools.

1. Awards and grants by local education authorities.—(1) Section 1 of the Education Act 1962 (a) (local education authority (*) awards for designated first degree courses or comparable courses) shall apply also to such courses at universities, colleges or other institutions in Great Britain and Northern Ireland as may for the time being be designated by or under regulations (b) made for the purposes of that section as being—

(*a*) full-time courses for the diploma of higher education or the higher national diploma; or

(*b*) courses for the initial training of teachers.

(2) Paragraph (*b*) of subsection (1) of the said section 1 (eligibility for award dependent on possession of requisite educational qualifications) shall apply only in relation to courses for the time being designated for the purposes of that section as being comparable to first degree courses.

(3) Section 2 (1) of the said Act of 1962 (local education authority awards for courses of further education not falling within section 1 of that Act) shall apply also to any course for the training of teachers (whether held in Great Britain or elsewhere) to which section 1 of that Act does not apply including, in relation to a person undergoing training as a teacher, any course which he attends as such training and which is for the time being designated under section 4 of the Education Act 1973 (b) (postgraduate courses).

(4) Subsections (2) and (3) of section 4 of the said Act of 1962 (regulations under sections 1 to 3 of that Act) shall apply also in relation to subsection (1) above; and subsection (6) of that section (meaning of " training " and " person undergoing training " in section 2 of that Act) shall apply also in relation to subsection (3) above.

NOTES

(*) For the meaning of " local education authority ", see p. 68, *ante*.

(a) **" Education Act 1962 ".**—For ss. 1–4 of the Act of 1962, and the notes thereto, see pp. 240 *et seq.*, *ante*.

(b) **" Regulations ".**—At the time of going to press, no regulations had been made under this section.

(c) **" Education Act 1973 ".**—For s. 4 of that Act, see p. 278 *ante*.

2. Awards by Secretary of State for students at adult education colleges.—[*This section amends s.* 3 *of the Education Act* 1962, *which is printed as so amended at p.* 244, *ante.*]

3. Contributions and grants for aided and special agreement schools.—[*This section amends ss.* 102 *and* 103 *of the Education Act* 1944, *and s.* 1 (2) *of the Education Act* 1967. *These sections are printed as so amended at pp.* 176, 177, 255, *ante.*]

4. Repeals.—The enactments mentioned in the Schedule to this Act are hereby repealed to the extent specified in the third column of that Schedule.

5. Citation, interpretation, commencement and extent.—(1) This Act may be cited as the Education Act 1975.

(2) The Education Acts 1944 to 1973 (a) and this Act may be cited together as the Education Acts 1944 to 1975.

(3) Any reference in this Act to any enactment is a reference to that enactment as amended by any subsequent enactment.

(4) Subsection (2) of section 1 above shall not come into force until 1st September 1975; and subsection (3) of that section and Part I of the Schedule to this Act shall not come into force until the first regulations made by virtue of subsection (1) (*b*) of that section come into operation.

(5) Nothing in section 3 above or in Part II of the Schedule to this Act affects contributions or grants in respect of expenditure on work which was begun before 6th November 1974 or on the provision of the site on which, or buildings to which, any such work was done.

(6) This Act does not extend to Scotland or Northern Ireland.

NOTES

(a) **" Education Acts 1944 to 1973 ".**—For the citation of the Education Acts generally, see the General Note to the Education Act 1944, p. 73, *ante*.

SCHEDULE

REPEALS

PART I

[*Amends s.* 2 *of the Education Act* 1962, p. 244, *ante and ss.* 1 *and* 8 *of the Local Government Act* 1974, as from the date when regulations come into operation: see s. 5 (4), *supra*.]

PART II

[*Amends s.* 1 (1) *of the Education Act* 1967, *p.* 258, *ante*.]

THE EDUCATION (SCHOOL-LEAVING DATES) ACT 1976

(1976 c. 5)

An Act to make further provision with respect to school-leaving dates; and for connected purposes [25th March 1976]

1. Alteration of summer school-leaving date

(1) For subsections (3) and (4) of section 9 of the Education Act 1962 (under which a person who attains the age of 16 between the end of January and the beginning of September is deemed to attain the upper limit of compulsory school age at the end of the summer term) there shall be substituted—

" (3) If he attains that age (a) after the end of January but before the next May school-leaving date, he shall be deemed not to have attained that age until that date.

(4) If he attains that age after the May school-leaving date and before the beginning of September next following that date, he shall be deemed to have attained that age on that date. "

(2) After subsection (7) of that section there shall be added—

" (8) In this section " the May school-leaving date " means the Friday before the last Monday in May. "

NOTE

(a) **" Attains that age ".**—A person attains a given age at the beginning of the relevant anniversary of the date of his birth; see the Family Law Reform Act 1969.

* * * * *

3. Citation, repeals, commencement and extent

(1) This Act may be cited as the Education (School-leaving Dates) Act 1976.

(2) The Education Acts 1944 to 1975 (a) and this Act may be cited together as the Education Acts 1944 to 1976.

(3) The enactments mentioned in the Schedule to this Act (which include provisions that are spent in consequence of the Raising of the School Leaving Age Order 1972 (b)) are hereby repealed to the extent specified in the third column of that Schedule.

(4) Section 21 (2) of the Child Benefit Act 1975 (repeals consequential on the introduction of child benefit) shall have effect as if section 2 (1) to (3) above were included among the enactments mentioned in Part I of Schedule 5 to that Act.

(5) Section 2 (4) above and so much of the Schedule to this Act as relates to the Social Security Act 1975 shall not come into force until 6th April 1976.

(6) This Act does not extend to Northern Ireland; and section 1 above does not extend to Scotland.

NOTES

(a) **Education Acts 1944 to 1975.**—For the Acts that may be cited together by this collective title, see the General Note to the Education Act 1944, p. 73, *ante*.

(b) **Raising of the School Leaving Age Order 1972.**—S.I. 1972 No. 444, *post*. That order was made under the Education Act 1944, s. 35, *ante*.

SCHEDULE

Section 3 (3)

REPEALS

Chapter	Short Title	Extent of Repeal
7 & 8 Geo. 6. c. 31	The Education Act 1944	Section 38 (1). In section 114, in subsection (1) in the definition of " compulsory school age " the words " subject to the provisions of section thirty-eight of this Act " and subsection (6).
10 & 11 Eliz. 2. c. 12	The Education Act 1962	In section 9, the proviso to subsection (5), subsection (6) and in subsection (7) the definition of the " the appropriate summer term " (together with the word " and " immediately preceding it) and the words " or month of September (as the case may be) ".
1964 c. 82	The Education Act 1964	Section 2. In section 5 (3) and (6) the words " and 2 ".

* * * * *

PART II

STATUTES

DIVISION B

OTHER RELEVANT ENACTMENTS

SUMMARY

THE REPRESENTATION OF THE PEOPLE ACT, 1949

(12, 13 & 14 Geo. 6c 68)

ARRANGEMENT OF SECTIONS

* * * * *

* * * * *

An Act to consolidate certain enactments relating to parliamentary and local government elections, corrupt and illegal practices and election petitions.

GENERAL NOTE

The two sections printed below provide for the use of schools at times of parliamentary and local government elections.

As to the use of school rooms as polling stations, see Schedule 2 of the Act (11 Halsbury's Statutes (3rd Edn.) 736, 737).

* * * * *

Election meetings

82. Right to use certain schools and halls for meetings at parliamentary elections.—(1) Subject to the provisions of this section a candidate at a parliamentary election shall be entitled for the purpose of holding public meetings in furtherance of his candidature to the use at reasonable times between the receipt of the writ and the date of the poll of—

(*a*) a suitable room in the premises of any school to which this section applies;

(*b*) any meeting room to which this section applies.

(2) This section applies—

(*a*) in England and Wales, to county schools and voluntary schools of which the premises are situated in the constituency or an adjoining constituency; and

(*b*) [*Relates to Scotland*];

but a candidate shall not be entitled under this section to the use of a room in school premises outside the constituency if there is a suitable room in other premises in the constituency which are reasonably accessible from the same parts of the constituency as those outside and are premises of a school to which this section applies.

(3) This section applies to meeting rooms situated in the constituency, the expense of maintaining which is payable wholly or mainly out of public funds or out of any rate, or by a body whose expenses are so payable.

(4) Where a room is used for a meeting in pursuance of the rights conferred by this section, the person by whom or on whose behalf the meeting is convened—

(*a*) may be required to pay for the use of the room a charge not exceeding the amount of any actual and necessary expenses incurred in preparing, warming, lighting and cleaning the room and providing attendance for the meeting and restoring the room to its usual condition after the meeting; and

(*b*) shall defray any damage done to the room or the premises in which it is situated, or to the furniture, fittings or apparatus in the room or premises.

(5) A candidate shall not be entitled to exercise the rights conferred by this section except on reasonable notice; and this section shall not

authorise any interference with the hours during which a room in school premises is used for educational purposes, or any interference with the use of a meeting room either for the purposes of the person maintaining it or under a prior agreement for its letting for any purpose.

(6) The provisions of the Seventh Schedule (a) to this Act shall have effect with respect to the rights conferred by this section and the arrangements to be made for their exercise.

(7) For the purposes of this section (except those of paragraph (*b*) of subsection (4) thereof), the premises of a school shall not be taken to include any private dwelling house, and in this section—

(*a*) the expression " meeting room " means any room which it is the practice to let for public meetings; and

(*b*) the expression " room " includes a hall, gallery or gymnasium.

(8) This section shall not apply to Northern Ireland.

NOTE

(a) **" Seventh Schedule ".**—See 11 Halsbury's Statutes (3rd Edn.) 797, 798. The Schedule makes detailed provisions as to the use of school premises, *e.g.*, that any arrangement for the use of a room in school premises shall be made with the local education authority maintaining the school; that questions arising as to such use shall be determined by the Secretary of State for Education and Science; that every local authority shall prepare for their area lists of rooms which candidates are entitled to use; that such lists shall be revised from time to time, and shall be kept by the registration officer, etc.

83. Right to use certain schools and rooms for meetings at local government elections.—(1) Subject to the provisions of this section, a candidate at a local government election shall be entitled for the purpose of holding public meetings in furtherance of his candidature to use free of charge, at all reasonable times, during the period commencing on the day on which the notice of election is given, and ending on the day preceding the day of election—

(*a*) in England or Wales, any suitable room in the premises of a county or voluntary school (a) situated in the electoral area for which he is a candidate, or . . . in a parish in part comprised in that electoral area;

(*b*) [*Relates to Scotland.*]

(2) Where a room is used for a meeting in pursuance of the rights conferred by this section, the person by whom or on whose behalf the meeting is convened shall defray any expense incurred by the persons having control over the room or any damage done to the school premises or to the furniture, fittings or apparatus therein.

(3) A candidate shall not be entitled to exercise rights conferred by this section except on reasonable notice; and this section shall not authorise the use of any room used as part of a private dwelling house or any interference with the hours during which the school premises are used for educational purposes.

(4) Any question arising under this section as to what is reasonable or suitable shall be determined in England or Wales by the [Secretary of State for Education and Science (b)] and in Scotland, where the question arises in relation to a room in the premises of a school by the persons having control of the school, and, in the case of a room maintained by a district council, by that council.

NOTES

(a) **" School ".**—As to the election of councillors of the Greater London Council and of the chairman of the Greater London Council, reference should be made to rule 18 of the Greater London Council Election Rules 1970, S.I. 1970 No. 92, which similarly provides for the free use of a school room for the purpose of taking the poll or of counting votes.

(b) **" Secretary of State for Education and Science ".**—See note (b) to s. 1 of the Education Act, 1944, p. 74, *ante*.

As to the use of schoolrooms for parish or community meetings, see section 134 of the Local Government Act 1972, p. 306, *post*.

THE LONDON GOVERNMENT ACT, 1963

1963 c. 33

GENERAL NOTE

This Act received the Royal Assent on 31st July, 1963, though most of it came into force on 1st April, 1965. The Act made new provisions with respect to local government in what is called by the Act " Greater London ", *viz.*, the administrative county of London, virtually the whole of the administrative county of Middlesex, and certain areas in Essex, Hertfordshire, Kent and Surrey.

Greater London, by this Act, consists of the City of London, the Inner and Middle Temples, and thirty-two " London boroughs ", twelve of which (all in the former county of London) are called " inner London boroughs " and the remainder of which are called " outer London boroughs ".

The Greater London Council has much more limited powers than had the London County Council, while the Common Council of the City of London and the councils of the London boroughs have much wider powers than had formerly the Common Council and the councils of the metropolitan boroughs.

Part IV of the Act, which is reproduced below, deals with education and the youth employment Service in Greater London. Section 30 deals with local education authorities in inner London and outer London; section 31 with primary, secondary and further education in Greater London; section 32 with the co-ordination of school and other health services in inner London; section 33 with the continuance of existing educational grants; and section 34 with the youth employment service in Greater London.

The appointment of officers, and the taking of other action, before 1st April, 1965, by the Greater London Council, and the outer London borough councils under this Part of the Act, was facilitated by the London Government (Education) (Interim Action) Order, 1964, S.I. 1964 No. 1293, which provided that provisions for such appointment, etc., under Part IV should be deemed to have been operative as from the passing of the Act.

* * * * *

PART IV

EDUCATION AND YOUTH EMPLOYMENT SERVICE

30. Local education authorities.—(1) As from 1st April, 1965, any reference in the Education Acts, 1944 to 1962 (a) or in any other Act to the local education authority (b) (*) shall be construed—

(*a*) in relation to any outer London borough (c), as a reference to the council of that borough;

(*b*) . . . in relation to the remainder of Greater London (c) (which remainder shall be known as the Inner London Education Area) as a reference to the Greater London Council (c) acting by means of a special committee thereof constituted as mentioned in subsection (2) of this section;

and the Greater London Council, when acting as aforesaid as the local education authority for the said Area, shall, except for the purposes of any document of title, be known as the Inner London Education Authority, and any reference in this or any other Act to a member or officer of that Authority or, in relation to that Authority, to a member or officer of a local education authority shall be construed as a reference to a member of the special committee aforesaid or, as the case may be, an officer appointed for the purposes of the functions of the Greater London Council as a local education authority.

(2) The special committee aforesaid shall consist of—

(*a*) such of the councillors of the Greater London Council as have been elected by local government electors for an inner London borough or the City;

(*b*) one representative of each inner London borough council appointed by that borough council from among the members thereof;

(*c*) one representative of the Common Council appointed by the Common Council from among the members thereof;

and any person appointed in pursuance of paragraph (*b*) or (*c*) of this subsection shall, unless re-appointed, retire on the fourteenth day after the ordinary day of retirement of London borough councillors falling next after his appointment, but may resign his membership of the Inner London Education Authority at any time by notice in writing to the clerk of the council by whom he was appointed thereto.

(3) The Greater London Council shall not act by means of the special committee aforesaid for the purpose of issuing any precept or borrowing any money, but shall so act for the purpose of determining—

(*a*) the amount for which the Council are to precept upon rating authorities in the Inner London Education Area in respect of expenditure of the Inner London Education Authority; and

(*b*) what amount, if any, is to be borrowed by the Council in respect of such expenditure,

and for the purpose of the making of the arrangements for the handling of receipts and payments required by section 58 of the Local Government Act, 1958 (d) so far as those arrangements relate to moneys paid or payable in connection with the functions of the Greater London Council as a local education authority, and shall also so act for the purpose of the appointment of any officer employed solely for the purposes of those functions, and in particular the appointment of the officer referred to in subsection (4) of this section.

(4) The officers to be appointed by the Greater London Council under paragraph 12 of Schedule 2 to this Act shall include a chief education officer of the Inner London Education Authority; and section 88 of the Education Act, 1944 (e) shall apply to the appointment of that officer as it applies to the appointment of any similar officer under the Local Government Act 1933 (f).

(5) Part II of Schedule 1 to the Education Act, 1944 (g) shall have effect in its application to the Inner London Education Area as if—

(*a*) paragraph 7 from " or has been " onwards and paragraph 11 were omitted;

(*b*) in paragraph 8, the reference to the power to borrow money or to raise a rate included a reference to the power to make such a determination as is referred to in subsection (3) of this section;

and Part III of the said Schedule 1 (g) (which relates to the delegation of functions of local education authorities to divisional executives) shall not apply to Greater London.

(6), (7) [*Repealed* (h)].

(8) In section 97 of the Children and Young Persons Act, 1933 (i), in proviso (*b*), for the words " London County Council as local authority " there shall be substituted the words " local education authority ".

NOTES

As from 1st April, 1965, this section established the local education authorities for Greater London. As regards the outer London boroughs (see General Note, p. 289, *ante*), these are to be the councils of such boroughs; as to the remainder of Greater London, the Greater London Council (acting by a special committee) is to be the authority and known for that purpose as the Inner London Education Authority.

(a) **" Education Acts, 1944 to 1962 ".**—These are the Education Act, 1944, the Education Act, 1946, the Education (Miscellaneous Provisions) Act, 1948 (with the exception of certain parts relating only to endowed schools), the Education (Miscellaneous Provisions) Act, 1953 (except section 5 thereof), the Education Act, 1959, and the Education Act, 1962. With the Education Act, 1964, the Education Act, 1967, the Education Act, 1968, and the Education (No. 2) Act, 1968, the Education (Handicapped Children) Act 1970, the Education (Milk) Act 1971, the Education Act 1973, the Education (Work Experience) Act 1973, and the Education Act 1975, they may be cited as the Education Acts, 1944–1975. All the Acts mentioned are printed in Part I, *ante*.

(b) **" Local education authority ".**—Defined by sections 6 (1) and 114 (1) of the Education Act, 1944, *ante*.

(c) **" Outer London borough "; " Greater London "; " Greater London Council ".**—See General Note, p. 289, *ante*.

(d) **" Section 58 of the Local Government Act, 1958 ".**—See 19 Halsbury's Statutes (3rd Edn.) 799.

(e) **" Section 88 of the Education Act, 1944 ".**—This section, which deals with the appointment of chief education officers of local education authorities, is printed at p. 169, *ante*.

(f) **" Local Government Act, 1933 ".**—See 19 Halsbury's Statutes (3rd Edn.) 393.

(g) **" Parts II, III of Schedule I to the Education Act 1944 ".**—See p. 198, *ante*. Part III is now repealed.

(h) Subsections (6), (7) were repealed by the Local Government (Termination of Reviews) Act 1967. The subsections had provided for a review of the administration of education in the Inner London Education Area and the possible transfer of functions of local education authorities.

(i) **" Children and Young Persons Act, 1933.**—See 17 Halsbury's Statutes (3rd Edn.) 510.

31. Primary, secondary and further education in Greater London.—(1) For the purposes of the Education Acts, 1944 to 1962 (a)—

(*a*) the development plan (*) under section 11 of the Education Act, 1944 (b) in force for the county of London immediately before 1st April, 1965, so far as it relates to the Inner London Education Area (c), shall continue on and after that date to be the development plan approved by the [Secretary of State for Education and Science] (d) for that Area;

(*b*) until replaced by a revised development plan submitted to and approved by the said [Secretary of State] (d) under subsection (2) of this section, any development plan under the said section 11 in force immediately before 1st April, 1965, which relates, or so far as it relates, to the area of any outer London borough shall, or, if more than one, shall together, constitute as from that date the development plan approved by the said [Secretary of State] (d) for that borough;

(*c*) subject to subsection (4) of this section, any scheme of further education (*) under section 42 of the said Act of 1944 (e) in force immediately before 1st April, 1965, which relates, or so far as it relates, to the Inner London Education Area or to the area of any outer London borough, shall, or, if more than one, shall together, continue to be, or, as the case may be, constitute, on and after that date the scheme of further education approved by the [Secretary of State for Education and Science] (d) under the said section 42 for that Education Area or, as the case may be, that borough.

(2) The council of each outer London borough shall, by 1st April, 1966, or within such period thereafter as the [Secretary of State for Education and Science] (d) may in any particular case allow, prepare and submit to that [Secretary of State] (d) a revised development plan (f) for the borough for the purposes of the said Acts of 1944 to 1962 which shall be in such form and contain such particulars with respect to existing primary (*) and secondary (*) schools in their area and as to the action the authority propose to take to secure that there shall be sufficient schools available for their area as that [Secretary of State] (d) may require; and subsections (3) to (5) of section 11 of the said Act of 1944 shall apply to any revised development plan submitted under this subsection as they apply to a development plan submitted under subsection (1) of that section.

(3) Before preparing a revised development plan for their borough under subsection (2) of this section, the council of each outer London borough shall consult with any other local education authority whose area is contiguous with that borough with a view to ensuring that the revised plan has regard both to the use made of schools outside that borough by children resident therein and to the use of schools within that borough by children resident outside it.

(4) Within such period as the [Secretary of State for Education and Science] (d) may allow, the council of each outer London borough shall for the purposes of section 42 of the said Act of 1944 submit to that [Secretary of State] (d) a restatement of the scheme or schemes of further education referred to in subsection (1) (*c*) of this section so far as relating to that borough; and that restatement when submitted to that [Secretary of State] (d) shall be deemed for the purposes of the said section 42 to be a scheme of further

education which has been submitted to that [Secretary of State] (d) under subsection (1) of that section.

(5) As from 1st April, 1965, it shall be the duty of the local education authority for any area in Greater London to maintain, and that authority shall not except in accordance with [the Education Acts 1944 to 1968 (g)] or subsection (6) of this section cease to maintain, any county or voluntary school maintained immediately before that date by the former local education authority for that area, being a school which is situated in that area or of which that former local education authority were, or in case of dispute are determined by the [Secretary of State for Education and Science] (d) to have been, the main user immediately before that date.

(6) Any authority who by virtue of section 30 (1) of this Act are, or are to become, the local education authority for any area in Greater London may agree with any other local education authority for the maintenance by that other authority of any school which under subsection (5) of this section would otherwise fall to be maintained by the first-mentioned authority.

(7) In the case of any school maintained immediately before 1st April, 1965, by a local education authority who in consequence of this Act will not continue to maintain it on and after that date—

(*a*) any instrument or rules of management or instrument or articles of government made by an order under section 17 of the said Act of 1944 (h) and any arrangement made under section 20 (h) of that Act, being an order or arrangement in force immediately before that date, shall continue in force on and after that date, subject to any further such order or arrangement and to any agreement under subsection (6) of this section, as if—

(i) any reference therein to that local education authority were a reference to the authority by whom by virtue of subsection (5) or (6) of this section the school falls to be maintained on and after that date or, if there is no such authority or if there is any doubt as to the identity of that authority, such local education authority as the [Secretary of State for Education and Science] (d) may direct;

(ii) any reference therein to any other existing local authority, being the council of a metropolitan borough, non-county borough or urban district to whom section 3 (1) (*b*) of this Act applies, were a reference, if the school falls to be maintained by the council of a borough, to that council or, in any other case, to the council of the London borough which includes the area of that existing authority or, if different parts of that area are included in different London boroughs, the council of such of those boroughs (or, if more than one, the councils thereof acting jointly) as appears to the local education authority to be served by the school;

(*b*) any direction of the local education authority under section 22 (i) of the said Act of 1944 and any agreed syllabus of religious instruction under section 29 (i) of that Act, being a direction or syllabus in force immediately before that date, shall continue in force on and after that date until replaced by a further direction under the said section 22 or, as the case may be, by the adoption of a new syllabus under the said section 29.

(8) For the purposes of any duty imposed by or under the Education Acts 1944 to 1962 [or section 4 (2) of the Local Government Act 1966] (j) with respect to the admission of pupils to—

(*a*) county or voluntary schools; or

(*b*) institutions maintained or assisted by local education authorities for the purpose of providing further education,

it shall not be a ground for refusing a pupil admission to, or excluding a pupil from, any such school or institution maintained or assisted by a local education authority in Greater London that the pupil resides in the area of some other local education authority if that area is within, or is contiguous with any part of, Greater London; and where any provision for further education is made by a local education authority in Greater London in respect of a pupil who resides in Greater London, or in some other local education authority's area which is contiguous with any part of Greater London, but belongs to the area of a local education authority other than the providing authority, and the [Secretary of State for Education and Science] (d) is satisfied that, having regard to all the circumstances of the case, it is right so to do, that [Secretary of State] (d) may on the application of the providing authority direct that section 7 (1) of the Education (Miscellaneous Provisions) Act, 1953 (j) (which relates to the recoupment of the providing authority by the authority to whose area the pupil belongs), shall apply notwithstanding that the last-mentioned authority have not consented to the making of the provision.

(9) Section 7 (4) and (5) of the Education (Miscellaneous Provisions) Act, 1953 (k) (which relate to the determination of the local education authority to whose area any pupil belongs for the purposes of further education), shall apply for the purposes of subsection (8) of this section as they apply for the purposes of the said section 7.

(10) In relation to any school maintained by the Inner London Education Authority, the expression " minor authority " (*) in the said Act of 1944 shall be construed as a reference to any of the following councils whose area appears to that Authority to be served by the school, that is to say, the councils of the inner London boroughs and the Common Council; and before approving any proposals submitted to him under section 13 of the said Act of 1944 with respect to any school which is, or is to be, situated within the City or an inner London borough, the [Secretary of State for Education and Science] (d) shall afford to the Common Council or, as the case may be, the borough council, an opportunity of making representations to him with respect to the proposal.

(a) **" Education Acts, 1944 to 1962 ".**—See note (a) to section 30, p. 290, *ante*.

(b) **" Section 11 of the Education Act, 1944 ".**—See p. 85, *ante*.

(c) **" Inner London Education Area ".**—See General Note, p. 289, *ante*.

(d) **" Minister of Education ".**—Now Secretary of State for Education and Science. See note (b) to section 1 of the Education Act, 1944, p. 74, *ante*.

(e) **" Section 42 of the Act of 1944 ".**—See p. 136, *ante*.

(f) In *Wood* v. *London Borough of Ealing*, [1966] 3 All E.R. 514; [1967] Ch. 364 it was held that where the revision of a development plan was being carried out pursuant to this subsection, parents had no general right to be consulted, any such right being negatived by s. 11 of the Education Act, 1944.

(g) The words in square brackets in sub-s. (5) were substituted by the Education Act, 1968, Sch. 1.

(h) **" Sections 17, 20 of the Act of 1944 ".**—See pp. 100, 108, *ante*.

(i) **" Sections 22, 29 of the Act of 1944 ".**—See pp. 110, 121, *ante*.

(j) The words omitted in sub-s. (8) were removed by the Statute Law (Repeals) Act 1975. The words in square brackets were added by the Local Government Act 1966, s. 43, Sch. 5.

(k) **" Section 7 of the Education (Miscellaneous Provisions) Act, 1953 "**—See p. 232, *ante*.

32. Co-ordination of school and other health services in inner London.—(1)–(6) [*Repealed.*]

(7) In its application to the Inner London Education Authority, section 54 (4) of the Education Act, 1944 (c), shall have effect as if for the words " the council of any county district in the area of the authority " there were substituted the words " the council of any inner London borough or the Common Council of the City of London ".

NOTES

Sub-sections (1)—(6) were repealed by the National Health Service Reorganisation Act 1973.

33. Provision for continuance of existing educational grants.— (1) Where, in the case of any grant made before 1st April, 1965, under section 50, 61 (2) or 81 of the Education Act, 1944 (a), section 6 of the Education (Miscellaneous Provisions) Act, 1953 (b) or section 1 or 2 of the Education Act, 1962 (c), in respect of a pupil who has not completed his course by that date, the local education authority (*) by whom that grant was made—

(*a*) cease on that date in consequence of this Act to be a local education authority; or

(*b*) if the authority's area at the date of the making of the grant had been the same as on 1st April, 1965, would not have been the appropriate authority to make it,

it shall on and after 1st April, 1965, be the duty of the authority specified in subsection (2) of this section to make the remaining payments in pursuance of that grant, subject to the same conditions, if any, as to satisfactory work, financial need or other matters as were attached to the grant or as would be attached to such a grant by the authority specified as aforesaid, whichever are the most favourable.

(2) The authority referred to in the foregoing subsection shall be—

(*a*) the local education authority to whose area the pupil would have belonged (or, in the case of an award under section 1 of the Education Act, 1962 (c) in whose area he would have been ordinarily resident) at the date immediately before the grant was made if at that date the changes taking place under Parts I and IV of this Act on 1st April, 1965, had already taken place; or

(*b*) if there is no local education authority to whose area the pupil would have belonged (or, as the case may be, in whose area he would have been ordinarily resident) as aforesaid, then, without prejudice to any right to recoupment, such local education authority as the [Secretary of State for Education and Science (a)] may determine;

and section 6 (2) to (4) of the Education (Miscellaneous Provisions) Act, 1948 (e) or section 7 (4) and (5) of the Education (Miscellaneous Provisions) Act, 1953 (b) (which relate to the determination of the local education authority to whose area any pupil belongs for the purposes of primary or secondary education or, as the case may be, further education), or Schedule 1 to the said Act of 1962 (c) (which relates to the determination of ordinary residence for the purposes of the said section 1), as the case may be, shall apply for the purposes of this subsection as they apply for the purposes of the said Act of 1948, the said section 7 or the said section 1, as the case may be.

NOTES

(a) **" Education Act, 1944, sections 50, 61 (2), 81 ".**—See pp. 142, 150, 166, *ante*.

(b) **" Education (Miscellaneous Provisions) Act, 1953, sections 6, 7 ".**—See pp. 231, 232, *ante*.

(c) **" Education Act, 1962, sections 1, 2, Schedule I ".**—See pp. 242, 244, 249, *ante*.

(d) **" Secretary of State for Education and Science ".**—See note (b) to s. 1 of the Education Act, 1944, p. 74, *ante*.

(e) **" Education (Miscellaneous Provisions) Act, 1948, section 6 ".**—See p. 222, *ante*.

THE INDUSTRIAL TRAINING ACT, 1964

1964 c. 16

ARRANGEMENT OF SECTIONS

An Act to make further provision for industrial and commercial training; to raise the limit on contributions out of the National Insurance Fund towards the expenses of the Minister of Labour in providing training courses; and for purposes connected with those matters [12th March, 1964]

GENERAL NOTE

This Act, of which four sections are printed below, provides for the setting up, by order of the Minister of Labour (now Secretary of State for Employment and Productivity) of industrial training boards, with the functions of providing (or securing the provision) of courses and other facilities for the training of persons for industry, etc.

Section 2 sets out the functions of industrial training boards, *i.e.*, boards established under section 1 of the Act or by the Cotton Board. Powers of local education authorities are defined in section 16.

The Act was modified and amended by the Employment and Training Act 1973, which Act (*inter alia*) inserted sections 2A, 2B.

* * * * *

2. Functions of industrial training board.—(1) For the purpose of encouraging adequate training of persons employed or intending to be employed in the industry an industrial training board—

(*a*) may provide or secure the provision of such courses and other facilities (which may include residential accommodation) for the training of those persons as the board considers adequate having regard to any courses of facilities otherwise available to those persons;

(*b*) may approve such courses and facilities provided by other persons;

(*c*) may from time to time consider such employments in the industry as appear to require consideration and publish recommendations with regard to the nature and length of the training for any such employment and the further education to be associated with the training, the persons by and to whom the training ought to be given, the standards to be attained as a result of the training and the methods of ascertaining whether those standards have been attained;

(*d*) may apply or make arrangements for the application of selection tests and of tests or other methods for ascertaining the attainment of any standards recommended by the board and may award certificates of the attainment of those standards;

(*e*) may assist persons in finding facilities for being trained for employment in the industry;

(*f*) . . .

(*g*) may carry on or assist other persons in carrying on research into any matter relating to training for employment in the industry.

(*h*) may provide advice about training connected with the industry.

(2) An industrial training board may enter into contracts of service or apprenticeship with persons who intend to be employed in the industry and to attend courses or avail themselves of other facilities provided or approved by the board.

(3) An industrial training board may—

(*a*) at the request of another industrial training board provide advice for the other board and courses and other facilities for the training of persons employed or intending to be employed in the industry for which that other board is established;

(*b*) at the request of the Commission provide such other advice, and such other courses and facilities for training, as are mentioned in the request;

(*c*) at the request of an employer in the industry provide for him advice about training connected with activities carried on in Northern Ireland or outside the United Kingdom which, if they were carried on in Great Britain, would be included in the industry;

(*d*) enter into agreements with persons for the making by them of payments to the board in respect of the exercise by the board of any of its functions;

(*e*) take part in any arrangements made in pursuance of section 2 (1) or (2), 3 (4) or 8 of the Employment and Training Act 1973 (which relate to arrangements for persons to select, train for and obtain suitable employments and to obtain suitable employees);

but any expense incurred by the board in pursuance of paragraph (*c*) of this subsection shall not be defrayed out of sums received by the board by way of levy.

(4) An industrial training board may—

(*a*) pay maintenance and travelling allowances to persons attending courses provided or approved by the board;

(*b*) make grants or loans to persons providing courses or other facilities approved by the board, to persons who make studies for the purpose of providing such courses or facilities and to persons who maintain arrangements to provide such courses or facilities which are not for the time being in use;

(*c*) pay fees to persons providing further education in respect of persons who receive it in association with their training in courses provided or approved by the board.

(*d*) make payments to persons in connection with arrangements under which they or employees of theirs make use of courses or other facilities provided or approved by the board.

(5) An industrial training board shall exercise its functions under this section in accordance with proposals submitted to the Commission and approved by the Commission under section 7 of this Act.

(6) An industrial training board shall give to the Commission such information or facilities for obtaining information with regard to the exercise of its functions, in such manner and at such times as the Commission may reasonably require.

NOTE

This section is printed as modified and amended by the Employment and Training Act 1973, and as set out in Sch. 2, Part II, to that Act. The Commission referred to is the Manpower Services Commission, one of three bodies set up under section 1 of the Act of 1973, which is empowered to provide services in the employment and training field.

2A. Control of Agricultural Training Board by the Minister.—(1) The Minister may give to the Agricultural Training Board such directions as he thinks fit with respect to the performance by the Board of its functions; and it shall be the duty of the Board, notwithstanding anything in any other provision of this Act, to comply with the directions.

(2) Any such directions may require the said Board to exercise on behalf of the Minister functions exercisable by the Minister, whether by virtue of an

enactment or otherwise, which are connected with the provision of training or advice for persons employed or intending to be employed in agriculture or in agriculture or horticulture business within the meaning of section 64 of the Agriculture Act 1967 (excluding a function of making regulations or any other instrument having the force of law).

2B. Disclosure of information to Agricultural Training Board.—The Minister of Agriculture, Fisheries and Food and the Secretary of State may, for the purpose of assisting the Agricultural Training Board in planning and carrying out activities (including research) connected with the functions conferred on it by section 2 (1) (*a*) of this Act, disclose to the Board any information about—

(*a*) the kind of crops grown on any land and the areas of land on which crops of any kind are grown; and

(*b*) the number and description of persons employed on any land and employed on disposing of the produce of any land; and

(*c*) the kinds of machinery used on any land,

which has been furnished to him in pursuance of section 78 of the Agriculture Act 1947.]

* * * * *

16. Powers of education authorities.—The facilities for further education that may be provided by a local education authority under section 41 of the Education Act, 1944 (a), or by an education authority in Scotland under section 1 of the Education (Scotland) Act, 1962, shall be deemed to include and always to have included facilities for vocational and industrial training.

NOTE

(a) **" Section 41 of the Education Act, 1944 ".**—See p. 135, *ante*.

THE LOCAL GOVERNMENT ACT 1966

(1966 c. 42)

NOTE

This Act (now restricted by the Local Government Act 1974) makes provision, in relation to England and Wales, with respect to (*inter alia*) the payment of grants to local authorities.

Up to and including the financial year 1966–67, education was included among the services covered by the general grant paid by the Ministry of Housing and Local Government under Part I of the Local Government Act, 1958. That Act, further, conferred power upon the Secretary of State for Education and Science to make regulations for certain categories of educational expenditure to be pooled and shared amongst all local education authorities by adjustment of the general grant. Power was also conferred upon the Secretary of State to prescribe, by regulations, standards and requirements for schools, etc., which if not observed might result in reduction of the general grant.

The present Act replaced those provisions in the following way:—

(1) Section 12 thereof provided that general grants under Part I of the Local Government Act, 1958 should not be payable for the year 1967–68 and subsequent years.

(2) Section 14 further provided that grants under s. 100 (1) (*a*) (i) and (ii) of the Education Act, 1944 (which related to the provision of milk and meals) should not be payable for the year 1967–68 or any subsequent year.

For present pooling arrangements see the Rate Support Grants (Pooling Arrangements) Regulations, 1967, S.I. 1967 No. 467, as amended by the Rate Support Grants (Pooling Arrangements) (Amendment) Regulations, 1969, S.I. 1969 No. 1107, p. 378, *post*.

For the relevant part of the Local Government Act 1974, see p. 315, *post*.

THE GENERAL RATE ACT 1967

(1967 c. 9)

An Act to consolidate certain enactments relating to rating and valuation in England and Wales. [22nd March 1967]

GENERAL NOTE

Section 30 is the only section of the Act which it is necessary to print here. The section deals with the rating of county and voluntary school premises.

30. County and voluntary school premises.—(1) For the purpose of the application of section 19 (2) of this Act [ascertainment of rateable value] to county and voluntary schools (a), the Minister and the Secretary of State for Education and Science (hereinafter in this section together referred to as " the Ministers ") may make regulations providing that the gross value of such schools of any prescribed class shall be ascertained in accordance with provisions of the regulations—

(*a*) requiring the Secretary of State to certify the amount estimated by him, by reference to such factors as appear to him to be relevant, to be the average cost of providing a place for one pupil in a school of that class completed not less than one year before the coming into force of the valuation lists to which the regulations apply;

(*b*) providing for the determination for any school of that class of an amount equal to the product of—

(i) a standard gross value for each such place, being a prescribed percentage of the amount certified under paragraph (*a*) of this subsection; and

(ii) the number of places determined in accordance with the regulations to be available for pupils in that school; and

(*c*) providing for taking as the gross value for any such school the amount arrived at under paragraph (*b*) of this subsection as adjusted in the prescribed manner by reference to the age, lay-out and construction of the buildings, the facilities and amenities provided at the school, and such other factors of any description as may be prescribed.

(2) The Ministers may by regulations provide that land of any prescribed description forming part of, or occupied with, a county or voluntary school shall in such cases as may be prescribed be treated for rating purposes as a separate hereditament and not as forming part of the school or its appurtenances.

(3) Before making any regulations under this section the Ministers shall consult (b) with such associations of local authorities as appear to them to be concerned and with any local authority with whom consultation appears to them to be desirable.

(4) In this section " county school " and " voluntary school " have the same meanings respectively as in the Education Act 1944 (c), and " prescribed " means prescribed by regulations (d) under this section.

NOTES

(a) **" County and voluntary schools ".**—Voluntary schools were formerly exempted from rates by virtue of the Education Act, 1944, s. 64. That section was repealed as from 1st April 1963 by the Rating and Valuation Act, 1961, ss. 12 (2), 29 (2) and Sch. 5, Part I, but the liability of voluntary schools for rates was temporarily limited by s. 12 (4) of that Act (repealed).

County schools, which were formerly valued on a rental basis, are now valued according to a formula agreed by the various bodies concerned, and the present section enables the Minister of Housing and Local Government and the Secretary of State for Education and Science to make regulations which will put a similar formula on a legal basis for the purposes of valuing both county schools and voluntary schools.

(b) **" Consult ".**—On what constitutes consultation, see, in particular, *Rollo* v. *Minister of Town and Country Planning*, [1948] 1 All E.R. 13, C.A., and *Re Union of Whippingham and East Cowes Benefices*, *Derham* v. *Church Commissioners of England*, [1954] 2 All E.R. 22; [1954] A.C. 245, P.C.

(c) **" Education Act, 1944 ".**—For the meaning of " county school " and " voluntary school ", see s. 9 (2) of that Act, p. 82, *ante*.

(d) **" Regulations under this section ".**—No regulations had been made under this section at the time of going to press.

THE CHRONICALLY SICK AND DISABLED PERSONS ACT 1970

(1970 c. 44)

ARRANGEMENT OF SECTIONS

* * * * *

* * * * *

An Act to make further provision with respect to the welfare of chronically sick and disabled persons [29th May 1970]

8. Access to, and facilities at, university and school buildings.—(1) Any person undertaking the provision of a building intended for purposes mentioned in subsection (2) below shall, in the means of access both to and within the building, and in the parking facilities and sanitary conveniences to be available (if any), make provision, in so far as it is in the circumstances both practicable and reasonable, for the needs of persons using the building who are disabled.

(2) The purposes referred to in subsection (1) above are the purposes of any of the following:—

(*a*) universities, university colleges and colleges, schools and halls of universities;

(*b*) schools within the meaning of the Education Act 1944, teacher training colleges maintained by local education authorities in England or Wales and other institutions providing further education pursuant to a scheme under section 42 of that Act;

(*c*) (*applies to Scotland.*)

NOTES

"**Commencement**".—This section came into force on 29th November, 1970.

"**Education Act, 1944**".—For s. 42 of that Act, see *ibid.*, p. 136.

25. Special educational treatment for the deaf-blind.—(1) It shall be the duty of every local education authority to provide the Secretary of State at such times as he may direct with information on the provision made by that local education authority of special educational facilities for children who suffer the dual handicap of blindness and deafness.

(2) The arrangements made by a local education authority for the special educational treatment of the deaf-blind shall, so far as is practicable, provide for the giving of such education in any school maintained or assisted by the local education authority.

(3) (*Applies to Scotland.*)

NOTES

"**Commencement**".—This section came into force on 29th August, 1970.

"**Local education authority**".—For meaning, see the Education Act, 1944, s. 114 (1), p. 184, *ante*. By the London Government Act, 1963, s. 30, p. 289, *ante*, as from 1st April 1965 any reference in the Education Acts, 1944 to 1975, or in any other Act to the local education authority is to be construed in relation to any outer London Borough (as defined by s. 1 (1) (*b*) of the Act of 1963) as a reference to the council of that borough, and in relation to the remainder of Greater London (as defined by *ibid.*, s. 2 (1)) as a reference to the Greater London Council acting by means of a special committee known as the Inner London Education Authority constituted as mentioned in *ibid.*, s. 30 (2), *ibid.*, p. 289, *ante*.

"**Special educational treatment**".—Similar provisions in respect of special educational treatment are made by s. 26, *infra*, in relation to children suffering from autism and other forms of early childhood psychosis, and by s. 27, p. 301, *post*, in relation to children suffering from acute dyslexia.

26. Special educational treatment for children suffering from autism, &c.—(1) It shall be the duty of every local education authority to provide the Secretary of State at such times as he may direct with information on the provision made by that local education authority of special educational facilities for children who suffer from autism or other forms of early childhood psychosis.

(2) The arrangements made by a local education authority for the special educational treatment of children suffering from autism and other forms of early childhood psychosis shall, so far as is practicable, provide for the giving of such education in any school maintained or assisted by the local education authority.

(3) (*Applies to Scotland.*)

NOTES

"**Commencement**".—This section came into force on 29th August 1970.

"**Local education authority**".—See the note to s. 25, *ante*.

"**Special educational treatment**".—Similar provisions in respect of special educational treatment are made by s. 25, *ante*, in relation to children suffering from the dual handicap of deafness and blindness, and by s. 27 p. 301, *post*, in relation to children suffering from acute dyslexia.

27. Special educational treatment for children suffering from acute dyslexia.—(1) It shall be the duty of every local education authority to provide the Secretary of State at such times as he may direct with information on the provision made by that local education authority of special educational facilities for children who suffer from acute dyslexia.

(2) The arrangements made by a local education authority for the special educational treatment of children suffering from acute dyslexia shall, so far as is practicable, provide for the giving of such education in any school maintained or assisted by the local education authority.

(3) (*Applies to Scotland.*)

NOTES

"**Commencement**".—This section came into force on 29th August, 1970.

"**Local education authority**".—See the note to s. 25, *ante*.

"**Special educational treatment**".—Similar provisions in respect of special educational treatment are made by s. 25, *ante*, in relation to children suffering from the dual handicap of deafness and blindness, and by s. 26, *ante*, in relation to children suffering from autism or other forms of early childhood psychosis.

THE CHILDREN AND YOUNG PERSONS ACT 1969

(1969 c. 54)

An Act to amend the law relating to children and young persons; and for purposes connected therewith [22nd October 1969]

ARRANGEMENT OF SECTIONS

GENERAL NOTE

The main purpose of this Act was to give effect to the proposals in a White Paper, *Children in Trouble*, 1968 (Cmnd. 3601). The first Part makes changes in legal proceedings involving children and young persons and in the power of the courts. Below are printed ss. 1, 2, which deal with care proceedings in juvenile courts.

* * * * *

1. Care proceedings in juvenile courts.—(1) Any local authority, constable or authorised person who reasonably believes that there are grounds for making an order under this section in respect of a child or young person may, subject to section 2 (3) and (8) of this Act, bring him before a juvenile court.

(2) If the court before which a child or young person is brought under this section is of opinion that any of the following conditions is satisfied with respect to him, that is to say—

(*a*) his proper development is being avoidably prevented or neglected or his health is being avoidably impaired or neglected or he is being ill-treated; or

(*b*) it is probable that the condition set out in the preceding paragraph will be satisfied in his case, having regard to the fact that the court or another court has found that that condition is or was satisfied in the case of another child or young person who is or was a member of the household to which he belongs; or

(*c*) he is exposed to moral danger; or

(*d*) he is beyond the control of his parent or guardian; or

(*e*) he is of compulsory school age within the meaning of the Education Act 1944 (a) and is not receiving efficient full-time education suitable to his age, ability and aptitude; or

(*f*) he is guilty of an offence, excluding homicide,

and also that he is in need of care or control which he is unlikely to receive unless the court makes an order under this section in respect of him, then, subject to the following provisions of this section and sections 2 and 3 of this Act, the court may if it thinks fit make such an order.

(3) The order which a court may make under this section in respect of a child or young person is—

(*a*) an order requiring his parent or guardian to enter into a recognisance to take proper care of him and exercise proper control over him; or

(*b*) a supervision order; or

(*c*) a care order (other than an interim order); or

(*d*) a hospital order within the meaning of Part V of the Mental Health Act 1959 (b); or

(*e*) a guardianship order within the meaning of that Act.

(4) In any proceedings under this section the court may make orders in pursuance of paragraphs (*c*) and (*d*) of the preceding subsection but subject to that shall not make more than one of the orders mentioned in the preceding subsection, without prejudice to any power to make a further order in subsequent proceedings of any description; and if in proceedings under this section the court makes one of those orders and an order so mentioned is already in force in respect of the child or young person in question, the court may discharge the earlier order unless it is a hospital or guardianship order.

(5) An order under this section shall not be made in respect of a child or young person—

(*a*) in pursuance of paragraph (*a*) of subsection (3) of this section unless the parent or guardian in question consents;

(*b*) in pursuance of paragraph (*d*) or (*e*) of that subsection unless the conditions which, under section 60 of the said Act of 1959, are required to be satisfied for the making of a hospital or guardianship order in respect of a person convicted as mentioned in that section are satisfied in his case so far as they are applicable;

(*c*) if he has attained the age of sixteen and is or has been married.

(6) In this section " authorised person " means a person authorised by order of the Secretary of State to bring proceedings in pursuance of this section and any officer of a society which is so authorised, and in sections 2 and 3 of this Act " care proceedings " means proceedings in pursuance of this section and " relevant infant " means the child or young person in respect of whom such proceedings are brought or proposed to be brought.

NOTES

This section sets out all the circumstances in which a child or young person may be brought before a juvenile court and dealt with as in need of care or control. If also specifies the orders which the court may make, including " care orders " and " supervision orders ".

(a) **" Compulsory school age ".**—Now from five years to sixteen years. See section 35 of the Education Act 1944, *ante*.

(b) **Mental Health Act 1959.**—25 Halsbury's Statutes (3rd Edn.) 42.

2. Provisions supplementary to s. 1.—(1) If a local authority receive information suggesting that there are grounds for bringing care proceedings in respect of a child or young person who resides or is found in their area, it shall be the duty of the authority to cause enquiries to be made into the case unless they are satisfied that such enquiries are unnecessary.

(2) If it appears to a local authority that there are grounds for bringing care proceedings in respect of a child or young person who resides or is found in their area, it shall be the duty of the authority to exercise their power under the preceding section to bring care proceedings in respect of him unless they are satisfied that it is neither in his interest nor the public interest to do so or that some other person is about to do so or to charge him with an offence.

(3) No care proceedings shall be begun by any person unless that person has given notice of the proceedings to the local authority for the area in which it appears to him that the relevant infant resides or, if it appears to him that the relevant infant does not reside in the area of a local authority, to the local authority for any area in which it appears to him that any circumstances giving rise to the proceedings arose; but the preceding provisions of this subsection shall not apply where the person by whom the notice would fall to be given is the local authority in question.

(4) Without prejudice to any power to issue a summons or warrant apart from this subsection, a justice may issue a summons or warrant for the purpose of securing the attendance of the relevant infant before the court in which care proceedings are brought or proposed to be brought in respect of him; but subsections (3) and (4) of section 47 of the Magistrates' Courts Act 1952 (a) (which among other things restrict the circumstances in which a warrant may be issued) shall apply with the necessary modifications to a warrant under this subsection as they apply to a warrant under that section

and as if in subsection (3) after the word " summons " there were inserted the words " cannot be served or ".

(5) Where the relevant infant is arrested in pursuance of a warrant issued by virtue of the preceding subsection and cannot be brought immediately before the court aforesaid, the person in whose custody he is—

(*a*) may make arrangements for his detention in a place of safety for a period of not more than seventy-two hours from the time of the arrest (and it shall be lawful for him to be detained in pursuance of the arrangements); and

(*b*) shall within that period, unless within it the relevant infant is brought before the court aforesaid, bring him before a justice;

and the justice shall either make an interim order in respect of him or direct that he be released forthwith.

(6) Section 77 of the Magistrates' Courts Act 1952 (b) (under which a summons or warrant may be issued to secure the attendance of a witness) shall apply to care proceedings as it applies to the hearing of a complaint.

(7) In determining whether the condition set out in subsection (2) (*b*) of the preceding section is satisfied in respect of the relevant infant, it shall be assumed that no order under that section is to be made in respect of him.

(8) In relation to the condition set out in subsection (2) (*e*) of the preceding section the references to a local authority in that section and subsections (1), (2) and (11) (*b*) of this section shall be construed as references to a local education authority; and in any care proceedings—

(*a*) the court shall not entertain an allegation that that condition is satisfied unless the proceedings are brought by a local education authority; and

(*b*) the said condition shall be deemed to be satisfied if the relevant infant is of the age mentioned in that condition and it is proved that he—

(i) is the subject of a school attendance order which is in force under section 37 of the Education Act 1944 (c) and has not been complied with, or

(ii) is a registered pupil at a school which he is not attending regularly within the meaning of section 39 (d) of that Act, or

(iii) is a person whom another person habitually wandering from place to place takes with him,

unless it is also proved that he is receiving the education mentioned in that condition;

but nothing in paragraph (*a*) of this subsection shall prevent any evidence from being considered in care proceedings for any purpose other than that of determining whether that condition is satisfied in respect of the relevant infant.

(9) If on application under this subsection to the court in which it is proposed to bring care proceedings in respect of a relevant infant who is not present before the court it appears to the court that he is under the age of five and either—

(*a*) it is proved to the satisfaction of the court, on oath or in such other manner as may be prescribed by rules under section 15 of the Justices of the Peace Act 1949 (e) that notice of the proposal to bring the proceedings at the time and place at which the application is made was served on the parent or guardian of the relevant infant at what appears to the court to be a reasonable time before the making of the application; or

(*b*) it appears to the court that his parent or guardian is present before the court the court may if it thinks fit, after giving the parent or guardian if he is present an opportunity to be heard, give a direction under this subsection in respect of the relevant infant; and a relevant infant in respect of whom such a direction is given by a court shall be deemed to have been brought before the court under section 1 of this Act at the time of the direction, and care proceedings in respect of him may be continued accordingly.

(10) If the court before which the relevant infant is brought in care proceedings is not in a position to decide what order, if any, ought to be made under the preceding section in respect of him, the court may make an interim order in respect of him.

(11) If it appears to the court before which the relevant infant is brought in care proceedings that he resides in a petty sessions area other than that for which the court acts, the court shall, unless it dismisses the case and subject to subsection (5) of the following section, direct that he be brought under the preceding section before a juvenile court acting for the petty sessions area in which he resides; and where the court so directs—

(*a*) it may make an interim order in respect of him and, if it does so, shall cause the clerk of the court to which the direction relates to be informed of the case;

(*b*) if the court does not make such an order it shall cause the local authority in whose area it appears to the court that the relevant infant resides to be informed of the case, and it shall be the duty of that authority to give effect to the direction within twenty-one days.

(12) The relevant infant may appeal to [the Crown Court] (f) against any order made in respect of him under the preceding section except such an order as is mentioned in subsection (3) (*a*) of that section.

(13) Such an order as is mentioned in subsection (3) (*a*) of the preceding section shall not require the parent or guardian in question to enter into a recognisance for an amount exceeding fifty pounds or for a period exceeding three years or, where the relevant infant will attain the age of eighteen in a period shorter than three years, for a period exceeding that shorter period; and section 96 of the Magistrates' Courts Act 1952 (which relates to the forfeiture of recognisances) shall apply to a recognisance entered into in pursuance of such an order as it applies to a recognisance to keep the peace.

(14) For the purposes of this Act, care proceedings in respect of a relevant infant are begun when he is first brought before a juvenile court in pursuance of the preceding section in connection with the matter to which the proceedings relate.

NOTES

This section contains provisions supplementary to s. 1. Further supplementary provisions are contained in s. 3 of the Act (not printed in this volume). See 40 Halsbury's Statutes (3rd Edn.) 855. The further provisions relate only to those cases where the child has been guilty of an offence.

(a) **" Section 47 of the Magistrates' Courts Act 1952 ".**—21 Halsbury's Statutes (3rd Edn.) 226.

(b) **Ibid., section 77.**—21 Halsbury's Statutes (3rd Edn.) 250.

(c) **" Section 37 of the Education Act 1944 ".**—See p. 129, *ante*.

(d) **Ibid., section 39.**—See p. 132, *ante*.

(e) **" Section 15 of the Justices of the Peace Act 1949 ".**—21 Halsbury's Statutes (3rd Edn.) 120.

(f) The words in square brackets in sub-s. (12) were substituted by the Courts Act, 1971, s. 56 (2), Sch. 9, Part I.

* * * * *

THE CHILDREN ACT 1972

1972 c. 44

An Act to secure that the minimum age at which children may be employed is not affected by any further change in the school-leaving age. [27th July 1972]

GENERAL NOTE

This Act, which came into force on receiving the Royal Assent on 27th July, 1972, provides that the age of thirteen remains the minimum age at which children may be employed, despite the raising of the school leaving age to sixteen on 1st September, 1972, by the Raising of the School Leaving Age Order, 1972, S.I. 1972 No. 444, *post*, made under s. 35 of the Education Act 1944, *ante*). The Act does not apply to Northern Ireland.

The powers of a local authority to make byelaws raising the minimum age, or permitting children under thirteen to be employed in light agricultural or horticultural work by their parents or guardians, are not affected by the Act.

1. Minimum age of employment.—(1) Notwithstanding any change in the age governing the time when children may leave school, the minimum age at which, under section 18 (1) of the Children and Young Persons Act 1933 (a) . . . it is lawful for a child to be employed shall remain the age of 13 years.

(2) Accordingly in each of those sections for subsection (1) (*a*) there shall be substituted the paragraph—

" (*a*) so long as he is under the age of thirteen years ";

and in subsection (2) (a) (which allows the general rules in subsection (1) to be modified by local authority bye-laws) for paragraph (*a*) (i) there shall be substituted the sub-paragraph—

" (i) the employment of children under the age of thirteen years (notwithstanding anything in paragraph (*a*) of the last foregoing subsection) by their parents or guardians in light agricultural or horticultural work ".

NOTE

(a) **" Section 18 (1), (2) of the Children and Young Persons Act 1933 ".**—17 Halsbury's Statutes (3rd Edn.) 448. The section has been amended by the Employment of Children Act 1973 The words omitted in subsection (1) relate only to Scotland.

SCHEDULE

[*Repeal of enactments*]

THE LOCAL GOVERNMENT ACT 1972

1972 c. 70

ARRANGEMENT OF SECTIONS

* * * * *

An Act to make provision with respect to local government and the functions of local authorities in England and Wales . . . [26th October, 1972.]

GENERAL NOTE

Various sections of this Act are concerned with teachers and schools.

Firstly, s. 80 deals with disqualifications for election and holding office as a member of a local authority. Section 81 (3), however, provides that nothing in s. 80 shall operate to disqualify any person from being (*a*) chairman, vice-chairman, deputy chairman or an alderman of the Greater London Council; or (*b*) a councillor of the Greater London Council for an electoral area in an outer London borough; or (*c*) a member of the council of an inner London borough, by reason of his being a teacher in any school, etc., maintained or assisted by the Inner London Education Authority. Section 81 (4) further provides that a person shall not be disqualified from being a member of a district council or a county council by reason of being a teacher. These sections are not printed here; see 42 Halsbury's Statutes (3rd Edn.) 917–920.

Secondly, s. 134, *infra*, makes provision for the use of a schoolroom in a parish or community where no other suitable public room is available.

Thirdly, s. 192, *infra*, makes further provisions as to local education authorities and amends the Education Act 1944.

* * * * *

134. Use of schoolroom, etc. in parish or community.—(1) If in a parish there is no suitable public room vested in the parish council or the parish trustees, as the case may be, which can be used free of charge, a suitable room in premises of a school maintained by the local education authority or a suitable room the expenditure of maintaining which is payable out of any rate may, subject to subsection (3) below, be used free of charge at all reasonable times and after reasonable notice for any of the following purposes, that is to say, for the purpose of—

(*a*) a parish meeting or any meeting of the parish council, where there is one; or

(*b*) meetings convened by the chairman of the parish meeting or by the parish council, where there is one; or

(*c*) the administration of public funds within or for the purposes of the parish where those funds are administered by any committee or officer appointed by the parish council or parish meeting or by the county council or district council.

(2) If in a community there is no suitable public room vested in the community council which can be used free of charge or there is no community council, a suitable room in premises of a school maintained by the local education authority or a suitable room the expenditure of maintaining which is payable out of any rate may, subject to subsection (3) below, be used free of charge at all reasonable times and after reasonable notice for any of the following purposes, that is to say, for the purpose of—

(*a*) a community meeting or any meeting of the community council, where there is one; or

(*b*) meetings convened by the community council, where there is one; or

(*c*) the administration of public funds within or for the purposes of the community where those funds are administered by any committee or officer appointed by the community council, where there is one, or by the county council or district council.

(3) Nothing in this section shall authorise—

(*a*) the use of a room used as part of a private dwelling; or

(*b*) any interference with the hours during which a room in the premises of a school is used for educational purposes; or

(*c*) any interference with the hours during which a room used for the purposes of the administration of justice, or for the purposes of the police, is used for those purposes.

(4) If, by reason of the use of a room for any of the purposes mentioned in subsection (1) or (2) above, any expense is incurred by persons having control of the room, or any damage is done to the room or the building of which it is part or to its appurtenances, or to the furniture of the room or any teaching aids, the expense or the cost of making good the damage shall be defrayed as an expense of the parish or community council or parish or community meeting.

(5) If any question arises under this section as to what is reasonable or suitable, it may be determined by the Secretary of State.

NOTE

As to the use of schoolrooms at election times, see the Representation of the People Act 1949, ss. 82, 83, pp. 287, 288, *ante*.

* * * * *

192. Education.—(1) The local education authority for each non-metropolitan county shall be the council of the county and the local education authority for each metropolitan district shall be the council of the district.

(2) No scheme of divisional administration shall be made under Part III of Schedule 1 to the Education Act 1944 and that Part of that Schedule shall cease to have effect.

(3) Section 52 of the Local Government Act 1958 shall cease to have effect on the passing of this Act.

(4) [*Substitutes a new definition of " minor authority " in s.* 114 (1) *of the Education Act* 1944 (a).]

(5) Subject to subsection (6) below any instrument made by an existing local education authority for an area outside Greater London in connection with the discharge of any of their functions, and any other thing done by or to or in relation to such an authority in connection therewith, shall be treated as having been made by, or done by or to or in relation to, the new local education authority to whom those functions are transferred by or by virtue of this Act, and any instrument relating to the exercise of those functions, or to things done in their exercise or property held or maintained for the purposes of those functions shall, so far as it so relates, have effect as if any reference to a specified existing local education authority for an area outside Greater London by whom those functions were exercisable or to the area of such an authority were a reference to the new local education authority to whom those functions are so transferred or to so much of the area of the new authority as includes the area of the existing authority, as the case may be.

(6) Subsection (5) above is without prejudice to any express provision made by, or by any instrument made under, this Act, but has effect subject to any provision to the contrary so made and in particular may be excluded from applying, either wholly or to any specified extent, in any particular case by an order made by the Secretary of State.

NOTES

(a) **Education Act 1944, section 114 (1).**—See p. 184, *ante*.

* * * * *

THE EMPLOYMENT OF CHILDREN ACT 1973

(1973 c. 24)

An Act to make further provision with respect to restrictions on the employment of persons under the upper limit of school age and to the means of imposing and enforcing such restrictions; and for connected purposes. [23rd May 1973]

GENERAL NOTE

This Act strengthens the legislation restricting the employment of children in part-time work and during holidays by protecting all children under school-leaving age. The Act authorises the Secretary of State to require children to obtain a permit from their local education authority before they take up any employment (s. 1, Sch. 1).

Section 2, *infra*, enables local education authorities to obtain in advance details of proposed employment from parents and employers, and gives them power to prevent a child from taking a job which is unsuitable, or is prejudicial to his education.

* * * * *

2. Supervision by education authorities.—(1) The following powers shall be exercisable in England and Wales by a local education authority and, in Scotland, by an education authority in cases where the authority have reason to suppose that a child is, or is to become, employed (whether or not in the authority's area).

(2) The authority may by a notice served—

(*a*) on the child's parent or guardian or a person who has actual custody of the child; or

(*b*) on a person appearing to have the child in his employment or to be about to employ him,

require the person served to furnish to the authority, within such period as may be specified in the notice, particulars of how the child is, or is to be, employed and at what times and for what periods.

(3) If it appears to the authority that a child is for the time being, or is to become, employed in ways, or at times or for periods, which are not unlawful apart from this section but are unsuitable for the child, by reference to his age or state of health, or otherwise prejudicial to his education, they may, by a notice served on any such person as is mentioned in paragraph (*a*) or (*b*) of subsection (2) above as one on whom a notice may be served, either—

(*a*) prohibit the child's employment in any manner specified in the notice; or

(*b*) require his employment in any manner so specified to be subject to such conditions (specified in the notice and to be complied with by the person served with it) as the authority think fit to impose in the interests of the child.

(4) Any person who—

(*a*) being served with a notice under subsection (2) above—

(i) fails to furnish the particulars required by the notice within the period specified thereby, or

(ii) in purported compliance with the notice, makes any statement which he knows to be false in a material particular, or recklessly makes any statement which is false in a material particular; or

(*b*) being served with a notice under subsection (3) prohibiting a child's employment in any manner specified in the notice, employs or causes or permits the child to be employed in that manner contrary to the prohibition; or

(*c*) being served with such a notice requiring compliance by him with any conditions, wilfully fails to comply with them,

shall be guilty of an offence.

(5) A person guilty of an offence under subsection (4) above shall be liable on summary conviction—

(*a*) in the case of an offence under paragraph (*a*) of the subsection, to a fine of not more than £20 or, if he has previously been convicted of an offence under that paragraph, to a fine of not more than £50;

(*b*) in the case of an offence under paragraph (*b*) or (*c*) of the subsection, to a fine of not more than £50, or if he has previously been convicted of an offence under either paragraph, to a fine of not more than £100.

(6) For purposes of this section, a person who assists in a trade or occupation carried on for profit shall be deemed to be employed notwithstanding that he receives no reward for his labour.

* * * * *

THE NATIONAL HEALTH SERVICE REORGANISATION ACT 1973

(1973 c. 32)

An Act to make further provision with respect to the national health service in England and Wales . . . and for purposes connected with those matters.

[5th July 1973.]

GENERAL NOTE

Section 3 of this Act, *infra*, transfers to the Secretary of State for Social Services the functions of local education authorities relating to the medical and dental inspection and treatment of pupils.

* * * * *

3. Medical and dental service for pupils.—(1) It shall be the duty of the Secretary of State to make provision for the medical and dental inspection at appropriate intervals of pupils in attendance at schools maintained by local education authorities and for the medical and dental treatment of such pupils.

(2) Without prejudice to the powers of the Secretary of State apart from this subsection, he may—

(*a*) by arrangement with any local education authority, make provision for any medical or dental inspection or treatment of—

(i) senior pupils in attendance at any educational establishment, other than a school, which is maintained by the authority and at which full-time further education is provided, or

(ii) any child or young person who, in pursuance of special arrangements made for him by the authority by virtue of section 56 of the Education Act 1944 (a) is receiving primary or secondary education otherwise than at a school;

(*b*) by arrangement with the proprietor of any educational establishment which is not maintained by a local education authority, make any such provision in respect of junior or senior pupils in attendance at the establishment.

(3) A local education authority shall not make an arrangement in pursuance of the preceding subsection in respect of such an establishment as is mentioned in paragraph (*a*) (i) of that subsection except by agreement with the governors of the establishment; and an arrangement made in pursuance of paragraph (*b*) of the preceding subsection may include provision for the making of payments by the proprietor in question.

(4) It shall be the duty of the local education authorities by which schools (other than voluntary schools) are maintained and of the managers or governors of voluntary schools to make available to the Secretary of State such accommodation as is appropriate for the purpose of assisting him to make such provision as is mentioned in subsection (1) of this section for pupils in attendance at the schools.

(5) In this section expressions to which meanings are assigned by section 114 (1) of the Education Act 1944 (b) have those meanings.

NOTES

(a) **" Section 56 of the Education Act 1944 ".**—See p. 148, *ante*.

(b) **" Section 114 (1) of the Education Act 1944 ".**—See p. 183, *ante*.

* * * * *

THE EMPLOYMENT AND TRAINING ACT 1973

(1973 c. 50)

ARRANGEMENT OF SECTIONS

* * * * *

An Act to . . . amend the law relating to the provision by education authorities of services relating to employment; and for purposes connected with those matters.

[25th July, 1973.]

GENERAL NOTE

Sections 8–10 of the Act, *infra*, deal with the establishment of careers services by local education authorities.

* * * * *

Careers services of education authorities

8. Provision of services by education authorities.—(1) Subject to subsections (3) to (5) of this section, it shall be the duty of each local education authority—

(*a*) to make arrangements for the purpose of assisting persons who are attending, either full-time or part-time, educational institutions in Great Britain other than universities—

(i) to determine what employments will, having regard to their capabilities, be suitable for them and available to them when they leave the institutions, and

(ii) to determine what training will then be required by them and available to them in order to fit them for those employments;

(*b*) to make arrangements for the purpose of assisting persons leaving institutions mentioned in the preceding paragraph to obtain such employments and training as are so mentioned; and

(*c*) to make the arrangements made in pursuance of the preceding paragraphs available to persons who seek to make use of them and are either such persons as are mentioned in those paragraphs or persons attending or leaving universities in Great Britain;

and it shall also be the duty of each local education authority to arrange for officers of the authority to be appointed to administer the arrangements made by the authority in pursuance of this subsection.

(2) A local education authority may, and shall so far as the Secretary of State directs it to do so, make arrangements in accordance with the following subsection—

(*a*) for the purpose of assisting persons (other than those mentioned in paragraphs (*a*) and (*b*) of the preceding subsection) who are seeking employment or different employment to determine—

(i) what employments are suitable for persons having their capabilities, and

(ii) what training they require and is available to them in order to fit them for those employments; and

(*b*) for the purpose of assisting those persons to obtain such employments and training as are mentioned in the preceding paragraph.

(3) The arrangements made in pursuance of subsection (1) or (2) of this section shall be arrangements—

(*a*) for the giving of assistance by collecting and furnishing information about persons seeking and offering employment and persons providing facilities for training; and

(*b*) for providing advice and guidance for the purposes mentioned in that subsection,

and may include arrangements for the provision of services calculated to facilitate the carrying out of arrangements made in pursuance of paragraph (*a*) or (*b*) of this subsection.

(4) Subject to the following subsection, it shall be the duty of local education authorities to consult and co-operate with one another to the extent appropriate for the purpose of securing that the functions conferred on them by subsections (1) and (2) of this section are performed efficiently; and, without prejudice to the powers exercisable by an authority for the purpose of performing that duty, any two or more local education authorities may make arrangements on such terms as they think fit (which may include terms as to the making of payments by one authority to another)—

(*a*) for any of the authorities to perform any of those functions on behalf of another of the authorities as respects the whole or part of the other authority's area;

(*b*) for the authorities to act jointly in performing any of those functions as respects the whole or parts of their areas.

(5) The Commission and any local education authority may make arrangements for the performance by the Commission on behalf of the authority of any function conferred on the authority by virtue of subsection (1) of this section or the preceding subsection so far as it relates to subsection (1), and any such arrangements—

(*a*) may be made in respect of the whole or part of the area of the authority; and

(*b*) except in a case in which the Secretary of State has authorised the Commission to disregard this paragraph, must include provision for the making by the authority to the Commission of payments intended to defray the expenditure incurred by the Commission by virtue of the arrangements;

and the preceding provisions of this subsection shall have effect during any period when this subsection is in force before the establishment of the Employment Service Agency as if paragraph (*b*) were omitted and for any reference to the Commission there were substituted a reference to the Secretary of State.

(6) The Secretary of State may by order provide that the preceding subsection, subsection (5) of the following section, this subsection and any arrangements in force by virtue of the preceding subsection or the said subsection (5) shall cease to have effect on a day specified in the order; and different days may be specified in pursuance of this subsection in relation to Scotland and the rest of Great Britain.

(7) The reference to part-time attendance in paragraph (*a*) of subsection (1) of this section does not include—

(*a*) part-time attendance where none of the relevant classes begins on any day before five o'clock in the evening; and

(*b*) any other part-time attendance as to which the Secretary of State directs that it shall be disregarded for the purposes of that paragraph;

except that the said reference does not include part-time attendance by persons who satisfy the local education authority in question that their attendance is with a view to employment.

NOTE

This section requires local education authorities to make arrangements for providing a vocational guidance service for people attending educational institutions (other than universities) and an employment placing service for people leaving such institutions, requires them to make these services available to people attending or leaving universities who seek to make use of the services and requires them to arrange for officers to be appointed to administer these services (sub-ss. (1), (3)). It also enables them to provide such services for other people and requires them to do so when directed by the Secretary of State (sub-ss. (2), (3)). These requirements do not apply in the case of people attending evening classes only and in the case of such other part-time students as the Secretary of State may direct, except where such attendance is with a view to employment (sub-s. (7)). Local education authorities are required to consult and co-operate with each other so as to perform their functions efficiently and are enabled to operate a joint service (sub-s. (4)). They are also enabled to arrange for the Commission (*i.e.* the Manpower Services Commission set up under the Act) to perform their functions until such time as the Secretary of State may determine by order (sub-ss. (5) and (6)).

9. Records of vocational advice.—(1) It shall be the duty of each local education authority to keep records of the vocational advice given on behalf of the authority to such persons as are mentioned in subsection (1) (*a*) of the preceding section.

(2) Where a person ceases to attend an educational institution (other than a university) in the area of an authority and begins to attend such an institution in the area of another authority it shall be the duty of the first-mentioned authority, on the request of the other authority, to furnish to the other authority any records relating to that person which have been kept by the first-mentioned authority in pursuance of the preceding subsection or transmitted to that authority in pursuance of this subsection and any records of vocational advice given to that person by the Secretary of State which have been transmitted to the first-mentioned authority by the Secretary of State.

(3) Where to the knowledge of an authority a person ceases to attend a school in the area of the authority otherwise than with a view to attending another school in the area of that or another authority, then, subject to the following subsection, it shall be the duty of the authority—

(*a*) to give him a written summary of any vocational advice already given to him on behalf of the authority and of any vocational advice relating to him of which records were transmitted to the authority in pursuance of the preceding subsection or by the Secretary of State; and

(*b*) to keep a copy of the summary for two years beginning with the date on which he ceased to attend the school in question; and

(*c*) to comply with a request for a copy of the summary which during that period is made to the authority by him; and

(*d*) to comply with a request for a copy of the summary which, during that period and at a time when the person to whom it relates is under the age of eighteen, is made to the authority by his parent or guardian;

but an authority shall not be required by virtue of paragraph (*c*) or (*d*) of this subsection to furnish more than one copy of the summary to the person to whom it relates or more than one copy of it to a parent or guardian of his.

(4) An authority shall not be required by virtue of paragraph (*a*) of the preceding subsection to furnish a person with the summary mentioned in that paragraph in a case where the authority has, or the authority and other authorities and the Secretary of State between them, have already furnished him with written statements which together contain the information which apart from this subsection would fall to be included in the summary; and that subsection shall have effect in such a case as if paragraph (*a*) were omitted and any reference to the summary in any other provision of that subsection were a reference to the statements.

(5) Subsection (5) of the preceding section shall have effect in relation to any function conferred on an authority by virtue of the preceding provisions of this section as it has effect in relation to any function mentioned in that subsection.

(6) In this section—

" authority " means local education authority;

" school " in relation to England and Wales, has the meaning assigned to it by section 114 (1) of the Education Act 1944 (a) . . .; and

" vocational advice " means advice and guidance given in pursuance of arrangements made for the purposes of subsection (1) (*a*) of the preceding section or in pursuance of the Employment and Training Act 1948 (b).

NOTES

This section requires local education authorities (and, by virtue of sub-s. (5) above, the Commission when it is carrying out an authority's functions) to keep records of vocational advice given to the persons mentioned in s. 8 (1) (*a*), *ante* (sub-s. (1)), and makes provision for the transfer of those records where the person moves into the area of another authority (sub-s (2)). It also requires an authority, where it is aware that a person has left school, to give him a summary of the vocational advice previously given, to keep a copy of the summary for two years and to provide on demand copies of the summary in specified circumstances (sub-s. (3)). The duty to give a summary does not apply if written statements of the advice which have been given have already been supplied (sub-s. (4)).

(a) **" Section 114 (1) of the Education Act 1948 ".**—See p. 185, *ante*.

(b) **" Employment and Training Act 1948 ".**—The whole Act is repealed by the present Act, s. 14 (2), Sch. 4 (43 Halsbury's Statutes (3rd Edn.) 454, 488).

10. Control of education authorities by Secretary of State.—(1) It shall be the duty of each local education authority—

(*a*) to perform the functions conferred on the authority by sections 8 and 9 of this Act in accordance with such guidance of a general character as the Secretary of State may give to the authority; and

(*b*) to provide the Secretary of State, in such manner and at such times as he may specify with such information and facilities for obtaining information as he may specify with respect to the performance by the authority of those functions.

(2) The Secretary of State may make arrangements with one or more other Ministers of the Crown—

(*a*) for constituting a body consisting of officers of his and of the other Ministers and of such other persons, if any, as may be determined in pursuance of the arrangements; and

(*b*) for the performance by that body on behalf of the Secretary of State of functions conferred on him by the preceding subsection.

NOTE

This section requires local education authorities to perform their functions under the Act in accordance with general guidance given by the Secretary of State and to provide him with such information as he requests (sub-s. (1)). The Secretary of State is empowered to set up a body, consisting of officers of his and of other Ministers and possibly other persons, to perform his functions under this section (sub-s. (2)).

* * * * *

THE LOCAL GOVERNMENT ACT 1974

(1974 c. 7)

An Act to make further provision, in relation to England and Wales, with respect to the payment of grants to local authorities . . . and for connected purposes. [8th February, 1974.]

* * * * *

8. Specific grants for purposes not covered by rate support grants.—(1) . . . (2) For the year 1974–75 and each subsequent year the Secretary of State shall pay to each local education authority a grant equal to 90 per cent. of the aggregate amount paid in that year by the authority—

(*a*) in pursuance of awards bestowed under section 1 (1) of the Education Act 1962 (a) (for persons attending first degree university courses and comparable courses; and

(*b*) by way of grants under section 2 (3) (a) of that Act (to or in respect of persons undergoing training as teachers).

(3) Payments of grants under . . . subsection (2) above shall be made at such times as the Secretary of State may, with the consent of the Treasury, determine. . . .

NOTE

(a) **" Education Act 1962, sections 1 (1), 2 (3) "**.—See pp. 242, 244, *ante*.

* * * * *

SEX DISCRIMINATION ACT 1975

(1975 c. 65)

An Act to render unlawful certain kinds of sex discrimination and discrimination on the ground of marriage, and establish a Commission with the function of working towards the elimination of such discrimination and promoting equality of opportunity between men and women generally; and for related purposes. [12th November, 1975]

ARRANGEMENT OF SECTIONS

* * * * *

PART III

* * * * *

GENERAL NOTE

This Act, which received the Royal Assent on 12th November, 1975, gives effect to the principles enunciated in the White Paper *Equality for Women* (Cmnd. 5724). It renders unlawful certain kinds of sex discrimination and discrimination on grounds of marriage. It also establishes the Equal Opportunities Commission.

Part III relates, amongst other matters, to discrimination in the field of education (ss. 22–28). Its provisions came into force on 29th December, 1975; see the Sex Discrimination (Commencement) Order 1975, S.I. 1975 No. 1485.

* * * * *

PART III

DISCRIMINATION IN OTHER FIELDS

Education

22. Discrimination by bodies in charge of educational establishments.—It is unlawful in relation to an educational establishment falling within column 1 of the following table, for a person indicated in relation to the establishment in column 2 (the " responsible body ") to discriminate against a woman—

(*a*) in terms on which it offers to admit her to the establishment as a pupil, or

(*b*) by refusing or deliberately omitting to accept an application for her admission to the establishment as a pupil, or

(*c*) where she is a pupil of the establishment—

(i) in the way it affords her access to any benefits, facilities or services, or by refusing or deliberately omitting to afford her access to them, or

(ii) by excluding her from the establishment or subjecting her to any other detriment.

TABLE

Establishment	*Responsible body*
ENGLAND AND WALES	
1. Educational establishment maintained by a local education authority.	Local education authority or managers or governors, according to which of them has the function in question.
2. Independent school not being a special school.	Proprietor.
3. Special school not maintained by a local education authority.	Proprietor.
4. University.	Governing body.
5. Establishment (not falling within paragraphs 1 to 4) providing full-time or part-time education, being an establishment designated under section 24 (1).	Governing body.

* * * * *

NOTES

The provisions omitted at the end of the Table (indicated by dots) apply only to Scotland.

As to the date of commencement of this Part, see General Note, *supra*.

Special schools are not defined in the Act; see s. 9 (5) of the Education Act 1944, *ante*.

23. Other discrimination by local education authorities.—(1) It is unlawful for a local education authority in carrying out such of its functions under the Education Acts 1944 to 1975 as do not fall under section 22, to do any act which constitutes sex discrimination.

(2) [*Applies to Scotland.*]

NOTE

For the Acts which may be cited together by the collective title Education Acts 1944 to 1975, see the General Note to the Education Act 1944, at p. 73, *ante*.

24. Designated establishments.—(1) The Secretary of State may by order designate for the purposes of paragraph 5 of the table in section 22 such establishments of the description mentioned in that paragraph as he thinks fit.

(2) An establishment shall not be designated under subsection (1) unless—

(*a*) it is recognised by the Secretary of State as a polytechnic, or

(*b*) it is an establishment in respect of which grants are payable out of money provided by Parliament, or

(*c*) it is assisted by a local education authority in accordance with a scheme approved under section 42 of the Education Act 1944, or

(*d*) it provides full-time education for persons who have attained the upper limit of compulsory school age but not the age of nineteen.

(3) A designation under subsection (1) shall remain in force until revoked notwithstanding that the establishment ceases to be within subsection (2).

NOTES

A person attains a given age (*e.g.* nineteen) at the commencement of the relevant anniversary of the date of his birth: see the Family Law Reform Act 1969, s. 9.

For the Education Act 1944, s. 42, see p. 136, *ante*.

For an order under this section, see the Sex Discrimination (Designated Educational Establishments) Order 1975, S.I. 1975 No. 1902, p. 444, *post*.

25. General duty in public sector of education.—(1) Without prejudice to its obligation to comply with any other provision of this Act, a body to which this subsection applies shall be under a general duty to secure that facilities for education provided by it, and any ancillary benefits or services, are provided without sex discrimination.

(2) The following provisions of the Education Act 1944, namely—

(*a*) section 68 (power of Secretary of State to require duties under that Act to be exercised reasonably), and

(*b*) section 99 (powers of Secretary of State where local education authorities etc. are in default),

shall apply to the performance by a body to which subsection (1) applies of the duties imposed by sections 22 and 23 and shall also apply to the performance of the general duty imposed by subsection (1), as they apply to the performance by a local education authority of a duty imposed by that Act.

(3) [*Applies to Scotland.*]

(4) The sanctions in subsections (2) and (3) shall be the only sanctions for breach of the general duty in subsection (1), but without prejudice to the enforcement of sections 22 and 23 under section 66 or otherwise (where the breach is also a contravention of either of those sections).

(5) [*Applies to Scotland.*]

(6) Subsection (1) applies to—

(*a*) local education authorities in England and Wales;

(*b*) [*Applies to Scotland.*]

(*c*) any other body which is a responsible body in relation to—

(i) an establishment falling within paragraph 1, 3 or 7 of the table in section 22;

(ii) an establishment designated under section 24 (1) as falling within paragraph (*a*) or (*c*) of section 24 (2);

(iii) an establishment designated under section 24 (1) as falling within paragraph (*b*) of section 24 (2) where the grants in question are payable under section 100 of the Education Act 1944.

NOTE

For the Education Act 1944, ss. 68, 69, 100, see pp. 155, 156, 175, *ante*.

Section 66 of the present Act deals with the enforcement of claims under Part III by way of civil proceedings for damages, a declaration or an injunction in the county court.

26. Exception for single-sex establishments.—(1) Sections 22 (a) and (b) and 25 do not apply to the admission of pupils to any establishment (a " single-sex establishment ") which admits pupils of one sex only, or which would be taken to admit pupils of one sex only if there were disregarded pupils of the opposite sex—

(*a*) whose admission is exceptional, or

(*b*) whose numbers are comparatively small and whose admission is confined to particular courses of instruction or teaching classes.

(2) Where a school which is not a single-sex establishment has some pupils as boarders and others as non-boarders, and admits as boarders pupils of one sex only (or would be taken to admit as boarders pupils of one sex only if there were disregarded boarders of the opposite sex whose numbers are comparatively small), sections 22 (a) and (b) and 25 do not apply to the admission of boarders and sections 22 (c) (i) and 25 do not apply to boarding facilities.

(3) Where an establishment is a single-sex establishment by reason of its inclusion in subsection (1) (b) the fact that pupils of one sex are confined to particular courses of instruction or teaching classes shall not be taken to contravene section 22 (c) (i) or the duty in section 25.

27. Exception for single-sex establishments turning co-educational.—(1) Where at any time—

(*a*) the responsible body for a single-sex establishment falling within column 1 of the table in section 22 determines to alter its admissions arrangements so that the establishment will cease to be a single-sex establishment, or

(*b*) section 26 (2) applies to the admission of boarders to a school falling within column 1 of that table but the responsible body determines to alter its admissions arrangements so that section 26 (2) will cease so to apply,

the responsible body may apply in accordance with Schedule 2 for an order (a " transitional exemption order ") authorising discriminatory admissions during the transitional period specified in the order.

(2) Where during the transitional period specified in a transitional exemption order applying to an establishment the responsible body refuses or deliberately omits to accept an application for the admission of a person to the establishment as a pupil the refusal or omission shall not be taken to contravene any provision of this Act.

(3) Subsection (2) does not apply if the refusal or omission contravenes any condition of the transitional exemption order.

(4) Except as mentioned in subsection (2), a transitional exemption order shall not afford any exemption from liability under this Act.

(5) Where, during the period between the making of an application for a transitional exemption order in relation to an establishment and the determination of the application, the responsible body refuses or deliberately omits to accept an application for the admission of a person to the establishment as a pupil the refusal or omission shall not be taken to contravene any provision of this Act.

NOTE

As to transitional exemption orders, see Sch. 2, *post*.

28. Exception for physical training.—Sections 22, 23 and 25 do not apply to any further education course being—

(*a*) a course in physical training, or
(*b*) a course designed for teachers of physical training.

* * * * *

SCHEDULE 2

TRANSITIONAL EXEMPTION ORDERS FOR EDUCATIONAL ADMISSIONS

Public sector (England and Wales)

1. Where under section 13 of the Education Act 1944 (as set out in Schedule 3 to the Education Act 1968) a responsible body submits to the Secretary of State, in accordance with subsection (1) or (2) of that section, proposals for an alteration in its admissions arrangements such as is mentioned in section 27 (1) of this Act the submission of those proposals shall be treated as an application for the making by the Secretary of State of a transitional exemption order, and if he thinks fit the Secretary of State may make the order accordingly.

2. Regulations under section 33 of the Education Act 1944 may provide for the submission to the Secretary of State as an application for the making by him of a transitional exemption order in relation to a special school, and for the making by him of the order.

3. Regulations under section 100 of the Education Act 1944 may provide for the submission to the Secretary of State of an application for the making by him of a transitional exemption order in relation to an establishment—

(*a*) which is designated under section 24 (1), and
(*b*) in respect of which grants are payable under subsection (1) (b) of the said section 100,

and for making by him of the order.

4. Regulations under section 5 (2) of the Local Government Act 1974 may provide for the submission to the Secretary of State of an application for the making by him of a transitional exemption order in relation to any educational establishment maintained by a local education authority and not falling within paragraphs 1 to 3, and for making by him of the order.

Private sector (England and Wales)

5.—(1) In the case of an establishment in England or Wales not falling within paragraphs 1 to 4 the responsible body may submit to the Equal Opportunities Commission set up under Part VI an application for the making by the Commission of a transitional exemption order in relation to the establishment, and if they think fit the Commission may make the order accordingly.

(2) An application under this paragraph shall specify the transitional period proposed by the responsible body to be provided for in the order, the stages by which within that period the body proposes to move to the position where section 22 (b) is complied with, and any other matters relevant to the terms and operation of the order applied for.

(3) The Commission shall not make an order on an application under this paragraph unless they are satisfied that the terms of the application are reasonable having regard to the nature of the premises at which the establishment is carried on, the accommodation, equipment and facilities available, and the financial resources of the responsible body.

NOTE

For the Education Act 1944, ss. 13, 33, 100, see pp. 90, 122, 175, *ante*. For s. 5 (2) of the Local Government Act 1974, see 44 Halsbury's Statutes (3rd Edn.) 646.

* * * * *

SCHEDULE 6

[*Repeals* s. 24 (3) *of the Education Act 1944*]

PART III

STATUTORY INSTRUMENTS

CONTENTS OF PART III

SOCIAL AND PHYSICAL TRAINING GRANT REGULATIONS, 1939

November 23, 1939

1. The Department of Education and Science (a) may make grants for any of the following purposes to an association recognised by them under these Regulations:—

(*a*) the maintenance of facilities for social and physical training in England or Wales, including the payment of leaders, instructors and wardens and the hiring and equipping of premises;

(*b*) the training of leaders, instructors and wardens for the carrying on of such facilities as aforesaid;

(*c*) the defraying of incidental expenses of organisation and administration.

2. An association seeking recognition under these Regulations may be a national association, or a local branch of a national association, or some other local association or committee (not being a local education authority), and the Department must be satisfied as to its constitution, financial standing, and generally as to its fitness to receive grant. Recognition may be withdrawn at the Department's discretion.

3. The amount of the grant to be paid to an association in respect of any period will be determined by the Department after consideration of the character, efficiency, volume and cost of the work, and of the aggregate sums available to the Department for grants under these Regulations; and the Department may pay such instalments during the period in question as they think fit having regard to the proposals of the association. The grants will be subject to such reductions (if any) in respect of broken periods as the Department think fit, and the Department may withhold or make a deduction from grant if the requirements of these Regulations are not fulfilled.

4. No grant will be paid for a purpose which in the opinion of the Department is attributable to a service in respect of which payments are made by the Department otherwise than under these Regulations or by another Government Department.

5. A person must not be required, as a condition of taking advantage of any facilities or training for which aid is sought under these Regulations, to attend or abstain from attending any Sunday School, place of religious worship, religious observance or instruction in religious subjects.

6. All work for which aid is sought under these Regulations, and the premises in which it is carried on, must be open to inspection by one of [Her] Majesty's Inspectors or any other person employed by the Department for the purpose of inspection.

7. Such registers and records must be kept, and such information and returns must be furnished from time to time, as the Department may require.

8. If any question arises as to the interpretation of these Regulations, or as to whether any of the requirements thereof are fulfilled, or as to the amount of any grant payable thereunder, the decision of the Department shall be final.

9. These Regulations may be cited as the Social and Physical Training Grant Regulations, 1939.

* * * * *

NOTE

(a) By virtue of section 121 of the Education Act 1944, p. 196, *ante*, these Regulations, which were made by the Board of Education under section 118 of the Education Act, 1921, have effect as though they were made under the Education Act, 1944. They also have effect as if (as here printed) for the original references to the Board of Education, there were substituted references to the Department of Education and Science. See the Secretary of State for Education and Science Order, 1964, S.I. 1964 No. 490, *post*.

SCHOOL ATTENDANCE ORDER REGULATIONS, 1944

S.R. & O. 1944 *No.* 1470
December 29, 1944

1. In pursuance of section 37 of the Education Act, 1944, the form set out in the Schedule hereto is hereby prescribed as the form in which a school attendance order shall be served upon the parent of a child of compulsory school age by a Local Education Authority.

2. These Regulations may be cited as the School Attendance Order Regulations, 1944.

* * * * *

SCHEDULE

EDUCATION ACT, 1944

School Attendance Order

....Local Education Authority.

Whereas .... (hereinafter called "the child") is a child of compulsory school age in the area of the above-named Authority:

And whereas you........................ of .... the parent* of the child, have failed to satisfy the Authority in accordance with the requirements of the notice served on you by the Authority on...............that the child is receiving efficient full-time education suitable to his[her] age, ability and aptitude either by regular attendance at school or otherwise:

And whereas, in the opinion of the Authority, it is expedient that the child should attend school:

Now therefore you are hereby required to cause the child forthwith to become a registered pupil at the following school:—

.... being the school selected by you [determined by a direction of the Secretary of State for Education and Science (a)] as the school to be named in this Order.

[Insert full name and address of school; and omit the whole or part of the following words as the case requires.]

Signed ....
.... to the ....
Local Education Authority
(County Council) (County Borough Council)

Dated ....

[*In this Order the expression "parent" in relation to the child, includes a guardian and every person who has the actual custody of the child.]

NOTE

(a) Secretary of State for Education and Science. See S.I. 1964 No. 490, *post*.

CENTRAL ADVISORY COUNCILS FOR EDUCATION REGULATIONS, 1945

S.R. & O. 1945 *No.* 152
February 7, 1945

NOTE

In these Regulations (as here printed) references to "Minister of Education" and "Minister" have been replaced by references to "Secretary of State for Education and Science" and Secretary of State" respectively. See S.I. 1964 No. 490, *post*.

Whereas Section 4 of the Education Act, 1944, provides for two Central Advisory Councils for Education, one for England and the other for Wales and Monmouthshire, hereinafter referred to as the English Council and the Welsh Council respectively:

And whereas the said Section provides for the appointment by the Secretary of State for Education and Science of a Chairman and other members for each

Council and requires the Secretary of State to make Regulations providing as to the term of office and conditions of retirement of the members and for periodical or other meetings of the Councils but, subject to such Regulations, provides that the meetings and procedure of each Council shall be such as may be determined by them:

And whereas the Secretary of State in pursuance of the said Section has appointed:—

(*a*) a Chairman and twenty-one other members for the English Council; and

(*b*) a Chairman and eighteen other members for the Welsh Council:

Now therefore the Secretary of State, in accordance with the requirements of the said Section, hereby provides as follows:—

1.—[(1) Subject as hereinafter provided, the term of office of the Chairman and of any other member of each Council shall be three years.]

(2) The term of office of any member may be prolonged by the Secretary of State by such further period as the Secretary of State may determine.

(3) The Chairman or any other member going out of office may be re-appointed.

NOTE

Paragraph (1) was substituted by the Central Advisory Councils for Education Amending Regulations, 1951, S.I. 1951 No. 1742, *post*, the object of the substitution being to provide for a uniform initial term of office of three years for all members of Central Advisory Councils.

2. Of the first members other than the Chairman of each Council who have been appointed as hereinbefore recited, seven members of the English Council and six members of the Welsh Council to be named by the Secretary of State shall hold office for four years, and a further seven members of the English Council and six members of the Welsh Council to be named by the Secretary of State shall hold office for two years. The terms of office of the first members of each Council shall begin with the date on which the Council in question first meets.

3. If a member of either Council is absent from three consecutive meetings of the Council except for some reason approved by the Secretary of State, his office shall become vacant.

4.—[*Revoked by the Central Advisory Councils for Education Amending Regulations*, 1951, *S.I.* 1951 *No.* 1742, post.]

5. The Secretary of each Council shall notify the Secretary of State as soon as possible of every vacancy in the office of a member.

6. Each Council shall hold ordinary meetings on such dates as may be fixed by them. Other meetings of each Council shall be determined by the Council concerned.

7.—(1) The Chairman of each Council shall preside at every meeting of the Council at which he is present.

(2) At a meeting of the English Council eight, and at a meeting of the Welsh Council seven, shall be a quorum.

(3) No act or proceeding of either Council shall be questioned on account of any vacancy in their body.

8. Each Council may appoint such committees as they think fit and may with the consent of the Secretary of State include among the persons appointed persons who are not members of the Council.

9. The Interpretation Act, 1889, applies to the interpretation of these Regulations as it applies to the interpretation of an Act of Parliament.

10. These Regulations may be cited as the Central Advisory Councils for Education Regulations, 1945.

* * * * *

REGULATIONS FOR SCHOLARSHIPS AND OTHER BENEFITS, 1945

S.R. & O. 1945 *No.* 666
May 17, 1945

NOTE

In these Regulations (as here printed) references to " Minister of Education " and " Minister " have been replaced by references to " Secretary of State for Education and Science " and " Secretary of State " respectively. See S.I. 1964 No. 490, *post*.

1. In these Regulations unless the context otherwise requires—

(*a*) " The Act " means the Education Act, 1944.

" The Secretary of State " means the Secretary of State for Education and Science.

" Authority " means local education authority.

" Approved " where it relates to fees or expenses which require the approval of the Secretary of State under other Regulations made under the Act means approved by the Secretary of State under those Regulations and subject thereto means approved by the Secretary of State for the purpose of these Regulations.

" School " includes any school within the definition of the Act and any course of instruction forming part only of the work of a school or conducted separately.

" Direct-grant school " means a school in respect of which grants are paid by the Secretary of State under Section 100 (1) (*b*) of the Act.

" Place of further education " includes an institution of technology, commerce, art or music and an institution providing full-time courses of liberal education for older students.

(*b*) Other expressions which have meanings assigned to them by the Act shall have the same respective meanings for the purposes of these Regulations.

2. Subject to the conditions prescribed by these Regulations, every authority may, for the purpose of enabling pupils to take advantage without hardship to themselves or their parents of any educational facilities available to them—

(*a*) defray such expenses of children attending county schools, voluntary schools or special schools as may be necessary to enable them to take part in any school activities ;

(*b*) pay the approved fees of children attending direct-grant schools, whether within or without the area of the authority, at which fees are payable ;

(*c*) defray the expenses payable in respect of children attending direct-grant schools, whether within or without the area of the authority, at which fees are payable ;

(*d*) pay the whole or part of the approved fees and expenses of children attending schools, whether within or without the area of the authority, which are not in receipt of direct grant and at which fees are payable ;

(*e*) grant scholarships, exhibitions, bursaries or other allowances in respect of—

(i) pupils over compulsory school age attending schools ;

(ii) students other than those to whom the next following sub-paragraph applies who are pursuing a course of education at a university, university college or other like institution or at any place of further education ; and

(iii) students pursuing an approved course of training as teachers ; and

[(iv) students pursuing approved correspondence courses in subjects of further education.]

(*f*) grant allowances in respect of any children in respect of whom any scholarship, exhibition, bursary or other allowance had been granted by a former authority before the 1st April, 1945.

[(*g*) grant maintenance allowances in respect of pupils, being registered pupils at special schools, who are by virtue of section 38 (1) of the Act deemed to be of compulsory school age but who, apart from the said section 38 (1), would be over compulsory school age.]

NOTES

Sub-paragraph (iv) of paragraph (*e*) was added by the Scholarships and Other Benefits Amending Regulations No. 1, 1948, S.I. 1948 No. 688, *post*. The object of the sub-paragraph is to enable Local Education Authorities, with the approval of the Secretary of State, to assist students to take suitable correspondence courses in subjects of further education in cases where the student cannot obtain the instruction which he needs in a local institution of further education and cannot, owing to the location of his employment or for other sufficient reason, attend an institution at a distance.

Paragraph (*g*) was added by the Scholarships and Other Benefits Amending Regulations, 1964, S.I. 1964 No. 1294 (11th August, 1964), p. 375, *post*.

In Circular No. 312 (11th September, 1956) correspondence courses are suggested as a useful means of providing further education for hospital patients, and it is stated that where necessary use may be made of courses provided by certain professional bodies and educational establishments or by private correspondence colleges.

As to the effect of the phasing out of direct grant grammar schools, see regulation 6 of the Direct Grant Grammar Schools (Cessation of Grant) Regulations 1975, S.I. 1975 No. 1198, *post*.

3. The following conditions apply to the exercise by the authority of the powers prescribed by these Regulations:—

(*a*) the authority shall at such times and in such form as the Secretary of State may require submit for his approval particulars of their arrangements for the exercise of the powers aforesaid;

[(*b*) the expenses defrayed by the authority under paragraph (*a*) of Regulation 2 shall not include expenditure on clothing which the authority are authorised to provide by or under the provisions of Section 5 of the Education (Miscellaneous Provisions) Act, 1948;]

(*c*) payments under paragraph (*b*) or paragraph (*d*) of Regulation 2 may include the whole or part of any fees payable for boarding or lodging a child: provided that the authority shall pay—

(i) the whole of such fees if in their opinion education suitable to the age, ability and aptitude of the child cannot otherwise be provided by them; and

(ii) the whole or part of such fees if in their opinion the payment thereof by the person otherwise liable for such payment would involve financial hardship to him;

(*d*) the courses of education in respect of which the benefits are provided shall be suitable for the pupils and the authority must be satisfied that the pupils will pursue a suitable course for a definite period;

(*e*) the benefits shall not cover activities which in the opinion of the Secretary of State are within the purview of another government department unless the Secretary of State otherwise approves.

NOTE

Paragraph (*b*) was substituted by the Scholarships and Other Benefits Amending Regulations No. 2, 1948, S.I. 1948 No. 2223, *post*, the substitution being consequential on the consolidation in section 5 of the Education (Miscellaneous Provisions) Act, 1948, p. 221, *ante*, of powers of local authorities with regard to the provision of clothing.

4. These Regulations shall have effect as from the 1st April, 1945.

5. These Regulations may be cited as the Regulations for Scholarships and Other Benefits, 1945.

* * * * *

EDUCATIONAL SERVICES AND RESEARCH GRANT REGULATIONS, 1946

S.R. & O. 1946 *No.* 424
March 22, 1946

NOTE

In these regulations (as here printed) references to " Minister of Education " and " Minister " have been replaced by references to " Secretary of State for Education and Science " and " Secretary of State " respectively. See S.I. 1964 No. 490, *post*.

1. In these Regulations—

" The Secretary of State " means the Secretary of State for Education and Science.

" Recognised " means recognised by the Secretary of State for the purposes of payment of grant.

" Approved " means approved by the Secretary of State for the purposes to which the context relates.

" Inspector " means one of [Her] Majesty's Inspectors or any other person employed by the Secretary of State for the purpose of inspection.

" Research " means educational research.

" Service " means any educational service within the scope of paragraphs (*a*) and (*b*) of Regulation 2.

2. The Secretary of State may, subject to the conditions hereinafter prescribed, make grants to any recognised persons other than Local Education Authorities in respect of expenditure incurred or to be incurred by them for any of the following purposes, and purposes incidental thereto, that is to say—

(*a*) the development of special educational methods ;
(*b*) the maintenance of special educational services of an advisory or organising character ; and
(*c*) research.

3. Persons seeking recognition under these Regulations shall satisfy the Minister as to the precise purposes for which the service or research is or is to be conducted, as to their financial standing, and generally as to their fitness to receive grant. Recognition may be withdrawn at the discretion of the Secretary of State.

4.—(1) The amount of grant to be paid in respect of any approved service or research will be determined by the Secretary of State after consideration of its character and cost and of the aggregate sums available to the Secretary of State for grants under these Regulations.

(2) Any grant may be paid in one sum or by instalments on such date or dates as may be determined by the Secretary of State, who may withhold or make a deduction from grant if the requirements of these Regulations are not fulfilled.

5. In assessing grant for any purpose, the Secretary of State will have regard to payments made by him otherwise than under these Regulations or by another Government Department and if, having regard to such other payments, the Secretary of State considers that payment of grant or payment of grant in full for this purpose would not be proper, he may withhold or reduce the grant.

6. Any premises or other thing used for any service or research shall be open to inspection by an Inspector who shall be afforded all the facilities he requires for informing himself as to that service or research.

7. Such records shall be kept, and such information and returns shall be furnished from time to time, as the Secretary of State may require.

8.—(1) The Interpretation Act, 1889, applies to the interpretation of these Regulations as it applies to the interpretation of an Act of Parliament.

(2) If any question arises as to the interpretation of these Regulations, or as to whether any of the requirements thereof are fulfilled, or as to the amount of any grant payable thereunder, the decision of the Secretary of State shall be final.

9. The Educational Research Grant Regulations, 1945, are hereby repealed.

10. These Regulations may be cited as The Educational Services and Research Grant Regulations, 1946.

* * * * *

SCHOLARSHIPS AND OTHER BENEFITS AMENDING REGULATIONS NO. 1, 1948

S.I. 1948 *No.* 688

April 1, 1948

NOTE

These Regulations amend the Regulations for Scholarships and Other Benefits, S.R. & O. 1945 No. 666, which are printed as amended, p. 327, *ante*.

PROVISION OF CLOTHING REGULATIONS, 1948

S.I. 1948 *No.* 2222

October 4, 1948

NOTE

These Regulations are made under Section 5 of the Education (Miscellaneous Provisions) Act, 1948, which consolidates and amends the provisions of the Education Acts of 1944 and 1946 with regard to the provision of clothing. The Regulations prescribe the conditions in which a right of property or a right of user only in the clothing provided shall be conferred and the circumstances in which Local Education Authorities shall or shall not, or may at their discretion, require parents to pay according to their means a sum not exceeding the cost to the Authority of providing the clothing.

Circular No. 183, p. 449, *post*, should be read with the Regulations.

1. These Regulations may be cited as the Provision of Clothing Regulations, 1948, and shall come into operation on the fifth day of October, 1948.

2.—(1) The Interpretation Act, 1889, shall apply to the interpretation of these Regulations as it applies to the interpretation of an Act of Parliament.

(2) In these Regulations the expression " the Act " means the Education (Miscellaneous Provisions) Act, 1948, and other expressions, to which meanings are assigned by the Education Acts, 1944 to 1948, shall have the same meanings for the purposes of these Regulations.

3.—[(1) Where a Local Education Authority provide clothing for a pupil under subsection (1), other than paragraphs (*b*) and (*c*) thereof, of Section 5 of the Education (Miscellaneous Provisions) Act, 1948, as amended by the Education (Miscellaneous Provisions) Act, 1953, they may require the parent of the pupil to pay such sum, if any, as they think fit, not exceeding such sum as, in the opinion of the Authority, he is able without financial hardship to pay:

Provided that any sum which the parent may be required to pay under this paragraph shall not exceed the cost to the Local Education Authority of the provision of the clothing.]

(2) Where a Local Education Authority provide clothing under sub-paragraph (*b*) or (*c*) of sub-section (1) of Section 5 of the Act, for a pupil at a Day Nursery School maintained by the Authority, or for a pupil in a Nursery Class at any day school so maintained, then if a right of property in the clothing is conferred on the pupil the Local Education Authority shall require the parent of the pupil to pay such sum, if any, as in the opinion of the Authority he is able without financial hardship to pay, not exceeding the cost to the Authority of the provision of the clothing and if the pupil is given a right of user only of the clothing the parent of the pupil shall not be required to pay any sum in respect of the clothing.

NOTE

Paragraph (1) was substituted by the Provision of Clothing Amending Regulations, 1956, S.I. 1956 No. 559, *post*.

4. Where a Local Education Authority provide clothing under sub-section (2) of Section 5 of the Act, then—

(*a*) if the school is a county school or a voluntary school for day pupils, the Local Education Authority shall require the parent of the pupil to pay such sum, if any, as in the opinion of the Authority he is able, without financial hardship, to pay, and a right of property in the clothing shall be conferred on the pupil;

(*b*) if the school is a Special School for day pupils *or a Residential Special School not maintained by a Local Education Authority*, the Local Education Authority may require the parent of the pupil to pay such sum, if any, as they think fit, not exceeding such sum as in the opinion of the Authority he is able, without financial hardship, to pay:

Provided that any sum which a parent may be required to pay under paragraph (*a*) or (*b*) of this Regulation shall not exceed the cost to the Local Education Authority of the provision of the clothing.

NOTE

The words printed in italics in paragraph (*b*) were directed to be omitted by the Provision of Clothing Amending Regulations, 1956, S.I. 1956 No. 559, *post*.

5. A Local Education Authority may provide free of charge—

(*a*) for pupils at a school maintained by them, or at a county college or other establishment for further education so maintained, and

(*b*) for persons who make use of facilities for physical training made available for them by the Authority under sub-section (1) of Section 53 of the Education Act, 1944,

the articles of clothing, suitable for physical training, specified in the Schedule to these Regulations:

Provided that pupils who are provided with clothing under this Regulation shall be given a right of user only of the clothing.

6. The Physical Training (Clothing) Regulations, 1945, are hereby revoked.

SCHEDULE

Plimsolls	Shorts	Cardigans
Running shoes	Knickers	Bathing suits
Football boots	Singlets	Bathing slips
Hockey shoes or boots	Sports blouses	Bathing caps
Cricket boots	Jerseys	

SCHOLARSHIPS AND OTHER BENEFITS AMENDING REGULATIONS NO. 2, 1948

S.I. 1948 *No.* 2223

NOTE

These Regulations amend reg. 3 of S.R. & O. 1945 No. 666, which is printed as so amended, p. 327, *ante*.

LOCAL AUTHORITIES AND LOCAL EDUCATION AUTHORITIES (ALLOCATION OF FUNCTIONS) REGULATIONS, 1951

S.I. 1951 *No.* 472
March 20, 1951

NOTE

These Regulations, which were made by the Secretary of State and the Minister of Education (now Secretary of State for Education and Science; see *infra*), under section 21 of the Children Act, 1948 (17 Halsbury's Statutes (3rd Edn.) 556), were issued with the following Explanatory Note:—

" Under Part II of the Children Act, 1948, which is concerned with the treatment of children in the care of local authorities, these authorities have certain functions concurrent with those of local education authorities as such. These regulations determine by which authority these functions are to be exercised, and, where the local education authority must,

in the exercise of their functions, have regard to the resources of a child's parent, determine whether a child in the care of a local authority shall be treated as a child of parents of sufficient resources or of parents without resources."

The Regulations should be read in conjunction with Circular No. 232 (31st March, 1951), p. 450, *post*. References to " Minister of Education " have been replaced, in the Regulations as here printed, by references to " Secretary of State for Education and Science ". See S.I. 1964 No. 490, *post*.

1. These Regulations may be cited as the Local Authorities and Local Education Authorities (Allocation of Functions) Regulations, 1951, and shall come into operation on the first day of May, 1951.

2.—(1) The Interpretation Act, 1889, shall apply to the interpretation of these Regulations as it applies to the interpretation of an Act of Parliament.

(2) In these Regulations, unless the context otherwise requires:—

" the Act " means the Children Act, 1948;

" child " has the meaning assigned to that expression by subsection (1) of Section 59 of the Act, and the expression " child who is in the care of a local authority under the Act " means any child in relation to whom the provisions of Part II of the Act apply;

" compulsory school age " has, subject to the provisions of Section 8 of the Education Act, 1946, the meaning assigned to that expression by Section 35 of the Education Act, 1944, or, in relation to registered pupils at special schools, by subsection (1) of Section 38 of the said last mentioned Act;

" local authority " means the council of a county or county borough in England or Wales, the council of a London borough or the Common Council of the City of London (as amended by the London Government Order (S.I. 1965 No. 654).

" local education authority " has the meaning assigned to that expression by subsection (1) of Section 114 of the Education Act, 1944;

" school " has the meaning assigned to that expression by subsection (1) of Section 114 of the Education Act, 1944;

" special educational treatment " has the meaning assigned to that expression by paragraph (*c*) of subsection (2) of Section 8 of the Education Act, 1944.

3. As respects the functions of the local education authority under Regulation 10 of the Provision of Milk and Meals Regulations, 1945, as amended by the Provision of Free Milk Regulations, 1946, the Milk and Meals (Amending) Regulations, 1949, and the Milk and Meals (Amending) Regulations, 1951, made by the Secretary of State for Education and Science under Section 49 of the Education Act, 1944 (which Regulation relates to payment for meals or other refreshment), a child who is in the care of a local authority under the Act shall be treated as a child of parents of sufficient resources to pay the whole of any sum payable under the said Regulation.

4. Where the local education authority are of opinion that a child who is in the care of a local authority under the Act should be provided with board and lodging to enable him to attend a particular county school, voluntary school or special school, or to receive special educational treatment, they shall inform the local authority accordingly, and where the child attends any such school as aforesaid or receives such special educational treatment, the function of providing any such board and lodging shall be exercised by the local authority under the Act, and not by the local education authority under Section 50 of the Education Act, 1944, as amended by the Education Act, 1946, and by the Education (Miscellaneous Provisions) Act, 1948.

5. Where it is necessary for payment to be made of the reasonable travelling expenses of a child who is in the care of a local authority under the Act to enable him to attend school or any establishment for further education, such payments shall be made by the local authority under the Act, and accordingly the local education authority shall not exercise their functions under subsection (2) of Section 55 of the Education Act, 1944, in respect of such child.

6. Where a child who is in the care of a local authority under the Act is provided under subsection (2) of Section 61 of the Education Act, 1944, by the local education authority with board and lodging at a school maintained by a local education authority, the child shall be treated as a child of parents without resources, and accordingly the local education authority shall remit the whole of the boarding fees.

7.—(1) As respects the functions of the local education authority under the Regulations for Scholarships and Other Benefits, 1945, made by the Secretary of State for Education and Science under Section 81 of the Education Act, 1944, a child who is in the care of a local authority under the Act shall be treated—

(*a*) for the purposes of paragraph (*a*) of the said Section 81, as a child of parents of sufficient resources, and accordingly the local education authority shall not exercise their functions under the said paragraph in respect of such a child;

(*b*) for the purposes of paragraph (*b*) of the said Section 81, as a child of parents without resources, and accordingly the local education authority shall pay the whole of the fees and expenses of such a child;

(*c*) for the purposes of paragraph (*c*) of the said Section 81, as a child of parents without resources, and accordingly the local education authority shall pay the whole of the cost of any such scholarships, exhibitions, bursaries or other allowances as are mentioned in the said paragraph (*c*):

Provided that the Local Education Authority shall not exercise their functions under the said paragraph (*c*) so far as those functions relate to the payment of maintenance allowances to parents in respect of pupils over compulsory school age attending school.

(2) The functions of a local authority under Section 20 of the Act in relation to a person who has attained the age of eighteen, and who is in receipt of education or training, shall only be exercised to the extent that the exercise of the functions of the local education authority under paragraph (*c*) of the said Section 81 does not meet the needs of such a person.

8. As respects the functions of the local education authority under Section 5 of the Education (Miscellaneous Provisions) Act, 1948, a child who is in the care of a local authority under the Act, shall, for the purposes of the Provision of Clothing Regulations, 1948, made by the Secretary of State for Education and Science under subsection (6) of the said Section 5, be treated as a child of parents of sufficient resources to pay the whole of any sums which under the Regulations the local education authority either shall be obliged to require, or may require, a parent to pay.

CENTRAL ADVISORY COUNCILS FOR EDUCATION AMENDING REGULATIONS, 1951

S.I. 1951 *No.* 1742

September 27, 1951

NOTE

These Regulations amend the Central Advisory Councils for Education Regulations, 1945, S.R. & O. 1945 No. 152, which are printed as amended, p. 325, *ante*.

LOCAL EDUCATION AUTHORITIES (RECOUPMENT) REGULATIONS, 1953

S.I. 1953 *No.* 507

March 23, 1953

NOTE

These Regulations were issued with the following Explanatory Note:—

" These Regulations consolidate and amend the Local Education Authorities (Recoupment) Regulations, 1949, and the Local Education Authorities (Recoupment) Amending Regulations, 1950. The most important change relates to pupils attending boarding schools who will be regarded as not belonging to the area of any Local Education Authority if their parents change their place of ordinary residence after the pupils have begun their boarding school career. Provision is also included in regard to children of members of visiting armed forces."

In the Regulations as here printed references to " Minister of Education " and " Minister " have been replaced by references to " Secretary of State for Education and Science " and " Secretary of State " respectively. See S.I. 1964 No. 490, *post*.

1.—(1) These Regulations may be cited as the Local Education Authorities (Recoupment) Regulations, 1953, and shall come into operation on the 1st day of April, 1953, and shall extend to any provision for primary or secondary education made before that date in so far as the cost of the provision is attributable to any period after the 31st day of March, 1952.

(2) The Local Education Authorities (Recoupment) Regulations, 1949, as amended by the Local Education Authorities (Recoupment) Amending Regulations, 1950, hereinafter called " the existing Regulations ", are hereby revoked without prejudice to the previous operation of, or anything duly done under, those Regulations.

(3) The Interpretation Act, 1889, shall apply to the interpretation of these Regulations as it applies to the interpretation of an Act of Parliament.

(4) In these Regulations, unless the context otherwise requires:—

(*a*) " the Act " means the Education Act, 1944, as amended by any subsequent enactments;

" the Act of 1948 " means the Education (Miscellaneous Provisions) Act, 1948;

" Authority " means Local Education Authority;

" Secretary of State " means Secretary of State for Education and Science;

" parents " means father and mother or surviving father or surviving mother, or where a pupil is ordinarily in the charge of one only of his parents, then the father or mother as the case may be;

" charitable institution " means any establishment in which persons are boarded and lodged from motives of charity;

" holiday home " means any establishment in which pupils are boarded and lodged for payment during holidays;

" handicapped pupil " means a handicapped pupil as defined by Regulation 1 (*a*) of the Handicapped Pupils and School Health Service Regulations, 1945;

" Visiting Force " means any body, contingent or detachment of the forces of a country to which the Visiting Forces Act, 1952, applies, being a body, contingent or detachment for the time being present in England or Wales on the invitation of Her Majesty's Government in the United Kingdom; and

" year " means financial year; and

(*b*) other expressions which have meanings assigned to them by the Act shall have the same respective meanings for the purposes of these Regulations.

NOTE

The Handicapped Pupils and School Health Service Regulations, 1945, S.R. & O. 1945 No. 1076, have been revoked. " The categories of pupils, called handicapped pupils, requiring special Educational treatment " are now defined by Regulation 4 of the Handicapped Pupils and Special Schools Regulations, 1959, S.I. 1959 No. 365, *post*.

2.—(1) Every claim by an Authority for recoupment in respect of the provision by them of primary or secondary education for a pupil who belongs to the area of some other Authority shall be sent to that Authority within eighteen months after the end of the year during which the attendances on which the claim is based were made.

(2) [*Revoked.*]

NOTE

Paragraph (2) was revoked by the Local Education Authorities Recoupment (Primary, Secondary and Further Education) Amending Regulations, 1959, S.I. 1959 No. 448, *post*.

3. [*Spent.*]

NOTE

This Regulation was substituted by the Local Education Authorities Recoupment (Primary, Secondary and Further Education) Amending Regulations, 1959, S.I. 1959 No. 448, *post*, the object whereof was to provide that the expenditure of local education authorities in educating pupils who did not belong to the area of any authority should be shared amongst all local education authorities by means of adjustments of the general grant formerly payable under section 1 of the Local Government Act, 1958. See now the Note to the Local Government Act, 1966, *ante*.

4.—(1) Notwithstanding any other provision in these Regulations, where a local Authority under the Children Act, 1948 receive into their care under that Act a child as defined in that Act, that child shall be treated for the purposes of these Regulations as belonging to the area of the local Authority responsible for meeting the expenses incurred in respect of that child under that Act.

(2) Notwithstanding any other provision in these Regulations, where a local Authority as aforesaid is appointed as a fit person under the Children and Young Persons Act, 1933, as amended by any subsequent enactment, for a child or young person, that child or young person shall be treated for the purposes of these Regulations as belonging to the area of that local Authority.

(3) A pupil, not falling into any of the categories specified in Regulation 5 of these Regulations, who is provided by an Authority with board and lodging otherwise than at school under Section 50 (1) of the Act, shall, whether or not he spends his holidays at the place where he has been boarded out, be treated as belonging to the area of the Authority in which the person, with whom the pupil would habitually reside but for the fact that he has been boarded out by the Authority, ordinarily resides.

(4) Where the person with whom a pupil, not being a pupil falling into any of the categories specified in Regulation 5 of these Regulations, ordinarily resides, makes arrangements for the pupil to reside during terms with another person and to attend school as a day pupil, both the aforesaid persons being resident in the area of the same Authority, the pupil shall be treated as belonging to the area of that Authority.

(5) A handicapped pupil, not falling into any of the categories specified in Regulation 5 of these Regulations, who is sent by an Authority to a boarding school, and does not spend his holidays with the person with whom he habitually resided immediately before he was sent to the boarding school, shall nevertheless be treated as belonging to the area of the Authority in which the said person ordinarily resides.

(6) A pupil, not falling into any of the categories specified in Regulation 5 of these Regulations, who resides as a patient in a hospital [or in a nursing home, hostel or other establishment for the care of handicapped children] and who receives primary or secondary education therein, shall be treated as belonging to the area of the Authority in which the person, with whom the pupil would habitually reside but for the fact that he is in hospital [or other establishment], ordinarily resides.

(7) Notwithstanding any other provision in these Regulations, where immediately before the commencement of these Regulations an Authority were making payments under paragraph (4) of Regulation 4 of the existing Regulations (which continued in certain circumstances the effect of Section 106 of the Act) to another Authority in respect of a pupil, then, so long as the first-mentioned Authority would have continued to make such payments if the said Section had remained in force, the pupil shall be treated as belonging to their area.

NOTE

The words in square brackets in paragraph (6) were inserted by the Local Education Authorities (Recoupment) (Amendment) Regulations 1973, S.I. 1973 No. 1676.

5.—[(1) Where a pupil, not being a pupil falling into any of the categories hereinafter specified in this Regulation or falling to be dealt with under Section 6 (2) (*b*) of the Act of 1948, has either—

(*a*) become a boarder at a school maintained by an Authority, or

(*b*) received a grant from an Authority in respect of the whole or part of the fees at any other school to enable him to become, or to remain, a boarder thereat

and thereafter the person with whom the pupil habitually resides during holidays—

(*a*) changed his place of ordinary residence between 1st September, 1949, and 31st March, 1952, to the area of another Authority, or

(*b*) after 31st March, 1952, changes his place of ordinary residence as aforesaid,

then as from 1st April, 1952, in the former case, or as from the date of the change in the latter case, the pupil shall be treated as not belonging to the area of any Authority and shall continue to be so treated while he remains a boarder at the same school:

Provided that the foregoing provisions of this paragraph shall not apply to a handicapped pupil.]

(2) The following categories of pupils, not being pupils included in the categories specified in paragraphs (1), (2) and (7) of the last foregoing Regulation, shall be included among the categories of pupils treated as not belonging to the area of any authority:—

(*a*) pupils whose parents are ordinarily resident, or are resident for the time being, outside England and Wales, or whose parents, though resident for the time being in England or Wales, were formerly resident in, and may be expected to return as soon as possible to, Gibraltar or Malta;

(*b*) pupils resident for the time being in England or Wales by virtue of their having entered England or Wales with members of a Visiting Force;

(*c*) pupils who habitually reside in holiday homes as inmates thereof;

(*d*) pupils who parents, being aliens, are resident for the time being in hostels or camps in England or Wales;

(*e*) pupils whose parents have no fixed abode; and

(*f*) pupils who are resident in charitable institutions or boarded out by such institutions or sent from such institutions to residential schools:

Provided that a pupil shall only be treated as resident in a charitable institution if he is boarded and lodged therein during both terms and holidays.

(3) A pupil who is educated as a boarder at a boarding school and who, by virtue of these Regulations or of Section 6 (2) (*b*) of the Act of 1948, has, after the 31st day of March, 1952, been treated as not belonging to the area of any Authority, shall continue to be so treated while he remains a boarder at the same school.

NOTE

Paragraph (1) was substituted by the Local Education Authorities (Recoupment) Amending Regulations, 1954, S.I. 1954 No. 991, *post*. Its effect is to provide for the treatment of boarding pupils as pupils not belonging to the area of any Authority in cases where the person with whom the pupil habitually resides during holidays changed his place of residence between 1st September, 1949, and 31st March, 1952, or changes his place of residence after the latter date.

LOCAL EDUCATION AUTHORITIES RECOUPMENT (FURTHER EDUCATION) REGULATIONS, 1954

S.I. 1954 *No.* 815

June 21, 1954

NOTE

These Regulations were issued with the following Explanatory Note:—

"These Regulations prescribe conditions governing the recoupment to local education authorities in accordance with the provisions of section 7 of the Education (Miscellaneous Provisions) Act, 1953, of the cost of providing further education for students not belonging to their area, and specify categories of students to be treated as students not belonging to the area of any authority".

In the Regulations as here printed references to "Minister of Education" and "Minister" have been replaced by references to "Secretary of State for Education and Science" and "Secretary of State" respectively. See S.I. 1964 No. 490, *post*.

1.—(1) These Regulations may be cited as the Local Education Authorities Recoupment (Further Education) Regulations, 1954, and shall come into operation on the 29th day of June, 1954, and shall extend to any provision for further education made before that date in so far as the cost of the provision is attributable to any period after the 13th July, 1953.

(2) The Interpretation Act, 1889, shall apply to the interpretation of these Regulations as it applies to the interpretation of an Act of Parliament.

(3) In these Regulations unless the context otherwise requires:—

(*a*) "the Act" means the Education Act, 1944, as amended by any subsequent enactment;

"the Act of 1948" means the Education (Miscellaneous Provisions) Act, 1948;

"the Act of 1953" means the Education (Miscellaneous Provisions) Act, 1953;

"academic year" means the period of twelve months beginning with 1st August in any year and ending with 31st July in the next following year;

"Authority" means Local Education Authority;

"Secretary of State" means Secretary of State for Education and Science;

"parents" means father and mother or surviving father or surviving mother, or where a pupil is ordinarily in the charge of one only of his parents, then the father or mother as the case may be;

"charitable institution" means any establishment in which persons are boarded and lodged from motives of charity;

"child" means a person under the age of eighteen years;

"Visiting Force" means any body, contingent or detachment of the forces of a country to which the Visiting Forces Act, 1952, applies, being a body, contingent or detachment for the time being present in England or Wales on the invitation of Her Majesty's Government in the United Kingdom;

"young person" means a person who has attained the age of fourteen years and is under the age of seventeen years; and

(*b*) other expressions which have meanings assigned to them by the Act shall have the same respective meanings for the purposes of these Regulations.

2.—(1) Every claim by an Authority for recoupment in respect of the provision by them of further education for a pupil who belongs to the area of some other Authority, that other Authority having consented to the making of the provision, shall be sent to that Authority within eighteen months after the end of the academic year during which the provision was made.

(2) [*Revoked.*]

3.—(1) Where an Authority provide further education for a pupil who belongs to the area of some other Authority, that other Authority having consented to the making of the provision, the providing Authority shall be entitled to recoupment from the other Authority of [the whole] of the amount of the cost to the providing Authority of the provision.

[(2) Where an Authority provide further education for a pupil who does not belong to the area of any Authority, the cost of the provision shall be recouped to the Authority, and the aggregate amount of the cost of recouping all Authorities who make such provision apportioned amongst all Authorities, in accordance with the General Grants (Pooling Arrangements) Regulations, 1959.]

NOTE

The words in square brackets in paragraph (1) were substituted for "seven-eighths" by the Local Education Authorities Recoupment (Further Education) Amending Regulations, 1965, S.I. 1965 No. 512. The providing authority is thus now recouped the whole cost of provision of education for a pupil belonging to the area of another local education authority.

Paragraph (2) was substituted by the Local Education Authorities Recoupment (Primary, Secondary and Further Education) Amending Regulations, 1959, S.I. 1959 No. 448, *post*.

4.—(1) Notwithstanding any subsequent provision in these Regulations, other than paragraph (3) of Regulation 5, where immediately before the 14th July, 1953, an Authority was either—

(*a*) making payments under Section 6 (5) (*b*) of the Act of 1948 to another Authority in respect of the full-time further education of a pupil, or

(*b*) making payments to a pupil to assist him to receive full-time further education

then, so long as the pupil continues to receive the further education aforesaid, he shall be treated as belonging to the area of the first-mentioned Authority.

(2) Notwithstanding any subsequent provision in these Regulations. other than paragraph (3) of Regulation 5, where a child is in the care of a local Authority under the Children Act, 1948, that child shall be treated for the purposes of these Regulations as belonging to the area of the local Authority responsible for meeting the expenses incurred in respect of that child under that Act.

(3) Notwithstanding any subsequent provision in these Regulations, other

than paragraph (3) of Regulation 5, where a local Authority as aforesaid is appointed as a fit person under the Children and Young Persons Act, 1933, as amended by any subsequent enactment, for a young person, that young person shall be treated for the purposes of these Regulations as belonging to the area of that local Authority.

[(4) Subject to regulation 5, for the purposes of these regulations there shall, in the case of any pupil who changes his place of residence after 31st December 1971, be disregarded any residence in the area of any authority in which he becomes ordinarily resident for the purpose of attending a full-time course of further education.]

(5) A pupil who is provided by an Authority with part-time further education shall be treated as belonging to the area of the Authority in which he is for the time being residing.

(6) A pupil, not being a pupil falling into any of the categories specified in Regulation 5 of these Regulations, or falling to be dealt with under Section 7 (4) (*b*) of the Act of 1953, [on whom an authority have resolved to bestow an award in respect of his attendance at a course of full-time education shall be treated as belonging to the area of that authority for so long as he attends the course.]

[Provided that the payment by an Authority to a pupil as aforesaid of a sum to meet, or assist in meeting, travelling expenses to enable him to attend a course as aforesaid, shall be deemed not to be a grant for the purpose of this paragraph.]

[(7) Notwithstanding any other provisions of these regulations, a pupil who is pursuing a course of study provided by the Open University shall, in respect of any calendar year in which he pursues that course,—

(*a*) [[subject to sub-paragraph (*b*),]] if on the 31st October preceding that year he is ordinarily resident within the area of a local education authority, be treated as belonging to the area of that authority; and

(*b*) if on that date he is not so resident, or if although so resident he falls within any of the categories described in paragraphs (1), (2) and (3) of regulation 5 below, be treated as not belonging to the area of any local education authority.]

NOTES

The words in square brackets in paragraph (4) were added by the Local Education Authorities Recoupment (Further Education) Amending Regulations, 1955, S.I. 1955 No. 222, *post*. The proviso to paragraph (6) was added by the Local Education Authorities Recoupment (Further Education) Amending Regulations, 1956, S.I. 1956 No. 1588, *post*.

The words in square brackets in paragraph (6) were substituted by the Local Education Authorities Recoupment (Further Education) (Amendment) Regulations 1975, S.I. 1975 No. 1569.

Paragraph (7) was added by the Local Education Authorities Recoupment (Further Education) (Amendment) Regulations 1971, S.I. 1971 No. 701.

Paragraph (4), and the words within double square brackets in paragraph (7) (*a*), were respectively substituted and inserted by the Local Education Authorities Recoupment (Further Education) (Amendment No. 2) Regulations 1971, S.I. 1971 No. 1821.

5.—(1) The following categories of pupils who are provided by Authorities with full-time further education, not being pupils included in the categories specified in paragraphs (1), (2) and (3) of the last foregoing Regulation, shall be included among the categories of pupils treated as not belonging to the area of any Authority:—

(*a*) pupils whose parents would ordinarily reside in England and Wales but for the fact that they are employed for the time being outside England and Wales;

(*b*) pupils resident for the time being in England or Wales by virtue of their having entered England or Wales with members of a Visiting Force;

(*c*) pupils resident for the time being in hostels or camps for aliens in England or Wales; and

(*d*) pupils resident in charitable institutions or boarded out by such institutions:

Provided that a pupil shall only be treated as resident in a charitable institution if he is boarded and lodged therein during both terms and holidays.

(2) A pupil who is provided by an Authority with full-time further education and who at the time he ceased to receive secondary education had been

treated, under Section 6 of the Act of 1948, or the Regulations made thereunder, as not belonging to the area of any Authority shall continue to be so treated.

(3) Notwithstanding any other provision in these Regulations, a pupil who resides as a patient in a hospital and who receives further education therein, shall be treated as not belonging to the area of any Authority.

(4) A pupil who by virtue of these Regulations, or of Section 7 (4) (*b*) of the Act of 1953, has been treated as not belonging to the area of any Authority shall continue to be so treated while he is provided by an Authority with full-time further education.

LOCAL EDUCATION AUTHORITIES (RECOUPMENT) AMENDING REGULATIONS, 1954

S.I. 1954 *No.* 991

July 23, 1954

NOTE

These Regulations amend retrospectively Regulations 2 and 5 of the Local Education Authorities (Recoupment) Regulations, 1953, S.I. 1953 No. 507, which are printed as amended at p. 333, *ante*.

LOCAL EDUCATION AUTHORITIES RECOUPMENT (FURTHER EDUCATION) AMENDING REGULATIONS, 1955

S.I. 1955 *No.* 222

February 7, 1955

NOTE

These Regulations amend Regulation 4 of the Local Education Authorities Recoupment (Further Education) Regulations, 1954, S.I. 1954 No. 815, which is printed as amended on p. 336, *ante*.

PUPILS' REGISTRATION REGULATIONS, 1956

S.I. 1956 *No.* 357

March 14, 1956

NOTE

These Regulations were issued with the following Explanatory Note:—

" These Regulations consolidate and amend the Pupils' Registration Regulations, 1948, and the Pupils' Registration Amending Regulations, 1948. Two changes are made:—

(i) When a pupil leaves an independent or direct grant school, his name must be removed from the register without reference to any other grounds specified in Regulation 4;

(ii) When a pupil has been permanently excluded from a maintained school his name must be removed from the register."

In the Regulations as here printed references to " Minister of Education " and " Minister " have been replaced by references to " Secretary of State for Education and Science " and " Secretary of State " respectively. See S.I. 1964 No. 490, *post*.

The Regulations were made under s. 80 of the Education Act, 1944, p. 165, *ante*, as amended by the Education (Miscellaneous Provisions) Act 1948, s. 4 and Sch. 1.

Citation

1. These Regulations may be cited as the Pupils' Registration Regulations 1956, and shall come into operation on the third day of April, 1956.

Interpretation

2.—(1) In these Regulations unless the context otherwise requires:—

(*a*) " the Act " means the Education Act, 1944, as amended by any later enactment;

" Authority " means Local Education Authority;

" Secretary of State " means Secretary of State for Education and Science;

(*b*) other expressions which have meanings assigned to them by the Act shall have the same respective meanings for the purposes of these Regulations.

(2) The Interpretation Act, 1889, shall apply to the interpretation of these Regulations as it applies to the interpretation of an Act of Parliament.

Registers to be kept by Proprietors

3.—(1) The proprietor of every schoool shall cause to be kept:—

(*a*) an Admission Register; and

(*b*) except in the case of an independent school of which all the pupils are boarders, an Attendance Register.

(2) The Admission Register shall contain an index in alphabetical order of all the pupils at the school and shall also contain the following particulars in respect of every such pupil:—

(*a*) Name in full;

(*b*) Sex;

(*c*) Name and address of parent;

(*d*) Day, month and year of birth;

(*e*) Day, month and year of admission or re-admission;

(*f*) Name and address of the school last attended, if any.

(3) In the case of every school which includes boarding pupils a statement as to whether each pupil of compulsory school age is a boarder or a day pupil shall be added to the particulars specified in paragraph (2) of this Regulation.

(4) There shall be recorded in the Attendance Register at the commencement of each morning and afternoon session the presence or absence of every pupil whose name is entered in and not deleted from the Admission Register:

Provided that it shall not be necessary to record in the Attendance Register the presence or absence of any pupil who is a boarder in an independent school.

Deletions from Admission Register

4. The following grounds are hereby prescribed as those on which the name of a pupil is to be deleted from the Admission Register, that is to say—

(*a*) if the pupil is of compulsory school age, any of the following grounds:—

(i) where the pupil is registered at the school in accordance with the requirements of a School Attendance Order, that another school is substituted for that named in the Order or the Order is revoked on the ground that arrangements have been made for the child to receive efficient full-time education suitable to this age, ability and aptitude otherwise than at school;

(ii) in a case not falling within sub-paragraph (i) of this paragraph, that he has been registered as a pupil of another school;

(iii) in a case not falling within sub-paragraph (i) of this paragraph, that he has ceased to attend the school at which he is registered and his parent has satisfied the Authority that he is receiving efficient full-time education suitable to his age, ability and aptitude otherwise than by attendance at school;

(iv) except in the case of a boarder, that his ordinary residence has been transferred to a place whence the school at which he is registered is not accessible with reasonable facility;

(v) that he is certified by the School Medical Officer as unlikely to be in a fit state of health to attend school before becoming legally exempt from the obligation so to attend;

(vi) that he has been continuously absent from school for a period of not less than four weeks and the proprietor of the school has failed, after reasonable enquiry, to obtain information of the cause of absence;

(vii) that the proprietor has ascertained that the pupil has died;

(viii) that he will cease to be of compulsory school age before the school next meets and intends to discontinue in attendance thereat;

(ix) in the case of a boarder, or of a pupil at a school not maintained by an Authority, that he has ceased to be a pupil of the school; or

(x) where the pupil is registered at a school maintained by an Authority, that he has been excluded, other than temporarily, therefrom by the Authority or by the Managers or Governors of the school:

Provided that if in the result of an appeal by the parent of the pupil against such exclusion the Secretary of State determines that the pupil has been excluded on other than reasonable grounds, the name of the pupil shall forthwith be reinstated in the Admission Register:

Provided that in a case not covered by sub-paragraph (i) of this paragraph, the name of a child who has under arrangements made by an Authority become a registered pupil at a special school shall not be removed from the Admission Register of that school without the consent of that Authority or, if that Authority refuse to give consent, without a direction of the Secretary of State; or

(*b*) if he is not of compulsory school age, on any of the following grounds:—

(i) that he has ceased to attend the school or, in the case of a boarder, that he has ceased to be a pupil of the school;

(ii) that he has been continuously absent from school for a period of not less than four weeks and the proprietor of the school has failed, after reasonable enquiry, to obtain information of the cause of absence; or

(iii) that the proprietor has ascertained that the pupil has died.

Inspection of Registers

5. The Admission Register and Attendance Register of every school shall be available for inspection during school hours by Inspectors appointed by Her Majesty and by persons authorised by the Secretary of State under Section 77 (2) of the Act:

Provided that in the case of every school maintained by an Authority the said Registers shall also be open to inspection by officers authorised by the Authority for that purpose.

Extracts from Registers

6. The persons authorised by the last foregoing Regulation to inspect the Admission Register and Attendance Register of any school shall be permitted to make extracts therefrom for the purposes of the Act.

Returns

7. The proprietor of every school shall make to the Authority for the area to which the pupil in question belongs, at such intervals as may be agreed between the proprietor and the Authority, or as may be determined by the Secretary of State in default of agreement, a return giving the full name and address of every registered pupil of compulsory school age not being a boarder who fails to attend the school regularly or who has been absent from the school for a continuous period of not less than two weeks and specifying the cause of absence, if known to the proprietor:

Provided that this Regulation shall not have effect with respect to any absence from the school due to sickness of the pupil in respect of which a Medical Certificate has been furnished to the Headmaster.

Method of making Entries

8. Every entry in an Admission Register or Attendance Register shall be written in ink and any correction shall be made in such a manner that the original entry and the correction are both clearly distinguishable.

Preservation of Registers

9. Every entry in an Admission Register or Attendance Register shall be preserved for a period of three years after the date on which it was last used.

Revocation

10. The Pupils' Registration Regulations, 1948, as amended by the Pupils' Registration Amending Regulations, 1948, are hereby revoked.

PROVISION OF CLOTHING AMENDING REGULATIONS, 1956

S.I. 1956 *No.* 559

April 13, 1956

NOTE

These Regulations amend Regulations 3 and 4 of the Provision of Clothing Regulations, 1948, S.I. 1948 No. 2222, which are printed as amended *ante*.

LOCAL EDUCATION AUTHORITIES RECOUPMENT (FURTHER EDUCATION) AMENDING REGULATIONS, 1956

S.I. 1956 *No.* 1588

October 9, 1956

NOTE

These Regulations amend Regulation 4 of the Local Education Authorities Recoupment (Further Education) Regulations 1954, S.I. 1954 No. 815, which are printed as amended, *ante*.

INDEPENDENT SCHOOLS REGISTRATION REGULATIONS, 1957

S.I. 1957 *No.* 929

May 28, 1957

NOTE

These Regulations were issued with the following Explanatory Note:—

" These Regulations prescribe the particulars to be furnished to the Registrar of Independent Schools by proprietors applying to register their schools under Part III of the Education Act, 1944. They also provide for notification of any changes in those particulars, and for the removal from the register of any school in default."

In the Regulations as here printed references to " Minister " and " Ministry of Education " have been replaced by references to " Secretary of State " (*i.e.*, Secretary of State for Education and Science) and " Department of Education and Science ". See S.I. 1964 No. 490, *post*.

1. These Regulations may be cited as the Independent Schools Registration Regulations, 1957, and shall come into operation on the 30th day of September, 1957.

2.—(1) In these Regulations, unless the context otherwise requires, the expression "proprietor" means the person or body of persons responsible, or proposing to be responsible, for the management of an independent school; and the expression "independent school" means any school at which full-time education is provided for five or more pupils of compulsory school age (whether or not such education is also provided for pupils under or over that age), not being a school maintained by a Local Education Authority or a school in respect of which grants are made by the Secretary of State to the proprietor of the school or an independent school of a class which is for the time being exempted from registration by an order made under section 70 of the Education Act, 1944.

(2) Other expressions to which meanings are assigned by the Education Acts, 1944 to 1953 shall have the same meanings for the purpose of these Regulations.

(3) The Interpretation Act, 1889, shall apply to the interpretation of these Regulations as it applies to the interpretation of an Act of Parliament.

SCHEDULE

RETURN TO BE MADE FOR THE PURPOSES OF REGISTRATION UNDER SECTION 70 OF THE EDUCATION ACT, 1944, AND THE INDEPENDENT SCHOOLS REGISTRATION REGULATIONS, 1957

1. Name of School..
2. Full Postal Address..
3. Responsible Body or Proprietor..
4. Number of full-time pupils at the date when this form is signed:—

Age last Birthday	2	3	4	5	6	7	8	9	10	11	12	13	14	15	16	17	18	19	TOTAL
Boys																			
Girls																			
TOTAL																			

5. Number of boarders included in 4, above: Boys............ Girls............
6. Teaching staff:—

	Surname (including maiden name in case of married woman)	First names	Qualifications (e.g. University Degrees, Diploma or Certificate)	Date of birth in full
(i) Head Master/ Mistress				
(ii) Full-time Assistants			Continue overleaf if necessary	
(iii) Part-time Assistants			Continue overleaf if necessary	

I certify the above particulars to be correct and hereby apply under section 70 (1) of the Education Act, 1944, for the above-named school to be registered.

Date.................... Signature..

3. Every application by a proprietor for the registration of his independent school shall be made in writing addressed to the Registrar of Independent Schools, Department of Education and Science (a), Curzon Street, London, W.1 (hereinafter referred to as the Registrar), and shall contain the particulars specified in the Schedule to these Regulations.

4.—(1) In January, 1959, and thereafter in each succeeding January, a proprietor shall communicate in writing to the Registrar particulars of any changes in the school since the date of the particulars last furnished by him, in relation to—

(*a*) the number of pupils by sex and age groups;
(*b*) the number of boarders, if any, by sex groups; and
(*c*) the teaching staff.

(2) If there is any change in the proprietorship or postal address of the school, particulars of the change shall immediately be furnished in writing to the Registrar by the proprietor.

5. If at any time it appears to the Registrar that a proprietor has failed to comply with the requirements of the preceding Regulation, he may by notice in writing require the proprietor to furnish such particulars in relation to the matters mentioned in that Regulation as he may specify; and if the proprietor fails to comply with the terms of such notice within two months from the date thereof, the Secretary of State may order the name of the school to be deleted from the register.

INDEPENDENT SCHOOLS (EXEMPTION FROM REGISTRATION) ORDER, 1957

S.I. 1957 *No.* 1173

July 3, 1957

NOTE

In this Order as here printed the reference to " Minister " has been replaced by a reference to " Secretary of State " (for Education and Science). See S.I. 1964 No. 490, *post.*

1. This Order may be cited as the Independent Schools (Exemption from Registration) Order, 1957, and shall come into operation on the thirtieth day of September, 1957.

2. A school which has received or receives from the Secretary of State a notification that he recognises it as efficient shall, unless and until the notification is withdrawn, be exempt from registration under the said Section 70.

3. The following schools shall also be exempted from registration:—

The Royal Marines School of Music, Deal.
The Duke of York's Royal Military School, Dover.

INDEPENDENT SCHOOLS TRIBUNAL RULES, 1958

S.I. 1958 *No.* 519

March 25, 1958

NOTE

These Rules were issued with the following Explanatory Note:—

" These Rules prescribe the procedure to be followed in proceedings before an Independent Schools Tribunal set up under section 72 of the Education Act, 1944, to hear appeals against a notice of complaint served by the [Secretary of State for Education and Science (see *infra*)] on the proprietor of an independent school or against a refusal of the Secretary of State to remove a disqualification imposed as the result of such a notice."

In these Rules as here printed references to " Minister of Education " and " Minister " have been replaced by references to " Secretary of State for Education and Science " and " Secretary of State " respectively. See S.I. 1964 No. 490, *post.*

Citation, Commencement and Interpretation

1.—(1) These Rules may be cited as the Independent Schools Tribunal Rules, 1958, and shall come into operation on the first day of April, 1958.

(2) The Interpretation Act, 1889, shall apply to the interpretation of these Rules as it applies to the interpretation of an Act of Parliament.

(3) In these Rules, unless the context otherwise requires—

" The Act " means the Education Act, 1944;

" The Secretary of State " means the Secretary of State for Education and Science;

" Notice of complaint " means a notice served by the Secretary of State under section 71 of the Act;

" The tribunal " means an Independent Schools Tribunal constituted in accordance with the provisions of the Sixth Schedule to the Act.

Notice of Appeal

2.—(1) An appeal to the tribunal shall be instituted by sending to the Secretary of State a written notice of appeal signed by the appellant, setting out the grounds of appeal and stating an address to which communications regarding the appeal should be sent.

(2) The notice shall be sent to the Secretary of State—

(i) in the case of an appeal against a notice of complaint, within the time limited by that notice; or

(ii) in the case of an appeal against a refusal of the Secretary of State to remove a disqualification imposed by an order under Part III of the Act, within one month after the communication of the refusal to the appellant.

(3) Where the appeal is against a notice of complaint alleging that a teacher is not a proper person to be employed as a teacher in any school, the appellant shall at the same time send a copy of the notice of appeal to the proprietor of the school or to the teacher, as the case may be.

Constitution of Tribunal

3.—(1) On receipt of a notice of appeal the Secretary of State shall forthwith request the Lord Chancellor and the Lord President of the Council respectively to appoint the chairman and members of the tribunal to hear the appeal.

(2) The Lord Chancellor shall appoint a person to act as secretary of the tribunal for the purposes of the appeal and the Secretary of State shall as soon as may be send four copies of the notice of appeal to the secretary so appointed.

Time and Place of Hearing

4. The chairman of the tribunal shall fix a date, time and place for the hearing of the appeal and shall cause to be served upon the appellant, not less than twenty-eight days before the date so fixed, a notice in the form set out in the First Schedule hereto and shall at the same time send a copy of the notice to the Secretary of State and, where the appeal is against a notice of complaint alleging that a teacher is not a proper person to be employed as a teacher in any school, to the proprietor of the school or to the teacher, as the case may be.

Abandonment of Appeal

5. [If an appellant at any time before the hearing gives notice in writing to the secretary of the tribunal that he desires to withdraw his appeal, the tribunal shall hear and determine the appeal in his absence.]

NOTE

This rule was substituted by rule 2 of the Independent Schools Tribunal (Amendment) Rules 1972, S.I. 1972 No. 42.

Default of Appearance

6. [If an appellant or the Secretary of State fails to appear at the time fixed for the hearing of the appeal, the tribunal may hear and determine the appeal in his absence.]

NOTE

This rule was substituted by rule 2 of the Independent Schools Tribunal (Amendment) Rules 1972, S.I. 1972 No. 42.

Right of Audience

7.—(1) An appellant may appear and be heard—

(i) in person,

(ii) by counsel or solicitor,

(iii) if a partnership, by a partner,

(iv) if a company, by a duly authorised director or officer of the company, or

(v) by any other person allowed by the tribunal to appear on behalf of the appellant.

(2) The Secretary of State may appear and be heard by counsel or solicitor or by any officer of his department.

Hearing

8. The hearing of an appeal shall take place in public unless the tribunal determines that there are exceptional reasons which make it desirable that the hearing or some part of it should take place in private.

Procedure at Hearing

9.—(1) An appellant and the Secretary of State shall have the right to address the tribunal and call witnesses, who shall be subject to cross-examination and to re-examination.

(2) The tribunal may require the attendance of further witnesses in addition to those called by or on behalf of the appellant and the Secretary of State.

(3) The tribunal may permit evidence to be given by affidavit, but may at any stage of the proceedings require the personal attendance of any deponent for examination and cross-examination.

(4) The tribunal shall not reject any evidence on the ground only that such evidence would be inadmissible in a court of law.

(5) After the evidence has been concluded, the Secretary of State and the appellant shall have the right to address the tribunal if they so desire.

Application of Arbitration Act, 1950

10. The provisions of section 12 of the Arbitration Act, 1950, with respect to the administration of oaths and the taking of affirmations, the summoning, attendance and examination of witnesses, and the production of documents shall apply to proceedings before the tribunal as they apply to an arbitration where no contrary intention is expressed in the arbitration agreement.

Decision of Tribunal

11.—(1) The decision of the tribunal on the appeal shall, in the event of disagreement, be the decision of the majority and may be given orally at the hearing or in writing as soon as may be after the hearing.

(2) The secretary shall send a copy of the order made by the tribunal, together with a statement of its findings and of the reasons for the decision, to every appellant and to the Secretary of State.

Extension of Time

12. The time appointed by these Rules for doing any act in connection with an appeal may be extended by the tribunal or by the chairman upon such terms (if any) as may seem just, notwithstanding that the time appointed has expired before an application for extension is made.

Remuneration and Allowances of Tribunal

13.—(1) The chairman of the tribunal shall be remunerated at the rate of [£40] and the members at the rate of [£16] for each day on which the tribunal sits.

(2) The chairman and members of the tribunal shall be paid the allowances specified in the Second Schedule hereto in respect of travelling and subsistence expenses incurred by them in connection with the performance of their duties.

[(3) When under rule 15 the chairman of the tribunal gives directions of an interlocutory nature without a hearing by the tribunal, he shall be remunerated at the following rate:—

(i) if no party has appeared before the chairman: £10;

(ii) for each day on which a party appears—

for a hearing lasting not more than 3 hours: £20;

for a hearing lasting more than 3 hours: £40.]

NOTES

The figure of £40 in rule 13 (1) was substituted by the Independent Schools Tribunal (Amendment) Rules 1975, S.I. 1975 No. 854; that of £16 by the Independent Schools Tribunal (Amendment No. 2) Rules 1975, S.I. 1975 No. 1298.

Paragraph (3) was added by the Independent Schools Tribunal (Amendment) Rules 1972, S.I. 1972 No. 42, but the figures of £10, £20 and £40 respectively were substituted by the Independent Schools Tribunal (Amendment) Rules 1975, S.I. 1975 No. 854.

Power to Regulate Procedure

14.—(1) Subject to the provisions of the Act and these Rules, the tribunal shall have power to regulate its own procedure.

(2) Failure to comply with any requirements of these Rules shall not invalidate any proceedings unless the tribunal so directs.

Interlocutory Applications

15.—(1) An application for directions of an interlocutory nature in connection with any appeal may be made by the Secretary of State or any appellant to the chairman of the tribunal appointed for the purposes of that appeal.

(2) The application shall be in writing and shall be sent to the secretary of the tribunal appointed for the purposes of the appeal and shall state the grounds upon which the application is made.

(3) If the application is made with the consent of the Secretary of State or an appellant, it shall be accompanied by consents signed by or on behalf of the Secretary of State or the appellant, as the case may be.

(4) If the application is not made with such consent, then, before it is made, a copy of it shall be sent to the appellant or the Secretary of State, as the case may be, and the application shall state that this has been done.

(5) If the appellant or the Secretary of State, within 7 days after receiving a copy of the application, sends to the secretary of the tribunal and to the Secretary of State or the appellant, as the case may be, written notice of objection, the chairman of the tribunal shall, before giving any direction on the application, consider such objection and, if he considers it necessary for the proper determination of the application, shall give the appellant and the Secretary of State an opportunity of appearing before him.

(6) The chairman of the tribunal shall communicate his decision in writing to the Secretary of State and the appellant.

(7) If at any stage the chairman of the tribunal decides that an application involves a question which ought to be decided by the tribunal, he shall fix a time, date and place for a hearing by the tribunal and shall cause the Secretary of State and the appellant to be notified thereof, not less than 14 days before the date fixed.]

NOTE

This rule was inserted by the Independent Schools Tribunal (Amendment) Rules 1972, S.I. 1972 No. 42.

Rule 4

FIRST SCHEDULE

NOTICE OF HEARING

THE EDUCATION ACT, 1944

TAKE NOTICE that your appeal against the Secretary of Education and Science's notice of complaint dated the day of , 19 , alleging that (*here insert short statement of grounds of complaint*) [*or* against the Secretary of State for Education and Science's refusal to remove the disqualification imposed on (*here insert description of disqualification*) under Part III of the Education Act, 1944,] will be heard by the Independent Schools Tribunal sitting at on the day of , 19 , at o'clock. If for any reason you do not wish, or are unable, to attend at the above time and place, you should IMMEDIATELY inform me in writing at the address mentioned at the head of this notice stating the reasons for your inability to attend.

(Signed)

Secretary.

Rule 13 (2)

SECOND SCHEDULE

TRAVELLING AND SUBSISTENCE ALLOWANCES OF THE TRIBUNAL

There shall be paid to the chairman and members of the tribunal—

(1) travelling expenses actually incurred by them in attending a hearing including the cost of first class return railway fares;

(2) where, for the purpose of attending the hearing, the chairman or member—

(*a*) is absent from home for a period of more than five but less than ten hours, [£0·85]; or for a period exceeding ten hours, [£1·80];

(*b*) spends one or more nights away from home.

(i) for each night spent within 4 miles of Charing Cross, [£16·55];

(ii) for each night spent elsewhere [£14·65].

Note: The allowance specified in paragraph (*a*) above is not payable for any period of twenty-four hours for which the allowance specified in paragraph (*b*) is payable.

NOTE

The amounts payable under para. (2) of the above Schedule were increased by r. 3 of the Independent Schools Tribunal (Amendment No. 2) Rules 1975, S.I. 1975 No. 1298.

HANDICAPPED PUPILS (BOARDING) REGULATIONS, 1959

S.I. 1959 *No.* 362

March 4, 1959

NOTE

These Regulations, made under s. 3 (4) of the Local Government Act, 1958, were issued with the following Explanatory Note:—

" These regulations replace the regulations which prescribe the conditions for grant to local education authorities in respect of handicapped pupils boarded by them otherwise than at boarding schools, viz., Part IV of the School Health Service and Handicapped Pupils Regulations, 1953 (S.I. 1953 No. 1156), revoked by the Special Schools and Establishments (Grant) Regulations, 1959 (S.I. 1959 No. 366). The regulations are no longer grant regulations and considerable modifications have been made in the [then] Minister's requirements: provisions requiring his approval of boarding homes, and enabling him to impose specific conditions as to the number and classes of pupils to be boarded there, have been omitted."

In the regulations as here printed references to " Minister of Education " and " Minister " have been replaced by references to " Secretary of State for Education and Science " and " Secretary of State " respectively. See S.I. 1964 No. 490, *post.*

1. These regulations may be cited as the Handicapped Pupils (Boarding) Regulations, 1959, and shall come into operation on the first day of April, 1959.

2. These regulations prescribe the requirements to be observed by local education authorities in respect of board and lodging provided by them for handicapped pupils otherwise than at boarding schools.

3. In these regulations—

" authority " means a local education authority as defined in the Education Act, 1944;

" boarding home " means a home maintained by an authority for the purpose of providing board and lodging for handicapped pupils;

" handicapped pupils " means pupils falling within one or more of the categories defined by regulation 4 of the Handicapped Pupils and Special Schools Regulations, 1959;

" Secretary of State " means the Secretary of State for Education and Science.

4. An authority shall secure—

(*a*) that the premises of a boarding home conform as closely as is practicable with the standards prescribed by the regulations relating to boarding accommodation contained in Parts VI and VII of the Standards for School Premises Regulations, 1954, and any regulations amending or replacing the same;

(*b*) that the premises are kept in a proper state of repair, cleanliness and hygiene, and that adequate arrangements are made for the safety of the pupils and staff in case of fire; and

(*c*) that every boarding home is in general suitably designed and equipped for pupils of the category boarded there, and that the accommodation provided is suited to the number, age and sex of the pupils.

5. Before new premises are provided for a boarding home, or alterations made to existing premises, the approval of the Secretary of State shall be obtained, which approval may be given either generally, or in a particular case.

6. A boarding home shall be open to inspection by Her Majesty's Inspectors or some other person appointed for the purpose by the Secretary of State.

7. Where a handicapped pupil is boarded and lodged by an authority elsewhere than in a boarding home, the place where he is boarded and lodged shall be suitable for the needs of the pupil, and the authority shall arrange for it to be inspected before the admission of the pupil and regularly while he is there.

8. An authority shall make provision for the medical and dental care of handicapped pupils boarded and lodged in a boarding home or other place as aforesaid.

9. An authority shall make provision, so far as practicable, for every handicapped pupil boarded and lodged in a boarding home or other place as aforesaid to attend religious worship and receive religious instruction in accordance with the wishes of his parent, and no pupil shall be required to attend religious worship or receive religious instruction contrary to the wishes of his parent.

SCHOOLS REGULATIONS, 1959

S.I. 1959 *No.* 364

March 5, 1959

NOTE

These Regulations were issued under s. 3 (4) of the Local Government Act, 1958, with the following Explanatory Note:—

" These regulations impose, in respect of schools (other than special schools) maintained by local education authorities, standards and general requirements to replace the provisions contained in the existing regulations for grant, viz. Part II of the Schools Grant Regulations, 1951. A number of regulations have been simplified, particularly those relating to length of terms and hours of attendance (regulations 9 to 12) and there are the following further changes—

(*a*) regulation 16 (2) and the First Schedule now specify the principal courses of training for teachers wishing to be qualified teachers;

(*b*) regulation 20 specifies the requirements to be observed in respect of handicapped pupils receiving special educational treatment at ordinary schools (some of these were formerly in the School Health Service and Handicapped Pupils Regulations, 1953 (S.I. 1953/1156));

(*c*) regulation 19 of the existing regulations, relating to the employment as teachers ot ministers of religion, has been omitted."

In the regulations as here printed references to " Minister " have been replaced by references to " Secretary of State " (for Education and Science). See S.I. 1964 No. 490, *post.*

1. These regulations may be cited as the Schools Regulations, 1959, and shall come into operation on the first day of April, 1959.

2. These regulations prescribe standards and general requirements to be observed in respect of schools, other than special schools, maintained by local education authorities.

3.—(1) In these regulations, unless the context otherwise requires—

"authority" means a local education authority as defined in the Education Act, 1944;

"nursery class" means a class mainly for children who have attained the age of three years but have not attained the age of five years;

"school" means a school, other than a special school, maintained by an authority;

and other expressions have the same meaning as in the Education Acts, 1944 to 1953.

(2) The Interpretation Act, 1889, shall apply for the interpretation of these regulations as it applies for the interpretation of an Act of Parliament.

Premises

4.—[(1) The premises of a school shall be kept in a proper state of repair, cleanliness and hygiene and adequate arrangements shall be made for the health and safety of the pupils and staff in case of danger from fire and other causes.]

(2) Before new premises are provided for a school, or alterations made to existing premises, the approval of the Secretary of State shall be obtained, which approval may be given either generally, or in a particular case.

NOTE

Paragraph (1) was substituted by regulation 3 of the Schools Amending Regulations, 1965, S.I. 1965 No. 3, p. 439, *post*.

5. Classrooms and other rooms used for instruction shall not be overcrowded.

Size of Classes

6. [*Revoked.*]

NOTE

This regulation, which formerly limited the number of pupils on the register of a class to (*a*) 30 for a nursery class, (*b*) 30 for a class mainly of senior pupils in a primary school, (*c*) 40 for any other class in a primary school and (*d*) 30 for any class in a secondary school, was revoked by the Schools (Amendment No. 2) Regulations, 1969, S.I. 1969 No. 1174.

Admission

7.—(1) A pupil shall not be refused admission to or excluded from a school on other than reasonable grounds.

(2) A pupil shall not, unless exceptional circumstances require it, be admitted to a nursery school under the age of two years or to a nursery class under the age of three years, nor be retained in a nursery school or class after the end of the term in which he attains the age of five years.

8. Whenever a pupil ceases to attend a school and becomes a pupil at any other school or place of education or training, such educational information concerning him as the authority considers reasonable shall be supplied to the person conducting the other school or place, if so requested by that person.

School Year, Terms and Sessions

9. [*Revoked.*]

NOTE

Regulation 9 was revoked by regulation 2 (*a*) of the Schools Amending Regulations, 1966, S.I. 1966 No. 1577, *post*.

10.—(1) On every day on which a school meets there shall be provided for the pupils—

(*a*) in a nursery school or nursery class, at least three hours of suitable activities,

(*b*) in a school or class mainly for pupils under eight years of age, at least three hours of secular instruction, and

(*c*) in a school or class mainly for pupils of eight years of age and over, at least four hours of secular instruction, divided into two sessions, one of which shall be in the morning and the other in the afternoon unless exceptional circumstances make this undesirable:

Provided that—

(*a*) in a school which meets on six days in the week there may be on two of those days one session only of half the appropriate period of time prescribed by this paragraph; and

(*b*) it shall be sufficient to provide one-and-a-half hours of suitable activities for pupils attending a nursery school or nursery class for half a day only.

(2) For the purposes of this regulation, time occupied in marking the registers shall not be counted towards the required periods of activities or instruction, but there may be counted—

(*a*) in a voluntary school, the time required for the purposes of the inspection of religious instruction in accordance with subsection (5) of section 77 of the Education Act, 1944; and

(*b*) in any school, the necessary time for recreation, and any time occupied by the medical examination, inspection and treatment and dental treatment of pupils.

11. A school shall, apart from some unavoidable cause, meet for at least four hundred sessions in each . . . year, from which may be deducted a number not exceeding twenty in respect of occasional school holidays granted during term.

NOTE

The omitted word (" school ") was deleted by regulation 2 (*b*) of the Schools Amending Regulations, 1966, S.I. 1966 No. 1577, *post.*

12.—(1) Leave of absence shall not be given to enable a pupil to undertake employment, whether paid or unpaid, during school hours, except—

(*a*) in accordance with arrangements, approved by the Secretary of State, permitting employment temporarily in the interests of the general welfare of the community; or

(*b*) in accordance with a licence granted under section [37 of the Children and Young Persons Act, 1963, or

(*c*) in accordance with a licence granted under section 25 of the Children and Young Persons Act, 1933 as amended by section 42 of the Children and Young Persons Act, 1963.]

(2) Leave shall not be given to a pupil to take his holiday during term, except a period not exceeding two weeks in any calendar year to enable him to accompany his parent on the annual holiday of the latter.

NOTE

The amendments in square brackets in paragraph (1) were made by regulation 2 of the Schools (Amendment) Regulations, 1969, S.I. 1969 No. 231, *post.*

Instruction and Examinations

13. The instruction given in a school shall be efficient and appropriate to the needs of the pupils attending it.

13A. [No instruction shall be given in a school involving the use of—

(*a*) radioactive material, other than a compound of potassium, thorium or uranium used as a chemical agent, or

(*b*) apparatus in which electrons are accelerated by a potential difference of five kilovolts or greater, other than apparatus used only for the purpose of receiving visual images by way of television and sounds connected therewith

unless the Secretary of State has given his approval to the giving of such instruction, which approval he may withdraw if at any time he is of opinion that the arrangements made for the health and safety of the pupils and staff are inadequate.]

NOTE

This Regulation was inserted by regulation 4 of the Schools Amending Regulations, 1965, S.I. 1965 No. 3, *post.*

14. There shall be a time-table showing—

(*a*) the time at which the school sessions begin and end on each day; and

(*b*) the place of any instruction regularly given elsewhere than on the ordinary premises of the school.

15. A pupil shall not be entered for any external examination unless—

[(*a*) he has completed or is about to complete his fifth school year of a course of secondary education; or]

(*b*) he will have attained the age of sixteen on or before the 1st September in the year in which the examination is held; or

(*c*) if the examination is the General Certificate Examination, the head teacher certifies that it is desirable on educational grounds to enter him earlier, and that he has pursued a course of study with such competence that it is probable he will pass the examination in the subjects for which it is proposed to enter him.

NOTE

Paragraph (*a*) of this regulation was inserted by the Schools (Amending) Regulations, 1963, S.I. 1963 No. 1468, *post*. The two following paragraphs, formerly paragraphs (*a*) and (*b*) are consequently re-lettered (*b*) and (*c*).

Teachers

16.—(1) There shall be—

(*a*) . . .

(*b*) in every . . . school or department a head teacher, who shall take part in the teaching; and

(*c*) in every school a staff of assistant teachers suitable and sufficient in number to provide full-time education appropriate to the ages, abilities and aptitudes of the pupils:

Provided that if the Secretary of State, having regard to the number oι teachers available in England and Wales as a whole, considers it necessary to do so in order to secure a fair distribution, he may, in respect of any authority, fix maximum numbers of teachers to be employed.

(2) A teacher shall, subject to paragraph (3) of this regulation and to regulations 17 and 18, be a qualified teacher, that is to say, [any of the following:—

(*a*) a person who has successfully completed either—

(i) a course for the degree of Bachelor of Education, or a Certificate in Education or comparable qualification, of a university in the United Kingdom or the CNAA which is approved by the Secretary of State for the purpose of this regulation as a course for the initial training of teachers; or

(ii) a course (whether within the United Kingdom or elsewhere) approved by the Secretary of State for the purpose of this regulation as comparable to such a course;

(*b*) a person who possesses a special qualification . . . approved by the Secretary of State for the purposes of these regulations;

(*c*) a person recognised by, or eligible for recognition by, the Board of Education as an uncertificated teacher who has completed 20 years service as a teacher;

(*d*) a supplementary teacher who has completed 20 years service as a teacher;

(*e*) a person who possesses such a qualification, and has completed 10 years (or such shorter periods as may for special reasons be approved) of such service as a teacher, or such experience, as may on the recommendation of an authority be approved by the Secretary of State for the purposes of this sub-paragraph;

[(*f*) a person who has obtained the Diploma and has subsequently completed five years service in training children classified under section 57 of the Education Act 1944 as unsuitable for education at school or as a teacher in a special school or partly in such training and partly as such a teacher;

(*g*) a person who has obtained the Diploma by virtue of having been awarded a diploma in the teaching of mentally handicapped children by the National Association of Mental Health or the council of the county of

Middlesex and has, since being awarded such a diploma, completed such service as is described in sub-paragraph (*f*);

(*h*) a person who has obtained the Declaration and has subsequently completed five years service as a teacher in a special school.]]

and (in each case) has been accepted by the Secretary of State as a qualified teacher] [[[provided that a person who is eligible for acceptance as a qualified teacher by virtue only of sub-paragraph (*b*) above—

(i) may not be accepted as a teacher in a primary school (but, subject to sub-paragraph (ii) below, may be accepted as a teacher in a secondary school) if his qualification was acquired after 31st December 1969;

(ii) may be accepted as a teacher in a secondary school if his qualification was acquired after 31st December 1973 only where it is one for the time being recognised by the Secretary of State as a qualification in a subject for teachers of which there is a special need.]]]

(3) Notwithstanding the provisions of the preceding paragraph—

(*a*) a teacher who was in service at any time before 1st April, 1945, in a school which was maintained or aided by a former authority or was in receipt of grant from the Secretary of State may, though not a qualified teacher, be employed in any school, but subject to the approval of Her Majesty's Inspector if the teacher is a supplementary teacher and there has been a break in his service;

(*b*) . . .

(*c*) a person who has completed a course of instruction in the care of young children, may, though not a qualified teacher, be appointed with the Secretary of State's approval to the assistant staff of a nursery school or to the staff of a nursery class.

NOTES

Sub-paragraph (*a*) in paragraph (2) was substituted by the Further Education Regulations 1975, S.I. 1975 No. 1054, *post*.

The words in the outer square brackets in paragraph (2) were substituted by the Schools (Qualified Teachers) Regulations 1969, S.I. 1969 No. 1777.

The words in the inner double square brackets (sub-paragraphs (*f*)–(*h*)) were added by the Qualified Teachers and Teachers in Special Schools Regulations 1971, S.I. 1971 No. 342.

The word " Diploma " means the Diploma awarded to teachers of mentally handicapped children by the Training Council for Teachers of the Mentally Handicapped, and " Declaration " means the Declaration of Recognition of Experience Awarded by that Council (*ibid*., reg. 1 (3)).

The words omitted were revoked, the proviso to paragraph (2) (treble square brackets) inserted, and the words " or such experience, as may on the recommendation of an authority be" substituted, by the Schools (Qualified Teachers) Regulations 1973, S.I. 1973 No. 2021.

17.—(1) A person who is not a qualified teacher may with the approval of the Secretary of State be employed as a [student] teacher if he is eighteen years of age and has passed one of the examinations specified in [paragraph 3 of Schedule 2 to the Training of Teachers Regulations, 1967].

(2) Such employment shall not be for a period exceeding two years unless the Secretary of State approves employment for a longer period.

NOTE

The amendments shown in square brackets were made by regulation 2 of the Schools (Amendment) Regulations, 1968, S.I. 1968 No. 1281, *post*.

The amendment did not prevent the employment, up to 31st August 1970, of an unqualified temporary assistant teacher who was so employed at any time before 1st September 1968.

18. A person who is not a qualified teacher may be employed to give instruction in any art or skill or in any subject or group of subjects (including any form of vocational training) the teaching of which requires special qualifications or experience if, in the case of each such appointment,—

(*a*) he satisfies the authority as to his qualifications or, as the case may be, experience and as to his health and physical capacity for teaching; and

(*b*) no qualified teacher is available to give the instruction.

NOTE

This regulation was substituted by the Schools (Amendment) Regulations, 1968, S.I. 1968 No. 1281, *post*.

The regulation did not prevent the employment, up to 31st August, 1970, of an occasional teacher in accordance with the former regulation, provided that such person had been so employed at any time before 1st September, 1968.

19. The provisions of Schedule II to these regulations shall have effect in relation to the terms of employment of teachers.

Handicapped Pupils

20.—(1) Where an authority provides special educational treatment for any category of handicapped pupils, as defined by regulation 4 of the Handicapped Pupils and Special Schools Regulations, 1959, in a school which is not a special school, the following provisions shall have effect.

(2) If there is a special class for such pupils the authority shall comply as regards that class with the requirements of regulation 7 of the said regulations as to the special educational treatment to be given . . .

(3) Teachers of classes for partially deaf pupils, except classes in practical instruction, shall, in addition to possessing such qualifications as are required by these regulations, have passed the examination for the Teacher's Diploma of the National College of Teachers of the Deaf, or the final examination of the Course of Training for Teachers of the Deaf at Manchester University, or possess an equivalent qualification approved by the Secretary of State.

(4) If handicapped pupils are educated otherwise than in a special class the authority shall comply with the requirements specified in paragraph (2) of this regulation so far as it is practicable to do so.

NOTE

The words omitted in paragraph (2) were revoked partly by the Schools (Amendment No. 2) Regulations 1969, S.I. 1969 No. 1174 and partly by the Handicapped Pupils and Special Schools (Size of Classes) Regulations 1973, S.I. 1973 No. 340.

General

21. Any approval given by the Secretary of State under any regulation contained in Part II of the Schools Grant Regulations, 1951, shall have effect as if given under the corresponding regulation contained in these regulations.

SCHEDULES

SCHEDULE I

[*Revoked.*]

NOTE

This Schedule was revoked by the Schools (Qualified Teachers) Regulations, 1969, S.I. 1969 No. 1777.

SCHEDULE II

(regulation 19)

EMPLOYMENT OF TEACHERS

1. Subject to the provisions of the Disabled Persons (Employment) Acts, 1944 and 1958, every teacher shall, on first employment as a qualified teacher or [student teacher] in a maintained school, satisfy the Secretary of State of his health and physical capacity for teaching, unless he has already done so for the purposes of the Scheme of 11th October, 1926, made under the Teachers (Superannuation) Act, 1925.

2.—(*a*) The initial period of service of a teacher as a qualified teacher shall be a probationary period [which in the case of a full-time teacher who has satisfactorily completed [[any such course of training (other than a course outside the United Kingdom) as is mentioned in Regulation 16 (2) (*a*)]] shall be one year and in the case of any other teacher shall be two years] during which he may be required to satisfy the Secretary of State of his practical proficiency as a teacher, but in exceptional cases the Secretary of State may approve a probationary period which is less or more than one year, [or as the case may be two years] or dispense with it entirely.

(*b*) During his probationary period a teacher shall be employed in such school and under such supervision and conditions of work as shall be suitable to a teacher on probation.

(*c*) If at the end of the probationary period the Secretary of State determines the teacher to be unsuitable for further employment as a qualified teacher he shall not [without the approval of the Secretary of State] be so employed [and in the case of any teacher whose further employment is approved by the Secretary of State under this sub-paragraph the preceding provisions of this paragraph shall apply to the initial period of such further employment as if it were the initial period of his service as a qualified teacher].

3.—(*a*) A teacher, not being [a person employed by virtue of regulation 18], shall be employed under a written agreement, or, in the case of a teacher appointed by an authority, either under a written agreement or under a minute of the authority.

(*b*) The agreement or minute shall, either expressly or by reference to specified regulations or minutes, define the conditions of service and indicate whether the teacher is employed in full-time service exclusively in the capacity of a teacher, or in part-time service in the capacity of a teacher, or partly in the capacity of a teacher and partly in another capacity.

(*c*) The agreement or minute, unless it relates to employment partly in the capacity of a teacher and partly in another capacity or in a school in which pupils are boarded, shall provide that the teacher shall not be required to perform any duties except such as are connected with the work of the school or to abstain outside the school hours from any occupations which do not interfere with the due performance of his duties.

(*d*) A teacher shall be furnished with a copy of the agreement or minute under which he is employed; and he shall also be furnished with a copy of any specified regulations or minutes referred to in the agreement or minute under which he is employed, unless facilities are otherwise afforded to him for acquainting himself with their contents.

4. A person who is on grounds of misconduct or conviction of a criminal offence determined by the Secretary of State to be unsuitable for employment as a teacher or suitable for employment as such only to a limited extent, shall not be employed as a teacher or, as the case may be, shall be employed as such only to the extent determined by the Secretary of State.

5. If the engagement of a teacher is terminated whether by dismissal or resignation on account of misconduct or conviction of a criminal offence, the facts shall be reported to the Secretary of State.

6. The Secretary of State may, after consultation with the authority, the managers or the governors as the case may be, at any time on educational or medical grounds require that the employment of a teacher be suspended or terminated or made subject to such conditions or qualifications as the Secretary of State may determine; but before so requiring the Secretary of State shall use every available means of informing the teacher of the grounds of the proposed action and of giving him an opportunity of making representations on the subject.

NOTES

Paragraph 5 of Schedule II, *supra*, was substituted by the Schools Amending Regulations, 1964, S.I. 1964 No. 1311, *post*.

The words in square brackets in paragraph 1 were substituted by regulation 2 (*c*) of the Schools (Amendment) Regulations, 1968, S.I. 1968 No. 1281, *post*.

The words in square brackets in paragraph 2 (*a*) were substituted by regulation 4 (1) of the Regulations of 1968, *supra*, and the words in double square brackets, within the single brackets, were substituted by the Qualified Teachers and Teachers in Special Schools Regulations 1971, S.I. 1971 No. 342.

The words in square brackets in paragraph 2 (*c*) were added by regulation 4 (2) of the Regulations of 1968, *supra*.

The words in square brackets in paragraph 3 (*a*) were substituted by regulation 2 (*d*) of the Regulations of 1968, *supra*.

New paragraphs 4 and 5 were substituted by regulation 5 of the Regulations of 1968, *supra*.

HANDICAPPED PUPILS AND SPECIAL SCHOOLS REGULATIONS, 1959

S.I. 1959 *No.* 365

March 5, 1959

NOTE

These Regulations were issued with the following Explanatory Note:—

" These regulations replace the existing regulations, contained in Parts III, V and VI of the School Health Service and Handicapped Pupils Regulations, 1953, which define the categories of pupils requiring special educational treatment, and prescribe the requirements to be observed in respect of special schools. No alteration of any substance has been made in the regulations."

In Circular 4/61 (27th March, 1961) p. 461, *post*, the then Minister announced that as from 1st January, 1961, an independent school which was not recognised as efficient under Rules 16, would, subject to exceptions in particular cases, be regarded as unsuitable for providing special Educational treatment.

In the regulations as here printed references to " Minister of Education " and " Minister " have been replaced by references to " Secretary of State for Education and Science " and " Secretary of State " respectively. See S.I. 1964 No. 490, *post*.

PART I

INTRODUCTORY

1. These regulations may be cited as the Handicapped Pupils and Special Schools Regulations, 1959, and shall come into operation on the first day of April, 1959.

2.—(1) Part II of these regulations defines the several categories of pupils requiring special educational treatment, and Parts III, IV and V make provision as to the requirements to be complied with as a condition of approval of a school by the Secretary of State for Education and Science as a special school.

(2) If any requirement applicable to a special school under these regulations, or under any provision of the Education Acts, 1944 to 1953, is not complied with, the Secretary of State may withdraw his approval of the school as a special school.

3. The Interpretation Act, 1889, shall apply for the interpretation of these regulations as it applies for the interpretation of an Act of Parliament.

PART II

CATEGORIES OF HANDICAPPED PUPILS

4. The categories of pupils, called handicapped pupils, requiring special educational treatment, are defined as follows:—

(*a*) blind pupils, that is to say, pupils who have no sight or whose sight is or is likely to become so defective that they require education by methods not involving the use of sight;

(*b*) partially sighted pupils, that is to say, pupils who by reason of defective vision cannot follow the normal regime of ordinary schools without detriment to their sight or to their educational development, but can be educated by special methods involving the use of sight;

[(*c*) deaf pupils, that is to say, pupils with impaired hearing who require education by methods suitable for pupils with little or no naturally acquired speech or language;

(*d*) partially hearing pupils, that is to say, pupils with impaired hearing whose development of speech and language, even if retarded, is following a normal pattern, and who require for their education special arrangements or facilities though not necessarily all the educational methods used for deaf pupils.]

(*e*) educationally sub-normal pupils, that is to say, pupils who, by reason of limited ability or other conditions resulting in educational retardation, require some specialised form of education wholly or partly in substitution for the education normally given in ordinary schools;

(*f*) epileptic pupils, that is to say, pupils who by reason of epilepsy cannot be educated under the normal regime of ordinary schools without detriment to themselves or other pupils;

(*g*) maladjusted pupils, that is to say, pupils who show evidence of emotional instability or psychological disturbance and require special educational treatment in order to effect their personal, social or educational readjustment;

(*h*) physically handicapped pupils, that is to say, pupils not suffering solely from a defect of sight or hearing who by reason of disease or crippling defect cannot, without detriment to their health or educational development, be satisfactorily educated under the normal regime of ordinary schools;

(*i*) pupils suffering from speech defect, that is to say, pupils who on account of defect or lack of speech not due to deafness require special educational treament; and

(*j*) delicate pupils, that is to say, pupils not falling under any other category in this regulation, who by reason of impaired physical condition need a change of environment or cannot, without risk to their health or educational development, be educated under the normal regime of ordinary schools.

NOTE

Paragraphs (*c*) and (*d*) were substituted by the Handicapped Pupils and Special Schools Amending Regulations, 1962, S.I. 1962 No. 2073 (17th September, 1962), *post*.

PART III

SPECIAL SCHOOLS

Premises

5.—(1) The premises of a special school shall be kept in a proper state of repair, cleanliness and hygiene, and adequate arrangements shall be made for the safety of the pupils and staff in case of fire.

(2) Before new premises are provided for a school, or alterations made to existing premises, the approval of the Secretary of State shall be obtained, which approval may be given either generally, or in a particular case.

Organisation

6. A school shall be organised for the purpose of providing special educational treatment suitable for handicapped pupils of such number, category, age and sex as the Secretary of State shall approve.

[**6A.**—(1) The Secretary of State may, on the application of the managers or governors of a school which is a single sex establishment within the meaning of the Sex Discrimination Act 1975 or a school to which section 26 (2) of the Act applies make an order authorising discriminatory admissions to the school during the period specified in the order.

(2) An application for an order under this regulation shall specify—

(*a*) whether the school is a single sex establishment or a school to which section 26 (2) applies;

(*b*) the transitional period during which the managers or governors propose that discriminatory admissions should be authorised by the order;

(*c*) the stages by which the managers or governors propose that the school should move to a position where section 26 ceases to apply to it; and

(*d*) any other matters relevant to the terms and operation of the order applied for.]

NOTE

This Regulation was added by the Special Schools (Transitional Exemption Orders) Regulations 1975, S.I. 1975 No. 1962.

7. The special educational treatment given in a school shall be efficient and suited to the age, ability and aptitude of the pupils, with particular regard to their disability of mind or body.

8. Provision shall be made for every pupil, so far as practicable, to attend religious worship and receive religious instruction in accordance with the wishes of his parent, and no pupil shall be required to attend religious worship or receive religious instruction contrary to the wishes of his parent.

9. [*Revoked.*]

NOTE

Regulation 9, which dealt with the number of pupils on the register of a class in a special school, was revoked by the Handicapped Pupils and Special Schools (Size of Classes) Regulations 1973, S.I. 1973 No. 340, *post*.

10. Whenever a pupil ceases to attend any school and becomes a pupil at any other school or place of education or training, such educational information concerning him as is reasonable shall be supplied to the person conducting the other school or place, if so requested by that person.

Admission and Sessions

11.—(1) The number of pupils on the register of a school shall not exceed the number approved by the Secretary of State for that school.

(2) No pupil shall be admitted to a school or retained in it unless it is suitable for him, having regard to his age and sex and to the nature of his handicap, but in case of doubt whether a school is suitable for a pupil he may be admitted for a period of trial.

(3) If a pupil can properly be given a place in a school in accordance with this regulation, he shall not be refused admission to or excluded from it, except on reasonable grounds.

12.—(1) [*Revoked.*]

(2) [The school shall, except for some unavoidable cause, meet on at least two hundred days in each year:

Provided that mid-term or other occasional holidays during term not exceeding in the aggregate ten days in each year may be granted.]

NOTE

This regulation was amended, as shown by square brackets, by regulation 2 of the Handicapped Pupils and Special Schools Amending Regulations, 1966, S.I. 1966 No. 1576. There is thus no longer any obligation to divide the year into a specified number of terms; and the number of occasions on which a special school is to meet is determined by reference to the calendar year instead of by reference to a school year beginning in August.

13.—(1) On every day on which a school meets there shall be at least three hours of secular instruction for a school or class for pupils mainly under the age of eight, and at least four hours of such instruction for a school or class for pupils mainly over that age, divided into morning and afternoon sessions, unless exceptional circumstances make two sessions undesirable:

Provided that in a school which meets on six days in the week there may be on two of those days one session only of half the appropriate period of time prescribed by this paragraph.

(2) In reckoning any period for the purposes of this regulation the necessary time for recreation, and any time occupied by the medical examination, inspection and treatment and dental treatment of pupils, may be included.

14. Leave shall not be given to a pupil to take a period of holiday during term, except a period not exceeding two weeks in any calendar year, to enable him to accompany his parent on the annual holiday of the latter.

Teachers

15.—(1) There shall be in every school a head teacher, who shall take part in the teaching, and a staff of assistant teachers able to provide full-time education suitable to the ages, abilities and aptitudes of the pupils.

(2) Subject to the provisions of this and [regulations 16 and 16A], such teachers shall be qualified teachers within the meaning of regulation 16 (2) of the Schools Regulations 1959 [as amended] and if they are teaching blind, deaf, or partially deaf children, they shall have such further qualifications as the Secretary of State may require.

(3) Notwithstanding the foregoing provisions of this regulation—

(*a*) a teacher who was recognised by the Board of Education before the 1st April, 1945, may continue to be employed in the capacity and in the type of special school in which he was so recognised, and if he was recognised as a teacher of the blind he may also be employed in any school for partially sighted pupils;

(*b*) any person who taught in a secondary school for blind pupils before the said date may be employed in any school for blind pupils.

[(*c*) a person who holds the Diploma or the Declaration but has not completed such service as is described in sub-paragraph (*f*), (*g*) or (*h*), as the case may be, of regulation 16 (2) of the Schools Regulations 1959 as amended, may be employed in any special school.]

NOTES

The words in square brackets in paragraph (2) were substituted by the Qualified Teachers and Teachers in Special Schools Regulations 1971, regulation 3 (1), S.I. 1971 No. 342.

Sub-paragraph 3 (*c*) was added by *ibid.*, regulation 3 (2).

" *Diploma*," " *Declaration* ". These mean the Diploma awarded to teachers of mentally handicapped children by the Training Council for Teachers of the Mentally Handicapped; and Declaration of Recognition of Experience awarded by that Council (*ibid.*, regulation 1 (3)).

In regulation 15 (2), the reference to regulation 16 (2) of the Schools Regulations 1959, as amended, is to be subject to the *substitution* for the proviso to the latter of the following:

" provided that a person who is eligible for acceptance as a qualified teacher by virtue only of sub-paragraph (*b*) above may not be accepted as a teacher in a special school if his qualification was acquired after 31st December 1969."

See regulation 3 (1) of the Schools (Qualified Teachers) Regulations 1973, S.I. 1973 No. 2021.

16. The provisions of regulations 17 and 18 of the Schools Regulations, 1959, regarding the employment of temporary and occasional teachers, and the provisions of the Second Schedule to those regulations, regarding the terms of employment of teachers, shall apply in relation to teachers in special schools.

NOTE

The references, in the above regulation, to regulations 17 and 18 and Sch. 2 to the Schools Regulations, 1959 are to be construed as references to those provisions as amended by the Schools (Amendment) Regulations, 1968, S.I. 1968 No. 1281, *post*.

[**16A.**—(1) A person may be employed as a teacher in any special school if he was employed before 1st April 1971 by or under a local health authority or a regional hospital board in training, or in assisting a person engaged in training, children classified under section 57 of the Education Act 1944 as unsuitable for education at school.

(2) A person whose employment as a teacher in a special school is not authorised by the preceding provisions of these regulations may be so employed if—

(*a*) the authority or (in the case of a school not maintained by a local education authority) the managers of the school are satisfied that he is fitted, by reason of his qualifications, experience or otherwise, to teach children requiring special educational treatment; and

(*b*) no person whose employment is so authorised is available for appointment at the school.]

NOTE

This regulation was inserted by the Qualified Teachers and Teachers in Special Schools Regulations 1971, S.I. 1971 No. 342.

17.—(1) No woman shall be disqualified for employment as a teacher in a special school, or be dismissed from such employment, by reason only of marriage.

(2) No person shall be disqualified by reason of his religious opinions, or of his attending or omitting to attend religious worship, from being a teacher in a special school, or from being otherwise employed for the purposes of such a school; and no teacher in any such school shall be required to give religious instruction or receive any less emolument or be deprived of, or disqualified for, any promotion or other advantage by reason of the fact that he does or does not give religious instruction or by reason of his religious opinions or of his attending or omitting to attend religious worship:

Provided that, save in so far as they require that a teacher shall not receive any less emolument or be deprived of, or disqualified for, any promotion or other advantage by reason of the fact that he gives religious instruction or by reason of his religious opinions or his attending religious worship, the provisions of this paragraph shall not apply with respect to a teacher in a special school not maintained by a local education authority.

(3) A teacher shall not be dismissed without an opportunity of appearing in person before the body of managers, or, if there is no such body, the local education authority, accompanied, if he so desires, by a friend.

PART IV

FURTHER REQUIREMENTS RELATING TO NON-MAINTAINED SPECIAL SCHOOLS

18. The requirements of this Part of these regulations shall apply only to special schools not maintained by a local education authority.

19.—(1) A school shall be under the direction of a body of managers composed of a sufficient number of suitably qualified persons, and no member of the staff shall be a manager.

(2) The school shall not be conducted for profit, and no member of the staff may have any financial interest in it.

20. The premises shall conform as closely as is practicable with the regulations made from time to time by the Secretary of State under section 10 of the Education Act, 1944.

21. Any fees charged to a local education authority for pupils sent by it to the school shall be such as may be approved by the Secretary of State.

22.—(1) Provision shall be made for the periodical medical (including dental) inspection and adequate medical and dental care of the pupils, including provision for their examination and treatment by a medical practitioner possessing special experience of the disability from which they suffer.

(2) Medical and dental records in a form approved by the Secretary of State shall be kept for every pupil attending the school.

23.—(1) Milk to drink shall be provided for day pupils free of charge.

(2) Mid-day meals shall be provided for day pupils at such charge as the Secretary of State shall approve, but the charge shall be remitted or reduced if a parent is unable to pay it without financial hardship.

24.—(1) A teacher shall not be employed after he attains the age of 65 years except with the Secretary of State's approval.

(2) Teachers shall be paid adequate remuneration.

25.—(1) The managers shall furnish the Secretary of State with such information and returns relating to a school, and keep such registers and records, as he shall require.

(2) The accounts of the school shall be kept in a form approved by the Secretary of State, and shall be duly audited.

(3) Copies of the accounts shall be sent to the Secretary of State annually; and copies shall be sent to any local education authority or other body sending pupils to the school on request by such authority or body, and on payment of a reasonable charge for copying.

PART V

SUPPLEMENTAL

26. If a special school is in a hospital the requirements contained in Parts III and IV of these regulations shall apply to it with such modifications as are required to meet the conditions obtaining in the hospital.

27. These regulations shall have effect in the Isles of Scilly with such modifications as are required to meet the special circumstances there obtaining.

28. Parts III, V and VI, of the School Health Service and Handicapped Pupils Regulations, 1953, and the Schedules to those Regulations, are hereby revoked:

Provided that any approval or determination given, or requirement imposed, by the Secretary of State under any regulation hereby revoked shall have effect as if given, or imposed, under the corresponding provision of these regulations.

SPECIAL SCHOOLS AND ESTABLISHMENTS (GRANT) REGULATIONS, 1959

S.I. 1959 *No.* 366

March 5, 1959

NOTE

These Regulations were issued with the following Explanatory Note:—

" These regulations revoke the existing regulations providing for grant in respect of all special schools and establishments for the further education and training of disabled persons, and replace them by provisions limited to grant in respect of schools and establishments of this kind maintained by bodies other than local education authorities. No change of substance has otherwise been made."

In the regulations as here printed references to " Minister of Education " and " Minister " have been replaced by references to " Secretary of State for Education and Science " and " Secretary of State " respectively. See S.I. 1964 No. 490, *post.*

1. These regulations may be cited as the Special Schools and Establishments (Grant) Regulations, 1959, and shall come into operation on the first day of April, 1959.

2. These regulations make provision for payment by the Secretary of State for Education and Science of grant in respect of special schools, and establishments for the further education and training of disabled persons, maintained or proposed to be maintained by bodies other than local education authorities, and prescribe the conditions on which grant will be paid.

3. The Interpretation Act, 1889, shall apply for the interpretation of these regulations as it applies for the interpretation of an Act of Parliament.

Grant

4.—(1) The Secretary of State may pay

(*a*) capital grant in respect of expenditure on the acquisition of any interest in land or buildings, or the provision of buildings, furniture or equipment, for the purpose of a special school [or of an establishment for the further education and training of disabled persons], if such expenditure has been approved by the Secretary of State; and

(*b*) maintenance grant in respect of the maintenance of a special school or establishment for the further education and training of disabled persons,

of an amount to be determined by him.

(2) In determining whether to pay grant under this regulation, and the amount of grant, the Secretary of State will take into consideration the character and cost of the school or establishment, and the financial resources of the body responsible for it, including, in respect of capital grant, any sums which may accrue from the disposal of land or buildings, and, in respect of maintenance grant, any sums which may be received from any Government Department or local authority, or as fees from pupils.

(3) The Secretary of State shall not pay grant under this regulation unless he is satisfied that the body responsible for the school or establishment is properly constituted, and financially sound.

NOTE

The words in square brackets in paragraph 1 (*a*) of this regulation were inserted by the Special Schools and Establishments (Grant) Amending Regulations, 1964, S.I. 1964 No. 1083 (14th July, 1964), *post.*

5. [*Revoked.*]

NOTE

Regulation 5 was revoked by the Special Schools and Establishments (Grant) (Amendment) Regulations, 1969, S.I. 1969 No. 410, *post.*

Conditions of Grant

6.—(1) Grant in respect of a special school will be paid on condition that it observes the requirements applicable to it contained in the Handicapped Pupils and Special Schools Regulations, 1959.

(2) The Secretary of State may impose the following further conditions on paying capital grant in respect of a special school—

(*a*) he may require two or more schools to be combined for the more efficient provision of facilities for the treatment of handicapped pupils;

(*b*) he may impose such conditions for securing the continuity of the school as he shall think necessary;

(*c*) he may require the body receiving grant to undertake in writing to repay such portion of the grant as the Secretary of State may require in the event of the school either ceasing to exist, or failing, in his opinion, to be carried on efficiently.

7. Grant in respect of an establishment for the further education and training of disabled persons will be paid on condition that it observes the requirements contained in regulations 5, 10, 11, 17, 19, 20, 21, 22, 24 and 25 of the Handicapped Pupils and Special Schools Regulations, 1959, and in the Second Schedule to the Schools Regulations, 1959 (except paragraph 2 thereof), as if those requirements applied to such establishments, and to the students and teachers therein.

8. Grant in respect of such an establishment will be paid on the following further conditions—

(*a*) the establishment shall provide courses of training for persons suffering from disability of mind or body, in preparation for their employment;

(*b*) the courses shall be such as are approved by the Secretary of State, and they shall be appropriate to the disability of the students, and include provision for their general education and for their physical training and recreation;

(*c*) students shall not be admitted if under the upper limit of compulsory school age;

(*d*) there shall be a staff of teachers able to provide the courses of training required; and

(*e*) the establishment shall be carried on with efficiency, and be open to inspection by Her Majesty's Inspectors or some other person appointed for the purpose by the Secretary of State.

9. When a condition is imposed by or under these regulations on the payment of grant, and the condition is not, in the opinion of the Secretary of State, complied with, he may withhold, or make a deduction from, grant.

Revocation

10. Parts I, II, IV, VII and VIII of the School Health Service and Handicapped Pupils Regulations, 1953, and the School Health Service and Handicapped Pupils Amending Regulations, 1954, are hereby revoked.

LOCAL EDUCATION AUTHORITIES RECOUPMENT (PRIMARY, SECONDARY AND FURTHER EDUCATION) AMENDING REGULATIONS, 1959

S.I. 1959 *No.* 448

March 16, 1959

NOTE

These Regulations amend the Local Education Authorities (Recoupment) Regulations, 1953, S.I. 1953 No. 507, as amended by the Local Education Authorities (Recoupment) Amending Regulations, 1954, S.I. 1954 No. 991 (which Regulations are printed as amended at pp. 333 *et seq., ante*), and the Local Education Authorities Recoupment (Further Education) Regulations, 1954, S.I. 1954 No. 815, as amended by the Local Education Authorities Recoupment (Further Education) Amending Regulations, 1955, S.I. 1955 No. 222, and the Local Education Authorities Recoupment (Further Education) Amending Regulations, 1956, S.I. 1956 No. 1588 (which Regulations are printed as amended at pp. 336 *et seq., ante*). The effect of the amendments was to provide that the expenditure of local education authorities in educating pupils who did not belong to the area of any authority should be shared amongst all local education authorities by means of adjustments of the general grant formerly payable under s. 1 of the Local Government Act, 1958, from 1st April, 1959, instead of by adjustment of the main education grant, which ceased to be payable from that date.

DIRECT GRANT SCHOOLS REGULATIONS, 1959

S.I. 1959 *No.* 1832

October 29, 1959

NOTE

These Regulations were issued with the following Explanatory Note:—

" These regulations (relating to schools receiving direct grant from the Minister [now Secretary of State; see *infra*] revoke and replace all provisions of the Schools Grant Regulations, 1951, and amending regulations, which were left unrevoked by the Schools Regulations, 1959. The provisions of the old regulations have been much simplified; but the only substantial change is an increase in the rate of sixth-form grant payable to grammar schools from £50 to £66 in respect of each pupil " (for latest figures see reg. 4, *infra*).

In the regulations as here printed references to " Minister " have been replaced by references to " Secretary of State " (for Education and Science). See S.I. 1964 No. 490, *post*.

These Regulations and the Direct Grant Grammar Schools (Cessation of Grant) Regulations 1975, S.I. 1975 No. 1198, *post*, are to be construed together.

PART I

GENERAL

1. These regulations may be cited as the Direct Grant Schools Regulations, 1959, and shall come into operation on the 6th day of November, 1959.

2. These regulations make provision for payment by the Secretary of State of direct grant in respect of schools (other than special schools) not maintained by local education authorities, and prescribe the conditions relating to grant.

3.—(1) In these regulations, unless the context otherwise requires—

" authority " means the local education authority, or, where there is more than one such authority, the local education authorities, for the area served by the school;

" educational year " means the year beginning on the 1st August;

" school " does not include a school maintained by an authority, or any special school;

" upper school " means such of the forms in a school as are accepted by the Secretary of State as providing education mainly for senior pupils.

(2) The Interpretation Act, 1889, shall apply for the interpretation of these regulations as it applies for the interpretation of an Act of Parliament.

Grant to Grammar Schools

4.—(1) The Secretary of State may recognise a grammar school for the purpose of receiving grant under this regulation and may pay to the proprietors of the school, for the period for which it is so recognised, yearly grant as follows:—

(*a*) capitation grant at a rate not exceeding [£79] in respect of every pupil in the upper school on the 1st March in any year, who on or before the 31st July in that year will have attained the age of eleven but will not have attained the age of twenty;

(*b*) sixth-form grant at a rate not exceeding [£84] in respect of every pupil in the sixth form on the 1st March in any year who on or before the 31st July in that year will not have attained the age of twenty, and who either will have attained the age of seventeen on or before the date last-mentioned, or intends to take at least two subjects in the examination for the General Certificate of Education at Advanced Level during either that or the following educational year;

(*c*) grant equal to the amount of fees and charges remitted to the parents of pupils in accordance with regulation 18 of these regulations;

(*d*) grant in respect of any special or experimental work at the school involving extraordinary expenditure, and approved by the Secretary of State.

(*e*) in respect of the educational year beginning on the 1st August 1964, supplementary capitation grant at a rate not exceeding £2 6*s*. 8*d*. [£2·33] in respect of every pupil in the upper school on the 1st March 1965 who on or before the 31st July 1965 had attained the age of eleven but had not attained the age of twenty.

(2) Grant shall be paid under this regulation in respect of the educational year.

(3) A school in respect of which grant is paid under this regulation shall fulfil the conditions contained in Part II of these regulations, and if in the opinion of the Secretary of State any condition is not fulfilled he may withhold or make a deduction from grant.

NOTE

The amount of £79 was substituted in sub-paragraph (*a*) by the Direct Grant Schools (Amendment) Regulations 1973, No. 1535.

The amount of £84 in sub-paragraph (*b*) was substituted by the Direct Grant Schools Amending Regulations, 1963, S.I. 1963 No. 1379.

Sub-paragraph (*e*) was added by the Direct Grant Schools Amending Regulations, 1965, S.I. 1965 No. 1978.

Grant ceases to be payable under regulation 4 (1) to the proprietors of a school which ceases to be recognised as a grammar school: see regulation 2 of the Direct Grant Grammar Schools (Cessation of Grant) Regulations 1975, S.I. 1975 No. 1198, *post*. These regulations provide for the phasing out of grants to grammar schools.

Grant to Schools not Grammar Schools

5.—(1) The Secretary of State may recognise for the purpose of receiving grant under this regulation—

(*a*) any nursery school;

(*b*) any other school which was at the time of the coming into operation of these regulations in receipt of grant under regulation 51 or regulation 52 of the Schools Grant Regulations, 1951,

and he may pay to the proprietors of any such school, for the period for which it is recognised for grant, yearly grant as follows:—

(*a*) in respect of a nursery school, grant not exceeding one half of the net cost of maintaining the school as approved by the Secretary of State, excluding any sums received from an authority and payments made on behalf of pupils;

(*b*) in respect of a school in receipt of grant under the said regulation 51, grant in respect of each pupil at the school at such rate, and in respect of a school in receipt of grant under the said regulation 52, grant of such an amount, as the Secretary of State shall determine, having regard to the rate or amount, as the case may be, paid in respect of the school for the year which ended on the 31st March, 1959.

(2) Grant shall be paid under this regulation in respect of the financial year.

(3) A school in respect of which grant is paid under this regulation shall fulfil the conditions contained in or applicable under Part III of these regulations, and if in the opinion of the Secretary of State any such condition is not fulfilled he may withhold or make a deduction from grant.

5A.—(1) The Secretary of State may, on the application of the governors of a school which is a single sex establishment within the meaning of the Sex Discrimination Act 1975 or a school to which section 26 (2) of the Act applies make an order authorising discriminatory admissions to the school during the period specified in the order.

(2) An application for an order under this regulation shall specify—

(*a*) whether the school is a single sex establishment or a school to which section 26 (2) applies;

(*b*) the transitional period during which the governors propose that discriminatory admissions should be authorised by the order;

(*c*) the stages by which the governors propose that the school should move to a position where section 26 ceases to apply to it; and

(*d*) any other matters relevant to the terms and operation of the order applied for.]

NOTE

This Regulation was added by the Direct Grant Schools (Transitional Exemption Orders) Regulations 1975, S.I. 1975 No. 1964.

Revocation

6.—(1) Parts I, IV, V and VI of the Schools Grant Regulations, 1951, the Schools Grant Amending Regulations No. 3, 1952, the Schools Grant Amending Regulations No. 5, 1954, the Schools Grant Amending Regulations No. 9, 1959, and the Schools Grant Amending Regulations No. 10, 1959, are hereby revoked.

(2) Any approval given, or requirement imposed, by the Secretary of State under any regulation hereby revoked shall have effect as if given or imposed under the corresponding regulation contained in these regulations.

PART II

CONDITIONS APPLICABLE TO GRAMMAR SCHOOLS

Governors

7.—(1) A grammar school shall be conducted by a body of governors, and—

(*a*) either one-third of the governors shall be appointed by the authority (if more than one authority, in such proportions as the Secretary of State shall approve); or

(*b*) if the proprietors of the school so prefer, the majority of the governors shall be representative governors as defined in paragraph (2) of this regulation.

(2) A representative governor shall be a person who is—

(*a*) a Member of Parliament, a Mayor, a chairman or vice-chairman or member of a local authority as defined in the Local Government Act, 1933, or a chairman or vice-chairman of an education committee of an authority, or of a parish meeting; or

(*b*) appointed by a local authority as above defined or by members of such an authority elected for part of the area of the authority, by an education committee, or by a parish meeting.

NOTE

As regards any school to whose proprietors grant has ceased to be payable in respect of pupils admitted to the school in any educational year beginning after 1975, the governing body shall be constituted in such manner as appears to the Secretary of State to be appropriate: see regulation 4 (*a*) of the Direct Grant Grammar Schools (Cessation of Grant) Regulations 1975, S.I. 1975 No. 1198, *post*.

8. Except in such special circumstances as the Secretary of State may approve a governor shall not have any interest, otherwise than as a trustee, in property belonging to the school, or any interest in the doing of work for or the supply of goods to the school, or receive any remuneration from the school.

Premises

9.—(1) [The premises of a school shall be kept in a proper state of repair, cleanliness and hygiene and adequate arrangements shall be made for the health and safety of the pupils and staff in case of danger from fire and other causes.]

(2) The premises shall be convenient for teaching purposes, adapted to the circumstances of the school, and provided with equipment adequate for the curriculum; and the rooms shall not be overcrowded.

(3) Before new premises are provided or alterations made to existing premises the approval of the Secretary of State shall be obtained, and any application to the Secretary of State for such approval shall be accompanied by plans, and an estimate of cost, of the work proposed.

NOTES

Paragraph (1) was substituted by regulation 3 of the Direct Grant Schools Amending Regulations, 1965, S.I. 1965 No. 1, p. 439, *post*.

Paragraph (3) ceases to apply as regards any school to whose proprietors grant has ceased to be payable in respect of pupils admitted to the school in any educational year beginning after 1975: see regulation 4 (b) of the Direct Grant Grammar Schools (Cessation of Grant) Regulations 1975, S.I. 1975 No. 1198, *post*.

General conduct of the school

10.—(1) The school shall be kept on a level of efficiency satisfactory to the Secretary of State, and shall not be conducted for profit.

(2) [No instruction shall be given in the school involving the use of—

(*a*) radioactive material other than a compound of potassium, thorium or uranium used as a chemical agent, or

(*b*) apparatus in which electrons are accelerated by a potential difference of five kilovolts or greater, other than apparatus used only for the purpose of receiving visual images by way of television and sounds connected therewith

unless the Secretary of State has given his approval to the giving of such instruction, which approval he may withdraw if at any time he is of opinion that the arrangements made for the health and safety of the pupils and staff are inadequate.]

NOTE

Paragraph (2) was added by regulation 4 of the Direct Grant Schools Amending Regulations, 1965, S.I. 1965 No. 1, *post*.

11. The number of pupils on the register of a class shall not exceed thirty unless, owing to unavoidable circumstances, it is not possible to comply with this regulation, in which case the number of pupils shall be such as is reasonable.

12.—(1) A pupil shall not be entered for any external examination unless either—

(*a*) he will have attained the age of sixteen on or before the 1st September in the year in which the examination is held; or

(*b*) if the examination is the General Certificate Examination, the head teacher certifies that it is desirable on educational grounds to enter him earlier, and that he has pursued a course of study with such competence that it is probable he will pass the examination in the subjects in which it is proposed to enter him.

(2) The examination fee in respect of any pupil entered for the General Certificate Examination in accordance with this regulation shall be paid by the governors.

13.—(1) Adequate provision shall be made, either by arrangement with the authority under section 78 (2) of the Education Act, 1944, or otherwise, for—

(*a*) the medical inspection of all pupils and the medical care of boarders; and

(*b*) for the supply to day-pupils of . . . mid-day meals.

(2) No charge shall be made for medical inspection . . .

(3) The charges for mid-day meals to day-pupils shall be such as the Secretary of State shall approve, and shall be wholly or partly remitted to parents unable to pay them in accordance with arrangements approved by the Secretary of State.

NOTES

The omitted words were revoked by the Direct Grant Schools (Amendment) Regulations, 1968, S.I. 1968 No. 1148, proprietors of a grammar school being no longer required to provide milk for day-pupils.

Paragraph (3) is not applicable in respect of any pupils admitted to a school in respect of whom grant has ceased to be payable: see regulation 4 (*c*) of the Direct Grant Grammar Schools (Cessation of Grant) Regulations 1975, S.I. 1975 No. 1198, *post*.

14. Such records shall be kept (in addition to the register required by section 80 of the Education Act, 1944), and such information and returns furnished to him, as the Secretary of State shall require.

15. Whenever a pupil ceases to attend the school and becomes a pupil at any other school or place of education or training, such educational and medical information concerning him as is reasonable shall be supplied to the person conducting the other school or place, if so requested by that person.

Admission

16. Places in the upper school shall, in respect of each educational year, be allocated in accordance with the following provisions:

(*a*) a number of free places, equal at least to one quarter of the total number of pupils admitted to the upper school during the preceding educational year, shall be allotted by the governors either directly, or by putting them at the disposal of the authority, to pupils who have attended for at least two years a primary school which was either maintained by a local authority or in receipt of grant out of Government funds;

(*b*) such further number of places, called reserved places, shall be put at the disposal of the authority as it may need for pupils who are suitably qualified whether or not they have attended a primary school as aforesaid, so long as the authority specifies the number of reserved places it requires at least six months before the beginning of the educational year;

(*c*) the total number of free and reserved places shall not, unless the governors otherwise agree, exceed one half of the total number of pupils admitted to the upper school during the preceding educational year;

(*d*) the whole of the fees payable in respect of the education provided for pupils given free places directly by the governors shall be remitted in full, or met out of the funds of an endowed foundation, for the whole period the pupils remain in the upper school; and in respect of places put at the disposal of the authority, the fees shall be paid by the authority as provided by s. 6 of the Education (Miscellaneous Provisions) Act, 1953;

(*e*) for the residuary places, that is places other than free and reserved places, fees shall be payable in accordance with regulation **18**.

NOTE

Regulations 16, 17 and 18 are not applicable in respect of any pupils admitted to a school in respect of whom grant has ceased to be payable: see regulation 4 (*c*) of the Direct Grant Grammar Schools (Cessation of Grant) Regulations 1975, S.I. 1975 No. 1198, *post*.

17.—(1) A pupil shall not be admitted to a school, or retained in it, unless he is capable of profiting from the education there; and, so far as is compatible with the provisions of regulation **16**, with any scheme or other instrument relating to the conduct of the school, and with any arrangements made by the governors with the authority, preference shall be given to pupils who by reason of their ability and aptitude are most likely to profit from being at the school.

(2) The minimum educational standard qualifying a pupil for admission to or retention in a school shall be the same for all pupils of similar age.

(3) Subject to the provisions of regulation 16 and of paragraph (1) of this regulation, a pupil shall not be refused admission to or excluded from a school on other than reasonable grounds.

NOTE

See note to Regulation 16, above.

Fees

18.—(1) The fees payable in respect of the education provided at a school, and any boarding or other charges, shall be such as the Secretary of State shall approve.

(2) Fees and charges payable in respect of day pupils in the upper school shall be wholly or partly remitted to parents unable to pay them in accordance with arrangements approved by the Secretary of State.

NOTE

See note to Regulation 16, above.

Religious worship and instruction

19.—(1) On every school day there shall, subject to the next following regulation, be collective worship on the part of all pupils at the school.

(2) Religious instruction shall be given in accordance with the provisions of the trust deed, or, if there are no provisions relating to religious instruction, in accordance with the practice already observed in the school.

(3) No pupil shall be required to attend or abstain from attending any Sunday school or place of religious worship elsewhere than on the school premises.

20.—(1) A pupil shall, if his parent so requests, be excused from attendance at religious worship or religious instruction at the school, or both, and be allowed to attend elsewhere for the purpose of receiving religious instruction of a kind not provided in the school, so long as this will not interfere unreasonably with his work at the school.

(2) A pupil who is a boarder shall, if his parent so requests, be given reasonable facilities to attend religious worship on Sundays and other days exclusively set apart for religious observance by the religious body to which the parent belongs, and to receive religious instruction outside school hours in accordance with the tenets of a particular denomination; and such worship or instruction

may be on the school premises or elsewhere, but the governors shall not be required to incur expense in connection therewith.

Teachers

21.—(1) The teachers shall be sufficient in number and have the qualifications necessary for providing adequate instruction in each subject of the school curriculum.

(2) The teachers shall be paid salaries which are adequate and reasonable.

(3) A teacher shall not receive any less emolument or be deprived of or disqualified for promotion or other advantage on the ground that he does or does not give religious instruction, or by reason of his religious opinions or of his attending or omitting to attend religious worship.

(4) A teacher shall not be dismissed without an opportunity of appearing in person before the governors accompanied, if he so desires, by a friend.

22. A teacher, other than an occasional teacher, shall be employed under a written agreement, which shall define the conditions of service and indicate whether the teacher is employed in full-time service exclusively in the capacity of a teacher, or in part-time service in the capacity of a teacher, or partly in the capacity of a teacher and partly in another capacity.

[**23.** A person who is on grounds of misconduct or conviction of a criminal offence determined by the Secretary of State to be unsuitable for employment as a teacher or suitable for employment as such only to a limited extent, shall not be employed as a teacher or, as the case may be, shall be employed as such only to the extent determined by the Secretary of State.

24. If the engagement of a teacher is terminated whether by dismissal or resignation on account of misconduct or conviction of a criminal offence, the facts shall be reported to the Secretary of State.]

NOTE

Regulations 23 and 24 were substituted by regulation 5 of the Direct Grant Schools (Amendment) Regulations, 1968, S.I. 1968 No. 1148.

PART III

CONDITIONS APPLICABLE TO SCHOOLS NOT GRAMMAR SCHOOLS

25. A school that is not a grammar school shall fulfil the conditions contained in regulations 8, 9, 10, 13, 14, 15, 18 (except paragraph (2)) and 21 (except paragraph (1)), and (except in the case of a nursery school) regulations 12, 19 and 20 of these regulations, and shall comply with the requirements contained in regulation 6 (relating to the size of classes), regulation 7 (relating to admission) and regulations 16, 17 and 18 and Schedules I and II (relating to teachers) of the Schools Regulations, 1959.

26. A school that is not a grammar school shall fulfil the following further conditions—

(*a*) the number of pupils on the register shall not exceed such number as the Secretary of State shall approve;

(*b*) it shall, if a primary school, be conducted by a body of managers, and if a secondary school by a body of governors, to which shall be appointed, so far as the Secretary of State so requires, representatives of an authority, not however exceeding one-third of the total number of managers or governors unless the proprietors of the school otherwise agree; and

(*c*) there shall be reserved for pupils from the area in which the school is situated, and from any other area normally served by the school, such number of places as may be agreed between the managers or governors and the authorities for those areas, or, failing agreement, as may be determined by the Secretary of State.

HANDICAPPED PUPILS (CERTIFICATE) REGULATIONS, 1961

S.I. 1961 *No.* 476

March 16, 1961

1.—(1) These regulations may be cited as the Handicapped Pupils (Certificate) Regulations, 1961, and shall come into operation on the 24th day of March, 1961.

(2) The Handicapped Pupils (Certificate) Regulations, 1953, are hereby revoked.

2. The form of certificate to be issued under section 34 (5) of the Education Act, 1944, shall be that set out in the Schedule hereto.

SCHEDULE

Certificate prescribed by the now Secretary of State under Section 34 (5) *of Education Act*, 1944

1. Name, date of birth and address of child submitted for medical examination:—

....

....

....

[2. I have examined this child and I certify that in my opinion—
*the child is not suffering from any disability of mind or body
*the child is suffering from a disability of mind/body of the following nature and extent:—

....

....

....

....]

Signed..............................
Medical Officer of the Local Education Authority.

Dated.......................

*Delete whichever is inappropriate

NOTE

Paragraph 2 of the certificate was substituted by the Handicapped Pupils (Certificate) (Amendment) Regulations 1975, S.I. 1975 No. 328.

HANDICAPPED PUPILS AND SPECIAL SCHOOLS AMENDING REGULATIONS, 1962

S.I. 1962 *No.* 2073

September 17, 1962

NOTE

These Regulations were issued with the following explanatory note: " These regulations amend the definitions of pupils handicapped by impaired hearing in order to take account of the greater use of residual hearing made possible by improved electronic aid and new techniques of special educational treatment ". The Regulations were made by the then Minister of Education under powers conferred on him by section 33 of the Education Act, 1944, *ante*.

The Handicapped Pupils and Special Schools Regulations, 1959, S.I. 1959 No. 365 (5th March, 1959), as so amended, are printed at p. 356, *ante*.

STATE AWARDS REGULATIONS, 1963

S.I. 1963 *No.* 1223

July 11, 1963

NOTE

These Regulations were issued with the following explanatory note: " These regulations authorise the Minister of Education [now Secretary of State; see *infra*] to make two types of State Award, namely State Scholarships for Mature Students and State Studentships. The former are awarded to selected students over the age of 25 to enable them to take university degree courses in liberal studies which they were unable to embark upon at the normal age. The latter are awarded for full-time advanced postgraduate study in Arts and Social Studies. These regulations specify the courses for which these two kinds of awards are tenable, prescribe the conditions to which they are subject and allow for the payment of appropriate grants in respect of fees and maintenance ".

The Regulations were made under the powers conferred by section 3 of the Education Act, 1962, p. 294, *ante*.

In the Regulations references to " Minister of Education " and " Minister " have been replaced by references to " Secretary of State for Education and Science " and " Secretary of State " respectively. See S.I. 1964 No. 490, *post*.

1.—(1) These regulations may be cited as the State Awards Regulations, 1963, and shall come into operation on 1st September, 1963.

(2) In these regulations, unless the context otherwise requires—

" the Secretary of State " means the Secretary of State for Education and Science;

" university " includes a university college and a constituent college or school of a university.

(3) The Interpretation Act, 1889 (a), shall apply for the interpretation of these regulations as it applies for the interpretation of an Act of Parliament.

2. These regulations authorise the Secretary of State to bestow awards, hereinafter called " State Awards ", of the following types—

(*a*) State Studentships, being awards to persons in respect of their attendance at such courses at universities, colleges or other institutions, whether in England or Wales or elsewhere, as are designated by or under the next following regulation;

(*b*) State Scholarships for Mature Students, being awards to persons, qualified as to age as hereinafter provided, in respect of their attendance at such courses at universities, colleges or other institutions, whether in England or Wales or elsewhere, as are designated by or under the next following regulation as being first degree courses or comparable to first degree courses;

[(*c*) State Bursaries, being awards to persons in respect of their attendance at such courses at universities, colleges or other institutions, whether in England or Wales or elsewhere, as are designated under regulation 3.

(*d*) State Bursaries for Adult Education, being awards to persons, qualified as to age as is provided by regulation 4 (3) below, in respect of their attendance at courses at any institution which is designated by the schedule to these regulations.]

NOTE

Paragraph (*c*) of this regulation was added by the State Awards (Amendment) Regulations, 1969, S.I. 1969 No. 554, *post*.

Paragraph (*d*) was added by the State Awards (Amendment) Regulations 1975, S.I. 1975 No. 940.

3.—(1) The courses designated for the purposes of paragraph (*a*) of the last foregoing regulation shall be the following full-time courses in [the Humanities]:—

(*a*) [at a university or other institution in England or Wales in preparation for a doctorate, a master's degree or a degree of bachelor of letters or of bachelor of philosophy;]

(*b*) [*Revoked.*]

(*c*) such other full-time courses in [the Humanities], being postgraduate courses or comparable to postgraduate courses, at universities, colleges or other institutions in the United Kingdom or, if the Secretary of State thinks fit in special circumstances, abroad, as the Secretary of State may from time to time designate under this paragraph of this regulation.

(2) The courses designated for the purposes of paragraph (*b*) of the last foregoing regulation shall be the following full-time courses:—

(*a*) at universities in the United Kingdom or, if the Secretary of State thinks fit in special circumstances, abroad, in preparation for a first degree in Economics, English, History or Sociology, not restricted to students already holding first degrees; and

(*b*) such other full-time courses, being first degree courses, or comparable to first degree courses, in the field of liberal studies at universities, colleges or other institutions in the United Kingdom or, if the Secretary of State thinks fit in special circumstances, abroad, not restricted to students already holding first degrees, as the Secretary of State may from time to time designate under this paragraph of this regulation.

[(3) The courses designated for the purposes of paragraph (*c*) of regulation 2 shall be such full time courses (not being courses designated for the purposes of paragraph (*a*) of regulation 2) being postgraduate courses or comparable to postgraduate courses, at universities, colleges or other institutions in the United Kingdom, as the Secretary of State may from time to time designate under this paragraph.]

NOTE

Sub-paragraph (*a*) was substituted, sub-paragraph (*b*) revoked, and paragraph 3 added, by the State Awards (Amendment) Regulations, 1969, S.I. 1969 No. 554, *post*.

4.—(1) Candidates for State Awards shall [unless they are candidates for State Bursaries of Adult Education] satisfy the Secretary of State as to their educational qualifications and the Secretary of State may require the submission of such evidence of the fitness of candidates as he may think necessary and may require candidates to attend interviews.

(2) A candidate for a State Scholarship for Mature Students shall have attained the age of 25 before the 31st August next following the date of his application.

[(3) A candidate for a State Bursary for Adult Education shall have attained the age of 20 before the 1st September in the year in which the course in question begins or (in the case of a course which began before the commencement of these regulations) began.]

NOTE

The words in square brackets in paragraph (1) were inserted, and paragraph (3) was added, by the State Awards (Amendment) Regulation 1975, S.I. 1975 No. 940.

5. A State Award shall be tenable for the duration of the designated course, subject to the Secretary of State being satisfied as to the holder's attendance, conduct and progress:

Provided that in the case of a State Scholarship for Mature Students the Secretary of State may, if he thinks fit, extend the period of tenure in respect of the holder's attendance at an additional course.

6. The Secretary of State may pay to the holder of a State Award such grants as he thinks fit towards—

(*a*) the fees for the holder's course;

(*b*) the holder's maintenance including, where appropriate, the maintenance of dependants;

(*c*) the holder's travelling expenses during the course; and

(*d*) such other expenses of the holder as may be approved by the Secretary of State:

Provided that in determining the amount of such grants the Secretary of State may take account of any income of the holder, including any other awards, and of any dependants, and for that purpose every successful candidate shall submit a written statement of the income, or expected income, of himself and of any dependants.

NOTE

In their application to State Bursaries the references in the proviso to "dependants" shall be construed as including references to the holders' parents. See regulation 6 of the State Awards (Amendment) Regulations, 1969, S.I. 1969 No. 554, p. 388, *post*.

7.—(1) Every holder of a State Award shall, as soon as possible, submit a written statement of any change in the financial circumstances of himself or of any dependant.

(2) A State Award may be suspended or cancelled if the Secretary of State is not satisfied with the holder's attendance, conduct or progress.

NOTE

The word "dependant" in paragraph (1), *supra*, is to be construed as including "parent" in the case of a State Bursary. See Note to regulation 6, *supra*.

[SCHEDULE

Adult Education Colleges

The following are designated as colleges providing long-term residential courses of full-time education for adults:—

Co-operative College, Loughborough
Fircroft College, Birmingham
Hillcroft College, Surbiton
Plater College, Oxford
Ruskin College, Oxford
Coleg Harlech, Harlech, Wales
Newbattle Abbey, Dalkeith, Scotland.]

NOTE

The Schedule was added by the State Awards (Amendment) Regulations 1975, S.I. 1975 No. 940.

DIRECT GRANT SCHOOLS AMENDING REGULATIONS, 1963

S.I. 1963 *No.* 1379

August 8, 1963

NOTE

These Regulations, which were made by the Minister of Education (now Secretary of State for Education and Science) in exercise of the powers conferred on him by section 100 of the Education Act, 1944, and which came into operation on 17th August, 1963, were issued with the following explanatory note: "These Regulations raise from £43 to £45 and from £81 to £84 the yearly capitation grant payable in respect of upper school pupils and the yearly grant in respect of sixth-form pupils respectively, at direct-grant grammar schools".

The Direct Grant Schools Regulations, 1959, S.I. 1959 No. 1832 (29th October, 1959), are set out, as so amended, *ante*. But see the Direct Grant Schools (Amendment) Regulations 1973, S.I. 1973 No. 1535, *post*.

SCHOOLS (AMENDING) REGULATIONS, 1963

S.I. 1963 *No.* 1468

August 26, 1963

NOTE

These Regulations were issued with the following explanatory note: "These regulations amend the conditions under which school pupils may be entered for public examinations. They may now be entered for an examination if they have completed or are about to complete their fifth year of secondary education".

The Schools Regulations, 1959, S.I. 1959 No. 364 (5th March, 1959) are printed as so amended *ante*.

SECRETARY OF STATE FOR EDUCATION AND SCIENCE ORDER, 1964

S.I. 1964 *No.* 490
March 26, 1964

NOTE

This Order was issued with the following explanatory note: " This Order in Council, made under the Ministers of the Crown (Transfer of Functions) Act, 1946, transfers to the Secretary of State for Education and Science all the functions of the Minister of Education and the Minister for Science, and certain residuary research functions of the Lord President of the Council. The Order also dissolves the Ministry of Education and the Office of the Minister for Science ".

Whereas Her Majesty has been pleased to appoint a principal Secretary of State by the style and title of Secretary of State for Education and Science (in this Order referred to as the Secretary of State):

And whereas it is expedient that all functions of the Minister of Education and of the Minister for Science, and certain other functions hereinafter described be transferred to the Secretary of State:

And whereas copies of the draft of this Order have been laid before Parliament in pursuance of section 3 of the Ministers of the Crown (Transfer of Functions) Act, 1946 (a), and each House has presented an Address to Her Majesty praying that the Order be made:

Now, therefore, Her Majesty, in pursuance of section 1 of the said Act, is pleased, by and with the advice of Her Privy Council, to order, and it is hereby ordered, as follows:—

Citation, interpretation and commencement

1.—(1) This Order may be cited as the Secretary of State for Education and Science Order, 1964.

(2) The Interpretation Act, 1889 (b), applies for the interpretation of this Order as it applies for the interpretation of an Act of Parliament.

(3) In this Order " instrument " (without prejudice to the generality of that expression) includes in particular Royal Charters, Orders in Council, Letters Patent, judgments, decrees, orders, rules, regulations, schemes, byelaws, awards, contracts, memoranda and articles of association, certificates and other documents.

(4) This Order shall come into operation on 1st April, 1964.

NOTES

(a) 6 Halsbury's Statutes (3rd Edn.) 737.
(b) 32 Halsbury's Statutes (3rd Edn.) 434.

Transfer of functions and dissolution of existing departments

2.—(1) There are hereby transferred to the Secretary of State all functions of the Minister of Education and all functions of the Minister for Science; and the Ministry of Education and the Office of the Minister for Science are hereby dissolved.

(2) Without prejudice to the foregoing paragraph, the Secretary of State is hereby substituted for the Minister of Education and the Minister for Science respectively as member or chairman of any council, committee or other body, and as trustee of any trust, of which either of the said Ministers was by virtue of his office a member or chairman or trustee, as the case may be, immediately before the coming into operation of this Order.

(3) There are also hereby transferred to the Secretary of State the functions of the Lord President of the Council under paragraph 6 of Part I of Schedule 3 to the Agriculture Act, 1957 (a), and under the constitution of any research institute or other body in receipt of a grant from the Agricultural Research Council under section 1 of the Agricultural Research Act, 1956 (b).

(4) With the functions hereby transferred, there are also hereby transferred to the Secretary of State all property, rights and liabilities to which the Minister of Education and the Minister for Science were respectively entitled or subject immediately before the date of the coming into operation of this Order subject, in the case of property held in a fiduciary capacity, to the trusts affecting that property immediately before that date.

NOTES

(a) 1 Halsbury's Statutes (3rd Edn.) 294.
(b) 1 Halsbury's Statutes (3rd Edn.) 268.

Amendment, repeal and adaptation of enactments and instruments

3.—(1) The enactments described in Part I of the Schedule to this Order shall have effect subject to the amendments set out in relation thereto in column 2 of that Part; and the enactments described in Part II of that Schedule are hereby repealed to the extent specified in column 3 of that Part.

(2) Subject to paragraph (1) of this Article, any enactment or instrument in force at the coming into operation of this Order shall have effect, so far as may be necessary for the purpose or in consequence of the foregoing provisions of this Order, as if—

(*a*) for any reference to the Minister of Education, the Minister for Science or the Lord President of the Council (including any reference which is to be construed as such a reference) there were substituted a reference to the Secretary of State; and

(*b*) for any reference to the Ministry of Education or any officer of the Minister or Ministry of Education (including any reference which is to be construed as such a reference) there were substituted a reference to the department of the Secretary of State or, as the case may be, an officer of that department.

Supplemental

4.—(1) This Order shall not affect the validity of anything done by or in relation to the Minister of Education or the Minister for Science before the coming into operation of this Order; and anything which, at the time of the coming into operation of this Order, is in process of being done by or in relation to either of those Ministers (including in particular any legal proceedings then pending to which either of them is a party) may be continued by or in relation to the Secretary of State.

(2) Any authority, appointment or direction given or made by the Minister of Education or the Minister for Science, or given or made by the Lord President of the Council in the exercise of any functions transferred by this Order, shall, if in force at the coming into operation of this Order, continue in force and have effect as if given or made by the Secretary of State.

(3) Nothing in this Order affects the construction of any reference to the Secretary of State in the Charities Act, 1960, or in any other enactment or instrument in force at the coming into operation of this Order which applies or refers to a Secretary of State as well as to the Minister of Education or the Minister for Science.

SCHEDULE

AMENDMENTS AND REPEALS

PART I

ENACTMENTS AMENDED

The Documentary Evidence Act, 1868 (c. 37).	The Act shall apply in relation to the Secretary of State for Education and Science as if references to orders and regulations included references to any instrument, and as if the officers as mentioned in Schedule 2, column 2, included any officer authorised to act on behalf of the Secretary of State.
The Ministers of the Crown Act, 1937 (c. 38).	In Schedule 2, for the words " Board of Education " there shall be substituted the words " Department of Education and Science ".
The Education Act, 1944 (c. 31).	In section 1 (1), for the words from the beginning to " whose duty it shall be " there shall be substituted the words " It shall be the duty of the Secretary of State for Education and Science ". For section 1 (2) there shall be substituted the following: (2) The Secretary of State for Education and Science shall for all purposes be a corporation sole under the name of Secretary of State for Education and Science.

In section 3 (1) to (3), for the words " the Minister " and the words " the Ministry of Education " or " the Ministry ", wherever those words occur, there shall be substituted respectively the words " the Secretary of State for Education and Science " and the words " the Department of the Secretary of State ".

PART II

ENACTMENTS REPEALED

Chapter	Short Title	Extent of Repeal
1 Edw. 8 & 1 Geo. 6. c. 38.	The Ministers of the Crown Act, 1937.	In Schedule 1, the words " President of the Board of Education ".
7 & 8 Geo. 6. c. 31.	The Education Act, 1944	Section 1 (3) and (4). Section 3 (4), except in relation to documents issued before the coming into operation of this Order.
5 & 6 Eliz. 2. c. 20.	The House of Commons Disqualification Act, 1957.	In Schedule 2, Part I, the words " Minister of Education ". In Schedule 2, Part II, the words " Parliamentary Secretary to the Ministry of Education ".
9 & 10 Eliz. 2. c. 6.	The Ministers of the Crown (Parliamentary Secretaries) Act, 1960.	Section 2. In Schedule 1, the amendment of the Education Act, 1944.

SPECIAL SCHOOLS AND ESTABLISHMENTS (GRANT) AMENDING REGULATIONS, 1964

S.I. 1964 *No.* 1083
July 14, 1964

NOTE

These Regulations, which were made by the Secretary of State for Education and Science in exercise of the power conferred upon him by section 100 of the Education Act, 1944, p. 175, *ante*, were issued with the following explanatory note: " These regulations empower the Secretary of State to pay capital grant to establishments maintained by bodies other than local education authorities for the further education of disabled persons in the same way as he is already empowered to make such grants to special schools maintained by such bodies ".

The Special Schools and Establishments (Grant) Regulations, 1959, S.I. 1959 No. 366 5th March, 1959), are printed as hereby amended, *ante*.

SCHOLARSHIPS AND OTHER BENEFITS AMENDING REGULATIONS, 1964

S.I. 1964 *No.* 1294
August 11, 1964

NOTE

These Regulations, which were made by the Secretary of State for Education and Science under section 81 (*c*) of the Education Act, 1944, p. 166, *ante*, were issued with the following explanatory note: " These Regulations give effect to section 2 of the Education Act, 1964, by enabling local education authorities to pay maintenance allowances in respect of pupils at special schools at the same age as pupils attending ordinary schools, notwithstanding the higher leaving age imposed by section 38 of the Education Act, 1944, on pupils in special schools ".

The Regulations for Scholarships and Other Benefits, 1945, are printed as hereby amended at p. 327, *ante*.

SCHOOLS AMENDING REGULATIONS, 1964

S.I. 1964 *No.* 1311

August 13, 1964

NOTE

These Regulations were made by the Secretary of State for Education and Science in exercise of his powers under section 3 (4) of the Local Government Act, 1958, and were issued with the following explanatory note: " These regulations remove a drafting ambiguity in the existing paragraph 5 of Schedule II but otherwise closely reproduce the existing terms of paragraph 5 ".

The Schools Regulations, 1959, S.I. 1959 No. 364, are reproduced as hereby amended at p. 349, *ante*.

DIRECT GRANT SCHOOLS AMENDING REGULATIONS, 1964

S.I. 1964 *No.* 1312

August 13, 1964

NOTE

The above Regulations were made by the Secretary of State for Education and Science in exercise of his powers under section 100 of the Education Act, 1944, p. 175, *ante*, and were issued with the following explanatory note: " These regulations remove a drafting ambiguity in the existing regulation 24, but otherwise closely reproduce the existing terms of regulation 24 ".

The Direct Grant Schools Regulations, 1959, S.I. 1959 No. 1832, are reproduced as hereby amended, *ante*.

DIRECT GRANT SCHOOLS AMENDING REGULATIONS, 1965

S.I. 1965 *No.* 1

January 1, 1965

NOTE

These regulations were issued with the following explanatory note: " These regulations, which apply to schools in receipt of direct grants from the Secretary of State, prescribe, first, that adequate arrangements be made for the protection of staff and pupils against danger not only from fire (as at present) but also against other dangers to health and safety; second, that in the interests of health and safety the Secretary of State's approval shall be required for the giving of instruction involving the use of radioactive substances and equipment, other than television sets, producing X-rays ".

The regulations were made by the Secretary of State for Education and Science in exercise of his powers under s. 100 of the Education Act, 1944, *ante*.

The Amendments made hereby have been incorporated in the Direct Grant Schools Regulations 1959, *ante*.

SCHOOLS AMENDING REGULATIONS, 1965

S.I. 1965 *No.* 3
January 1, 1965

NOTE

These regulations were issued with the following explanatory note: "These regulations, which apply to schools, other than special schools, maintained by local education authorities, prescribe, first, that adequate arrangements be made for the protection of staff and pupils against danger not only from fire (as at present) but also against other dangers to health and safety; second, that in the interests of health and safety the Secretary of State's approval shall be required for the giving of instruction involving the use of radioactive substances and equipment, other than television sets, producing X-rays."

The amendments have been incorporated in the Schools Regulations, 1959, *ante*.

LOCAL EDUCATION AUTHORITIES RECOUPMENT (FURTHER EDUCATION) AMENDING REGULATIONS, 1965

S.I. 1965 *No.* 512
April 26, 1965

NOTE

These Regulations were issued with the following explanatory note: "These regulations provide that where a local education authority provides further education for a pupil who belongs to the area of another local education authority, the providing authority shall be recouped by the latter authority the whole cost of the provision of the education instead of only $\frac{7}{8}$ths of the cost".

See the principal regulations as thus amended, *ante*.

DIRECT GRANT SCHOOLS AMENDING REGULATIONS, 1965

S.I. 1965 *No.* 1978
November 29, 1965

NOTE

These Regulations raised the capitation grant payable under regulation 4 of the Direct Grant Schools Regulations, 1959, S.I. 1959 No. 1832, p. 363, *ante*, and also provided for payment of a supplementary grant for pupils in their last educational year.

The capitation grant has again been changed by S.I. 1973, No. 1535.

HANDICAPPED PUPILS AND SPECIAL SCHOOLS AMENDING REGULATIONS, 1966

S.I. 1966 *No.* 1576
January 1, 1967

NOTE

These Regulations were issued with the following explanatory note: "These Regulations provide for the number of occasions on which a special school shall meet to be determined by reference to the calendar year, instead of by reference to a school year beginning in August, and remove the obligation to divide the year into a specified number of terms.

For the amendments made by these regulations to regulation 12 of the Handicapped Pupils and Special Schools Regulations, 1959, see p. 358, *ante*.

SCHOOLS AMENDING REGULATIONS, 1966

S.I. 1966 *No.* 1577

January 1, 1967

NOTE

These regulations, made under s. 3 (4) of the Local Government Act, 1958, were issued with the following explanatory note: " These regulations amend the Schools Regulations, 1959 so as to provide for the number of occasions on which a school shall meet to be determined by reference to the calendar year, instead of by reference to a school year beginning in August, and remove the obligation to divide the year into a specified number of terms. They also make a drafting amendment to those regulations ".

The Schools Regulations, 1959, S.I. 1959 No. 364, are printed as so amended, *ante*.

RATE SUPPORT GRANTS (POOLING ARRANGEMENTS) REGULATIONS, 1967

S.I. 1967 *No.* 467

April 1, 1967

NOTE

These Regulations, which were made by the Secretary of State for Education and Science, under powers conferred on him by Sch. 1, para. 13, to the Local Government Act 1966 (see Notes to that Act on p. 298, *ante*), provide for the pooling, for the purposes of rate support grants paid under the Act of 1966, of expenses incurred by local education authorities on teacher training, advanced further education, the education of pupils who do not belong to the area of any authority and on the training of persons as educational psychologists.

Citation, commencement and interpretation

1.—(1) These regulations may be cited as the Rate Support Grants (Pooling Arrangements) Regulations 1967 and shall come into operation on 1st April 1967.

(2) The Interpretation Act 1889 shall apply for the interpretation of these regulations as it applies for the interpretation of an Act of Parliament.

Ascertainment of expenditure

2.—(1) Every local education authority shall in each year, in relation to expenditure incurred by the authority to which these regulations apply, make to the Secretary of State in such form as he may direct—

(*a*) not later than 21st October an estimate of—

(i) the expenditure incurred for the previous financial year;

(ii) the expenditure likely to be incurred for the current financial year;

(iii) the expenditure likely to be incurred for the ensuing financial year; and

(*b*) as soon as practicable after the authority's accounts have been audited, an account of the expenditure incurred for the year to which the audit relates.

(2) These regulations do not apply to any capital expenditure from revenue exceeding £10,000 in respect of any one college or other institution for the training of teachers or any one establishment of further education, but subject thereto apply to the following:—

(*a*) expenditure incurred in establishing, maintaining or assisting colleges or other institutions for the training of teachers or in providing or assisting the provision of other facilities specified in directions under section 62 of the Education Act 1944;

(*b*) (i) grants made in accordance with arrangements approved by the Secretary of State under section 2 (3) of the Education Act 1962;

(ii) salaries, employers' superannuation and national insurance contributions of seconded teachers taking full-time courses of training approved by the Secretary of State for the purposes of the regulations for the time being in force relating to the training of teachers;

(*c*) expenditure incurred in the provision and in assisting the provision in establishments of further education of:—

(i) any course to which regulation 10 (2) (*a*), (*b*) and (*c*) of the Further Education (Local Education Authorities) Regulations 1959 as amended applies;

(ii) such facilities in connection with any such course as the Secretary of State may direct;

(iii) facilities for research;

(*d*) expenditure incurred in the making of provision for primary, secondary or further education of pupils not belonging to the area of any local education authority;

[(*e*) expenditure incurred after 31st August 1969 in respect of persons who are being trained as educational psychologists].

NOTE

Sub-paragraph (*e*) of regulation 2 (2) was substituted by the Rate Support Grants (Pooling Arrangements) (Amendment) Regulations, 1969, S.I. 1969 No. 1107.

Apportionment of expenditure

3.—(1) The expenditure to which these regulations apply shall be so apportioned among local authorities that each authority's share of the whole of the expenditure to which regulation 2 (2) (*a*), (*b*), (*d*) and (*e*) applies and of one-half the expenditure to which regulation 2 (2) (*c*) applies shall be in the ratio in which in the relevant financial year the school population of the authority stands to the aggregate of the school populations of all authorities; and each authority's share of the other half of the expenditure to which regulation 2 (2) (*c*) applies shall be in the ratio in which in that year the rateable value of the area of the authority stands to the aggregate of the rateable values of the areas of all authorities.

(2) The school population of an authority shall be treated as the aggregate of the numbers of—

(*a*) pupils belonging to the area of the authority whose names are on the register of a school maintained or assisted by any authority or who receive education otherwise than at school in accordance with arrangements made under section 56 of the Education Act 1944;

(*b*) pupils not belonging to the area of any authority whose names are on the register of a school maintained or assisted by the authority; and

(*c*) pupils at other schools the fees for whose education are paid by the authority.

(3) The rateable value of the area of an authority shall be treated as the difference between—

(*a*) the aggregate of the rateable values as ascertained in the relevant financial year for the purposes of paragraph 2 (2) (*b*) of Schedule 5 to the General Rate Act 1967 of the areas of rating authorities within the area of the authority; and

(*b*) the aggregate, as certified by the valuation officer, of the rateable values in that year of the dwelling houses within the meaning of that Act in those areas.

Adjustment of needs element

4. The needs element payable to each authority for any year shall be increased or decreased by the amount by which the expenditure of the authority for that year respectively exceeds or falls short of the share attributable to that authority for that year by virtue of regulation 3.

Certificates of needs element

5.—(1) The Secretary of State shall in each year certify to the Minister of Housing and Local Government—

(*a*) not later than 31st December, the estimated amount of the increases and decreases of the needs element which ought to be made for—

(i) the preceding financial year;
(ii) the current financial year;
(iii) the ensuing financial year; and

(*b*) as soon as practicable after he has received the audited accounts of each local education authority, the actual amount of those increases and decreases.

(2) In making any estimate for the purposes of sub-paragraph (*a*) above the Secretary of State may modify any estimate submitted by an authority under regulation 2 (1) (*a*) if, after consulting the authority, he is satisfied that, in respect of any class of expenditure, the expenditure likely to be incurred by the authority is substantially more or less than the amount shown in the estimate.

TRAINING OF TEACHERS REGULATIONS, 1967

S.I. 1967 *No.* 792
June 6, 1967

NOTE

The whole of these Regulations, except for regulation 34, were revoked by the Further Education Regulations 1975, S.I. 1975 No. 1054, *post.*

Grants to students

34.—(1) Subject to paragraphs (2) and (3), the Secretary of State may pay grants to a recognised student undergoing training as a teacher at any university, university department of education or other voluntary institution in respect of expenditure incurred or to be incurred by him on his tuition, board and other maintenance.

(2) The amount of grant paid to any person under this regulation shall not exceed the amount that would be payable to him as an award under the regulations for the time being in force under section 1 of the Education Act 1962 (which relates to awards bestowed by authorities); and accordingly the provisions of those regulations which relate to the computation of such awards shall apply with the necessary modifications to the computation of grants under this regulation.

(3) No grant shall be paid under this regulation in respect of any expenditure in respect of which a grant is payable to the student by an authority under section 2 (3) of the Education Act 1962 (which empowers authorities to pay grants in accordance with arrangements approved by the Secretary of State).

INDEPENDENT SCHOOLS TRIBUNAL (AMENDMENT) RULES, 1968

S.I. 1968 *No.* 588
April 25, 1968

NOTE

These Rules increase the subsistence allowances payable to the chairmen and members of Independent Schools Tribunals as originally laid down in the Second Schedule to the Independent Schools Tribunal Rules 1958, S.I. 1958 No. 519. For the new rates see p. 348, *ante*.

COUNTY AND VOLUNTARY SCHOOLS (NOTICES) REGULATIONS, 1968

S.I. 1968 *No.* 615
April 24, 1968

NOTE

These Regulations, which were made under s. 13 (3) of the Education Act 1944, were issued with the following explanatory note: " These regulations prescribe the manner in which public notice must be given of proposals for the establishment, discontinuance or alteration of county and voluntary schools ".

Citation, commencement and interpretation

1.—(1) These regulations may be cited as the County and Voluntary Schools (Notices) Regulations 1968 and shall come into operation on 24th April 1968.

(2) The Interpretation Act 1889 shall apply for the interpretation of these regulations as it applies for the interpretation of an Act of Parliament.

Public notices

2. Public notice shall be given in the following manner of any proposals to which section 13 (3) of the Education Act 1944 (public notice of proposals relating to schools) applies:—

(*a*) by publishing the notice in at least one newspaper circulating in the area served or, as the case may be, to be served by the school;

(*b*) by posting the notice in some conspicuous place or places within that area;

(*c*) in the case of an existing school, by posting the notice at or near any main entrance to the school; and

(*d*) in such other manner, if any, as appears to the authority or persons by whom the proposals were submitted to be desirable for giving publicity to the notice.

Revocation

3. The County and Voluntary Schools (Notices) Regulations 1945 and the County and Voluntary Schools (Notices) Amending Regulations 1953 are hereby revoked.

DIRECT GRANT SCHOOLS (AMENDMENT) REGULATIONS, 1968

S.I. 1968 *No.* 1148
August 1, 1968

NOTE

These Regulations, which came into operation on 1st August 1968, amend the provisions of the Direct Grant Schools Regulations 1959, S.I. 1959 No. 1832, relating to the payment of capitation grant to, and the provision of milk in, direct grant grammar schools, and to the dismissal and exclusion of teachers from direct grant schools generally.

For the amendments made to the principal regulations, see p. 363, *ante*.

SCHOOLS (AMENDMENT) REGULATIONS, 1968

S.I. 1968 *No.* 1281
September 1, 1968

NOTE

These Regulations were issued with the following explanatory note:—
" These provisions amend the regulations relating to the employment as teachers in county and voluntary schools and special schools of persons who are not qualified teachers. They permit the employment of certain student teachers and specialists and, subject to transitory provisions, bring to an end the provisions for the employment of temporary assistant teachers and occasional teachers. They also extend the period of probationary service for certain teachers and make drafting amendments to the provisions relating to the dismissal and exclusion of teachers ".

For the amendments made to the Schools Regulations 1959, S.I. 1959 No. 364, see p. 349, *ante*.

SCHOOLS (AMENDMENT) REGULATIONS, 1969

S.I. 1969 *No.* 231
March 3, 1969

NOTE

These Regulations, which were issued by the Secretary of State in exercise of powers conferred on him by s. 3 (4) of the Local Government Act, 1958, amend the Schools Regulations, 1959, S.I. 1959 No. 364. Those principal regulations, as so amended, are printed at p. 349, *ante*.

SPECIAL SCHOOLS AND ESTABLISHMENTS (GRANT) (AMENDMENT) REGULATIONS, 1969

S.I. 1969 *No.* 410
April 1, 1969

NOTE

These regulations were made by the Secretary of State under s. 100 (1) (*b*) and (3) of the Education Act, 1944. They revoke regulation 5 of the principal Regulations (p. 361, *ante*), thus terminating the Secretary of State's power to pay grants towards an employee's superannuation contribution in respect of teachers in contributory service in a special school, etc.

The Secretary of State for Education and Science, in exercise of the powers conferred upon him by section 100 (1) (*b*) and (3) of the Education Act 1944 as amended by the Secretary of State for Education and Science Order 1964, hereby makes the following regulations:—

Citation, commencement and interpretation

1.—(1) These regulations may be cited as the Special Schools and Establishments (Grant) (Amendment) Regulations 1969 and shall come into operation on 1st April 1969.

(2) The Interpretation Act 1889 shall apply for the interpretation of these regulations as it applies for the interpretation of an Act of Parliament.

Amendment of 1959 *Regulations*

2. Regulation 5 of the Special Schools and Establishments (Grant) Regulations 1959 (grant in respect of employer's superannuation contribution) is hereby revoked.

PROVISION OF MILK AND MEALS REGULATIONS, 1969

S.I. 1969 *No.* 483
April 7, 1969

NOTE

These Regulations were issued with the following explanatory note:—

" These regulations consolidate with amendments the regulations which impose upon local education authorities the duty to provide milk, meals and other refreshment for pupils attending schools maintained by them. The principal amendments are—

(*a*) the provisions for determining the parent's capacity to pay the charge for school dinner (regulation 10 (4) and schedule 1); and

(*b*) the omission of the provision for the remission of that charge in respect of children belonging to large families ".

The Secretary of State for Education and Science, in exercise of the powers conferred upon him by section 49 of the Education Act 1944 as amended by the Secretary of State for Education and Science Order 1964 and section 3 of the Public Expenditure and Receipts Act 1968, hereby makes the following regulations:—

Citation, commencement and interpretation

1.—(1) These regulations may be cited as the Provision of Milk and Meals Regulations 1969 and shall come into operation on 7th April 1969.

(2) The Interpretation Act 1889 shall apply for the interpretation of these regulations as it applies for the interpretation of an Act of Parliament.

Revocation

2. The regulations specified in schedule 2 are hereby revoked.

Duty of local education authority

3.—(1) It shall be the duty of every local education authority (in these regulations called " authority "), subject to and in accordance with these regulations, to provide so far as is reasonably practicable such milk, meals and other refreshment as are required by day pupils in attendance at schools maintained by them.

(2) The duty imposed by paragraph (1) above shall include the duty to provide such premises, equipment and transport and such incidental and ancillary facilities and services as appear to the authority to be necessary; and for the purposes of this regulation the duty to provide premises shall include the duty to make alterations to the school buildings, including such consequential alterations as are necessary to secure that the school premises conform to the prescribed standards.

Provision of milk

4.—(1) On every school day one third of a pint of milk shall be provided for—

[(*a*) every pupil in every special school;

(*b*) every pupil in every primary school until the end of the summer term ending next after the date on which he attains the age of seven; and

(*c*) every other pupil in a primary school, and every junior pupil in an all-age school or a middle school, in respect of whom there is for the time being in force a certificate given by a medical officer of the authority stating that his health requires that he should be provided with milk at school.]

(2) On any school day a further third of a pint of milk may be provided in any special school for any delicate pupil within the meaning of the Handicapped Pupils and Special Schools Regulations 1959 (a) as amended (b).

[(3) On any school day milk may be provided for any pupil in any school whether or not milk is provided for him under paragraph (1) or (2) above.]

(4) The authority shall provide milk—

(*a*) which is pasteurised or ultra heat treated or, if no such milk is obtainable, designated for sale as untreated; and (*b*) from sources and of a quality approved for the purposes of these regulations by the medical officer of health for the area of the authority after consultation with the medical officer of health for any county district concerned and the school medical officer.

(5) If it is not reasonably practicable for the authority to comply with the requirements of paragraph (4) (*b*) above, they shall provide full-cream dried milk prepared for drinking or milk tablets.

[(6) In these regulations—

" primary school " means a school for providing primary education;

" all-age school " means a school which is deemed to be a primary school by virtue only of section 114 (3) of the Education Act 1944;

" middle school " means a school which is deemed to be a primary school or a secondary school by virtue of an order under section 1 (2) of the Education Act 1964.]

NOTE

The words in square brackets in paragraphs (1), (3) and (6) were respectively substituted, inserted and added by the Provision of Milk and Meals (Amendment No. 2) Regulations 1971, S.I. 1971 No. 1368.

Provision of meals and other refreshment

5.—(1) On every school day there shall be provided, and on any other day there may be provided, for every pupil as a midday dinner a meal suitable in all respects as the main meal of the day.

(2) On any school day there may be provided such other meals and refreshment as the authority consider appropriate.

Exceptions and saving

6.—(1) The authority shall not be under any duty to provide milk under regulation 4 (1) or as the case may be a meal under regulation 5 (1) for any pupil who takes it so rarely or irregularly that unreasonable expense is involved in catering for him.

(2) These regulations shall be without prejudice to the exercise by the head teacher of a school, under the articles of government or rules of management for the school, of any function relating to the internal discipline of the school.

Duties of managers and governors

7. The managers or governors of every school shall afford to the authority such facilities as are required by the authority to enable them to carry out their duties under these regulations and for that purpose shall allow the authority to make such use of the premises and equipment of the school, and to make such alterations to the school buildings, as the authority consider necessary.

Organisers of school meals

8. [*Revoked.*]

NOTE

Regulation 8 was revoked by the Provision of Milk and Meals (Amendment) Regulations 1974, S.I. 1974 No. 1125.

Supervision of pupils

9. The authority shall ensure that suitable arrangements are made for the supervision and social training of pupils during meals.

Expenses

10.—(1) Subject to the provisions of this regulation, the expense incurred in providing milk, meals and other refreshment under these regulations shall be defrayed by the authority.

[(2) The authority shall make arrangements for securing that the expense of providing milk under regulation 4 (3) is defrayed by the pupil or his parent.]

(3) The authority shall make arrangements for the payment by the parent of—

(*a*) a charge of [[15p]] for every meal provided in [a nursery school or] a county or voluntary school under regulation 5 (1);

(*b*) such a charge (if any) as they consider appropriate for any meal provided in a special school under regulation 5 (1); and

(*c*) such charges as they consider appropriate for meals and refreshment provided under regulation 5 (2).

(4) The arrangements made by the authority under paragraph (3) above shall include provision for the remission of the charge [under sub-paragraphs (*a*) and (*b*)] in the case of any parent who satisfies them that he is unable to pay it without hardship [[and may include provision for the remission of the charge under sub-paragraph (*c*) in the case of any parent in whose case the charge under sub-paragraph (*b*) is remitted in pursuance of this paragraph.]]

(5) For the purposes of paragraph (4) above, a parent who is in receipt of a supplementary pension or a supplementary allowance under section 4 of the Ministry of Social Security Act 1966 [or a benefit under the Family Income Supplements Act 1970] shall be treated as unable to pay the charge without hardship; and in the case of the charge under paragraph (3) (*a*) above, the question whether any parent not in receipt of such benefit is so unable to pay shall be determined in accordance with schedule 1.

[(6) Subject to paragraph (7) below the parent shall for the purposes of paragraph (4) above be treated as having satisfied the authority that, as regards any child, he is unable to pay the charge under paragraph (3) (*a*) above without hardship for a period of twelve months beginning on the first day on which the charge is, or as the case may be was last, remitted in pursuance of paragraph (4) by virtue of schedule 1; and this paragraph shall have effect notwithstanding any increase in the net income of the parent, and any decrease in the size of the family, during that period.

(7) Paragraph (6) above shall not apply if the authority are satisfied that the inability of the parent, immediately before the commencement of the period of twelve months referred to, to pay the charge without hardship was due to a temporary reduction in his income.]

NOTES

The words in square brackets in paragraphs (2), (3), (4) and (5) were inserted or substituted by the Provision of Milk and Meals (Amendment No. 2) Regulations 1971, S.I. 1971 No. 1368.

The amount of 15p in double square brackets in paragraph (3) (*a*) was substituted by the Provision of Milk and Meals (Amendment) Regulations 1975, S.I. 1975 No. 311.

Paragraphs (6), (7) were added by the Provision of Milk and Meals (Amendment) Regulations 1973, S.I. 1973 No. 271.

The words in double square brackets at the end of paragraph (4) were added by the Provision of Milk and Meals (Amendment No. 2) Regulations 1973, S.I. 1973 No. 1299.

Inspection

11. All the facilities (including buildings and equipment) provided under these regulations shall be open to inspection by any person authorised by the Secretary of State for that purpose.

Regulation 10 (4)

SCHEDULE 1

DETERMINATION OF FINANCIAL HARDSHIP

Net income scale

1. Where the net weekly income of the parent of a family of any size specified in Part A of the following table is less than any amount shown in the corresponding entry in Part B, the number of children in respect of whom the charge shall be remitted is the number at the head of the column in Part B in which there appears the lowest amount in that entry which exceeds his income.

Part A	Part B					
Size of Family	Net weekly income in £·p					
	1	2	3	4	5	6
1	23·90					
2	29·30	28·55				
3	34·70	33·95	33·20			
4	40·10	39·35	38·60	37·85		
5	45·50	44·75	44·00	43·25	42·50	
6	50·90	50·15	49·40	48·65	47·90	47·15

For larger families, in respect of each child—

(*a*) [£5·40] is to be added at each incremental point in every additional line;

(*b*) [£0·75] is to be deducted at each incremental point in every additional column.

For the purposes of this paragraph the expression "size of family" means the number of dependent children in the family who have not attained the age of 19.

NOTE

A new table, and the amounts in square brackets in the notes, were substituted by the Provision of Milk and Meals (Amendment No. 2) Regulations 1975, S.I. 1975 No. 1619.

Calculation of net income

2. In calculating the net income of the parent there shall be taken into account his income (reduced by income tax and national insurance contributions but including any benefit in kind other than a dwelling) from all sources, but there shall be disregarded the resources specified in paragraph 3 below and a deduction shall be made in respect of the expenses specified in paragraph 4 below.

Resources to be disregarded

3.—[(1) £4 of any income to which this sub-paragraph applies; provided that there shall not be disregarded more than £1 of any payments of a kind to which paragraph 25 of schedule 2 to the Supplementary Benefit Act 1966 (as substituted by paragraph 5 of schedule 3 to the Social Security Benefits Act 1975 (occupational pensions) applies.

(2) sub-paragraph (1) applies to all income except—

(*a*) earnings;

(*b*) benefit under the National Insurance Acts 1965 and 1966;

(*c*) industrial injury benefit under the National Insurance (Industrial Injuries) Acts 1965 and 1966;

(*d*) family allowances;

(*e*) payments for maintenance (including any marriage allowance); and

(*f*) any rent received in respect of accommodation whether let furnished or unfurnished;

but for the purposes of sub-paragraph (1) the amount of—

(i) a war widow's pension; and

(ii) a widow's pension under section 19 (3) of the National Insurance (Industrial Injuries) Act 1965 or an analogous payment—

shall be reduced by the amount of the rate of pension payable to a widow under schedule 3 to the National Insurance Act 1965.]

(3) [[£4]] of the earnings of a mother or female guardian.

(4) [[£2]] of the casual earnings of an unemployed father or male guardian.

(5) Any maternity grant under section 23 of the National Insurance Act 1965.

(6) Any death grant under section 39 of the National Insurance Act 1965.

(7) Any payment in respect of a pupil under the Regulations for Scholarships and Other Benefits 1945 as amended.

(8) [£1·25] of any income if one parent is blind.

(9) [£2] of any income if both parents are blind.

(10) One-tenth of the rent received in respect of accommodation let unfurnished.

(11) One-quarter of the rent received in respect of accommodation let furnished.

(12) [Any income] received as a contribution towards the expenses of the household from any other member of, or person living with, the family.

[(13) Any attendance allowance under section 4 of the National Insurance (Old persons' and widows' pensions and attendance allowance) Act 1970.]

NOTES

The words or figures in single square brackets in sub-paragraph (3) were substituted by the Provision of Milk and Meals (Amendment No. 2) Regulations 1971, S.I. 1971 No. 1368.

Sub-paragraphs (1) and (2) of paragraph (3) were substituted by the Provision of Milk and Meals (Amendment No. 2) Regulations 1975, S.I. 1975 No. 1619, as were the figures in double square brackets in paragraphs 3 (3), 3 (4) and 4 (6).

Sub-paragraph (13) was added by the Provision of Milk and Meals (Amendment) Regulations 1972, S.I. 1972 No. 1098.

Expenses to be deducted

4.—(1) The amount of any premium on a policy of assurance on the life of either parent.

(2) Any expenses reasonably incurred in the provision of necessary household assistance and necessary day care for a child below compulsory school age where—

(*a*) the parent is widowed, divorced or permanently separated from the other party to the marriage;

(*b*) either parent is incapacitated;

(*c*) the parent is an unmarried women.

(3) Any expenses necessarily incurred in the course of the parent's employment, including travelling expenses, trade union subscriptions and superannuation contributions.

(4) The amount of any rent, general and water rates and mortgage payments in respect of the home and of any hire purchase payments in respect of any caravan or houseboat which is the permanent home of the family.

(5) Any payment made—

(*a*) for the maintenance of a former wife or her child;

(*b*) under an affiliation order;

(*c*) under a contribution order in respect of a child in the care of a local authority.

(6) [[£1·35]] of the cost of any special diet prescribed by a registered medical practitioner.

SCHEDULE 2

Regulation 2

REVOCATIONS

NOTE

This Schedule revokes all previous Milk and Meals Regulations (1945–1968).

STATE AWARDS (AMENDMENT) REGULATIONS, 1969

S.I. 1969 *No.* 554

April 25, 1969

NOTE

These Regulations were made by the Secretary of State under s. 3 of the Education Act, 1962. They extend the Secretary of State's powers to make State Awards so as to include State Bursaries, to be awarded in respect of postgraduate courses designated under the regulations.

The amendments made by regulations 4 and 5 have been incorporated in the principal regulations, p. 370, *ante*.

Citation, commencement and interpretation

1.—(1) These regulations may be cited as the State Awards (Amendment) Regulations 1969 and shall come into operation on 25th April 1969.

(2) The Interpretation Act 1889 shall apply for the interpretation of these regulations as it applies for the interpretation of an Act of Parliament.

Effect of regulations

2. The State Awards Regulations 1963 (in these regulations called " the principal regulations ") shall, as respects any course beginning after 31st August 1969 to which these regulations apply, have effect subject to these regulations.

State Bursaries

3. In regulation 2 of the principal regulations the word " and " at the end of paragraph (*a*) shall be omitted and at the end of the regulation there shall be added—

" and

(*c*) State Bursaries, being awards to persons in respect of their attendance at such courses at universities, colleges or other institutions, whether in England or Wales or elsewhere, as are designated under regulation 3 ".

Courses designated for State Studentships

4. In regulation 3 (1) of the principal regulations—

(*a*) for the expression " Arts and Social Studies " in both places where it occurs there shall be substituted the expression " the Humanities ";

(*b*) for sub-paragraph (*a*) there shall be substituted—

" (*a*) at a university or other institution in England or Wales in preparation for a doctorate, a master's degree or a degree of bachelor of letters or of bachelor of philosophy ";

and

(*c*) sub-paragraph (*b*) shall be omitted.

Courses designated for State Bursaries

5. In regulation 3 of the principal regulations there shall be added as a new paragraph (3)—

" (3) The courses designated for the purposes of paragraph (*c*) of regulation 2 shall be such full-time courses (not being courses designated for the purposes of paragraph (*a*) of regulation 2), being postgraduate courses or comparable to postgraduate courses, at universities, colleges or other institutions in the United Kingdom, as the Secretary of State may from time to time designate under this paragraph ".

Parental contribution

6. In determining the amount of grant to the holder of a State Bursary the Secretary of State may take account of any income of the holder's parent and accordingly the references in the proviso to regulation 6 and in regulation 7 (1) of the principal regulations to the holder's dependants shall, in their application to State Bursaries, be construed as including references to his parent.

RATE SUPPORT GRANTS (POOLING ARRANGEMENTS) (AMENDMENT) REGULATIONS, 1969

S.I. 1969 *No.* 1107

August 13, 1969

NOTE

These Regulations, which were made by the Secretary of State for Education and Science under powers conferred upon him by Sch. 1, para. 13, to the Local Government Act, 1966, amend the Rate Support Grants (Pooling Arrangements) Regulations, 1967, S.I. 1967 No. 467. Those Regulations, as so amended, are printed at p. 378, *ante*.

SCHOOLS (AMENDMENT No. 2) REGULATIONS, 1969

S.I. 1969 *No.* 1174
September 1, 1969

NOTE

These regulations removed restrictions on the size of classes in county and voluntary schools. See the Note to the revoked regulation 6 of the Schools Regulations, 1959, S.I. 1959 No. 364, *ante*.

SCHOOLS (QUALIFIED TEACHERS) REGULATIONS, 1969

S.I. 1969 *No.* 1777
January 1, 1970

NOTE

These Regulations amend the definition of the expression " qualified teacher " in the Schools Regulations, 1959, p. 349, *ante*, so that from 1st January, 1970 a person shall be eligible for appointment as a qualified teacher in a maintained primary school or a special school by virtue of a special qualification only if he acquired it before that date.

Citation, commencement and interpretation

1.—(1) These regulations may be cited as the Schools (Qualified Teachers) Regulations 1969 and shall come into operation on 1st January 1970.

(2) The Interpretation Act 1889 shall apply for the interpretation of these regulations as it applies for the interpretation of an Act of Parliament.

Teachers in County and Voluntary Schools

2. [*Redefines " qualified teacher ".*]

NOTE

See regulation 16 (2) of the Schools Regulations, 1959, *ante*.

Teachers in Special Schools

3. [*Revoked.*]

NOTE

Regulation 3 was revoked by the Schools (Qualified Teachers) Regulations 1973, S.I. 1973 No. 2021, *post*.

EDUCATION OF HANDICAPPED CHILDREN (TRANSFER OF STAFF AND PROPERTY) ORDER 1971

S.I. 1971 *No.* 341
March 12, 1971

NOTE

This Order made provision for the transfer of staff and property to local education authorities, on the discontinuance of the classification of handicapped children as unsuitable for education at school. The Order also provided for the protection of the interests of staff affected by the Order.

QUALIFIED TEACHERS AND TEACHERS IN SPECIAL SCHOOLS REGULATIONS 1971

S.I. 1971 *No.* 342

April 1, 1971

NOTE

These Regulations amended the Schools Regulations 1959 and the Handicapped Pupils and Special Schools Regulations 1959, consequential upon the coming into operation of the Education (Handicapped Children) Act 1970.

The regulations, as so amended, will be found at pp. 349, 356, *ante*.

LOCAL EDUCATION AUTHORITIES RECOUPMENT (FURTHER EDUCATION) (AMENDMENT) REGULATIONS 1971

S.I. 1971 *No.* 701

May 7, 1971

NOTE

These Regulations, made under s. 7 (4) of the Education (Miscellaneous Provisions) Act 1953, amend the Local Education Authorities Recoupment (Further Education) Regulations 1954, by adding a new paragraph 4 (7) thereto: see p. 336, *ante*.

PROVISION OF MILK AND MEALS (AMENDMENT NO. 2) REGULATIONS 1971

S.I. 1971 *No.* 1368

September 1, 1968

NOTE

These Regulations, made under s. 49 of the Education Act 1944, and s. 1 of the Education (Milk) Act 1971, amend regulations 4 and 10 of, and Sch. 1 to, the Provision of Milk and Meals Regulations 1969, S.I. 1969 No. 483. These principal regulations, as so amended, will be found at p. 383, *ante*.

LOCAL EDUCATION AUTHORITIES RECOUPMENT (FURTHER EDUCATION) (AMENDMENT NO. 2) REGULATIONS 1971

S.I. 1971 *No.* 1821

January 1, 1971

NOTE

These Regulations, made under s. 7 (4) of the Education (Miscellaneous Provisions) Act 1953, amend the Local Education Authorities Recoupment (Further Education) Regulations 1954, S.I. 1954 No. 815. Those regulations, as so amended, will be found at p. 336, *ante*.

INDEPENDENT SCHOOLS TRIBUNAL (AMENDMENT) RULES 1972

S.I. 1972 *No.* 42
February 21, 1972

NOTE

These Regulations, made under s. 75 (1) of the Education Act 1944, after consultation with the Council on Tribunals in accordance with s. 10 of the Tribunals and Inquiries Act 1971, amend the Independent Schools Tribunal Rules 1958, S.I. 1958 No. 519. These principal rules, as so amended, will be found at p. 344, *ante*.

EDUCATION (NO. 2) ACT 1968 (COMMENCEMENT NO. 3) ORDER 1972

S.I. 1972 *No.* 212 (c. 3)
February 15, 1972

NOTE

This Order, made under s. 4 (1) of the Education (No. 2) Act 1968, provides for the coming into force of that Act for the purposes of establishments of further education. Local education authorities had, by the day appointed, to make instruments and articles of government for such establishments.

1. This Order may be cited as the Education (No. 2) Act 1968 (Commencement No. 3) Order 1972.

2.—(1) The appointed day for the coming into force of the Education (No. 2) Act 1968 for the purposes of establishments of further education shall be 1st September 1972.

(2) In this Order " establishment of further education " means an institution, other than a college of education, providing full-time education pursuant to a scheme of further education approved under section 42 of the Education Act 1944.

RAISING OF THE SCHOOL LEAVING AGE ORDER 1972

S.I. 1972 *No.* 444
September 1, 1972

NOTE

This Order in Council raised the upper limit of the compulsory school age from fifteen to sixteen years.

Whereas Her Majesty, in pursuance of the Regency Acts 1937 to 1953, was pleased, by Letters Patent dated the fourth day of February 1972, to delegate to the following Counsellors of State (subject to the exceptions hereinafter mentioned) or any two or more of them, that is to say, His Royal Highness The Prince Philip, Duke of Edinburgh, Her Majesty Queen Elizabeth The Queen Mother, His Royal Highness The Prince Charles, Prince of Wales, Her Royal Highness The Princess Anne, Her Royal Highness The Princess Margaret, Countess of Snowdon, and His Royal Highness The Duke of Gloucester, full power and authority during the period of Her Majesty's absence from the United Kingdom to summon and hold on Her Majesty's behalf Her Privy Council and to signify thereat Her Majesty's approval for anything for which Her Majesty's approval in Council is required:

And whereas Her Majesty was further pleased to except from the number of the said Counsellors of State His Royal Highness The Prince Philip, Duke of Edinburgh, His Royal Highness The Prince Charles, Prince of Wales, Her Royal Highness The Princess Anne and Her Royal Highness The Princess Margaret, Countess of Snowdon, while absent from the United Kingdom:

And whereas the Secretary of State for Education and Science and the Secretary of State for Wales are satisfied that it has become practicable to raise to sixteen the upper limit of the compulsory school age:

And whereas a draft of this Order has lain before Parliament for a period of 40 days in accordance with the proviso to section 35 of the Education Act 1944 and section 6 (2) of the Statutory Instruments Act 1946 and neither House of Parliament has resolved that the draft be not submitted to Her Majesty:

Now, therefore, Her Majesty Queen Elizabeth The Queen Mother and Her Royal Highness The Princess Anne, being authorised thereto by the said Letters Patent, and in pursuance of the said section 35, do hereby, by and with the advice of Her Majesty's Privy Council, on Her Majesty's behalf order, and it is hereby ordered, as follows:—

Citation and commencement

1. This Order may be cited as the Raising of the School Leaving Age Order 1972 and shall come into operation on 1st September 1972.

Raising of the School Leaving age

2. The definition in section 35 of the Education Act 1944 of the expression " compulsory school age " shall have effect as if for the references therein to the age of fifteen years there were substituted references to the age of sixteen years.

PROVISION OF MILK AND MEALS (AMENDMENT) REGULATIONS 1972

S.I. 1972 *No.* 1098

September 1, 1972

NOTE

These Regulations, made under s. 49 of the Education Act 1944, as amended by s. 1 of the Education (Milk) Act 1971, added a new sub-paragraph (13) to paragraph 3 of the Provision of Milk and Meals Regulations 1969, S.I. 1969 No. 483. For these principal regulations, as so amended, see p. 383, *ante*.

STANDARDS FOR SCHOOL PREMISES REGULATIONS 1972

S.I. 1972 *No.* 2051

February 1, 1973

NOTE

These Regulations, which were made under s. 10 of the Education Act 1944, were issued with the following explanatory note: " These regulations consolidate with amendments the regulations which prescribe the standards to which the premises of schools maintained by local education authorities are to conform. The regulations substitute metric units for the imperial measures in the Standards for School Premises Regulations 1959, and make other amendments of a minor or drafting character. "

The Regulations of 1959, and their amending regulations, are revoked.

PART I

GENERAL

Citation, commencement and interpretation

1.—(1) These regulations may be cited as the Standards for School Premises Regulations 1972 and shall come into operation on 1st February 1973.

(2) In these regulations, unless the context otherwise requires—

" approved " means approved by the Secretary of State;

" boarding accommodation " means any premises provided solely for the use of boarding pupils attending a school other than a nursery school;

" daylight factor " means the ratio of the illumination, including light reflected from interior and exterior surfaces, at a given point inside a building when measured on a horizontal plane at that point, to the illumination simultaneously existing on a horizontal plane under an unobstructed sky of uniform luminance;

" fittings " includes closets and urinal stalls;

" hard porous surface " means a loosely compacted surface, consisting of cinder-ash, brick dust, blaes or similar material or a bitumen bound surface, through which water can penetrate;

" infant " means a child who has attained the age of five but has not attained the age of eight;

" infant school " means a school wholly or mainly for infants;

" internal area " means the area calculated by measuring from the internal faces of external walls to the centre line of internal walls and partitions;

" junior " means a child who has attained the age of eight but has not attained the age of twelve;

" junior school " means a school wholly or mainly for juniors;

" middle school " means a school in respect of which the Secretary of State has given a direction under section 1 (2) of the Education Act 1964;

" nursery class " means a class in a primary school wholly or mainly for children who have attained the age of three but have not attained the age of five;

" paved area " means an area of land having a hard impervious surface constructed of materials such as tarmacadam or concrete;

" primary school " includes a middle school to which children under the age of ten are admitted but does not include a special school;

" school " means a school maintained by a local education authority and a department of a school having a separate head teacher shall be treated as a school;

" secondary school " includes a middle school to which children under the age of ten are not admitted but does not include a special school;

" teaching accommodation " means all the internal space in a school so designed and equipped as to be suitable for teaching.

(3) References to the number of pupils are, as regards any school, references to the number of pupils for whom the school is designed; and where the context so requires " unit ", in the expression " unit of pupils ", includes part of a unit.

(4) In these regulations the abbreviations in the first column below are used to denote the expressions in the second column:—

ha	hectare
mm	millimetre
m	metre
m^2	square metre
m^3	cubic metre
cd/m^2	candela per square metre
C	Celsius

(5) The Interpretation Act 1889 shall apply for the interpretation of these regulations as it applies for the interpretation of an Act of Parliament.

Application of regulations and revocations

2.—(1) Subject to these regulations—

(*a*) Part II applies to primary schools;
(*b*) Part III applies to secondary schools;
(*c*) Part IV applies to nursery schools and nursery classes;
(*d*) Part V applies to special schools;
(*e*) Part VI applies to boarding accommodation;
(*f*) Part VII applies to all schools and all boarding accommodation.

(2) The Standards for School Premises Regulations 1959 to 1972 shall cease to have effect and accordingly the regulations specified in the schedule are hereby revoked.

PART II

PRIMARY SCHOOLS

Sites

3.—(1) (*a*) Subject to sub-paragraphs (*b*) and (*c*) below the minimum area of the site shall be—

Number of pupils	*ha*
Not more than 25	0·2
26–50	0·25
51–80	0·3

and for every additional unit of 40 pupils the minimum area shall be increased by 0·05 ha.

(*b*) In its application to a middle school to which children under the age of ten are admitted sub-paragraph (*a*) shall have effect subject to the addition to the minimum area of 0·05 ha for every unit of 60 pupils over the age of eleven.

(*c*) In its application to a primary school which contains a nursery class sub-paragraph (*a*) shall have effect subject to the addition to the minimum area of 0·1 ha and a further 0·05 ha for every unit of 20 pupils in excess of 40 in the class.

(2) (*a*) The site shall include a paved area, laid on suitable foundations, properly graded and drained.

(*b*) The minimum area of the paved area shall be—

	Number of pupils	m^2
(i) Infant schools	Not more than 100	300
	101—280	612
	281—400	1,032
	401—480	1,224
(ii) Infant and Junior schools	Not more than 25	300
	26—80	420
	81—170	612
	171—280	1,122
	281—440	1,734
	441—480	2,244
(iii) Junior schools	Not more than 140	612
	141—280	1,122
	281—360	1,734
	361—480	2,244
(iv) Middle schools to which pupils under the age of ten are admitted	Not more than 140	612
	141—280	1,122
	281—360	1,734
	361—420	2,244
	421—600	3,180
	More than 600	3,180, plus 465 for each unit of 150 pupils in excess of 600.

Playing Fields

4.—(1) Subject to paragraphs (2) and (3) below every school except an infant school shall have a playing field of the following minimum area—

	Number of junior pupils	ha
(i) Junior Schools and Infant and Junior Schools	Not more than 50 ..	0·2
	51—120	0·4
	121—200	0·6
	201—280	0·9
	More than 280 ..	1·2
	Number of pupils aged eight and over	*ha*
(ii) Middle schools to which pupils under the age of ten are admitted	Not more than 150	0·6
	151—200	0·9
	201—280	1·4
	281—320	1·8
	321—480	2·4
	481—600	2·8
	More than 600 ..	3·4

(2) The minimum area of the playing fields may be reduced to such extent as may be approved for any school in whose case—

(*a*) the teaching accommodation includes an area designed for the playing of indoor games;

(*b*) facilities for physical training and recreation elsewhere are made available.

(3) For the purposes of this regulation a field with a hard porous surface large enough for the playing of team games shall be reckoned as twice its area.

Teaching Accommodation

5.—(1) The minimum internal area of the teaching accommodation shall be—

Number of Pupils	m^2
Not more than 25	3·7 per pupil.
26—75	93, plus 2·1 for each pupil in excess of 25.
76—119	227, plus 2 for each pupil in excess of 75.
More than 119	312, plus 1·575 for each pupil in excess of 120.

(2) This regulation does not apply to a middle school.

(3) Any part of the dining accommodation provided under regulation 14 which is designed also for teaching may be treated as forming part of the teaching accommodation for the purposes of this regulation.

Storage of Teaching Apparatus, Equipment and Materials

6. Sufficient and suitable facilities shall be provided, in or near the teaching accommodation, for the storage of apparatus, equipment and materials required for teaching.

Storage of Pupils' Outdoor Clothing

7. Sufficient and suitable facilities shall be provided for storing and drying pupils' outdoor clothing and for storing pupils' other belongings.

Sanitary Accommodation for Pupils

8.—(1) (*a*) Closets shall be provided.

(*b*) Urinal stalls may be provided in a school attended by boys under 8 and shall be provided in a school attended by boys of 8 and over.

(2) The minimum number of fittings shall be—

(*a*) not more than 50 pupils: 2, and 2 for every unit of 40 pupils;

(*b*) more than 50 pupils: 4, and 2 for every unit of 40 pupils;

and in a school attended by boys not less than one-third of the number of fittings provided for them shall be closets.

Washing Accommodation for Pupils

9. The number of washbasins shall be not less than the number of fittings specified in regulation 8.

Staff Rooms

10.—(1) A common room shall be provided for the teaching staff.

(2) In a school for more than 120 pupils a separate room shall be provided for the head teacher.

(3) A separate room shall be provided—

(*a*) in a school for 280 or more infants and juniors, for the teacher in charge of the infants;

(*b*) in a school for 320 or more juniors of both sexes, for the senior assistant teacher.

Cloakroom, Sanitary and Washing Accommodation for Adults

11. Sufficient and suitable cloakroom, washing and sanitary accommodation, separate from the accommodation provided for the pupils, shall be provided for the teaching staff and the staff engaged in the provision of milk, meals and other refreshments.

Facilities for Medical Inspection and Treatment

12.—(1) Suitable accommodation shall be provided so as to be immediately available at any time during school hours for the inspection and treatment of pupils by doctors, dentists and nurses.

(2) Effective provision shall be made for securing sufficient and suitable lighting and heating.

(3) The accommodation shall be conveniently accessible to a closet, and every room shall include a washbasin with a supply of hot and cold water.

Storage Facilities for School Stocks, Maintenance Equipment, Furniture and Fuel

13.—(1) Sufficient and suitable facilities shall be provided for the storage of stationery, materials, maintenance equipment and furniture.

(2) Separate and conveniently situated accommodation shall where necessary be provided for the storage of fuel.

Accommodation for Meals

14.—(1) Accommodation designed for dining and available for so long as is necessary to prepare and serve the meal and clear up afterwards shall be provided.

(2) Subject to paragraph (3), the minimum area of the accommodation provided under paragraph (1) above shall be—

(*a*) where there are two sittings, 0·4m² per person; and

(*b*) where there is one sitting, 0·8m² per person.

(3) In its application to a middle school to which children under the age of ten are admitted paragraph (2) shall have effect subject to the substitution, in respect of each senior pupil, of references to 0·5m² and 1·0m² respectively for the references to 0·4m² and 0·8m².

(4) Sufficient and suitable kitchens shall be provided.

(5) If the meals are cooked off the school premises, sufficient accommodation shall be provided for receiving and serving the meals and for washing up.

PART III
SECONDARY SCHOOLS

Sites

15.—(1) The minimum area of the site shall be—

Number of pupils	*ha*
Not more than 150	0·6
151—210	0·7
211—300	0·8
301—360	0·9
361—420	1·0
421—450	1·2

and for every additional unit of 50 pupils the minimum area shall be increased by 0·1 ha.

(2) (*a*) The site shall include a paved or hard porous area, suitable for lawn tennis, net ball, basket ball or other appropriate games, laid on suitable foundations and properly graded and drained.

(*b*) The minimum area of the paved or hard porous area of a school for either boys or girls of not more than 180 pupils shall be 970m² and of any other school as follows:—

Number of pupils	*m²*
Not more than 420	1,850
421—600	3,180
More than 600	3,180, plus 465 for every additional unit of 150 pupils.

Playing Fields

16.—(1) Every school shall have a playing field either separately or jointly with another school or schools.

(2) Subject to the provisions of this regulation the minimum area of the playing field under paragraph (1) above for any school or schools shall be as follows:—

Total number of pupils		*ha*
(*a*) Boys	Not more than 150	1·8
	151—300	3·0
and for every additional unit of 150 pupils the area shall be increased by		0·6
(*b*) Girls	Not more than 150	1·6
	151—300	2·6
	301—450	3·4
and for every additional unit of 150 pupils the area shall be increased by		0·4
(*c*) Boys and Girls	Not more than 150	1·8
	151—300	2·8
	301—600	4·0
and for every additional unit of 300 pupils the area shall be increased by		1·2

(3) The minimum area of the playing field may be reduced by such extent as may be approved for any school in whose case—

(i) approved facilities for regular instruction in swimming are provided;
(ii) buildings are provided for instruction in outdoor sports;
(iii) facilities for physical training and recreation elsewhere are made available.

(4) For the purposes of this regulation accommodation with a hard porous surface large enough for the playing of team games shall be reckoned as three times its area.

Teaching Accommodation

17.—(1) The minimum internal area of the teaching accommodation shall be determined in accordance with the following table:—

Number of pupils under 16	Area per pupil in m²			
	Under 11	11 and 12	13 and 14	15 and over
Not more than 150		3·72	4·65	5·20
151— 300	2·14	3·62	4·55	5·11
301— 450	2·04			
451— 520	1·95			
521— 700	1·86	3·53	4·46	5·02
701— 800		3·48	4·41	4·97
801— 900		3·39	4·32	4·88
901—1,050		3·25	4·18	4·74
1,051—1,200		3·21	4·13	4·69
1,201—1,350		3·16	4·09	4·65
1,351—1,500		3·10	4·02	4·58
1,501—1,650		3·07	3·99	4·55
1,651—1,800		3·04	3·97	4·52
1,801—1,950		2·99	3·92	4·48
1,951—2,100		2·97	3·90	4·46

Notes:

1. In the application of this table to a school wholly or mainly for pupils who have attained the age of sixteen the heading to the first column is to be read without the words " aged under 16 ".

2. The reference to the age of the pupils is a reference to their ages on 1st September.

(2) This regulation applies to all middle schools.

(3) Any part of the dining accommodation provided under regulation 27 which is designed also for teaching may be treated as forming part of the teaching accommodation for the purposes of this regulation.

Storage of Teaching Apparatus, Equipment and Materials

18. Sufficient and suitable facilities shall be provided in or near the teaching accommodation, for the storage of apparatus, equipment and materials required for teaching.

Storage of Pupils' Outdoor Clothing and Belongings

19. Sufficient and suitable facilities shall be provided for storing and drying pupils' outdoor clothing, and for storing pupils' other belongings.

Sanitary Accommodation for Pupils

20.—(1) Closets and, in any school attended by boys, urinal stalls shall be provided.

(2) (*a*) Subject to sub-paragraph (*b*) below, the number of fittings shall be not less than two for every unit of 30 pupils.

(*b*) The number of fittings in a school for more than 1,000 pupils shall be such as may be approved in each case.

(3) In a school attended by boys, not less than one third of the number of fittings provided for their use shall be closets.

Washing Accommodation for Pupils

21. The number of washbasins shall be not less than the number of fittings specified or approved under regulation 20 above.

Changing Rooms and Showers

22. Sufficient and suitable changing rooms and showers shall be provided near the gymnasium or other space used for physical education.

Staff Rooms

23.—(1) A common room shall be provided for the teaching staff and a separate room shall be provided for the head teacher.

(2) A separate room shall be provided for the senior assistant teacher in any school for 450 or more pupils and in any school for pupils of both sexes.

Cloakroom, Washing and Sanitary Accommodation for Adults

24. Sufficient and suitable cloakroom, washing and sanitary accommodation, separate from the accommodation provided for the pupils, shall be provided for the teaching staff and the staff engaged in the provision of milk, meals and other refreshments.

Facilities for Medical Inspection and Treatment

25.—(1) Suitable accommodation shall be provided so as to be immediately available at any time during school hours for the inspection and treatment of pupils by doctors, dentists and nurses.

(2) Effective provision shall be made for securing sufficient and suitable lighting and heating.

(3) The accommodation shall be conveniently accessible to a closet, and every room shall include a washbasin with a supply of hot and cold water.

Storage Facilities for School Stocks, Maintenance Equipment, Furniture and Fuel

26.—(1) Sufficient and suitable facilities shall be provided for the storage of stationery, materials, maintenance equipment and furniture.

(2) Separate and conveniently situated accommodation shall where necessary be provided for the storage of fuel.

Accommodation for Meals

27.—(1) Accommodation designed for dining and available for so long as is necessary to prepare and serve the meal and clear up afterwards shall be provided.

(2) The minimum area of the accommodation provided under paragraph (1) above shall be—

(*a*) where there are two sittings, 0·5m² per person;

(*b*) where there is one sitting, 1m² per person.

(3) The accommodation provided under paragraph (1) above shall be separate for any gymnasium or combined hall and gymnasium.

(4) If the meals are cooked off the school premises, sufficient accommodation shall be provided for receiving and serving the meals and for washing up.

PART IV

NURSERY SCHOOLS AND NURSERY CLASSES

Sites

28. The minimum area of the site shall be 0·1 ha for a school of not more than 40 pupils; and for every unit of 20 pupils above 40 the area shall be increased by 0·05 ha.

Garden Playing Space

29. The site of a nursery school shall include, and there shall be available to a nursery class, a garden playing space of a minimum area of 9·3m² per pupil of which not less than 3·7m² per pupil shall be paved.

Playroom Accommodation

30.—(1) Playroom accommodation of a minimum internal area of 2·3m² per pupil shall be provided.

(2) Teaching accommodation shall be provided for the pupils over the age of five in accordance with regulation 5 above.

Storage of Children's Outdoor Clothing

31. Sufficient and suitable facilities shall be provided for storing and drying pupils' outdoor clothing.

Washing and Sanitary Accommodation for Children

32.—(1) At least one washbasin shall be provided for every five pupils under the age of five where more than half the pupils regularly stay for a midday meal and for every ten pupils in any other case, and at least one closet shall be provided for every ten pupils under the age of five.

(2) One deep sink shall be provided for every 40 pupils under five years of age.

Staff Room

33.—(1) In a nursery school one room shall be provided for the superintendent and one room for the remainder of the teaching staff, together with cloakroom, washing and sanitary accommodation suitable for adults.

(2) One of the rooms provided under paragraph (1) shall be available for use also as a medical inspection and isolation room.

Storage of Apparatus, Equipment and Fuel

34.—(1) Sufficient and suitable facilities shall be provided for the storage of apparatus and equipment including in particular the storage of beds and large toys.

(2) In a nursery school separate and conveniently situated storage accommodation shall where necessary be provided for fuel.

Kitchen

35.—(1) Sufficient and suitable kitchens shall be provided for cooking a midday meal for pupils attending full time.

(2) A sink and a means of heating drinks shall be available in a school wholly for pupils attending part time and in a nursery class.

PART V

SPECIAL SCHOOLS

Sites

36.—(1) (*a*) Subject to sub-paragraphs (*b*) and (*c*), the minimum area of the site shall be—

Number of pupils	*ha*
Not more than 25	0·2
26—50	0·25
51—80	0·3

and for every additional unit of 40 pupils, the minimum area shall be increased by 0·05 ha.

(*b*) The minimum area prescribed by sub-paragraph (*a*) above shall, in the case of a school for senior pupils, be increased as follows:—

Number of senior pupils	*ha*
Not more than 50	0·05
51—120	0·1
121—160	0·15
More than 160	0·2

(*c*) The minimum area of the site of any school for some or all of whose pupils boarding accommodation is provided shall be such as may be approved in each case.

(2) (*a*) The site shall include a paved area, laid on suitable foundations and properly graded and drained:

provided that in a school for more than 120 senior pupils this requirement may be satisfied by the provision of a hard porous area suitable for team games, laid on suitable foundations and properly graded and drained, or partly by the provision of such a paved area and partly by the provision of such a hard porous area.

(*b*) The minimum area of the area provided under sub-paragraph (2) (*a*) shall be—

	Number of pupils	m^2
(i) Schools for infants and juniors	Not more than 105	612
	More than 105	910
	Number of senior pupils	m^2
(ii) All-age schools and schools for seniors	Not more than 50	910
	51—120	1,122
	More than 120	1,850

Playing Fields

37.—(1) Every school for educationally sub-normal day pupils of both sexes and all ages shall have a playing field, which shall unless otherwise approved adjoin the site.

(2) The minimum area of the playing field provided under paragraph (1), shall be—

Number of pupils	*ha*
Not more than 120	0·5 or such smaller area as may for special reasons be approved in the case of any school.
121—200	1·0

(3) In the case of any other school the area of the playing field shall be such as may be approved in each case.

Teaching Accommodation

38.—(1) In a school for not more than 200 educationally sub-normal pupils—

(*a*) the minimum internal area of the teaching accommodation shall be 520m² for the first unit of 100 pupils plus 56m² for each additional unit of 20 pupils or such smaller area as may for special reasons be approved in the case of any school; and

(*b*) there shall be a hall, and for each class a room of an area of not less than 28m² for the first unit of ten pupils plus 2·2m² for each additional pupil.

(2) In the case of any other school the teaching accommodation shall be such as may be approved in each case.

Sanitary and Washing Accommodation for Pupils

39.—(1) (*a*) Closets shall be provided.

(*b*) Urinal stalls may be provided in a school attended by boys under 8 and shall be provided in a school attended by boys of 8 and over.

(2) The minimum number of fittings shall be one for every ten pupils; and in a school attended by boys not less than one third of the fittings provided for them shall be closets.

(3) At least one washbasin shall be provided for every ten pupils.

Other Accommodation

40. Every school shall conform to the standards prescribed in the following regulations—

14 (accommodation for meals)
18 (storage of teaching apparatus, equipment and materials)
19 (storage of pupils' outdoor clothing and belongings)
23 (1) (staff room)
24 (cloakroom, washing and sanitary accommodation for adults)
25 (facilities for medical inspection and treatment)
26 (storage facilities for school stocks, maintenance equipment, furniture and fuel)—

and regulation 22 (changing rooms and showers) shall apply to any school for senior pupils.

PART VI

BOARDING ACCOMMODATION

Sites

41. The area of the site shall be such as may be approved in each case.

Dormitories and Cubicles

42.—(1) The floor area of any dormitory shall be not less than 5m² for each of the first two beds plus not less than 4·2m² for each additional bed; and the area shall be sufficient to permit a space of 900mm between any two beds.

(2) Where a separate cubicle is provided for a pupil, the dubicle shall have a window and its floor area shall be not less than 5m².

(3) Where a separate bedroom is provided for a pupil, its floor area shall be not less than 6m².

(4) Separate dormitories shall be provided for boys and girls respectively over the age of eight.

Washing and Sanitary Accommodation

43.—(1) There shall be provided not less than—

for every ten pupils	..	1 slipper bath or shower bath
for the first 60 pupils	..	1 washbasin to every 3 pupils
for the next 40 pupils	..	1 washbasin to every 4 pupils
for every additional 5 pupils		1 washbasin
for every 5 pupils ..	..	1 closet

Provided that—

(i) at least half the baths shall be slipper baths; and

(ii) in any case where any of the washing or sanitary accommodation for the day pupils in the school is both accessible to and suitable for the boarders the requirements of this paragraph may be reduced to such extent as may be approved.

(2) Baths, showers, washbasins and closets shall be suitably dispersed throughout the building, regard being had in particular to their accessibility from the dormitories.

Accommodation for Meals

44. Sufficient accommodation shall be provided for the cooking and serving of meals for the boarders.

Day Room Space

45.—(1) Subject to paragraph (2) day room space of an internal area of not less than 2·3m² for each pupil shall be provided.

(2) The requirements of this regulation may be reduced to such extent as may be approved in each case:—

(*a*) where all or part of the day school accommodation is adjacent to the boarding accommodation and is suitable for use as day room space;

(*b*) where the boarding accommodation is provided in some manner other than dormitories and common rooms;

(*c*) where the boarding accommodation is for weekly boarders only.

Sick Rooms

46.—(1) (*a*) All boarding accommodation shall include a sick room and, where the total number of boarders exceeds 40, a separate isolation room;

(*b*) The total number of beds in the sick room and isolation room shall be on the scale of one bed for every unit of 20 boarders.

(2) Separate sick room accommodation shall be provided for boys and for girls.

(3) Suitable and sufficient bathing, washing and sanitary accommodation shall be provided for use in connection with the sick room accommodation.

(4) In every sick room adequate cross ventilation shall be provided, and any cubicle provided shall have a window.

(5) The floor area shall be not less than 7·4m² for each bed and shall be sufficient to allow a space of 1·8m between any two beds.

(6) Sufficient bedrooms, baths and washing and sanitary accommodation shall be provided for the use of the nursing staff.

Staff Accommodation

47. Such residential accommodation, including sufficient dining, washing and sanitary accommodation, for the teaching and domestic staff shall be provided as may be approved in each case.

Other Accommodation

48. A sewing room, an airing room and sufficient and suitable storage space for bedding, equipment and pupils' personal belongings shall be provided.

PART VII

GENERAL REQUIREMENTS FOR SCHOOLS AND BOARDING ACCOMMODATION

Structural Loadings

49. The load bearing structure shall be such as to be capable of safely sustaining and transmitting dead load and imposed loads and the horizontal and inclined forces to which it is likely to be subjected.

Protection against the Weather

50. The building shall be so designed and constructed as adequately to resist the penetration of rain, snow, wind and moisture rising from the ground.

Precautions for Health and Safety

51. In all parts of the buildings the design, the construction, the limitation of the surface flame spread, the fire resistance of the elements of the structure and the properties of the materials shall be such that the health and safety of the occupants, and in particular their safe escape in the event of fire, shall be reasonably assured.

Lighting

52.—(1) The lighting, both natural and artificial, of each room or other space shall be appropriate to the normal use for which the room or other space is designed.

(2) In teaching accommodation and kitchens the lowest level of maintained illumination and the minimum daylight factor, on the appropriate plane in the area of normal use, shall be 110 lux and 2 per cent. respectively:

provided that if in the case of any particular teaching room or space the Secretary of State is satisfied that, regard being had to its proposed use, sufficient lighting can be provided by a combination of permanent supplementary artificial lighting and daylight at less than a 2 per cent. daylight factor, the minimum daylight factor shall be such lower percentage as may be approved.

(3) In teaching accommodation and kitchens no luminous part of any lighting unit, or mirrored image thereof, having a maximum brightness greater than 5,100 cd/m^2 or an average brightness greater than 3,400 cd/m^2, shall be visible to any occupant in a normal position within an angle at the eye of 135 degrees from the perpendicular from the eye to the floor.

(4) A sufficient part of the light emitted from the lighting fittings shall illuminate the ceiling and upper parts of the walls so as to prevent excessive contrast between the fittings and their background.

Ventilation and Heating

53.—(1) Every room shall be provided with means of ventilation capable of securing that the fresh air available shall be as follows:—

Cubic space per person for whom the room is designed m^3	*Appropriate number of air changes per hour*
Not more than 5	6
5—5·7	5
5·8—7	4
7·1—8·5	3
More than 8·5	1½

(2) Adequate measures shall be taken to prevent condensation in, and to expel noxious fumes from, every kitchen and other room in which there may be steam or fumes.

(3) The heating system shall be such as to secure that, when the outside temperature is 0°C and the heating system is heating air at the rates specified below, the temperature at a height of not more than three feet from the floor in any room or space specified below shall be as so specified or as near as may be thereto:—

Type of room or space	*Number of air changes per hour to be heated by the heating system*	*Temperatures °C*
Convalescent sitting rooms	3	18·5
Medical inspection rooms	3	18·5
Changing rooms, bathrooms and shower rooms	3	18·5
Teaching rooms	2	17
Nursery playrooms	2	17

Type of room or space	*Number of air changes per hour to be heated by the heating system*	*Temperatures °C*
Common rooms	2	17
Staff rooms	2	17
Sanatoriums and sickrooms	3	14·5
Halls	1½	14
Dining rooms	2	14
Gymnasiums	2	14
Cloakrooms	2	13
Corridors	1½	13
Dormitories	2	11

Acoustics

54. In every part of a school building the acoustic conditions and the insulation against disturbance by noise shall be appropriate to the use of that part.

Water Supply

55.—(1) Sufficient and wholesome water shall be provided.

(2) The premises shall, where reasonably practicable, be connected to a supply of water in pipes.

(3) Where a supply of water under pressure is available, running water shall be laid on to the washbasins, baths and showers.

(4) Sufficient warmed and cold water shall be available to satisfy the following requirements:—

(*a*) every washbasin shall have an adequate supply of warmed water; and

(*b*) all baths and showers shall have a supply of water warmed on emission to a temperature of not less than 38°C and not more than 43·5°C.

Gas and Electric Power

56. The premises shall, where reasonably practicable, be connected to gas and electricity supplies and, where they are so connected, sufficient and suitable gas and electric power points shall be provided.

Washing and Sanitary Accommodation

57.—(1) The washing and sanitary accommodation shall be soundly designed and constructed, and shall be reasonably accessible to the persons for whose use it is provided.

(2) All urinal stalls shall be constructed of glazed material and shall be fitted with a flushing apparatus.

(3) Each closet shall be provided with a door and with a partition so constructed as to secure privacy.

(4) Each water closet provided shall be capable of being flushed separately.

(5) The surfaces of the floors of washing and sanitary accommodation, including bath and shower compartments, and of the walls to a height of not less than 1·8m shall be finished with a material which resists the penetration of water and which can be easily cleaned.

Drainage and Sewage Disposal

58.—(1) Where a system of public sewers and a constant water supply under pressure are available, water closets shall be provided and the waste matter (" sewage "), together with the liquid waste (" drainage ") from urinals, baths, showers, washbasins and sinks shall be conveyed into the public sewer by means of drains.

(2) Where a supply of water under pressure is available but no public sewers are available, closets shall be provided and the sewage and drainage shall be discharged either into a cesspool or into a treatment plant comprising a settlement tank and either a filter or surface land irrigation.

(3) Where public sewers are available but no water supply under pressure is available, the drainage shall be discharged into the public sewer and earth or chemical closets shall be provided.

(4) Where neither public sewers nor a water supply under pressure are available, the drainage shall be discharged either into a cesspool or into a treatment plant comprising a settlement tank and either a filter or surface land irrigation, and earth or chemical closets shall be provided.

(5) Adequate provision shall be made for the disposal of rain water.

Regulation 2 (2)

SCHEDULE

[*Revoked previous regulations.*]

PROVISION OF MILK AND MEALS (AMENDMENT) REGULATIONS 1973

S.I. 1973 *No.* 271

April 1, 1973

NOTE

These Regulations, made under s. 49 of the Education Act 1944, as amended by s. 1 of the Education (Milk) Act 1971, add two new paragraphs to regulation 10 of the Provision of Milk and Meals Regulations 1969, S.I. 1969 No. 483. For these principal regulations as so amended see p. 383, *ante*.

HANDICAPPED PUPILS AND SPECIAL SCHOOLS (SIZE OF CLASSES) REGULATIONS 1973

S.I. 1973 *No.* 340

April 1, 1973

NOTE

These Regulations, made under s. 33 (3) of the Education Act 1944, and s. 3 (4) of the Local Government Act 1958, amended the Handicapped Pupils and Special Schools Regulations 1959, S.I. 1959 No. 365, as to sizes of classes in special schools, and the Schools Regulations 1959, S.I. 1959 No. 364, as to sizes of classes for handicapped pupils in county and voluntary schools. Those Regulations, as so amended, will be found at p. 356 and p. 349, *ante*.

POSTGRADUATE, ETC., COURSES (EXCLUSION FROM DISCRETIONARY AWARDS) REGULATIONS 1973

S.I. 1973 *No.* 1232

September 1, 1973

NOTE

These Regulations, made under s. 4 of the Education Act 1973, were issued with the following explanatory note: " These Regulations designate the courses to which section 2 (1) of the Education Act 1962 (which enables local education authorities to bestow awards on persons over compulsory school age attending courses of further education) is not to apply ".

Citation and commencement

1. These regulations may be cited as the Postgraduate, etc. Courses (Exclusion from Discretionary Awards) Regulations 1973 and shall come into operation on 1st September 1973.

Designated courses

2. There are hereby designated for the purposes of section 4 of the Education Act 1973 (exclusion of postgraduate courses from grants under section 2 (1) of the Education Act 1962 as postgraduate courses or comparable to postgraduate courses—

(*a*) any full-time course at a university or other institution in Great Britain or Northern Ireland in preparation for a doctorate, or a degree of bachelor of letters or bachelor of philosophy;
(*b*) any full-time course at a university or other institution in Great Britain or Northern Ireland in preparation for a master's degree which is not a course to which section 1 (1) of the Education Act 1962 applies;
(*c*) any course at the Royal College of Art in preparation for a master's degree or a diploma of the College;
(*d*) any art and design course at an establishment of further education within the meaning of the Further Education Regulations 1969 maintained by a local education authority in preparation for the Higher Diploma in Art or the Higher Diploma in Design; and
(*e*) any other full-time course (whether in Great Britain or elsewhere) which is for the time being designated by the Secretary of State under these regulations.

NOTE

The Further Education Regulations 1969 were revoked by the Further Education Regulations 1975, reg, 4. p. 412, *post*.

PROVISION OF MILK AND MEALS (AMENDMENT NO. 2) REGULATIONS 1973

S.I. 1973 *No.* 1299
September 1, 1973

NOTE

These Regulations, made under s. 49 of the Education Act 1944, as amended by s. 1 of the Education (Milk) Act 1971, amend regulation 10 (4) of the Provision of Milk and Meals Regulations 1969, S.I. 1969 No. 483. For those principal regulations, as so amended, see p. 383, *ante*.

DIRECT GRANT SCHOOLS (AMENDMENT) REGULATIONS 1973

S.I. 1973 *No.* 1535
December 1, 1973

NOTE

These Regulations, made under s. 100 (1) (*b*) of the Education Act 1944, increased the capitation grant payable to direct grant schools. See the amendment to regulation 4 (1) (*a*) of the Direct Grant Schools Regulations 1959, S.I. 1959 No. 1832, p. 363, *ante*.

EDUCATION ACT 1973 (COMMENCEMENT) ORDER 1973

S.I. 1973 *No.* 1661 (c. 51)
September 28, 1973

NOTE

This Order, made under s. 1 (5) of the Education Act 1973, appointed February 1, 1974, as the day on which the functions of the Secretary of State for Education and Science and the Secretary of State for Wales under the Charities' Act 1960, ceased to be exercisable by them.

LOCAL EDUCATION AUTHORITIES (RECOUPMENT) (AMENDMENT) REGULATIONS 1973

S.I. 1973 *No.* 1676

November 9, 1973

NOTE

These Regulations, made under s. 6 of the Education (Miscellaneous Provisions) Act **1948**, amend regulation 4 (6) of the Local Education Authorities (Recoupment) Regulations **1953**, S.I. **1953** No. **507**, p. 333, *ante*.

SCHOOLS (QUALIFIED TEACHERS) REGULATIONS 1973

S.I. 1973 *No.* 2021

January 1, 1974

NOTE

These Regulations, which were made under section 4 (2) of the Local Government Act 1966, and section 33 (3) of the Education Act 1944, were issued with the following explanatory note:

"These Regulations provide that from 1st January 1974 a person shall be eligible for appointment as a qualified teacher in a maintained secondary school by virtue of a special qualification only if he acquired it before that date or it is in a subject for teachers of which there is a special need. They also make minor amendments to the provisions of the regulations which regulate the employment of teachers in maintained schools."

These provisions were made by way of amendments to the Schools Regulations **1959**, S.I. **1959** No. **364**, which will be found, as so amended, *ante*.

A consequential amendment is also made to the Handicapped Pupils and Special Schools Regulations **1959**, S.I. **1959** No. **365**, *ante*.

LOCAL GOVERNMENT (VOLUNTARY SCHOOLS AND EDUCATIONAL CHARITIES) ORDER 1973

S.I. 1973 *No.* 2025

April 1, 1974

NOTE

This Order, which was made under section 254 (1), (2) (*b*) of the Local Government Act 1972, was issued with the following explanatory note:

"This Order makes provision consequential upon the Local Government Act 1972 with regard to the composition of the managing bodies of voluntary primary schools; the terms of office of managers and governors of voluntary schools and of trustees of educational charities who are appointed by local education authorities; and the construction of references to the chief education officers of certain bodies which will cease to exist as a result of the repeal by the Act of Part III of Schedule 1 to the Education Act 1944."

Citation, commencement and interpretation

1.—(1) This Order may be cited as the Local Government (Voluntary Schools and Educational Charities) Order 1973 and shall come into operation on 1st April 1974.

(2) In this Order, except where the context otherwise requires—

"educational charity" means a charity, not being a charity incorporated under the Companies Acts or by charter, registered in the register established under section 4 of the Charities Act 1960 in a part of the register which immediately before 1st February 1974 is maintained by the Secretary of State by virtue of section 2 of the Charities Act 1960 or excepted from registration by virtue of the Charities (Exception of Voluntary Schools from Registration) Regulations 1960;

"instrument" means an instrument of government or of management made under section 17 (2) of the Education Act 1944;

"representative", in references to a manager or governor, means a manager or governor who is not a foundation manager or governor;

"trust deed" includes any instrument regulating a charity, except an instrument of government or of management made under section 17 (2) of the Education Act 1944;

"Wales" means the area comprising the counties named in Part I of Schedule 4 to the Local Government Act 1972 and "England" does not include any part of that area;

other expressions have the meanings assigned to them by the Education Acts 1944 to 1973.

(3) The Interpretation Act 1889 shall apply for the interpretation of this Order as it applies for the interpretation of an Act of Parliament.

Managers of primary schools

2.—(1) The instrument for any voluntary primary school maintained by the council of an existing county which as from 1st April 1974 will not serve the area of any minor authority shall have effect as if it provided for all the representative managers of the school to be appointed by the local education authority; and any manager of such a school who was appointed by an existing minor authority shall vacate his office on 1st April 1974.

(2) The instrument for any voluntary primary school maintained by the council of an existing county borough which as from 1st April 1974 will serve the area of a minor authority shall have effect as if it provided for the appointment by that minor authority of one third of the number of representative managers or, if the number of such managers is not divisible by three, of one half of that number; and the representative managers of all such schools shall vacate their offices on 1st April 1974.

Terms of office of managers and governors

3.—(1) There shall be substituted for any provision in an instrument relating to the term of office of the representative managers or governors of a voluntary school which—

(*a*) is maintained by the council of an existing county borough; and
(*b*) as from 1st April 1974 will be maintained by the council of a non-metropolitan county—

a provision that any such manager or governor shall hold office until the appointment of his successor, which may be made at any time after the ordinary day of election of county councillors next after his appointment; and the representative managers and governors of all such schools who are in office immediately before 1st April 1974 shall, unless article 2 (2) above applies to them, hold their offices for the terms for which they were respectively appointed.

(2) There shall be substituted for any provision in an instrument relating to the term of office of the representative managers or governors of a voluntary school which—

(*a*) is maintained by the council of an existing county; and
(*b*) as from 1st April 1974 will be maintained by the council of a metropolitan district—

a provision that any such manager or governor shall hold office for a period of three years.

(3) There shall be substituted for any provision in an instrument relating to the term of office of the representative managers or governors of a voluntary school which—

(*a*) is maintained by the council of an existing county; and
(*b*) as from 1st April 1974 will be maintained by the council of a non-metropolitan county—

a provision that any such manager or governor shall hold office until the appointment of his successor, which may be made at any time after the ordinary day of election of county councillors next after his appointment.

Construction of references to officers

4. Any reference (in whatever terms) contained in an instrument, or in articles of government, for a voluntary school to the chief education officer of a divisional executive or the council of an excepted district shall, unless the context otherwise requires, be construed as a reference to the chief education officer of the local education authority by which the school is maintained.

Educational charities

5. Article 8 of the Local Government (New Councils, etc.) Order 1973 and article 3 above shall, with the necessary adaptations, apply to a provision contained in a trust deed of an educational charity which specifies the term of office of any trustee appointed by a local education authority as they apply to any provision in the instrument for a voluntary school which specifies the term of office of any manager or governor so appointed (references to the authority having the power of appointment being substituted for references to the authority maintaining the school).

REMUNERATION OF TEACHERS (BURNHAM COMMITTEES) ORDER 1974

S.I. 1974 *No.* 959

September 1, 1974

NOTE

This Order, made under s. 1 (3), (4) of the Remuneration of Teachers Act 1965, ended the representation of the Association of Education Committees and the Inner London Education Authority on the Burnham Committees.

PROVISION OF MILK AND MEALS (AMENDMENT) REGULATIONS 1974

S.I. 1974 *No.* 1125

August 1, 1974

NOTE

These Regulations revoked regulation 8 of the Provision of Milk and Meals Regulations 1969, S.I. 1969 No. 483, *ante.*

INDEPENDENT SCHOOLS TRIBUNAL (AMENDMENT NO. 3) RULES 1974

S.I. 1974 *No.* 1972

December 30, 1974

NOTE

These Rules, made under s. 75 (1) of the Education Act 1944, amend paragraph (2) of Sch. 2 to the Independent Schools Tribunal Rules 1958, S.I. 1958 No. 519, *ante.*

PROVISION OF MILK AND MEALS (AMENDMENT) REGULATIONS 1975

S.I. 1975 *No.* 311
April 7, 1975

NOTE

These Regulations, made under s. 49 of the Education Act 1944, as amended by s. 1 of the Education (Milk) Act 1971, increased the charge for school dinners in nursery schools and in county and voluntary schools from 12p to 15p, and amended the provisions for the calculation of a parent's income for the purposes of determining his entitlement to remission of the charge.

For the Provision of Milk and Meals Regulations 1969, S.I. 1969 No. 483, as accordingly amended, see p. 383, *ante*.

HANDICAPPED PUPILS (CERTIFICATE) (AMENDMENT) REGULATIONS 1975

S.I. 1975 *No.* 328
April 5, 1975

NOTE

These Regulations, made under s. 34 (5) of the Education Act 1944, substitute a new paragraph in the form of certificate issued by a medical officer of health of a local education authority showing whether a child is suffering from any disability of mind or body. See the form of certificate, as so amended, in the Handicapped Pupils (Certificate) Regulations 1961, S.I. 1961 No. 476, *ante*.

INDEPENDENT SCHOOLS TRIBUNAL (AMENDMENT) RULES 1975

S.I. 1975 *No.* 854
June 20, 1975

NOTE

These Rules, made under s. 75 (1) of the Education Act 1944, amend rule 13 of the Independent Schools Tribunal Rules 1958, S.I. 1958 No. 519, *ante*.

STATE AWARDS (AMENDMENT) REGULATIONS 1975

S.I. 1975 *No.* 940
July 4, 1975

NOTE

These Regulations, made under s. 3 of the Education Act 1962, as amended by s. 2 of the Education Act 1975, empower the Secretary of State for Education and Science to bestow awards on students attending long-term residential courses at colleges of adult education. The new provisions are made by way of amendments to the State Awards Regulations 1963, S.I. 1963 No. 1223, *ante*.

FURTHER EDUCATION REGULATIONS 1975

S.I. 1975 *No.* 1054

August 1, 1975

NOTE

These Regulations, made under powers conferred by s. 100 (1) (*b*), (*c*) of the Education Act 1944, s. 2 (4) of the Rent Act 1968 and s. 5 (2) of the Local Government Act 1974, were issued with the following explanatory note:

" These Regulations consolidate with amendments the existing regulations relating to the training of teachers and the provision of further education. The principal amendments are the provisions relating to the control of fees (regulation 6), the government of voluntary establishments (regulation 22), the payment of capital grant at the rate of 85 per cent. in certain cases (regulation 19 (2)) and payments to the Secretary of State out of the proceeds of the disposal of premises and equipment purchased with the assistance of grants (regulation 27 (2) (*d*)). Regulation 3 contains transitional provisions relating to the assimilation of facilities for the training of teachers with facilities for the provision of further education."

The " existing Regulations " referred to above (the Training of Teachers Regulations 1967, and their amendment regulations) are revoked, as are the Further Education Regulations 1969, and their amendment regulations.

PART I

GENERAL

Citation, commencement and interpretation

1.—(1) These regulations may be cited as the Further Education Regulations 1975 and shall come into operation on 1st August 1975.

(2) The Interpretation Act 1889 shall apply for the interpretation of these regulations as it applies for the interpretation of an Act of Parliament.

Definitions

2.—(1) In these regulations, unless the context otherwise requires—

" authority " means a local education authority;

" establishment " means an establishment of further education and " establishment of further education " includes a college of education and the Cambridge Institute of Education but, in its application to voluntary institutions, does not include any institution to which grants in aid of university education are paid out of moneys provided by Parliament or any college of a university except Goldsmiths' College;

" maintained " means provided by an authority;

" national association " means a voluntary national association having as one of its principal objects the promotion of liberal education for adults;

" premises " includes a hostel or other residential accommodation;

" responsible body " means a university, a university college, a committee of a university or university college, a national association or a district committee of a national association;

" Secretary of State " means the Secretary of State for Education and Science; and

" voluntary " means provided by a body other than an authority.

(2) References to expenditure incurred in connection with the provision of an institution shall, in relation to the power to pay grants in respect of such expenditure, be construed as references to expenditure incurred in the provision, replacement, extension, improvement, furnishing or equipment of the premises of the institution.

Transitional provisions

3.—(1) This regulation shall have effect for the purpose of facilitating the reorganisation of the facilities for the training of teachers for service in schools and in colleges and other educational establishments, whether maintained or voluntary, that is to say, the assimilation of those facilities with the facilities for further education provided by local education authorities in pursuance of schemes of further education approved under section 42 of the Education Act 1944 and by persons other than local education authorities in pursuance of these regulations.

(2) An authority or (in the case of a voluntary establishment) the governing body shall comply with any direction by the Secretary of State given after consultation with them and expressed to be given for the purpose of facilitating the reorganisation referred to in paragraph (1) above—

(*a*) as to the discontinuance of any course or courses for the training of teachers; or

(*b*) as to the numbers and categories of students to be admitted for the purpose of attending such courses at—

(i) any institution provided by them which immediately before 1st August 1975 was conducted as a training establishment within the meaning of the Training of Teachers Regulations 1967 as amended; or

(ii) any other institution provided by them which includes a department which immediately before 1st August 1975 was conducted as is described in sub-paragraph (i).

(3) Any grant that would apart from this paragraph be payable under these regulations to the governing body of a voluntary establishment shall, notwithstanding that the governing body have fulfilled any conditions imposed by or under these regulations as to the conduct of the institution, cease to be payable if the Secretary of State is satisfied that it is necessary for the purpose of facilitating the reorganisation referred to in paragraph (1) above that facilities for the training of teachers should cease to be provided at that institution.

NOTE

The Training of Teachers Regulations 1967, (except rule 34) and their amendment regulations are revoked; see rule 4, *infra.*

Revocations, savings and consequential amendments

4.—(1) There are hereby revoked—

(*a*) the Training of Teachers Regulations 1967 (except regulation 34) together with the training of Teachers (Amendment) Regulations 1969; and

(*b*) the Further Education Regulations 1969 together with the Further Education (Amendment) Regulations 1970.

(2) Paragraph (1) (*a*) above does not affect any power to pay grants under regulations 28, 31 and 33 of the Training of Teachers Regulations 1967 in respect of tuition or board and lodging provided in the academic year ending last before September 1975.

(3) Any approval, direction or other authorisation however described given under a provision of the regulations revoked by paragraph (1) which is reproduced with or without amendment by these regulations shall have effect as if it had been given under the relevant provision of these regulations.

(4) [*Substitutes new paragraph* (2) (*a*) *in the* Schools Regulations 1959, S.I. 1959 No. 364, *ante.*]

(5) [*Amends regulation* 2 *of the* Protected Tenancies (Exceptions) Regulations 1974.]

NOTE

The Protected Tenancies (Exceptions) Regulations 1974 contain a list of various types of educational institution; tenancies granted by such institutions to their students or prospective students do not fall within the definition of "protected tenancy"

Application of regulations

5.—(1) Part II, except regulation 18, applies to maintained establishments.

(2) Part III applies to voluntary establishments.

PART II

MAINTAINED ESTABLISHMENTS

Fees

6. An authority shall comply with any direction given by the Secretary of State after consultation with representatives of local education authorities as to the fees that may be charged by them for tuition in any course designated for the purposes of section 1 of the Education Act 1962 as amended by section 1 of the Education Act 1975, or for board and lodging at any establishment.

[**6A.**—(1) The Secretary of State may, on the application of the authority maintaining an establishment which is a single sex establishment within the meaning of the Sex Discrimination Act 1975, make an order authorising discriminatory admissions to the establishment during the transitional period specified in the order.

(2) An application for an order under this regulation shall specify—

(*a*) the transitional period during which the authority propose that discriminatory admissions should be authorised by the order;

(*b*) the stages by which the authority propose that the establishment should move to a position where section 26 (1) of the Sex Discrimination Act 1975 ceases to apply to it; and

(*c*) any other matters relevant to the terms and operation of the order applied for.]

NOTE

This Regulation was added by the Further Education (Transitional Exemption Orders) Regulations 1975, S.I. 1975 No. 1929.

Co-ordination with neighbouring authorities

7. Every authority shall in consultation where appropriate with the Regional Advisory Council for Further Education secure that so far as may be reasonable—

(*a*) the courses provided by the authority do not duplicate the courses provided in the areas of neighbouring authorities; and

(*b*) any fees charged by them which are not subject to the directions of the Secretary of State under regulation 6 do not differ substantially from the corresponding fees charged in those areas.

Courses subject to approval of the Secretary of State

8. The provision of—

(*a*) full-time courses for the further training of teachers of not less than 4 weeks' duration and of part-time courses of such training of equivalent length; and

(*b*) the courses specified in schedule 1—

shall be subject to the approval of and (where approval is granted subject to conditions) in accordance with conditions imposed by the Secretary of State; and the provision of any such course shall be discontinued if the Secretary of State so directs.

Instruction involving use of radioactive materials, etc.

9. No instruction which involves the use of—

(*a*) radioactive material, other than a compound of potassium, thorium or uranium used as a chemical agent; or

(*b*) apparatus in which electrons are accelerated by a potential difference of not less than five kilovolts, other than apparatus used only for the purpose of receiving visual images by way of television and sounds connected therewith

shall be given without the approval of the Secretary of State.

Premises

10.—(1) Premises shall be suitable for the purposes of the establishment.

(2) Without prejudice to the generality of paragraph (1), effective and suitable provision shall in particular be made with regard to—

(*a*) the lighting, heating, sanitation and ventilation of the premises;

(*b*) the provision of safeguards against danger from fire and accident;

(*c*) the maintenance of the premises in good repair and their cleanliness; and

(*d*) the equipment of the premises.

Provision of premises and equipment

11.—(1) The provision of new premises and the alteration of existing premises shall be subject to the approval of the Secretary of State.

(2) No installation or article of equipment costing £2,500 or more shall be provided for teaching or research without the approval of the Secretary of State.

Teaching staff

12. The teachers shall be sufficient in number and have the qualifications necessary for the adequate instruction of the students in the courses provided.

Employment and remuneration of teachers

13.—(1) A teacher, not being an occasional teacher or a teacher employed for not more than a year as a part-time teacher, shall be employed under a written agreement or a minute of the authority appointing him to a post specified in the agreement or minute.

(2) The agreement or minute shall define the conditions of service of the teacher and shall in particular specify whether the teacher is employed in full-time service in the capacity of a teacher, in part-time service in the capacity of a teacher or partly in the capacity of a teacher and partly in another capacity.

(3) Remuneration in accordance with scales approved by the Secretary of State shall be paid to any teachers employed in institutions to which regulation 3 (2) (*b*) above applies whose remuneration is not paid in accordance with the Remuneration of Teachers Act 1956.

Restrictions on employment of teachers on grounds of misconduct

14. A person who is on grounds of misconduct or conviction of a criminal offence determined by the Secretary of State to be unsuitable for employment as a teacher or suitable for employment as such only to a limited extent, shall not be employed as a teacher or, as the case may be, shall be employed as such only to the extent determined by the Secretary of State.

Restriction on employment of teachers on medical grounds

15. A teacher shall not be employed, or as the case may be shall be employed upon conditions approved by the Secretary of State, if, after consulting the authority and offering the teacher an opportunity of making representations to him, the Secretary of State is satisfied that it is on medical grounds desirable that the teacher should not be employed or should be employed on such conditions.

Reporting of termination of employment of teachers

16. If the engagement of a teacher is terminated whether by dismissal or resignation on account of misconduct or conviction of a criminal offence, the facts shall be reported to the Secretary of State.

Application of regulations 14 *to* 16 *to wardens, etc.*

17. Regulations 14 to 16 shall apply to wardens of community centres, leaders of youth clubs, youth workers and youth and community workers as they apply to teachers, and to youth workers and youth and community workers employed by an authority otherwise than on the staff of an establishment as they apply to such workers so employed on such staff.

Assistance to voluntary institutions

18.—(1) Where an authority assist a voluntary establishment by means of recurrent grants or other regular payments they shall require as a condition of their assisting the establishment that—

(*a*) the preceding provisions of these regulations; and
(*b*) the provisions of section 68 (reasonable exercise of functions), 77 (inspection) and 92 (reports and returns) of the Education Act 1944—

are, subject to the necessary modifications, treated as having effect as if the governing body of that establishment were an authority and the establishment a maintained establishment.

(2) This regulation shall not apply to any voluntary establishment in respect of which grants are paid under Part III.

PART III

VOLUNTARY ESTABLISHMENTS

Grants to voluntary establishments

19.—(1) The Secretary of State may pay to the governing body of any voluntary establishment—

(*a*) subject to paragraph (2), a grant not exceeding any expenditure incurred by them in connection with the provision of the establishment;

(*b*) grants not exceeding the expenditure incurred by them in maintaining the establishment;

(*c*) a loan not exceeding 15 per cent. of any expenditure in respect of which a grant is made under sub-paragraph (*a*) above to the governing body of a voluntary college of education to which paragraph (2) below applies.

(2) A grant under paragraph (1) (*a*) above shall not exceed 85 per cent. of the expenditure incurred if it appears to the Secretary of State that either—

(*a*) a majority of the governing body has been appointed to represent the interests of a particular religious denomination; or

(*b*) the property in respect of which the expenditure was incurred is held upon trusts which provide that, on the discontinuance of the establishment, it may be applied for the purposes of such a denomination.

(3) The payment of a grant to the governing body of any institution named in Schedule 2 shall be subject to such conditions as the Secretary of State may direct; and accordingly regulations 21 to 27 shall not apply to those institutions.

General conditions of grant

20. If the Secretary of State is satisfied that the governing body are not conducting the establishment efficiently or are in default in respect of any duty imposed upon them by or under these regulations, he may withhold or reduce the grant otherwise payable to them.

Application of regulations to voluntary establishments

21. Regulations 6, [6A] and 8 to 16 above, and regulations 22 to 26 below, shall apply (with, in the case of regulations 6 and 8 to 16, any necessary modifications) to voluntary establishments in respect of which grants are paid under regulation 19 (1) (*b*), and any reference to an establishment in regulations 22 to 26 below is to be read as a reference to such a voluntary establishment.

NOTE

The amendment in square brackets was inserted by the Further Education (Transitional Exemption Orders) Regulations 1975, S.I. 1975 No. 1929.

Government of voluntary establishments

22. The governing body of every establishment shall be constituted, and the establishment shall be conducted, in accordance with arrangements (whether incorporated in a charter, trust deed or other instrument) approved for the purposes of these regulations by the Secretary of State which shall in particular determine the functions to be exercised in relation to the establishment by the body providing it, the governing body, the academic board (if any) and the principal.

Conduct of voluntary establishments

23. The provisions relating to the reasonable exercise of functions and the making of reports and returns respectively contained in section 68 and 92 of the Education Act 1944 shall apply in relation to the governing bodies of voluntary establishments and the exercise of their functions as such as they apply to authorities and the exercise of their functions under the Education Acts 1944 to 1975; and the provisions relating to inspection contained in section 77 of the Education Act 1944 shall apply to voluntary establishments as they apply to maintained establishments.

Provision of courses

24. The governing body shall comply with any direction given by the Secretary of State requiring his approval to the provision of any course of instruction to which regulation 8 (as applied by regulation 21) does not apply.

Fees at voluntary establishments

25. The governing body shall comply with any direction given by the Secretary of State as to the approval by him of arrangements for the charging and remission of any fees which are not subject to his directions under regulation 6.

Provisions as to religious faith and instruction

26.—(1) The governing body of an establishment shall not reject or invite the withdrawal of the application of a student for admission on the ground of his religious faith—

(*a*) if the establishment is for the time being recognised by the Secretary of State as one to which regulation 19 (2) applies, in respect of one-half of the places;

(*b*) if it is not such an establishment, at all.

(2) The governing body of an establishment shall not require a student to undertake either to attend or not to attend any place of religious worship or any religious observance or instruction in the establishment or elsewhere, or to take an examination in religious knowledge; and no student shall be required, as a condition of entering or remaining in an establishment, to comply with any rule of the establishment as to attendance at religious worship, observance or instruction.

(3) In its application to an establishment to which paragraph (1) (*a*) above applies, paragraph (2) shall be read as referring only to a student who is not a member of the denomination in question.

Particular requirements relating to capital grant

27.—(1) The governing body of an establishment in respect of which grant is paid under regulation 19 (1) (*a*) shall comply with any requirement of the Secretary of State to which this regulation applies.

(2) This regulation applies to—

(*a*) a requirement imposing conditions for securing the continuity of the institution;

(*b*) a requirement that the books and other documents relating to the accounts of the establishment shall be open to inspection by persons appointed for the purpose by the Secretary of State;

(*c*) a requirement that they will undertake to repay to the Secretary of State so much as he may require of any grant paid under regulation 19 (1) (*a*) on the discontinuance of the establishment;

(*d*) a requirement that they will undertake to pay the Secretary of State, on the disposal of any premises, equipment or other thing in respect of the purchase of which grant was paid under regulation 19 (1) (*a*), so much as is determined by him to be just of the proceeds of that disposal, reduced by any expenses or other charges incurred in connection with it and the amount of any payment made in pursuance of sub-paragraph (*c*).

PART IV

OTHER VOLUNTARY INSTITUTIONS AND ORGANISATIONS

Grants to responsible bodies

28.—(1) Subject to the provisions of this regulation, the Secretary of State may pay a grant to a responsible body towards the cost of providing tuition in any course of liberal adult education included in a programme approved by him for the purposes of these regulations.

(2) The amount of any such grant shall be determined by reference to the general standard of the courses included in the programme (having regard to

the syllabuses, the quality of teaching, the length of courses and the arrangements for written work, reading under guidance and other forms of private study to be carried out between meetings), the needs of the area, the activities of other bodies providing further education in the area and the fees paid by students.

(3) It shall be a condition of grant under this regulation that the appointment of full-time lecturers and tutor organisers for any such programme shall be subject to the approval of the Secretary of State; and regulation 23 shall apply in respect of any course included in the programme as it applies in respect of courses provided by voluntary establishments.

Grants to national associations

29. The Secretary of State may pay to any national association grants towards expenditure incurred by them in providing educational services otherwise than in or in connection with the provision of courses to which regulation 28 (1) applies.

Grants for village halls and community centres

30. The Secretary of State may pay a grant to the trustees or other persons responsible for the management of any village hall or community centre in respect of capital expenditure incurred by them in connection with the provision of any such hall or centre.

Grants for training youth leaders

31. The Secretary of State may pay grants to the governing body of any university department of education and to any national voluntary youth organisation in respect of expenditure incurred by them in providing courses for the training of youth leaders and community centre wardens.

Grants for recreation and leisure-time activities

32. The Secretary of State may pay grants to any organisation in respect of expenditure incurred by them, whether as part of wider activities or not, in providing, or in connection with the provision of, facilities for further education within the meaning of section 41 (*b*) of the Education Act 1944.

Conditions of grant under Part IV

33.—(1) Regulation 20 shall apply to institutions and organisations in respect of which grants are paid under this Part as it applies to establishments in respect of which grants are paid under Part III.

(2) The payment of grant under regulations 29 to 33 shall be subject to such conditions as the Secretary of State may prescribe.

Regulation 8

SCHEDULE 1

COURSES SUBJECT TO APPROVAL OF SECRETARY OF STATE

This Schedule applies to any full-time course of more than one month's duration and any part-time course occupying more than forty hours, being—

(*a*) a course of post-graduate or post-diploma instruction;

(*b*) a course of study in preparation for a degree, a Diploma of Higher Education, a Higher National Diploma, a Higher National Certificate, a Diploma in Management Studies, or a final professional examination of a standard above that of the examination for the Ordinary National Certificate or General Certificate of Education (advanced level);

(*c*) a course of study of at least two years' duration if part-time other than block release or of equivalent length if full-time or block release, following an initial course of not less than one year's duration or equivalent length respectively, in preparation for an Advanced or Final Certificate or a Full Technological Certificate of the City and Guilds of London Institute or any other course for which the possession of such an Advanced or Final Certificate is a minimum qualification for entry;

(*d*) any other course in preparation for an examination of a standard above that of the examination for the Ordinary National Certificate or General Certificate of Education (advanced level) for which the normal age of entry is not less than 18 years and the normal minimum qualification for entry is, or is of a standard not below, one of the following:—

(i) an Ordinary National Certificate;
(ii) five passes in examination for Certificates of Education being passes at the ordinary level in the examination for the General Certificate of Education or at the grade 1 level in the examination for the Certificate of Secondary Education;
(iii) two passes in the examination for the General Certificate of Education, one of which is at the advanced level.

Regulation 19 (3)

SCHEDULE 2

NAMED INSTITUTIONS

Cranfield Institute of Technology.
Royal Academy of Music.
Royal College of Art.
Royal College of Music.

DIRECT GRANT GRAMMAR SCHOOLS (CESSATION OF GRANT) REGULATIONS 1975

S.I. 1975 *No.* 1198

August 21, 1975

NOTE

These Regulations, which were made under ss. 81 (*b*), 100 (1) (*b*), (*c*), of the Education Act 1944, provide for the cessation by stages of the payment of grants to the proprietors of direct grant grammar schools, thus obliging such schools either to join the State-run comprehensive system or to become independent fee-paying schools. For the principal regulations, see p. 363, *ante*.

Citation, commencement, construction and interpretation

1.—(1) These regulations may be cited as the Direct Grant Grammar Schools (Cessation of Grant) Regulations 1975 and shall come into operation on 21st August 1975.

(2) These regulations shall be construed together with the Direct Grant Schools Regulations 1959 as amended (" the principal regulations ").

(3) The Interpretation Act 1889 shall apply for the interpretation of these regulations as it applies for the interpretation of an Act of Parliament.

Cessation of Grant

2. Grant shall cease to be payable under regulation 4 (1) of the principal regulations to the proprietors of a school which ceases to be recognised as a grammar school for the purpose of that regulation by reason of—

(*a*) the school becoming maintained by a local education authority as a county or voluntary school; or

(*b*) the school ceasing to have any pupils in respect of whom grant is payable under sub-paragraphs (*a*), (*b*) and (*c*) (" the principal grant provisions ") of regulation 4 (1)—

whichever first occurs, and the principal regulations shall thereupon cease to apply to the school.

Phasing out of grant under principal grant provisions

3.—(1) Grant shall be payable under the principal grant provisions in respect of a pupil who is admitted to a school in the educational year beginning in 1976 only if the proprietors have before 1st January 1976 satisfied the Secretary of State that—

(*a*) they intend that the school should be maintained by a local education authority specified by them (" the authority ") as a county or voluntary school where the arrangements for the admission of pupils are not based (wholly or partly) on selection by reference to ability or aptitude; and

(*b*) they have notified the authority of their intention to consult the authority with regard to the submission of proposals under section 13 of the Education Act 1944 for that purpose.

(2) Grant shall be payable under the principal grant provisions in respect of a pupil who is admitted to a school in any educational year after 1976 only if on 1st January preceding that year the Secretary of State is satisfied that it continues to be the intention of the proprietors that the school should be maintained as mentioned in paragraph (1) (*a*) above and before that date—

(*a*) the proprietors have consulted the authority with regard to the submission of proposals for that purpose; and

(*b*) the authority have not notified the proprietors that they are unwilling either to submit proposals to the Secretary of State relating to the school under section 13 (1) (*b*) of the Education Act 1944 or to concur in the submission of proposals by the proprietors under section 13 (2) of that Act; and

(*c*) either—

(i) proposals that the school should be maintained by the authority have been submitted to the Secretary of State under section 13 of the Education Act 1944 and not rejected by him; or

(ii) the proprietors have satisfied the Secretary of State that, regard being had to all the circumstances, neither they nor the authority could reasonably have been expected to submit such proposals to him before that date—

and if the grant ceases to be payable by virtue of this paragraph in respect of pupils admitted to the school in any educational year it shall not be payable in respect of pupils admitted to the school in any subsequent year.

(3) References in this regulation to a school being maintained by a local education authority are to be read as including references to the premises of the school becoming the premises of a school so maintained, whether by the significant enlargement of the premises of an existing school or by the establishment of a new school in those premises; and references to the submission of proposals to the Secretary of State under section 13 of the Education Act 1944, and to the persons by whom those proposals are or are to be submitted, shall be construed accordingly.

Application of principal regulations during phasing out

4. As regards any school to whose proprietors grant has ceased to be payable under the principal grant provisions in respect of pupils admitted to the school in any educational year beginning after 1975—

(*a*) for the provisions relating to the constitution of the governing body contained in regulation 7 (1) of the principal regulations there shall be substituted a requirement that that body shall be constituted in such manner as, regard being had to the cessation of the grant payable in respect of the school, appears to the Secretary of State after consultation with the proprietors to be appropriate;

(*b*) regulation 9 (3) (provision and alteration of premises) of those regulations shall cease to apply;

(*c*) regulations 13 (3) (school dinners), 16 and 17 (admission) and 18 (fees) of those regulations shall not apply in respect of any pupils admitted to the school in respect of whom grant has ceased to be payable under the principal grant provisions in accordance with regulation 3.

Grants for schools becoming maintained

5. Where the Secretary of State has approved proposals submitted to him under section 13 of the Education Act 1944 that a school recognised as a grammar school for the purpose of regulation 4 (1) of the principal regulations should be maintained by an authority as a county or voluntary school, or that its premises should become the premises of such a school, he may pay to the proprietors of the school grants not exceeding—

(*a*) the sums required to discharge any liability incurred by them before 11th March 1975 in relation to capital expenditure in connection with the provision of premises or equipment for the purposes of the school which was met by borrowing;

(*b*) 85 per cent. of any expenditure incurred by them after 10th March 1975 on the provision or alteration of premises which was approved by him under regulation 9 (3) of the principal regulations;

(c) any expenditure out of income which he is satisfied was necessarily incurred by them by reason of the school ceasing to be recognised as a grammar school for the purpose of the said regulation 4 (1) and becoming maintained as a county or voluntary school or, as the case may be, of the premises of the school becoming the premises of a school so maintained.

Consequential amendment

6. The reference in regulation 2 (*b*) of the Regulations for Scholarships and Other Benefits 1945 to the approved fees of children attending direct grant schools shall be construed as including the whole or part of any fees of children in respect of whom, by reason of regulation 4 (*c*) above, regulation 18 of the principal regulations does not apply.

LOCAL EDUCATION AUTHORITIES AWARDS REGULATIONS 1975

S.I. 1975 *No.* 1207
September 1, 1975

NOTE

These Regulations, which were made under s. 1 of the Education Act 1962, as amended by s. 1 of the Education Act 1975, were issued with the following explanatory note:

" These Regulations consolidate with amendments the existing provisions regulating the duty of local education authorities to bestow awards on students attending first degree and comparable courses and extend them to students attending courses for the initial training of teachers, the Diploma of Higher Education and the Higher National Diploma. The principal amendments involve the removal of all provisions which discriminate between students on grounds of sex, increases in the sums treated by schedule 1 as the student's requirements and the modification of the provisions of schedule 2 relating to the parental and spouse's contribution."

The former Awards (First Degree, etc. Courses) Regulations 1971, and their amendment regulations are revoked.

* * * * *

PART I

GENERAL

Citation, commencement and interpretation

1.—(1) These regulations may be cited as the Local Education Authorities Awards Regulations 1975 and shall come into operation on 1st September 1975.

(2) The Interpretation Act 1889 shall apply for the interpretation of these regulations as it applies for the interpretation of an Act of Parliament.

(3) Without prejudice to paragraph (2) above, section 37 (exercise of powers before commencement) of the Interpretation Act 1889 shall apply in relation to these regulations as it applies in relation to an Act; and section 38 (2) (effect of repeals) of that Act shall have effect in relation to the regulations revoked by these regulations as if they were enactments repealed by an Act.

Definitions

2.—(1) In these regulations, unless the context otherwise requires—

" academic authority " means governing body, or other body having the function in question, of an establishment;

" authority " means local education authority;

" award " includes an award bestowed under previous awards regulations;

" Certificate in Education " includes Teacher's Certificate;

" course ", in relation to any designated course except one designated under regulation 6 (1) (*d*) (ii) or (iii), includes a course of full-time study and a sandwich course within the meaning of paragraph 1 of schedule 5;

" designated course " has the meaning assigned to it by paragraph (2) below;

" establishment " means a university or establishment of further education and " establishment of further education " includes a college of education;

" high-cost country " means Austria, Belgium, Denmark, Federal Republic of Germany, France, Luxembourg, Netherlands, Norway, Sweden, Switzerland or the United States of America;

" ordinarily resident " is to be construed in accordance with schedule 1 to the Education Act 1962;

" prescribed fraction " has the meaning assigned to it by paragraph 1 of schedule 5;

" previous awards regulations " means the Awards (First Degree, etc. Courses) Regulations 1971 as amended (" the 1971 regulations ") and any regulations superseded by those regulations;

" sandwich year " has the meaning assigned to it by paragraph 1 of schedule 5;

" statutory award " means any award bestowed or grant paid under the Education Act 1962 as amended by the Education Act 1975 or any comparable grant which is paid out of moneys provided by Parliament;

" student " means a person upon whom an award has been bestowed under these regulations or previous awards regulations;

" university " means a university in the United Kingdom and includes a university college and a constituent college, school or hall of a university;

" year ", as regards any course, means the period of twelve months beginning on 1st January, 1st April or 1st September according as the academic year of the course in question begins in the spring, the summer or the autumn respectively; and references to the first year of a designated course shall be construed accordingly.

(2) "Designated course " means a course prescribed by or under regulation 6 and any reference otherwise unqualified to such a course shall as the context requires be construed as a reference to a designated course which the person in question attends or has applied to attend.

(3) References to payments made to a student include references to payments made to the academic authority in respect of a student by virtue of regulation 21 (2).

(4) In calculating a person's income for any year any reduction for income tax is to be made by calculating the tax payable on the income received in that year as if the year were a year of assessment within the meaning of the Income Tax Acts (the necessary apportionment being made in any case where the relevant provisions of those Acts change during the year).

(5) For the purposes of these regulations a person's marriage is to be treated as having been terminated, not only by the death of the other spouse or the annulment or dissolution of the marriage by an order of a court of competent jurisdiction, but also by virtue of the parties to the marriage ceasing to live together, whether or not an order for their separation has been made by any court.

Revocations

3. The regulations specified in schedule 6 are hereby revoked.

PART II

AWARDS

Duty to bestow awards

4. Subject to and in accordance with these regulations, it shall be the duty of every authority to bestow an award on any person who is ordinarily resident in their area in respect of his attendance at—

(*a*) any designated course beginning after 31st August 1975; and

(*b*) any designated course beginning before 1st September 1975 which was not designated under previous awards regulations.

Modification of provisions for determining ordinary residence

5.—(1) This regulation shall have effect for modifying paragraph 2 of schedule 1 to the Education Act 1962 in the case of a person who, apart from this regulation, would be treated by virtue of that paragraph as having been ordinarily resident in the area of more than one authority within the period of twelve months ending with the date on which the course is due to begin.

(2) Any such person as is described in paragraph (1) above shall be treated as being ordinarily resident in the area of the authority in which he was so resident on the last day of the month of October, February or June preceding the beginning of the course according as the course begins in the spring, the summer or the autumn respectively.

Designated courses

6.—(1) The following are prescribed as designated courses—

(*a*) as a first degree course (" a first degree course ")—

(i) a course by an establishment for a first degree of a university or for the degree of Bachelor of Medicine or an equivalent degree;

(ii) a course provided by an establishment of further education for a first degree of the Council for National Academic Awards;

(*b*) as a course for the Diploma of Higher Education (" a Dip HE course ")

(i) a course provided by an establishment for the Diploma of Higher Education;

(ii) a course provided by an establishment for the Diploma of Higher education or a first degree as the student may elect after the commencement of the course;

(*c*) as a course for the Higher National Diploma (" an HND course "), a course provided by an establishment of further education for the Higher National Diploma;

(*d*) as a course of initial training for teachers ("a teacher training course")—

(i) a course for the initial training of teachers (other than a course for the degree of Bachelor of Education) provided by an establishment;

(ii) a part-time day course of teacher training, involving not less than 3 days' attendance a week during the course, for the time being prescribed for the purposes of this provision by the Secretary of State;

(iii) any other course of teacher training, whether part-time or partly full-time and partly part-time, for the time being so prescribed;

(*e*) as a course comparable to a first degree course—

(i) a course of at least 3 years' duration provided by a university for a certificate or diploma;

(ii) a course for the time being prescribed for the purposes of this provision by the Secretary of State.

(2) In this regulation references to an establishment and an establishment of further education do not include references to establishments of further education which are neither maintained, nor assisted by recurrent grants, out of public funds.

NOTE

As to courses of initial training for teachers under paragraph (1) (*d*) (iii), see further the Local Education Authorities Awards (Amendment) Regulations 1975, S.I. 1975 No. 1697, *post*, which makes a saving for grants which would otherwise be reduced.

Conditions

7.—(1) Subject to paragraph (3), the duty of an authority to bestow an award shall be subject to the conditions that—

(a) an application in writing for the award reaches the authority before the date on which the course is due to begin; and

(*b*) the applicant gives the authority a written undertaking that, where any sum is paid, whether as a provisional payment or not, in pursuance of the award before the end of the year in respect of which the sum is payable, he will if called upon to repay the amount by which the sums paid during the year exceed (for whatever reason) the grant payable in respect of that year.

(2) If the applicant is a minor, paragraph (1) (*b*) shall have effect, with the necessary modifications, as if the references to the applicant were references to the applicant or his parent.

(3) Paragraph (1) (*a*) above shall not apply in respect of any course beginning before 1st September 1975 which is designated by or under paragraph (1) (*b*) (*c*) or (*d*) of regulation 6 above.

Exceptions relating to attendance at previous courses

8.—(1) An authority shall not bestow an award on a person in respect of his attendance at a course if it is their duty to transfer an award already bestowed on him so that it is held in respect of his attendance at that course.

(2) Subject to paragraph (5) below, an authority shall not be under a duty to bestow an award on a person in respect of his attendance at a course if—

(*a*) (in the case of a person who has not attained the age of 25 before the first year) he has previously attended a full-time course of further education of not less than two years' duration or successfully completed a part-time course of such education of equivalent duration or attended or, as the case may be, successfully completed a comparable course outside the United Kingdom; or

(*b*) (in the case of a person who has attained the age of 25 before the first year) he has previously attended a full-time course of not less than two years' duration to which schedule 1 of the Further Education Regulations 1975 applies or successfully completed a part-time course course of equivalent duration to which that schedule applies or attended or, as the case may be successfully completed a comparable course outside the United Kingdom—

unless (in either case) the course which he previously attended or, as the case may be, completed either—

(i) was a course for the Diploma of Higher Education, the Higher National Diploma or a qualification prescribed by Schedule 4; or

(ii) was provided by a college designated by the Schedule to the State Awards Regulations 1963 as amended (colleges providing long term residential courses of full-time education for adults).

(3) Subject to paragraph (5) below, an authority shall not be under a duty to bestow an award on a person in respect of his attendance at a course designated by or under regulation 6 (1) (*a*), (*d*) or (*e*) if he has previously—

(*a*) attended a course designated by or under regulation 6 (1) (*a*), (*d*) (i) or (*e*) or successfully completed a course designated under regulation 6 (1) (*d*) (ii) or (iii); or

(*b*) attended a course designated by regulation 6 (1) (*b*) (ii) in a case where after the commencement of the course he elected to attend a course of a first degree.

(4) An authority shall not be under a duty to bestow an award on any person in respect of his attendance at any course designated by regulation 6 (1) (*b*) or (*c*) if he has previously—

(*a*) attended a full-time course of initial training as a teacher or successfully completed a part-time course of such training; or

(*b*) attended any other designated course;

or has before the commencement of these regulations attended a course for the Diploma of Higher Education or the Higher National Diploma: provided that nothing in this paragraph shall affect the duty of an authority to bestow an award on a person in respect of his attendance at a course for the Diploma of Higher Education or the Higher National Diploma beginning before 1st September 1975 which he was attending immediately before that date.

(5) Nothing in paragraphs (2) and (3) above shall affect the duty of an authority to bestow an award on a person—

(*a*) in respect of his attendance at a course for the post-graduate Certificate in Education (or a comparable qualification) or for the Art Teacher's Certificate or Diploma (or a comparable qualification);

(*b*) in respect of his attendance at any one year full-time course of initial training as a teacher, or a comparable part-time course, not within sub-paragraph (*a*) above unless he has for more than three years held a statutory award in respect of his attendance at a full-time course to which schedule 1 to the Further Education Regulations 1975 applies or a comparable course outside England and Wales;

(*c*) in respect of his attendance at a course for the degree of Bachelor of Education to which he is admitted on or before the completion of a course for the Certificate of Education;

(*d*) in respect of his attendance at a course of initial training for teachers of the deaf to which he is admitted on the completion of a course for the Certificate in Education or the degree of Bachelor of Education.

(6) For the purposes of this regulation a person shall be treated as having attended a course if he has attended any part of that course.

Other exceptions

9. An authority shall not be under a duty to bestow an award—

(*a*) upon a person who has not been ordinarily resident in the United Kingdom for the three years immediately preceding the first year, unless the authority are satisfied that he has not been so resident only because he, his wife (or, in the case of a woman student, her husband) or his parent was for the time being employed outside the United Kingdom;

(*b*) upon a person who has, in the opinion of the authority, shown himself by his conduct to be unfitted to receive an award;

(*c*) in respect of his attendance at a course designated by or under regulation 6 (1) (*e*), upon a person who does not possess a qualification prescribed by schedule 4.

Transfer of awards

10.—(1) Subject to paragraph (2) below, an award shall be transferred by the authority so as to be held in respect of attendance at a course other than that in respect of which it was bestowed in any case where—

(*a*) on the recommendation of the academic authority made before the expiry of two months after the end of the first year, the student commences to attend another course at the establishment;

(*b*) with the consent of the academic authority of both establishments concerned, given on educational grounds before the expiry of two months after the end of the first year, the student commences to attend a course at another establishment;

(*c*) on the completion of the Dip HE course the student is admitted to a course designated by or under regulation 6 (1) (*a*), (*d*) or (*e*);

(*d*) after commencing a course for the Certificate of Education, the student is, on or before the completion of that course, admitted to a course for the degree of Bachelor of Education;

(*e*) on the completion of a course for the Certificate of Education or the degree of Bachelor of Education, the student is admitted to a course of initial training for teachers of the deaf.

(2) The authority may, after consultation with the academic authority, refuse to transfer the award under paragraph (1) (*a*) or (*b*) above if they are satisfied that when the student applied for it he did not intend to complete the course to which the application related.

(3) It shall be the duty of the authority to transfer the award under sub-paragraphs (*c*), (*d*) or (*e*) of paragraph 1 whether or not the second course is provided by the same establishment as the first.

Termination of awards

11.—(1) The award shall terminate on the expiry of the period ordinarily required for the completion of the course:

provided that—

(*a*) if the academic authority refuse to allow the student to complete the course, the authority shall terminate the award forthwith;

(b) if the student does not complete the course within the period ordinarily required, the authority—
  (i) may extend the award until the student has completed the course; and
  (ii) shall extend it for a period equivalent to any period in respect of which they have made any payment under regulation 22 (1) below.

(2) The authority may, after consultation with the academic authority, terminate the award if they are satisfied that the student has shown himself by his conduct to be unfitted to hold it.

Supplementary provisions

12. The authority may require the student to provide from time to time such information as they consider necessary for the exercise of their functions under this Part; and if in the case of any student the authority are satisfied that he has wilfully failed to comply with any such requirement, they may terminate the award or withhold any payments due under it as they see fit.

PART III

PAYMENTS

Ordinary cases

Payments

13. Except in a case to which any of regulations 16 to 20 below inclusive applies the authority shall, subject to regulations 22 and 23 (2) below and to schedule 3, in respect of each year pay in pursuance of the award either the sum of £50 (in these regulations called " minimum payment ") or a grant calculated in accordance with regulation 14, whichever is the greater.

Calculation of grant

14. The grant payable to the student in any year shall be the amount by which his resources fall short of his requirements, and for the purpose of ascertaining that amount—

(a) the requirements of any student shall be taken to be the aggregate of such of the amounts specified in schedule 1 as are applicable to his case;

(b) the resources of any student shall be taken to be the aggregate of his income for the year calculated in accordance with Part 1 of schedule 2 and any contribution applicable to his case by virtue of Part 2 or 3 of that schedule.

Assessment of requirement and resources

15. The requirements and resources of the student shall be assessed by the authority, and for the purpose of the exercise of their functions under this regulation the authority shall require the student to provide from time to time such information as they consider necessary as to the resources of any person whose means are relevant to the assessment of his requirement and resources.

Special cases

Sandwich courses

16. In the case of a sandwich course—

(a) the authority shall—
  (i) in respect of a sandwich year, pay a grant calculated in accordance with regulation 14 above as modified by virtue of schedule 5; and
  (ii) in respect of a year in which there are no periods of experience within the meaning of paragraph 1 of schedule 5, make a payment in accordance with regulation 13 above; and

(b) in respect of a year in which there are no periods of full-time study no payment shall be made.

Members of religious orders

17.—(1) Subject to paragraph (2) and regulation 18 below, there shall in each year be paid in pursuance of an award to a student who is a member of a religious order the aggregate of the appropriate sum specified under paragraph (3) below and the sums specified by paragraphs 1 and 9 of schedule 1.

(2) As respects any sandwich year in which the period of full-time study does not exceed 30 weeks, paragraph (1) above shall have effect with the substitution for the reference to the appropriate sum specified under paragraph (3) below of a reference to the prescribed fraction of that sum.

(3) The sum referred to in paragraphs (1) and (2) above is—

if the student resides at his parent's home or in a house of the order of which he is a member	£315
if the student resides elsewhere—	
in the case of a student attending a course at the university of London or any other establishment within the area comprising the City of London and the Metropolitan Police District, or at an institution outside the United Kingdom which is not a high cost country	£445
in the case of a student attending an institution in a high cost country	£510
in the case of a student attending a course elsewhere ..	£405

Part-time courses of teacher training

18.—(1) There shall be paid in each year to a student attending a course designated under regulation 6 (1) (*d*) (ii) whichever is the greater of the minimum payment and a grant equal to the amount by which the aggregate of his requirements under paragraph 1 of schedule 1 and three-quarters of his requirements under the other provisions of that schedule exceed three-quarters of his resources under schedule 2.

(2) There shall be paid in each year to a student attending part-time a course designated under regulation 6 (1) (*d*) (iii) the aggregate of any relevant sum specified by paragraph 1 (fees) of schedule 1 and—

(*a*) (if he is employed full-time as a teacher) the amount of such travelling expenses as are mentioned in paragraph 7 of that Schedule; or

(*b*) (if he is not so employed) any relevant sum specified by that paragraph and £180.

Assisted students

19. Notwithstanding anything in the preceding provisions of these regulations, no payment shall be made in any year to a student to whom there is in respect of that year paid an amount which is not less than the aggregate of the requirements for fees and ordinary maintenance prescribed as applicable to his case either—

(*a*) by way of remuneration (except remuneration paid to a person whose case falls within regulation 18 (2) above) paid in respect of any period when he has leave of absence from his employment to attend the course; or

(*b*) in pursuance of any scholarship, bursary or similar allowance in respect of his attendance at the course; or

(*c*) partly by way of such remuneration and partly in pursuance of such a scholarship, bursary or allowance.

Students provided with free board and lodging

20. In its application in any year to a student whose case falls within paragraph 2 (4) of schedule 1, regulation 13 above shall have effect as if there were omitted the words " either the sum of £50 (in these regulations called " minimum payment ") or " and " whichever is the greater ".

General

Method of payment

21.—(1) The authority shall make any payment due under these regulations in such instalments (if any) and at such times as they consider appropriate; and in the exercise of their functions under this paragraph the authority may in particular make provisional payments pending the final calculation of the grant.

(2) Any payment in respect of such fees as are described in Part 1 of schedule 1 may be made to the academic authority but subject thereto all payments shall be made to the student.

Discretionary payments

22.—(1) In respect of any period during which the student repeats any part of the course, the authority shall pay in pursuance of the award such sums (if any) as they consider appropriate, being sums not exceeding the amount of any payment that would, apart from this regulation, be payable to that student in respect of that period.

(2) In any case where an award is bestowed on, or transferred in pursuance of regulation 10 (1) (*c*) to, a student who has previously attended a course for the Diploma of Higher Education or the Higher National Diploma ("the first course") in respect of his attendance at a course designated by or under regulation 6 (1) (*a*), (*d*) or (*e*) above ("the designated course"), then, if the academic authority do not treat his attendance at the first course as excusing him from attending the whole of the first two years of the designated course, paragraph (1) above shall apply in respect of so much of those first two years as he is not excused from attending.

Suspension, etc. of payments

23.—(1) The authority may withhold any payment to any student who is for the time being in default of any requirement to provide such information as is described in regulation 15.

provided that, in the case of a student in respect of whom apart from this paragraph a grant (other than a grant in respect of a sandwich year or a grant to a student to whom regulation 20 above applies) would be payable, the authority shall in respect of any year in which he remains in default pay a grant of a sum not less than the minimum payment.

(2) Any payment otherwise due under these regulations shall be reduced by an amount equal to the sum specified by paragraph (3) below in respect of—

(*a*) any period after the termination of the award; and

(*b*) any period during which the student is excluded from attendance at the course by the academic authority or is absent without leave;

and in respect of any other period during which the student does not attend the course (other than a period of not more than 28 days due to his illness) they may reduce the payment by such amount not exceeding that sum as, having regard to all relevant circumstances, they consider appropriate.

(3) The sum referred to in paragraph (2) above is in the case of a student in respect of whom apart from this paragraph a minimum payment would be payable, the appropriate proportion of the minimum payment, and in the case of any other student the aggregate of—

(*a*) fees otherwise due that are not payable by reason of the student not attending the course; and

(*b*) the appropriate proportion of the balance of the grant.

SCHEDULE 1

Regulation 14 (a)

REQUIREMENTS

PART 1

FEES

1. The amount of the following fees—

(*a*) except in the case of a college to which sub-paragraph (*b*) applies, sessional or tuition fees, which in the case of a composition fee shall not include the element of the fee attributable to maintenance;

(*b*) so much as does not exceed £325 of the sessional or tuition fees of a college of a university (other than a college of the university of Oxford or Cambridge) which is a college in respect of which no grant is paid out of moneys provided by Parliament to the university to which it belongs;

(*c*) special fees, including lecture fees, laboratory fees and any fees in respect of such courses as are mentioned in Part 3 of this schedule;
(*d*) fees for admission or registration;
(*e*) fees for matriculation or matriculation exemption and graduation;
(*f*) fees for examination taken as part of a course;
(*g*) at any university which is organised on a collegiate basis, university and college dues;
(*h*) where a sum representing the subscription to a students' union, junior common room or similar body is not included in the fee charged under sub-paragraph (*a*), (*b*) or (*d*) above—
 (i) the fee charged for such membership at the university of Durham, the university of Newcastle, any college of the universities of Oxford and Cambridge or any establishment designated by the Secretary of State as a Polytechnic;
 (ii) at any other establishment, the subscription to any one such body membership of which is obligatory by virtue of any requirement contained in, or having effect under, the instruments regulating the conduct of the establishment.

PART 2

ORDINARY MAINTENANCE

2.—(1) This Part shall apply for the ascertainment of the student's requirements for his ordinary maintenance.

(2) Subject to sub-paragraph (4), the lower rate prescribed by paragraph 3 (3) below shall be applicable to the case of—

(*a*) any student who resides at his parents' home, unless his case falls within sub-paragraph (3) (*c*) below; and
(*b*) any student whose case falls within the exception to sub-paragraph (3) (*b*) below.

(3) Subject to sub-paragraph (4), the appropriate higher rate prescribed by paragraph 3 below shall be applicable in the case of—

(*a*) any student who, on the recommendation of the academic authority, resides in the establishment or in a hostel administered by the academic authority;
(*b*) any other student who does not reside at his parent's home, unless he can in the opinion of the authority conveniently attend the course from his parent's home and the authority, after consultation with the academic authority, consider that in all the circumstances the lower rate would be appropriate; and
(*c*) any student residing at his parent's home whose parents by reason of age, incapacity or otherwise cannot reasonably be expected to support him and in respect of whom the authority are satisfied that in all the circumstances the higher rate would be appropriate.

(4) The special rate prescribed by paragraph 3 (6) below shall be applicable in the case of any student who is provided with board and lodging by the academic authority in accordance with arrangements under which fees for board and lodging are charged only to those students whose resources exceed their requirements.

(5) In this part of this Schedule references to the parent's home include, in the case of a student whose spouse attends a full-time course in any establishment, the home of the parent of the student's spouse.

3.—(1) Higher rate for the university of London and any other establishment within the City of London and the Metropolitan Police District ..	£810
(2) Higher rate for any other establishment in the United Kingdom ..	£740
(3) Lower rate	£570
(4) Higher rate for an institution in a high cost country in respect of attendance required as part of a course	£930
(5) Higher rate for any other institution outside the United Kingdom in respect of attendance required as part of a course	£810
(6) Special rate	£315

PART 3

SUPPLEMENTARY MAINTENANCE, ETC.

4.—(1) Subject to sub-paragraph (3) below, for each additional week or incomplete part of an additional week in attendance at the course—

if the student resides at his parent's home .. .. £8·40

if the student does not reside at his parent's home—

in the case of a student attending a course at the university of London or any other establishment within the area comprising the City of London and the Metropolitan Police District, or at an

institution outside the United Kingdom which is not in a high cost country .. .. £16·10
in the case of a student attending a course at an institution in a high cost country .. .. £18·90
in the case of a student attending a course elsewhere £14

(2) For the purposes of this paragraph attendance at the course in any year is additional if it is in excess of 25 weeks 3 days at the university of Oxford or Cambridge or in excess of 30 weeks 3 days at any other establishment or an institution outside the United Kingdom.

(3) This paragraph does not apply to a student whose case falls within paragraph 2 (4) above.

5. In the case of a student who attends the course for not less than 45 weeks, for each week or incomplete part of a week during the vacation in respect of which paragraph 4 (1) above does not apply . . . the sum prescribed as appropriate to his case by paragraph 4 (1) above.

6.—(1) Subject to sub-paragraph (2) and paragraph 8, in the case of a student attending a course at an establishment of further education which is not wholly maintained out of public funds—

(*a*) for each day in respect of vacation study on the recommendation, and under the guidance, of the academic authority—
if the student resides at his parent's home .. .. .. £1·20
if the student does not reside at his parent's home—
in the case of study at the university of London or otherwise within the area comprising the City of London and the Metropolitan Police District, or at an institution outside the United Kingdom which is not a high cost country .. .. .. £2·30
in the case of study at an institution in a high cost country .. £2·70
in any other case £2

(*b*) in respect of vacation study, undertaken on the recommendation of the academic authority by a student studying modern languages, in a country whose language is a main language of the course, for each day on which he resides with a family approved for the purposes of this paragraph by the academic authority—
if the country is a high cost country .. .. £2·70
in any other case .. .. £2·30

(*c*) for each day in respect of any additional expenditure on his maintenance incurred for the purpose of attending, as part of the course, a period of residential study during term away from the establishment . . . so much of the expenditure as does not exceed £2·30.

(2) Sub-paragraph (1) (*a*) and (*b*) above does not apply to any case to which paragraph 5 above applies.

7.—(1) Subject to paragraph 8, in respect of any expenditure which he is obliged to incur—

(*a*) within the United Kingdom for the purpose of attending the establishment;
(*b*) within or without the United Kingdom, for the purpose of attending any period of study to which paragraph 3 (4) or (5) or 6 applies;
(*c*) (in the case of a student attending a course at an establishment of further education which is not wholly maintained out of public funds) on any other travel within the United Kingdom in connection with the course during term—
the amount by which the expenditure exceeds £22.

(2) In the case of a student whose home is for the time being outside the United Kingdom, in respect of expenditure necessarily incurred at the beginning and end of term on travel between his home and the establishment . . . such sum (if any) as the authority consider appropriate.

8. Paragraphs 6 (1) (*a*) and (*c*) and 7 (1) (*b*) above shall apply in relation to a period of study or, as the case may be, travel outside the United Kingdom only where the academic authority certify that if the student did not attend or, as the case may be, did not travel he would not be eligible to complete the course; and where no such certificate is given the student's requirements shall be treated as such a sum (if any) not exceeding the amount specified in the relevant paragraph as the authority consider appropriate.

9.—(1) In respect of expenditure necessarily incurred on the purchase of special equipment for the course by a student attending a course to which this paragraph applies . . . so much of the expenditure as does not during the course exceed £30.

(2) This paragraph applies to courses in architecture, art and design, domestic science, landscape architecture, medicine, music, ophthalmic optics, physical education, town and country planning and veterinary science or medicine and to courses in which any of these is a principal subject.

10. In the case of any student who in the opinion of the authority would otherwise suffer undue hardship, in respect of any week during the vacation in respect of which

no sum is prescribed by the preceding provisions of this Part . . . such sum (if any) not exceeding £10 as, regard being had to the means of the student, the authority consider appropriate.

11. In the case of any disabled student in respect of whom the authority are satisfied that he is obliged by reason of his disability to incur additional expenditure in respect of his attendance at the course . . . such sum not exceeding £120 as the authority consider appropriate.

PART 4

MAINTENANCE OF DEPENDANTS

12.—(1) In this Part—

references to provisions of the 1971 Regulations include references to provisions to the like effect contained in arrangements made under section 2 (3) of the Education Act 1962 and " award " shall be construed accordingly;

" child " includes a person adopted in pursuance of adoption proceedings and a stepchild;

" dependant " means spouse or qualified dependant;

" income " means income for the year from all sources less income tax, national insurance contributions and family allowances and, in the case of the spouse the amount of any payment made by the student in pursuance of an obligation reasonably incurred before the first year;

" qualified dependant " means a person dependent on the student whose income does not exceed the relevant sum prescribed by sub-paragraph (5) below by £160 or more;

a person shall not be treated as dependent on the student during any period when he holds a statutory award in respect of his attendance at a full-time course to which Schedule 1 to the Further Education Regulations 1975 applies, or a comparable course outside England and Wales, or a course designated under Regulation 6 (1) (*d*) (ii).

(2) The requirements of a student to whom this paragraph applies for the maintenance of persons in the United Kingdom who are dependent on him shall be—

(*a*) if the student's spouse holds a statutory award and in calculating payments under it account is taken of the spouse's dependants, one half of any sum more than nil which is ascertained in accordance with the formula in sub-paragraph (4) below;

(*b*) in any other case, subject to paragraph 13, the whole of any such sum.

(3) This paragraph applies to a student who married before the first year and—

(*a*) supported himself out of his earnings for any three years preceding the first year (any period not exceeding six months during which he was registered under section 11 of the Supplementary Benefit Act 1966 or in receipt of benefit under section 14 (1) (*a*) of the Social Security Act 1975, or any period during which he held a State Studentship or comparable award, being treated as a period during which he so supported himself); or

(*b*) attained the age of 25 before the year for which his requirements fall to be ascertained; or

(*c*) held an award bestowed in respect of attendance at a course beginning before 1st September 1975 and is a person to whom paragraph 10 of Schedule 1 to the 1971 regulations applied by virtue of sub-paragraph 2 (*c*) of that paragraph:

provided that in its application to sub-paragraph (5) (*a*) (ii) and paragraph 14 below this sub-paragraph is to be read without the words " married before the first year and ".

(4) The formula referred to in sub-paragraph (2) above is—

$$X-(Y-Z)$$

where X is the aggregate of the relevant sums prescribed by sub-paragraph (5) below; Y is the aggregate of the income of the student's dependants; and Z is so much of the sum ascertained by multiplying the number of those dependants by £160 as does not exceed Y.

(5) The relevant sums referred to in sub-paragraph (3) above are—

(*a*) (i) spouse; or
(ii) one other adult dependant; or
(iii) the first child £380

(*b*) except where sub-paragraph (*a*) (iii) above applies, first child .. £165

(*c*) any other child £85

13. Except in the case which falls within paragraph 12 (2) (*a*) above, the requirements under this Part of a student upon whom an award was bestowed in respect of his attendance at a course beginning before September 1975 shall while he holds that award be whichever is the greater of the sum ascertained in accordance with Part 4 of

schedule 1 to the 1971 regulations and the sum ascertained in accordance with paragraph 12 above.

14. The requirements of a student to whom paragraph 12 applies for the maintenance in the United Kingdom, at a place other than that at which he resides during the course, of a home for himself and any such dependant as is mentioned in that paragraph shall be £135.

15. The requirements of a student to whom paragraph 12 applies, for the maintenance of any dependant outside the United Kingdom shall be such sum not exceeding the amount that would be treated as constituting his requirements if his case fell within paragraph 12 as the authority, having regard to all the circumstances, consider reasonable.

PART 5

OLDER STUDENTS

16.—(1) The requirements of any student to whom this paragraph applies shall include the sum of £57 for every complete year not exceeding five by which his age at the beginning of the first year exceeds 25.

(2) This paragraph applies to any student who attained the age of 26 before the first year and either—

(*a*) was in full-time employment for a total of three of the six years immediately preceding that year and whose gross earnings in any one year of those six amounted to a sum which exceeded by not less than one-quarter the aggregate of £740 and any relevant sum specified in respect of his dependants by paragraph 12 (5); or

(*b*) held an award (or was in receipt of a grant under arrangements made under section 2 (3) of the Education Act 1962) in respect of his attendance at a previous course and is a person to whom sub-paragraph (2) (*a*) above or paragraph 14 (1) of schedule 1 to the 1971 regulations (or provision to the like effect in such arrangements) applied in respect of that course.

NOTE.—Any reference in this Schedule to a requirement, expenditure or attendance in respect of which no period of time is specified is to be construed as a reference to such a requirement expenditure or attendance for the year.

SCHEDULE 2

Regulation 14 (*b*)

RESOURCES

PART 1

STUDENT'S INCOME

Calculation of student's income

1. In calculating the student's income there shall be taken into account his income (reduced by income tax and national insurance contributions) from all sources, but there shall be disregarded the following resources—

(*a*) the first £160 of income;

(*b*) in the case of a student who—

(i) has no parent living; and

(ii) is not such a person as is described in sub-paragraph (*a*), (*b*) or (*c*) of paragraph 3 below—

£320 of any such income as is described in paragraph 5 (2) below: provided that the amount disregarded under this sub-paragraph shall not, together with the amount disregarded under sub-paragraph (*a*) above, exceed £320;

(*c*) any disability pension not subject to income tax;

(*d*) any bounty received as a Reservist with the Armed Forces;

(*e*) remuneration for work done in vacations;

(*f*) in the case of a student in respect of whom a parental contribution is by virtue of Part 2 of this schedule treated as forming part of his resources, any payment made under covenant by his parent;

(*g*) any payment made for a specific educational purpose not treated by schedule 1 as a requirement for the purposes of these regulations;

(*h*) family allowances;

(*i*) any benefit under the Supplementary Benefit Act 1966;

(*j*) any attendance allowance under section 35 of the Social Security Act 1975;

(*k*) any allowance granted to him in pursuance of a scheme under section 19 of the Housing Finance Act 1972;

and in the case of any such student as is described in sub-paragraph (*a*), (*b*) or (*c*) of paragraph 3 below there shall be deducted a sum equivalent to any payment made by him in pursuance of an obligation reasonably incurred by him before the first year unless a deduction in respect of the payment has been made under paragraph 12 of schedule 1

PART 2

PARENTAL CONTRIBUTION

Definitions

2.—(1) In this Part—

" child " includes a person adopted in pursuance of adoption proceedings but, except in paragraph 4 (2) below, does not include a child who holds a statutory award nor, except in paragraph 6 (1) and (11) below, a stepchild; and " parent " shall be construed accordingly;

" gross income " has the meaning assigned to it by paragraph 5 below;

" income of the student's parent " means the total income of the parent from all sources computed as for income tax purposes, except that no deduction shall be made which is of a kind for which provision is made by paragraph 6 below;

" residual income " means, subject to sub-paragraph (2) below, the balance of gross income remaining in any year after the deductions specified in paragraph 6 below have been made.

(2) Where, in a case not falling within the proviso to paragraph 5 (1) below, the authority are satisfied that the income of the parent in any financial year is as a result of some event beyond his control likely to be and to continue after that year to be not more than four-fifths of his income in the financial year preceding that year, they may, for the purpose of enabling the student to attend the course without hardship, ascertain the parental contribution for the academic year in which that event occurred by taking as the residual income the average of the residual income for each of the financial years in which that academic year falls.

Application of Part 2

3. A parental contribution ascertained in accordance with this Part shall be applicable in the case of every student except any of the following—

(*a*) a student who for any three years preceding the first year supported himself out of his earnings (any period not exceeding six months during which he was registered under section 11 of the Supplementary Benefit Act 1966 or in receipt of benefit under section 14 (1) (*a*) of the Social Security Act 1975, or any period during which he held a State Studentship or comparable award, being treated as a period during which he so supported himself);

(*b*) a student who attained the age of 25 before the year for which the grant falls to be ascertained;

(*c*) a student who held an award bestowed, or was in receipt of a grant under arrangements made under section 2 (3) of the Education Act 1962, in respect of his attendance at a course beginning before 1st September 1975, and in whose case no contribution was applicable by virtue of previous awards, regulations or such arrangements;

(*d*) a student in respect of whom the authority are satisfied that his parents cannot be found.

Parental contribution

4.—(1) Subject to sub-paragraphs (2) and (3) below, the parental contribution shall be—

(*a*) in any case in which the residual income is more than £2,199 but less than £3,400, £30 with the addition of £1 for every complete £5 by which it exceeds £2,200; and

(*b*) in any case in which the residual income is not less than £3,400, £270 with the addition of £1 for every complete £10 by which it exceeds £3,400;

and in any case in which the residual income is less than £2,200 the parental contribution shall be nil.

(2) For any year in which more than one child of the parent holds a statutory award, the parental contribution for each student shall be such proportion of the parental contribution, ascertained in accordance with this Part, as the authority consider just.

(3) For any year in which the parent holds a statutory award and a contribution is applicable under Part 3, the parental contribution shall be such sum, not exceeding the amount ascertained in accordance with the preceding provisions of this paragraph, as the authority consider just.

Gross income

5.—(1) Subject to the provisions of this paragraph " gross income " means the income of the student's parent in the financial year preceding the year in respect of which the resources of the student fall to be assessed: provided that, where the authority are satisfied that the income of the parent in the next succeeding financial year is likely to be not more than four-fifths of that income, they may for the purpose of calculating the parental contribution ascertain the gross income by reference to that next succeeding financial year; and in that case the above definition shall have effect accordingly both in relation to that year and, if the authority so determine, the year following that year and any subsequent year.

(2) Where trustees of property held in trust for a student or for any other person dependent on the parent pay, by virtue either of section **31** (1) of the Trustee Act **1925** or of the trust instrument, any income of that property to the parent or otherwise apply it for or towards the maintenance, education or other benefit of the beneficiary the amount so paid or applied shall be treated as part of the gross income of the parent.

(3) Any dividends or interest paid or credited to the parent by a building society which has entered into arrangements with the Commissioners of Inland Revenue under section **343** (1) of the Income and Corporation Taxes Act **1970** shall be deemed to have been received by him after deduction of income tax at the reduced rate determined under those arrangements for the year of assessment in which the dividends or interest are paid or credited; and the amount deemed to have been so deducted shall be treated as part of his gross income.

(4) There shall be treated as part of the gross income all income arising from an office or employment which by virtue of any enactment is as such exempt from tax.

(5) There shall be disregarded any income of the student which is treated as income of the parent in accordance with any provision of the Income Tax Acts relating to the aggregation of the income of unmarried minors not regularly working.

(6) Where the parents do not ordinarily live together the parental contribution shall be ascertained by reference to the income of whichever parent the authority consider the more appropriate in the circumstances.

Deductions

6.—(1) In respect of any child dependent on the parent during the year for which the contribution falls to be ascertained . . . the amount by which the relevant sum specified below exceeds the child's income in that year:

Age of child immediately before beginning of academic year	Sum
Under 11	£310
11 or over but under 17	£320
17 or over	£400

(2) In respect of any other person, other than a spouse, dependent on the parent during the year for which the contribution falls to be ascertained . . . the amount by which £400 exceeds the income of that person in that year.

(3) The amount of any sums paid as interest (including interest on a mortgage) in respect of which relief is given under the Income Tax Acts or as interest under the option mortgage scheme.

(4) The amount of any contribution to a dependants' pension scheme being a contribution in respect of which relief is given under the Income Tax Acts.

(5) So much of the aggregate of the amount of any other contribution to a pension or superannuation fund or scheme (excluding national insurance and graduated pensions contributions) and any premium on a policy of life assurance being a contribution or premium in respect of which relief is given under the Income Tax Acts as does not exceed fifteen per cent. of the gross income.

(6) Where the parents are living together and are gainfully employed . . . the cost in wages of domestic assistance not exceeding whichever is the less of £320 and the emoluments of the parent who earns the less.

(7) Where the parents ordinarily live together and one of them is incapacitated . . . so much of the cost in wages of domestic assistance as does not exceed £320.

(8) Where a parent whose marriage has terminated either is gainfully employed or is incapacitated . . . so much of the cost in wages of domestic assistance as does not exceed £320.

(9) In respect of additional expenditure incurred by reason of the fact that the parent lives in a place where the cost of living is higher than that cost in the United Kingdom . . . such sum (if any) as the authority consider reasonable in all the circumstances.

(10) In the case of a parent who holds a statutory award . . . the amount by which the aggregate of his requirements for his ordinary maintenance and £160 exceeds the sum payable in pursuance of that award.

(11) In the case of any student who holds an award bestowed in respect of his attendance at a course beginning before September **1975**, so much of any expenditure in respect of a child or covenant as—

(*a*) would have been deductible by virtue of sub-paragraph (10), (11) or (12) of paragraph 6 of schedule 2 to the 1971 regulations (or provisions to the like effect contained in arrangements made under section 2 (3) of the Education Act 1962); and

(*b*) does not exceed the amounts respectively deducted in respect of that child or covenant in ascertaining the parental contribution for the year ending last before September 1975.

PART 3

SPOUSE'S CONTRIBUTION

Application of Part 3

7. A spouse's contribution ascertained in accordance with this Part shall be applicable in the case of every man student living with his wife and every woman student living with her husband if (in either case) no parental contribution is applicable by virtue of paragraph 3 (*a*), (*b*) or (*c*) above.

Spouse's contribution

8.—(1) Subject to sub-paragraphs (2) and (3) below, Part 2 above, except paragraphs 3, 4 (2), 5 (6) and 6 (8), shall apply with the necessary modifications for the ascertainment of the spouse's contribution as it applies for the ascertainment of the parental contribution, references to the parent being construed except where the context otherwise requires as references to the student's spouse.

(2) If the student marries during any year for which the contribution falls to be ascertained the contribution for that year shall be the fraction of the sum ascertained in accordance with the provisions of sub-paragraph (1) above of which the denominator is 52 and the numerator is the number of complete weeks between the date of the marriage and whichever is the earlier of the end of that year and the end of the course.

(3) If the student's marriage terminates during any year for which the contribution falls to be ascertained the contribution for that year shall be the fraction of the sum ascertained in accordance with the provisions of sub-paragraph (1) above of which the denominator is 52 and the numerator is the number of complete weeks between the beginning of that year and the termination of the marriage.

SCHEDULE 3

Regulation 13

WIDOWS, WIDOWERS, DIVORCED PERSONS, ETC.

1. In its application to a student whose marriage terminates during the course, regulation 14 shall have effect subject to the proviso that the grant shall be payable to him after the termination of his marriage at a rate not lower than that at which it was payable before its termination.

2. If the student has dependants within the meaning of paragraph 12 of schedule 1 and that paragraph applies to him, then, whether his marriage terminated before or during the course—

(*a*) the sum to be disregarded under paragraph 1 (*a*) of schedule 2 shall be £400 instead of £160; or

(*b*) his requirements under paragraph 12 of schedule 1 shall be treated as increased by the sum of £240; or

(*c*) in the case of a student to whom paragraph 16 of schedule 1 applies, his requirements shall be treated as including the sum specified by that paragraph—

whichever is the most favourable to him.

3. A student whose marriage has terminated may elect that the sum specified as his requirements under Part 4 of schedule 1 shall be disregarded and that instead there shall in calculating his income be disregarded £550 in respect of his first dependent child and £240 in respect of every other dependent child.

SCHEDULE 4

Regulation 9 (*c*)

EDUCATIONAL QUALIFICATIONS

1. A foundation credit of the Open University obtained by a student who had attained the age of 21 at the beginning of the Open University course in question.

2. A pass at advanced level in two subjects in the examination for the General Certificate of Education.

3. An Ordinary National Certificate or Diploma, in the examination for which the holder obtained either a mark of not less than 60 per cent. in any two final year subjects or an average mark of not less than 60 per cent. in any three final year subjects.

4. A pass in two principal subjects in the examination for the Higher School Certificate.

5. An Attestation of Fitness of the Scottish Universities Entrance Board.

6. A pass in three subjects in the higher grade gained at not more than two sittings of the Scottish Universities Preliminary Examination, the Scottish Certificate of Education Examination or the examination for the Scottish Leaving Certificate.

7. A pass at advanced level in two subjects in the Northern Ireland General Certificate or Senior Certificate of Education Examination.

8. The European Baccalaureate awarded by any establishment to which the European Communities (European Schools) Order 1972 applied at the time when it was awarded.

9. Any other qualification for the time being prescribed by the Secretary of State or the purposes of these regulations.

SCHEDULE 5

Regulation 16

SANDWICH COURSES

1. In this Schedule—

(*a*) " sandwich course " means a course consisting of alternate periods of full-time study in an establishment and associated industrial, professional or commercial experience (in this Schedule called " periods of experience ") at a place outside the establishment so organised that, taking the course as a whole, the student attends the periods of full-time study for an average of not less than 19 weeks in each year; and for the purpose of calculating his attendance the course shall be treated as beginning with the first period of full-time study and ending with the last such period;

" periods of experience " does not include unpaid service in a hospital, with a local authority acting in the exercise of their functions relating to health, welfare or the care of children and young persons or with a voluntary organisation providing facilities or carrying out activities of a like nature, teaching practice or unpaid research in an establishment;

" sandwich year " means, as respects any student, any year of a sandwich course which includes periods of both such study and such experience as are described above;

" prescribed fraction " means the fraction of which the denominator is 30 and the numerator is the number of weeks in the year for which the student in question attends the establishment;

" modified fraction " means the fraction of which the denominator is 52 and the numerator is the number of weeks in the year in which there are no periods of experience for the student in question; and

(*b*) in the application of this schedule to a student whose marriage has terminated, references to schedules 1 and 2 are to be construed as references to those schedules as modified in accordance with schedule 3.

2. The provisions of schedule 1 shall, as respects any sandwich year, have effect subject to the following modifications—

(*a*) where the period of full-time study does not exceed 30 weeks 3 days, the student's requirements for his maintenance shall be the prescribed fraction of the appropriate amount specified by Part 2;

(*b*) where the period of full-time study exceeds 30 weeks 3 days, the student's requirements for his maintenance shall be the aggregate of the appropriate amount specified in Part 2 and the appropriate amount specified by paragraph 4 of Part 3;

(*c*) the student's requirements for travelling expenses under paragraph 7 (1) of Part 2 shall be the amount by which the expenditure incurred exceeds the prescribed fraction of £22;

(*d*) the student's requirements for the maintenance of a dependant shall be the modified fraction of the sum specified by Part 4; and

(*e*) if the student is a person to whom paragraph 16 of schedule 1 applies, his requirements under that paragraph shall be the prescribed fraction of the amount specified by it.

3. The provisions of schedule 2 shall, as respects any sandwich year, have effect subject to the following modifications—

(*a*) the sum to be disregarded under paragraph 1 (*a*) shall be the prescribed fraction of £160 and the reference in the proviso to paragraph 1 (*b*) to £320 shall be construed as a reference to the aggregate of £160 and that prescribed fraction;

(*b*) in calculating the student's income there shall be disregarded any payment made to him by his employer in respect of any period of experience;

(c) the amount of the parental contribution applicable to his case shall be the prescribed fraction of the contribution ascertained in accordance with Part 2 of the schedule; and

(d) the amount of the spouse's contribution applicable to his case shall be the prescribed fraction of the contribution ascertained in accordance with Part 3 of the schedule.

SCHEDULE 6 Regulation 3

REVOCATIONS

[*Revokes previous regulations and their amending regulations.*]

STUDENTS' DEPENDANTS' ALLOWANCES REGULATIONS 1975

S.I. 1975 *No.* 1225
September 1, 1975

NOTE

These Regulations, which were made under section 3 (*a*) of the Education Act 1962, and s. 3 of the Education Act 1973, were issued with the following explanatory note:

" These Regulations reproduce with amendments the regulations which enable the Secretary of State to pay allowances in respect of the wife, husband or child, of a student attending a course to which Section 1 of the Education Act 1962 applies who is not entitled to any payment in respect of his or her dependants under the provisions regulating the payment of grants to students attending such courses. These regulations increase the rate of allowance payable in respect of the children of a one-parent family; they also contain provisions consequential on the Local Education Authorities Awards Regulations 1975 and make other minor changes."

Citation, commencement, construction and interpretation

1.—(1) These regulations may be cited as the Students' Dependants' Allowances Regulations 1975 and shall come into operation on 1st September 1975.

(2) These regulations (except regulation 7) shall be construed together with the Local Education Authorities Awards Regulations 1975 (" the principal regulations ").

(3) In these regulations " spouse " includes a woman who cohabits with a man student as his wife and a man who cohabits with a woman student as her husband.

(4) The Interpretation Act 1889 shall apply for the interpretation of these regulations as it applies for the interpretation of an Act of Parliament; and section 38 (2) (effect of repeals) of that Act shall have effect in relation to the regulations revoked by these regulations as if they were enactments repealed by an Act.

Power to pay allowances

2.—(1) Subject to regulation 3 below, the Secretary of State may pay an allowance in respect of any eligible dependant to a student to whom paragraph 12 of schedule 1 to the principal regulations does not apply.

(2) References in these regulations to the eligible dependant of a student mean—

(a) a wife or husband with whom the student is living if—

(i) they have a dependent child; and

(ii) the wife or husband does not hold a statutory award;

(b) a wife or husband with whom the student is living and in respect of whom there is for the time being in force a certificate by a registered medical practitioner that she or he is incapable of being gainfully employed for a period of at least eight weeks;

(c) a child who is dependent on the student, unless either—

(i) the parents do not live together and the child resides with the parent; or

(ii) the student's spouse holds a statutory award and in calculating payments under it account is taken of that child.

Exceptions

3. No allowance shall be payable to a student if by virtue of regulation 23 (1) proviso (withholding of payment to student in default) of the principal regulations a grant equal to the minimum payment is paid to him or if by virtue of regulation 19 (assisted students) of those regulations no payment is made to him under those regulations.

Amount of allowance

4.—(1) Subject to paragraphs (4) and (5) below, an allowance shall be payable at the weekly rate specified below for any week or incomplete part of a week in which—

(a) the student attends the course at the establishment or is pursuing any course of study of a kind mentioned in paragraph 6 of Schedule 1 to the principal regulations (" weeks of attendance "); and

(b) there is an eligible dependant of the student:

provided that this paragraph shall be read without sub-paragraph (a) in its application to a student who is not living with a spouse.

(2) The weekly rate of an allowance shall, subject to paragraph (3) below, be the amount by which the aggregate of—

(a) one fifty-second of the amount for the time being prescribed by any appropriate provision of the principal regulations as the requirements of a student for the maintenance of a wife, husband or child; and

(b) (if a student maintains a home for himself and an eligible dependant in the United Kingdom at a place other than that at which he resides during the course) the sum equal to the fraction of which the numerator is the amount for the time being prescribed by the principal regulations as the requirements of a student who maintained such a home for himself and a dependant to whom these regulations apply and the denominator is the number of weeks of attendance in the year—

exceeds one fifty-second of the annual income of the student's family (within the meaning of regulation 5 below).

(3) If an allowance is payable by virtue of these regulations to both the student and the student's spouse the weekly rate shall be half the amount ascertained in accordance with paragraph (2) above.

(4) In the case of any student to whom the minimum payment is paid by virtue of regulation 13, 16 (a) (ii) or 18 (1) of the principal regulations, the rate of the allowance shall be reduced—

(a) if his requirements as assessed in accordance with the principal regulations exceed his resources as so assessed, by one fifty-second of the amount by which the excess falls short of £50;

(b) if those requirements do not exceed those resources, by 96p.

(5) No allowance shall be paid for any week in which the capital resources of the student's household (assessed in accordance with Part III of Schedule 2 to the Supplementary Benefit Act 1966) amount to £1,200 or more.

(6) For the purposes of this regulation a student shall be treated as having attended at an establishment, or as having pursued a course of study, for a part of a week if he attends at an establishment, or pursues such a course, on four consecutive days; and, in determining whether he has attended the establishment or pursued the course, any period during which he is absent on account of illness shall be ignored.

Income of student's family

5.—(1) For the purposes of these regulations the income of the student's family in any year shall be taken to be the aggregate of—

(a) any sums which are disregarded in calculating the student's income for the purposes of the principal regulations, except—

(i) the first £160 of any scholarship, bursary or similar endowment awarded in respect of his attendance at the establishment;
(ii) remuneration for work done in vacations;
(iii) any benefit under the Supplementary Benefit Act 1966;
(iv) family allowances;
(v) (in the case of a sandwich student) any payment made to him by his employer in respect of any period of experience;
(iv) any attendance allowance under section 35 of the Social Security Act 1975; and
(vii) any allowance granted to him in pursuance of a scheme under section 19 of the Housing Finance Act 1972;

(*b*) the income (reduced by income tax, family allowances and national insurance contributions and disregarding the income specified in paragraph (2) below) of a spouse or child who is a member of the same household; and

(*c*) (in the case of any student to whom the minimum payment is paid) the amount (if any) by which his resources as assessed in accordance with the principal regulations exceed his requirements as so assessed.

(2) The income referred to in paragraph (1) (*b*) above is—

(*a*) except in a case falling within sub-paragraph (*c*) below, in respect of the earned income of the spouse whichever is the less of £160 and half that income;

(*b*) any payment under a statutory award; and

(*c*) all income of a person who attends a course designated by or under any provision of the principal regulations except regulation 6 (1) (*d*) (iii) or a full-time course of further education which is not designated by or under those regulations.

Supplementary

6.—(1) An allowance may be paid in instalments.

(2) An allowance, and an instalment of an allowance, may be paid before the end of the year by reference to which, in accordance with regulation 4 above, it falls to be assessed; and any overpayment in any year may, and any underpayment in any year shall, be corrected by way of deduction from or addition to any allowance payable in the next following year or, if no such allowance is payable, by repayment to or payment by the Secretary of State.

Application to recognised students

7. These regulations shall apply to a person to whom a grant is for the time being paid in pursuance of regulation 34 (1) of the Training of Teachers Regulations 1967 (grants to recognised students) and in its application to such a person any reference above to a provision of the principal regulations shall be construed as a reference to that provision as applied by regulation 34 (2) of the Training of Teachers Regulations 1967.

Revocation of regulations

8. The Students' Dependants' Allowances Regulations 1973 are hereby revoked.

REMUNERATION OF TEACHERS (FURTHER EDUCATION) NO. 2 ORDER 1975

S.I. 1975 *No.* 1226
July 26, 1975

NOTE

This Order, made under section 2 of the Remuneration of Teachers Act 1965, was issued with the following explanatory note:

" This Order brings into operation the scales and other provisions relating to the remuneration of full-time teachers in establishments for further education (other than farm institutes) maintained by local education authorities set out in a document published by Her Majesty's Stationery Office. This document gives effect to recommendations agreed by the Committee constituted under the Remuneration of Teachers Act 1965 for the consideration of the remuneration of such teachers. The Order has retrospective effect from 1st March 1975 by virtue of section 7 (3) of the Remuneration of Teachers Act 1965."

See also the limitation of increments imposed by the Remuneration of Teachers (Further Education) No. 2 (Amendment) Order 1975, S.I. 1975 No. 1417, *post*.

Whereas—

(1) in pursuance of section 2 (2) of the Remuneration of Teachers Act 1965 ("the Act") the Committee constituted under section 1 of the Act for the purpose of considering the remuneration of teachers in establishments for further education (other than farm institutes) maintained by local education authorities ("the Committee") have transmitted to the Secretary of State for Education and Science ("the Secretary of State") certain recommendations agreed on by them with respect to the remuneration of such teachers;

(2) in pursuance of section 2 (3) of the Act, the Secretary of State has prepared a draft document setting out the scales and other provisions required for determining the remuneration of teachers of the description aforesaid in the form in which, in his opinion, those scales and provisions should be so as to give effect to the recommendations;

(3) the Secretary of State, as required by section 2 (4) of the Act, has consulted the Committee with respect to the draft document and made such modifications thereof as were requisite for giving effect to representations made by the Committee; and

(4) The Secretary of State has arranged for a document setting out the requisite scales and other provisions in the form of the draft as modified as aforesaid to be published by Her Majesty's Stationery Office on 24th July 1975 under the title "SCALES OF SALARIES FOR TEACHERS IN ESTABLISHMENTS FOR FURTHER EDUCATION, ENGLAND AND WALES 1975".

Now, therefore, the Secretary of State, in pursuance of section 2 (4) of the Act, hereby orders as follows:—

Citation and Commencement

1. This Order may be cited as the Remuneration of Teachers (Further Education) No. 2 Order 1975 and shall come into operation on 26th July 1975.

Interpretation

2. The Interpretation Act 1889 shall apply for the interpretation of this Order as it applies for the interpretation of an Act of Parliament; and section 38 (2) (effect of repeals) of that Act shall have effect in relation to the Order specified in Article 4 of this Order as if it were an enactment repealed by an Act.

Remuneration of Teachers

3. The remuneration payable from 1st March 1975 to full-time teachers in establishments for further education (other than farm institutes) maintained by local education authorities shall be determined in accordance with the scales and other provisions set out in the document published by Her Majesty's Stationery Office as aforesaid.

Revocation

4. The Remuneration of Teachers (Further Education) Order 1975 is hereby revoked.

REMUNERATION OF TEACHERS (FARM INSTITUTES) NO. 2 ORDER 1975

S.I. 1975 *No.* 1227
July 26, 1975

NOTE

This Order, made under s. 2 of the Remuneration of Teachers Act 1965, was issued with the following explanatory note:

" This Order brings into operation the scales and other provisions relating to the remuneration of full-time teachers in farm institutes and teachers of agricultural subjects on the staff of local education authorities set out in a document published by Her Majesty's Stationery Office. This document gives effect to the recommendations agreed by the Committee constituted under the Remuneration of Teachers Act 1965 for the consideration of the remuneration of such teachers. The Order has retrospective effect from 1st March 1975 by virtue of section 7 (3) of the Remuneration of Teachers Act 1965."

See also the limitation of increments imposed by the Remuneration of Teachers (Farm Institutes) No. 2 (Amendment) Order 1975, S.I. 1975 No. 1416, *post*.

Whereas—

(1) in pursuance of section 2 (2) of the Remuneration of Teachers Act 1965 (" the Act ") the Committee constituted under section 1 of the Act for the purpose of considering the remuneration of teachers in farm institutes and teachers of agricultural subjects on the staff of local education authorities (" the Committee ") have transmitted to the Secretary of State for Education and Science (" the Secretary of State ") recommendations agreed on by them with respect to the remuneration of such teachers;

(2) in pursuance of section 2 (3) of the Act, the Secretary of State has prepared a draft document setting out the scales and other provisions required for determining the remuneration of teachers of the description aforesaid in the form in which, in his opinion, those scales and provisions should be so as to give effect to those recommendations;

(3) the Secretary of State, as required by section 2 (4) of the Act, has consulted the Committee with respect to the draft document and the Committee have made no representations with respect thereto; and

(4) the Secretary of State has arranged for a document setting out the requisite scales and other provisions in the form of the draft to be published by Her Majesty's Stationery Office on 24th July 1975 under the title " SCALES OF SALARIES FOR THE TEACHING STAFF OF FARM INSTITUTES AND FOR TEACHERS OF AGRICULTURAL (INCLUDING HORTICULTURAL) SUBJECTS, ENGLAND AND WALES 1975."

Now, therefore, the Secretary of State, in pursuance of section 2 (4) of the Act, hereby orders as follows:—

Citation and Commencement

1. This Order may be cited as the Remuneration of Teachers (Farm Institutes) No. 2 Order 1975 and shall come into operation on 26th July 1975.

Interpretation

2. The Interpretation Act 1889 shall apply for the interpretation of this Order as it applies for the interpretation of an Act of Parliament; and section 38 (2) (effect of repeals) of that Act shall have effect in relation to the Order specified in Article 4 of this Order as if it were an enactment repealed by an Act.

Remuneration of Teachers

3. The remuneration payable from 1st March 1975 to full-time teachers employed as members of the teaching staff of farm institutes maintained by local education authorities or as teachers of agricultural subjects (including horticultural and related subjects) on the staff of local education authorities shall be determined in accordance with the scales and other provisions set out in the document published by Her Majesty's Stationery Office as aforesaid.

Revocation

4. The Remuneration of Teachers (Farm Institutes) Order 1975 is hereby revoked.

INDEPENDENT SCHOOLS TRIBUNAL (AMENDMENT NO. 2) RULES 1975

S.I. 1975 *No.* 1298
August 30, 1975

NOTE

These Rules, made under s. 75 (1) of the Education Act 1944, amend the Independent Schools Tribunal Rules 1958, S.I. 1958 No. 519, *ante*.

REMUNERATION OF TEACHERS (FARM INSTITUTES) NO. 2 (AMENDMENT) ORDER 1975

S.I. 1975 *No.* 1416
August 27, 1975

NOTE

This Order, made under s. 2 of the Remuneration of Teachers Act 1975, prohibits the payment of increments to teachers in farm institutes, and teachers of agricultural subjects on the staff of local education authorities, whose total remuneration is £8,500 *per annum* or more.

* * * * *

Citation and Commencement

1. This Order may be cited as the Remuneration of Teachers (Farm Institutes) No. 2 (Amendment) Order 1975 and shall come into operation on 27th August 1975.

Interpretation

2. The Interpretation Act 1889 shall apply for the interpretation of this Order as it applies for the interpretation of an Act of Parliament.

Amendment of Document

3. (i) An increment shall not be paid if a teacher's rate of remuneration is £8,500 or more per annum, and if the payment of an increment in full would increase a teacher's rate of remuneration beyond £8,500 per annum such part only of that increment shall be paid as will increase the rate of remuneration to that amount.

(ii) For the purpose of this article remuneration means the total remuneration payable to a teacher under the Document, together with any remuneration for residential duties.

NOTE

The " Document " referred to in paragraph (ii) is the document published by Her Majesty's Stationery Office, on July 24, 1975, setting out scales of remuneration. See the preamble to the Remuneration of Teachers (Farm Institutes) No. 2 Order 1975, S.I. 1975 No. 1227, *ante*.

REMUNERATION OF TEACHERS (FURTHER EDUCATION) NO. 2 (AMENDMENT) ORDER 1975

S.I. 1975 *No.* 1417
August 27, 1975

NOTE

This Order, made under s. 2 of the Remuneration of Teachers Act 1965, prohibits the payment of increments to teachers in establishments for further education (other than farm institutes) whose total remuneration is £8,500 *per annum* or more.

Citation and Commencement

1. This Order may be cited as the Remuneration of Teachers (Further Education) No. 2 (Amendment) Order 1975 and shall come into operation on 27th August 1975.

Interpretation

2. The Interpretation Act 1889 shall apply for the interpretation of this Order as it applies for the interpretation of an Act of Parliament.

Amendment of Document

3. (i) An increment shall not be paid if a teacher's rate of remuneration is £8,500 or more per annum, and if the payment of an increment in full would increase a teacher's rate of remuneration beyond £8,500 per annum such part only of that increment shall be paid as will increase the rate of remuneration to that amount.

(ii) For the purpose of this article remuneration means the total remuneration payable to a teacher under the Document, together with any remuneration for residential duties.

NOTE

The " Document " referred to in paragraph (ii) is the document published by Her Majesty's Stationery Office, on July 24, 1975, setting out scales of remuneration. See the preamble to the Remuneration of Teachers (Further Education) No. 2 Order 1975, S.I. 1975 No. 1226, *ante*.

REMUNERATION OF TEACHERS (PRIMARY AND SECONDARY SCHOOLS) NO. 2 ORDER 1975

S.I. 1975 *No.* 1558

September 26, 1975

NOTE

This Order, made under s. 2 of the Remuneration of Teachers Act 1965, was issued with the following explanatory note:

" This Order brings into operation the scales and other provisions relating to the remuneration of teachers in primary and secondary schools maintained by local education authorities set out in a document published by Her Majesty's Stationery Office. This document gives effect both to the recommendations agreed by the Committee constituted under the Remuneration of Teachers Act 1965 for the consideration of the remuneration of such teachers and to the recommendations of arbitrators appointed under that Act.

The Order has retrospective effect from 1st March 1975 by virtue of section 7 (3) of the Act."

Whereas—

(1) in pursuance of section 3 (1) of the Remuneration of Teachers Act 1965 (" the Act ") certain matters in respect of which agreement had not been reached in the Committee constituted under section 1 of the Act for the purpose of considering the remuneration payable to teachers in primary and secondary schools maintained by local education authorities (" the Committee ") were referred to arbitration;

(2) in pursuance of section 2 (2) of the Act the Committee transmitted to the Secretary of State for Education and Science (" the Secretary of State ") recommendations agreed on by them with respect to certain other matters affecting the remuneration of such teachers;

(3) in pursuance of section 2 (3) of the Act, the Secretary of State has prepared a draft document setting out the scales and other provisions required for determining the remuneration of teachers of the description aforesaid in the form in which, in his opinion, those scales and provisions should be so as to give effect to the recommendations of the arbitrators and of the Committee;

(4) the Secretary of State, as required by section 2 (4) of the Act, has consulted the Committee with respect to the draft document and made such modifications thereof as were requisite for giving effect to representations made by the Committee; and

(5) the Secretary of State has arranged for a document setting out the requisite scales and other provisions in the form of the draft as modified as aforesaid to be published by Her Majesty's Stationery Office on 24th September 1975 under the title " SCALES OF SALARIES FOR TEACHERS IN PRIMARY AND SECONDARY SCHOOLS, ENGLAND AND WALES 1975 ".

Now, therefore, the Secretary of State, in pursuance of sections 2 (4) and 4 (1) of the Act, hereby orders as follows:—

Citation and Commencement

1. This Order may be cited as the Remuneration of Teachers (Primary and Secondary Schools) No. 2 Order 1975 and shall come into operation on 26th September 1975.

Interpretation

2. The Interpretation Act 1889 shall apply for the interpretation of this Order as it applies for the interpretation of an Act of Parliament; and section 38 (2) (effect of repeals) of that Act shall have effect in relation to the Order specified in Article 4 of this Order as if it were an enactment repealed by an Act.

Remuneration of Teachers

3. The remuneration payable from 1st March 1975 to teachers in primary and secondary schools maintained by local education authorities shall be determined in accordance with the scales and other provisions set out in the document published by Her Majesty's Stationery Office as aforesaid.

Revocation

4. The Remuneration of Teachers (Primary and Secondary Schools) Order 1975 is hereby revoked.

LOCAL EDUCATION AUTHORITIES RECOUPMENT (FURTHER EDUCATION) (AMENDMENT) REGULATIONS 1975

S.I. 1975 *No.* 1569

October 30, 1975

NOTE

These Regulations, made under s. 7 (4) of the Education (Miscellaneous Provisions) Act 1953, were issued with the following explanatory note:

"These Regulations provide that a person upon whom a local education authority have bestowed an award in respect of his attendance at a course of full-time education shall be treated for recoupment purposes as belonging to the area of that authority while he attends the course irrespective of any subsequent change in the area of his ordinary residence."

See the amendment to regulation 4 (6) of the Local Education Authorities Recoupment (Further Education) Regulations 1954, S.I. 1954 No. 815, *ante*.

PROVISION OF MILK AND MEALS (AMENDMENT NO. 2) REGULATIONS 1975

S.I. 1975 *No.* 1619

November 17, 1975

NOTE

These Regulations, made under s. 49 of the Education Act 1944, as amended by s. 1 of the Education (Milk) Act 1971, amend Sch. 1 to the Provision of Milk and Meals Regulations 1969, S.I. 1969 No. 483. Those principal regulations, as so amended, will be found at p. 383, *ante*.

LOCAL EDUCATION AUTHORITIES AWARDS (AMENDMENT) REGULATIONS 1975

S.I. 1975 No. 1697

November 20, 1975

NOTE

These Regulations, made under s. 1 of the Education Act 1962, as amended, make a saving for grants which would otherwise be reduced by the operation of the Local Education Authorities Awards Regulations 1975, payable to students attending certain courses of teacher training which began before September 1975.

Citation, commencement and interpretation

1.—(1) These regulations may be cited as the Local Education Authorities Awards (Amendment) Regulations 1975 and shall come into operation on 20th November 1975.

(2) The Interpretation Act 1889 shall apply for the interpretation of these regulations as it applies for the interpretation of an Act of Parliament.

(3) References to regulations are to the Local Education Authorities Awards Regulations 1975.

Part-time courses of teacher training

2. Notwithstanding any provision of the regulations the grant payable to a student in respect of his attendance at a course designated under regulation 6 (1) (*d*) (iii) beginning before 1st September 1975 shall, if grant was paid to him in respect of his attendance before that date in pursuance of arrangements made under section 2 (3) of the Education Act 1962 relating to part-time day courses, be not less than the grant that would be payable to him in respect of his attendance at a course designated under regulation 6 (1) (*d*) (ii).

NOTE

For Regulation 6 (1) (*d*) (ii), (iii) of the Local Education Authorities Awards Regulations 1975, S.I. 1975 No. 1207, see p. 422, *ante*.

SEX DISCRIMINATION (DESIGNATED EDUCATIONAL ESTABLISHMENTS) ORDER 1975

S.I. 1975 No. 1902

December 29, 1975

NOTE

This Order, made under s. 24 (1) of the Sex Discrimination Act 1975, designates establishments of further education in England and Wales and schools in England for the purposes of s. 22 of the Sex Discrimination Act 1975, which makes it unlawful for any establishment to which the section applies to discriminate on grounds of sex in the conduct of the establishment.

FURTHER EDUCATION (TRANSITIONAL EXEMPTION ORDERS) REGULATIONS 1975

S.I. 1975 *No.* 1929

December 29, 1975

NOTE

These Regulations, made under s. 100 of the Education Act 1944, as extended by paragraph 3 of Sch. 2 to the Sex Discrimination Act 1975 and by s. 5 (2) of the Local Government Act 1974, as extended by paragraph 4 of that Schedule, provide for the making of orders by the Secretary of State authorising discriminatory admission to single sex establishments of further education during a transitional period so as to enable them to become fully co-educational by stages.

See the addition of a new paragraph 6A to the Further Education Regulations 1975, S.I. 1975 No. 1054, *ante*.

SPECIAL SCHOOLS (TRANSITIONAL EXEMPTION ORDERS) REGULATIONS 1975

S.I. 1975 *No.* 1962

December 29, 1975

NOTE

These Regulations, made under s. 33 of the Education Act 1944, as extended by paragraph 2 of Sch. 2 to the Sex Discrimination Act 1975, provided for the making of orders by the Secretary of State authorising discriminatory admissions to single sex special schools during a transitional period so as to enable them to become fully co-educational by stages.

See the addition of a new Regulation 6A to the Handicapped Pupils and Special Schools Regulations 1959, S.I. 1959 No. 365, *ante*.

DIRECT GRANT SCHOOLS (TRANSITIONAL EXEMPTION ORDERS) REGULATIONS 1975

S.I. 1975 No. 1964

December 29, 1975

NOTE

These Regulations, made under s. 100 of the Education Act 1944, as extended by paragraph 3 of Sch. 2 to the Sex Discrimination Act 1975, provide for the making of orders by the Secretary of State authorising discriminatory admissions to single sex direct grant schools during a transitional period so as to enable them to become fully co-educational by stages.

See the addition of a new Regulation 5A to the Direct Grant Schools (Transitional Exemption Orders) Regulations 1975, S.I. 1975 No. 1964, *ante*.

PART IV

CIRCULARS AND ADMINISTRATIVE MEMORANDA

GENERAL NOTE

A very large number of circulars and administrative memoranda issued by the Department of Education and Science (before 1st April, 1964, by the Ministry of Education) are current. The limitations of size imposed on this volume make it impossible to print them all, and a selection has therefore had to be made. The circulars printed are, in the main, those which are explanatory of Statutory Instruments printed in Part III, *ante*, or which otherwise relate to the performance by local education authorities of duties under the Education Acts, 1944 to 1975. Except where otherwise indicated all circulars and memoranda are printed *in extenso*.

Notes to which reference is made by an asterisk (*) or a dagger (†) or by a numeral form part of the circulars to which they are appended; all other notes have been inserted by the editors of this volume.

The copyright in all the circulars and memoranda is the property of the Crown, and they are reproduced here by the permission of the Controller of Her Majesty's Stationery Office.

They now have effect as if for references to " Minister of Education ", " Minister " and " Ministry of Education " there were substituted references to " Secretary of State for Education and Science ", " Secretary of State " and " Department of Education and Science " respectively. See the Secretary of State for Education and Science Order, 1964, S.I. 1964 No. 490, *ante*.

LIST OF CIRCULARS, MEMORANDA, ETC.

CIRCULAR 183

October 8, 1948

PROVISION OF CLOTHING REGULATIONS

NOTE

Paragraphs 10 and 11 of, and the Appendix to, this Circular are omitted as being obsolete.

1. Section 5 of the Education (Miscellaneous Provisions) Act, 1948 (a), amends and consolidates the provisions of the 1944 and 1946 Acts relating to the provision of clothing by Local Education Authorities. It provides in sub-sections (5) and (6) for the Minister (b) to prescribe by regulation—

(i) the circumstances, if any, in which a right of property or of user only shall be conferred;

(ii) the circumstances in which Authorities shall, or shall not, or may at their discretion, require parents to pay, according to their means, for the clothing provided. (See footnote [p. 450, *post*].)

It also provides in sub-section (3) for the Minister to make regulations empowering Authorities to provide Physical Training clothing and specifying the clothing which they may so provide.

2. The Minister has now made these regulations (c) and a copy is enclosed. The main considerations which Authorities should bear in mind in applying them, are set out in the following paragraphs.

Pupils at Special Schools

3. Under Regulations 3 (1) and (4) (*b*), it is left to the discretion of the Authority, when clothing is provided for a pupil at a special school,

(*a*) whether a right of property in the clothing, or of user only, is conferred;

(*b*) what charge, if any, is made to the parent.

The arrangements to be adopted will vary according to circumstances. Regulations 3 (1) and 4 (*b*) are so drawn as to enable the Authority, if they so desire, either to charge a parent according to his means or to make a small flat-rate charge in those cases when they do not provide the clothing free of charge. The flat-rate method would obviate the need for meticulous examination of the child's wardrobe, and for an elaborate system of book-keeping to cover a miscellany of small items. It is assumed that no charge would be made for special clothing required, for instance, at an open-air school.

Pupils at day schools (*other than special schools*)

4. *County and voluntary Schools*.—Where clothing is provided for a day pupil at a county or voluntary school, the Authority are required by Regulation 4 (*a*) to charge the parent according to his means and to confer a right of property in the clothing.

Nursery Schools and Nursery Classes at County and Voluntary Schools.—Regulation 3 (2) empowers Authorities to provide clothing for pupils at maintained nursery schools and nursery classes at county and voluntary day schools on the same basis as for other pupils at county and voluntary schools. The special arrangements, however, for the free provision on loan of knickers and overalls for pupils at maintained nursery schools and classes will continue as described in Circular 3U.

Pupils at Boarding Schools (*other than Special Schools*)

5. Under Regulation 3 (1) it is left to the discretion of the Authority, when clothing is provided for a pupil who is a boarder at an educational institution maintained by an Authority—

(*a*) whether a right of property in the clothing, or of user only, is conferred;

(*b*) what charge, if any, is made to the parent.

It is assumed that in the case of pupils attending boarding schools otherwise

---

(a) Page 221, *ante*.

(b) See General Note to this Part, p. 447, *ante*.

(c) The Provision of Clothing Regulations, 1948, S.I. 1948 No. 2222, p. 330, *ante*, where they are printed as amended by the Provision of Clothing Amending Regulations, 1956, S.I. 1956 No. 559.

than for a short period only, their parents will be charged according to their means, and that a right of property in the clothing will be conferred. Where the pupil is attending for a short period only, any clothing he requires might be provided free of charge, or for a small flat-rate charge, on a user basis only.

Distinctive Clothing

6. The foregoing paragraphs relate to ordinary clothing. The provision of distinctive clothing will continue to be made under the Regulations for Scholarships and Other Benefits, 1945, made under Section 81 of the 1944 Act, and the Amending Regulations, Nos. 1 and 2. A copy of the Amending Regulations, No. 2, is enclosed. It will usually be more convenient, especially where a pupil attends a non-maintained boarding school, for such provision to take the form of payment of the expenses rather than the purchase by the Authority of the necessary clothing.

Protective Clothing

7. The provision of protective clothing for teachers, school nurses, nursery students, training college students and certain full-time students over 18, does not fall under Section 5 of the 1948 Act. Arrangements for the provision of such clothing will continue to be notified to Authorities, as occasion may require, by circular.

Physical Training Clothing

8. Regulation 5 extends the scope of the former Physical Training Clothing Regulations by empowering Authorities to provide Physical Training clothing free on loan for pupils at maintained establishments of Further Education and for persons who make use of facilities made available by the Authority under Section 53 (1) of the 1944 Act, as well as for pupils at maintained schools. The list of articles which may be provided has been amended and modified by the abolition of the former discrimination by age and sex.

Arrangements with non-maintained Schools

9. Section 5 (4) of the 1948 Act deals with arrangements for the supply of clothing to pupils at non-maintained schools. In making such arrangements, Authorities should secure that the proprietors of those schools impose on the parents such conditions as to property and payment as would have been applicable if the pupils were in attendance at maintained schools.

* * * * *

Footnote [forming part of the circular.]

Section 5 (6) (*a*) of the 1948 Act lays down that the charge made to parents for clothing shall not exceed the cost to the Authority of the provision of the clothing. This condition therefore attaches to any reference made in this Circular to a charge made to parents.

CIRCULAR 232

March 31, 1951

CHILDREN ACT, 1948

ALLOCATION OF FUNCTIONS AS BETWEEN LOCAL AUTHORITY AND LOCAL EDUCATION AUTHORITY

NOTE

This Circular was issued jointly by the Home Office and the Ministry of Education (now the Department of Education and Science (a)) and its Home Office reference is Circular 35/1951.

1. A copy is enclosed of the Local Authorities and Local Education Authorities (Allocation of Functions) Regulations, 1951 (S.I. 1951 No. 472), made

(a) See General Note to this Part, p. 447, *ante*.

by the Secretary of State and the Minister of Education under Section 21 of the Children Act, 1948 (b). The Regulations will come into operation on the 1st May, 1951.

2. The purpose of the Regulations is to provide, where a local authority under Part II of the Children Act and a local education authority as such have concurrent functions, by which authority the functions are to be exercised; and to determine, as respects the functions of a local education authority specified in the Regulations, whether a child in the care of a local authority is to be treated as a child of parents of sufficient resources or a child of parents without resources. The Regulations apply to all children to whom the provisions of Part II of the Act apply.

3. In framing the Regulations, the aim has been to secure that children in the care of local authorities should have the same educational benefits and opportunities as other children, including facilities for continued education at universities and other forms of further education and training; and to avoid as far as possible administrative processes which would distinguish between young people who are or have been in care, and others.

4. Regulations 4 and 5 provide that, in respect of a child who is in the care of a local authority:—

(*a*) the provision of board and lodging to enable him to attend a particular day county school, voluntary school or special school, or to receive special educational treatment, and

(*b*) the payment of reasonable travelling expenses (otherwise than under Section 55 (1) of the Education Act, 1944 (c)) to enable him to attend school or any establishment for further education,

are functions of the local authority.

5. Regulations 3, 7 (1) (*a*) and 8 provide that a child in the care of a local authority is to be treated as a child of parents of sufficient resources to pay:—

(*a*) the whole of any sum payable by a parent for meals or other refreshment provided by a local education authority;

(*b*) such expenses as may be necessary to enable a child attending a county school, voluntary school or special school to take part in any school activities; and

(*c*) such sums as a parent either shall or may be required to pay for clothing provided by a local education authority.

The effect is that expenditure in respect of these items will not be a charge on the local education authority. Such expenditure will in practice fall to be met by the local authority, who, whether or not they are regarded as a parent, as defined in Section 114 of the Education Act, 1944 (d), are responsible under the Children Act for the maintenance, accommodation and upbringing of a child in their care.

6. Regulations 6, 7 (1) (*b*) and 7 (1) (*c*) provide that a child in the care of a local authority is to be treated as a child of parents without resources as respects:—

(*a*) the payment of boarding fees at a maintained school (under Section 61 (2) of the Education Act, 1944);

(*b*) the payment of fees and expenses payable at a school at which fees are charged (where the Local Education Authority exercise their functions under Section 81 (*b*) of the Education Act, 1944);

(*c*) the cost of any scholarship, exhibition, bursary, or any other allowance granted to a pupil over the compulsory school age by the Local Education Authority (under Section 81 (*c*) of the Education Act, 1944 (e)).

The whole cost of these items will therefore fall to be met by the Local Education Authority.

7. Under the proviso to Regulation 7 (1) (*c*), a local education authority are debarred from paying maintenance allowances to parents in respect of

(b) 17 Halsbury's Statutes (3rd Edn.) 556.
(c) Page 147, *ante*.
(d) Page 184, *ante*. (e) Page 166, *ante*.

pupils over compulsory school age attending school, where the pupils are children in the care of a local authority.

8. Regulation 7 (2) provides that financial assistance under Section 20 of the Children Act (f) towards the cost of the maintenance, education or training of a person over the age of eighteen who is in receipt of education or training is to be given by a local authority only in so far as his needs are not met by the grant of scholarships, exhibitions, bursaries or other allowances by the local education authority. The contribution of the local authority will be limited therefore to the payment of such expenses as are not covered by local education authorities' powers to grant scholarships, etc.—e.g. fees for professional training as an architect or solicitor, and such supplementary sums as may be needed when the grant made by the local education authority is not large enough to cover expenses which parents might reasonably be expected to pay. In considering whether such supplementary assistance is needed, local authorities should consult the current standard figure of maintenance issued from time to time by the Ministry of Education. It is hoped that local education authorities, in making grants under Section 81 of the Education Act, 1944, will do all they can to avoid the need for young people over the age of eighteen who have been in care to receive supplementary assistance from the local authority.

9. Regulation 3 renders Regulation 10 (1) of the Provision of Milk and Meals Regulations, 1945 (g), inapplicable to children who are in the care of a local authority. The local education authority, therefore, cannot make any remission of the approved charges for school meals or other refreshments for any such child who is a day pupil at a maintained school. Where a child in the care of a local authority is maintained in a home provided by a local authority or in a voluntary home, the local education authority will accordingly look to the local authority in whose care the child is, for payment for the child's school meals or refreshments. If the child is in a home not provided by the local authority in whose care he is, payment may be made either direct by that authority or through the authority or persons providing the home, as may be convenient.

10. It is particularly desirable that where a child in the care of a local authority is boarded out with a foster parent, there should not appear to be any difference with regard to payment for school meals or other refreshment between the foster parent's own children and the foster children. Authorities are asked, therefore, to adopt arrangements on the following lines:—

(*a*) if the foster parent's own child or children are not eligible for free school meals, or if he has no children at school, the local education authority should obtain payment for the foster child's school meals from the foster parent;

(*b*) if the foster parent's own child or children are eligible for free school meals, the local education authority should obtain the payments due for the foster child's school meals from the local authority.

In some cases it may happen that the foster parent's own child or children would be eligible for free school meals (or for a reduction of the charge) under the authority's income scale but for the addition which the boarding out allowance of the foster child makes to the family income. In order to avoid anomalies, local education authorities are asked, in applying income scales under Regulation 10 (1) of the Provision of Milk and Meals Regulations, 1945 (g) to exclude children in care who are boarded out in reckoning the number in the family, and also to exclude boarding out allowances, in all cases where foster parents have a child or children of their own for whom a remission of the charge for school meals is made or is under consideration.

11. Similar principles should be followed with regard to expenses for school meals at non-maintained schools and with regard to the payment of these expenses by local education authorities under the Regulations for Scholarships and Other Benefits, 1945 (h).

12. Copies of this Circular are enclosed for the information of the Chief Financial Officer, and the Children's Officer.

(f) 17 Halsbury's Statutes (3rd Edn.) 556.
(g) Revoked. See now the Provision of Milk and Meals Regulations, 1969, p. 383, *ante*.
(h) S.R. & O. 1945 No. 666, p. 327, *ante*.

ADMINISTRATIVE MEMORANDUM 455

September 18, 1953

SECTION 12 OF THE EDUCATION (MISCELLANEOUS PROVISIONS) ACT, 1953

NOTE

The Appendix to this Memorandum is omitted as being largely out of date.

Section 12 of the Education (Miscellaneous Provisions) Act, 1953 (a), empowers a Local Education Authority to fill any vacant places in a motor vehicle provided under Section 55 (1) of the Education Act, 1944 (b), with other pupils and to charge them a reasonable fare. The Section neither removes nor adds to the powers and duties of Authorities in regard to the provision of free transport: it gives them a new power, which they may use or not at their discretion, in relation to pupils for whom free transport has not been provided.

Hitherto under the Road Traffic Act, 1930 (c), if an Authority had wished to charge fares to any pupils in a hired motor vehicle, a road service licence would first have had to be secured from the Licensing Authority for Public Service Vehicles; if the Local Education Authority owned and operated the vehicle certain other licences would also have been required. Section 12 simplifies this procedure considerably; only the written consent of the Licensing Authority is needed and this may be expected to be given readily where other transport facilities are not, or cannot readily be made, available to meet the reasonable needs of the fare-paying pupils.

In the rare cases where a route over which it is intended to carry fare-paying pupils runs through the Traffic Areas of two Licensing Authorities, applications will have to be made to both. The Traffic Areas are specified in the First Schedule to the Road and Rail Traffic Act, 1933 (d). In the " special area " (defined in Section 107 (1) of the London Passenger Transport Act, 1933 (e), as so much of the London Passenger Transport Area as lies within the London Traffic Area) the consent of both the Licensing Authority and the London Transport Executive will have to be obtained. The addresses of the London Transport Executive and of the Licensing Authorities in England and Wales are given in the Appendix to this Circular.

An application to a Licensing Authority should include the following particulars: the route to be followed; the seating capacity and type of vehicle to be used; how many seats will normally be filled by non-paying pupils; how many fare-paying pupils are to be picked up and at what places *en route,* and what the arrangements will be for identifying the fare-paying pupils in advance and for payment of their fares. Where the application relates to the " special area " similar particulars to those included in the application to the Licensing Authority should be sent to the London Transport Executive.

The Section lays down that the Licensing Authority shall not give their consent unless they are satisfied that there are no other transport facilities which meet the reasonable needs of the fare-paying pupils. For this purpose if there are any operators of public service vehicles who are likely to be affected by a Local Education Authority's proposals the Licensing Authority will notify them of the application and will consider any representations which they may make. If the operators wish to oppose the application, they will be required to show that alternative facilities are, or will shortly be made, available which will in practice meet the reasonable needs of the pupils concerned in all respects, including times and stopping places. The Licensing Authority may also wish to assure themselves that the proposals of the Local Education Authority

---

(a) Page 235, *ante*.
(b) Page 147, *ante*.
(c) 24 Halsbury's Statutes (2nd Edn.) 569. The Act is now largely repealed and replaced by the Road Traffic Act, 1960.
(d) This Schedule substituted a new Part I in the Third Schedule to the Road Traffic Act, 1930, which has since been repealed by section 267 of and the Eighteenth Schedule to the Road Traffic Act, 1960.
For the list of the Traffic Areas, see now section 119 (1) of the Road Traffic Act, 1960, and as to their boundaries, see *ibid.*, section 252. Note that the London Traffic Area is abolished by section 9 (6) of the London Government Act, 1963 (43 Halsbury's Statutes (2nd Edn.) 680).
(e) 24 Halsbury's Statutes (2nd Edn.) 932.

are generally satisfactory on such matters as the identification of the fare-paying pupils to be carried.

* * * * *

ADMINISTRATIVE MEMORANDUM 557

July 15, 1957

INTRODUCTION OF PART III OF THE EDUCATION ACT, 1944

1. Part III of the Education Act, 1944, will come into operation on the 30th September this year. A letter has been sent to the proprietors of all known independent schools inviting them to register their schools as soon as possible after 30th September, and a copy of it is attached to this memorandum for the information of the authority. Responsibility for the operation of Part III rests with the Minister, but there will be several ways in which the interests of local education authorities will be affected and many ways in which they can, and would no doubt wish to, give help to the independent schools. The purpose of this memorandum is to give information on several important questions.

Duty of parents to secure the education of their children

2. Section 36 of the Education Act, 1944, imposes on the parent of every child of compulsory school age the duty to cause him to receive efficient full-time education suitable to his age, ability and aptitude, either by regular attendance at school or otherwise. Section 37 of the Act requires a local education authority to take action if it appears to them that the parent of any child of compulsory school age in their area is failing in this duty. The Minister wishes to make it clear that the introduction of Part III of the Act neither intensifies nor lessens the responsibility of local education authorities in regard to sections 36 and 37.

3. The Act defines a school as an institution for providing primary or secondary education or both primary and secondary education, and the Minister will not regard an establishment as a school for the purposes of the Act unless it has the provision of primary or secondary education or both as its sole or one of its principal purposes. It may therefore happen that some establishments which have been popularly regarded as schools will fail to obtain a place on the Register.

4. Classification of establishments as schools or not schools for the purposes of Part III should not, however, influence the authority in any action they take in regard to sections 36 and 37. The fact that the Minister will not insist on some establishments submitting particulars to the Registrar of Independent Schools should not lead the authority ipso facto to conclude that they ought to take action under section 37 against the parents of any children of compulsory school age who may be attending them, just as the attendance of a child of compulsory school age at a registered school will not be evidence that the child in question is necessarily receiving efficient full-time education suitable to his age, ability and aptitude. The Minister hopes that in regard to any action they may contemplate under section 37 authorities will, as now, be guided by their own judgment in the light of the circumstances of each individual case.

H.M.I.s' Reports on Independent Schools

5. Authorities are not at present sent copies of reports made by H.M. Inspectors on independent schools recognised as efficient under Rules 16, but they are sent copies of reports on independent schools not so recognised. The Minister will continue this practice after 30th September whenever a copy of a report on an unrecognised independent school is sent to the proprietor. It will not, however, always be the case that a report will be issued following a visit by H.M.I. to an independent school for the purpose of advising the Minister whether or not to confirm registration of the school. Independent schools which are recognised by the Minister as efficient under Rules 16 will be exempted from registration under an Order made under section 70 (2) of the Education Act, 1944. A new edition of List 70 will be published shortly, and authorities will continue

to be notified by the Ministry as and when an independent school in their area is granted recognition under Rule 16 or ceases to be so recognised.

Pupils' Registration Regulations, 1956

6. In the letter inviting them to complete a form of application for registration the attention of independent school proprietors has once more been drawn to their responsibility under Regulation 7 of the Pupils' Registration Regulations, 1956, for agreeing with the authority arrangements for making a periodic return of registered day pupils of compulsory school age who fail to attend school regularly or who are absent for two weeks or more without a medical certificate.

General

7. The Minister's main concern under Part III is, so far as he can, to safeguard children and parents against abuses. He is also concerned, through H.M. Inspectorate to give the independent schools all the positive help that he can, and he hopes that a growing number of them will aim at securing recognition as efficient. He is confident that for their part local education authorities will be equally willing to give help when it is requested.

CIRCULAR 2/60

March 1, 1960

LAND QUESTIONS (a)

I. SCOPE OF THE CIRCULAR

1. The Town and Country Planning Act, 1959, came into force on 16th August, 1959. This circular takes account of the provisions of this Act (on which more detailed guidance is given in the Ministry of Housing and Local Government's Circulars 48/59 and 49/59) and of the Local Government Act, 1958, and consolidates current guidance on land transactions and land use Administrative Memorandum No. 260, Circulars 243 and 337 and paragraph 16 of Circular 350 are cancelled.

2. For the purposes of this circular, it is important to bear in mind the distinction between land transactions (which are dealt with in Part II) and land use (which is dealt with in Part III). Land transactions are actual dealings in land involving the transfer of an interest, whether by way of sale, lease, appropriation, exchange, or otherwise, from or to the local education authority or between one committee of the authority and another. Such dealings do not in themselves determine what use is to be made of the land, and it is this further question which raises the issues dealt with in Part III of the circular. Land transactions are governed, broadly, by the general law affecting all functions of local authorities. The use of land for educational purposes may, in addition, be affected by the terms of the Education Acts and the Minister's (b) regulations.

3. Under both heads, the changes brought into force by legislation and by this circular represent a substantial relaxation of statutory and administrative controls. Most acquisitions of land were freed from control by the introduction of the general grant; most disposals by Sections 23 and 26 of the Town and Country Planning Act, 1959; and most changes in use are given general approval in paragraph 10 of this circular.

4. Parts II and III of this circular do not deal with land transactions or land use by voluntary bodies. So far as voluntary schools are concerned, these are dealt with in Administrative Memorandum 1/60. Proposals affecting voluntary training colleges and non-maintained special schools require the Minister's specific approval.

5. In this circular, " land " includes land with buildings.

(a) The information contained in this Circular is now incorporated in the Building Code, as to which see generally Circular 6/62 (3rd September, 1962).

So far as projects carried out by local education authorities are concerned this Circular is, accordingly, superseded by the Building Code; but it remains in force so far as it relates to other aspects.

(b) Now Secretary of State. See General Note to this Part, p. 447, *ante*.

II. LAND TRANSACTIONS

6. *Approval.* Approval to land transactions by local education authorities is required only as follows:—

(*a*) compulsory acquisition is subject to the Minister's confirmation in accordance with the statutory procedure;

(*b*) the acquisition by agreement of land outside the area of the acquiring authority in advance of requirements requires the consent of the Minister;

(*c*) the acquisition or appropriation to education of land required solely for the school meals service requires the Minister's approval as a condition of grant;

(*d*) the appropriation to education* of open spaces, of allotments and cottage holdings, and of land acquired (directly or indirectly†) by compulsory powers and not subsequently appropriated for any purpose other than that for which it was so acquired, requires the consent of the Minister of Housing and Local Government, the Minister of Agriculture, Fisheries and Food, and the appropriate Minister, respectively;

(*e*) the disposal or appropriation from education of land acquired (directly or indirectly†) by compulsory powers for educational purposes and not subsequently appropriated for any other purpose, requires the consent of the Minister;

(*f*) loans will continue to require sanction from the Minister of Housing and Local Government, on the recommendation of the Minister of Education;

(*g*) the disposal of land held on charitable trusts remains subject to the law of charitable trusts.

7. *Procedure.* Guidance on procedure for compulsory acquisition is given in the Appendix to this circular. Other proposals requiring the Minister's approval should be accompanied by a District Valuer's report and, in the case of acquisition, a completed Form S.B.1 (Revised). Applications for loan sanction should be submitted to the Minister, and should be accompanied by a District Valuer's report unless the price has been determined by the Lands Tribunal.

8. *Finance.* The District Valuer will be ready to advise authorities on the price to be paid for land. The Minister will not normally recommend loan sanction, nor give his approval where this is required under paragraph 6 above, if the proposed price exceeds that recommended by the District Valuer or determined by the Lands Tribunal. When disposing of land** authorities are bound by Section 26 (4) of the Town and Country Planning Act, 1959, to obtain the best price, consideration or rent that can reasonably be obtained, unless the Minister of Housing and Local Government gives his consent to a lower figure; this does not, however, affect the re-sale to voluntary bodies of land acquired on their behalf (see paragraph 9 below).

9. *Acquisition on behalf of voluntary bodies.* Authorities may, under Section 90 (1) of the Education Act, 1944 (c), and Section 10 of the Education (Miscellaneous Provisions) Act, 1948, acquire land, whether compulsorily or by agreement, on behalf of voluntary bodies. Where land is acquired for the

---

* The reason why acquisition from other authorities of land in these categories is not mentioned here is that in such a case it will be the responsibility of the other authority and not of the local education authority to obtain the consent of the relevant Minister, particularly in view of Section 29 (1) (*b*) of the Town and Country Planning Act, 1959.

† The meaning of this expression is explained in Section 30 (5) of the Town and Country Planning Act, 1959, and in paragraph 37 of the memorandum annexed to the Ministry of Housing and Local Government's Circular 48/59.

** Except in the case of lettings for terms not exceeding seven years, which were not subject to the then Minister's approval before the coming into force of the Town and Country Planning Act, 1959, and are therefore not affected by Section 26 (4).

(c) The provisions of the Education Acts, 1944 to 1959, referred to in this Circular are:

*1. Regulation 4 (2) of the Schools Regulations, 1959, p. 350, *ante*.

2. Regulation 7 (1) of the Further Education (Local Education Authorities) Regulations, 1959 (revoked; see now the Further Education Regulations, 1975, p. 411, *ante*).

3. Regulation 9 of the Training of Teachers (Local Education Authorities) Regulations, 1959 (revoked; see the Further Education Regulations, 1975, p. 411, *ante*).

4. Regulation 5 (2) of the Handicapped Pupils and Special Schools Regulations, 1959, p. 357, *ante*.

5. Regulation 5 of the Handicapped Pupils (Boarding) Regulations, 1959, p. 349, *ante*.

purposes of a voluntary school, they are required to secure that this does not result in their bearing expenditure which would otherwise have been borne by the managers or governors, and the Minister expects that they will normally transfer the land immediately to the managers or governors for no more and no less than is necessary to cover the costs of the acquisition. Since the acquisition of the land by the managers or governors may be subject to the Minister's approval as a condition of grant under Section 102, 103 or 104 of the Education Act, 1944, or under the Education Act, 1959, authorities are asked in all such cases to consult the Ministry and submit a District Valuer's report and a completed Form S.B.1 (Revised), before acquiring land. Where authorities acquire land for voluntary schools in fulfilment of their own duty under the Education Acts (whether or not it is also their duty to convey the land to the managers or governors under the First Schedule to the 1946 Act) they need not seek approval except as in paragraph 6 above.

III. LAND USE

Alterations to schools and other establishments

10. The Minister's approval, either general or specific, is required by his regulations* to any alterations to existing premises (including sites). The Minister hereby approves, under the regulations appropriate to the type of establishment in each case, all alterations to premises undertaken by local education authorities which involve the taking into use or discontinuance of use of land or land with buildings, except:—

(*a*) those which he determines, under Section 67 (4) of the Education Act, 1944, to amount to the establishment of a new school;

(*b*) those involving building work requiring his specific approval in accordance with Part [II] or Part [III] of Administrative Memorandum 3/60;

(*c*) the addition to the premises of an institution of further education of a farm or other agricultural land to be used as such for teaching purposes;

(*d*) the discontinuance of the use as part of the premises of a school of land with or without buildings unless it is:—

(i) surplus to the requirements of the Standards for School Premises Regulations, 1959 (d); or

(ii) land without buildings less than 150 square yards in area.

11. The main purpose of this general approval is to make it unnecessary for authorities to obtain the Ministry's specific approval to individual proposals to extend sites or to take into use, temporarily or otherwise, additional or existing buildings, provided that no substantial amount of new building work is involved. It will also enable them to give up the use of small pieces of land for electricity sub-stations, road widening or similar purposes and of any land or building surplus to requirements, which in the case of schools (including special schools) are defined by regulations, but in the case of other establishments will be left in this respect to authorities' discretion.

12. Easements and rights of way are not alterations and do not require approval.

New schools and other establishments (including complete new premises for existing establishments)

13. In the case of new schools, other than special schools, including enlargements which he determines to amount to the establishment of a new school, the Minister must satisfy himself that the site complies with the requirements of the Standards for School Premises Regulations, 1959, and is capable of development within an appropriate limit of cost, before he approves specifications and plans under Section 13 (6) of the Education Act, 1944. In the case of new special schools, or complete new premises for existing schools of any kind, he feels bound to satisfy himself in the same way before giving his approval under Regulation 4 (2) of the Schools Regulations, 1959, or Regulation 5 (2) of the Handicapped Pupils and Special Schools Regulations, 1959. In the case of other establishments there are no prescribed standards,

---

(d) Revoked; see now the Standards for School Premises Regulations, 1972, p. 392, *ante*.

but the Minister nevertheless must satisfy himself that the site is suitable before giving his approval under the appropriate regulations quoted in the footnote to paragraph 10. In all types of case, building work requiring specific approval under Section 13 (6) or the Minister's regulations (see Parts [II] and [III] of Administrative Memorandum 3/60) will nearly always be involved and this approval will serve both purposes.

Suitability of sites

14. These arrangements leave in the hands of local education authorities a large degree of responsibility for ensuring that land is not acquired that will later prove to be unsuitable for educational use. In all cases the cost of developing a site for educational purposes must be taken into account at the time of acquisition, especially where site conditions may make it difficult to build within the Ministry's limits of cost. Particular care must be taken over sites for further education establishments and teacher training colleges. No general statutory standards such as apply to schools exist or are possible to guide authorities on the appropriate sizes of site in these cases. Whether or not and, if so, how much land is required for playing fields and what assumptions should be made about possible future expansions are both difficult but critical points to be resolved. The location of such sites, especially in the case of further education establishments, is another key consideration. There is a natural desire to seek a prominent central position for new establishments, especially when these are of major importance. But the advantages of central sites are neither automatic nor unqualified and, before they are acquired, proper weight must be given to both the present and future outlook with regard to the location of industry and residential areas and to transport facilities, both public and private.

15. Although no separate approval of the educational use of land is contemplated under the arrangements mentioned in paragraphs 10–13 above, authorities will no doubt wish to ensure that neither the nature, size, location nor cost of development of any site they propose to acquire will be a bar to the Minister's subsequent approval under his regulations. The Minister will welcome informal consultation at an early stage on any cases of difficulty and will be ready to give his advice on site questions provided that sufficient information can be given to show how the authority intend to develop any site they have in mind.

16. Authorities are reminded that, in accordance with [paragraphs 5–24 of Administrative Memorandum 3/60], site plans are required in all cases where the Minister's approval of plans is sought. Site plans should be drawn to a scale of 1 : 500 and should show areas, compass points, contour lines, sections of trial holes (if any), main services, roads and means of access. They should be accompanied, wherever necessary, by any relevant general notes on the character of the site with particular reference to special difficulties such as liability to subsidence or flooding.

IV. THE AVAILABILITY OF SITES

Town and Country Planning

17. All educational projects which can be clearly enough defined should be safeguarded by having sites allocated for educational purposes in the development plan submitted by the local planning authority to the Minister of Housing and Local Government, or in a subsequent amendment whether in the course of the five-yearly review or otherwise. The planning authority have powers to prevent any development inconsistent with the use for which a site has been allocated. Designation of land in the development plan as subject to compulsory acquisition should not normally be necessary and is not recommended.

18. Part IV of the Town and Country Planning Act, 1959, sets out the circumstances in which notices may be served on local education authorities requiring them to buy forthwith land allocated or designated in a development plan. Detailed guidance on these provisions is given in paragraphs 55–65 of the memorandum annexed to the Ministry of Housing and Local Government's Circular 48/59.

19. Planning permission for development by a local planning authority within its own area (including development by the authority in its capacity as local education authority) is normally deemed to be granted under the Town

and Country Planning (Development by Local Planning Authorities) Regulations, 1951 (e), as modified by the Town and Country Planning (Development Plans) Direction, 1954 (f). When a proposal does not come within the terms of these regulations the authority must apply to the Ministry of Housing and Local Government. An authority proposing to carry out development outside its own area must apply for planning permission to the local planning authority concerned and will have a right of appeal, if necessary, to the Minister of Housing and Local Government. If such an appeal is made, copies of all relevant documents should be sent at the same time to the Minister of Education.

20. Under Section 37 of the Town and Country Planning Act, 1959, owners of land and agricultural tenants have to be notified of planning applications in respect of their land, and under Section 36 certain applications have to be advertised. Guidance on these matters is given in paragraphs 42–51 of the memorandum annexed to the Ministry of Housing and Local Government's Circular 48/59.

Agriculture

21. Agriculture should be disturbed as little as possible. The Regional Land Commissioner of the Ministry of Agriculture, Fisheries and Food should be consulted when proposals affecting agricultural land are being formulated, i.e. before any formal step is taken in connection with planning permission or acquisition. He may be able to suggest alternative sites equally suitable for educational purposes, but less valuable for agriculture. At the stage when the authority seek the allocation of land for educational purposes, the local planning authority will be responsible for formally consulting the Regional Land Commissioner of the Ministry of Agriculture, Fisheries and Food.

22. Any agricultural land owned by local education authorities should continue in cultivation until required for educational purposes, and wherever possible existing tenancy arrangements should remain undisturbed. It will be understood that the right to terminate the occupation of agricultural land may be affected by the Agricultural Holdings Act, 1948 (g).

Restrictive Covenants

23. Where land subject to restrictive covenants is acquired by compulsory purchase, the provisions of the Lands Clauses Consolidation Act, 1845 (h), apply by virtue of the Second Schedule to the Acquisition of Land (Authorisation Procedure) Act, 1946 (j). Accordingly, the procedure described by Section 68 of the Act of 1845 (k) is available to any person who claims that his land, or any interest therein, has been injuriously affected by the execution of the works on the land compulsorily acquired. Where local education authorities propose to purchase by agreement, they will doubtless first consider whether the waiver of any restrictions can conveniently be obtained by agreement. Where this cannot be done, they will have to consider what alternative steps should be taken to secure waiver, e.g. by the use of compulsory purchase powers or by proceeding under Section 84 of the Law of Property Act, 1925 (l).

MARY SMIETON

APPENDIX (m)

COMPULSORY PURCHASE ORDER PROCEDURE

Scope of the Appendix

1. This Appendix reproduces the guidance given in the Appendix to Circular 243 and in Circular 337. It contains no new material.

Procedure before the public inquiry

2. Before a compulsory purchase order is made it is most desirable that the Ministry should be consulted as to the prima facie suitability of the site.

3. A compulsory purchase order should not be made until any necessary notices under Section 13 of the Education Act, 1944, have been published, and unless or until approval under Section 13 (4) has been given.

(e) S.I. 1951 No. 2069.
(f) Given by the Minister of Housing and Local Government on June 16, 1954.
(g) 1 Halsbury's Statutes (3rd Edn.) 685.
(h) 3 Halsbury's Statutes (2nd Edn.) 893.
(j) 3 Halsbury's Statutes (2nd Edn.) 1081.
(k) 3 Halsbury's Statutes (2nd Edn.) 919.
(l) 20 Halsbury's Statutes (2nd Edn.) 617.
(m) This Appendix is reproduced as Appendix 15 to the Building Code, as to which, see Circular 6/62 (3rd September, 1962).

4. Authorities should, as far as possible, give early notification of their proposals to those who may be affected.

5. The form of a compulsory purchase order and the various forms of notice to be used are prescribed by the Compulsory Purchase of Land Regulations, 1949 (S.I. 1949 No. 507).

6. The Minister is not prepared to give consideration to any compulsory purchase order in which the specific purpose for which the land is required is not incorporated. The inclusion of such a phrase as "for the purpose of the Education Acts" is not a sufficient description. If, for example, the object of the order is to acquire land for an extension to a school, it should be so stated in the order and the name of the school should be given.

7. Immediately the notice of compulsory purchase order has been published the following documents should be forwarded to the Ministry:—

(*a*) the compulsory purchase order, sealed with the seal of the Council and properly authenticated, together with one sealed copy;
(*b*) four unsealed copies for purposes of reference;
(*c*) four copies of the deposited map, to which reference is made in the order, of which two should be sealed;
(*d*) a completed Form S.B.1;
(*e*) the District Valuer's report (this can be forwarded later if it is not available at the time);
(*f*) a copy of the notice served on the owners, lessees and occupiers;
(*g*) two copies of the statement sent to all persons who receive the statutory notice. This statement, which should also normally be sent to any person who lodges a written objection, should give full and clear particulars of the case for acquisition, and should refer to any ministerial regulations or statements of policy of which the Authority have taken account in their proposals, including, for example, the appropriate provision in the Standards for School Premises Regulations, 1959, if applicable, and in any circular suggesting particular classes of projects for inclusion in building programmes.

8. Formal application for the confirmation of the order should not be made until the period allowed for objections to the order has expired. When it is made it should be accompanied by a certificate from the Clerk of the Council on Form 201aG, together with copies of the newspapers mentioned in the certificate.

9. Where compensation falls to be assessed in accordance with the provisions of the Town and Country Planning Acts, copies of a form of claim to accompany notices to treat may be obtained from H.M. Stationery Office.

Departmental witnesses

10. Where a Government Department other than the Ministry of Education has expressed positive views which form part of the Authority's case and are referred to as such in the written statement furnished by the Authority, a representative from the Department will attend the inquiry and be available to give evidence if any owner, lessee, or occupier of land affected by the order has, on receiving the statement, asked for the presence of such a witness at the inquiry.

11. This situation will not normally arise in respect of land included in the compulsory purchase order since it is not the function of, for example, the Ministry of Agriculture, Fisheries and Food to express positive views in favour of the acquisition of any piece of land for educational use. Positive views may, however, have been expressed by that Department about alternative sites which the Authority have rejected for agricultural rather than educational reasons. If so those may be quoted in the written statement, and the owners, lessees and occupiers who receive it should be informed that if they should decide to object and would wish a representative from the Ministry of Agriculture to attend at any inquiry, it will be necessary for them to inform the Authority. It should be explained at the same time that such a representative would not be liable to cross-examination on questions of ministerial policy but only on matters of fact and expert opinion.

12. On learning that the attendance of a Departmental representative is required, the Authority should at once notify the Department concerned, sending a copy of the notification to the Ministry of Education.

13. The views of any Department set out in an Authority's written statement should either be quoted verbatim from the Department's official letter or be in terms which have been agreed with the Department.

The public inquiry and the Inspector's report

14. The Minister appoints independent inspectors to hold public inquiries and sends their reports to the parties when he gives his decision.

15. The Minister instructs inspectors to divide their reports into two parts, the first consisting of a summary of evidence, findings of fact, and inference of fact. As soon as possible after the public inquiry this part will be sent to the parties if they so desire, and they will be given fourteen days in which to propose corrections.

The Minister's decision

16. If new factual evidence is brought to the Minister's notice after an inquiry, and if in his view it may be a material factor in the decision, he will give the parties an opportunity of commenting on it.

17. When giving his decision the Minister will explain his reasons for it in addition to sending the inspector's report.

CIRCULAR 4/61

March 27, 1961

THE USE OF INDEPENDENT SCHOOLS FOR HANDICAPPED PUPILS

1. The Committee on Maladjusted Children drew attention to the extensive use made by local education authorities of independent schools for the education of maladjusted pupils and to the large number of such pupils who were being maintained at schools not recognised as efficient. Although not doubting that some of these schools would receive recognition if they applied for it, the Committee considered that it was unsatisfactory that local education authorities lacked positive guidance as to the quality and suitability of individual schools. Accordingly, they recommended that local education authorities should be permitted to maintain maladjusted pupils only in those independent schools which are recognised as efficient.* The Minister (a) has accepted this recommendation and has decided to apply the same principle to all categories of handicapped pupils because he considers that the provision made for them should similarly reach a standard which he can regard as suitable.

2. Local education authorities are accordingly notified, under Section 33 (2) of the Education Act, 1944†, that as from 1st January, 1964, the Minister will regard an independent school which is not recognised as efficient under Rules 16**, as unsuitable for providing special educational treatment unless, upon receipt of an application from an authority‡, he decides to make an exception in the case of a particular school either generally or for a particular pupil or category of pupils.

3. The Minister is making this announcement now in order to give ample notice to the schools affected and to local education authorities. Between three and four dozen unrecognised schools cater wholly or mainly for handicapped pupils. The Minister believes that some of them will wish to consider making application for recognition as efficient under Rules 16 or for approval as non-maintained special schools under the Handicapped Pupils and Special Schools Regulations, 1959§. H.M. Inspectors and the Ministry's Medical Officers will be prepared to advise schools on the standards required for recognition or approval.

4. Local education authorities will need to find alternative places either in special schools or in independent schools recognised as efficient for pupils they might otherwise have sent to unrecognised schools. For the time being they will, no doubt, wish to await the result of any application that may be made for recognition or approval before ceasing to use an unrecognised independent

---

* Report of the Committee on Maladjusted Children 1955, Recommendation 75. "As from an appropriate date as soon as possible, local education authorities should be permitted to maintain maladjusted pupils only in those independent schools which are recognised by the Minister of Education as efficient".

(a) Now Secretary of State. See General Note to this Part, p. 447, *ante*.

† Education Act, 1944 as amended by the Education (Miscellaneous Provisions) Act, 1953. "33 (2). The arrangements made by a local education authority for the special educational treatment of pupils of any such category shall, so far as is practicable, provide for the education of pupils in whose case the disability is serious in special schools appropriate for that category, but where that is impracticable, or where the disability is not serious, the arrangements may provide for the giving of such education in any school maintained by a local education authority or in any school not so maintained, other than one notified by the Minister to the local education authority to be, in his opinion, unsuitable for the purpose".

** Department of Education and Science Rules 16 (p. 468, *post*).

‡ In suitable cases, the Minister may decide to accord provisional recognition. Unless and until provisional recognition is withdrawn from a school, local education authorities wishing to use it will not need to apply to the Minister for an exception to be made in the case of that school.

§ S.I. 1959 No. 365 (p. 356, *ante*).

school. Additional places will have to be provided, principally for maladjusted pupils who constitute about two-thirds of the total sent to unrecognised schools. Some authorities have already submitted proposals for establishing new schools for maladjusted children and others have proposals under consideration as a result of the request made to authorities in Circular 348 of March, 1959, as to review their provision for these pupils.

5. Authorities may still occasionally find it necessary, even after January, 1964, to use for handicapped pupils independent schools which have not qualified for recognition as efficient. There is the special case of particular children who for one reason or another (e.g. on account of an unusual combination of handicaps) cannot be placed satisfactorily either in a special school or in a school that has been recognised as efficient. There will also be the continuing need for experiment in the educational provision for handicapped pupils, with the resulting possibility that an authority may wish to send a child to a new school before it has been recognised as efficient. Furthermore, some authorities send severely handicapped pupils to schools outside England and Wales, to which Rules 16 do not apply. The notification in paragraph 2 of this Circular is made in such a way as to enable authorities to apply to the Minister for exceptions to be made in circumstances such as these.

CIRCULAR 4/62

April 18, 1962

The Education Act, 1962

1. The Education Act, 1962, received the Royal Assent on 29th March, 1962. The Act changes the system of awards to students and reduces the number of school leaving dates in the year. This Circular describes its main provisions so far as they relate to England and Wales and draws attention to some of their administrative consequences.

Section 1

2. Sub-sections (1) and (2) impose a duty upon local education authorities to make awards to students who:—

(*a*) are attending full-time courses, designated by the Minister (a), leading to a first degree, or of comparable standard, at universities and institutions of further education in the United Kingdom;
(*b*) possess certain educational qualifications, to be prescribed by the Minister; and
(*c*) are ordinarily resident in the area of the authority.

This duty will take effect in respect of awards for courses beginning on or after 1st September, 1962. Awards current at that date will continue under present arrangements.

3. It is the Minister's intention to designate for this purpose first degree courses at all universities in the United Kingdom, courses leading to the Diploma in Technology, and such other courses as he decides, after consulting the Standing Advisory Committee on Grants to Students, to regard as comparable. He intends to prescribe, as the standard educational qualification, two passes at Advanced level in the General Certificate of Education. Other equivalent qualifications, for instance, those gained in Scotland and those expressed in terms of the Higher School Certificate examination system, will also be prescribed together with the qualifications appropriate for courses leading to the Dip. Tech. and other comparable courses.

4. Regulations are being drafted to cover the matters referred to in subsections (1) and (2). Regulations will also prescribe the conditions and exceptions governing the performance by local education authorities of their duties, and the composition and amounts of the grants payable to students holding awards under this section, as provided in sub-section (3). These matters are

---

(a) Now Secretary of State. See the General Note to this Part, p. 447, *ante*.

currently under review by the Minister in the light of advice received from the Standing Advisory Committee, and the regulations will be laid before Parliament as soon as possible.

5. Sub-section (7) and the First Schedule, provide for the determination of questions of ordinary residence arising under this section, in accordance with the criteria used for the purposes of Section 7 of the Education (Miscellaneous Provisions) Act, 1953. Where, under those criteria, a student otherwise eligible for an award would fall to be regarded as not ordinarily resident in the area of any local education authority, the Minister may direct that he be treated as ordinarily resident in the area of a specified authority. This procedure will enable students of this kind, for example, those whose parents are employed abroad but intend to return eventually to England or Wales, to know for certain to which local education authority they should apply for an award. In order to remove any doubts about the responsibilities of local education authorities for students who change their area of residence during the twelve months immediately before their course begins, the Minister intends to specify 30th June as the date by reference to which, in any given year, these responsibilities are to be determined.

6. Sub-sections (4) and (5) empower local education authorities to make awards at their discretion to students who attend courses to which this section applies but who are not entitled to awards under the provisions of sub-sections 1 and 2, *e.g.* because they do not possess the requisite educational qualifications. Where an award is made to such a student, the amount of grant payable will be governed by the regulations to be made under sub-section (3).

7. As soon as possible after he has made the necessary regulations, the Minister will publish guidance for local education authorities in making awards under Section 1; this will supersede Circular 5/61.

Section 2

8. Section 2 empowers local education authorities to make awards to students attending courses which fall outside the scope of Section 1. During the passage of the Bill, the Minister undertook to bring to the attention of authorities the scope of their powers under this Section. It embraces awards not only for courses at further education institutions below the level comparable with degree courses, courses at adult residential institutions and courses of teacher training, but also awards for postgraduate courses at universities in the United Kingdom and courses of any level at universities and other institutions abroad. The Section applies also to part-time courses so far as assistance to students to meet the educational expenses arising from these courses is justified. The Minister hopes shortly to issue fresh guidance to local education authorities on the exercise of their powers to make awards to postgraduate students.

9. Local education authorities are not required to submit their arrangements under this Section for the Minister's approval, except in respect of grants to students training as teachers (see paragraph 12 below). The Minister would, however, be glad to receive copies from time to time of authorities' current schemes for the exercise of their powers.

10. While the powers conferred on authorities by Section 2 are to be exercised at their discretion, the Minister thinks it right to draw their attention to the concern which was expressed during the passage of the Bill at variations of practice among local education authorities, both in their award making policy for courses falling under this section, and also in the rates and conditions of their grants. The Minister made it clear that, because of the diversity in standards, length and other respects of these courses, and in the financial needs of the students attending them, it would be inappropriate to extend to awards in this field statutory requirements similar to those embodied in Section 1. He trusts that authorities will justify the confidence which he expressed in them by their preparedness to consider sympathetically the claims of students whose courses are within this discretionary field, and to apply to them, so far as is possible, consistent standards and rates of grant.

11. The Minister is advised that Section 2 confers no powers on local education authorities to make awards to students by way of loans rather than grants. He would expect that loans would only be made in future in exceptional cases and for purposes not covered by the grant.

12. Section 2 (3) empowers authorities to make grants to students training as teachers. These powers are to be exercised in accordance with arrangements

approved by the Minister. In practice this provision continues the present system of grants for students attending training colleges.

13. The provisions of Sections 1 and 2 replace the corresponding provisions of Section 81 of the Education Act, 1944, and of the Regulations for Scholarships and Other Benefits, 1945. That section and those regulations will remain in force with respect to the payment of fees, allowances and other expenses of pupils attending schools.

Section 3

14. This section of the Act re-defines the powers of the Minister to make awards and grants, and replaces the corresponding provisions of Section 100 (1) (*c*) of the Education Act, 1944. The Minister will continue to make grants to students attending University Departments of Education for courses of training as teachers, and to offer state studentships for advanced postgraduate study in arts subjects and state scholarships to selected older candidates for first degree courses.

15. As announced in A.M. 3/61 dated 8th February, 1961, the Minister will award General Certificate of Education, Supplemental and Technical state scholarships for the last time during the summer of 1962. These awards must be made before 1st September, 1962, and the closing date for the recommendation of candidates on Form 2 U.S. by university and college authorities has accordingly been advanced from 30th September, 1962, as announced in A.M. 3/61, to 31st July (exceptionally up to two weeks later).

16. The Minister has also decided to allow state scholarships awarded in 1962 to be postponed for *one* year only, until the autumn of 1963, not two years, as stated in A.M. 3/61. Scholarships awarded in 1962, whether taken up then or in 1963, together with those now current, will be tenable for the full duration of the students' approved course of study, subject to the usual conditions.

Section 7

17. This section authorises the adjustment of general grant for 1961-62 and 1962–63 in respect of additional expenditure already incurred, or likely to be incurred, by local education authorities as a consequence of the revised arrangements for awards and grants to students introduced by Circular 5/61 and Circular 7/61, and under the corresponding provisions of Section 1 and 2 of this Act. The Minister of Housing and Local Government will lay before Parliament in due course an Order increasing the aggregate amounts of general grant for 1961-62 and 1962-63 to take account of increases in prices, costs or remuneration, in accordance with the provisions of this Section and of Section 2 (4) of the Local Government Act, 1958.

SCHOOL LEAVING DATES

Section 9

[*Paragraphs* 18–21 *now obsolete.*]

[**Note.** The former provisions of the Education Act 1962, as to school leaving dates, have been amended by the Education (School Leaving Dates) Act 1976, which received the Royal Assent whilst this volume was about to go to press. The effect of the 1976 Act, as explained by Circular 4/76 (Wales, 58/76), is that it substitutes the Friday before the last Monday in May for the end of the summer term as the summer school leaving date in England and Wales. This means that pupils with sixteenth birthdays between 1st February and 31st August (inclusive) will from the summer of 1976 onwards be free to leave school at the May leaving date if they wish to do so. There is no change in the Easter leaving date. The Act applies equally to special school pupils.

The new summer term leaving date does not affect the structure of the school year, and it does not advance the end of the summer term. Those who are eligible to leave school at the new earlier summer leaving date may decide to continue to attend voluntarily, either because they wish to complete public examinations or because they intend to return to full-time education in the following September. Local education authorities still have a clear duty to make suitable provision for senior pupils who wish to continue in full-time education.]

ADDENDUM

October 10, 1969

Circular 4/62, *Addendum No.* 1

SCHOOL LEAVING DATES

The Family Law Reform Act 1969

1. The Family Law Reform Act 1969 received the Royal Assent on 25th July, 1969. On 7th August, in exercise of powers conferred on him by Section 28 (3) of the Act, the Lord Chancellor made an Order bringing into force on 1st January, 1970, among other provisions in the Act, Section 9 which provides that the time at which a person attains a particular age expressed in years shall be the commencement of the relevant anniversary of the date of his birth.

2. Local education authorities will recognise that this provision renders obsolete the legal ruling in the High Court case *In re Shurey* according to which a child attained a given age at the beginning of the day preceding his birthday. In paragraph 20 of Circular 4/62 of 18th April, 1962, authorities were reminded of this rule and of its relevance to the application of Section 9 of the Education Act 1962 which relates to school leaving dates.

3. The immediate effect of the new law on the application of Section 9 of the Education Act 1962 will be that children whose fifteenth birthday will fall on 1st February, 1970, will not be able to leave school until the end of the summer term 1970 and children whose fifteenth birthday will fall on 1st September, 1970, will not be able to leave school until the end of the spring term 1971. Children whose fifteenth birthday (or sixteenth birthday when the school leaving age is raised) falls on 1st February or 1st September in subsequent years will similarly be required to remain at school until the end of the subsequent summer or spring term, as the case may be.

4. It was also suggested in paragraph 20 of Circular 4/62 that authorities would need to follow the ruling in the case " In re Shurey " in transferring children from primary to secondary schools. Authorities will now no doubt wish to review their transfer arrangements in the light of the new law.

5. Paragraph 20 of Circular 4/62 is cancelled.

CIRCULAR 1/64

February 28, 1964

INDUSTRIALISED BUILDING AND EDUCATIONAL BUILDING CONSORTIA

1. In the White Paper " A National Building Agency " (Cmnd. 2228) attention was called to the importance of increasing rapidly the use of industrialised methods of building. In particular, paragraph 5 refers to the intention

to expand and develop the building consortia which have been established with the encouragement of the Ministry of Education (a).

2. The value of school and college projects to be started in 1965/66 and the years immediately afterwards will be about a third greater than in 1963/64. This increased effort will come at a time when the demand for new buildings of all kinds will be rising considerably. Within the building industry heavy demands will be made on trained manpower, both architectural staff and building labour, especially craftsmen. Long term forecasts suggest that these conditions will persist: the volume of demand for building is expected to rise by over 50 per cent. in the next ten years and the building labour force to expand only slightly.

3. These are the circumstances in which the Government are encouraging the wider use of industralised methods of building. One object is to secure that through the combination of skilful use of building systems and the bulk ordering of components authorities should be able to achieve worth-while economies in building costs and better value for money. It is no less important, however, to bring about a reudction both in the demand for site labour and particularly for building craftsmen, and in the time needed for planning and erection on site. For example, the use of one of the consortium systems has resulted on average in a saving of about one-quarter in site labour compared with traditional building and it is hoped to improve considerably on this as a result of current development work. Erection time may be up to 40 per cent. shorter.

4. There are now five groups of local education authorities in England and Wales concerned mainly with educational building but also with other types of public building. While there are variations in their organisation and aims, all have the common purpose of co-ordinating effort and pooling resources of skilled manpower in the interests of all the authorities in membership. There are also arrangements for associating authorities or managers or governors of voluntary schools with the consortia, often through the agency of this Ministry, with a view to allowing the benefits to be shared for a limited number of projects or even for a single one. Notes on the membership and constitution of the different groups concerned with educational building, their purposes and proposals for future development, are attached.

5. The Ministry is also compiling systematic information about proprietary systems of industrialised building commonly used for educational projects. It is intended to make this information available to authorities as well as the knowledge and experience gained by the Ministry's development group in using and, in some cases, assisting with the development of these systems.

6. The Minister recognises that local education authorities will wish to decide for themselves upon the methods to be adopted for building the increased number of projects in the years ahead but he believes that unless industrialised methods are used to a much greater extent than in the past building programmes will become seriously delayed. With the prospect of a continuing high level of work combined with longer notice of programmes, the situation is particularly favourable for industrialised building and especially for further development of the local authority consortia. The Minister hopes that those authorities which are not already members of a group will consider whether it would be to their advantage to join. Where an authority does not join such a group, owing perhaps to their having only a small programme, they may wish to consider using a proprietary system of industrialised building or using a consortium system through the agency of the Ministry or of another consortium member (see paragraph 4 above). These alternatives appear to offer ample opportunities for using industrialised methods of construction for schools and colleges. Whether the new arrangements set out in the White Paper are also required for school or college building will be considered later in the light of the use made of these existing alternatives.

7. The Minister hopes that promoters or managers and governors of voluntary aided and special agreement schools will also use industrialised methods of building for their projects. Consortium systems can usually be made available either through the agency of the Ministry or of another consortium member

---

(a) Now Department of Education and Science. See the General Note to this Part, p. 447, *ante*.

in whose area the school is situated and proprietary systems are also available. Promoters or managers and governors who have projects in building programmes are advised in the first instance to consult the appropriate Church authorities with whom discussions have been held.

8. The Ministry's Architects and Building Branch will be glad to discuss informally the possibilities with any local education authorities or with the Church authorities. Arrangements are being made to enable advice to be given on all aspects of greater productivity in educational building. In particular, a building productivity group is being established to give technical assistance with new and developing constructional systems as the need arises, and to work on such questions as dimensional co-ordination, the interchange of components between different systems and other productivity problems concerned both with industrialised and traditional building in the educational field. The experience and knowledge gained by this group will be at the disposal of authorities. Direct approaches may, of course, be made to the consortia through their officers whose names are given in the attached notes.

[*Detailed notes on Educational Building Consortia are printed as an appendix to this Circular. Various systems are described and such matters as arrangements for tendering, qualifications for membership, etc., are dealt with.*]

CIRCULAR 11/64

August 27, 1964

NOTE

This Circular, which was issued jointly by the Ministry of Housing and Local Government and the Department of Education and Science, outlines the measures which the Government is taking to encourage the further development of sport and to suggest ways in which local authorities, in co-operation with voluntary bodies and other interests, may be able to improve and extend facilities in their areas for children and young people and for the community at large.

Paragraphs 9 and 10 of the Circular, which deal with the dual use of facilities at educational establishments, are printed below.

PROVISION FOR FACILITIES FOR SPORT

* * * * *

Dual use of facilities at educational establishments

9. In assessing local needs and the resources to match them, it is appropriate to consider how far facilities for sport and physical education already provided, or in course of provision, at schools and other educational establishments can be shared with other users, or can be economically expanded to meet the needs. The provision of playing fields is normally related closely to the needs of the establishments themselves, but with good construction and maintenance some additional use even of grass pitches may be possible without undue wear; and hard-paved or porous areas (tennis courts, running tracks, hard pitches and jumping pits) and indoor facilities can often support use beyond the needs of the establishments themselves. Where facilities are made available for outside use, the need for supervision must be borne in mind. The Department of Education and Science will shortly be issuing a revised edition of Building Bulletin No. 10 ("School playing fields and hard-paved areas") which will contain advice on the dual use of playing field facilities.

10. In planning new, or replanning existing, sports provision for educational establishments, the needs of the community generally, as well as of pupils and students for both outdoor and indoor sports facilities should be borne in mind. Better value for money, and a wider range, may sometimes be obtained if combined provision can be made in an integrated scheme. Consultation and co-operation between the local education authority or other body responsible for the facilities, any other local authority concerned and, in appropriate cases, voluntary organisations will clearly be essential. The Departments will ensure that no unnecessary administrative difficulties are put in the way of a combined scheme.

* * * * *

RULES 16

(*Revised December,* 1965)

RECOGNITION OF SCHOOLS, ETC., AS EFFICIENT

NOTE

Rules 16 were further revised in December 1965. It was decided in November 1967 to apply the standards required for recognition as efficient to all boarding schools included in the register of independent schools, and such schools were so informed by the Secretary of State in 1968.

1. Recognition as efficient is a special mark of the Secretary of State's approval and is given to:—

(*a*) Schools and

(*b*) Establishments of Further Education which apply for it and fulfil the conditions indicated below.

2. In order to be eligible for recognition as efficient

(*a*) a *school* must provide a progressive general education suitable at all stages for pupils of an age-range of normally not less than three years between the ages of two and nineteen, and

(*b*) *an establishment of further education* must provide courses which are educationally sound, are suitable to the needs of students over the statutory school leaving age and have a content appropriate to their stated objectives.

3. A school or establishment of further education must comply with any requirements of the Education Acts 1944 to 1965, and the Regulations made under them.

4. A school or establishment of further education must be kept on a level of efficiency which is satisfactory, regard being had to the purposes for which it is conducted and to the level of efficiency which would be required in the case of any similar school or establishment aided by grant.

5. The instruction must be efficient and suitable and must be adequate in scope and character for the whole age-range of pupils.

6. The number of pupils must be sufficient for economical and effective organisation.

7. (i) The teaching staff must be suitable and sufficient in number and qualifications for providing adequate instruction at each stage of the course.

(ii) No person shall be employed as a teacher who the Secretary of State decides, or the Minister or the Board of Education previously decided, is unsuitable either on medical grounds or on grounds of misconduct or grave professional default. If it has been decided that a teacher is suitable for employment to a limited extent only, he shall be employed only to that extent.

(iii) If a teacher's engagement is terminated, whether by dismissal or resignation, on account of misconduct, grave professional default or conviction of a criminal offence, the facts must be reported forthwith to the Secretary of State.

(iv) Before a decision is made as to the unsuitability of a teacher he will be informed of the charges against him and will have an opportunity for explanation or making representations on the subject.

8. The premises must be adequate, suitable and properly equipped having regard to the number, ages and sex of the pupils. They must be kept in a proper state of repair, cleanliness and hygiene and adequate arrangements must be made for the health and safety of the pupils and staff in case of danger from fire and other causes.

9. No instruction shall be given involving the use of:

(i) radioactive material other than elemental potassium, thorium or uranium, or such compounds of them as are normally used as chemical reagents, or

(ii) apparatus in which electrons are accelerated by a potential difference of five kilovolts or greater, other than apparatus used only for the purpose of receiving visual images by way of television and sounds connected therewith until the Secretary of State has given his approval (except that further education establishments using quantities small enough to bring them within the exemption provisions of the Code need not seek his approval). He may withdraw his approval if at any time he is of opinion that the arrangements made for the health and safety of the pupils and staff are inadequate.

10. Such Registers and records must be kept and such information and returns must be furnished from time to time as the Secretary of State may require.

11. Failure to comply with the above conditions may lead to recognition being withheld or withdrawn.

12. The Secretary of State will notify the Local Education Authority and, where appropriate, the Divisional Executive, of the granting of recognition and also of the withdrawal of any such recognition.

CIRCULAR 6/70

April 8, 1970

THE EDUCATION ACT 1968

INTRODUCTION

1. This Circular deals with a number of questions of procedure which arise on Section 13 of the Education Act 1944 as amended. (Section 13 is reprinted with amendments as A of Schedule 3 to the Education Act 1968). It deals also with questions arising on determinations under Section 67 (4) of the Education Act 1944 as substituted by Paragraph 3 of Schedule 1 to the Education Act 1968. In this respect the Circular fulfils the undertaking given in paragraph 6 of Circular 12/68 [see p. 567, *ante*].

GENERAL PROCEDURE AFFECTING ALL SECTION 13 PROPOSALS

2. Local education authorities, governors and managers of voluntary schools and other persons making proposals under Section 13 of the Education Act 1944, as amended, are reminded that proposals must be submitted to the Secretary of State by the body specified in the Act before public notice of them is given under Section 13 (3). The Secretary of State's consent to the publication of notices is not required: publication must follow forthwith and as of course on the submission of proposals. The submission of a proposal cannot take the form of the supplying of a copy of notices as published, though it may, if this is convenient, take the form of the supplying of a copy of notices as prepared for publication. Authorities or promoters need not resubmit proposals for new schools or significant enlargements of existing schools which have been authorised in precise terms in the major building programme (preliminary list, design list or starts programme) subject to the outcome of notices.

3. All proposals and notices should be worded in the terms used in the Education Acts. This is particularly important for proposals since the Secretary of State's decision will be formulated in these terms and there must be no room for doubt as to what was intended by the proposer.

4. The formulation of proposals in terms of Section 13 for purposes of notices may in some cases, especially those which relate to a scheme of secondary reorganisation and/or involve the amalgamation of two or more schools (see paragraph 5 below), give an insufficient account to the public of what is intended to happen. One of the main purposes of the procedure of public notice is to give all those affected an understanding of what is afoot and a chance to object. Authorities and others concerned are asked to supplement the text of any notice whose full implications may not be readily apparent with an explanatory statement in untechnical language. An explanatory statement may properly describe what it is intended shall happen to schools other than those to which the particular

proposals relates or it may give a cross reference to another concurrent proposal. All Section 13 proposals and notices other than those for closures should give the numbers and sex of pupils and age range of new or significantly changed schools. For proposals which are to be implemented in stages over a period not exceeding five years the full intention should be made clear from the outset: the notice should relate to the final stage, the immediate stage or stages being dealt with in each case in an explanatory note. If the period will exceed five years a proposal should be submitted, and notices published, for each stage which constitutes a significant change or enlargement.

" AMALGAMATIONS " OF SCHOOLS

5. There is no statutory process of amalgamation as such and Section 13 proposals cannot be expressed in this term, though it may of course be used in the explanatory statement referred to in paragraph 4 above. Where it is proposed that one school should function in place of two or more there is a choice of procedures:

(*a*) both or all existing schools may be discontinued and a new school established in the premises of the old: or

(*b*) one school may be enlarged while the other (or others) is discontinued, and its premises used for purposes of enlargement.

Authorities and other bodies should use whichever procedure seems to them appropriate in the particular case.

DETERMINATIONS UNDER SECTION 67 (4) OF THE EDUCATION ACT 1944

6. Section 67 (4) of the Education Act 1944 as substituted by paragraph 3 of Schedule 1 to the Education Act 1968 is in the following terms:—

> " If in the case of a county or voluntary school a question arises whether a change in the character of the school or enlargement of the school premises would be a significant change or enlargement, that question shall be determined by the Secretary of State "

The paragraphs which follow are intended to give as full an indication as possible of the lines on which the Secretary of State will reach decisions under Section 67 (4).

SIGNIFICANT CHANGES IN CHARACTER

7. Section 13 (10) as added by Section 1 (2) of the 1968 Act specifies three changes in character. These are dealt with in turn in the following paragraphs.

CHANGES IN AGE RANGE:—EDUCATION BEGINNING OR CEASING TO BE PROVIDED FOR PUPILS ABOVE OR BELOW A PARTICULAR AGE

8. The extension or reduction of the age range of a school by a full year or more at either end will normally be regarded as significant (but see paragraph 9 below). Examples of significant changes are:—

(i) the conversion of primary or secondary schools into middle schools;

(ii) changes in the age range of primary schools (not internal changes between departments), e.g., from 5–11 to 5–7, 5–8, 5–9 or 7–11;

(iii) changes in the age range of secondary schools, e.g., from 11–16 to 11–13 or 13–18, from 11–18 to 12–18 or 13–18;

(iv) the conversion of a secondary school into a sixth form college and any consequential reduction in the age ranges of other schools.

9. The following are examples of changes which will not be regarded as significant:

(i) the provision of extended courses for pupils staying on voluntarily beyond the compulsory age in schools which did not previously cater for such pupils;

(ii) in the case of a primary school, the admission of pupils below the age of five years where this has not been the previous practice;

(iii) the exceptional admission or retention of individual pupils or small groups of pupils outside the normal age range of a school;

(iv) changes in the age range of any secondary school which are attributable solely to the raising of the school leaving age.

CHANGES IN THE SEX COMPOSITION OF SCHOOLS

10. All changes from single sex to mixed or *vice versa* are significant changes in character. It is not, however, intended to bring within the scope of Section 13 incidental arrangements for co-operation between single sex schools in order to widen the range of educational opportunity or to economise in staffing. These arrangements are likely generally to be on a comparatively minor scale. It is possible, however, that in particular cases they will be on a larger scale amounting to a significant change. Any case of doubt should be submitted to the Secretary of State for his determination.

CHANGES RESULTING FROM THE MAKING OR ALTERATION OF ARRANGEMENTS FOR THE ADMISSION OF PUPILS BY REFERENCE TO ABILITY OR APTITUDE

11. The great majority of changes in this category will result from or be associated with the introduction of a non-selective or partially non-selective pattern of secondary education. Changes may be made in the most obvious way, for example the elimination of any 11+ tests and the admission of all pupils at 11 to a secondary school or schools catering for all abilities and aptitudes. Or they may be made in other ways, for example the conversion of one school or schools from secondary modern with age range eleven to fifteen to a junior secondary comprehensive with age range eleven to fourteen and the complementary conversion of a grammar school into comprehensive school with age range fourteen to eighteen. All changes of this kind will be treated as significant.

OTHER CHANGES OF CHARACTER

12. The publication of the Report of the Central Advisory Council for Education (Wales) on Primary Education has drawn attention to the possibility of a change being made in the linguistic character of a maintained school in Wales. Such a change will be treated as significant. It is unlikely that there will be any other changes in the function of a school outside the three categories specified in Section 13 (10) of the 1944 Act.

SIGNIFICANT ENLARGEMENTS

13. The criteria for determining whether a proposed modification to existing school premises will involve a substantial change in the size of the school, i.e., will substantially increase the numbers of pupils for whom accommodation can be provided, cannot be reduced to a simple set of rules generally applicable. Among other reasons, a proposal to enlarge a school may accompany a proposal to change its character, e.g., by changing the age range, so that a straightforward comparison between existing and proposed accommodation is inappropriate; and account must be taken of a series of modifications over a period, none of which is substantial in isolation but whose cumulative effect is to produce a substantial increase in size. In these circumstances the Secretary of State has concluded that it is not practicable to do more than indicate in fairly general terms the types of enlargement which will not be treated as significant. These are set out in paragraph 14.

ENLARGEMENTS WHICH WILL PRIMA FACIE NOT BE SIGNIFICANT

14. (i) The modification of either:—

(*a*) a school in wholly postwar buildings which has not undergone any previous enlargement (other than with Section 13 approval), or

(*b*) a school in buildings, whether wholly or partly pre-war, which have been remodelled so as to bring them up to the prescribed standards,

to an extent which will increase the numbers of pupils who can be accommodated by up to 25 per cent. or full 2 form entry, whichever is the less, the pupils remaining of the same age range. For schools with accommodation for up to 200 pupils the extent of the increase can be 50 per cent. or 50 places, whichever is the less. The existing and proposed capacity of the school should be assessed by reference to the Standards for School Premises.

(ii) Any enlargement which is intended to last for a short and predetermined period by means of additional accommodation of either permanent or temporary construction. Such an enlargement would be to meet a situation where a school needs to cater for increased numbers for a short time, for example pending the completion of another school or a proposed but not yet implemented reduction to the age range of the school in question. The time limit should normally be three years.

(iii) An enlargement of a secondary school attributable solely to the effects of the raising of the school leaving age at that school.

(iv) Any enlargements attributable solely to the need to provide accommodation for pupils staying on voluntarily for courses beyond the compulsory upper age.

15. In cases not covered by the preceding paragraph (and in such cases if the Secretary of State is asked to make a determination) the Secretary of State will make formal determinations on the basis of the facts of each individual proposal and with the object of securing results which are not significantly different from those obtained previously. Authorities and governors and managers are asked to furnish information for each proposal to cover the following points as appropriate:—

(*a*) present numbers of pupils and proposed future numbers;
(*b*) area of present teaching accommodation, including the size of each teaching space, and date (approximate) of building if it is not postwar or remodelled up to prescribed standards;
(*c*) size, i.e., pupil numbers and teaching accommodation in square feet, of any enlargements made in the last five years without action under Section 13;
(*d*) present age range and proposed age range if any change is proposed.

16. If in any case the Authority or the governors or managers of a voluntary aided or special agreement school are satisfied that a proposed enlargement *is* significant and no question as to their decision is raised with the Secretary of State they should proceed under Section 13 accordingly. For voluntary controlled schools, however, there must be a prior reference to the Secretary of State under Section 1 (1) of the Education Act 1946, as amended.

CIRCULAR 11/70

July 30, 1970

AWARDS FOR POSTGRADUATE STUDY

* * * * *

Introduction

1. This circular supersedes Circular 14/66 and describes the respective responsibilities of central government departments, the research councils and local education authorities for postgraduate awards.

GENERAL

2. Awards are available from public funds to selected students wishing to undertake postgraduate courses. Following revised arrangements announced in 1969,* responsibility for these awards now rests solely with the central government except for those courses normally taken at the postgraduate stage which fall outside the scope of the categories listed in the Appendix to this Circular.

3. Some central government award-making bodies have policies which limit their awards to selected courses within their general areas of responsibility. In the case of courses not selected for support, awards will not be made by other central government award making bodies.

4. For most courses and subject areas there is only one source of student support. Occasionally, however, more than one central government body may wish to make awards to students attending the same course, or courses in the same subject area, and in these cases responsibility for individual awards will normally be determined by the subject of the applicant's first degree.

5. All postgraduate awards are made on a competitive basis or, in the case of local education authority awards (see paragraph 13 below), are at the discretion of the authority. Acceptance for a postgraduate course does not of itself qualify a student for an award.

AWARDS IN THE HUMANITIES

6. (*a*) The Department of Education and Science offers studentships on a competitive basis to students resident in England and Wales taking courses leading to a higher or further degree in the Humanities. Details of the scheme of awards are given in the booklet " Grants to Students 4 " obtainable from the Department of Education and Science, Elizabeth House, York Road, London, S.E.1.

(*b*) The Department also offers bursaries to institutions on a quota basis for students resident in England and Wales taking certain postgraduate courses, leading to a diploma or certificate and mainly of one year's duration. Details of the bursary scheme are given in the booklet " Grants to Students 3 " obtainable from the Department. A list of the courses covered by the scheme, the majority of which are in the Humanities, is also available from the Department.

(*c*) Residents of Scotland or Northern Ireland should apply for postgraduate awards in the Humanities to the Scottish Education Department, 2 South Charlotte Street, Edinburgh 2, or the Ministry of Education, Dundonald House, Upper Newtownards Road, Belfast 4, respectively.

AWARDS IN SCIENCE AND TECHNOLOGY

7. (*a*) The Science Research Council makes postgraduate awards in its field to enable promising young students, normally resident in Great Britain, to continue their training beyond a first degree.

---

* Awards for postgraduate courses: circular letter UF/45/01 dated 20th February, 1969, to local education authorities, U.K. universities, major establishments for further education and research councils.

It also makes higher awards to those who have already had postgraduate training. Awards are made for research or other postgraduate training in science and technology EXCLUDING the fields of:—

(i) agriculture (including horticulture), agricultural economics, agricultural engineering, and the more applied aspects of agricultural science;

(ii) the natural environment sciences, which may be defined broadly as geology and geophysics (including seismology and geomagnetism), meteorology, hydrology, oceanography, marine and fresh-water biology, and terrestrial ecology;

(iii) medicine;

(iv) social science,

but INCLUDING those aspects of psychology which are closely related to fundamental biology and to the engineering and biological aspects of ergonomics and cybernetics.

The S.R.C. will also consider applications, on behalf of eligible science and technology candidates, for awards in certain courses of business and industrial administration or management.

(*b*) Types of award are as follows:—

(i) Research Studentships provide for the maintenance of students while they are being trained in the methods of research.

(ii) Advanced Course Studentships provide for the maintenance of students taking suitable postgraduate courses of instruction.

(iii) The Award Scheme for Science, Industry and School Teaching (" Assist " awards) is intended to encourage new science or engineering graduates to gain experience in industry or teaching by providing a guarantee of support for subsequent postgraduate studies. The offer of an award is made on graduation; it can be taken up after one to five years in industry or in teaching in school or technical college. This scheme is not intended for students who have already established links with an industrial organisation since adequate provision is made for such students under the " Instant " awards scheme.

(iv) " Instant " Awards provide for an early decision on applications from those who, having had at least one year's acceptable postgraduate experience in industry, wish to return to university with a research studentship or an advanced course studentship.

(v) Industrial Studentships are Research or Advanced Course Studentships awarded under any S.R.C. scheme which have been supplemented in value by an industrial employer in agreement with the S.R.C. This scheme is intended to help eligible candidates with industrial experience to obtain postgraduate training without undue financial hardship.

Co-operative Awards in Pure Science are intended to encourage the development of collaboration between universities and industry and in particular to provide an opportunity for graduates working in pure science departments to undertake research of direct interest to industry.

(vii) Studentships for experimental schemes of postgraduate training are awarded by the S.R.C. as a means of encouraging experiments in providing a broad-based training fitted to the requirements of industry on the lines suggested in the Swann Report.* The Council, in conjunction with the Social Science Research Council, has set up a Joint Committee to deal with postgraduate training matters in cross-discipline areas of interest to the two Councils, and is making a number of studentships available to enable graduates to undertake such broader forms of training.

---

* The Flow into Employment of Scientists, Engineers and Technologists: Cmnd. 3760.

(viii) Industrial Fellowships are designed for those who have had valuable experience in industry and are rather older than other candidates. The awards are to enable industrial scientists and technologists resident in the United Kingdom to obtain further training in the methods of research or on suitable courses of instruction, generally at a postgraduate rather than postdoctoral level.

(ix) Research Fellowships are for promising young research workers resident in the United Kingdom who have completed the normal courses of postgraduate research training, have shown a special aptitude for original and independent research and are likely to benefit substantially from an opportunity to develop this aptitude further.

(*c*) Further details of these studentships and conditions of eligibility are contained in " S.R.C. Studentships and Fellowships " published annually, and obtainable from the Science Research Council, State House, High Holborn, W.C.1.

AWARDS IN THE SOCIAL SCIENCES

8. (*a*) The Social Science Research Council makes studentship awards to enable young graduates resident in Great Britain to spend a period on full-time postgraduate training. Training includes taught courses and research for a higher degree. There is also a limited number of fellowships for candidates resident in the United Kingdom who have already done postgraduate research training or are graduates who have worked in a professional capacity.

Awards are made in the following fields: area studies (where the major or majority of options are in the social science field), economic and social history, economic and social statistics (including demography), economics, education, human geography, management and industrial relations (including accountancy), planning, political science (including international relations), psychology, social anthropology (including ethnology related to social anthropology), sociology and social administration (including criminology).

Information is available in the Council's handbook " Postgraduate Training in the Social Sciences " which is published annually in January, and is obtainable from the Social Science Research Council, State House, High Holborn, W.C.1.

(*b*) The Social Science Research Council also makes awards under its Bursary Scheme to students resident in England and Wales for full-time postgraduate courses of a vocational rather than academic nature, leading to a diploma, mainly in the fields of planning and management. A booklet " S.S.R.C. Bursary Scheme " is published annually, and is obtainable from the Social Science Research Council.

AWARDS IN THE ENVIRONMENTAL SCIENCES

9. (*a*) The Natural Environment Research Council makes postgraduate awards to enable promising young scientists resident in Great Britain to continue their training beyond a first degree. It also makes higher awards to those who have had postgraduate research training.

Awards are made for research or other postgraduate training in five main fields, as follows:—

(i) The solid earth, its physical properties and mineral resources (geology, geophysics, geochemistry, and physiography).

(ii) The inland waters and their living resources (hydrology, freshwater biology, ecology and fisheries).

(iii) The terrestrial communities, their resources and amenities (ecology, forestry conservation and other scientific aspects of land use).

(iv) The seas and oceans, their behaviour and their living and mineral resources (oceanography, marine biology and ecology, and fisheries).

(v) The atmosphere (some aspects of meteorology).

(*b*) Types of award are as follows:—

(i) Research Studentships provide for the maintenance of students while they are being trained in the methods of research.

(ii) Advanced Course Studentships provide for the maintenance of students taking suitable postgraduate courses of instruction.

(iii) Industrial Fellowships are designed for men and women who have had valuable experience in industry and are rather older than other candidates. The awards are to enable industrial scientists to obtain further training either in the methods of research or on suitable courses of instruction, generally at a postgraduate rather than postdoctoral level.

(iv) Research Fellowships are for promising young research workers who have completed the normal course of postgraduate research training, have shown a special aptitude for original and independent research and appear likely to benefit substantially from an opportunity to develop this aptitude further.

(*c*) Detailed information is available in " N.E.R.C., Studentships and Fellowships " published annually, and obtainable from the Natural Environment Research Council, Alhambra House, 27–33 Charing Cross Road, W.C.2.

(*d*) N.E.R.C. Research Establishments.

There are opportunities for postgraduate training at the Council's Research Establishments, details of which are available from N.E.R.C.

AWARDS IN AGRICULTURE

10. (*a*) A limited number of postgraduate awards in agricultural subjects is made by the Ministry of Agriculture, Fisheries and Food to candidates resident in England and Wales either for advanced courses of instruction at postgraduate level or for training in research techniques, normally leading to a higher degree of a university. Minimum degree standards are required of applicants, the level of which depends on the course of study to be undertaken. Details of these awards are available from Ministry of Agriculture, Fisheries and Food, Room 277, Great Westminster House, Horseferry Road, London, S.W.1.

(*b*) A small number of training grants are available from the Agricultural Research Council to graduates in veterinary science.

(*c*) Residents of Scotland or Northern Ireland should apply for postgraduate awards in Agriculture to the Department of Agriculture and Fisheries, St. Andrews House, Edinburgh, or the Ministry of Agriculture for Northern Ireland, Dundonald House, Upper Newtownards Road, Belfast 4, respectively.

AWARDS IN MEDICINE AND DENTISTRY

11. (*a*) The Medical Research Council offers awards to medical, dental and science graduates of special promise resident in the United Kingdom who wish to prepare themselves for future medical research in the United Kingdom. The Council also entertains applications for awards to enable suitable candidates who intend to make their future careers in research to receive approved postgraduate instruction—as distinct from training in research methods—in a subject ancillary to their main research interest in the field of the medical or biological sciences. For example, the Council would be prepared to assist a medical graduate who wished to take a course in radiation biology and radiation physics or in engineering as applied to medicine, or a science graduate who

had a first degree in physiology and wished to take a postgraduate course in biochemistry; support may also be given in relation to certain postgraduate courses which are not specifically intended as an introduction to research.

(*b*) The Council are unable to support candidates who wish to take higher professional qualifications such as the F.R.C.S., M.R.C.P., M.R.C.O.G., F.D.S. or Diploma in Orthodontics. Postgraduate preparation for a career in a chosen field of medicine is often best carried out by hospital in-service training, augmented in appropriate cases by periods of formal training in subjects which cannot be covered in other ways. Through the provision of paid posts providing suitable training and through its study leave arrangements—which have recently been improved—the N.H.S. hospital service can provide both these aspects of preparation.

(*c*) Further information is contained in " Fellowships and Scholarships awarded by the Medical Research Council ", which is published by the M.R.C. and is obtainable from them at 20 Park Crescent, Regents Park, W.1.

AWARDS IN SOCIAL WORK AND RELATED SUBJECTS

12. Generally the responsible bodies are the Department of Health and Social Security and the Home Office who will consider assistance to students undertaking courses leading to either a basic or a professional postgraduate qualification. The Department of Health and Social Security offers awards, normally to students resident in England and Wales, in respect of courses taken in preparation for employment in one of the statutory health and welfare services or in related voluntary services: similar awards are made by the Home Office to students resident in the United Kingdom intending to work in the child care or probation services. A small number of bursaries are available from the Department of Education and Science for students resident in England and Wales following courses leading to a basic postgraduate qualification who do not come within the field of either the Department of Health and Social Security or the Home Office. Residents of Scotland or Northern Ireland should apply for information about postgraduate awards in Social Work to the Scottish Education Department, 2 South Charlotte Street, Edinburgh 2, or the Ministry of Education, Dundonald House, Upper Newtownards Road, Belfast 4, respectively.

LOCAL EDUCATION AUTHORITY AWARDS

13. (*a*) Local education authorities should not make awards to students following courses described in the Appendix to this Circular but the Secretary of State hopes that they will continue to consider sympathetically applications from students taking courses for which awards remain at their discretion, such as part-time courses leading to higher degrees and other postgraduate qualifications (see paragraph 2 (*a*), (*b*) and (*c*) of the Appendix) for which awards are not available from central government award-making bodies.

(*b*) Any awards made to students undertaking a second first degree course will fall under Section 1 (4) of the Education Act 1962. In such cases it will be necessary under the provisons of the University and Other Awards Regulations to apply undergraduate rates of grants and conditions. Most new awards will be made under Section 2 of the Act, but the Secretary of State takes the view that the same rates would normally be appropriate.

APPENDIX TO CIRCULAR 11/70

Courses for which Central Government Departments and Research Councils consider applications for Awards

1. All courses leading to higher degrees.

2. All courses where a degree is a necessary entry requirement, except:—

(*a*) courses for performers in music, drama and related subjects;
(*b*) courses leading to ordination as a Minister of religion;
(*c*) secretarial courses designed for graduates. Examples:—

Diploma, Millbank College of Commerce, Liverpool
R.S.A., Hatfield College of Technology
Diploma, University of Strathclyde

3. All courses at the Royal College of Art leading to the award of a Master's degree (M.A. (R.C.A.) or M.Design (R.C.A.) or Diploma of the College (Dip.R.C.A.)).

4. All art courses for which the entrance requirement is a Dip.A.D. or equivalent qualification and specifically a post Dip.A.D. course approved by the N.C.D.A.D.

5. In cases where non-graduate and post graduate courses lead to the same qualification those courses, or stages of courses, reserved exclusively for, or specifically designed for, graduates. Example:—

A.L.A., Newcastle upon Tyne Polytechnic
1 year course for graduates
(2½ years for non-graduates)

6. Courses for which entry requirements include qualifications other than a degree, but which are postgraduate in content and where students are predominantly graduate or of equivalent status. Examples:—

Diploma in Drama, University of Manchester
Diploma in Management Studies.

CIRCULAR 12/70

July 30, 1970

THE EDUCATION OF YOUNG CHILDREN WITH DEFECTS OF BOTH SIGHT AND HEARING

1. Enquiries by the Department of Education and Science show that in England and Wales there are approximately 200 children born since 1st January, 1962, known to have serious impairment of both sight and hearing. A quarter of these children are deaf/blind: the rest have some degree of sight or hearing or both. Many of these children have other mental or physical handicaps, some of them serious. Any decisions made about their education are, therefore, inevitably complex and particular attention needs to be given to assessing the individual requirements of each child. There is, however, some general advice which can be given on methods of meeting the needs of these handicapped children in their early years.

2. The first essential is to detect children who have defects of sight and hearing at the earliest possible moment so that comprehensive help and guidance can be given to them and to their families in good time and during the first stages of the child's development. Once a child appears not to be developing normally there should be prompt referral for as comprehensive assessment as possible of his medical and educational needs and of the needs of his family for social work support. As stated in paragraph 4 of Circular 11/69 (" Special Education for children handicapped by Spina Bifida ") it is important that Medical Officers of Health/Principal School Medical Officers should establish lines of communication if these do not already exist to ensure that they are informed of all children in their area with handicapping conditions and of movements in and out of the area. This information should be made available to the officers of the local education authority, and of the local social services department.

3. Early comprehensive assessment of these children should be accompanied by the prompt provision of advice and support for the parents. This can best be given by someone with a personal knowledge of the child and his family. To provide this service, continuing visits to the home will be necessary. The most appropriate person to visit might be a peripatetic teacher of the deaf, a nursery teacher or assistant, a part-time or visiting teacher, or a social worker, but whoever undertakes the work it is essential that it should be carefully co-ordinated to ensure that consistent advice is given and that the family is not distressed by a superfluity of visitors. The advice given in Circular 9/66, " Co-ordination of Education, Health and Welfare Services for Handicapped Children and Young

People ", is relevant in this and other connections. Some special training is essential for staff concerned with children with defective vision and hearing, and opportunities should be made for them to visit at least one of the existing centres for such children: the Pathways Unit, Condover Hall School, Shrewsbury, or any other class or unit where work has been proceeding for a number of years and which should be regarded as a source of continued help and advice.

4. The development of children with handicaps of sight and hearing is much slower than that of other children. It may be a number of years before a firm decision can be reached as to the kind of special educational treatment most suitable to the child's needs and the extent to which he is capable of benefiting from it. His development will need, therefore, to be carefully followed and his needs and capacity kept under review at regular intervals from an early age. Persons experienced in education, medicine and other appropriate disciplines should take part in this continuing assessment. Authorities should be aware of the facilities available at the specialist assessment centre at the Royal National Institute for the Blind unit at Condover Hall, where these children live at the unit for a short time whilst being assessed.

5. The small numbers of these children, as compared with the total school population, their scattered distribution and the variety of different types of care they need, make arrangements for their education very difficult. The most effective placement in the early stages will depend not only on the extent and nature of the child's disabilities but also on the location of his home. In densely populated urban areas it may be possible to assemble a number of children to form a special nursery or infant class, perhaps with other handicapped children, and possibly in association with an existing special school. Experience with existing groups of this kind suggests that they should consist of not more than six children with defects of sight and hearing, each group being in the charge of a suitably qualified teacher assisted by two ancillary workers. In areas where there are only one or two of these children, consideration may be given to placing them, subject to satisfactory arrangements being made, individually in ordinary nursery schools or classes, special schools or units, or (where they are suffering in addition from mental handicap) in junior training centres, utilising suitable specialist help that is locally available such as speech therapists, peripatetic teachers of the deaf, teachers from schools for the deaf, for the blind or partially sighted, or teachers of the deaf/blind. Where an existing nursery school or class, or training centre admits one of these children, consideration should be given to the addition of one person to the staff who would accept particular responsibility for the care of the child and all staff should be informed about the problems involved. If none of these alternatives is available or considered suitable, specialist educational support should be provided wherever possible for the child at home. It should be appreciated, however, that there is a cumulative strain, physical as well as mental, on parents looking after these children at home and every effort should be made to organise relief for them.

6. It is hoped that a considerable number of these children will be able in this way to receive special educational treatment in day groups near their homes at least until the age of about seven and often older for more severely handicapped children. Thereafter day provision may continue to be suitable for some children particularly where this can be provided in close association with an existing special school. Residential facilities will often be required for others who will continue to receive special educational treatment appropriate to their needs in boarding special schools or in hostels attached to special schools. Others again, who are suffering in addition from mental handicap, may by this stage have been found to require placement in junior training centres or placement in residential care for the subnormal.

7. Authorities are asked to review the provision currently available in their areas to see if it is meeting the needs of children with serious impairments of both sight and hearing. Authorities with a sufficient number of such children to warrant the establishment of special classes or groups will no doubt have already done so or have formed plans for doing so. The Department will be glad to have information by 1st October, 1970, about such groups, or plans for their establishment, with details of site, numbers and age range of children and staffing ratios. Authorities with a small number of children are also asked to inform the Department by the same date how they make provision for them.

CIRCULAR 14/70

August 27, 1970

IN-SERVICE COURSES FOR TEACHERS: FINANCIAL AND ADMINISTRATIVE ARRANGEMENTS

1. Circular 19/69, which set out the arrangements under which serving teachers could take the Bachelor of Education degree, referred to a wider examination of the financial and administrative framework for in-service training which was then in hand. This circular sets out the decisions which have been taken to widen somewhat the scope of the present arrangements for pooling expenditure on in-servicing training. It deals with general policy only and the administrative arrangements will be set out in more detail in an administrative memorandum when the Rate Support Grants (Pooling Arrangements) Regulations have been amended.

Full-Time Advanced Courses

2. At present serving teachers in schools may only be seconded under the pooling arrangements to courses leading to the B.Ed., advanced diplomas and higher degrees in education and the one year and one term supplementary courses in the Department's annual programme. A number of teachers have however been taking courses leading to other first degrees and some universities have introduced courses leading to higher degrees which involve the advanced study of education and another academic subject. For some teachers, depending on their experience and duties, it appears that such courses may well be more appropriate forms of further professional education than the traditional courses leading to diplomas and higher degrees in education. It has therefore been decided that the scope of the pooling arrangements should be widened to include support given towards one year of full-time study for all first and higher degree courses and advanced diplomas of universities and the Council for National Academic Awards. The tuition fees of teachers seconded to such courses will be met from the Department's vote.

Other Full-Time Courses

3. The one year supplementary courses have now fulfilled their original purpose and it is expected that demand for them will continue to dwindle, but they will be retained so long as they attract sufficient numbers of applicants to be viable. The one term courses in the Department's programme have attracted a poor attendance but they also will continue where individual courses can attract viable numbers of teachers. The pooling arrangements will continue to apply to teachers seconded to these courses and to expenditure incurred by authorities in supporting the attendance of their teachers at other courses approved by the Secretary of State under the Regulations. The pooling arrangements will not apply to the great bulk of in-service courses, of relatively short duration, organised by local education authorities at their own initiative.

4. In order to alleviate any personal hardship in individual cases which may arise as the result of the decision to phase out the employment of unqualified teachers, it has been decided that instructors who are admitted to one year shortened courses of initial training may, if they have more than five years' service, be seconded under the pooling arrangements. Other persons who have had less than five years' service, or whose qualifications and experience do not merit admission to courses of less than two years' duration, will be eligible to attend such courses under the normal grant arrangements.

Part-Time Courses

5. In many areas it is more convenient that further professional training should be gained through attendance at part-time courses rather than full time secondment. In future, to facilitate this, the travelling expenses and tuition fees of teachers attending part-time courses leading to any of the qualifications listed above, will be chargeable to the teacher training pool provided that the charge is limited to a period equivalent to not more than one year's full-time course. In view of this it has been decided that it would be anomalous to continue the

restriction laid down in paragraph 8 of Circular 19/69 on part-time courses leading to the B.Ed. degree; while the Secretary of State hopes that all universities will be able to open such courses to all qualified teachers in due course, irrespective of the origin of their certificates, this will no longer be a condition of charging to the teacher training pool the costs of such courses and of assistance to teachers attending them.

Approval of Courses

6. Although the extension of the pooling arrangements to all first and higher degree courses will remove the necessity for an approved list of such courses to which pooling arrangements apply, approval will continue to be necessary for other full-time courses of further training held at universities, colleges of education or further education establishments if the costs of mounting them or of the expenses of teachers attending them are to be met from the teacher training pool. At present, there is a lower limit of six weeks on the duration of courses the cost of which may be poolable, but it has been decided that this limit should be lowered and that in principle, subject to prior approval, the costs of courses lasting four weeks or more full-time or the equivalent part-time may be charged to the teacher training pool. It would however be anomalous if the costs of courses shorter than four weeks in length were to be charged to the pool if they were provided in colleges of education, while the costs of providing similar courses elsewhere or at teachers' centres were met locally. Where therefore courses shorter than four weeks in length are held at colleges of education the college accounts should be reimbursed, through fees or otherwise, for any ascertainable additional costs attributable to them.

POOLING OF SALARIES

7. It has now been decided that the arrangements announced in paragraph 3 of Circular 19/69, under which 75 per cent. of the expenditure by authorities on the salaries, superannuation and national insurance of seconded teachers will be poolable, shall apply only to courses of further training. Such expenditure incurred in respect of courses of initial training will be 100 per cent. poolable. As stated in Circular 19/69, this new arrangement will be kept under review.

SUBSISTENCE ALLOWANCES

8. There is at present no uniform system of subsistence allowances for teachers attending in-service courses nor is the cost of such allowances chargeable to the teacher training pool. It has been agreed that these questions should be the subject of further consultation between the local authorities' associations and the Department.

NOTE

See also Administrative Memorandum 26/70, p. 490, *post*.

CIRCULAR 15/70

September 22, 1970

THE EDUCATION (HANDICAPPED CHILDREN) ACT, 1970

RESPONSIBILITY FOR THE EDUCATION OF MENTALLY HANDICAPPED CHILDREN

1. The Education (Handicapped Children) Act received the Royal Assent on 23rd July, 1970. It makes provision to bring within the educational system those children who have or would previously have been determined as being unsuitable for education at school. From a date appointed by the Secretary of State for Education and Science the power to exclude such children from education will cease, and local health authorities will cease to have power to provide

training for them. Decisions made before that day determining a child as being unsuitable for education at school will apply as if they had been decisions that the child requires special educational treatment. No child within the age limits for education, therefore, will be outside the scope of the educational system. The Secretary of State has announced her intention to make 1st April, 1971, the date from which this extension of educational responsibility will operate.

2. The purpose of this Circular is to provide local education authorities with information and guidance to assist their planning in the coming months and in particular to draw their attention to steps which need to be taken before the assumption of this new educational responsibility. Copies are being sent also by the Department of Health and Social Security to local health authorities, regional hospital boards and hospital management committees. The Welsh Office will distribute copies to local health and hospital authorities in Wales.

3. The new responsibility is the natural consequence of the considerable advances already made by health and hospital authorities in meeting the educational needs of mentally handicapped children. Future provision will undoubtedly have to be built on the foundation already laid in recent years, and the legislation provides for staff, buildings, and facilities already in existence to pass to local education authorities. The staff, with their experience in this important field, will be a welcome addition to the education service, and the needs of the new area of responsibility will take their place, both centrally and locally, in the programme of educational development. Progress will necessarily be gradual, not only because of the general pressure on educational resources, but because of the nature of this particular field; but the Secretary of State has no doubt that as time passes the change will lead to real advances in the standards of education which even the most afflicted children can reach. The new statutory responsibility of local education authorities for these children will permit a greater flexibility in adapting the education available to each child at different stages in his development and according to his individual needs. In the case of children who are, at least for the time being, incapable of response to any form of educational stimulus—and there will always be some of these—education authorities will be responsible for seeing that such children are kept under regular review and freshly assessed from time to time, so that it is possible to respond without delay to any development of a child's capacity to benefit from educational processes.

4. From the Appointed Day the procedure for determining a child as ineducable will cease to be used. Children who would hitherto have been considered for determination under Section 57 of the Education Act 1944 will in future come under the provisions which apply generally to those requiring special educational treatment and in particular Section 34 of that Act.

5. The responsibilities to be assumed by local education authorities in respect of mentally handicapped children are those laid upon them by the Education Acts in respect of all children and in particular those requiring special educational treatment. As in any case where a child needs medical or social work care, local education authorities will need to work in close co-operation with those authorities responsible for providing such care.

6. The Secretary of State is aware that many local education authorities have already undertaken preliminary planning and entered into discussions with the authorities at present responsible for these children. Local education authorities will no doubt give early consideration to a broader strategy for the education of mentally handicapped children within their total provision for children in need of special education. Before however any such strategic thinking can be very far developed, there is the immediate task of taking the necessary steps in co-operation with local health authorities and hospital authorities to ensure a smooth transfer on the date appointed. This is the main concern of this Circular and the following paragraphs set out the issues that need to be settled before the transfer takes place.

FUTURE STATUS OF EXISTING ESTABLISHMENTS

7. Mentally handicapped children are at present being taught and cared for in a variety of ways: in junior training centres (some of which form part of

all-age training centres); in special care units, the majority of which are attached to junior training centres; and in hospitals for the mentally handicapped, where many, though by no means all, are given teaching. These children, however, are not at present considered as attending schools in terms of the Education Acts. A few children are receiving teaching provided by the local health authority at home. In addition, some children are placed in privately run training centres, residential homes or registered mental nursing homes. Information about existing arrangements in the areas of individual local education authorities can be obtained from local health authorities, Hospital Management Committees, and Regional Hospital Boards.

8. Local education authorities are asked, in co-operation with the authorities now responsible, to establish which are the services in their own areas for which they are to assume responsibility. (Authorities are not asked in this Circular to take any action on services provided by privately run establishments). Details of each centre or unit, including those in hospitals, should be set out in the form indicated at Appendix A. This information should be forwarded to the Secretary of State not later than 30th November, 1970, to serve as a proposal from the authority, for the Secretary of State's approval under Section 9 (5) of the Education Act 1944, to set up a new maintained special school or schools, as the case may be. The Secretary of State's approval will take effect on the Appointed Day. Some comments on each of the main types of existing provision is set out in the paragraphs below.

Junior Training Centres

9. It will normally be appropriate for local education authorities to propose to the Secretary of State that she should approve the establishment of a centre as a separate special school. In some cases, where sufficiently close links already exist with an adjoining special school, it may be appropriate for the authority to propose that centre and school should be combined to form a new special school. Where a junior training centre is part of an all-age centre, it will be necessary for the local authority (in Inner London, the Inner London Education Authority and the local health authority) to make an administrative division between the provision made for juniors and adults so as to allow for the establishment within the premises of a recognisable special school.

Special Care Units

10. Where a special care unit is part of an existing junior training centre, it should be included as part of the authority's proposal for that centre. Where a unit operates independently, the authority may prefer, if attachment to a school is not practicable, to propose that it should continue to operate independently, on the lines of the special classes and units which already exist within the provision now made for special education.

Schools in Hospitals for the Mentally Handicapped

11. Arrangements for the teaching of children in hospitals for the mentally handicapped should be reviewed in the light of the guidance given in Circular 312 "The Education of Patients in Hospitals". Whether the local education authority will wish to propose the establishment of a hospital special school, or arrangements for teaching under the terms of Section 56 of the 1944 Education Act, will depend upon the circumstances in each hospital: in general, it seems likely that the conditions applying in specialist hospitals for the mentally handicapped will justify the establishment of schools. Local education authorities should bear in mind that their responsibilities as defined by the Education Acts extend to the education of all children in hospitals for the mentally handicapped, including those who at present are not receiving teaching; this may in some cases mean some redeployment or strengthening of teaching staff.

Hostels

12. Some local health authority hostels have been established to provide a permanent home for children who cannot be cared for by their parents. Others provide boarding accommodation in term-time for children who live too far from a training centre to attend daily. Either type may also provide short-term care.

In most cases, it would appear appropriate that the administration of hostels should remain with the local health authority—and so pass in due course to the proposed social services department of the authority. The local education authority would then be responsible for arranging that the children resident there can take up day places in a special school. In some cases, a hostel providing boarding accommodation may be so closely linked with a junior training centre that the local education authority may wish to propose that they should take over the hostel also and establish a residential special school: the Secretary of State will be prepared to consider such proposals on their merits.

CHILDREN AT HOME

13. Local education authorities should find out how many children of compulsory school age in the care of their local health authority are living at home and not attending day centres, and whether or not they are at present receiving home training. It will be the authority's duty after the appointed day to ensure that at all times when any such child is capable of benefiting from education he or she should receive home tuition, always providing that it cannot be arranged that the child should attend a special school, whether on a day or residential basis.

BUILDINGS

14. Existing buildings housing junior training centres will normally belong to the local authority, and the transfer, save in the Inner London area, will merely give rise to internal administrative adjustments to building administration procedure. Although some children of compulsory school age will have to continue to be taught in buildings which provide also for the adult mentally handicapped, the Secretary of State expects local authorities to make separate provision for school-age children and for adults as early as possible. As in the case of hospital special schools at present, school buildings in hospitals for the mentally handicapped will remain the property of the hospital authority and charges will be made to the local education authority on the principles set out in paragraph 13 of Circular 312.

15. Resources allocated for future capital investment in junior training centres by the Department of Health and Social Security will after the transfer be made available to local education authorities as an addition to the special school building programme. Early in each financial year, the Secretary of State for the Social Services* issues to local health authorities a list of local authority mental health projects, at present including junior training centre projects, for which he hopes to be able to recommend loan sanction in that and the following two financial years. Where a project for the area of any local education authority is included in the list current at the date of transfer, the Department of Education and Science will be prepared to approve a building start for the project provided that the start can be made in the year for which the project has been listed by the Secretary of State for the Social Services. As an interim measure, all projects listed and started in the year indicated will be treated as major projects.

16. Educational provision for mentally handicapped children will of course no longer be included in lists of mental health projects drawn up by the Secretary of State for the Social Services after the date of transfer. For projects which are not covered in the preceding paragraph, the procedures for control of future special school building programmes, as set out in Circular 17/69 " Special schools and school clinics—major building programmes ", will apply. Major building projects will be defined in the normal way.

17. Projects nearing final approval at the time of the transfer will be scrutinised by the Department's Architects and Building Branch against the standards of provision and cost limits laid down in Local Authority Building Note 4 issued by the Department of Health and Social Security. Local health authorities with junior training centre projects included in the current 3-year list have been asked to draw local education authorities into the planning of these projects. Architects and Building Branch, in co-operation with the Department of Health and Social Security, will be prepared to advise local education authorities who expect to be submitting such projects to the Department of Education

* In the case of Wales, the Secretary of State for Wales.

and Science for approval. Local education authorities may wish to modify projects for what are now junior training centres in accordance with their overall plan for the provision of special education facilities: they are free to do so, although they will want to bear in mind the risk of delay to a project. Prior to the date of transfer, modifications will have to be agreed by the local health authority.

18. Local education authorities will be asked later this year whether they expect to be able in 1971/72 to start projects included for that year in the current three-year list of new junior training centre provision. Projects included at the time of transfer in the three-year list for later years will be assimilated into special school design lists and starts programmes at the appropriate time.

TRANSFER OF STAFF

19. The Act protects the interests of the staff who will be transferred to the education service by providing that they shall enjoy terms and conditions of employment not less favourable than those enjoyed immediately before the transfer date. Consideration is being given to the way in which these provisions should be implemented in regulations and in other ways and to other effects of the transfer on staff. Further guidance will be issued as necessary. Prospects for advancement within the service cannot be covered by statute, but the Secretary of State looks to authorities, on each occasion when they are making arrangements to fill higher posts, to give full weight not only to the underlying purpose of the Act to integrate the education of mentally handicapped children, and accordingly the staffing pattern, into the general framework of the education service, but also to the need to ensure that full account is taken of the training and experience of the existing staffs and to their reasonable career expectations.

20. Those who transfer will include all staff whose primary function is teaching. Although in the case of junior training centres and special care units it will usually be appropriate for all other staff to transfer as well, it is open to authorities, in the case for instance of an all-age centre, to decide to retain some or all of the non-teaching staff in the employment of the health authority. In hospitals, supervisors and assistant supervisors and possibly others who are mainly engaged in the education of child patients will be employed by the local education authority; all other staff should continue to be employed by the hospital authority. In some hospitals it may be difficult to identify staff for transfer and the local education and hospital authorities will need jointly to give special consideration to borderline cases.

TRAINING OF TEACHERS

21. The training of teachers of mentally handicapped children will be integrated as soon as possible into the ordinary teacher training system, and will consist of three year courses in colleges of education leading to a certificate in education, and to qualified teacher status on appointment. The minimum entrance qualifications will normally be five G.C.E. Ordinary level passes or the equivalent. To aid a smooth transition, special one year conversion courses will be available in selected colleges of education for those who have obtained the Diploma of the Training Council for Teachers of the Mentally Handicapped and who also satisfy the entrance requirements mentioned above. In addition it is hoped that for a limited period both two year and one year courses leading to the Training Council Diploma will continue to be available for those for whom the three year course is not appropriate. The Department of Health and Social Security issued a letter on 9th April, 1970, to local and hospital authorities, copies of which were sent by the Department of Education and Science to local education authorities on 15th April, giving details of arrangements for training made up to that time. Up to date details of the courses available and advice on the financial arrangements which have been agreed with the local authority associations will be issued shortly.

FINANCIAL PROVISION

22. Local authorities will need to establish what part of the funds within their own budgets should be transferred from the control of the health department to that of the education department from the beginning of the financial year

1971/72. Provision will have been made to cover administration, building upkeep and running costs, capital charges and staff costs. Authorities will need to modify their forecast expenditure a little to allow for higher salaries for those staff who become qualified teachers on the date of transfer; at the same time, authorities are asked to look for administrative savings in assimilating the provision for mentally handicapped children to the special school system that will so far as possible offset these additional costs. Local education authorities will take on additional charges in the form of expenditure on schooling in hospitals, which has previously been borne by the hospital authorities: this expenditure will be taken into account among authorities' relevant expenditure for rate support grant purposes when the grant for 1971/72 and 1972/73 is negotiated later this year.

SUMMARY

23. (*a*) Local education authorities are asked to examine, together with their colleagues in the hospital and local authority health services, the extent of the responsibility which they are to assume in their own areas for the education of mentally handicapped children with effect from 1st April, 1971.

(*b*) They are invited to forward, not later than 30th November, 1970, their proposals for the status after transfer of existing centres, units and hospital provision, for the approval of the Secretary of State under the terms of the Education Acts.

(*c*) They are advised to familiarise themselves with new building projects currently being planned for the education of mentally handicapped children so that they are prepared for the assimilation of these projects into the system of control applied to special school building programmes.

(*d*) They are encouraged to begin consideration now of what is to be their policy in the longer run towards mentally handicapped children in the context of special education.

APPENDIX A

Proposals for the Establishment of New Special Schools

1. Proposals for approval of new special schools to be established on the transfer of responsibility for the education of mentally handicapped children should be forwarded to the Department of Education and Science, Special Education Branch, Elizabeth House, York Road, London, S.E.1, not later than 30th November, 1970.

2. Proposals should be set out on Forms A1 and A2 (specimen copies attached) following the notes of guidance in paragraph 3 below. Supplies of Forms A1 and A2 will be available from the Department from 1st October, 1970, and local education authorities are invited to apply for the copies they will need, using the order slip attached.

Notes of Guidance for Forms A1 and A2

3. (*a*) A separate Form A1 should be completed for *each* proposed special school for which approval is sought.

(*b*) It is expected that schools will normally be approved for the education of educationally subnormal children.

(*c*) If the proposed school is to consist of more than one establishment existing before the date of transfer, please enter details for each of these in Section 1 of Form A1.

(*d*) Special care units which are to continue to operate as unattached units should each be entered on a separate Form A1 in order that a record can be made of them as provision under Section 56 of the Education Act 1944.

(*e*) A separate Form A2 should be completed for each hospital within the Authority's area admitting mentally handicapped patients of compulsory school age.

(*f*) Three copies of the appropriate form will be needed in each case: one to be retained by the Local Education Authority and two to be returned to the Department.

Forms Re-Numbering

Please note that since this Circular was issued the Forms A1 and A2 have been re-numbered Form 14M and Form 15M respectively.

EDUCATION (HANDICAPPED CHILDREN) ACT 1970: ESTABLISHMENT OF NEW SPECIAL SCHOOLS

To: Department of Education and Science, Special Education Branch (SE5), Elizabeth House, York Road, London SE1.

LEA ....

Address to which forms should be sent .... BLOCK LETTERS PLEASE

....

No of Forms A1 required ....

No of Forms A2 required ....

(Signed) ....

(Date) ....

For DES use:	
Date sent	Initials

FORM 14M (Circular No 15/70)

One copy of this form should be retained and two copies returned to the Department of Education and Science, Special Education Brahch (SE5) Elizabeth House, York Road, London SE1

LEA ....

DEPARTMENT OF EDUCATION AND SCIENCE

EDUCATION (HANDICAPPED CHILDREN) ACT, 1970

APPLICATION FOR APPROVAL OF A SPECIAL SCHOOL UNDER SECTION 9 (5) OF THE EDUCATION ACT 1944, AND FOR THE PURPOSES OF THE HANDICAPPED PUPILS AND SPECIAL SCHOOLS REGULATIONS 1959.

---

1. Name and full postal address before the date of transfer of each of the establishments which are to form the proposed new special school.

   Please specify: Junior Training Centre; part of All-age Training Centre; Special Care Unit, attached to JTC; Special Care Unit, unattached; existing Special School (where combination with a JTC is proposed); or Hostel (where a residential special school is proposed); and give reference number of each establishment as at present.

   ....

   ....

   ....

   ....

2. Name of proposed school after date of transfer ....

   ....

   ....

3. Postal address of proposed school in full ....

   ....

4. Category of Handicapped Pupils for whom the School will provide special educational treatment (see Regulation 4 of the Handicapped Pupils and Special Schools Regulations, 1959)

   ....

   ....

5. Proposed maximum number of a. Classes ....
   b. Pupils 1. Day
   2. Boarding ....

6. Sex of pupils ....

7. Age range of pupils defined by lower and upper ages of pupils normally accommodated (eg 5–16)

Boys	Girls

8. If, in the case of a boarding school, admissions are normally to be limited to children from the areas of certain Local Education Authorities, name the Authorities concerned:—

   ....

   ....

9. Name and qualifications of Head Teacher ....

   ....

   ....

I certify that the statements on this form are correct.

....
Authorising Officer of the Local Education Authority

FORM 15M (Circular No 15/70)

One copy of this form should be retained and two copies returned to the Department of Education and Science, Special Education Branch (SE5), Elizabeth House, York Road, London SE1

LEA ....

DEPARTMENT OF EDUCATION AND SCIENCE

EDUCATION (HANDICAPPED CHILDREN) ACT, 1970

APPLICATION FOR APPROVAL OF ARRANGEMENTS FOR PROVIDING EDUCATION IN A HOSPITAL FOR THE MENTALLY HANDICAPPED UNDER SECTION 9 (5) OR SECTION 56 OF THE EDUCATION ACT 1944, AND FOR THE PURPOSES OF THE HANDICAPPED PUPILS AND SPECIAL SCHOOLS REGULATIONS, 1959.

---

1. Name of hospital for the mentally handicapped admitting children of compulsory school age.

   ....

2. Postal address of hospital in full ....

   ....

3. Name of Regional Hospital Board or Hospital Management Committee

   ....

4. Does the Authority intend to provide education in the hospital

   a. by establishing a hospital special school?

      .... or

   b. by making special arrangements under the terms of Section 56 of the Education Act, 1944?

      ....

5. Maximum number of beds for patients under 16 ....

6. Name and qualifications of Head Teacher ....

   ....

   ....

I certify that the statements on this form are correct.

....
Authorising Officer of the Local Education Authority

ADMINISTRATIVE MEMORANDUM 26/70

September 11, 1970

IN-SERVICE COURSES FOR TEACHERS: FINANCIAL AND ADMINISTRATIVE ARRANGEMENTS

1. Circular 14/70 [see p. 480, *ante*] outlined certain changes, agreed in consultation with the local authorities' associations, in the arrangements for pooling expenditure on in-service courses for teachers. The provisions of The Rate Support Grants (Pooling Arrangements) (Amendment) Regulations 1970 enable effect to be given to those changes. This Administrative Memorandum sets out in more detail the conditions under which it has been agreed that expenditure on such courses should be pooled. These arrangements, which supersede those laid down in Circular 7/64 and 7/66, are the revised arrangements which it was stated in paragraph 7 of Administrative Memorandum 19/69 would be issued in an Addendum thereto. They will come into effect from 1st September, 1970.

General Provisions

2. Pooling of expenditure will only apply to courses of a minimum duration of four weeks if full-time, or of the equivalent if part-time, which are approved under one or other of the arrangements set out in paragraphs 5, 9, 11 and 12 below. For such courses the expenditure which may be pooled comprises:—

(*a*) *Tuition costs:* such costs incurred by a maintained college which provides the course; or the fees paid by an authority to a voluntary institution, together, where appropriate, with expenditure on registration and examination fees directly associated with the course.

(*b*) *Travelling expenses:* reimbursement to teachers of expenditure necessarily incurred, at not more than the second class rail fare, for terminal travel when the teacher is away from home or for daily travel from home when the authority is satisfied that such travel is reasonable.

(*c*) *Salaries, superannuation and national insurance of teachers seconded for training:* in respect only of any full-time period of four weeks' duration or more:—

(i) for courses of initial training, the whole of the expenditure incurred for the relevant full-time period;

(ii) for courses of further training, not more than 75 per cent. of the expenditure incurred for the time in which the teacher is out of service:

(*d*) *Subsistence allowances:* in respect of teachers attending courses abroad when seconded on salary, a cost of living addition the amount of which will be announced from time to time by the Department. . . .

3. The Secretary of State hereby approves, under Section 2 (3) of the Education Act 1962, the payment by authorities of grants to teachers in respect of one or more of the items of expenditure in paragraph 2 above.

4. To avoid misunderstandings, authorities are invited to note:—

(i) For the purpose of pooling expenditure on the salaries of teachers on part-time courses there is no provision for aggregating attendances for any number of days or periods each of which is less than four consecutive weeks.

(ii) The limitation of pooling to the cost of living addition referred to in paragraph 2 (*d*) does not debar an authority as employer from providing assistance, at its own expense, towards the extra costs incurred by a teacher attending a residential course in this country or abroad.

Courses Leading to Degrees or to Diplomas of Universities

5. One of the principal changes announced in Circular 14/70 is that the Department would discontinue the practice of approving individual courses leading to university degrees or advanced diplomas as courses of training for

teachers, and would replace it by a general dispensation covering all degree and advanced diploma courses. The new arrangements for teachers in schools are similar to those introduced for teachers in establishments of further education in Circular 7/66. The new arrangement places on individual local education authorities full responsibility for ensuring that the course proposed is appropriate to the teacher concerned: the authority must be satisfied that the course will not only benefit the teacher himself but is likely to enhance his value to the education service as a whole. In the latter context due regard should be paid to the fact that the teacher, on completion of his course, may seek employment under a different authority or in a different sphere of education.

6. The more detailed further conditions under which expenditure on such courses leading to a first or higher degree of a university or of the C.N.A.A. or to the advanced diploma of a university may be pooled are as follows:

(a) *Full-time courses*

(i) The authority must be satisfied that the teacher cannot reasonably attend an equivalent part-time course, having regard not only to the travelling distance to any such course centre but also to the teacher's personal circumstances.

(ii) The assistance given is limited to not more than one year, except that in the cases of such courses leading to the B.Ed. degree assistance may also be given in respect of preparatory courses.

(iii) The teacher must have had at least five years' teaching experience (subject to the special arrangements for the B.Ed. degree in paragraph 5 and 6 of Circular 19/69) and, in the case of courses leading to a first degree, the teacher must produce evidence of his progress thereto sufficient to indicate that he could reasonably sit the examination for the degree at the end of the one year course.

(b) *Part-time courses*

The assistance given must be limited to the part-time equivalent of a one year full-time course, except that in the case of such courses leading to the B.Ed. degree assistance may also be given in respect of preparatory courses.

7. The tuition costs and examination fees in respect of a teacher attending a full-time or part-time course at a college of education will be met as a charge to the account of the college. Responsibility for meeting the tuition and examination fees of teachers attending full-time or part-time courses at maintained establishments other than colleges of education, or attending part-time courses at universities or other voluntary establishments, will rest with the teachers' employing authority in the first instance. The Department will meet the fees for teachers attending full-time courses at universities or other voluntary establishments.

8. It will not be possible to list in the Department's annual programme of one year and one term courses all the degree or diploma courses brought within the ambit of pooling. The Department will publish this autumn a programme for the academic year 1971/72, in a form similar to that already published for 1970/71, and that programme will contain particulars of all advanced diploma courses individually approved up to 1st August, 1970. Consultations on the form of the future programmes are being initiated. The question whether courses not appearing in an annual programme published by the Department should attract the £50 addition to salary as a school-teacher would be a matter for the Burnham Committee.

Other Courses of Further Training

9. The Department will continue to approve on an individual basis other courses, not leading to a degree or to an advanced diploma of a university, for the purposes of the pooling regulations. Particulars of such courses will be included in the Department's annual programme or will be notified by circular letter.

10. It is proposed to amend The Training of Teachers Regulations 1967 to reduce from six to four weeks the minimum length of any course of further training in any training establishment which requires the approval of the Secretary of State for it to be established; any expenditure incurred by an authority in respect of any such course will be poolable. For courses in training

establishments of less than four weeks duration if full-time, or the equivalent if part-time, tuition fees should be charged, as a credit to the account of the establishment, to the extent necessary to cover ascertainable extra tuition costs arising from providing the course.

Courses for Teachers in Establishments of Further Education

11. For courses leading to degree or advanced diplomas of universities the provisions in Circular 7/66 will be replaced by those in paragraphs 6–8 above. The conditions in that Circular applying to other courses of a minimum of six weeks' duration if full-time, or the equivalent if part-time, will now apply to courses of a minimum of four weeks' duration if full-time (or the part-time equivalent): expenditure may be pooled where the employing authority is satisfied that the teachers' attendance at the course would enhance his value to the further education service.

Courses of Initial Training

12. Certain new forms of initial training have been proposed or are being developed for particular categories of teachers already in service. Where such a teacher is accepted by the relevant organisation for a one-year shortened course of initial training he may be seconded on salary at a charge to the pool. For full-time courses of initial training of two or more years the normal arrangement will be for the teacher to be supported on grant—at a charge to the pool in the usual way. Teachers accepted for a sandwich course or for a part-time course (which may include full-time periods), equivalent to a one-year full-time course, may be employed on salary throughout, the cost being chargeable to the pool in respect of any full-time periods of four weeks or more.

13. Courses of the forms outlined in the previous paragraph may be particularly appropriate for experienced but professional unqualified teachers of commercial subjects in schools. Special provisions will be required to cater for the proposed transfer of responsibility for teachers of the mentally handicapped; details thereof will be notified in due course.

14. Expenditure incurred by an employing authority in supporting the attendance of a serving graduate teacher at a part-time course leading to the postgraduate certificate in education may be charged to the pool under the conditions in paragraph 2. The Department will meet the tuition fees where such courses are provided by universities or the tuition costs if the course is provided by a voluntary college of education.

CIRCULAR 19/70

October 26, 1970

THE CHILDREN AND YOUNG PERSONS ACT 1969 AND THE ENFORCEMENT OF SCHOOL ATTENDANCE

1. The Children and Young Persons Act 1969 (referred to below as the 1969 Act) makes the amendments set out in paragraphs 2 and 3 below to the Education Acts and these amendments will be brought into force on 1 January, 1971.

2. The following subsections are substituted for subsections (2) to (5) of Section 40 of the Education Act 1944: [see the amendments on p. 134, *ante*.]

3. The following are repealed:

(*a*) Section 40A of the Education Act 1944.

(*b*) In Schedule I to the Education (Miscellaneous Provisions) Act 1948, the entries relating to Section 40 of the Education Act 1944, and

(*c*) Section 11 of the Education (Miscellaneous Provisions) Act 1953.

4. The effect of these amendments is that from 1 January 1971 proceedings in the juvenile court under Sections 40 and 40A of the Education Act 1944 will be replaced by care proceedings under Section 1 of the 1969 Act.

5. The attention of local education authorities is drawn particularly to the duty to be laid on them by Section 40(2) of the Education Act 1944, amended as in paragraph 2 above, to consider whether it would be appropriate in cases of offences against Sections 37 and 39 of the Act to bring the child in question before the juvenile court instead of, or as well as, instituting proceedings against the parents. Authorities will note the need to establish in care proceedings, not only that the child is not receiving efficient full-time education, but also that he is in need of care or control which he is unlikely to receive unless the court makes an order under Section 1(3) of the 1969 Act. Close consultation with the children's department (the social services department, when established) of the local authority will, as now, be desirable.

6. The effect of Section 2(8) of the 1969 Act is to preserve the position that the bringing of school attendance proceedings is a matter for the local education authority alone. But this provision does not prevent evidence about attendance at school being heard in care proceedings brought by other persons on other grounds.

7. A copy of " A Guide to Part I of the Children and Young Persons Act 1969 " prepared by the Home Office is being sent separately to each local education authority. The Guide includes particular references to the effect of the 1969 Act on proceedings in school attendance cases and to the desirability of local consultation.

ADMINISTRATIVE MEMORANDUM 1/73

January 10, 1973

THE STANDARDS FOR SCHOOL PREMISES REGULATIONS 1972

1. The Secretary of State for Education and Science and the Secretary of State for Wales have made Regulations prescribing standards for school premises (Statutory Instrument 1972 No. 2051). The Regulations come into force on 1 February 1973 and supersede the Standards for School Premises Regulations 1959 to 1972 .

2. The new Regulations consolidate the 1959 Regulations and subsequent amendments and standards are expressed in metric units... No other change has been made in the standards.

3. The general structure and numbering of the 1959 Regulations have been retained. The following minor changes have, however, been made: [*Minor changes noted.*]

Application to middle schools

4. The Parts which apply to middle schools are:

(i) Part II, for middle schools which admit pupils aged under ten years, except that Regulation 17, and not Regulation 5, applies for the calculation of the minimum teaching area for such a school;

(ii) Part III, for middle schools which do NOT admit pupils under the age of ten years;

(iii) Part VII and the relevant definitions in Part I for all middle schools.

Plans and specifications in Imperial units

5. Paragraph 2(c) of Administrative Memorandum No. 14/68 called upon local education authorities and others responsible for educational building to ensure that projects expected to start on or after 1 April 1972 were designed in metric units. If it is necessary to submit plans and specifications in Imperial units on or after 1 February 1973 for the Secretary of State's approval, the Imperial dimensions in the 1959 Regulations, as amended, will be applied.

CIRCULAR 1/73

January 16, 1973

(Wales, 22/73)

LOCAL GOVERNMENT ACT 1972
REORGANISATION OF LOCAL GOVERNMENT: THE EDUCATION FUNCTION

Introduction

1. The Local Government Act, which implements the Government's proposals* for the reorganisation of local government in England and Wales, received the Royal Assent on 26 October 1972. Circular No. 121/72 issued by the Department of the Environment on 28 November 1972 indicates the main features of the new system for England and outlines the further stages of implementation. Welsh Office Circular No. 238/72 dated 29 November, 1972 does the same for Wales. The purpose of this circular is to consider the effects of the Act on the discharge by authorities of their education function and where appropriate to offer guidance on practical issues likely to arise during the transition from the existing to the new structure and for a period thereafter. The circular is issued after consultation with the associations of local authorities and the staff interests chiefly concerned. It does not deal with the provisions of the Act affecting libraries or museums and art galleries; these will be the subject of separate circulars.

2. References in this circular to " the Act ", and to sections and schedules, are references to the Local Government Act 1972 and its provisions unless otherwise stated. References to " the Secretary of State " are to be read as references both to the Secretary of State for Education and Science and to the Secretary of State for Wales where this is appropriate in the context. Similarly, references to " the Department " should be read as references to the Welsh Education Office as well as to the Department of Education and Science.

The new structure

3. Outside the Greater London area the local education authorities from 1 April, 1974 will be the councils of non-metropolitan counties and the councils of districts in metropolitan counties. Schedules 1 and 4 of the Act give details, for England and Wales respectively, of the area covered by each. The new county and district councils will be elected in April and May, 1973 respectively, but they will not assume responsibility for services until 1 April 1974. Until that date the existing local authorities will continue to be statutorily responsible for all local government services. The period from the 1973 elections until 1 April, 1974 is referred to in this circular as " the transitional period ".

4. Section 192 contains the provisions relating to the allocation of the education function in the new local government system. Besides stipulating which new councils are to be local education authorities, this section abolishes all statutory schemes of divisional administration and ends provision for new applications for excepted district status; it amends the definition of " minor authority " for the purposes of section 18 and associated sections of the Education Act 1944 (management of primary schools); and it continues in relation to a new local education authority anything having effect in relation to an existing authority or authorities in connection with the discharge of their functions insofar as these relate to all or part of the new authority's area. The Secretary of State has power under the Act to provide by order that this last provision shall not apply in a particular case, and to make whatever modifications are necessary or desirable in the circumstances.

The transitional process

5. Existing authorities retain full responsibility for the education service in their areas during the transitional period. Each new local education authority will on 1 April, 1974 assume the functions hitherto discharged by the authority or authorities responsible until then for the education service in the whole or any

* " Local Government in England ": Cmnd. 4584. " Reform of Local Government in Wales ": Consultative Document. February 1971.

part of its area; and it will, subject where appropriate to the changes indicated in paragraph 4 above, exercise these functions by reference to all acts and instruments governing the former authority or authorities at the time of transfer. The Secretary of State is conscious of the burden that will fall to authorities and their officers before, during and following the transitional period in maintaining the impetus, continuity and standards of all parts of the service. This will apply particularly where, as in most cases, the area of a new authority is to consist of the whole or part of the areas of more than one existing authority.

6. Section 264 of the Act provides that committees of existing authorities must be set up to prepare for the changeover to the new system, and this provision came into effect on the date of Royal Assent insofar as it relates to the areas of the new local education authorities. These joint committees, which have been operating informally in many areas for some time, enable existing authorities to discuss educational matters of common concern to them arising in connection with local government reorganisation. During the transitional period the new authorities will appoint their senior staff, prepare for the transfer of property and other staff from the authorities they are to replace, and generally take all steps necessary to be ready for the full assumption of the education function on 1 April, 1974. The comprehensive preparatory work which the Secretary of State is aware has already been undertaken by many existing authorities, and collaboration between existing and new authorities, should provide an effective basis for this. Particular attention will no doubt be paid to collecting information on, and detailed records relating to, all aspects of education in the various parts of existing authorities' areas which go to make up a new authority's area; to collating this information to produce a comprehensive statement relating to education in the new authority's area as a whole; and to formulating a draft programme of action with appropriate priorities.

Transfer of staff and property

7. General guidance about the transfer of staff and of property is being issued by the Department of the Environment, the Welsh Office and, in the case of staff, by the Local Government Staff Commissions for England and Wales. The Secretary of State will if necessary supplement this with advice specific to the education service.

Education committees

8. By virtue of section 101 the new local authorities will be required to set up education committees in accordance with the provisions of Part II of the First Schedule to the Education Act 1944. They will no doubt do this as soon as is practicable after they are elected. The arrangements by each authority for setting up its committee will require the Secretary of State's approval under paragraph 1 of Part II of the First Schedule to the Education Act 1944. It may assist authorities, and speed the process of submission and approval of arrangements, if guidance is available on the constitution and membership of education committees, and the Secretary of State is consulting the associations of local authorities and teachers and other interests involved with a view to making such guidance available in the near future.

9. There will be no elections outside the Greater London area in 1973 for existing councils which are local education authorities. In consequence some existing authorities may find that their approved arrangements for the establishment of their education committees, in particular those which are dependent on what has hitherto been the cycle of local elections, are not entirely appropriate in 1973–4. This circular may be regarded as conferring the Secretary of State's approval to whatever amendments of their arrangements are needed to ensure continuity until 31 March, 1974.

Chief Education Officers

10. Section 112 continues the requirement of section 88 of the Education Act 1944 that each local education authority shall appoint a chief education officer. The appointment or designation of a chief education officer and his senior supporting staff will be among a new authority's first priorities after it is elected. The Local Government Staff Commissions are considering arrangements for the recruitment and transfer of staff, including chief officers, and the new authorities will have appropriate guidance to assist them in making these appointments.

11. Schedule 30 repeals from 1 April 1974 the provision of section 88 of the Education Act 1944 which requires each local authority to submit to the Secretary of State a list of the persons from whom it is proposed to appoint a chief education officer. Steps will be taken under the relevant provisions of the Act to ensure that this requirement does not apply to appointments made by the new authorities before 1 April, 1974.

Joint education committees

12. Paragraph 2 of Part II of the First Schedule to the Education Act 1944 enables two or more education authorities, with the Secretary of State's approval, to set up a joint committee to consider questions of common interest. This provision is repealed from 1 April 1974, being no longer required in view of the general provision in section 102(4) for the appointment by local authorities of joint committees to advise them on any matters relating to the discharge of their functions. No prior approval will be required for the establishment of such committees.

13. Paragraph 3 of Part II of the First Schedule to the 1944 Act, which empowers the Secretary of State to establish by order a joint education committee of two or more education authorities for the purpose of exercising some but not all of their functions, remains in force. The Welsh Joint Education Committee is established by order under this provision, as are a number of joint education committees set up to administer certain colleges of education, polytechnics and various other educational establishments. Section 192(5) provides for the continued application of these orders after 1 April, 1974, with references in them to specified existing local education authorities thereafter being regarded as references to the appropriate successor authorities. In some cases no amendment may be needed to existing orders. In others, however, amendment to some of the detailed provisions will be needed fully to reflect the new pattern of authorities, and in such cases it would clearly be desirable for amending orders to be made in time to become effective on 1 April, 1974. A new order will be required in the case of the Welsh Joint Education Committee. New authorities concerned with other joint education committees will wish to consider whether an amending order appears necessary in their case; if so, they should submit full details to the Secretary of State as soon as possible during the transitional period and in any event not later than the end of 1973.

Decentralised administration

14. The Act contains no provisions requiring a new authority to decentralise its administration of the education service, but for the purpose of providing a better service many authorities may wish to establish branch offices. In this connection attention is drawn to the power in section 101(1) and (10) for authorities to arrange for the discharge of functions by officers, and to that in section 102(4) to appoint committees to advise on matters relating to the discharge of functions. The Secretary of State is advised that each of these powers may be exercised on an area as well as on any more general basis. It is open to local education authorities to arrange for the discharge of functions by officers without appointing an associated advisory committee; similarly it is open to them to appoint advisory committees which have no association with an officer discharging functions. Some local education authorities may, however, regard it as appropriate to appoint an officer to discharge functions for part of their area and an area committee to advise him. Since the Act specifies no restriction as to the membership of committees appointed under section 102(4), area committees of this kind can be composed of suitable local persons, including teachers and other persons with a special interest in education, and where appropriate members of district councils.

15. Committees appointed by a local education authority under section 102(4) are distinct from sub-committees set up by the education committee of an authority under paragraph 10 of Part II of the First Schedule to the Education Act 1944. The former can be only advisory in character, while the latter may be authorised by the education committee to exercise the committee's functions subject only to any restriction imposed by the authority. The Secretary of State is advised, however, that the provisions of paragraph 10 do not enable an education committee (whose powers continue to be governed by the Education Act 1944 and are not in this respect affected by section 101 of the Act) to set up sub-committees on an area basis and delegate functions to them.

16. In delineating areas for the purpose of decentralised administration, the new authorities will doubtless have regard to the grouping of schools in a locality, and the relationship between these schools and further education establishments, rather than to pre-existing boundaries established for different purposes. Within this general principle, however, places where former education authorities, including divisional executives and excepted districts, have had their offices, and which are in consequence regarded as centres of local educational interest and administration, may be thought suitable locations for area offices. Similarly, new districts in non-metropolitan counties may form suitable areas. Opportunities may arise in decentralising administration for sharing of accommodation and other services between the education and other authorities, as indicated in the recent report " The New Local Authorities; Management and Structure " *

Managing and governing bodies

17. The period of office of certain members appointed by local education authorities to managing and governing bodies of schools would in the normal course terminate in 1973 following local elections, as provided for in the relevant instruments. Since elections will not be held that year for existing authorities outside the Greater London area, it will be necessary to amend the instruments to permit the extension of the period of office of such members to 1974. The necessary amendment can be effected, in the case of county schools, by a resolution of the local education authority. In the case of voluntary schools, the necessary amendment will be made by order under the Act.

18. Section 192(4) amends the definition of " minor authority " for the purpose of section 18 and related sections of the Education Act 1944. This may entail alterations to the composition of managing bodies of maintained primary schools in a number of cases after 1 April 1974. Other such alterations may be needed as a result of changes in boundaries or the abolition under section 192(2) of divisional executives. The new local education authorities will wish to consider as soon as practicable whether the managing bodies of their primary schools reflect the provisions of section 192(2) and (4). Nothing in the Act calls for any special action to be taken by the new authorities in relation to the generality of governing bodies of secondary schools, but in the case of those in the areas of former divisional executives some modification of the constitutional structure may be required arising from section 192(2).

19. Nor will it be generally necessary in consequence of the Act to make any changes in membership of governing bodies established under the Education (No. 2) Act 1968. In some cases where an institution is maintained by more than one authority it will be necessary for the new maintaining authorities to consider whether the membership reflects the new structure of authorities and to make such changes as may in consequence be required. There is no question of new instruments of government being generally required as a consequence of the Act, although authorities may need to amend individual instruments in due course to reflect the new situation.

Schools serving areas affected by boundary changes

20. Some of the new local education authority boundaries will cross what were previously the boundaries of a single authority and in some cases this will mean that schools will for the first time serve the population of more than one authority. Thus some pupils in schools affected by boundary changes will become extra-district pupils. Special provision was made in the London Government Act 1963 to safeguard the interests of parents and pupils in a similar connection. Although there is no comparable statutory provision for the rest of the country, the Secretary of State expects the same principles to be applied by the new authorities. There should be no question of children being deprived of places at schools which would in other circumstances have served the areas in which the parents live solely on the ground that, by virtue of reorganisation, they no longer live in the area of the maintaining authority. Admissions across the new boundaries should be as flexible as possible.

Proposals under section 13 *of the Education Act* 1944 (*as amended*)

21. The effect of section 192(5) is that any undecided statutory proposal submitted by an existing authority will be regarded as from 1 April 1974 as having

* Report of a Study Group on Local Authority Management Structures: August 1972 (H.M.S.O.).

been submitted by the new authority for the area concerned. It is particularly important that transition in this field should be as smooth as possible for it is one which affects the whole of the provision which authorities make for primary and secondary education. Consultation during the transitional period will be crucial in this respect, not least because the approval and implementation of statutory proposals are sometimes substantially separated in time. The Secretary of State will expect the existing and new authorities to examine together the implications and timing of all current proposals.

Development plans: schemes of further education

22. Development plans and schemes of further education made by existing authorities under sections 11 and 42 respectively of the Education Act are, by virtue of section 192(5), regarded as having been made, in whole or in part as appropriate, by the new authority responsible for the whole or part of the area to which the plan or scheme applies. The new authorities are not therefore required to take any action in regard to either of these provisions of the 1944 Act. They will, however, need to give early consideration to the reconstitution of the Regional Advisory Councils for Further Education (which provide the main means for inter-authority consultations on further education matters of common concern) so as to avoid any serious disruption of timetables for course approvals and other important developments.

Aid to pupils and students

23. Where its area comprises all or part of the areas of more than one existing authority, a new authority may find that there are differences between the existing authorities in their award-making policies and practices where they have discretion as to the making or the amount of an award, or both. It will be necessary for the new authority in such cases to consider at an early stage how to reconcile these differences within the policy it intends to adopt on such awards. Unless this policy is formulated and publicised in good time before 1 April 1974 students entering courses in the academic year 1974–5 may be left in a state of uncertainty. The new authorities will no doubt ensure that the position of existing award-holders is safeguarded. The same principles apply to benefits provided at an authority's discretion in respect of certain pupils in attendance at school, e.g. maintenance allowances, clothing grants, assistance with independent and boarding school fees.

Building programme

24. Existing authorities (and voluntary bodies as appropriate) will be responsible for the planning and starting of all major projects in the 1973–4 starts programme. They will also be responsible for carrying out as far as possible preparatory work (including the acquisition of sites and the design of the buildings) on projects in the 1973–4 design lists. When these design lists are converted in the autumn of 1973 to starts programmes for 1974–5 the Department will inform authorities of the projects by reference to the areas of the new authorities. The replenishment of the preliminary lists (consisting mainly of projects to start in 1975–6), on which work is now in progress in the Department, will be settled early in 1973 in terms of existing authorities, but details of the projects to go forward to the 1974–5 design lists will be determined in consultation with both new and existing authorities and notified in the autumn of 1973.

25. Minor works allocations for 1973–4 are the responsibility of existing authorities. Allocations for 1974–5, announced in the summer of 1972, will in some cases need to be divided or adjusted to take account of the new areas. The Secretary of State looks to existing and new authorities to agree to any necessary re-allocation on this basis and notify the Department of the results by 30 September, 1973. The Department will be glad to provide any assistance that may be needed for this purpose. Allocations for 1975–6, to be settled during 1973, will be made in terms of the new authorities. There will be no change in the existing arrangements for allocations to aided schools made direct by the Department.

26. Block allocations for 1974–5 already made to five existing authorities will not be affected, except that two of the allocations will become the responsibility of a single new authority. Block allocations for 1975–6 to these five authorities and to a further 19 existing authorities will be made early in 1973.

Where two or more of these 24 existing authorities are to be combined in April 1974 the authorities concerned should aim at producing consolidated lists of projects which, in the autumn of 1973, will form the 1974–5 design list.

27. Existing and new authorities will share the Secretary of State's concern that the impetus of educational building should not be lost during reorganisation. Early in the transitional period it will be important for new authorities to ascertain which projects, under construction and projected, they will become responsible for on 1 April, 1974. The professional staff necessary to handle this commitment should be designated and assigned by consultation between existing and new authorities as quickly as possible in the transitional period so that they can continue in full and effective control when responsibility passes to the new authority.

Charities

28. Some local education authorities are trustees of, or exercise other powers (e.g. of appointment) in relation to, charitable trusts. Provision for these is made by section 210. If the trust is registered on the parts of the register of charities maintained by the Secretary of State the authority's rights and powers will devolve on the new local education authority; if it is registered on the part maintained by the Charity Commissioners they will devolve on the new county council where the existing authority is a county council; otherwise they will devolve on the community or parish council where the existing authority is the council of a borough or urban district. Where there is no such council for the area of the borough or urban district or where the existing authority is a rural district council they will devolve on the new district council. There are corresponding provisions for the devolution of the rights and powers exercisable by local office-holders. [*See now, however, the Education Act* 1973.]

Allocation of new reference numbers to authorities and establishments

29. The Department propose to allocate a new 3 digit code number to each of the new local education authorities, and in necessary cases to re-number individual educational establishments within the present 4-digit bands (e.g. 1000–1999 for nursery schools, 2000–3999 for maintained primary schools). As a first step in this operation the Department will send to existing authorities lists of the establishments in their areas and ask them to indicate into which new authority area each establishment will fall. Further details will be sent to authorities as soon as possible.

Statistical returns

30. By allocating new reference numbers to authorities and educational establishments well in advance of 1 April, 1974 the Department aim to devise a system whereby statistical returns submitted by existing authorities can be retabulated to relate to the post-April 1974 structure. Similarly, statistical returns from the new authorities after April 1974 will be capable of being retabulated if necessary to the pre-April 1974 structure. It is hoped by these means to keep the need for special returns to a minimum.

Teachers' records

31. Authorities will appreciate the importance of maintaining the continuity of teachers' records. The Department will in due course issue notes for guidance on the up-dating and handling of the service cards for teachers during the transitional period and for making retrospective entries.

Consultation and Publicity

32. The changes in the pattern of local education authorities are likely to affect many educational establishments, and individual pupils, students, parents and teachers, in one way or another. It will be important for authorities to consult with each other and with teaching and other interests concerned at all appropriate stages in the changeover process, and to keep the general public fully informed of developments in educational policies, practices and administration which are likely to affect them.

CIRCULAR 8/73

March 29, 1973

(Wales, 86/73)

LOCAL GOVERNMENT REORGANISATION ARRANGEMENTS FOR THE ESTABLISHMENT OF EDUCATION COMMITTEES

Introduction

1. As explained in paragraph 8 of Department of Education and Science Circular No. 1/73 (*ante*) the new local education authorities are required under section 101 of the Local Government Act 1972 to establish education committees in accordance with the provisions of Part II of the First Schedule to the Education Act 1944 (referred to as " Part II " in the rest of this circular).

2. The arrangements made by each authority for setting up its education committee require the Secretary of State's approval under paragraph 1 of Part II, as will any subsequent amendments to arrangements so approved. While the new authorities will not be responsible for functions until 1 April, 1974, they will have competence to act in relation to certain matters, including the setting up of their education committee, as from the date of their election, and they may apply to the Secretary of State for approval of their arrangements for doing so as soon as may be after they are elected. Authorities in Wales should address their applications to the Welsh Education Office.

3. Elections for the new councils which are to be local education authorities will be held on 12 April and 10 May, 1973 for county councils and metropolitan district councils respectively. The Secretary of State believes that they will see as one of their first tasks the early establishment of their education committee so that a start can be made to the formulation of educational policies and priorities for their areas, and to consideration of the many detailed issues that will face them even before they assume responsibility for functions.

4. The Secretary of State hopes that the following guidance on the composition and membership of education committees, which is issued after consultation with the associations of local authorities and teachers and organisations representing voluntary bodies, will be of assistance to the new authorities in framing their arrangements and in speeding the processes of their submission and approval.

Form and scope of the arrangements

5. The arrangements should be based on a formal resolution of the council. A sealed scheme is not necessary.

6. Arrangements submitted for the Secretary of State's approval must contain proposals, in accordance with the statutory requirements in Part II, for the composition of education committees. These requirements are recalled and further guidance given in paragraphs 10–13.

7. A number of matters affecting the education committee's constitution, membership and procedures are not however governed by the Education Acts, and the arrangements submitted for approval need not cover them. Such matters include the term of office of members, first meeting of the committee, frequency of meetings and quorums, the filling of casual vacancies, the resignation of members and disqualification from office. These and similar matters affect other committees besides the education committee and, save where the matter is specifically regulated by statute (e.g. disqualification), appropriate provisions relating to them would in the normal case best be made in the council's standing orders. To deal with them in this way rather than within the approved arrangements for the education committee has the added advantage of dispensing with the need to seek the approval of the Secretary of State whenever an authority wishes to make minor or procedural changes in the composition of the education committee or the conduct of its business.

8. As a general principle the Secretary of State does not consider it appropriate that arrangements affecting the education committee which depend on the exercise of an authority's discretion should be subject to approval. For this

reason it will not be necessary for an authority's arrangements to describe the functions delegated to the education committee under Part II, or to give details of the number and composition of proposed sub-committees. The Secretary of State trusts, however, that in practice all authorities will provide for appropriate delegation of functions to their education committee so as to ensure the most effective operation of the service in their area.

9. In regard to the discharge of functions, it will be noted that the effect of section 101(9) and (10) of the Local Authority Act 1972 is that a local authority which is a local education authority may not arrange for the discharge of any of its functions in respect to education by any committee or sub-committee other than its education committee or a sub-committee of its education committee.

Council members

10. The composition of an education committee must meet the requirement of paragraph 6 of Part II that council members must form at least a majority of its membership. Subject to this, the number of council members on the committee may be fixed as a single figure or expressed as lying between a given minimum and maximum. The flexibility of the latter may prove an advantage, obviating the need for authorities to seek approval for any small change in the number of council members. An authority which wishes to follow the practice of appointing all members of the council to membership of the education committee is free to do so.

11. Where they are not already effected by the Council's standing orders (in which case the submission should be noted to that effect), the arrangements should include requirements that the chairman of the education committee shall be an elected member of the council, and that at any of its meetings a majority of members present and voting shall be elected members of the council.

Other members

12. The composition of an education committee must also meet the requirement of paragraph 5 of Part II, that it shall include persons of experience in education and persons acquainted with the educational conditions prevailing in the authority's area. It has invariably been found in practice that this requirement can be satisfactorily met only by appointing to the education committee members from outside the council and all arrangements submitted for approval should include provision for the appointment of a reasonable proportion of such members. The Secretary of State does not have in mind any fixed proportion to be followed by all authorities irrespective of local circumstances, but given the range of interests referred to below, it is believed that authorities will wish to think in terms of a non-council membership of between a quarter and a third of the total. These members should be appointed for their personal experience of education or knowledge of and interest in educational conditions in the authority's area rather than as representatives of particular organisations, but authorities will no doubt wish to take the views of appropriate organisations before making appointments in particular categories.

13. In connection with the appointment of outside members, the new authorities should consider including particularly members nominated by the teaching profession and the churches and also, insofar as this may be necessary having regard to the existing composition of the governing bodies of educational institutions, members with knowledge and experience of industry and commerce, agriculture and the universities. Concerning the teaching profession and the churches specifically, they will no doubt take into account the following considerations:

(a) *Teachers*. Teachers employed by an authority are disqualified from being elected to the authority itself, but under section 104 (2) (*a*) of the Local Government Act 1972 they may be appointed members of its education committee. The Secretary of State considers that the professional expertise of serving teachers equips them well to make an effective contribution to the work of education committees, and therefore commends to the new authorities the practice of making specific provision in their committee arrangements for the appointment of serving teachers as non-council members. It is further recommended that this category of membership should adequately reflect the various stages of education by having teachers with current knowledge and experience of primary, secondary and further education. In view of the substantial reorganisation to be effected over the coming years, the knowledge and experience of teachers in colleges of education should also be borne in mind in this connection. Procedures for selecting teacher members should be agreed between the authority and teachers in the area but there is no need for these procedures to form part of the arrangements submitted for approval.

(b) *Churches.* The Secretary of State is also of the opinion that it would be desirable to have in the arrangements specific provision for appointment of members nominated by the churches in view of the important role they have to play in education. The number of such members on any education committee will of course depend on local circumstances. The Secretary of State suggests that where appropriate nominations should be sought from the Diocesan Education Committee in the case of the Church of England or the Church in Wales, from the Bishop of the Diocese in the case of the Roman Catholic Church, and from the local Free Church Federal Council or Federation in the case of the Free Churches. Where an authority's area covers all or part of more than one Diocese or analogous area of jurisdiction, joint nominations would no doubt be sought from all the committees concerned.

Area advisory committees

14. Authorities may, if they wish, as part of their arrangements for decentralising the administration of education functions, set up area advisory committees under Section 102 (4) of the Local Government Act 1972. Some authorities may wish to provide for members of the education committee to be made the chairmen of such advisory committees.

Area health authorities

15. Subject to enactment of the relevant Bill now before Parliament, the National Health Service will be reorganised with effect from 1 April, 1974 [*see the National Health Service Reorganisation Act* 1973]. As a result, responsibility for inspection and treatment aspects of the school health service will on that date pass to new area health authorities whose areas of operation will be co-terminous with those of the new local education authorities. Area health authorities will also be under an obligation to provide local education authorities with the medical and other professional services required for their special education and other education functions. Each area health authority will include members appointed by the local authorities operating in the same area. There will in addition be provision for joint consultative committees consisting of members appointed by the area health authority and by local authorities in the area, including the local authority responsible for education. The Secretary of State believes that local education authorities will for their part wish to consider the desirability of providing for the appointment of area health authority members to the education committee or, perhaps more appropriately, to sub-committees of the education committee established to deal with relevant aspects of the service.

Local education authorities in Greater London

16. The provisions of the Local Government Act 1972 do not entail any special action by local education authorities in the Greater London area with regard to their education committee, but such authorities may wish to reconsider their existing approved arrangements in the light of this circular, in particular the preceding paragraph, and where they consider it necessary or desirable to submit in due course revised arrangements for the Secretary of State's consideration.

CIRCULAR 1/74

January 4, 1974

THE NATIONAL HEALTH SERVICE REORGANISATION ACT 1973 FUTURE ARRANGEMENTS FOR THE PROVISION OF SCHOOL HEALTH SERVICES AND OF HEALTH ADVICE AND SERVICES TO LOCAL EDUCATION AUTHORITIES

1. This circular summarises changes in the provision of health services affecting local education authorities resulting from the National Health Service Reorganisation Act 1973.

2. [*This referred to a Circular " Child Health Services (including School Health Services) " prepared by the Department of Health and Social Security in consultation with the Department of Education and Science.*]

3. Under Section 3 of the National Health Service Reorganisation Act 1973 the Secretary of State for Social Services will become responsible on 1 April, 1974 for the medical and dental inspection and treatment services at present provided by local education authorities, and under Section 11 of that Act he will be required to make available the services of doctors, dentists and nurses and other staff including speech therapists and members of the professions supplementary to medicine and other health services " in so far as is reasonably necessary and practicable, to enable local education authorities to discharge their education functions ". He will in effect delegate these responsibilities to area health authorities under Section 7 of the Act.

4. The main changes are:

(i) Sections 48 (1) and (2) and (3) of the Education Act 1944 and Section 4 of the Education (Miscellaneous Provisions) Act 1953 are repealed by the NHS Reorganisation Act 1973, but LEAs retain their duty under Section 48 (4), as amended by the NHS Reorganisation Act 1973, to encourage and assist pupils to take advantage of the medical and dental inspection and treatment services provided under Section 3 of that Act. They and the managers or governors of voluntary schools are also required under Section 3 to make accommodation available for the medical and dental inspection and treatment of school children.

(ii) The definition of the term " medical officer " contained in Section 114 of the Education Act 1944 has been amended by Schedule 4 of the N.H.S. Reorganisation Act 1973 to include those whose services are made available to the local education authority by the Secretary of State for Social Services.

(iii) The Medical Examinations (Subnormal Children) Regulations 1959 will lapse but similar regulations are to be made under paragraph 10 of Schedule 1 of the N.H.S. Reorganisation Act 1973.

5. Local education authorities will retain their present obligations under Section 34 of the Education Act 1944 to arrange for medical examinations for children who may require special educational treatment and their obligations to secure medical examinations under the provision of the Milk and Meals (Amendment No. 2) Regulations 1971, and under Section 54 of the Education Act 1944. The services of medical practitioners will be made available to local education authorities by the Secretary of State for Social Services (in practice by area health authorities).

6. Section 10 of the N.H.S. Reorganisation Act requires health authorities and local authorities to co-operate with one another to secure and advance health and welfare and requires that joint consultative committees shall be established between local authorities and area health authorities. The Secretary of State has no doubt that local education authorities will be prepared to play an active part through the joint consultative machinery in the arrangements for the provision of services and advice and for liaison between health and education staff.

7. This circular with the D.H.S.S. circular has been sent to new local education authorities. Copies of both circulars have also been sent for information to existing local education authorities and to Chief Education Officers, Principal School Medical Officers and Principal School Dental Officers. In view of the

reference in paragraph 4 to the duty placed on local education authorities and on the managers or governors of voluntary schools to make accommodation available for medical and dental inspection and treatment purposes copies of the circular are also being sent to the managers and governors of voluntary aided and special agreement schools.

CIRCULAR 4/74

April 16, 1974

(Wales, 112/74)

THE ORGANISATION OF SECONDARY EDUCATION

Principles

1. The Government have made known their intention of developing a fully comprehensive system of secondary education and of ending selection at eleven plus or at any other stage. The Secretary of State looks to local education authorities (and to school governors*) to secure under his control and direction the effective execution of this policy. Circular 10/70 is accordingly withdrawn.

2. Local education authorities and governors will be expected to direct their efforts not only to planning the organisation of their secondary schools in such a way as to avoid the need for selection, but also towards the development of the education provided in them so that it is generally accepted as meeting the needs of all their pupils. Authorities will no doubt continue to have due regard to parents' wishes in respect of their children's education, e.g. in denominational schools where these are available. In Wales this issue may arise in the context of bilingual schools. It is not essential for a comprehensive school to be of very great size. There is no single ideal size for a comprehensive school. Experience has shown that some large schools work well but equally some authorities, teachers and parents prefer small schools. What is important is to ensure that the organisation adopted makes the maximum use of existing buildings and available resources.

Past progress

3. Substantial progress with reorganisation has already been made. In January 1973 38 per cent of all secondary schools in England and Wales, housing 48.4 per cent of the pupils, were already designated comprehensive. Of the 163 authorities totally on comprehensive lines, 76 had reorganised in part, and only 15 had received no approval to reorganise. Of the 104 authorities in existence on 1 April, 1974 only one has not reorganised any of the county schools in its area. These figures show the considerable efforts already made by many authorities. But the completion of the job must be accelerated.

Type of organisation

4. Since the issue of Circular 10/65 and with growing experience of comprehensive schools, local education authorities have developed three main types of organisation:

(i) All-through schools with an age range from 11 to 18.

(ii) Schools with an age range of 11 to 16, leading to separate colleges for those over 16 (which have in a few cases been combined with further education establishments).

(iii) Middle schools for the age range 8 to 12, or 9 to 13, leading to upper schools from 12 to 13 to 18.

Some authorities have adopted other forms of organisation involving a break in the period of secondary education between lower and upper tier comprehensive schools; and there are other possibilities.

---

* The contents of this Circular are addressed both to Authorities and to school governors according to their respective roles under the Education Acts.

5. The relevant advantages of the various types of organisation in any given area will depend to a great extent on practical considerations of the buildings and staff available, the geography of the area, the distribution of the population and whether it is increasing, static or declining. It is only right that authorities and voluntary school governors should have regard to these considerations. In addition there are other purely educational considerations—for example, the deployment of staff and the arrangements for sixth form work—which involve an important element of judgement. The Secretary of State regards these considerations as a proper matter for individual local education authorities, after due consultation with local interests (on which see paragraph 8), always subject to the overriding need to eliminate all forms of selection at all stages.

The new local education authorities

6. The new local education authorities which assumed responsibilities on 1 April, 1974, as well as the existing authorities in the Greater London area, will be faced with widely differing problems in secondary organistaion. Where areas have not been substantially changed, the problem remaining will already be familiar to the authorities concerned. In other cases authorities may have inherited different patterns of organisation in different parts of their area, from predecessor authorities. These authorities will, no doubt, already have given preliminary consideration to the new problem with which this situation will confront them, and the action which may be needed. They will be aware from paragraph 21 of Circular No. 1/73 (D.E.S.) (*ante*), that any undecided statutory proposal submitted by an authority existing before 1 April, 1974 is regarded as having been submitted by the new authority for the area concerned.

Next steps

7. While the Secretary of State is anxious to avoid placing undue burdens on new authorities at a time of transition, he is determined that all necessary steps should be taken to give effect to the Government's policy. Thanks to the impetus given by Circular 10/65, the progress already achieved makes it unnecessary in 1974 for all authorities to prepare and submit detailed plans; but the Secretary of State requires information as soon as possible and in any event not later than by the end of 1974 about the successive measures which will be taken to complete the process of reorganisation in those areas where selection procedures are still operated. The Department's territorial officers and the Welsh Education Office will be writing to the authorities concerned for this information. It should be provided by authorities after consultation with voluntary schools in their area.

8. The Secretary of State intends to expedite the process for examining and deciding upon proposals submitted to him under Section 13. He wishes to emphasise the need to ensure adequate and thorough consultation and explanation locally of schemes of reorganisation before a proposal is submitted to him and before the publication of statutory Notices. Teachers, preferably through their local associations, and parents in particular should be informed and have the opportunity of making their views known while proposals are being formulated and before they are submitted. The position of pupils at present in unreorganised schools should be safeguarded, so far as this is compatible with the progressive admission, without regard to ability, of pupils coming from primary or middle schools.

9. As a result of local government reorganisation in April 1974, there are now many new local education authorities in whose areas the schools have been organised in different patterns. It is a matter for local choice whether the pattern could remain varied or whether within one authority's area a homogeneous system should gradually be introduced. The Secretary of State leaves it to authorities and the governors of voluntary schools to decide what proposals, if any, to submit with this intention, subject to the development of a fully comprehensive system of secondary education.

Voluntary schools

10. In Circular 10/65 the Government of the day indicated that, while the plans which authorities were requested to prepare should embrace voluntary schools, it was not essential that the same pattern should be adopted for denominational and other voluntary schools in any given area as was employed for

that area's county schools. In many instances the governors of voluntary schools and Diocesan authorities have responded constructively by making proposals for the purpose of ensuring that their schools, while retaining their distinctive characteristics, become comprehensive. In some cases they have been readier than the relevant local education authorities to make proposals. In other cases, however, the governors of voluntary schools have stood out against the wishes of local education authorities who maintain their schools to attain a fully comprehensive system throughout their area. The Secretary of State asks these governors to reconsider their attitude in the light of the Government's policy.

11. In the case of voluntary controlled schools, the majority of the governors are appointed by the local education authority and it would seem entirely appropriate that they should represent the authority's point of view and that, when the authority intend to implement reorganisation, they, as the majority on the governing body, should themselves propose a change of character. Such proposals will fall to be considered in the usual way under Section 13. In the case of voluntary aided schools the governors cannot expect to continue to receive the substantial financial aid which their schools enjoy through being maintained by the local education authority, if they are not prepared to co-operate with that authority in settling the general educational character of the school and its place in a local comprehensive system.

Direct grant schools

12. It is not the purpose of this Circular to enter into a discussion of the direct grant schools as such. There may however be circumstances in which a direct grant school, because of the role it already plays in providing places for local education authorities, could readily fit into a scheme of comprehensive reorganisation; in such circumstances its present status should not be regarded as an obstacle.

Resources

13. The Secretary of State recognises that careful planning and consultation will be needed to effect the complete elimination of selection and he will not be prepared to give his approval under Section 13 to proposals which are manifestly unsuitable. He is convinced that authorities and voluntary school governors can expedite the transformation of many existing schools into parts of a coherent and fully comprehensive system without special building allocations, and he expects the fullest use to be made of the available resources to facilitate reorganisation. For this purpose he would not rule out, without due consideration, proposals for a school to function as an interim measure on more than one site. In considering future proposals for individual major projects at secondary schools he will take account of the contribution they will make to reorganisation. He does not propose to include in future building programmes projects at non-comprehensive schools, whether grammar, technical or modern, except where such projects are necessary to enable the schools to become comprehensive.

Consultation

14. The Secretary of State wishes to make it clear that the officers of his Department are always ready to assist local education authorities, voluntary school governors, denominational representatives and direct grant school governors, if they wish to have informal discussions. Such discussions may be particularly useful when proposals (whether in response to this Circular or under Section 13 of the Education Act 1944, as amended) are being formulated and before a decision has been taken to submit them formally to the Department. The educational system is a partnership and the Government are determined to make it work smoothly.

CIRCULAR 5/74

May 21, 1974

THE EDUCATION OF MENTALLY HANDICAPPED CHILDREN AND YOUNG PEOPLE IN HOSPITAL

Summary

This Circular, which is addressed to both health and education authorities, gives advice on various matters in regard to the education of mentally handicapped and other long stay children in hospital. It is mainly concerned with standards of practice but refers also to some questions of administration.

Introduction

1. Local education authorities assumed responsibility, in consequence of the Education (Handicapped Children) Act 1970, for the education of mentally handicapped children on 1 April, 1971 and the necessary changes in management arrangements that the transfer of responsibility brought about are now complete. Experience has shown the need for some further guidance, some of which concerns the administration of the service and some with promoting a high standard of practice to ensure that children in hospitals for the mentally handicapped receive, under suitable conditions, the education to which they are now entitled.

2. Much of the under-lying thinking in this Circular on ways of promoting good practice is relevant to the education of other children in hospital, particularly long-stay patients. On questions relating to administrative matters which are dealt with in paragraphs 11–15 (hospital school building programme), 27–28 (furniture and equipment), 22–25 (milk and meals), 26 (transport) and 37 (managing bodies), the advice given applies to all kinds of hospitals where there are children. The new arrangements described in paragraph 11 in respect of capital building programmes have already been put into effect.

Basic principles

3. Wherever children in hospital receive their education, it is important to preserve the idea that they go out to school. Experience in some hospitals has shown that, even where children are severely handicapped physically as well as mentally, only in extremely few cases need the nature or extent of their handicaps prevent them leaving the ward for their education. Even if education has to take place in the ward, the idea of going to school can be preserved to some extent by moving the children to a particular part of the ward and making it clear that while " school " is in progress it should not be interrupted by ward routine.

4. Wherever practicable, children should go out to a special school serving the community at large. The next best arrangement is for them to go to specially provided educational premises which form part of a hospital special school, that is an organisation concerned with all primary and secondary education provided within the confines of the hospital for children in it (though it may also take some day pupils from outside). Where educational premises do not exist or are inadequate the children should be taught in suitable hospital accommodation normally used for other purposes or, very exceptionally, in the wards themselves. The use of such accommodation for educational purposes will also be required in a few cases where it proves necessary to provide education " otherwise than at school " under Section 56 of the Education Act 1944. Arrangements under Section 56 should normally obtain only where the number of children to receive education falls below 25 or is likely to do so within the foreseeable future.

5. In the past there have been doubts about the ability of the most severely mentally handicapped children to respond to any form of educational stimulus. If, however, children when young are exposed to such stimulus over a period of time, there is now evidence to suggest that they will all be found capable of benefiting from some form of education which is now their right. At the earliest stages of development this may consist essentially of good child care, but with learning experiences for each child carefully planned in conjunction with teachers to evoke a growing range of responses. The educational character of the environment where these activities are undertaken is also very important, since the nature of the setting helps to determine the expectations of the children themselves. As

a child develops the teacher's role will assume increasing importance, and he/she should be in a position to adjust quickly and perceptively to the changing needs of the individual child.

6. Where there is a hospital special school, the head teacher should be responsible not only for the education of children in hospital premises as well as in the school, but also for making the arrangements for any children who can attend school outside the hospital. Decisions about which children can attend an outside school should be reached through consultation between the head teacher and the hospital staff. Where there is no hospital special school, the local education authorities should designate one teacher as in charge of educational arrangements for children in the hospital.

7. More than with any children in special schools in the community, the quality of the education received by children in hospital depends on close and harmonious relationships between the teachers and other staff who have contact with the children. The complementary roles of hospital nurses and teachers are discussed in more detail in paragraphs 18–20.

Comprehensive assessment

8. The duty which local education authorities have to ascertain pupils for whom special education is necessary calls for medical and educational assessment of each child's handicaps and capabilities. But this should not be regarded as a separate and distinct process from the assessment needed to plan the child's medical treatment, care and social development. The physical, emotional, social and educational needs of mentally handicapped—as of other handicapped—children must be considered as a whole; a multi-disciplinary approach to assessment is essential. For particular children or at particular times one aspect may be of special importance, but the complete picture must always be borne in mind and a team approach adopted. The general role of comprehensive assessment services for all handicapped children is mentioned in paragraph 37 of D.H.S.S. Circular H.R.C. (74) 5 " Child Health Services (including school health services) " . . .

9. Ideally all children who enter hospital will have undergone initial comprehensive assessment, but until such services are built up this will not always be the case. In the meantime, it is especially important for the health, social services and education authorities to co-operate fully to ensure that information which may be relevant to a child's education is passed on when he is admitted to or discharged from hospital. In particular, any previous school which a child admitted to hospital has attended should pass records about him to the hospital school (or the teacher in charge of educational arrangements for children in the hospital), and health authorities should keep L.E.A.s informed of movement in and out of hospital.

10. It is important that children in hospital should be assessed and kept under review by a multi-disciplinary team. The aim should be to include a paediatrician, psychiatrist, social worker, teacher, psychologist, nurse and other staff as appropriate. The younger and the more severely handicapped a child is, the more important it is for his response to education to be regularly assessed so that his programmes can be adjusted to suit changing needs. The expertise of an educational psychologist will be particularly important when the education of individual children is being planned. Other specialist educational staff employed by the L.E.A. may have a contribution to make, e.g. teachers of the deaf in the assessment of children with impaired hearing.

Premises

11. In the past the practice has been for Regional Hospital Boards to include hospital school buildings in their capital building programmes. Now responsibility rests with the local education authorities to programme hospital schools and to ensure that suitable premises are provided for the education of children in hospital. The authority may fulfil its responsibilities either by providing premises itself or by the use of health services premises made available under Section 11 (3) of the National Health Service Reorganisation Act 1973. As local education and hospital authorities were informed by a circular letter dated 17 April, 1973, responsibility for capital investment in educational premises in hospital now normally rests with L.E.A.'s and projects will be included in special school building programmes.

12. Major changes in the pattern of hospital services for the mentally handicapped are being planned by health authorities in consultation with local social services authorities following publication in June 1971 of Cmnd 4683 " Better Services for the Mentally Handicapped ". These plans envisaged that some existing hospitals will be closed, others will be reduced in size and a number of new, smaller hospitals will be built. These factors need to be taken into account by local education authorities in planning how to meet their new responsibilities for the education of mentally handicapped children in hospitals; and it is extremely important therefore for L.E.A.s to be kept informed about progress with the forward planning of services for the mentally handicapped.

13. Accordingly, before a local education authority builds or extends a hospital special school, it will be important to consider how far the need for such premises is likely to be temporary and whether it might be met by using existing hospital accommodation or by the local education authority providing suitable temporary accommodation in the hospital grounds; in such cases a formal lease to the L.E.A. will usually not be necessary. Where it is decided that a new building is required specifically for a hospital special school, it should be planned and sited in such a way that as far as possible the local education authority or health authority can put it to alternative use if it is no longer needed for the education of hospital children. Where a permanent building is provided it may be appropriate for the local education authority to acquire for the purpose, by lease or purchase, a suitable part of the hospital site.

14. In some situations, however, there may be advantage in the health and local education authority planning jointly a building or group of buildings designed both to serve as a school and also to provide, linked to it, hospital facilities —e.g. physiotherapy—required by the children. Shared use of some administrative accommodation might also be sensible. In the case of a jointly planned development both authorities should normally contribute their due proportion of capital and maintenance costs as they occur. In exceptional cases, however, it may be agreed that the health authority will meet the total capital cost of a scheme without reimbursement at the time, and the health authority would then include the cost of the entire project on its capital programme and charge the local authority an economic rent (i.e. a rent which includes not only actual outgoings but also a sum representing the notional loan charges on the capital cost involved.) The site might be in the ownership of either authority but a long-term agreement should be entered into covering the use by both authorities.

15. Apart from such developments, detailed arrangements will also need to be agreed to cover any substantial use of hospital premises for educational purposes and vice versa. Such arrangements should include provision for payments to be made by the using authority. The principles which govern payments are as follows:—

(*a*) where the premises have been provided or converted by one authority specifically for purposes which have become the responsibility of the other authority, an economic rent should be charged;

(*b*) where one authority makes rooms available to the other on a regular basis, payments should be directly related to the outgoings of the authority owning the premises, for heating, lighting, cleaning, etc.; and

(*c*) for occasional use, payments need cover only any special additional costs where these are significant.

Teaching staff

16. It is important that the education of all children in hospital, whether or not they attend a school, should be seen as a whole with their teachers flexibly deployed to meet changing needs. In general, however, staffing ratios in hospital schools will need to be somewhat more generous than those in day special schools in the community. A young and very severely handicapped child will need, for part of the day at least, the undivided attention of one adult, whereas at other times play activities in small groups of 3 or 4 children may be suitable. Older children will also need individual attention for some part of the day but at other times they may perhaps be taught in groups of 9 or 10, provided that ancillary educational staff in suitable numbers are available. Where there are children with defects of sight or of hearing a specialist teacher will be needed, either full or part-time.

17. Staffing ratios for children who have to be taught elsewhere than in a school will depend on the circumstances in which teaching takes place. Where, as is desirable, children can be grouped according to their educational needs, the staff ratios required will be similar to those prevailing in hospital schools. Where only a heterogeneous group is possible or where the children are more scattered, this will probably call for a higher ratio of staff.

The roles of nurses and teachers

18. Nursing and teaching are distinct professions with distinct skills, for which special and separate training is required, though the roles of teachers and nurses inevitably overlap and some areas of their work have much in common. The greatest benefit to the child will result from the two professional groups working together in harmony. Hospital nurses need to understand how teachers can develop the capabilities and enrich the lives of their patients and what conditions are required for an effective educational programme. In turn, the teachers should realise how the nurses' responsibility for the care and training of the children complements their work.

19. There is a variety of situations in which nurses and teachers need to work closely. In day-to-day care of children the nurse's professional role includes functions comparable with those of a parent. Like the parent, the nurse is presented with many excellent opportunities for helping the child to learn, and the influence of " home " background is just as crucial to the child in hospital as it is to the child living in the parental home. It is, therefore, hoped that teachers and nurses will establish a relationship akin to that between teachers and parents. However, there is also a need for a professional relationship since the management of some handicaps requires nursing care even in school. More generally, regular discussions between nurses and teachers about individual children will ensure that both are working to a common aim and that there is consistency of approach between the school and the hospital.

20. Where possible, hospital and school activities should be planned in such a way as to foster co-operation between staff. Head teachers and senior nursing officers, in consultation with those responsible for nurse training, should together provide joint training programmes designed to help teachers and nurses to understand what each other's role is and how they can best work together to promote the children's development. For teachers and nurses in training, colleges of education and nurse training schools whould arrange joint sessions to help them understand the conditions under which they will each work and how each can make a distinctive contribution to common objectives. Nursing staff should be encourage to join teachers in their class and participate in activities, whilst teachers should gain some experience of life on the ward. Joint common rooms, canteens and use of recreational facilities can help to encourage mutual understanding.

Health services

21. After 1 April, 1974 responsibility for the school health service will be transferred to area health authorities, who will decide how to continue to make available the services of medical, dental, nursing and other health staff, either from resources available within the hospital or otherwise. Where a school is situated in, or close to, the hospital many of these services will be available from the hospital, for example hospital nurses will normally provide the required nursing support in the school; but some specialist services, e.g. audiology and speech therapy, may not be available on site and there is clear need for health authorities and local education authorities to collaborate to ensure that the needs of children in hospital are fully met.

School meals and milk

22. Children receiving education in hospital special schools are regarded as day pupils, and a local education authority has the same duty under the Provision of Milk and Meals Regulations to provide school dinners and milk for them as for other pupils in its day special schools. The hospital for its part is regarded for dietary purposes as in loco parentis, and will decide which of the children should take school dinners provided by or on behalf of the local education authority, and which should, for medical or other reasons, take the mid-day meal as part of the hospital's own arrangements for their treatment and care. The L.E.A. will

be responsible for meeting the cost of providing the school dinners, while the health authority will be responsible for meeting the charge normally made to parents by the L.E.A. for school dinners provided in special schools in its area. To avoid elaborate calculations of cost, it is suggested that when the meal is supplied by the hospital the reimbursement by the L.E.A. should be based on the unit cost of providing a school dinner at other schools in the authority's area, rather than on the hospital's actual cost. The L.E.A. will also be responsible for the cost of milk supplied to the pupils under the milk-in-schools scheme.

23. Where children attend a special school outside the hospital which caters for the community at large, they will in most cases be provided, along with the other pupils in the school, with school dinners and milk for which the local education authority normally makes arrangements, and the L.E.A. will debit the health authority with the normal charge for the number of meals so provided. Where the special school is within the hospital, the normal arrangements will be for the L.E.A. to contract with the hospital for the supply of the necessary mid-day meals and school milk, and to arrange for the meals to be taken in a school dining-room or in suitable hospital accommodation made available for the purpose. Where it is decided that a child should not take the school dinner, the L.E.A. will have no responsibility, financial or otherwise, for his mid-day meal.

24. Meals in special schools for mentally handicapped children have a very valuable educational function, and play an important part in social training. It is, therefore, very important that sufficient auxiliary help should be available at meal times. Where a school meal is taken in a school building, whether inside or outside the hospital, or in hospital accommodation made specially available, the normal arrangements for supervision should be followed and sufficient auxiliary helpers appointed by the local education authority to ensure that the needs of the children are met.

25. This broad statement regarding the discharge of responsibility for school milk and meals is given for the general guidance of local education authorities and health authorities. It is emphasised, however, that these authorities have full discretion, in consultation with one another, to make whatever arrangements they agree are the most suitable to meet the needs of the children concerned, having regard to their respective statutory powers and responsibilities and the circumstances obtaining in any particular locality.

Transport

26. Section 55 of the Education Act 1944 enables local education authorities to make such arrangements as they consider necessary for the purpose of facilitating the attendance of pupils at school. Where children from hospital go to a school outside, it is for the local education authority to provide transport and, if necessary, escorts for the children. Where children attend a school within the hospital grounds, it is more appropriate for the hospital administration to arrange any transport and escorts that may be required, but teachers should co-operate with nurses in assisting the children.

Equipment

27. The provision of furniture and equipment for educational purposes in hospital is the responsibility of the local education authority, while provision for the care of children outside school is the responsibility of the health authority. To serve these different purposes very similar equipment is often needed, particularly for outdoor play activities. In order to avoid unnecessary duplication and to ensure that resources are used to the best advantage, it is hoped that the two authorities will consult together about the range of equipment each will provide. A rich variety of toys, materials and apparatus, including mobiles, musical instruments and large coloured building blocks and balls, is required to provide stimulation and to encourage movement. Where children cannot move about easily, the aim should be to provide objects such as wheels which they can make to move and things which they can look at where they are. For older boys materials for craftwork should be provided, and for older girls household equipment. In providing equipment the needs of further and adult education should also be borne in mind (see paragraph 39).

28. Some ideas about furniture and equipment that would be suitable for severely handicapped children, either in hospital or in day special schools, are

given in paragraphs 6 and 7 of D.E.S. Design Note No. 10 on " E.S.N. Special Schools: Designing for the Severely Handicapped ", which was issued in September 1972.

School holidays

29. All children benefit from a break in attendance at school, but the less retentive memories and lack of resourcefulness of severely handicapped children make long holidays a disadvantage. This particularly applies to children in long stay hospitals who may not have the opportunities for experiences that are available to children living at home. Holidays for mentally handicapped children should preferably last no longer than 3–4 weeks in the summer and 1–2 weeks at other holiday times. During such times responsibility for providing programmes of suitable activities and experiences to divert and stimulate the children will lie with the hospital staff. In order to make teaching available during the extended terms, local education authorities will need either to appoint additional teachers to the staff (to make possible some staggering of their holidays) or to employ part-time teachers or to employ student teachers under suitable professional supervision.

30. Holiday periods and programmes will place an increased burden on hospital staff; and it may be necessary for the hospital temporarily to augment its staff or its cadre of voluntary helpers. Students and other young people are often available at these times for temporary employment or voluntary work. Students on field and residential social work and teacher training courses are among those most likely to be interested. School groups and exchange and visiting foreign students may also wish to help.

31. Lack of day space in the hospital may be a problem during holiday periods and at weekends. Local education authorities are asked to respond whenever possible to requests from the hospital administration to make school premises available at these times. School halls in particular may be of value. Wherever possible, experience provided during the holidays should be different from everyday activities; group holidays in camps or caravans have been arranged successfully by some hospitals, often with the help of voluntary organisations.

Voluntary help

32. Just as in the hospital itself, there is considerable scope for well-briefed volunteers to work in the school. Voluntary helpers can make a regular and sustained contribution, and nurses and teachers should be encouraged to accept them as partners in the care of children. Other volunteers may be prepared to repair and maintain toys and equipment or to help in similar indirect but valuable ways.

33. Many hospitals for the mentally handicapped have appointed full-time organisers of voluntary help to develop and co-ordinate the services of volunteers throughout the hospital, and the number of such posts is still increasing. There should be close liaison between the organisers and the teachers so that suitable opportunities are grasped for voluntary helpers to supplement the services of teachers and nurses, both in and out of school hours.

Contact with parents

34. A child's good relationship with his family is of great importance to his development and therefore to his education. It is most desirable that parents should be encouraged to make regular visits to the hospital and school. Advance notice of such visits is a help to staff but visiting should not be restricted to particular hours. Visits by children to their homes should so far as possible be arranged so as not to interfere with their education.

35. In certain circumstances, as explained in paragraph 26 of HM (71) 51, parents visiting children in hospital can be helped with their travelling expenses under the Supplementary Benefits scheme. If the visitor is in a household receiving supplementary benefit this may already include a sufficient margin to provide for the cost of fares, but where it does not some addition can normally be made. If the visitor is not receiving supplementary benefit, he may nevertheless, depending upon his financial circumstances, be eligible for assistance with travelling expenses but this would normally be limited to help with the cost of an

emergency visit or with the expense of an occasional long journey where the child is a long-stay patient. Specific advice in relation to an individual's own circumstances can be obtained from the local Social Security Office.

36. Local education authorities are also reminded that, as explained in D.E.S Administrative Memorandum 6/66, they may pay part or all of the parents' travelling and other expenses incurred in visiting children who are boarded away from home to enable them to receive special educational treatment " if they are satisfied that without a visit the child's special educational treatment would be impaired and that the parents cannot afford the cost ". This should be taken as applying also to children where, in the view of the L.E.A., the child's educational needs constitute a significant part of the reason for the child's stay in hospital. It would be for the authority where the parents were normally resident to consider giving this form of assistance.

Managing bodies

37. Local education authorities are reminded that they have a statutory obligation under Section 2 of the Education (No. 2) Act 1968, to appoint governors for maintained hospital schools. Non-maintained hospital schools are required under The Handicapped Pupils and Special School Regulations 1959 to appoint a body of managers. It may be found helpful if these bodies include a representative of the health authority.

In-service training

38. Hospital schools have hitherto been somewhat remote from the mainstream of education, and there is a danger that teachers of mentally handicapped children in hospital may feel isolated if steps are not taken to associate them closely with the education system of which they have so recently become a part. Local education authorities are asked to consider making courses of in-service training available to these teachers in company with teachers in other schools. Head teachers have an important role to play not only in encouraging their staff to take part in courses of these types but also in initiating and leading discussion and experiment within the school itself.

Education over the age of 16

39. By the age of 16 some mentally handicapped young people are making faster progress in developing their capacities than at an earlier stage, and it is important that the progress they are making should not be interrupted by any rigidity about the age at which they leave school. Some will be ready when they are 16 to go on to the special training and work or educational programme provided for mentally handicapped adults by hospitals and local social services authorities; others who are less mature can benefit from staying on at school a little longer, possibly up to the age of 19. But even after they leave school many mentally handicapped young people can benefit from some form of continuing part-time education, whether in the form of further education or by provision of adult education linked to, or supplementing, the hospital's or the social services department's training programme. In some areas local education authorities are already providing courses specially for mentally handicapped people in one of their colleges of further education, youth centres, adult education centres, or, if appropriate, in the hospital.

Action

Health and local education authorities are asked to ensure that the Circular is brought to the attention of all staff concerned with the care and education of mentally handicapped children and other long stay children in hospital as well as to all those with relevant administrative responsibilities.

CIRCULAR 7/74

June 14, 1974

WORK EXPERIENCE

1. This Circular explains the provisions of the Education (Work Experience) Act 1973 and gives general guidance on work experience schemes.

2. The Act is concerned only with pupils of compulsory school age. There will no doubt continue to be work experience schemes in which pupils over compulsory school age will take part. Although these pupils are not subject to the provisions of the Act, the Secretary of State would expect that any arrangements which were made for them would take account of the general considerations set out in paragraphs 7 to 19 below concerning educational aims and the safety and welfare of pupils.

The provisions of the Act

3. In recent years, a number of schools have arranged for pupils to take part in the work of industrial and commercial concerns, or in public services, as part of their general education. Because of the statutory restrictions on the employment of children (which in this context means pupils below the upper limit of compulsory school age) the great majority of such schemes were available only for pupils over compulsory school age; in practice, schemes were devised mainly for pupils between the ages of 15 and 16.

4. The effect of raising the school leaving age was to extend by one year the period during which pupils are subject to the law relating to the employment of children, and thus to exclude those pupils between the ages of 15 and 16 from most work experience schemes. Subject to certain safeguards (dealt with in paragraph 5 below), the Act restores the former situation by allowing pupils to participate in such schemes in the last 12 months of compulsory schooling. The effect is that pupils who will cease to be of compulsory school age at the end of the spring term, 1975, have been eligible to take part in schemes since the end of the spring term, 1974; those who will cease to be of compulsory school age at the end of the summer term, 1975 will be eligible from the end of the summer term, 1974; and similarly in subsequent years.

5. The substantive provisions of the Act are contained in the first three sub-sections of Section 1.

(*a*) The effect of sub-section 1 is that the enactments which prohibit or regulate the employment of children will not apply to the employment of a pupil in the last 12 months of his compulsory schooling which is in pursuance of arrangements made or approved by the local education authority as part of an educational programme;

(*b*) Sub-section 2 prohibits work experience where the work concerned is subject to a statutory restriction based on age limits expressed in terms of a specified number of years or where work in ships is involved (in which case the prohibitions contained in the appropriate sections of the Employment of Women, Young Persons and Children Act 1920 and the Merchant Shipping Act 1970 will continue to apply); and

(*c*) Sub-section 3 forbids the making of arrangements for work experience for children in circumstances where it would be unlawful to employ young persons and applies the statutory restrictions relating to the employment of young persons to pupils employed in schemes of work experience under the Act.

6. The requirement in Section 1 (1) of the Act that arrangements should be made or approved by the local education authority is not intended to affect the responsibility for the curriculum of individual schools. In considering for approval arrangements made by voluntary aided, direct grant or non-maintained schools, including special schools, local education authorities may reasonably assume, in the absence of evidence to the contrary, that any arrangements submitted for their approval have been devised as part of the education of the pupils affected; they need concern themselves only with the suitability of the particular form of employment proposed.

The aims of work experience schemes

7. The principle which should underlie any work experience scheme is that pupils should be given an insight into the world of work, its disciplines and relationships. This principle, and the requirement of the Act that schemes for pupils of compulsory school age must form part of an educational programme, would not be satisfied by arrangements made, whether in school or elsewhere, whose purpose was specifically or mainly to assess individuals for particular forms of employment, or to occupy pupils in producing articles for sale. Schemes should include provision within the school curriculum for preparation before the pupils take part in work experience and for following up and discussing the experience gained. Employers should be made fully aware of the aims of the scheme and should be invited to plan their part in co-operation with the schools.

8. Work experience should have value for pupils of varying ability and aptitudes and should neither be designed as vocational training nor aimed at a limited range of pupils only. If it is possible to arrange for a variety of types of work to be available the opportunity for drawing comparisons will obviously be increased. It would, however, be undesirable if the time spent by an individual pupil in any place of work were so short as to give only a superficial impression. The total amount of time spent out of school on work experience schemes, and its distribution, will necessarily vary according to local and individual circumstances. In deciding how much time is appropriate, schools and local education authorities will need to take account of the time needed for supporting studies in schools and to satisfy themselves that the total amount of time spent is appropriate within the educational programme of the pupils.

Consultation

9. If such schemes are to be successful they need to be devised from the beginning in the fullest possible co-operation with all the interested parties. In the early stages the careers officer will be able to give advice, from his local knowledge, about suitable employers to approach and may be able to act as an intermediary between the school and the organisation. It is desirable that the preparatory discussions should include not only the management but also representatives of the employees, since the pupils will be under supervision and care of individual employees who will need to know the purpose of these schemes and to be aware of their responsibilities towards the pupils.

10. There may be some danger that parents will misunderstand the functions of work experience schemes unless they are carefully explained to them. It is therefore suggested that the nature and purpose of any scheme should be described to parents beforehand; authorities may think it desirable to obtain the individual consent of parents to their children taking part in such schemes.

Safety

11. Special attention should be given to the safety. health and welfare aspects of any scheme for participating in employment. There should be consultation, depending upon the type of employment envisaged, with H.M. Inspector of Factories, with the Inspectors appointed by the local authority for the purposes of the Offices, Shops and Railway Premises Act and with Regional Safety Inspectors of the Ministry of Agriculture, Fisheries and Food. Some successful work experience schemes have in the past included training sessions on the safety precautions observed in the particular industry and the reasons for them. Such a course might well form part of the introduction to any period of work experience.

12. In addition to the normal safeguards which apply to the employment of children and young persons no pupil should be allowed to undertake work which might be unsuitable for him on medical grounds (e.g. because of asthma, colour blindness, epilepsy or some other disability). School medical officers will normally be able to give advice based both on the pupils' previous medical records, and on the consideration that they will be giving at this stage of the pupils' school careers in order to identify any departure from normal health which might affect their choice of employment. The Employment Medical Adviser of the Department of Employment will be available to advise if there is doubt on medical grounds about whether a pupil should do any particular job. Special attention should be given to handicapped pupils between the ages of 15 and 16 at special schools, who become eligible to take part in work experience schemes for the first time under the provisions of the Act.

13. Some occupations are recognised as undesirable for young people, although not necessarily physically dangerous. Part-time employment of children in such occupations is generally prohibited by local bye-laws. The Employment of Children Act 1973 provides for these bye-laws to be replaced by regulations made by the Secretary of State for Social Services. So long as the bye-laws are in force, authorities and schools should have regard to their spirit and intention when selecting occupations for work experience schemes.

Teachers

14. The value of work experience schemes may be enhanced if the teachers who are helping the pupils with their preparation and follow-up studies have themselves had some experience in industry or commerce and are able to discuss the schemes with the pupils against that background. In this connection, authorities and schools may like to be reminded of the scheme which the Confederation of British Industry have been running for some years whereby teachers can be seconded to an industrial or commercial organisation for a short period. A description of this scheme was given in D.E.S. Circular 9/69 and further details may be obtained from the Confederation of British Industry at 21 Tothill Street, London SW1H 9LP.

15. The school will wish to supervise the progress of pupils while they are out of school, by making arrangements for teachers to visit the places where they are working and to keep in touch with the individuals in the organisations who are co-operating in the schemes.

16. Although work experience schemes should not be regarded primarily as vocational guidance they should make some contribution towards the individual pupil's knowledge of particular jobs and may influence his choices: this is a further reason for offering a variety of experience. Not only careers officers but also the teachers responsible for careers education within the schools will need to be closely associated with the development of schemes.

Payment

17. As work experience is part of the pupils' education, employers should make no payment to the pupils, the school or the authority. There may, however, be certain expenses, such as extra fares or the cost of meals taken out of school, which would normally be met by the school or authority as part of the cost of operating the scheme. There would be no objection to employers' assisting with such expenses either directly or, for instance, by extending the benefits of any welfare schemes for their employees to pupils engaged on work experience.

Insurance

18. Particular care will need to be taken to ensure that compensation is available if injury or damage is caused by accident. The provisions of the Act are intended to secure that proper safety arrangements are made. It must be recognised, however, that pupils will be working in unfamiliar conditions and that errors of judgement may arise. Any accident causing injury to persons or damage to property may, if responsibility is proved, render the local education authority or the school liable for damages to teachers, pupils or other persons affected. As pupils participating in work experience are not employed under a contract of service they are not entitled to the benefit of the National Insurance (Industrial Injuries) Act in the event of injury through accident; nor is the employer under an obligation under the Employers' Liability (Compulsory Insurance) Act 1969 to insure against his liability to them. Authorities and schools are advised to make certain that their insurance cover or other provision for compensation offers adequate protection against possible legal liabilities.

19. There may well be circumstances in which liability cannot be determined and in which an injured party might have no legal redress. Some authorities already maintain personal accident insurance schemes which provide compensation in these circumstances. If the existing insurance cover does not provide such protection it is advisable to make suitable arrangements before embarking upon any work experience schemes.

Administrative Memorandum 12/69

20. This Circular supersedes AM 12/69, which is withdrawn.

CIRCULAR 11/74

November 6, 1974

(Wales, 226/74)

HEALTH AND SAFETY AT WORK ETC. ACT 1974

1. The Health and Safety at Work Etc. Act 1974, which received the Royal Assent on 31 July, provides enabling legislation covering the main recommendations of the Committee on Safety and Health at Work (the Robens Committee). Parts I, II and IV are being brought into effect in three stages in the period up to 1 April, 1975 by Order of the Secretary of State for Employment (Statutory Instrument 1974/1439):

(i) 1 October, 1974, the Health and Safety Commission created by the new Act was set up.

(ii) 1 January, 1975, the Health and Safety Executive, responsible for enforcing statutory requirements on health and safety, will become operative. The staffs of the main health and safety inspectorates (Factories, Mines and Quarries, etc.) will then be transferred to the new executive.

(iii) 1 April, 1975, the general obligations of the Act on all employers and persons at work will come into force.

2. At that point, some five million people who are not at present covered by health and safety legislation will be brought within the scope of the Act. This will include all teachers and other employed persons in schools and other educational establishments. Students and schoolchildren are not included in the category of persons " at work " as defined in Section 52 (1) of the Act but come within the category of persons other than employees liable to be affected.

3. Local Authorities under the Commission's guidance will enforce the legislation in some areas of employment, including many covered by health and safety legislation for the first time. In general, these will relate broadly to " non-industrial " activities. Allocations of responsibilities will be made in regulations after consultation.

4. Employers are to ensure the health and safety of their employees at work by maintaining safe plant, safe systems of work, and safe premises; and also by ensuring adequate instruction, training and supervision. Employers are to prepare written safety policies and make them known. In addition regulations may be made prescribing certain circumstances in which safety representatives from among the employees may be appointed by trade unions, or elected by employees, or both, to represent the employees in consultations about health and safety. In prescribed circumstances the employer must establish a safety committee if requested by the safety representatives.

5. The aim is that employers should look at the conduct of their undertakings as a whole to ensure both the safety of their employees, and also that the general public are not adversely affected by their activities. This same obligation is placed upon the self-employed.

6. Designers, manufacturers, installers, erectors, importers, or suppliers of " articles and substances " for use at work are to ensure that, insofar as they are responsible, risks to health and safety are eliminated and that the articles or substances are safe when properly used.

7. Employees will have a duty to take reasonable care to avoid injury to themselves or to others by their work activities, and they are to co-operate with employers and others in meeting statutory requirements.

8. It should be noted that existing health and safety legislation will remain in force after 1 April, 1975 until such time as it is progressively repealed and replaced by improved and updated regulations made under the new Act, and by approved codes of practice. Regulations and codes of practice to be applied to the educational sector will be approved by the Health and Safety Commission only after full consultation with the Department of Education and Science and the Welsh Office, and with the appropriate education interests.

9. Part III of the Act deals with building regulations and attention is drawn to the enclosed Circular, issued jointly by the Department of the Environment

and the Welsh Office.* Section 61 of the Act extends the coverage of building regulations to maintained schools and colleges, at present exempt under Section 71 of the Public Health Act 1936. The provision of this part of the Act will be brought into force by statutory instrument on dates to be determined later. The preparation of the necessary new or amended building regulations will involve extensive consultation, and it should be noted that none of the new provisions will be in force until the appropriate commencement order has been made.

10. It should be emphasised that for the present nothing in the Act or the D.o.E./Welsh Office circular affects the validity of the Administrative Memorandum issued on 24 May, 1973 on Constructional Standards for Maintained and Direct Grant Educational Building in England and Wales (D.E.S. A.M. 11/73, W.E.O. A.M. 7/73). As modified by A.M. 4/74 (W.E.O. A.M. 1/74 this provides for certain parts of the Building Regulations 1972 to be applied to educational buildings for an experimental period from 1 July, 1975. Provision is made for the Department to grant exemptions if an authority wishes to depart from the standards indicated. Neither plans nor buildings in the course of construction will be subject to inspection by authorities responsible for the enforcement of the Building Regulations 1972 (i.e. the district councils).

CIRCULAR 5/75

July 18, 1975

THE REORGANISATION OF HIGHER EDUCATION IN THE NON-UNIVERSITY SECTOR: THE FURTHER EDUCATION REGULATIONS 1975

Introduction

1. The . . . regulations, which were laid before Parliament on 9 July, 1975 and will come into operation on 1 August, 1975, replace the Further Education Regulations 1969 and the Training of Teachers Regulations 1967 as amended.

2. The new regulations reflect the policy that, outside the universities, teacher education and higher and further education should be assimilated into a common system. The legal foundations for this reform will be further extended by the new awards Regulations made under the 1975 Education Act, which will provide for a common system of awards to students, including those following courses of teacher education.

General

3. The provisions of the previous regulations covered broadly the following areas:—

Teacher Training Regulations

(*a*) Provision for the overall supervision of teacher training through Area Training Organisations, including advice to the Secretary of State on the approval of persons as teachers in schools;

(*b*) Provisions relating to the management of maintained and voluntary establishments, the finance of the latter and the control of courses;

(*c*) Provisions for grant to students;

Further education regulations

(*d*) Provisions comparable to those at (*b*) above relating to the management of establishments and the control of courses;

(*e*) Provisions for grants to other voluntary institutions and organisations.

4. The new regulations bring together and modify the provisions relating to establishments and the control of courses (Parts II and III) and continue in Part IV, subject to minor modifications, the provisions relating to other voluntary institutions and organisations. Provision for teacher training student awards will in future be made in the Awards Regulations. The new arrangements for the supervision of teacher education and the approval of persons as teachers in

---

* Joint Circular No. 127/74 (Department of the Environment) and 194/74 (Welsh Office).

schools, which will be non-statutory except in so far as they depend on the amendment of the Schools Regulations 1959 effected by regulation 4 (4) of the new regulations, are set out in paragraphs 7 to 11 below.

5. *Transitional provisions: Regulation* 3.

This regulation provides, in connection with the reorganisation of higher education initiated by Circular 7/73, for directions to be given, after consultation with the maintaining authority or governing body, for the purpose of reorganising institutions which were conducted as training establishments under the Training of Teachers Regulations 1967, or which include a department which was so conducted. Staff of such institutions who become redundant as the result of directions given under regulation 3 will be eligible for compensation in accordance with the provisions of the Colleges of Education (Compensation) Regulations 1975* which were laid before Parliament on 15 July. The present intention is that such directions should normally be given each year in relation to decisions on the intake for the next academic year of students to concurrent courses of teacher training, as the reorganisation proceeds and the teacher training system contracts. It is intended that the regulation should be revoked as soon as the need for it expires.

6. *Revocation of teacher training regulations: Regulation* 4.

Apart from the provision for teacher training awards the most important provisions to lapse are those relating to:—

(*a*) the constitution and functions of Area Training Organisations,

(*b*) the duration, standards and academic supervision of courses of initial training, and

(*c*) the eligibility of students for admission to training.

The Government's intentions as to how these matters should be provided for in future are set out in the immediately following paragraphs.

7. *Qualified teacher status*

As a corollary to the revocation of the Teacher Training Regulations and the disappearance of the Area Training Organisations which were responsible for advising the Secretary of State on the approval of persons as teachers in schools, it has been necessary to amend the provisions of the Schools Regulations relating to qualified teacher status. This is done by regulation 4 (4) which amends the definition of the expression " qualified teacher " in regulation 16 (2) of the Schools Regulations to include a person who has successfully completed a course for the degree of Bachelor of Education, or a Certificate in Education or comparable qualification, of a U.K. university or the C.N.A.A. which has been approved by the Secretary of State as a course for the initial training of teachers, and who has been accepted by the Secretary of State as a qualified teacher. In relation to such acceptance the Secretary of State will be guided by the advice of the institution providing the course as to the suitability of the person concerned for employment as a teacher.

8. In approving courses for the purpose of the new Schools Regulation 16 (2) (*a*) (i) the Secretary of State will wish to satisfy himself that the body awarding the degree or certificate has established a committee or delegacy on which members of the teaching profession and their employers are suitably represented to advise, inter alia, on the professional aspects of such courses, including their duration, standard and academic supervision and the adequacy of the arrangements of the institutions providing them for recommending suitability for the teaching profession. These committees will therefore have a supervisory function over courses leading to qualified teacher status and over arrangements for recommending suitability for the teaching profession comparable with that exercised by the former Area Training Organisations.

9. It is not intended at the present time to lay down as a condition of recognition of courses any provisions as to their duration or the minimum academic qualifications or age of entry. The institution of courses which overlap and may lead to either a B.Ed. or a B.A. or a Dip.H.E. would make such provisions difficult if not impossible to administer. It will, however, be important that the institutions concerned should continue to ensure that persons who are unsuitable on grounds of character or health are not admitted to courses which include practical experience in schools. These matters will be within the purview of the Committees referred to in paragraph 8 above.

* S.I. 1975/1092.

10. *Regional organisations*

The Department is consulting separately those concerned about proposals made by the Council of Local Education Authorities for the establishment of new regional advisory machinery which through a series of committees would:—

(1) subsume the functions of the existing Regional Advisory Councils for Further Education,
(2) advise on the provision of courses of initial education and training for teachers, and
(3) be responsible for the promotion, co-ordination and review of in-service training for teachers and an improved system of induction.

The Advisory Committee on the Supply and Training of Teachers has already recommended that interim regional committees should be established as soon as possible for the third of the above functions.

11. It will be some time before decisions are reached on these proposals. In the meanwhile regulation 7 continues to provide for co-ordination between authorities, where appropriate in consultation with the existing Regional Advisory Councils for Further Education. It is hoped that universities responsible for Area Training Organisations will continue their existing co-ordinating activities in relation to in-service education and training of teachers until new regional committees are established.

12. *Other changes introduced by the* 1975 *regulations*

Regulation 6: *Fees.* The power in the 1967 Teacher Training Regulations to prescribe fees for tuition and board at teacher training establishments has been modified and extended to cover tuition fees for any course which attracts mandatory awards (in view of the fact that 90 per cent of the latter fees is met by central government grant) and fees for board and lodging at any establishment. It is, however, at present intended to exercise the powers conferred by this regulation only in respect of fees for board and lodging at establishments where it is provided in lieu of part of the normal student maintenance grant.

Regulation 8 *and Schedule* 1. Regulation 8 (a) reduces from six weeks to four the minimum length of courses of teacher education for which the Secretary of State's approval is required. This is in accordance with the decision announced in Circular 14/70 that the costs of providing approved full-time courses of four weeks or more and part-time courses of equivalent duration should be poolable. It also brings practice in relation to courses of teacher education more nearly into line with that applied to other advanced further education courses by regulation 8 and Schedule 1.

Regulation 11 (2): *Equipment.* Regulation 11 (2) raises from £1,000 to £2,500 the level above which the provision of items of equipment for teaching or research requires the approval of the Secretary of State. The change reflects increases in the costs of equipment.

Regulation 17: *Youth and community workers.* Regulation 17 extends to community centre wardens, youth club leaders, youth workers and youth and community workers the restriction on employment on medical grounds which applies to teachers.

Regulation 19: *Capital grant.* This regulation provides for capital grant of up to 100 per cent of expenditure in respect of assets which are neither under denominational control nor liable to revert to denominational use. It thereby extends to all non-denominational institutions the provision for 100 per cent grant which under the previous teacher training regulations was restricted to Goldsmiths' College. In the case of new voluntary institutions created by the amalgamation of a maintained college and a voluntary college, the provision of capital grant will be a matter for discussion between the Department and the Local Education Authority concerned.

Regulation 27 (2) (*d*): *Capital grant.* This regulation permits the Secretary of State to require undertakings from establishments receiving capital grant that they will pay to the Secretary of State a just part of the net proceeds of the disposal of any assets in respect of which grant was paid. Such undertakings will be framed so as to ensure that the Government benefits equitably from any change in the value of the assets as the result of inflation or otherwise.

CIRCULAR 7/75

July 30, 1975

(Wales, 126/75)

PHASING OUT OF DIRECT GRANTS TO GRAMMAR SCHOOLS

Introduction

1. The Direct Grant Grammar Schools (Cessation of Grant) Regulations 1975 were made by the Secretary of State for Education and Science and the Secretary of State for Wales on 21 July, 1975 and will come into operation on 21 August, 1975. The regulations, a copy of which is being sent with this Circular to local education authorities and the governors of direct grant grammar schools, give effect to the intention of the Government, announced by the Secretary of State for Education and Science in the House of Commons on 11 March, 1975, to end the present system of direct grants to grammar schools. The purpose of this Circular is to bring the new regulations to the attention of local education authorities and the proprietors of direct grant grammar schools and to offer guidance on their main provisions.

Effects of the new regulations

Cessation of Grant

2. Regulation 2 of the new regulations provides that grant shall cease to be payable to the proprietors of a direct grant grammar school when it becomes a maintained school or when it ceases to have any pupils in respect of whom grant is payable, whichever is the sooner. " Grant " includes capitation, sixth form and fee-remission grant, and also where applicable grant for special or experimental work, which will continue so long as other elements of the grant are payable in respect of pupils in the school. Until grant ceases completely to be payable, the school will continue to be recognised as a direct grant grammar school and remain subject to certain requirements of the Direct Grant Schools Regulations 1959; but some such requirements are modified or disapplied during the grant phasing-out period in the case of schools which are not going to enter the maintained system (see paragraph 9 below).

Grant for pupils admitted in 1976–7

3. Paragraph 1 of regulation 3 prescribes new conditions for the payment of grant in respect of pupils admitted in the educational year 1976–7. Grant may be paid to a school in respect of such pupils only if the proprietors have satisfied the Secretary of State by the end of 1975 that they intend the school to become a maintained comprehensive school and have notified a local education authority of their intention to consult the authority about statutory proposals to this effect.

4. All direct grant grammar schools have already been supplied with copies of a form of declaration of intent which, if completed on the authorisation of a school's governors and sent before 31 December, 1975 to the Secretary of State and to a local education authority specified by the governors, will satisfy these conditions and thus ensure that grant is payable in respect of pupils admitted to the school in 1976–7. The Secretary of State will welcome an early indication of each school's intentions, whether or not the governors intend it to become part of the maintained system. A local education authority receiving a completed declaration of intent may expect the governors of the school concerned to follow it up at an early date by initiating or continuing discussions on the practical possibilities of the school's finding a place in the authority's system (see paragraph 13 onwards).

5. A direct grant school becoming maintained will, in the normal way, retain its identity as a separate institution. In certain cases, however, it may be more appropriate that the school should enter the maintained system in amalgamation with another non-maintained school or with an existing maintained school. In terms of the statutory proposals required to bring it about, the latter course would involve either a significant enlargement of the premises of the existing maintained school to take in those of the former direct grant school, or the formal closure of the maintained school and the establishment of a single new maintained

school in the two sets of premises. By virtue of regulation 3 (3) and corresponding provisions elsewhere in the new regulations a direct grant school whose premises become in any of these ways part of the premises of a maintained school will be regarded, for the purposes of the new regulations, as becoming maintained. Governors who intend their school to follow such a course may therefore make a declaration of intent in the standard terms, and the remainder of this Circular should be read accordingly.

Grant for pupils admitted in subsequent years

6. Paragraph 2 of regulation 3 prescribes further conditions for the payment of grant in respect of pupils admitted in any educational year subsequent to 1976–7. Grant will be payable to a school in respect of such pupils only if the Secretary of State is satisfied on 1 January preceding the beginning of the relevant educational year that the proprietors' intention as declared in 1975 still holds good and that—

(*a*) the proprietors are in consultation with the specified local education authority and the authority are not unwilling to maintain the school; and

(*b*) either the necessary statutory proposals have been submitted to (and not rejected by) the Secretary of State or he is satisfied that there is good reason why they have not yet been submitted.

7. The Secretary of State expects to have received not later than the end of 1976 appropriate statutory proposals in respect of the generality of schools which have expressed the intention of coming into the maintained system. No grant will be payable to any school in respect of pupils admitted after the education year 1976–7 if by the end of 1976 proposals have already been submitted and rejected; nor will it be payable to a school for which proposals have not by then been submitted unless the governors are able to satisfy the Secretary of State in a particular case that there are special reasons why this could not have been done. In each such case he will expect the proposals to be made at the earliest appropriate opportunity in 1977. The Secretary of State will carry out a further review at the end of 1977 to determine whether there is any remaining school whose circumstances are so exceptional that proposals could not by then have reasonably been submitted; if not there will be no further deferment of the phasing-out of grants.

8. Once grant has ceased to be payable in respect of any one year's intake, it will not be payable in respect of any subsequent year's intake. Thus, once the phasing-out of grant to a school has commenced, it will continue until in due course the payment of grant ceases altogether and the school as a result ceases to be a direct grant school.

Removal of controls

9. Regulation 4 makes provision to remove or disapply certain controls imposed by the Direct Grant Schools Regulations 1959 in respect of schools in which the phasing-out of grants has commenced. In the case of such a school:

(*a*) the provisions of the 1959 Regulations as regards the constitution of the governing body are replaced by a requirement for the governing body to be constituted as may appear appropriate to the Secretary of State after consultation with the proprietors. This will permit the governing body of a school to be re-constituted by order made by the Secretary of State under section 1 (2) (*c*) of the Education Act 1973 without impairing the right of the proprietors to apply to the Charity Commissioners for a new scheme if they prefer;

(*b*) the approval of the Secretary of State to the provision or alteration of premises will no longer be required;

(*c*) the requirement of the 1959 Regulations as regards charges for school dinners, arrangements for admission (including free and reserved places) and the approval and remission of fees will apply only in respect of pupils for whom grant is still payable, so long as any such pupils remain in the school.

Grants to schools becoming maintained

10. Regulation 5 enables the Secretary of State, when a direct grant grammar

school becomes a county or voluntary school, to pay grants to the proprietors in order to cover:

(*a*) the outstanding balance of certain capital debts incurred before 11 March, 1975 in connection with the provision of premises or equipment. Grant will be paid only in respect of debts which have been serviced from tuition fees approved by the Secretary of State;

(*b*) 85 per cent of any expenditure incurred on approved building projects undertaken after 10 March, 1975 and before the school becomes maintained. Only expenditure on approved building work undertaken to meet emergency or other exceptional circumstances during this period will be considered for grant under this head;

(*c*) any expenses necessarily incurred in connection with the school becoming maintained. In particular, this will enable the Secretary of State to make grants, if necessary, to meet unavoidable deficits attributable to expenditure of one kind or another from income (e.g. compensatory or redundancy payments to staff) for purposes connected with the transition to the maintained system. The Secretary of State will exercise his discretion to make grants under this head only if he is satisfied that the expenditure was essential and of such a nature that without it the governors would not have been able to make, or look for the concurrence of the local education authority in making, the formal proposal to become maintained.

Assistance with fees

11. Regulation 6 has the effect that, for the purposes of the Regulations for Scholarships and Other Benefits 1945, pupils taking up places at direct grant schools for which grant is no longer payable may be treated in the same way as pupils taking up places at independent schools. The new Regulations leave unchanged the powers and obligations of authorities under Section 6 of the Education (Miscellaneous Provisions) Act 1953.

Entry to the maintained system

General

12. Entry to the maintained system is effected by the approval of the Secretary of State of formal proposals made to him under section 13 of the Education Act 1944 (as amended). If the proposal is that the direct grant school should be maintained as a county school, it must be made by the local education authority under section 13 (1) (*b*); if it is that the direct grant school should be maintained as a voluntary school (whether controlled or aided), it must be made by the proprietors, after consultation with the local education authority, under section 13 (2). A straightforward proposal for the maintenance of a direct grant grammar school as a voluntary school, if made with the concurrence of the local education authority, the proprietors and any trustees with a vested interest in the school premises, is exempted by the proviso to section 13 (3) from the public notice and objection provisions of that sub-section. If, however, the proposal involves amalgamation of the direct grant school with an existing school (see paragraph 5 above) this exemption does not apply unless the other school is also a direct grant school.

13. Where an authority are approached with a view to a direct grant school's finding a place in their system the Secretary of State hopes they will give it the most serious consideration, and do everything they can to facilitate the transition for any school willing to make it. He recognises that in some cases the acceptance of generally small and hitherto selective schools, some with a boarding element, into local comprehensive systems will present problems, but he hopes that both sides will make every effort to reach agreement wherever possible on the statutory proposals to be submitted to him at the appropriate time.

14. The Secretary of State wishes to emphasise that the Department will be ready to offer all possible help in any discussions between authorities and schools. He asks authorities to inform the Department if they propose to notify the governors of a school that they will not support statutory proposals by the governors or make such proposals themselves. Such notification would, by virtue of paragraph 3 (2) (*b*) of the new regulations, make it impossible for the Secretary of State to pay grant in respect of pupils admitted to the school subsequently,

and he would wish to satisfy himself that, in all the circumstances, it was reasonable for the authority to proceed with it.

Proposed admission arrangements

15. To conform with the Government's policy on the organisation of secondary education as set out in Circular 4/74, the regulations provide (paragraph 3 (1) (*a*)) that the proprietors' intention should be that their school should be maintained as a county or voluntary school where the admission of pupils is not based wholly or partly on selection by reference to ability or aptitude, and no formal proposal which does not meet this condition will be approved by the Secretary of State. If, after a school has become maintained casual vacancies arise in forms which were admitted while the school was a selective school, they may be filled on a suitably selective basis. In other respects the arrangements for admission to a maintained school which was formerly a direct grant school will be those specified in the articles of government which will be made in the normal way in accordance with the requirements of the Education Acts.

Premises

16. The Secretary of State will not withhold approval from a proposal that a direct grant school should be maintained as a county or voluntary school solely on the ground that the premises of the school are not, or in their proposed new function would not be, of the standard required by the Standards for School Premises Regulations 1959. It will be for governors or local education authorities, as the case may be, to bring the premises up to the prescribed standard as soon as may be. No special allocation of resources will be made for this purpose in building programmes. It will be for the maintaining authority to deal with the building requirements of maintained schools which were formerly direct grant schools on the same basis, both as to priorities and programming procedures, as other maintained schools. Responsibility for the cost of any such building work, and any associated financial arrangements, will be those appropriate to the type and classification of the maintained school.

Staff

17. Questions affecting the staff of direct grant schools which enter the maintained system may arise in connection with qualified teacher (Q.T.) status, salaries and further employment.

18. While no guarantee can be given that Q.T. status will automatically be granted to teachers entering the maintained system who do not already possess it, the Department will be ready to consider an application from a local education authority for Q.T. status on the basis of service and experience and qualifications in respect of any teacher without that status; the procedure is set out in paragraphs 15 and 16 of Circular 11/73. The Department will also be ready to receive enquiries on this subject from individual teachers; any such enquiry should be made in writing, addressed to Teachers' Salaries and Qualifications Division, D.E.S., Mowden Hall, Staindrop Road, Darlington, Co. Durham, and should make clear that it concerns a person who is teaching in a direct grant grammar school. For teachers with Q.T. status who have not completed a period of probation, the Department will be prepared to waive probation on the recommendation of the local education authority.

19. The provisions in the Burnham Salaries document which relate to safeguarding of salaries do not apply to staff hitherto employed in direct grant schools; but the Secretary of State hopes that, where a direct grant school enters the maintained system, arrangements can be made to maintain as far as possible the salary and position which each member of staff had before the change in status of the school. Similarly the Secretary of State hopes that the local education authority will make every effort to find appropriate employment for all members of staff either in the school or elsewhere in the authority's service. Where this does not prove to be possible, the issue of compensation for termination of employment by the school governors will arise: this matter is under consideration by the Department.

Boarding schools

20. It will be open to the governors of any direct grant boarding school to propose, after consultation with the local education authority, that the school

shall enter the maintained system as a boarding school. The Secretary of State hopes that such proposals will be made whenever, in the view of the governors and the authority, there is a continuing boarding need which would be met by the school. As with proposals for day schools, proposals for boarding schools must also provide for the admission of pupils to be without reference to ability or aptitude.

General

21. It is the hope of the Secretary of State that the schools and local education authorities will, as quickly as is consistent with a proper consideration of the courses of action open in particular cases, reach decisions of principle and carry them into effect so that prolonged uncertainty about the future of the schools can be avoided in the interests of all concerned.

CIRCULAR 2/76

January 20, 1976

(Wales, 20/76)

SEX DISCRIMINATION ACT 1975

1. The Sex Discrimination Act 1975 received Royal Assent on 12 November, 1975. Apart from certain transitional arrangements which are set out in Schedule 4, the provisions of the Act making discrimination unlawful were brought into operation by Order* on 29 December, 1975 with the exception of those parts of the education provisions which relate to admissions, where the appointed day will be 1 September, 1976.

2. The Act implements with some amendments the proposals set out in the White Paper " Equality for Women " published in September 1974 and incorporates additional provisions such as those relating to educational charities and to discriminatory training. It makes sex discrimination unlawful in employment, training and related matters (where discrimination against married women is also dealt with), in education and in the provision of housing and goods, services and facilities to the public. The Act applies to discriminatory advertising in these areas. The Equal Opportunities Commission has been established to ensure effective enforcement of the legislation in the public interest and to promote equal opportunities between the sexes.

3. The purpose of this Circular is to draw to the attention of local education authorities, and other bodies responsible for the provision of education, the new duties and obligations imposed by the Act and the consequent need to examine current practices and arrangements in the light of the Act. Appendix I explains the statutory definition of discrimination on grounds of sex and describes briefly the provisions dealing with employment; education; goods, services and facilities; general exceptions; the handling of individual complaints and the role of the Equal Opportunities Commission. It refers specifically to the position of single sex educational establishments and boarding accommodation. Appendix II describes the educational establishments which are covered by the education provisions of the Act. These are for convenience separated, as they are in Schedule 2 of the Act, into public and private sectors. (The separation relates essentially to enforcement of the Act—public sector establishments are subject to the Secretary of State's powers under the Education Acts; private sector establishments are not.) The education provisions give certain duties and responsibilities to the Secretary of State for Education and Science (or to the Secretary of State for Wales, in respect of those education fields for which he is responsible). Throughout this Circular, the term " Secretary of State " should therefore be taken to mean either the Secretary of State for Education and Science or the Secretary of State for Wales, as appropriate, except where otherwise indicated.

---

* The Sex Discrimination Act 1975 (Commencement) Order (S.I. 1975 No. 1845 C.51).

The effects of the educational provisions

4. It is neither practicable nor desirable (because any complainant has the right of access to the county courts) to attempt to interpret definitively the provisions of the Act or to forecast what decisions the Secretary of State, in exercising his role of enforcement of the education provisions in the public sector, would take in the case of any particular complaint. It will be the responsibility of local education authorities and managers, governors and proprietors of educational establishments to examine their existing practices and arrangements to ensure that any current practices made unlawful by the Act are discontinued.

5. Subject to the exception for single sex establishments, it will be unlawful to refuse to admit a girl or boy to an educational establishment in circumstances where a pupil of the other sex would be admitted. (This applies where appropriate to men and women students). Local education authorities and other responsible bodies may therefore need to consider their admission arrangements including, where selection procedures continue, the basis on which selective places should be allocated to boys and girls. The principle to be observed is, of course, that of ensuring equal opportunity irrespective of sex. The lines on which this principle can best be worked out in practice will need to emerge in due course from experience. The Department's view, however, is that equal opportunity does not necessarily imply, and may well be incompatible with, the maintenance of any particular balance of sexes in the intake of a school or the make-up of a class; the sex of a particular pupil will be irrelevant to his or her claim for admission, except in the case of a single-sex establishment.

6. Local education authorities will have not only an obligation not to discriminate in respect of existing education establishments but also a duty to secure that the facilities for education provided by them are provided without sex discrimination. The effect of the general duty under Section 25 is to require local education authorities to plan their future provision on the principle of equality of opportunities for boys and girls. Planning in education has to take account of the future numbers of pupils and of students and of their needs. This has implications for the organisation of institutions and for the courses which are provided within them.

7. It will, for example, be unlawful to refuse to allow girls in a co-educational school to join a course or class to which boys are admitted and similarly to refuse to admit boys to a course or class to which girls are admitted. This has particular relevance to those subject classes which in some schools have traditionally been mainly or even exclusively reserved for boys and girls, e.g. technology and home economics classes. It will, however, not be unlawful to refuse a pupil access to a facility which is already being so fully used that any further applicants would have to be refused whether they were boys or girls. The Act does not prohibit the continuance of separate facilities for boys and girls where these are considered appropriate, provided that the facilities afforded to each sex can justifiably be regarded as equal. For example, a co-educational school will not necessarily be obliged to provide mixed classes in physical education (a specific exception is made under which further education courses which are courses in physical training or courses designed for teachers of physical training may be provided separately for men and women). Nor does the Act oblige an educational establishment to provide a facility or course that is not already being provided in that establishment.

Curriculum

8. The attention of local education authorities and other responsible bodies is drawn to Education Survey 21 " Curricular Differences for Boys and Girls ", not only in respect of primary schools but more generally with regard to the conclusions as follows:

> " The prevailing picture is of traditional assumptions being worked out through the curricular patterns of secondary schools, and of support for and acceptance of these patterns by the majority of teachers, parents and pupils. It may be that society can justify the striking differences that exist between the subjects studied by boys and girls in secondary schools, but it is more likely that a society that needs to develop to the full the talents and skills of all its people will find the discrepancies disturbing. Whatever differences that may continue to exist ought to be based on genuine choice:

choice openly offered to all who reveal the necessary interest, ability and determination, and not choice based on traditional assumptions about the 'proper' spheres of interest and influence of men and women.

If all secondary schools were to carry out an analysis of both content and organisation of the curriculum from the first year onwards and to ensure that choices made later were based, as nearly as is practicable, on a real equality of access to experience, to information and to guidance, that would be one step towards eradicating prejudices about the roles of men and women which frustrate individual development and cause a wastage of talent a country can ill afford."

9. Although these conclusions relate to secondary schools, the principle is one of general application. Responsibility for evaluating curriculum to provide equal access to experience, information and guidance rests with local education authorities, managers and governors, and, most important of all, the teachers. While the Secretary of State will not hesitate to use his powers to stop any particular act of discrimination, he does not control the curriculum and it is important for teachers, with the support of local education authorities, to take a hard look at the organisation of the curriculum and to consider whether the materials and techniques they use, and the guidance they give, especially in the early years, inhibit free choice later.

Careers guidance

10. Careers education and guidance given by teachers is subject to the education provisions of the Act. Local education authorities also have a specific obligation placed on them by Section 15 of the Act not to discriminate in the performance of their functions under Section 8 of the Employment and Training Act 1973, that is, in the provision of advice and assistance through the careers service.

11. The principle of providing careers guidance without discrimination has been well established among careers officers for a number of years and is particularly important now that the expanded careers service is responsible for careers advice in further education establishments, including the polytechnics, as well as in schools. The fact that discrimination on the part of employers is made unlawful by the Act will assist careers officers in the task of overcoming traditional attitudes and assumptions about careers.

12. Local education authorities will no doubt have regard to the recommendations of the Survey by H.M. Inspectors "Careers Education in Secondary Schools" (Education Survey 18). It is important that curriculum in schools should enable boys and girls to keep subject options open. Pupils, parents, teachers and careers officers all have a part to play in ensuring that traditional attitudes and assumptions are examined at every stage in a pupils' education.

Discriminatory training

13. Section 47 provides that it is not unlawful for certain training bodies to discriminate by restricting training to one sex only when the training is for work in which over the past 12 months no persons, or comparatively few persons, of that sex have been engaged (whether nationally or in a particular area of Great Britain). There is also an exception for discrimination in the provisions of training to people who are in particular need of it because they have not been in employment for domestic or family reasons. Industrial Training Boards, the Manpower Services Commission, the Employment Service Agency and the Training Services Agency may all discriminate under this section. Other bodies may take advantage of the exception only if they are designated for the purpose in an Order made by the Secretary of State, (the Secretary of State for Employment or one of the Education Ministers). Further education colleges already provide courses designed to meet the needs of women who, for domestic or family reasons, have not been in employment, and it is hoped that local education authorities and colleges will encourage the development of such courses. If they are satisfied that it is desirable or necessary to restrict such courses, or courses in work previously dominated by the other sex, to persons of one sex, the Secretary of State will be prepared to consider making an Order under Section 47 on receipt of an application for designation.

14. It would not be unlawful for a further education college or other responsible body to provide a course of training restricted to members of one sex to meet the same special needs at the request of Industrial Training Boards, the Manpower Services Commission, the Employment Services Agency, the Training Services Agency or any other body designated by the Secretary of State for Employment under Section 47.

Enforcement provisions and the treatment of complaints

15. Local education authorities and other responsible bodies may have complaints made against them on the basis of alleged discrimination. Complaints alleging breaches of the employment provisions of the Act (including Section 15 which makes discrimination under the Employment and Training Act 1973 unlawful) would be brought before an industrial tribunal if no settlement can be reached through the services of a conciliation officer of the Advisory, Conciliation and Arbitration Service. Complaints alleging a breach of the obligations imposed by the education provisions of the Act would be brought before the county courts as civil actions.

16. However, a complaint in respect of a public sector education institution which is subject to the duty imposed by Section 25 must in the first place be made to the Secretary of State, who will deal with the complaint under the powers conferred by Sections 68 and 99 of the Education Act 1944 as extended by the present Act. Local education authorities and other responsible bodies should advise complainants in respect of public sector education institutions to address their complaints to the Permanent Under Secretary of State, Department of Education and Science (Room 10/9), Elizabeth House, York Road, London SE1 7PH, or to the Secretary for Welsh Education, Welsh Education Office, 31 Cathedral Road, Cardiff, CF1 9UT, as appropriate. Such complaints cannot be brought before the courts until two months after the complaint has been made to the Secretary of State unless, before the end of two months, the Secretary of State has reached a conclusion. If he has not done so within two months he will, without prejudice to the complainant's right to bring proceedings in the courts, continue his consideration of the complaint and notify his decision as quickly as possible.

17. The Equal Opportunities Commission may, in the course of a formal investigation, find that an unlawful discriminatory act or a breach of the Equal Pay Act has been committed, in which case it may issue a " non-discrimination notice ", enforceable by injunction, requiring that the offending acts cease. Where however the discriminatory act relates to a public sector educational institution, and the latter can be dealt with by the Secretary of State under his powers under Sections 68 and 99 of the 1944 Act, the Equal Opportunities Commission is not empowered to issue a non-discrimination notice but is instead to notify the Secretary of State.

Transitional exemption orders

18. The Act provides that it would not be unlawful for a single sex educational establishment to discriminate as regards admissions only during a period in which it was moving to full co-education where a transitional exemption order has been made by the Secretary of State (for the public sector) or by the Equal Opportunities Commission (for the private sector).

19. In the case of maintained schools, an application under Section 13 of the Education Act 1944 whereby a school moved from single sex to co-educational status over a period will be treated as an application for a transitional exemption order under Section 27 (1) of the Sex Discrimination Act. There is thus no need for two separate applications.

20. In the case of all public sector education establishments, other than maintained schools, regulations will be made to cover the submission to the Secretary of State of an application for, and the making by him of, a transitional exemption order.

21. Private sector establishments (independent schools, independent colleges and universities) should address applications for transitional exemption orders to the Equal Opportunities Commission. In considering an application, the Commission will need to be satisfied that the terms of the application are

reasonable, having regard to the nature of the premises at which the establishment is carried on, the accommodation, equipment and facilities available, and the financial resources of the responsible body.

22. The transitional exemption arrangements also apply to a co-educational school with boarding accommodation for pupils of one sex only, which decides to admit boarders of the opposite sex but wishes to move to complete non-discrimination in its boarding admissions over a period.

Finance

23. The Secretary of State expects that most local education authorities will be able to comply with the requirements of the Act by making appropriate administrative arrangements without incurring significant extra expenditure. If, however, any authorities find that their existing arrangements imply some unlawful discrimination within the terms of the Act and that in consequence some extra expenditure is unavoidable, they will be expected to contain that expenditure within budgets which are consistent with the Government's general advice on local authority expenditure. It will be the responsibility of local education authorities and other responsible bodies to ensure that their existing facilities and resources are so used as to ensure that there shall be no discrimination on grounds of sex.

APPENDIX 1

SEX DISCRIMINATION ACT 1975

Definition

1. Part I of the Act defines discrimination. Though the Act is drafted in terms of discrimination against women, it applies equally to discrimination against men. References in the Act to women and to men are construed as including references to girls and boys. Discrimination covers both " direct discrimination " and " indirect discrimination ". It is direct discrimination to treat a woman, on the grounds of her sex, less favourably than a man is, or would be, treated. Unfavourable treatment only amounts to discrimination where, as respects the circumstances relevant for the purposes of the provisions of the Act, the circumstances of the woman and of the man correspond as nearly as may be. Indirect discrimination occurs where, in order to determine who shall and who shall not receive some particular treatment, a person applies to men and women alike a condition or requirement which:

(i) is such that a considerably smaller proportion of women than men can comply with it and
(ii) which he cannot show to be justifiable irrespective of the sex of the person to whom it is applied,

where non-compliance with the condition or requirement constitutes a disadvantage to the woman to whom it is applied. Where the treatment accorded to men differs according to their marital status, the treatment accorded to a woman is to be compared with the treatment accorded to a man of the same marital status. In the field of employment only, it is discrimination to treat a married person less favourably than a single person of the same sex or to impose a condition or requirement which has the effect of discriminating against married people. The Act also covers discrimination by way of victimisation; i.e., treating one person less favourably than another because that person had, for example, asserted her rights under the Sex Discrimination Act, or had helped another person to assert their rights.

Employment

2. Part II of the Act applies to employment and related matters. It is unlawful under the Act for an employer to discriminate in the recruitment of new employees and in the treatment of his existing employees. The Act specifically refers to discrimination in the context of promotion, transfer, or training and also covers dismissal or other detrimental action by an employer. It complements the

Equal Pay Act 1970 by dealing with the non-contractual aspects of employment and contractual situations (other than the contractual payment of money) not covered by the 1970 Act, which is amended so that the two pieces of legislation do not overlap.

3. There are a number of exceptions to the employment provisions. Three of the exceptions deal respectively with provision made in relation to death or retirement, acts done under statutory authority (i.e. acts which are necessarily done in order to comply with a statutory requirement) and cases where sex is a genuine occupational qualification for a job. It is not unlawful under the Act for there to be difference of treatment between men and women in respect of pensions. No unlawful discrimination will be involved in the appointment of men and women teachers in order to comply with the requirements of the Burnham Salaries Documents (e.g. the provision in paragraph 5 of the 1975 Primary and Secondary document) because any acts which must be done in order to comply with legislation existing at the dat of the Act are excluded from its provisions.

4. Employers may discriminate on grounds of sex in recruitment or training for, and in promotion or transfer to, employment where being of a particular sex is a genuine occupational qualification. The Act lays down criteria for establishing whether a particular job satisfies this exception. The exception applies also to a job where only some of the duties satisfy any of the criteria, except where the employer has other employees who can reasonably and without undue inconvenience be expected to carry out such duties. The criterion under the genuine occupational qualification exception which is most relevant in the field of education, is that dealing with certain forms of social, welfare, educational and similar work. Where the sex of the individual providing personal services may have a bearing on the effectiveness of those services (Section 7 (2) (e)) it will be open to a local education authority or other employer in education to claim that a particular teaching post should be filled by a man or woman where that post involves a measure of pastoral care or counselling to pupils of one sex which cannot reasonably be provided by other members of the appropriate sex already employed. Section 7 (2) (e) does not provide a total exception. It would not prevent a complaint of discrimination being made to an industrial tribunal, but the body against whom the complaint is made could argue in front of the industrial tribunal that the act complained of did not constitute discrimination because it fell within the criterion set out in Section 7 (2) (e) as modified by Section 7 (4). It will be necessary for any body against which a complaint is made before an industrial tribunal to show that the criteria set out in Section 7 (2) apply to the particular job in question.

5. Single sex educational establishments are excluded from the education provisions of the Act but there is no exception from the employment provisions for the staff of such establishments. It would therefore be unlawful to discriminate in the appointment of staff to a single sex educational establishment if the discrimination is not otherwise permitted (c.f. paragraph 4 above) under the Act.

Education

6. The provision of education, and of goods, services and facilities is dealt with in Part III. Section 22 makes it unlawful for the " responsible body " for an educational establishment specified in Section 22 to discriminate on grounds of sex. The educational establishments specified are those maintained by a local authority, independent schools which are not special schools, special schools which are not maintained by a local education authority, and universities, and certain other establishments designated under Section 24. The Secretary of State has made an Order designating under Section 24 certain educational establishments. (The Sex Discrimination (Designated Educational Establishments) Order 1975—S.I. 1975 No. 1902).

7. Discrimination in the field of education covers:—

(*a*) the terms of admission to an establishment;

(*b*) the refusal or deliberate omission to accept an application for admission;

(*c*) where a person has already been admitted to the establishment, the way in which it affords him or her access to any benefits, facilities or services; or refusal or deliberate omission to afford such access; and exclusion from the establishment.

8. Section 23 makes it unlawful for a local education authority to discriminate in the performance of its other functions under the Education Acts. Examples of these functions are the award of discretionary grants under Section 2 of the Education Act 1962 and the provision of facilities for social and physical recreation under Section 53 of the Education Act 1944.

9. In addition to the obligation not to discriminate, Section 25 places on the responsible bodies in the public sector a general duty to secure that the facilities for education provided by them, and any ancillary benefits or services, are provided without sex discrimination. (The powers of the Secretary of State under Sections 68 and 99 of the Education Act 1944 are applied in the public sector both to the enforcement of the duties imposed by Sections 22 and 23 and to the general duty imposed by Section 25).

Single sex education establishments

10. Admissions to existing and future single sex establishments are excluded from the provisions of the Act by Section 26. Single sex establishments include not only those which admit pupils or students of one sex only but also those institutions whose essential single sex character is unchanged by the fact that they admit small numbers of pupils of the opposite sex. The admission of pupils of the opposite sex must however either be exceptional or be confined to particular courses of instruction or teaching classes. An example of the first criterion would be the admission to a women's college of education of mature men students who lived locally and who would otherwise have to leave home to attend a course at a mixed college. Examples of the second criterion are those girls' schools which admit boys to the infant or junior classes only and those boys' schools which admit girls to the sixth form only.

Boarding accommodation

11. A co-educational school (and exception relates only to schools and not to other educational establishments) which has boarding provision only for pupils of one sex, is excepted from the education provisions of the Act, so far as its boarding facilities are concerned.

12. No such exception is made for schools and other education establishments which provide boarding accommodation for both sexes. Section 46 of the Act provides however that it is not unlawful to discriminate as regards admission to residential accommodation, which includes shared sleeping or sanitary facilities which, for reasons of propriety and privacy, need to be reserved to men or to women, provided that men and women are treated as fairly and equitably as possible given the exigencies of the situation. However, there is a need in such a case, having regard to the frequency of the demand, to consider how far it would be reasonable to expect that the accommodation should be added to or altered.

13. Section 27 provides that single sex establishments, or establishments with single sex boarding facilities, which wish to move to full co-education over a period, may apply for a " transitional exemption order ". In the case of public sector establishments, the application would be to the Secretary of State; in the case of all other educational establishments, the application would be to the Equal Opportunities Commission.

14. Section 28 excludes from the education provisions of the Act further education courses in physical training and courses for teachers of physical training.

15. Only the establishments specified in Section 22 or in an Order made under Section 24 (i) are subject to the education provisions of the Act. Any other establishment which provides services of an educational nature to the public or a section of the public (such as a commercial school of languages) will be subject to the requirements of Section 29. However, under Section 34, voluntary bodies may restrict their membership to one sex, and where the objects of the body require it, may restrict the benefits they provide (which may include education or training) to one sex.

Goods, services and facilities

16. Discrimination in the provision to the public or a section of the public of goods, services and facilities, including for example loans, finance, mortgages

and educational services not covered by Sections 22 to 28, is made unlawful by Section 29. Discrimination in the disposal and management of premises is dealt with in Section 30. There are, however, exceptions for small dwellings; for single sex hospitals or other establishments for persons requiring special care, attention or supervision; where provision on a single sex basis is required by religious doctrine or to comply with the main object of a voluntary body: for the constitutional or organisational arrangements of political parties; and for situations where questions of decency and privacy arise.

General exceptions

17. Part V of the Act specifies certain general exceptions to its scope, for example, for acts done in order to comply with existing legislation; in relation to sporting activities in which by reason of physique women are at a disadvantage to men; or, in the life assurance and similar fields, on the basis of reliable actuarial or statistical data. Acts done in compliance with the terms of charitable instruments are also exempt but the legislation makes special provision to enable educational trusts at present benefiting one sex, if they so wish, to apply to the Secretary of State for a scheme or order enabling the trust to open its funds to both sexes.

Equal opportunities commission

18. The Act establishes the Equal Opportunities Commission, whose members will be appointed by the Home Secretary, with the following responsibilities:—

(i) to work towards the elimination of discrimination;
(ii) to promote equality or opportunity between men and women; and
(iii) to keep under review the working of the Act and of the Equal Pay Act and, either at the request of the Secretary of State or if it thinks fit, to draw up and submit to the Secretary of State proposals for amending the Act.

In its enforcement role, the Commission will be able to investigate unlawful discriminatory practices and issue " non-discrimination notices " requiring the cessation of these practices, which will be enforceable in the courts, by way of injunction. The Commission will be able to assist individuals in cases where special considerations arise, including cases raising questions of principle. It will be able to conduct formal investigations required by any Secretary of State or where the terms of reference of the investigation state that the Commission considers that named persons have committed unlawful discriminatory acts or acts in breach of the Equal Pay Act for any purpose connected with the carrying out of its duties. It will be open to the Commission to investigate any aspect of the educational system. For the purpose of a formal investigation the Commission has power to require information to be provided. The Commission also has an educative function.

Individual complaints

19. Individuals will have direct access to the courts and, in employment, training and related cases, to industrial tribunals. In the case of those educational bodies in respect of which the Education Ministers have powers of direction under the Education Acts (in the main, primary, secondary and further education in the public sector), complaints other than complaints in the employment field will go first to the Education Ministers so that they may consider the use of their powers. The remedies available from tribunals will be compensation (including damages for injured feelings), a declaration of rights and a recommendation of a particular course of action. The remedies available from the courts will be damages (including damages for injured feelings), a declaration of rights and an injunction. Compensation and damages will not be available however in respect of indirect discrimination where it can be shown that the condition or requirement concerned was not imposed with the intention of discriminating.

APPENDIX II

EDUCATION ESTABLISHMENTS COVERED BY THE EDUCATION PROVISIONS OF THE SEX DISCRIMINATION ACT

DESCRIPTION OF ESTABLISHMENT	RESPONSIBLE BODY FOR THE PURPOSES OF SECTION 22
PUBLIC SECTOR	
1. Establishments maintained by a local education authority (i.e. county and voluntary schools, maintained special schools, and establishments of further education including colleges of education).	Local education authority or managers or governors according to which of these have the function in question.
2. Special schools not maintained by a local education authority.	Proprietor
3. Polytechnics designated under Section 24 (1) of the Act (i.e. North London, South Bank, City of London, Central London and Thames Polytechnics).	Governing Body
4. Establishments in receipt of grant under Section 100 of the Education Act 1944 designated under Section 24 (1) (i.e. direct grant schools and grant aided establishments of further education including voluntary colleges of education).	Governing Body
5. Establishments assisted by local education authorities under a scheme approved under Section 42 of the Education Act 1944 which are designated under Section 24 (1).	Governing Body
PRIVATE SECTOR	
6. Independent schools (other than special schools).	Proprietor
7. Universities	Governing Body
8. Establishments in respect of which grants are payable out of money provided by Parliament designated under Section 24 (1) other than those covered by (4) above (e.g. London University Graduate School of Business Studies and University of Manchester Institute of Science and Technology).	Governing Body
9. Establishments providing full-time further education for 16–19 year-olds designated under Section 24 (1) (e.g. independent establishments of further education recognised as efficient).	Governing Body

PART V

CASES ON THE LAW OF EDUCATION

GENERAL NOTE

Leading cases arising out of the Education Acts are dealt with in the annotated statutes (Part II, *ante*). This part sets out summaries of cases taken from the common law relevant to the administration of education.

PART V
CASES ON THE LAW OF EDUCATION

A. Negligence of the Education Authority

1. Defective state of playground.]—In a case under the repealed Education Act 1902, the defendants were held liable where a child, playing in a playground attached to a school, caught his foot in a hole in the ground and sustained injury.—*Ching* v. *Surrey County Council*, [1910] 1 K.B. 736, C.A.

2. Dangerous door.]—In a case under the repealed Education Act 1902, a child was injured by having her fingers caught in a heavy swing door with a powerful spring. The door was held not suitable for use by young children, and the defendants were guilty of negligence.—*Morris* v. *Carnarvon County Council*, [1910] 1 K.B. 840, C.A.

3. ——.]—The Schools Grants Regulations, 1951, reg. 5 provided that schools should be kept " on a satisfactory level of efficiency." By reg. 6: " (1) . . . the premises of the school shall be . . . kept in a proper state of repair . . ." The plaintiff, then a pupil at a school maintained by the defendant authority, sustained injuries to his hand and wrist when it went through a glass panel in a swing door on the school premises. The plaintiff had attempted to push open a door leading to a changing-room. Another pupil, as a prank, stopped the door with his foot, and the plaintiff's hand slid off the woodwork of the door and went through the glass. The door was a wooden door, the upper half of which was glass-panelled. Each piece of glazing measured approximately twelve inches by eight inches. The glass used was ordinary one-eighth inch thick sheet glass. The plaintiff claimed damages against the authority for personal injuries, alleging negligence and breach of statutory duty. The authority denied negligence:—*Held:* the common law duty of a school master to his pupils—namely, that of a prudent parent, bound to take notice of the ordinary nature of boys and their tendency to do mischievous acts, not in the context of the home but in the circumstances of school life—extended not merely to how the pupils conducted themselves but also to the state and condition of the school premises; glass which would be suitable in domestic circumstances was not necessarily suitable in the rough-and-tumble of school life; in the circumstances, the one-eighth inch glass was, as the defendants knew or ought to have known, too thin and accordingly the plaintiff had established negligence.—*Lyes* v. *Middlesex County Council* (1962), 61 L.G.R. 443.

4. ——.]—The plaintiff was a pupil at a school which was controlled and maintained by the defendants, a local education authority. She put out her hand towards a swing door that was swinging towards her and her hand went through the glass panel of the door and she was injured. The glass of the panel was one-eighth inch thick and was not toughened. The plaintiff claimed damages for breach of statutory duty under the Education Act 1944, s. 10 (2), and the Standards for School Premises Regulations 1959, reg. 51, in that the "construction and properties" of the materials, *viz.*, the glass panel, were not such that the " safety of the occupants " should be " reasonably assured " as required by reg. 51:—*Held:* the defendants were liable in damages because (1) an action lay for breach of statutory duty under s. 10 (2) and reg. 51, which imposed an absolute duty of which the test of breach was an objective test, *viz.*, that there would be breach of duty if safety were not reasonably assured, and, on the facts, safety had not been reasonably assured; (2) on the facts, negligence on the part of the defendants, or breach of their common duty of care under the Occupiers' Liability Act 1957, s. 2 (2), was established.—*Reffell* v. *Surrey County Council*, [1964] 1 All E.R. 743.

5. Conveyance of children to school.]—An education authority provided a vehicle to convey certain children to and from their school. A child who lived nearer to the school, but was not one of those for whom the vehicle was provided, was conveyed in it with the consent of the education authority, and, while getting out of it, fell and was injured, in consequence of there being no second person in addition to the driver to help the children to get in and out:—*Held:* there was evidence of negligence on the part of the education authority, and they were liable for the injury to the child. A person who provides anything for the use of another is bound to provide a thing reasonably safe for the purpose for which it is intended, even though the person using it does so only by the permission or consent of the person providing it and has no legal claim to such use.—*Shrimpton* v. *Hertfordshire County Council* (1911), 104 L.T. 145, H.L.

6. ——.]—A deaf and dumb child aged eight years travelled home from a special school in a school bus provided by the local education authority. The children on the bus were in the care and under the charge of an employee of the authority. The child was seen off the bus by the employee who gave him certain instructions. He was put on the pavement where he stood for a moment and then went to cross the road. As he emerged from the offside of the bus at the rear he was knocked down by a van coming at a substantial speed from the opposite direction to the bus and received injuries. In an action for damages for personal injuries, the judge held that the owners and driver of the van were eighty per cent. and the local authority, through the negligence of their employee, twenty per cent. responsible for the accident and awarded the child £2,000 general damages. On appeals by the plaintiff on the amount of damages awarded and cross-appeals by the defendants on the issue and apportionment of liability:—*Held:* (1) dismissing the cross-appeals of the defendants, in the circumstances the employee had a duty of acting as a reasonable parent and the judge was justified in assessing the small degree of fault on the part of the employee in not ascertaining the presence of the van or giving more definite instruction as to look out to the child at twenty per cent., the main cause of the accident being the excessive speed of the van; (2) damages increased to £3,000.—*Ellis* v. *Sayres Confectioners, Ltd.* (1963), 107 Sol. Jo. 252, C.A.

7. ——.]—The plaintiff, a boy of fourteen, was travelling in a school bus provided by the local education authority when his eye was injured by a paper or lead pellet. There was no adult supervisor but a senior boy and a senior girl had been appointed prefects to be in charge. Occasionally things were thrown about the bus or paper pellets flicked, but such conduct was generally stopped by the prefects and on the whole the boys on the bus were controlled fairly well. There was no evidence that metal pellets had even been used. There was insufficient evidence to prove that any particular pupil had fired the pellet which hit the plaintiff in the eye. The plaintiff brought an action against the education authority alleging negligence:—*Held:* the duty of the education authority was to see that the bus was reasonably safe for the children travelling in it, including the provision of supervision if necessary. The standard of care was that of a reasonably prudent parent applying his mind to school life, where there was a greater risk of skylarking. As there was no evidence that the group of pupils on the bus were particularly boisterous or undisciplined, the education authority had not failed in their duty in leaving the supervision to prefects. Action against the authority dismissed.—*Jacques* v. *Oxfordshire County Council* (1967), 66 L.G.R. 440.

8. Young children sent home before arrival of parents.]—The appellant, a five-year-old girl, attended a school run by the respondent local education authority. At the end of the day the appellant and other five-year-old children (other than those going home by school bus) were let out of the playground by one of the teachers to meet their parents. No effort was made by the teachers to pair the children with their parents but the children were told to return to the playground if they were expecting to be met but could not find their respective parents. There was a main road a short distance from the school.

On the day in question the five-year-old children were released five minutes earlier than usual. The appellant left the playground and was knocked down and injured on the main road. No blame attached to the vehicle driver concerned. The appellant's mother, who arrived at the usual leaving time, would, in normal circumstances, have met the appellant before she reached the main road:—*Held:* the appellant was entitled to damages. The period of five minutes was not a negligible one in the circumstances and the release of the children roughly five minutes before the scheduled time amounted to negligence on the part of the school authorities.—*Barnes* (*infant*) v. *Hampshire County Council,* [1969] 3 All E.R. 746, H.L.

9. **Unguarded machine.**]—Technical classes were provided by the defendants, a borough council. The plaintiff, a nineteen-year-old pupil, used an electrically-driven circular saw with no guard, and injured his hand. The plaintiff admitted that he knew the saw was dangerous and would be less dangerous if guarded, but he had not suggested to the instructor that it should be guarded:—*Held:* the maxim *volenti non fit injuria* applied, and judgment was entered for the defendants.—*Smerkinich* v. *Newport Corpn.* (1912), 76 J.P. 454.

10. ——.]—The plaintiff, a printing apprentice, attended a school of further education for printing tuition. While operating an unguarded printing machine his hand was caught and injured:—*Held:* while the school was not a factory, so that the provisions of the Factories Acts did not apply, it was the duty of the education authority to provide for the safety of their pupils, and they had not adequately done so. The authority was therefore guilty of negligence.—*Butt* v. *Inner London Education Authority* (1968), 66 L.G.R. 379, C.A.

11. **Unguarded gas cooker.**]—The plaintiff attended a school maintained by the defendant authority. During a cookery class her apron caught fire from an unguarded gas cooker and she was injured:—*Held:* the danger was one that ought reasonably to have been anticipated, and one which a local authority ought to have taken precautions to prevent by the provision of a guard round the stove or otherwise.—*Fryer* v. *Salford Corporation* [1937] 1 All E.R. 617, C.A.

12. **Dangerous materials left in playground.**]—A contractor, who was to carry out repairs at a school left a quantity of materials (sand and lime) in a truck in a corner of the school playground. The headmaster of the school instructed the school caretaker to have the materials removed as he considered it dangerous. The caretaker telephoned the contractor but the materials were not removed. When the boys came out of school one of them threw some of the sand and lime at another, injuring his eye:—*Held:* both the education authority and the contractor had been guilty of negligence.—*Jackson* v. *London County Council and Chappell* (1912), 76 J.P. 217, C.A.

13. **Broken glass in playground.**]—The plaintiff, a schoolchild, fell in the school playground and injured her hand on a piece of broken glass. She alleged negligence against the education authority and claimed damages. The evidence showed that school milk was delivered in crates and left in a recess outside in the school playground. The crates were carried in by senior pupils and the milk distributed before the mid-morning break. The bottles were then replaced in the crates and the crates taken back to the recess. Slow drinkers had to take their bottles down to the recess and put them in the crates if there was room or else stand them alongside. The children played in the playground during their breaks and the empty bottles were collected by the milkman in the afternoon.

The caretaker swept the playground twice a day but said that there were often loose bottles standing by the crates and also pieces of glass in the playground:—*Held:* the defendants were liable in negligence, for the risk of an accident was reasonably foreseeable and should have been guarded against by making better arrangements for the disposal of empty bottles.—*Martin* v. *Middlesborough Corporation* (1965), 109 Sol. Jo. 576, C.A.

14. Lack of playground supervision.]—A borough council was the education authority for a school which the infant plaintiff, aged 6 years, attended. During the mid-day break the plaintiff and some fifty other children were playing in the playground which formed part of the school premises. There was an unlocked gate which led to the street and, if given permission, children could leave the playground by this gate to go home for lunch or to buy sweets or toys. From time to time one of the teachers would go into the playground to see that all was well; but there was no continuous supervision. On the day in question one of the pupils, a boy aged 10, left the playground and went across to a nearby shop and purchased some blunted pieces of bamboo made up in the form of a bow and arrow. Returning to the playground and unseen by the teachers, he discharged the arrow in close proximity to the infant plaintiff, the arrow struck the plaintiff's spectacles splintering the glass, and it was necessary to remove one eye. The infant plaintiff suing by her father as next friend brought an action for damages against the council on the ground that they were negligent by their servants in failing to maintain adequate supervision over the pupils in the playground: —*Held:* taking into consideration all the circumstances, it was not incumbent upon the council to have a teacher continuously present in the yard throughout the break, and the supervision had been adequate.—*Ricketts* v. *Erith Borough Council*, [1943] 2 All E.R. 629.

15. ——.]—The infant plaintiff was a pupil at a school under the care and management of the defendants. An unfenced heap of coke lay in one of the school's playgrounds and the infant plaintiff was injured by a piece of coke thrown at him by another boy. In an action for damages for negligence it was found that the school authorities had exercised adequate supervision over the boys:—*Held:* the duty owed by the defendants to the boys was to take such care of them as a careful parent would exercise in like circumstances; they were under no obligation to prevent the boys having access to the coke by erecting fencing or other similar means; their supervision of the boys had been held to be adequate; and, therefore, they were not liable to the plaintiff.—*Rich* v. *London County Council*, [1953] 2 All E.R. 376.

16. ——.]—The infant plaintiff went to his school on the last day of term when the prefects were absent and there was a general relaxation of discipline. In the course of the morning " break " the plaintiff and another boy wanted to get a sheath knife from a third boy who carried it in his belt. A scuffle ensued in which the third boy pulled out the knife, lunged with it, and unintentionally injured the leg of the plaintiff so that the leg had to be amputated. In an action for damages against the education authority and certain masters at the school it was contended on behalf of the plaintiff that the masters were negligent in that at least one of them knew that boys brought sheath knives to school, and there was an inadequate system of supervision on the day of the accident:—*Held:* the duty of a schoolmaster did not extend to the constant supervision of all the boys in his care all the time; only reasonable supervision was required; there was no evidence in the present case that there had been an absence of such supervision; and, therefore, the action failed.—*Clark* v. *Monmouthshire County Council* (1954), 118 J.P. 244, C.A.

17. ——.]—After his class had been dismissed one afternoon, a boy aged about five years and ten months went into the school playground, climbed up a water-pipe on to the roof of a lavatory, and fell through a glass roof, sustaining fatal injuries. No adult was present in the playground at the time. His father brought an action against the local education authority, alleging negligence in supervision and claiming damages. It was the practice of the school to instruct the children of five and upwards to remain in the playground until they were collected by a relative, and to report to a mistress if they were not collected within a short time, and these instructions were obeyed by the children. On the day of the accident, the mother of the deceased, who regularly called for him at the end of school hours, was late in arriving:—*Held:* dismissing the action, the school authorities had not failed to exercise reasonable care of the children; as they could not reasonably anticipate that children allowed to disperse into the playground would meet with such an accident, & it was not their duty under all circumstances to keep the children under such detailed observation as to prevent climbing.—*Jeffery* v. *London County Council* (1954), 119 J.P. 43.

18. ——.]—In a school of nine hundred girls and boys between 11 and 18, a length of discarded, powerful elastic was placed in a wastepaper bin in a place where pupils congregated in the playground. The elastic was taken from the bin by some of the younger children, and whilst they were indulging in horseplay one of them was hit by the elastic and seriously injured in the eye. The general standard of discipline at the school was high.

Two members of the staff were charged with supervisory duties during the break, but because of extraordinary circumstances neither was present in the playground at the time of the accident. The plaintiff brought an action for damages against the local education authority maintaining the school.—*Held:* (1) it was a headmaster's duty, bearing in mind the known propensities of boys and girls between the ages of 11 and 18, to take all reasonable and proper steps to prevent any of the pupils under his care from suffering injury from inanimate objects and the actions of fellow pupils; (2) it was unreasonable to put the powerful elastic in an open wastepaper bin, for the possibility was foreseeable that some physical injury might be caused by horseplay with the elastic if it were left there, so that the defendants were liable for the unforseen injury occurring. Since the horseplay would have been stopped before the accident occurred if the system of supervision had been working properly, the defendants had failed in their duty of care to the plaintiff and were liable to him in damages.—*Beaumont* v. *Surrey County Council* (1968), 112 Sol. Jo. 704.

19. ——.]—The infant plaintiff, aged eight, was a pupil in a local authority primary school. The children arrived at varying times after 8.15 a.m. each day, and they were left without supervision in the playground until 8.55 a.m. when school began. The playground was surrounded by a wall about 3 to 3½ feet high made of flints reaching to about 2¼ feet from the ground with a brick coping above. It had been standing for about 100 years and many of the houses and schools in the area had similar walls. While racing to this wall at about 8.50 a.m., the infant plaintiff tripped and struck his head against it, suffering injuries which were made more severe by the jagged nature of the flints. There was evidence before the trial judge of three previous accidents which had occurred many years before when pupils had fallen against the same wall in the ordinary course of play but it had never occurred to any parent to complain that the wall was dangerous. The staff of the school were aware that children were accustomed to race in the playground but the headmaster stated that he would not have prevented play of this nature had he been present. On appeal against the findings of the trial judge that the wall was inherently dangerous and that there had been insufficient supervision on the part of the local education authority:—*Held:* the local education authority was not liable to the infant plaintiff in negligence or for breach of statutory duty, because—(1) the fact that accidents in the ordinary course of play had occurred in connection with the wall did not prove it to be dangerous bearing in mind its nature, typicality and long standing in the area and the fact that complaints had never been made against it; (2) the accident having occurred in the ordinary course of play it was irrelevant that there was no supervision in the playground, it being impossible in any event so to supervise the children that they never fell down and hurt themselves.—*Ward* v. *Hertfordshire County Council*, [1970] 1 All E.R. 535, C.A.

20. Slippery floor.]—The plaintiff had joined a class in physical training organised by the defendant council, and had paid a small fee on joining. The exercises were performed in a hall which was used for dances and of which the floor was fairly highly polished. While performing an exercise the plaintiff slipped and suffered injury. The whole class at the time were wearing rubber shoes. It appeared in evidence that it had been discussed whether the floor should be covered with matting or a drugget:—*Held:* (1) the duty of the council was to provide a floor which was reasonably safe in the circumstances, and this they had failed to do; (2) the accident did not result from a risk which the plaintiff had agreed to take, and the defence of *volenti non fit injuria* was not available.—*Gillmore* v. *London County Council*, [1938] 4 All E.R. 331.

21. Scissors in class.]—The infant plaintiff was one of a class of thirty-seven girls between 9 and 10 years of age who were being taught geography in a primary school. The class were given pointed scissors to cut out illustrations and put them into scrapbooks. The experienced teacher in charge had said at the beginning of the class: " Put the scissors down except when you are using them ". While the teacher was looking at the work of one girl, another girl, who had scissors in her hand, whispered to the plaintiff. The plaintiff turned round. The point of the scissors went into the plaintiff's eye, causing serious injury. At the trial the of plaintiff's action for damages for negligence against the education authority evidence was given by the experienced teachers that pointed scissors were desirable educationally and that there was no fault in the system of issuing them. MOCATTA J. found that although the teacher was not at fault the system was at fault in not ensuring proper supervision. He awarded damages. On appeal by the defendants:—*Held:* the teacher was conducting her class properly and efficiently and there was no fault in the system of supervision; that since neither the school authorities nor the teacher were at fault for the accident, judgment must be entered for the defendants.—*Butt* v. *Cambridgeshire and Isle of Ely County Council* (1969), 68 L.G.R. 81, C.A.

22. Accident during game.]—The plaintiff, who was a pupil in one of the defendant's schools, was, under the supervision of a master, taking part in a game of " touch " which was being played in the hall of the school. One side of the hall consisted of glass partitions, with doors in them. The glass partitions began 3 ft. 2¾ in. from the ground. During the game, which involved rushing about, the plaintiff, while being chased by another boy, unwittingly put his hand through one of the glass partitions and in consequence suffered personal injury. In an action for damages it was held that a reasonable and prudent father would have contemplated that such an action might have happened if he had seen his children playing that game in those circumstances; the defendants were negligent in not having contemplated that such an accident might occur; and the plaintiff was accordingly entitled to damages. —*Ralph* v. *London County Council* (1947), 111 J.P. 548, C.A.

23. Gymnastic exercises.]—In the course of gymnastic training a schoolboy was required to vault over a horse. For some reason the boy landed " in a stumble " and was injured. The master in charge did nothing to assist the boy in landing:—*Held:* the master had not taken reasonable care and the education authority were liable in damages to the injured boy.—*Gibbs* v. *Barking Corporation*, [1936] 1 All E.R. 115, C.A.

24. ——.]—The plaintiff, a boy aged twelve years, was taking part in gymnastic exercises at a school managed and controlled by the defendants. He was in a party of ten boys who were engaged in the exercise of vaulting the " buck ". The ten boys, who had all had experience of the exercise, were vaulting one after the other, and it was the duty of the boy who was last over to wait at the receiving end of the buck to assist as necessary the next boy to come over. As the plaintiff was vaulting, the school bell denoting that play-time had arrived rang, and the boy at the receiving end of the buck ran off without waiting to receive the plaintiff who fell and sustained injuries. At the time of the accident the instructor was a little distance away supervising the activities of other classes. Evidence was given that it was the approved practice in schools to leave boys who had had a little practice to carry out the exercise by themselves, so as to give them self-confidence, but evidence was also given by a physical training instructor that he considered the practice dangerous. The plaintiff sued for damages, alleging that the defendants were negligent in failing to exercise reasonable care in not having an adult present at the receiving end of the buck:—*Held:* the test of what was reasonable care in ordinary everday affairs might well be answered by experience arising from practices adopted generally and followed successfully for many years; the evidence in the present case was that the defendants had adopted a generally approved practice; taking into account the nature of the activity in question, they had not been shown to have been negligent; and, accordingly, they were not liable in damages to the plaintiff.—*Wright* v. *Cheshire County Council*, [1952] 2 All E.R. 789, C.A.

25. Child ordered to attend to fire.]—The plaintiff, who was a child of fourteen years of age, was being educated at a provided school. One of the teachers of the school directed her to go to a room used in common by the teachers, and to attend to the fire in that room. The fire was used for cooking this particular teacher's food. While she was attending to the fire the plaintiff's clothes became alight and she was injured:—*Held:* (1) the teacher was liable; (2) the education authority were also liable on the ground that the teacher was put by them in a position in which it was intended that her orders should be obeyed by the children, and that the order given by her in the present case was therefore one for which the education authority were liable.—*Smith* v. *Martin and Kingston-upon-Hull Corporation*, [1911] 2 K.B. 775.

26. Child allowed to stray.]—A small boy, aged about four years, who was a pupil at a nursery school conducted by the appellants, the local education authority, was made ready with another child to go out for a walk with one of the mistresses. The mistress left them unattended in the classroom, she herself going to get ready. While out of the classroom she met another child who had cut himself and she bandaged him. During her absence of about ten minutes, the boy got out of the classroom and made his way out of the school playground through an unlocked gate down a lane into a busy highway where he caused the driver of a lorry to make the lorry swerve so that it struck a telegraph pole as a result of which the driver was killed. His widow brought an action for damages for negligence against the appellants:—*Held:* (1) in the circumstances of the case, there was no negligence on the part of the mistress concerned; (2) the presence of a child as young as the child in the present case wandering alone outside the school premises in a busy street at a time when he was in the care of the appellants indicated a lack of reasonable precautions on the part of the appellants, who had given no adequate explanation of the child's presence in the street, and, since it was foreseeable that such an accident as happened might result from the child being alone in the street, the appellants were guilty of negligence towards the deceased and were liable to the respondent in damages.—*Affirmed sub nom. Carmarthenshire County Council* v. *Lewis*, [1955] 1 All E.R. 565; [1955] A.C. 549; *Lewis* v. *Carmarthenshire County Council*, [1953] 2 All E.R. 1403, C.A.

27. Playing with toy.]—The plaintiff, a child of five years of age, was a scholar at a non-provided school. With the leave of the teacher another scholar had brought certain toy soldiers to the school. While playing with these soldiers, the plaintiff fell on a toy " lancer " with the result that the lance pierced his eye, which had subsequently to be removed. In an action against the school managers and the education authority for damages for negligence:—*Held:* the accident being one which might have happened in any nursery where children play with toy soldiers, there was no evidence of negligence and the defendants were entitled to succeed.—*Chilvers* v. *London County Council* (1916), 80 J.P. 246.

28. Playing dangerous game.]—The infant plaintiff, who was 17 years of age and was an unemployed person undergoing a compulsory course of instruction at a county council instruction centre, was ordered by the council's instructor, a man of experience, to take part in an organised game called " riders & horses," in which one boy mounted the back of another and endeavoured to bring to the ground the foot of the boy who was acting as " rider " in an opposing pair. During the game, the infant plaintiff, who was taking the part of a " horse," fell on the wooden floor and seriously injured his arm. In an action against the council for negligence, on the ground that the game was so dangerous in itself that to order a boy to play it amounted to negligence, the evidence of the instructor was that for 20 years he had seen the game played without serious accident:—*Held:* there was no evidence of negligence, and therefore the action failed.—*Jones* v. *London County Council* (1932), 96 J.P. 371, C.A.

29. Carrying dangerous article.]—The plaintiff, a boy of 12 years of age attending a school owned and conducted by the defendant council, was " trotting " from one classroom to another, when at a blind corner he collided with another boy, B., carrying an oil can. The spout of the oil can, about 6 ins. long, struck the plaintiff in the eye and severely injured him. The boy B., who was carrying the can in a perfectly proper way, had been told to take it from one room to another by a master. The plaintiff sued the council as the employer of the master, alleging that the latter was negligent in not taking special precautions when entrusting a boy with a dangerous article:—*Held:* the oil can was not an inherently dangerous thing, nor was it a dangerous thing in the special circumstances of a school for young children, and the master was under no duty in such a case to take special precautions.—*Wray* v. *Essex County Council,* [1936] 3 All E.R. 97, C.A.

30. Sufficiency of discipline.]—On 9th March, 1962, the plaintiff, who was a pupil at a school owned and administered by the defendant local authority, who employed the second defendant as a chemistry master, attended a chemistry class during which an experiment was conducted to test the reaction of certain oxides to an alkali, caustic soda. For the purposes of the experiment, beakers containing a weak solution of caustic soda were placed on the pupils' benches, but a beaker of double-strength solution, which was unlabelled, for use by those pupils who were to conduct the experiment with tin oxide, was placed on the master's demonstration bench. In accordance with his usual practice, the master first explained to the class the theory of the experiment and the way in which it was to be carried out and while so doing warned the class that the strong solution of caustic soda was dangerous. Teat pipettes were provided for the pupils to draw the strong solution from the beaker. The plaintiff, one of the group of pupils to experiment with tin oxide, who had paid no attention to the master's explanation, left his seat at the back of the class, and came to the master's bench where two girls were standing, to ask what the experiment was about. Both girls, thinking that the solution in the unlabelled beaker was water, squirted the liquid into the plaintiff's face and his eye was injured. In an action for damages for personal injuries the plaintiff alleged negligence against the chemistry master and against the local authority as being vicariously liable for his acts. There was evidence that discipline in the class was lax:—*Held:* (1) in the circumstances it was proper for the master to allow 15 year old pupils with the background this class had in the study of chemistry to draw the supplies of caustic soda without direct supervision, provided that they had been given adequate warning as to the danger and were supplied with adequate materials as was the case here; the failure to label the beaker containing the strong solution could not be criticised since at the material time there was no other liquid from which it had to be distinguished; (2) there was a distinction between enforcing discipline in the interests of safety and doing so merely to put down impertinence and high spirits; the standard of discipline maintained by the master was sufficient from a safety point of view and the conduct of the plaintiff and the irresponsible acts of the pupils which resulted in the accident were not reasonably foreseeable by the master approaching his duties as equivalent to those of a prudent and careful parent; accordingly, the allegations of negligence failed.—*Crouch* v. *Essex County Council* (1966), 64 L.G.R. 240.

31. Accident in judo class.]—The plaintiff enrolled for evening classes in judo conducted by the defendants, the local education authority. Under the system of teaching they were taught one or two throws in their first lesson and encouraged to engage in combat exercises at the end of the lesson. A highly experienced and qualified instructor was employed, although the first class which the plaintiff attended was also the instructor's first employment with the defendants. There were 16 pupils at the plaintiff's first class at which the instructor demonstrated and taught the O. throw. At the end of the lesson he divided the class into two teams and told them to practise what they had been taught by engaging in combat exercises with each other. He warned them that, if their opponent achieved domination, they should yield and allow themselves to be thrown, for otherwise they might suffer injury. The plaintiff in evidence said that the instructor told them " get your man down " and that he understood the instructor to mean " get your man down in any way you can ". While the plaintiff was in combat with his opponent and while both were tugging away at each other, neither recognised the other as having achieved domination and neither yielded, and in the course of further combat the plaintiff sustained injury. The plaintiff claimed damages in respect of his injuries. He alleged that the defendants were negligent in allowing him to engage in combat exercises at the end of his first lesson, but during the hearing he abandoned that allegation and relied only on negligent instruction or supervision by the instructor. The judge held that the instruction " get your man down " amounted to a licence to the class to conduct a free-for-all, and that the instructor was thereby negligent in allowing the class to develop into a rough and tumble. He accordingly awarded the plaintiff damages. On appeal:—*Held:* allowing the appeal, (1) even if the instructor had told the class " get your man down ", that could not reasonably be construed as a licence to the class to conduct a free-for-all, but was simply an instruction to practice the O. throw which they had been taught, and did not in the circumstances constitute negligence; (2) even if that instruction was a negligent instruction, it was not a cause of the accident, which resulted because of the failure of the plaintiff or his opponent in breach of the clear warning by the instructor, to yield and not resist further force; and accordingly, the plaintiff's claim failed.—*Conrad* v. *Inner London Education Authority* (1967), 111 Sol. Jo. 684, C.A.

32. Teacher and warden at pedestrian crossing.]—The infant plaintiff darted out onto a pedestrian crossing on a main road outside the primary school which he had just left and was hit by a van and severely injured. The defendant corporation, who were both highway and school authority, employed a crossing warden to help the children safely across the road. They also operated a system whereby classes of children left the school at intervals and were accompanied to the crossing by a teacher. At the time of the accident the crossing warden was standing on the pavement with his pole bearing the sign: " Stop: Children " in one hand and his arm outstretched, motioning the children back. The infant plaintiff, suing by his father and next friend, claimed damages against the van owners for the negligence of their driver. The van owners joined the corporation as third party and the corporation were also added as second defendants. BROWNE, J. dismissed the claim against the van owners and gave judgment for the infant plaintiff against the corporation, holding that their system was inadequate, alternatively, that their teacher was at fault, and that the crossing warden was negligent. On appeal by the corporation:—*Held:* no blame could be attached to the system of operation or to the teacher but the crossing warden was negligent in not doing enough to ensure that the children, including the infant plaintiff, stayed on the pavement, and on that ground only the judge had rightly held the corporation liable.—*Toole* v. *Sherbourne Pouffes, Ltd.* (1971), 70 L.G.R. 52, C.A.

33. Accident on ice in playground.]—A school began at 9 a.m. but was opened by the caretaker well before that time. Most children arrived ten minutes beforehand. A circular was sent out to all parents by the headmaster discouraging them from sending their children to school too early. The playground was not supervised at that time of day. M., a boy aged 14, arrived at the school at 8.55 a.m. when there was frost on the ground. He and his friends discovered a slide about 10 ft. long. He used it in an orderly manner, lost his balance and fell, suffering permanent brain damage. He claimed damages from the local authority on the ground that (1) the boys should not have been allowed to slide unsupervised; and (2) the playground should have been salted:—*Held:* the action failed. There was no evidence of disorder. No average prudent father in the playground at that time would have thought it necessary to stop the children playing on ice. Further, it would be quite impracticable to salt such a large area as a playground every time there was a frost. Again, unless the school voluntarily adopted responsibility for early arrivals, it was under no duty to provide supervision in the playground.—*Mays* v. *Essex County Council*, (1975), *Times*, 11th October.

B. Schoolmaster *in Loco parentis*

34. General rule.]—The duty of a schoolmaster in relation to his pupils is that of a careful father (DARLING, J.).—*Shepherd* v. *Essex County Council* (1913), 29 T.L.R. 303.

35. True parental authority prevails.]—The defendant's son was a pupil at the plaintiff's school, one of the rules of which, the defendant having notice of it, was that no "*exeat*" or permission to leave the school and remain away for one night, was allowed during Easter term. During Easter term the defendant requested that his son might be allowed to come home and remain for the night, which the plaintiff refused to allow; but subsequently, on the defendant repeating the request and sending a servant for the boy, the plaintiff allowed him to go home, writing to the defendant at the same time that he did so on the understanding that the boy returned the same night. On the boy reaching home, the defendant telegraphed to the plaintiff that it was not convenient to send the boy that day, but he could return the next morning, to which the plaintiff telegraphed in reply, that unless the defendant's son returned that night, he should not receive him back. In consequence of the last telegram the defendant did not send the boy back, and the present action was brought to recover the school fees due on the first day of Easter term, of which term less than three weeks had expired when the boy left. The defendant paid money into court with a denial of liability, and counter-claimed damages for breach of contract by the plaintiff:—*Held:* (1) the plaintiff's contract was to board, lodge and educate the defendant's son for the term on the condition that he should be at liberty to enforce with regard to the boy the rules of the school, or such of them as were known to the defendant; this condition having been broken by the defendant, the plaintiff had the right to refuse to complete his contract, and was consequently entitled to succeed in this action both on claim and counterclaim; (2) the parental authority in case of conflict must of course prevail, and the father might, no doubt, have had a *habeas corpus* if the master detained his son against his wish.—*Price* v. *Wilkins* (1888), 58 L.T. 680.

36. Authority of teacher to be exercised reasonably.]—(1) Although the master of a school has the same authority over the scholars as the parents would have, and, therefore, may impose reasonable restraints upon their persons, either by way of prevention, or punishment of disorderly conduct, yet he has not a discretionary power of expulsion; but only for reasonable cause. In judging of the cause, however, great regard must be had to his necessary discretion as to the enforcement of discipline; and the wilful breach of its reasonable rules may be sufficient cause, and the repetition of acts of disobedience, each in itself separately insufficient, may be sufficient as showing a persistent disregard of discipline, and a habit of disobedience. But, if the expulsion is justified on the ground of some particular act, or conduct, not only as likely to be seriously injurious to the peace and good order of the establishment, but as committeed with that object, it must appear that it was of that character, or the justification would fail; (2) a parent, when he places his child with a schoolmaster, delegates to him all his own authority, so far as it is necessary for the welfare of the child.—*Fitzgerald* v. *Northcote* (1865), 4 F. & F. 656.

C. Punishment of Pupils

37. Corporal punishment—Must be moderate and reasonable.]—A parent or a schoolmaster (who for this purpose represents the parent and has the parental authority delegated to him) may for the purpose of correcting what is evil in the child inflict moderate and reasonable corporal punishment, always, however, with the condition that it is moderate and reasonable. If it be administered for the gratification of passion or of rage, or if it be immoderate and excessive in its nature or degree, or if it be protracted beyond the child's powers of endurance, or with an instrument unfitted for the purpose and calculated to produce danger to life or limb; in all such cases the punishment is excessive, the violence is unlawful, and if evil consequences to life or limb ensure, then the person inflicting it is answerable to the law, and if death ensues it will be manslaughter.—*R.* v. *Hopley* (1860), 2 F. & F. 202.

38. —— Delegation to assistant teacher.]—An assistant teacher has authority to inflict corporal punishment on a pupil if the punishment inflicted is moderate, is not dictated by any bad motive, is such as is usual in the school, and such as the parent of the child might expect that the child would receive if it did wrong; and the fact that by the regulations of the school assistant teachers are forbidden to inflict corporal punishment will not of itself render the assistant teacher liable in an action by the pupil for assault.—*Mansell* v. *Griffin*, [1908] 1 K.B. 947, C.A.

39. —— Proper method.]—A magistrate, being of opinion that caning on the hand was attended by risk of serious injury, convicted a board schoolmaster of an assault for giving a pupil four strokes, though the boy deserved corporal punishment, and the caning was inflicted unobjectionably and did not cause serious injury:—*Held:* the magistrate was wrong in his reasons and the conviction must be quashed.—*Gardner* v. *Bygrave* (1889), 53 J.P. 743.

40. —— For misconduct outside school premises.]—The authority delegated by the parent of a pupil to a schoolmaster to punish a pupil is not limited to offences committed by the pupil on the premises of a school, but extends to acts done by such pupil while on his way to and from school.—*Cleary* v. *Booth*, [1893] 1 Q.B. 465.

41. —— ——.]—At a school for boys there was a rule prohibiting smoking by pupils during the school term, whether on the school precincts or in public. During the term a pupil rather less than sixteen years old, after having left the school for the day and returned home, smoked a cigarette in the public street, and next day the schoolmaster administered to him five strokes of the cane as a punishment for breach of the rule. On the hearing of an information against the schoolmaster for an alleged assault on the boy the justices found that the rule in question was reasonable, that the father of the boy by sending him to the school authorised the schoolmaster to administer reasonable punishment to the boy for breach of a school rule, and that the punishment administered was reasonable; and they dismissed the information. An order *nisi* having been obtained calling upon the justices to show cause why they should not state a case on a question of law:—*Held:* the decision of the justices was right, that no question of law arose on which they could state a case, and that the order *nisi* should be discharged.—*R.* v. *Newport* (*Salop*) *Justices, Ex parte Wright,* [1929] 2 K.B. 416.

D. Negligence of Teacher

42. Pupil allowed to use fireworks.]—A schoolmaster who permits an infant pupil under his care to make use of fireworks, is responsible in an action for the mischief which ensues.—*King* v. *Ford* (1816), 1 Stark. 421.

43. Golf in playground.]—The plaintiff, a schoolboy, whilst passing along a corridor in the school buildings from which an open doorway led to an asphalt playground, was hit in the eye by a golf ball flying through this doorway, which had been struck with a stick by a fellow pupil in the playground. In an action against the headmaster claiming damages for negligence, on the ground of lack of supervision, the plaintiff, in his evidence, said that he had never known a golf ball to be struck in the playground before. There was no express evidence given as to the amount and character of supervision in the playground, if any:—*Held:* this was not a case of *res ipsa loquitur.* There was no evidence of lack of supervision on the part of the headmaster and there was no evidence that, assuming there was such supervision, it would have prevented the accident.—*Langham* v. *Wellingborough School Governors and Fryer* (1932), 101 L.J.K.B. 513.

44. Accident in playground.]—A tip-up lorry in the charge of a single driver had delivered coke in a school playground, and was driving away when a number of boys jumped on to the rear of the lorry causing the tipping part to tip up. Another boy, the plaintiff, had jumped on to the lorry immediately behind the driver's cab, and when the tipping part of the lorry was suddenly released it came down on the plaintiff and crushed his leg. The headmaster of the school had left the boys to play in the playground and had returned into the school premises before the arrival of the lorry. He did not know of the arrival of the lorry. In an action for damages against the managers of the school, the headmaster and the owners of the lorry:—*Held:* (1) the headmaster was not negligent in leaving the boys in the playground without supervision, nor ought he to have taken steps to stop the lorry from coming during playtime. The headmaster and the managers were accordingly not liable; (2) the owners of the lorry had sent the lorry in the charge of a reasonable adult, and ought not reasonably to have anticipated interference; (3) the driver was not negligent in not looking to see if the boys had jumped on to the lorry, and he could not have anticipated sufficient weight to tip the lorry. The owners of the lorry were, therefore, not liable; (4) a lorry as such is not an allurement to children.—*Rawsthorne* v. *Ottley,* [1937] 3 All E.R. 902.

45. Boys helping farmer on half-holiday.]—On their half-holiday, a number of boys from a school were allowed by the headmaster to help a farmer by working in a field. As a result of horseplay among some of the boys, the infant plaintiff was struck on the forehead by a clod of earth, and one of his eyes was so badly injured that it had to be removed. In an action for damages for negligence against the headmaster, it was contended that he was under a duty to arrange for supervision of the boys while they were doing the work:—*Held:* in the circumstances of this case, the headmaster owed no duty to the infant plaintiff or his father to provide for the supervision of the boys.—*Camkin* v. *Bishop*, [1941] 2 All E.R. 713, C.A.

E. Miscellaneous Cases.

46. Dismissal of teacher.]—The plaintiff, who was a schoolmaster at an aided voluntary school maintained by the council, absented himself on 6th October, 1967 and refused to return to his duties at the school. On 19th December, his employment was terminated at a meeting of the school governors and he was given notice to take effect on 30th April, 1968, being the required period of notice under his contract. On 18th January, 1968, the staff sub-committee of the council met and held an inquiry whether the council should exercise its power under Education Act 1944, s. 24 (2) (*a*), to prohibit the dismissal of the plaintiff. This power was crystallised in the school's articles of government and the council's conditions of service of teachers (which included provision for the plaintiff to be given a hearing). The meeting of the sub-committee did not take the form of an appeal by the plaintiff from the decision of the governors to dismiss him. Three of the ten members of the sub-committee were governors of the school; none of them, however, had attended the meeting of the governors of the school on 19th December. The staff sub-committee resolved not to prohibit the plaintiff's dismissal, and this decision was later affirmed by the full council:—*Held:* (1) the decision of the staff sub-committee (which was admittedly exercising a quasi-judicial function) not to prohibit the dismissal of the plaintiff could not stand, because—(a) the fact that three governors of the school sat on the sub-committee gave rise to the possibility of bias; (b) no man could be a judge of his own cause; the three governors when acting as members of the sub-committee did not cease to be an integral part of the body whose action was being impugned, and it made no difference that they did not personally attend the meeting of the governors at which the plaintiff's employment was terminated; (2) the plaintiff was nevertheless not entitled to recover against the council for breach of contract on the ground of the council's failure to ensure that the hearing of the sub-committee was properly conducted, because—(a) the initial contract of service of the plaintiff was a contract by which the plaintiff was employed by the governors and the governors alone and there was no tripartite agreement including the council; (b) the plaintiff's right of hearing before the sub-committee was conferred by the articles of government; (c) there was no contract, either initial or subsequent, between the plaintiff and the council and his claim for breach of the supposed contract was totally misconceived.—*Hannam* v. *Bradford City Council* (*or Corporation*), [1970] 2 All E.R. 690, C.A.

47. ——.]—The plaintiff, a schoolteacher, claimed from his employer, the defendant council, his unpaid salary for the three and a half days when he was not permitted to attend at his school on account of his refusal to supervise school meals. The education officer, having been warned by the secretary of the National Union of Teachers that its members had been instructed to withdraw from their duties in respect of the supervision of school meals, had written a letter on 21st November, 1967 to all teachers in the defendant council's area stating that the teachers were required under their contract of service to supervise school meals, that if they refused to perform that duty they would have repudiated their contracts and would not be allowed to attend at school until they were prepared to carry out the whole of their duties, and that in the meantime no salary would accrue to them. The plaintiff refused to supervise school meals for several days, and consequently was not allowed at school during that period, Thereafter he resumed his full duties at the school and was reinstated. The defendant council contended that they were justified in refusing to pay the plaintiff his salary for the period when he did not attend because the plaintiff had repudiated his contract and the council had accepted the repudiation. The plaintiff contended that his conduct did not amount to a repudiation and that even if it did the council had no power to act on it without going through the procedure prescribed for terminating his employment, as set out in the agreement under which he was employed. He had, so he maintained, been suspended and the rule (incorporated in his contract) that payment of salary must be made for a period of suspension if that suspension was followed by reinstatement had not been observed:—*Held:* (1) since a local education authority had the power, under the Provision of Milk and Meals Regulations, 1945, reg. 14, to require teachers to supervise school meals, the order made, in pursuance of that regulation, that teachers in the defendant council's area should supervise school meals was a lawful order and the plaintiff's conduct in refusing to comply with it amounted to a direct repudiation of his contract with the defendant council, which the council was entitled to accept if they so wished; (2) the defendant council had not, however, acted on the repudiation for, on the evidence, they had not at the material time regarded the contract as at an end; they had merely regarded the plaintiff as temporarily " excluded ", a word which in the circumstances it was impossible to distinguish from " suspended "; (3) accordingly, the plaintiff was entitled to recover his salary for the three and a half days during which he was suspended. —*Gorse* v. *Durham County Council,* [1971] 2 All E.R. 666.

47. ——.]—*Ward* v. *Bradford Corporation* (1971), 115 Sol. Jo. 606, C.A.

48. ——.]—The appellant was formerly employed by the respondent Scottish education authority as a teacher. On 19th March, 1969, the respondents served on the appellant notice of dismissal, terminating his employment with them on 24th April, 1969. The notice followed a meeting of the respondents' education committee held on 18th March, 1969, at which the committee had passed a resolution dismissing the appellant from their employment on the ground that he was unregistered and that his continued employment was no longer lawful by virtue of the Schools (Scotland) Code, 1956, as amended, which provided by reg. 4 (2) that " every teacher employed by an education authority shall be a [registered] teacher holding the qualifications required by this Code for the post for which he is employed."

The appellant was a certificated teacher and prior to 1965 that was the recognised qualification for appointment to a teaching post by a Scottish education authority. The Teaching Council (Scotland) Act, 1965, however, established a General Teaching Council for Scotland and provided that it should, *inter alia,* be the duty of the council to establish a register of persons who were entitled to be registered and who applied to be registered. The appellant refused to register. The respondents were advised that, in view of this refusal, they had no option but to dismiss him. Prior to the meeting of the education committee the appellant had received a notice dated 20th February, 1969, informing him of his proposed dismissal. The Public Schools (Scotland) Teachers Act, 1882, s. 3 (substantially re-enacted in the Education (Scotland) Act, 1962, s. 85 (1)) provided, *inter alia,* that no resolution of a school board for the dismissal of a certified teacher was to be valid unless notice of the motion for his dismissal should have been sent to the teacher not less than three weeks previous to the meeting; further the resolution for dismissal was not to be valid unless agreed to by a majority of the full members of the board. In the 1882 Act the provisions were preceded by an explanation of their purpose, which was " to secure that no certificated teacher appointed by and holding office under a School Board in Scotland shall be dismissed from such office without due notice to the teacher and due deliberation on the part of the School Board ". The appellant sought the reduction of the resolution of the education committee and the notice of dismissal on the ground that, contrary to natural justice, the education committee had admittedly refused to receive his written representations or to afford him an opportunity to be heard before the resolution had been passed. The respondents contended: (a) that since, by virtue of the Education (Scotland) Act 1962, s. 82 (1) (substantially re-enacting the Education (Scotland) Act 1872, 2. 55), the appellant's appointment was during the respondent's pleasure, he was not entitled to be heard before being dismissed (prior to 1872 such an office was held *ad vitam aut culpam*); (b) that, even if in general a teacher had a right to be heard before being dismissed by an education authority, to have afforded the appellant a hearing would have been a useless formality because whatever he might have said they were legally bound to dismiss him; (c) that even if the appellant was entitled to a hearing he was not entitled to have their decision to dismiss him reduced or annulled:—*Held:* (1) had the status of such Scottish teachers been governed purely by common law a teacher, like the appellant, holding public office during the pleasure of a public authority would not be entitled to a hearing before being dismissed; the position, however, was different where, as here, the common law position had been fortified by statute and additional protection given. In such a case the court should examine the framework and context of the employment to see whether elementary rights were conferred on the employee either expressly or by necessary implication. The right of a man to be heard in his own defence was the most elementary protection of all and where a statutory form of protection would be less effective if it did not carry with it the right to be heard, it was not difficult to imply that right; (2) in the present instance the implication to be drawn from the requirement in the 1882 Act that three weeks' notice of a meeting to consider a motion for dismissal should be given to a teacher and the prohibition against dismissal without due deliberation was that a teacher was in appropriate circumstances accorded the right to be heard; the relevant provisions of that Act were only explicable on that basis; there could be no reason for the giving of notice unless it was to afford the teacher an opportunity to prepare his defence; without affording the teacher a hearing a responsible public body could not be said to reach a fair decision. Although the 1882 Act had been repealed and replaced by later Acts, there was nothing in those subsequent Acts which could reasonably be interpreted as taking away that elementary right; (3) to have afforded the appellant an opportunity to be heard would not have been a useless formality for there was an arguable case which the appellant might have made to the education authority committee and which might have influenced enough members to prevent a majority against him; he might, *inter alia*, have questioned the validity of the regulations requiring the dismissal of teachers who failed to acquire and pay for a new qualification such as registration, or he might have convinced a sufficient number of the education committee that reg. 4 (2) of the 1956 order, as amended, was ambiguous (on the ground, that " every teacher employed " could mean either " every teacher who is presently employed " or " every teacher who shall hereafter be taken into employment "; (4) where an employer failed to take the preliminary steps which the law regarded as essential he had no power to dismiss and any purported dismissal was a nullity; accordingly since in the present case the appellant had shown not only that his position was such that he had in principle the right to make representations before the decision to dismiss him was taken, but also that if admitted to state his case he had a case of substance to make, his appeal would be allowed and the case remitted to the Court of Session with a direction to reduce the resolution for dismissal and the consequent letter of dismissal.—*Malloch* v. *Aberdeen Corporation*, [1971] 2 All E.R. 1278.

49. Redundancy.]—The appellant had for ten years been employed by the respondent county council as headmaster of a boys' school which was to be amalgamated with another school and run on co-educational lines. As a result of this re-organisation the appellant's employment was terminated, *prima facie* on the ground of redundancy. The respondents made an offer to the appellant of alternative employment in a mobile pool of teachers serving for periods of one or two terms in schools with a shortage of staff, under the authority of the headmaster of each school, in an area some distance from the appellant's home. He was guaranteed the same salary, but he refused the offer. On the question whether the respondents had made an offer of alternative suitable employment within the Redundancy Payments Act 1965, s. 2 (4), which had unreasonably been refused:—*Held:* " suitable employment " meant employment which is substantially equivalent to the employment which had ceased; the offer of a position in a mobile pool of teachers to a headmaster with the appellant's qualifications, experience and status, and necessitating his moving house, was not suitable; nor could it be made so merely by guaranteeing the same salary.—*Taylor* v. *Kent County Council*, [1969] 2 All E.R. 1080; [1969] 2 Q.B. 560.

50. Duty to educate in accordance with parents' wishes.]—In 1968 the defendants in their capacity as education authority sent out a circular to all parents whose children were going to begin their secondary education in September, 1968. The circular emphasised that pupils who attended Roman Catholic primary schools would be considered only for Roman Catholic secondary schools so that parents of those children would not be able to opt for maintained county secondary schools. The reason for this was that, in the long term, maintained county secondary comprehensive schools would only have sufficient accommodation for pupils from county and Church of England primary schools. The circular stated that applications for pupils to attend secondary schools other than those to which they had been allocated would be considered only in exceptional cases and then only if there was accommodation in the alternative school when all the requirements of children within its area had been satisfied. The parents of a boy who had been sent to a Roman Catholic secondary school by the defendants in accordance with this policy and whose later application for him to go to a non-Roman Catholic secondary school was refused, claimed that the defendants had acted unlawfully in segregating the children into the two categories of Roman and non-Roman Catholic schools, in that they had failed to have regard to the wishes of the parents contrary to the Education Act 1944, s. 76, and were fettering the exercise of their discretion by laying down a policy as to which pupils should go to which secondary schools and applying that policy in disregard of the parents' wishes. A preliminary issue whether the parents' only remedy was by way of representations to the Minister under the Education Act 1944, ss. 68, 99, was ordered to be tried:—*Held:* (1) it could not be said that in issuing the circular the education authority were disregarding the parents' wishes in contravention of s. 76 of the 1944 Act; the parents' wishes were not the sole or overriding consideration, for there were other things to which the authority might have regard which might outweigh the wishes of the parents; (2) neither could it be said that, by laying down a policy as to which pupils should go to which secondary schools, the authority were fettering the exercise of the discretion which had been given to them, for it was perfectly legitimate for an administrative body, such as an education authority, to lay down a general policy which it proposed to adopt in cases coming before it, provided that the policy was not unreasonable or capricious but was one which, as in the present case, could reasonably be upheld for good educational reasons; (3) accordingly the education authority had not acted beyond their powers and the only remedy, if there were grounds for complaint, was to make representations to the Minister under s. 68 of the 1944 Act.—*Cumings* v. *Birkenhead Corporation*, [1971] 2 All E.R. 881; [1972] Ch. 12.

INDEX

MADE AND PRINTED IN GREAT BRITAIN BY
WILLIAM CLOWES & SONS, LIMITED, LONDON, BECCLES AND COLCHESTER